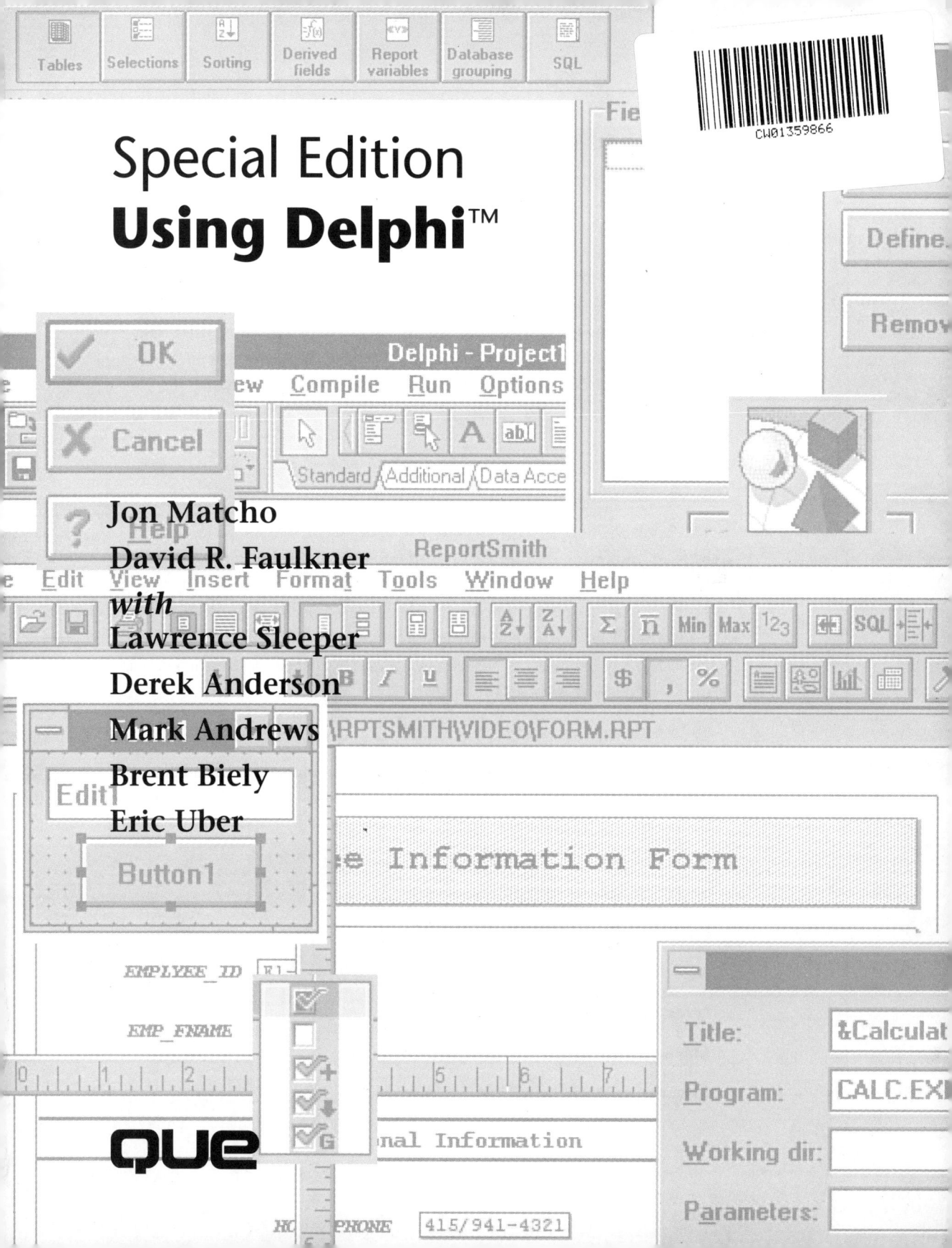

Special Edition
Using Delphi™

Jon Matcho
David R. Faulkner
with
Lawrence Sleeper
Derek Anderson
Mark Andrews
Brent Biely
Eric Uber

que

Special Edition Using Delphi

Copyright© 1995 by Que® Corporation.

All rights reserved. Printed in the United States of America. No part of this book may be used or reproduced in any form or by any means, or stored in a database or retrieval system, without prior written permission of the publisher except in the case of brief quotations embodied in critical articles and reviews. Making copies of any part of this book for any purpose other than your own personal use is a violation of United States copyright laws. For information, address Que Corporation, 201 W. 103rd Street, Indianapolis, IN 46290.

Library of Congress Catalog No.: 95-67676

ISBN: 1-56529-823-3

This book is sold *as is*, without warranty of any kind, either express or implied, respecting the contents of this book, including but not limited to implied warranties for the book's quality, performance, merchantability, or fitness for any particular purpose. Neither Que Corporation nor its dealers or distributors shall be liable to the purchaser or any other person or entity with respect to any liability, loss, or damage caused or alleged to be caused directly or indirectly by this book.

98 97 96 95   4 3 2 1

Interpretation of the printing code: the rightmost double-digit number is the year of the book's printing; the rightmost single-digit number, the number of the book's printing. For example, a printing code of 95-1 shows that the first printing of the book occurred in 1995.

This book is based on Delphi Version 1.

Publisher: Roland Elgey

Associate Publisher: Joseph B. Wikert

Director of Product Series: Charles O. Stewart III

Managing Editor: Kelli Widdifield

Director of Marketing: Lynn E. Zingraf

Dedication

To Amy and our own little work-in-progress, Weeser.

—JMM

To my beautiful bride, Sharon.

—DRF

Credits

Acquisitions Editor
Lori A. Jordan

Product Director
Bryan Gambrel

Development Editor
Richard Rhoades

Production Editor
Susan Shaw Dunn

Copy Editors
Patrick Kanouse
Jeff Riley

Assistant Product Marketing Manager
Kim Margolius

Technical Editor
Dan Dumbrill

Book Designer
Sandra Schroeder

Cover Designer
Dan Armstrong

Production Team
John Hulse
Daryl Kessler
Bob LaRoche
G. Alan Palmore
Kris Simmons
Scott Tullis

Indexer
Rebecca Mayfield

Operations Coordinator
Patricia J. Brooks

Acquisitions Coordinator
Angela C. Kozlowski

Editorial Assistant
Michelle R. Williams

Composed in *Stone Serif* and *MCPdigital* by Que Corporation

About the Authors

Jonathan Matcho began business programming in 1987 when he joined DZS Computer Solutions, Inc., an East Coast consulting firm. Since then, Jon has delivered a number of large multiuser database applications for various industries. After DZS, he joined Brickhouse Data Systems, Inc., to design and co-develop DueTime, a workgroup-based time and billing system. In 1993 he joined Professional Computer Solutions, Inc., to assist in the delivery of mission-critical database solutions. Jon can be reached at **71760.2720@compuserve.com**.

David R. Faulkner is the vice president of Silver Software, Inc., the premier Hawaii-based database development and training company, and a consultant with Brickhouse Data Systems, Inc., in New Jersey. Dave is a contributing editor to the *Paradox Informant* and has had several articles published in other magazines. He is the author of TxtView and Visage for Windows, Paradox-based add-ons, and is a co-founder of the Oahu Paradox users' group. He was a speaker at the fourth and fifth annual Borland International Conference and an author for Que's *Using Paradox 5.0 for Windows*, Special Edition.

Lawrence Sleeper is a senior analyst at Brickhouse Data Systems, Inc. He has designed, developed, maintained, and documented corporate database systems for 10 years. He has a B.A. in philosophy and English from Rutgers University in New Jersey. When not on a foreign continent, he can be reached at Brickhouse at (908) 563-6844.

Derek Anderson is the systems development manager for Haas Publishing Companies in Atlanta, Ga. He has been active in the PC development community for the past six years, spending the first three as an instructor of end-user PC applications before joining Haas. Currently he manages a programming staff that is developing wide area network applications. Derek is a frequent speaker at PC conferences and has must recently served as a contributing author for Que's *Using Paradox for Windows 5.0*, Special Edition.

Mark Andrews is a longtime technical writer and computer consultant who has written more than 20 books about computers and computer programming. For five years he was the nationally syndicated electronics columnist of the *New York Daily News*. Now he lives in the heart of Silicon Valley, where he has documented hardware and software products for companies including Apple, Borland, Microsoft, Hewlett-Packard, Amdahl, Tandem, and many more.

Brent Biely is a senior programmer/analyst at Brickhouse Data Systems, Inc., where he co-developed DueTime, a workgroup-based time and billing system. Before joining Brickhouse, Brent worked for American Cyanamid and the Port Authority of New York and New Jersey. He enjoys skiing and backpacking in the off time. Brent can be reached at (908) 563-6844.

Eric Uber, a technical engineer at Borland International, is currently a member of the Delphi team and participated in the development cycle of the product. Eric was also on the dBASE for Windows team and participated in its development process. A developer of several shareware utilities, Eric knows C and Pascal as well as Delphi's extended language and dBASE programming. He has provided sample programs and various other contributions, including technical reviews for various publications and technical manuals. He has also developed applications used in-house by staff at Borland International. Eric is highly knowledgeable in data modeling and manipulation, object-oriented theory, and Windows development.

Acknowledgments

Many thanks are in order for the contributions and sacrifices of the many people that made this book possible. From all of us, live long and prosper! Karen, Gerald, and Jen Matcho; Johnny B; Matthew Sleeper of Brickhouse; Pam & Wes Frueh; Angus; Susan Dunn, Lori Angelillo Jordan, Bryan Gambrel, Deborah Abshier, Lisa Wagner, and Jenny Watson at Macmillan Publishing; Eric Uber, Paul Dodds, David Intersimone, Walter Turney, Steven Segaliwicz, Phil Foti, Nan Borreson, Karen Giles, Arlette Lucchesi-Munoz, and Keith Bigelow of Borland; Ben Tandowski, Drew Wright, and Aaron Kornbluth of PCSI; Mitch Koulouris and Jerry Coffey of Informant Communications; Doron Steger and Robert Edwards at DZS; Chuck Raudonis; Alan Zenreich; Jim Kocis; Jim & Michelle Sleeper; AlphaGraphics #238; Ken Lang; Namir Shammas; and the entire Delphi development team for doing such a bang-up job.

Trademarks

All terms mentioned in this book that are known to be trademarks or service marks have been appropriately capitalized. Que cannot attest to the accuracy of this information. Use of a term in this book should not be regarded as affecting the validity of any trademark or service mark.

Delphi is a trademark of Borland International.

We'd Like to Hear from You!

As part of our continuing effort to produce books of the highest possible quality, Que would like to hear your comments. To stay competitive, we *really* want you, as a computer-book reader and user, to let us know what you like or dislike most about this book or other Que products.

You can mail comments, ideas, or suggestions for improving future editions to the address below, or send us a fax at (317) 581-4663. For the on-line inclined, Macmillan Computer Publishing has a forum on CompuServe (type **GO QUEBOOKS** at any prompt) through which our staff and authors are available for questions and comments. The address of our Internet site is **http://www.mcp.com** (World Wide Web).

In addition to exploring our forum, please feel free to contact me personally to discuss your opinions of this book: on CompuServe, I'm at 75230,1556, and on the Internet, I'm **bgambrel@que.mcp.com**.

Thanks in advance—your comments will help us continue publishing the best books available on computer topics in today's market.

Bryan Gambrel
Product Development Specialist
Que Corporation
201 W. 103rd Street
Indianapolis, Indiana 46290
USA

Contents at a Glance

Introduction	1
Essentials	**15**
1 Updating Pascal Programming to the Year 2000	17
2 Understanding the Environment	27
3 Understanding the Language	57

Components	**87**
4 Using Visual Components	89
5 Using Non-Visual Components	111
6 Using Data-Bound Components	127
7 Customizing and Reusing Components	153

Applications Development	**191**
8 Creating Forms	193
9 Creating Applications	217
10 Creating Database Applications	237
11 Using the Browser	279
12 Using the Database Desktop	307
13 Reporting with ReportSmith	355

Delivery	**385**
14 Handling Errors	387
15 Using Delphi's Debugging Features	415
16 Delivering Your Application	445

Appendixes	**459**
A Properties	461
B Events	503
C Methods	515
D Constants	541
Index	549

Table of Contents

Introduction **1**

   Who This Book Is For 2
      Programmers 2
      Project Leaders 4
      Managers 4
   Before You Begin 5
   Delphi Does Windows 6
   Delphi's Features 7
   Conventions Used in the Book 9
      Terms 9
      Variables 9
      Objects 11
      Constants 11
      Properties 12
      Procedures 12
   Examples Used in the Book 13
   Why Delphi Is for You 13

I Essentials   15

1 Updating Pascal Programming to the Year 2000   17

   Understanding Event-Driven Programming 18
   Understanding Object-"Based" Programming 20
   Understanding Objects 21
      What Are Objects? 21
      Creating Objects 22
   Understanding Properties 23
   Understanding Events 23
      What Is an Event? 24
      Objects and Events 25
   From Here… 26

2 Understanding the Environment   27

   Getting to Know the Delphi Environment 28
   Using the Main Window 30
      The Menu Bar 31
      The SpeedBar 32

xii   Contents

    The Component Palette 33
        Working with the Component Palette 34
        Getting Component-Specific Help 35
        Rearranging the Component Palette 35
        Adding Components to the Palette 37
    Using the Object Inspector Window 38
        Inspecting Properties 39
        Inspecting Events 40
    Using the Form and Code Editor Windows 42
        Adding Additional Forms to Your Application 43
        Adding Additional Units to Your Application 43
        Introducing the Project Manager Window 44
    Using the Environment to Build an Application 44
        Placing Objects 45
        Selecting Objects 46
        Setting Properties with the Object Inspector 47
        Attaching Code for Events 48
    Managing Delphi Project Files 49
        Saving Your Project 50
        Opening an Existing Project 51
        Running Your Application 53
    Navigating Delphi 53
    Configuring Delphi 54
    Suggestions for Effective Delphi Development 55
    From Here… 55

3 Understanding the Language   57

    The Pascal Language 58
        Data Types 59
            Type Compatibility 63
            Typecasting 63
        Procedures and Functions 65
        Program Blocks 67
    Extensions to Pascal 68
        The *Case* Statement 68
        Open Array Construction 69
        A Function's *Result* Variable 70
        A Function's Return Type 70
        The New Object Model 71
        Protected Parts 72
        Default Ancestor 72
        Reference Model 72
        Class Methods 73
        Method Pointers 74
    Programmed Properties 75
        Property Syntax 75
        Fields for Reading and Writing 76

Indexed Properties	76
Multiple-Index Properties	78
Read-Only and Write-Only Properties	79
Object References	79
Runtime Type Information	80
Virtual Constructors	80
Forward Class Declaration	80
Dynamic Methods	81
Abstract Methods	81
Override Directive	82
Message-Handling Methods	82
From Here…	85

II Components — 87

4 Using Visual Components — 89

Text-Related Components	89
Label Components	90
WordWrap and *AutoSize* Properties	90
OnClick Event and Focus Control	90
Edit, MaskEdit, and Memo Components	91
The *Autoselect* Property	91
The *PasswordChar* Property	91
The *ReadOnly* Property	91
The *MaxLength* Property	91
A Unique Property for the MaskEdit Component	92
Unique Properties for the Memo Component	92
List Box Components	93
Combo Box Components	93
String Grid Components	94
Button and Check Box Components	94
Button Components	95
BitBtn (Graphic Button) Components	95
Speed Button Components	95
Radio Button Components	96
Check Box Components	96
Grouping Components	97
Group Box Components	97
Panel Components	97
Tab Set Components	98
Notebook Components	98
Scrolling Components	99
Scrollbar Components	99
Scroll Box Components	99
Graphical Components	100
Image Components	100

Paintbox Components 100
Shape Components 101
Bevel Components 101
Outline Components 102
Color Grid Components 103
Draw Grid Components 103
Header Components 104
File and Directory Access Components 104
FileListBox Components 104
DirectoryListBox Components 105
DriveComboBox Components 106
FilterComboBox Components 106
Multimedia and OLE Components 107
Media Player Components 107
OLE Container Components 108
Common Component Properties 108
Popup Menus 108
The *TabStop* Property 108
Visual Basic Controls 109
Adding Visual Basic Controls 109
Using Delphi's Visual Basic Controls 109
BiSwitch 109
BiPict 110
BiGauge 110
TKChart 110
From Here… 110

5 Using Non-Visual Components   111

Creating Menus 111
Using the Menu Designer 112
Providing Menu Names and Captions 113
Including Separator Bars 113
Adding Accelerator and Shortcut Keys 114
Creating Submenus (Nested Menus) 115
Dragging and Moving Menu Items 115
Including Menu Hints 115
Controlling Menu Items at Runtime 116
Disabling Menu Items at Runtime 116
Toggling Menu Items at Runtime 117
Hiding Menu Items at Runtime 117
Using the Timer Component 117
Using DDE Components 118
DDE Client Conversation 119
DDE Client Item 119
DDE Server Conversation 120
DDE Server Item 120
Creating Dialogs 120
Open and Save Dialog Components 120

Contents **xv**

      Providing a Default Extension 121
      Designating File Edit Region Interface Styles 121
      Using the *FileName* Property 121
      Specifying File Masks 122
      Using the *FilterIndex* Property 122
      Using File Name History Lists 122
      Using the *Options* Property 123
   Color Dialog Component 123
      The *Color* Property 123
      Color Dialog Options 123
   Font Dialog Component 123
      Selecting and Configuring Fonts 124
      Using Font Dialog Options 124
      Using the *OnApply* Event 124
   Print and Print Setup Dialog Components 124
   Find and Replace Dialog Components 125
      Specifying the Text to Find 125
      Using the *OnFind* Event 125
      Specifying the Replacement Text 125
      Using the *OnReplace* Event 126
From Here… 126

6 Using Data-Bound Components   127

   Using Aliases 128
      Aliases and Local Data 129
      Aliases and Client/Server Data 130
   Using Non-Visual Data Components 132
      Using Tables 133
      Going Visual with the *DataSource* Component 134
   Querying Data 135
      Using SQL Off the Cuff 136
      Doing Power SQL with the Visual Query Builder 138
      Saving and Loading Visual Query Files 142
      Controlling *DataSource* Objects at Runtime 143
   Understanding One-to-Many Relationships 144
   Using Other Non-Visual Components 146
      Databases 146
      Stored Procedure Control 146
      Batch Move of Data 148
      Reports 148
   Using Visual Data Components 149
      DBGrid 149
      DBNavigator 150
      DBText 150
      DBEdit 150
      DBMemo 151
      DBImage 151
      Database List Components 151

Contents

      DBListBox 151
      DBComboBox 151
      DBCheckBox 151
      DBRadioGroup 151
    Database Lookup Components 152
      DBLookupList 152
      DBLookupCombo 152
  From Here… 152

7 Customizing and Reusing Components   153

  Introducing Component Libraries 153
    Details of DCL Files 154
    How to Manipulate DCL Files 155
      Customizing the Components on the Palette 158
      Removing Components from the DCL 161
    What DCL Files Are Made Of 163
  Introducing Component Writing 163
    How to Set Up a Project with the Component Expert 164
    Code the Component Expert Generates 167
    Source Sections for the Component's Declarations 168
    Component Registration 169
  Performing a Generic Install of Components 170
  Using Component Resources 172
    The DCR and Design-Time Bit Map 172
    Custom Help Files for Components 173
    Keywords and the KWD File 173
  Modifying Your First Component 173
    Overriding Standard Methods 175
    Inheriting Default Behavior 176
    Adding Properties or Events 177
      Adding Object Fields 177
      Adding and Overriding Methods 177
      Making Custom Properties Available
        to the Object Inspector 178
      Firing a Custom Event 178
    Changing Property Defaults... 179
      Changing the Default Values 179
      Overriding the Constructor 180
    Determining Design Time vs. Runtime 181
  Testing the Component 182
  Using VBX Controls 184
    Using VBX Controls in Delphi 185
    Installing VBX Controls 186
    Using the VBX Wrapper 188
  From Here… 189

III Applications Development — 191

8 Creating Forms — 193

Setting Form Properties 193
   ActiveControl 194
   AutoScroll 195
   Border Icons 195
   Border Styles 196
   ClientHeight and *ClientWidth* 198
   Color 198
   Ctl3D 198
   Cursor 199
   Enabled 199
   Font 200
   FormStyle 200
   HelpContext 201
   HorzScrollBar and *VertScrollBar* 202
   Icon 202
   KeyPreview 202
   Left and *Top* 203
   Menu 203
   Name 203
   PixelsPerInch and *Scaled* 203
   PopUpMenu 204
   Position 204
   Visible 205
   WindowMenu 205
   WindowState 205
Creating Projects with Multiple Forms 206
   Creating a Form with an About Box 206
   Using Autocreate Forms 207
   Using the Project Manager 208
Using Form Templates 209
   Configuring Delphi to Use Form Templates 209
   Using Default Templates 210
   Saving Your Own Templates 211
   Setting Gallery Options 212
Using Form Experts 213
From Here... 215

9 Creating Applications — 217

MDI Applications 218
   Setting Up MDI Parent and Child Forms 218
      Parent and MDI Child Form Project Units 218
      MDI Parent and Child Window Types 221

Referencing MDI Child Windows 221
Using Useful Properties for MDI
    Window Management 222
        Using Read- and Runtime-Only Properties 222
        Setting a Form's Type 223
        Controlling Form Visibility 223
    Incorporating MDI Window Methods 223
        Creating MDI Child Windows 224
        Arranging Icons 224
        Cascading MDI Windows 225
        Closing the Current Child Window 226
        Selecting the Next MDI Child 226
        Selecting the Previous MDI Child 227
        Tiling MDI Children 227
SDI Applications 228
    Controlling SDI Family Windows 228
    Manipulating Master SDI Window Objects 229
Application Templates 231
    Telling Delphi to Use Application Templates 232
    Using Application Templates 232
Advanced Coding Issues 234
    Where to Put the Code 234
    Shared Procedures 235
    Shared Event Handlers 235
From Here… 236

10 Creating Database Applications   237

Understanding Delphi Database Basics 238
    The Borland Database Engine 239
    Components, Controls, and Classes 240
    The Database Component Pages 241
    Database Components 242
    Non-Visual Components 243
        The *TField* Component 243
        The *TDataSet* Class 244
        The *TDataSource* Component 245
Creating a Customized DataGrid Application 245
    Designing a Customized DataGrid Application 245
    Creating a DataGrid Project Step by Step 246
    Testing Your Application 248
Improving the DataGrid Application 248
    Using the Customization Popup Menu
        and the DataSet Designer 249
    Using the Customization Popup Menu 249
    Using the DataSet Designer 250
        What You Can Do with the DataSet Designer 250
        Modifying a DataGrid Step by Step 251

Using SQL in Delphi Databases 254
   Getting Started with SQL 254
   Writing SQL Queries 255
   Using the *TDBNavigator* Component............................... 257
Designing an SQL Editor 259
   Building an SQL Editor Step by Step 259
   Adding Data-Access Controls 260
   Executing Queries 261
   Clearing Queries 262
   Writing and Executing SQL Commands 263
Creating a Data-Entry Form 263
   Using the *TDBEdit* Component 264
   Creating a Form for the DataForm Project 264
   Setting Component Properties 264
Creating the LineItem Application 266
   Designing the LineItem Form Step by Step 268
   Customizing Fields with the DataSet Designer 270
   Merging Information from Two Tables 272
   Reformatting Database Fields 273
   Calculating Values of Fields 274
   Linking a Table to a DBEdit Control 276
From Here… 278

11 Using the Browser   279

Compiling with Debug 280
Using the Browser Window 281
   Filters 281
      The Constants Filter 281
      The Functions/Procedures Filter 283
      The Types Filter 284
      The Variables Filter 284
      The Properties Filter 285
      The Inherited Filter 285
      The Virtual Filter 286
      The Private Filter 286
      The Protected Filter 286
      The Public Filter 286
      The Published Filter 286
   The Browser's SpeedMenu 287
      The Objects Command 287
      The Units Command 288
      The Globals Command 289
      The Symbol Command 292
      The Qualified Symbols Command 293
      The Sort Always Command 294
      The Show Hints Command 295
      The Info Line Command 295

Contents

The Previous Button	296
The History Button	296
The Scope Tab	296
The Inheritance Tab	298
The References Tab	298
Navigating the Browser	299
Typing to Find a Symbol	299
Using the Enter Key	299
Using Keyboard Shortcuts	300
Adjusting the Browser Panes	302
Configuring the Browser	303
From Here…	305

12 Using the Database Desktop — 307

Understanding the DBD Screen	308
Creating a Table	309
Starting a New Table	309
Working with Paradox Tables	310
Using the Field Roster	310
Setting Validity Checks	312
Specifying a Lookup Table	313
Specifying Secondary Indexes	314
Ensuring Referential Integrity	315
Setting Passwords	316
Specifying a Table Language	317
Listing Dependent Tables	318
Borrowing Table Structures	318
Naming the New Table	318
Working with dBASE Tables	319
Using the Field Roster	320
Creating Indexes	321
Locking Records	321
Working with InterBase Tables	322
Using the Field Roster	322
Creating Indexes	323
Naming the New Table	324
Restructuring Tables	324
Viewing a Table	325
Opening a Table	325
Adjusting Table Properties	326
Resizing Columns	326
Resizing Rows	327
Resizing the Table Header	328
Moving a Column	328
Rotating Columns	329
Using the Scroll Lock	329
Saving Table Properties	330

Contents   xxi

    Navigating a Table 331
Editing a Table 332
    Using Edit Mode 333
    Using Field View Mode 333
    Undoing Changes 334
    Inserting Records 335
    Deleting Records 335
    Locking Records 336
    Posting Records 336
Performing Queries 337
    Using QBE 337
    Setting ANSWER Table Properties 338
    Using Check Marks 339
    Applying Conditions 340
    Using Wild Cards 341
    Using Operators 341
    Performing Action Queries 342
    Using Example Elements 343
    Performing Multitable Joins 344
    Performing an ANSWER Table Sort 345
    Setting Execution Options 345
    Saving Queries 346
Using SQL Scripts 347
    Creating an SQL Script 347
    Saving Your SQL Statements 348
Using DBD Tools 348
    Add 348
    Copy 349
    Delete 350
    Empty 351
    Passwords 351
    Rename 352
    Sort 352
    Info Structure 353
    Subtract 354
From Here… 354

13 Reporting with ReportSmith   355

Starting ReportSmith 356
Understanding the ReportSmith Environment 357
    The Toolbar 358
    The Ribbon 359
    The Report Window 359
    Rulers 359
Creating Reports 360
    Choosing the Report Type 360
    Applying Report Styles 362

xxii Contents

Generating a Report Query 363
    Defining Tables 365
    Choosing a Sort Order 370
Formatting Your Report 374
    Making It Fit 374
    Reordering the Columns 376
    Changing the Text 377
        Selecting Text 377
        Changing Fonts and Attributes 378
        Changing and Adding Text 379
        Adding a Graphic 379
    Grouping Information 380
    Performing Mathematical Operations 382
    Changing the Sort Order 383
From Here… 383

IV Delivery   385

14 Handling Errors   387

Understanding Exceptions 388
    What Are Exceptions? 388
    When Are Exceptions Raised? 389
    Exception-Handling Syntax 389
    Exceptions and the Runtime Library 389
Programming with Exceptions 390
    Setting Up *try* Blocks 390
    Handling Exceptions in the IDE 391
    Terminating on Exceptions 392
    How to Handle Exceptions 393
        Using the *on..do* Construct 394
        Nesting *try* Blocks 396
    Raising Exceptions 398
Understanding Exceptions as Object Classes 399
    Defining the Exception Object's Default Constructors ... 400
    Using Properties of the *Exception* Object Class 402
    Descending Object Classes from *Exception* 402
    Handling Exceptions on the Class Level 403
    Using Members of the Exception Instance 404
    Exception Object Summary 405
Defining New Exceptions 405
A Healthy Example of Creating New Exceptions 406
Preventing Errors 412
From Here… 413

15 Using Delphi's Debugging Features   415

Understanding Delphi Bugs 416
    Syntax Errors 416

Letting Delphi Do the Work 417
Configuring Delphi to Find Syntax Errors 417
Finding Common Syntax Errors 419
Finding the Source of a Syntax Error 421
Use Help to Avoid Syntax Errors 422
Runtime Errors 423
Logic Errors 424
Using the Debugger 424
Configuring the Debugger 425
Using Breakpoints 427
The Breakpoint List Window 428
Breakpoint Pass Count 429
Conditional Breakpoints 430
Temporary Breakpoints 430
Letting Your Program Run 430
Run 431
Step Into 431
Step Over 432
Taking Advantage of Debugger Tools 432
The Watch List Window 433
Adding Variables to the Watch List Window 433
Using the Watch Properties Dialog 434
Simplifying Operations with the
  Watch List Window's SpeedMenu 434
The Evaluate/Modify Dialog 435
The Call Stack Window 437
Pause and Reset 438
Knowing When *Not* to Use Delphi's Debugging Tools 438
Using Other Borland Tools 439
Turbo Debugger 439
WinSight 441
WinSpector 443
From Here… 444

16 Delivering Your Application   445

Delivering Simple EXEs 446
Configuring the Linker 446
Setting Up Icons 447
Creating Your Own Icon 449
Hooking Up Your Icon 450
Including Help Files with Your Program 451
Delivering VBXs 453
Delivering Database Applications 453
Installing the BDE 454
Installing SQL Links 455
Adjusting Parameters to Use Paradox 456
Using ReportSmith Runtime 456
From Here… 458

Appendixes 459

A Properties 461

B Events 503

C Methods 515

D Constants 541
Built-In Named Constants 541

Index 549

Introduction

Welcome to *Special Edition Using Delphi*, a book on one of the most exciting new products in the computer industry today. Around the world, programmers are proclaiming that Delphi makes programming fun again. J.D. Hildebrand, editor of the Windows programming magazine *Windows Tech Journal*, has said about Delphi, "It's going to change our lives, you know." If you have the opportunity to learn and use the powerful development environment of Borland's Delphi, you may very well find this statement to be true. Delphi merges visual and object-oriented programming features into a programmer-friendly development environment, providing a reusable component-based architecture. This opens a new door for programming that allows rapid application development and deployment of high-speed Windows programs.

This book doesn't simply go through the Delphi menus choice by choice and describe what each does. Parts and chapters are structured so that if you need information on another topic, that topic's location can be quickly located. This book is divided into four logical parts with an appendix section. The parts are structured so that you can progress in a logical manner, according to your own skill level:

- *Part I, "Essentials."* This part of the book covers those items that you need to know before getting started with Delphi development. After reading the chapters in this section, you'll know how to navigate and use all the tools in Delphi.

- *Part II, "Components."* This part of the book organizes the components into logical chapters. Components are organized in the way you would think of them, not how they appear on the Component palette. All components are covered, with code examples for those that are more involved than a simple label component.

- *Part III, "Applications Development."* Like Part II, this part of the book was written with the application developer very much in mind. Issues involved with complete application development are discussed, along with what it takes to produce professional-quality results.

- *Part IV, "Delivery."* This part helps you prepare and deliver your Delphi application. Also discussed are the files necessary for delivery and shipment of a Delphi application. Don't let the term *files* worry you—Delphi programs can ship in a single executable file, but other programs can be quite complex.

- *Appendixes.* This part of the book is a bit more of a reference than the other parts. The appendixes contain tables of components and their associated properties, methods, and events. This way, you can quickly identify which properties, methods, and events apply to individual components.

Delphi promises to be an exciting product. With Delphi, application prototyping and full-scale development are entering another revolutionary age. At the same time "grass-roots" hard-core programmers are being given end-user visual development tools, more casual programmers can access the power of a compiled environment. You now have access to programming power and speed, before available only by sacrificing one for the other. Delphi puts power and speed in your hands in a state-of-the-art development environment. I hope that you'll enjoy the same amount of excitement I felt when being introduced to Delphi, which gives new meaning to the joy of programming!

Who This Book Is For

Delphi is a development tool targeted for programmers. While programmers will most likely become the most adept at using Delphi, they aren't the only ones who need to know what Delphi can do for them. This book was written to satisfy readers with intermediate- to advanced-level programming and development skills. This book doesn't cater to programmers only, nor does it limit the technical content. Some sections in this book may appeal more to a project leader than to a programmer. Ultimately, the authors hope to provide a bounty of information to quickly provide programmers with the necessary skills to leverage the power of Delphi and get started right away.

Programmers

This book is intended for intermediate- to advanced-level programmers who are familiar with a third-generation language (3GL)—preferably, but not necessarily, Pascal. This book isn't designed to teach you Pascal programming, but it is designed to teach you how to use visual and Pascal programming skills to develop Windows applications with Delphi. A basic knowledge of Pascal is beneficial but is only necessary to understand relatively small blocks of code. Delphi doesn't require you to write much code at all when simply controlling the user interface.

A number of chapters are for programmers who are coming from a development environment other than Pascal. The following chapters should be of particular interest:

- *Chapter 1, "Updating Pascal Programming to the Year 2000."* This chapter discusses how Windows programming has evolved and how it's performed today. This chapter ensures that you understand the topics that are assumed throughout the book. If you don't have experience with event-driven programming, reading this chapter is mandatory.

- *Chapter 2, "Understanding the Environment."* This chapter shows you how to move through Delphi's multiwindowed development environment (a single document interface). All the major external Delphi objects are discussed in this chapter.

- *Chapter 3, "Understanding the Language."* For those of you with Pascal experience, read this chapter as a Pascal "refresher." This chapter should also be the starting point for programmers wanting to migrate to Pascal from another programming language. If you have experience with a language other than Pascal, this chapter helps you apply what you know from that language to Delphi development.

- *Part II, "Components."* The chapters in this section of the book discuss all the components available in Delphi and how you can use them for development of your application.

- *Part III, "Applications Development."* All chapters in this section provide information on how applications are developed using Delphi. The chapters cover application fundamentals as well as Delphi's powerful object-oriented tools, such as the Browser, the Database Desktop, and ReportSmith.

- *Part IV, "Delivery."* The details involved with the delivery of a Delphi application are covered in this section. When it comes time to deliver your applications to your users, these chapters help you understand what you need to know to deliver a full-fledged Delphi application.

- *Appendixes*. Reference-type information for Delphi can typically be found in the appendixes. All appendixes should be of interest to programmers.

The examples in the book are fast-paced, with the overall goal to make you, the programmer, productive as soon as possible. This book isn't intended to replace the Delphi documentation or on-line help—in fact, references are made to the on-line help that is built into the Delphi product. Instead, this book is designed to bring you up to speed with Delphi in a logical and intuitive manner by providing insight on key features of Delphi. Many examples throughout the book highlight key features and techniques for effective Delphi development.

Project Leaders

Delphi has built-in support for team development. All programming groups, regardless of size, usually have some sort of project or technical leader who is responsible for overseeing design discussions and making final technical decisions. To be able to provide sufficient input as a project leader, you must be familiar with virtually all major Delphi features. This book is of great value in determining which features of Delphi can be used to produce the desired result in a manner suitable to your needs.

After reading this book, all project managers will have an understanding of what efforts are required to develop an entire application using Delphi. Ideas and suggestions are presented to guide you toward a result in a productive manner. You can always write a better program, and programs are never done, but you must first get that "version 1" out the door. Take a look at the suggested chapters for programmers and managers.

Managers

Programmers and project leaders tend to get mired down with the many technical details involved in developing an application, such as how to write the most optimal piece of code. While it's certainly impressive to have an intimate relationship with a development environment, this often prevents an accurate assessment or comparison of the environment with other products. Managers must make decisions on what environments will be used in the future within an organization and whether these environments are effective. Based on research, a new development environment may be chosen for development or evaluation. Once a development environment is implemented, further discussions and decisions are made as to whether the new environment works and whether it will continue to facilitate development with an advantage over other environments.

Delphi is an environment that includes the sophisticated features of component reuse and team development right out of the box. This book provides information that assists managers in understanding how Delphi can help their groups. For you to get the most out of this book, read the "Delphi's Features" section later in this introduction for a summary of the key features in Delphi. Also be sure to read the following chapters:

- *Chapter 2, "Understanding the Environment."* This chapter covers the major development tools in Delphi and how and when a programmer uses them. You'll be able to get a feel for those features that make Delphi stand out.

- *Part III, "Applications Development."* Learn what options are available for development of multiwindow and multidocument programs using Delphi. Accessing data is a standard requirement for today's applications. Chapter 10, "Creating Database Applications," is dedicated to showing you how a data-capable application is developed. Sections on accessing client/server data are also located in this chapter as well as in Chapter 6, "Using Data-Bound Components."

- *Part IV, "Delivery."* The chapters in this section help you prepare for and deliver your Delphi application. This section discusses the files necessary for delivery and shipment of a Delphi application. Fear not—simple programs ship in a single executable file, and even complicated data-driven programs ship with just a few more external files.

Before You Begin

The speed at which you acquire skills in a new third- or fourth-generation programming language is often greatly reduced if you have some degree of experience with a similar programming language. Delphi, with its Object Pascal core and visual development environment, is no different. A soon-to-be Delphi programmer benefits from experience with another language, preferably Pascal, but at the same time Pascal isn't absolutely necessary. Many other development environments provide ample amounts of comparable concepts and are often as beneficial as Pascal experience alone.

Chapter 3, "Understanding the Language," should be read by everyone and can be read quickly by those who have Pascal experience. If you know Pascal, read through this chapter anyway. Delphi's Object Pascal language descends from the Borland Pascal compiler. Along with Delphi's own Pascal language extensions, a number of other substantial "base" and object-oriented extensions have been added to the language since Borland Pascal Version 5.5.

Before sitting down to work with Delphi, the authors strongly suggest reading the remainder of this introduction and the following chapters, regardless of your skill level:

- *Chapter 1, "Updating Pascal Programming to the Year 2000."* This chapter discusses topics regarding development of Windows applications in general. Visual and event-driving programming in Windows is covered using Delphi terminology.

- *Chapter 2, "Understanding the Environment."* This chapter introduces you to all the available tools in Delphi. Take a look at this chapter to see what is available.

- *Chapter 3, "Understanding the Language."* This chapter is of interest for those coming from other 3GL, 4GL, or visual programming environments such as C, Paradox (PAL and ObjectPAL), or Visual Basic. Other non-typed languages are much more forgiving than the syntax-intensive nature of compiled languages, especially Pascal. To write effective code in Delphi, you need a basic understanding of the Pascal language structure. Use this chapter as a reference when adjusting your own programming guidelines.

Delphi Does Windows

Microsoft Windows supplies a graphical user interface (GUI) shell that provides a standard user and programming environment. While often thought of as an operating system, Windows 3.1x is actually just a DOS application and not actually an operating system.

Windows NT and future versions of Windows (Windows 95 and Cairo) will have functionality included directly in the operating system, providing increased performance. These operating systems run 32-bit programs, whereas programs on Windows 3.1x are 16-bit. Delphi can compile 32-bit programs for these new operating systems for extremely fast program execution.

GUIs offer a more sophisticated and user-friendly environment than a command-driven interface such as DOS. Windows works in an intuitive fashion, allowing you to easily switch tasks and share information between applications. Windows also offers task-switching, virtual memory management, drag-and-drop functionality, and standard conventions for common operations. Though overwhelmingly embraced by computer users everywhere, developers have traditionally been faced with the added burden of programming in the extremely complex Windows environment.

To make Windows programming available to the mass of developers, many major programming language vendors have released Windows versions of their popular compilers. Borland has launched Delphi to offer a visual compiler based on Borland's popular Pascal programming language. This book assumes that you're familiar with completing user-oriented tasks in Windows such as opening, closing, moving, and resizing windows. Before developing in Windows, you must first have a thorough understanding of how Windows programs look and feel. There are books on how to design Windows interfaces, but actual hands-on experience can have more value.

Delphi makes developing robust Windows applications a rapid and enjoyable process. Windows applications that used to require a roomful of highly skilled C++ programmers can now be written by a single programmer using Delphi.

Delphi's Features

Delphi contains a broad and ambitious set of features ranging from its form designer to transparent support of all the popular database formats. This book covers the following features of Delphi:

- *Reusable and extendible components.* Delphi eliminates the need for developers to program common Windows components such as labels, buttons, and even dialog boxes. In Windows, you often see the same "objects" time and time again between many different applications. The Choose File and Save File dialog boxes are examples of reusable components built directly into Delphi. Delphi comes with these and many more reusable components that allow you to take control of your Windows development effort. Delphi allows you to customize these components to work the way you need them to work for your application. See Chapter 7, "Customizing and Reusing Components," for more information on this topic.

    Predefined visual and non-visual objects including buttons, data objects, menus, and prebuilt dialog box objects are available. Data objects, for example, give the capability to display data with just a few mouse clicks and without any programming. This impressive list of objects places Delphi at the front of those development environments providing a reusable component architecture. Part II, "Components," is dedicated to components.

- *VBX support.* What would component reuse be without the capability to tap into the largest pool of "componentware" available, from third-party VBX vendors? Delphi supports packaging VBX objects directly into the Component palette for easy access to these objects and tools. Chapter 5, "Using Non-Visual Components," and Chapter 7, "Customizing and Reusing Components," discuss Delphi's VBX components.

- *Application and form templates.* Delphi provides prebuilt form and application templates that you can use to quickly get started developing entire applications. Also included are a number of commonly used dialog boxes. Chapter 8, "Creating Forms," and Chapter 9, "Creating Applications," offer an in-depth discussion of these topics.

- *Customizable development environment.* The Component palette, Code Editor, application templates, and form templates are just a few areas where Delphi can be completely customized. Chapter 2, "Understanding the Environment," shows you how to use Delphi's environment productively.

- *Compiled programs.* While other Windows visual development environments claim to "compile" programs, they usually compile only part of the program and then link an interpreter and pcode into the executable. This has worked in the past, but many programmers have run into a performance barrier with this structure. Delphi produces truly compiled executable programs with *no* interpreter and *no* pcode, thus making Delphi programs as fast as any 3GL and the fastest database development tool in the world. Simple Delphi programs can be shipped in a single executable without the need for ancillary DLLs required in other environments.

- *Robust data-access capabilities.* Built into Delphi is the Borland Database Engine (BDE). The BDE has matured over a number of generations. Formerly known as ODAPI, and then IDAPI, the BDE is now a standard layer of middleware that is used to access all the popular data formats available today. The BDE is also the key to transparent client/server access, with links to all the major client/server vendors, namely Sybase SQL Server, Microsoft SQL Server, Oracle, and Borland's InterBase. When compared to Microsoft's ODBC, the BDE shines, yielding substantial performance gains by having a closer link to the target database formats. Chapter 6, "Using Data-Bound Components," and Chapter 10, "Creating Database Applications," show you how use the BDE to present data in your applications.

Conventions Used in the Book

A common set of terms and naming conventions is recommended throughout this book to maximize the clarity of the information.

Terms

Every environment, whether a programming environment or a pool hall, has a set of terms and commonly accepted jargon. These terms enhance communication between participants in a particular environment. Imagine what it would be like telling someone to *break* the *racked balls* with the *cue stick* without using these common terms for a game of billiards. In this book, the following terms are used repeatedly:

- *Object.* Throughout the book, the authors use the term *object* interchangeably with *component*. In general, *object* tends to refer to a component—or even a group of components—as it exists at runtime. *Component* conveys a slightly different meaning for an object, with emphasis toward developmental tools. Components are available for inclusion in your programs through the Component palette (see Chapter 2) and are the foundation on which objects are built. A component at runtime is thought of more as an object than a component.

- *Environment.* This term is used in a few different contexts, including programming environment and development environment. There's not much of a difference between the contexts, except that *programming environment* may be used where the authors are referring to command- or "batch"-oriented compiler programs. Development environments are a step above in that they provide a comprehensive set of tools from within a single program.

- *Exception.* An exception is an error that hasn't been planned for. See Chapter 14, "Handling Errors," for a detailed discussion on exceptions and how to handle them.

Chapter 1, "Updating Pascal Programming to the Year 2000," is devoted to your understanding of many more terms and concepts associated with the Delphi development environment.

Variables

Delphi provides many different variable types for storing integer, real (floating point), Boolean (logical), char, string, and pointer values. Also, there are user-defined types, sets, records, and object variables. Since there are so many different types, reading programming code written by someone else can be confusing when confronted with obscure variable names. For example, consider the following assignment statement:

```
myVar := newVar;
```

What's being assigned here? How do you know whether you're not trying to perform an illegal type conversion? To find out what variable types `myVar` and `newVar` contain, you have to find out where they're defined in the program, which makes for inefficient maintenance.

Many examples in this book use a prefix naming convention. By using this convention, at a glance you immediately know the variable and object type that you're dealing with. You don't have to hunt until you find the file where it was declared. Using this naming convention, the previous line of code might look like the following:

```
realMyVar := intNewVar;
```

Notice the `real` and `int` portions being used to prefix the actual variable names. At a glance, you now can see that you're assigning an integer value to a real variable.

The prefix naming convention is used whenever possible, except when dealing with simple examples consisting of single object types. Some examples use Delphi's default naming convention in an effort not to distract you from the topic at hand. The following table lists suggested naming conventions for Delphi's many different data types:

Category	Data Type	Prefix	Example
Integer	Integer	int	intDaysInDecade
	Shortint	sint	sintDaysInMonth
	Longint	long	longDaysInMillenium
	Byte	byte	byteDaysInQuarter
	Word	word	wordDaysInCentury
Real	Single	sngl	snglMaxValue
	Double	dbl	dblPrecise
	Extended	ext	extMorePrecise
	Comp	comp	compMinValue
	Real	real	realDollarVal
Boolean	Boolean	bool	boolDone
Char	Char	char	charKeyPressed
String	String	str	strLastName
Pointer	Pointer	ptr	ptrAnyType
PChar	PChar	pc	pcFirstName

Objects

Objects behave much like variables. Objects have scope and type, and require similar naming conventions to ease development of your Delphi applications. Objects are perhaps the greatest reason to implement a prefix-style naming convention. Consider looking at a list of alphabetized object names for which you weren't shown the type. Imagine the difficulty you would have trying to remember which names in the object list were your buttons. You'd literally have to memorize the contents of your entire application.

The following table shows suggested naming conventions for some of the many different component types available in Delphi:

Class	Prefix	Example
TObject	obj	objUniversal
TForm	frm	frmMain, frmEntry
TTable	tbl	tblCustomer
TQuery	qry	qrySalesTotal
TStoredProc	sp	spGenSummaryData
TDataSource	dSrc	dSrcCustomer
TDBGrid	dbg	dbgCustomer
TButton	btn	btnOk, btnCancel
TRadioButton	rBtn	rBtnAppend, rBtnOverwrite
TMainMenu	mmob	mmobMainMenu, mmobMyMenu
TMenuItem	menu	menuFileOpen, menuFileSave

Constants

Borland has included a mass of constant names built directly into Delphi. For complete information on all Delphi constants, see Appendix D, "Constants." Borland has also chosen a prefix naming convention for Delphi's constant names, as shown in the following table:

Constant Type	Prefix	Example
Border icons	bi	biSystemMenu
Border style	bs	biSizeable
Color	cl	clGreen
Cursor	cu	cuArrow
Font style	fs	fsBold
Form style	fs	fsMDIChild
Window state	ws	wsMaximized

Remember that the preceding constant-naming conventions are Delphi's own. User-defined constants may be created by the programmer and named using any convention desired.

Throughout this book, constant names appear in a special font—for example, `fsMDIChild`.

Properties

Delphi provides default property names without a strict naming convention. Default property names are used throughout this book. When naming user-defined properties, similar naming conventions as those for the default properties are used.

Throughout this book, property names appear in a special font—for example, `Color`.

Procedures

Procedures are named so that they can be read in an English-like manner when used in `if..then` statements. No additional naming or syntactical conventions are applied to procedure names. For example, if you have a procedure that tests whether a user is logged into the network, you might name it `userIsLoggedIn()`. An `if..then` statement using this procedure would look like the following:

```
if userIsLoggedIn() then
    doSomething();
```

Named this way, code can be read more easily, increasing programming efficiency and overall maintainability.

Examples Used in the Book

A number of examples discussed in this book grow as the book progresses, providing an approach geared more toward hands-on application development as opposed to writing limited mini-demos. This saves the time that would be required to set up a new example for each feature of Delphi being discussed. If you don't understand a particular example, find where that example has been introduced.

Why Delphi Is for You

If you're skeptical about Delphi or just want to see what features Delphi has that its competitors don't, do yourself a favor and read this book. Delphi sets a standard for Windows development environments by which all environments will be compared. No other environment available today provides the ease of use, power, speed, and flexibility available with Delphi. Delphi fills a long-awaited gap between the 3GL and 4GL world, combining the benefits of each into a powerful yet extremely productive package.

Delphi provides a host of features that cater specifically to component reuse. Many aspects of Delphi are customizable, allowing the environment to grow along with the skills of your development team. When your team creates useful new objects, these objects—application templates, form templates, and components—can be made available for future development efforts.

Borland is betting that Delphi, a development tool designed with the next generation of Windows development in mind, will prove to be the tool of choice for years to come.

Part I

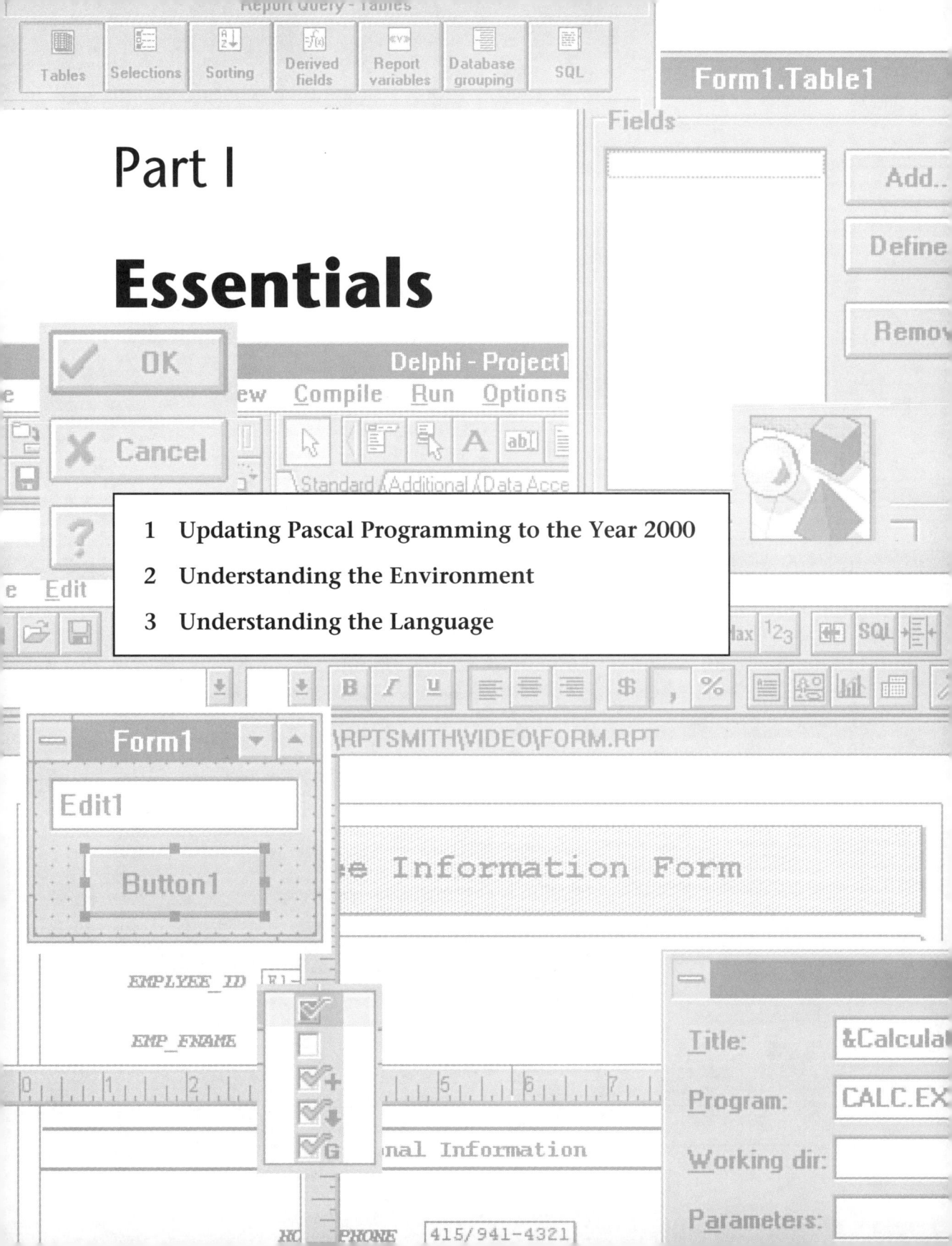

Essentials

1. Updating Pascal Programming to the Year 2000
2. Understanding the Environment
3. Understanding the Language

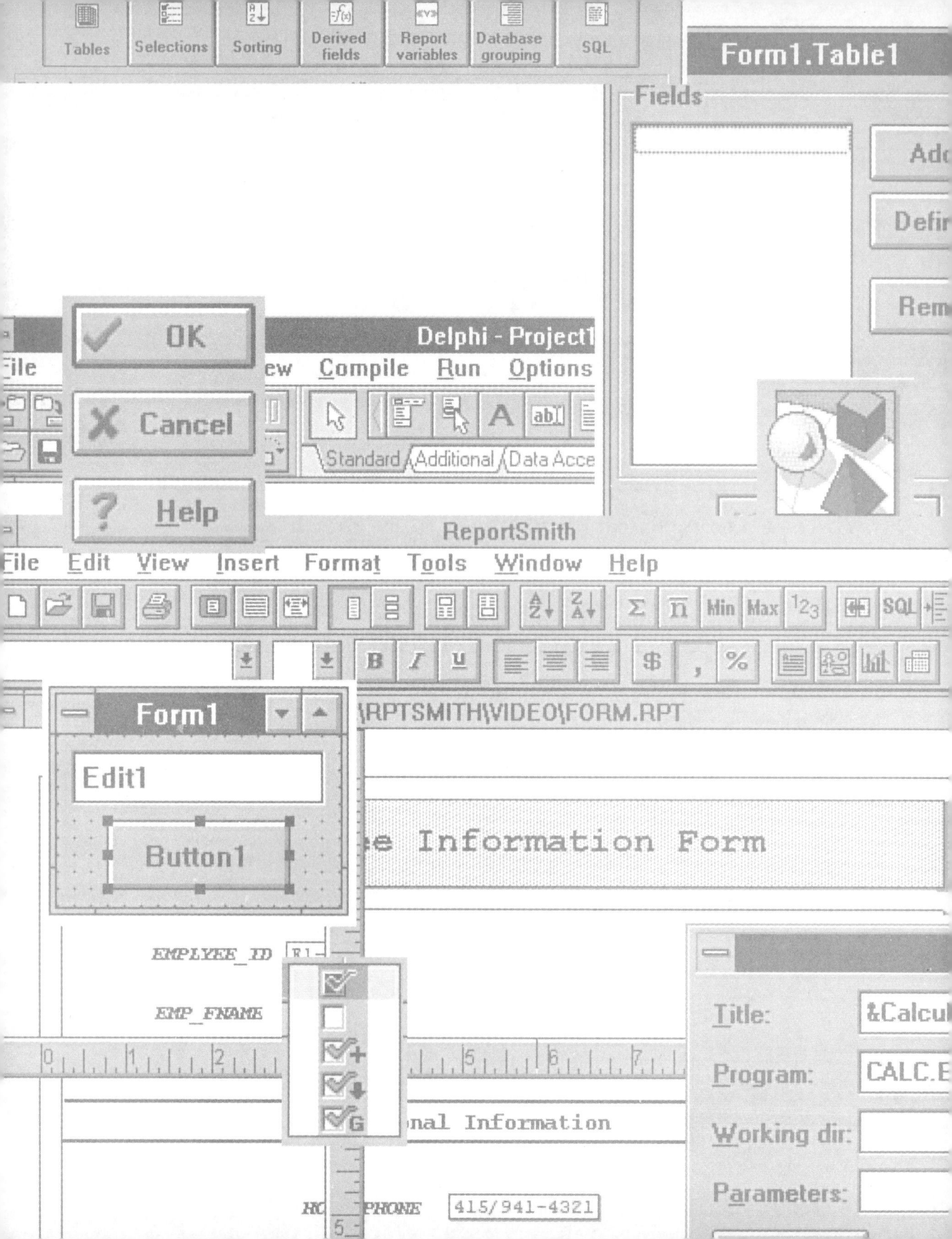

Chapter 1

Updating Pascal Programming to the Year 2000

Delphi is a development environment that uses many advanced features and concepts of the Microsoft Windows graphical user interface. Delphi allows you to provide extensive control of your application that's tightly linked to Windows itself. Since you're provided with this level of control, you should first be comfortable with how Windows works from a user's point of view. Once you become adept at how Windows operates, you'll be much better suited to effectively develop Windows applications.

This chapter discusses the basic concepts involved when developing Windows applications. Even if you're already familiar with Windows programming, this chapter is still beneficial since topics are discussed in Delphi's terms. In this chapter, you'll learn about:

- Event-driven programming concepts
- Objects: how they're created and used, and how they relate to events
- Object properties: what they are and what they do to objects

Visual programming environments use an assortment of terms and concepts to reference the many different "things" that make up an application. Luckily, many of these terms—including *object*, *property*, and *event*—have standard meanings across many visual programming environments, regardless of the underlying language. This chapter will help you sort through these terms and concepts with a discussion on how event-driven programming—not just Windows programming—has evolved to where it is today.

If you have experience with an event- or object-driven language or with a visual programming environment, this chapter will help you apply to Delphi what you've learned from working with these other programming environments. This chapter provides, in Delphi's terms, a fast-paced discussion on visual programming and concepts in a general sense. Your comfort with these concepts is vital to your understanding of how to work with Delphi.

Understanding Event-Driven Programming

Event-driven programming has been around well before the days of graphical user interfaces (GUIs) and is available to basically any programmer. Event-driven programming can be implemented in a number of ways. With the introduction of the mouse and the possibilities that it brings to the user interface, event-driven programming has just about become a requirement for users and developers alike.

Before event-driven programming environments, procedural top-down programming styles were considered state of the art. Top-down program design is very useful when building pieces of code that handle large amounts of processing. In fact, applications built using top-down programming techniques often result in elegant, maintainable code. Before event-driven programming, however, applications built using the top-down approach usually had overly complex menus and keystroke sequences that were linked tightly to application processing. Users of these applications were often required to have a more intimate relationship with the code than they may have desired.

Event-driven programming doesn't replace procedural programming, but complements it with a framework that provides better separation between user interface and business-specific processing. Delphi and other event-driven environments provide such frameworks that allow the programmer to concentrate more on the application-specific logic as opposed to worrying about how to handle and control user requests.

Real-life event-driven examples are everywhere you look. Consider the living room in your house. The following occurrences are actually events triggered (or driven) by other external events:

- Your TV turns on after you press the power button on your remote control.

- When the temperature dips below 70 degrees, the thermostat alerts the heating system to produce more heat. Here, the thermostat is triggering an event in response to another event. When the furnace receives this event from the thermostat, it instructs its system to burn more fuel to create heat.

- A friend calls. In response to the incoming signal, your telephone rings.

- You don't answer your phone. After counting four rings, your answering machine picks up the call and records a message.

- Your friend doesn't leave a message and instead decides to visit you. At the door, your friend rings the doorbell. In response to hearing this event, you rise from the couch to answer the door.

Events are real-time occurrences that result in one or more actions specific to the originating event. The key to event-driven programming is determining which events require special handling. Many events are triggered when working in Windows, but only those events that relate to your application need to be processed. Perhaps you don't care whether the user double-clicks a particular region of the screen, but you do want your application to do something whenever the user presses the Delete key. Event-driven environments, including Delphi, handle catching the keypress event and allow you to jump right into performing the logic you want to associate with the press of the Delete key.

Quite a few DOS-based development environments grew to offer event-driven interfaces and programming support without all the glitz of Windows itself. The resulting frameworks offered control over handling "Windows-like" events, such as window navigation, button presses, and other events not available before. In many cases, those who move from a DOS event-driven programming environment to Windows programming are better prepared than those who jump directly into Windows programming.

Delphi requires a fair amount of knowledge of event-driven programming concepts as well as Windows itself. Having event-driven programming experience is very helpful but not entirely necessary to begin programming in Delphi. You can learn event-driven programming, but what you can't learn through Delphi alone is how Windows behaves for the user. Delphi is actually a low-level language tightly linked to Windows' internal functions. Delphi packages and surfaces these functions into higher-level components, objects, and methods. Understanding standard Windows behavior will help you utilize Delphi's features in a standard Windows manner.

Understanding Object-"Based" Programming

The software industry goes through phases of promoting new technology and methodologies for program development. These promotions are often accompanied by a media blitz and the arrival of a new set of buzzwords. As a programmer, you're often challenged to sort through the hype and learn whether the new technology will make your complex tasks easier, especially if you're already attached to an environment that you feel is most productive. To move to another programming environment, the benefits would have to drastically outweigh the features of one's current environment. There's not much to be gained by moving to a different product that offers only incremental benefits. Delphi is the type of environment that once you arrive, you may never look back.

In the mid '80s, trade publications trumpeted artificial intelligence (AI) as the hot new wave to be involved with. The music shortly waned for one reason or another, perhaps in part from the software industry introducing the concept of object-oriented programming (OOP). Unlike the AI fad, OOP had a clearly defined set of objectives and has been capable of delivering what it has promised to software developers: tangible tools to facilitate reusable development. While some have argued that OOP is inefficient and incurs more overhead than traditional environments, compared to the alternatives, OOP is still highly attractive.

Object-oriented programming has been billed as superior to top-down programming in its capability to create reusable code and to better model real-world situations. The arrival of Microsoft Windows made moving to OOP languages a more rational decision, as OOP and GUI development compliment each other and have grown to the point where you don't have one without the other. Programming Windows applications using a popular non-OOP language such as C isn't a trivial task. Just to show a simple window with the message "Hello World!," you have to write excessive amounts of C code. The advocates of OOP argue that object-oriented languages make complex tasks easier by adding extensions to languages to encapsulate functions into "objects" necessary for Windows programming.

Software developers soon began paying more attention to object-oriented successors of current compilers, such as C++ from C. The late '80s witnessed the arrival of OOP language extensions to DOS-based Pascal and Modula-2 compilers. It was only a matter of time before various languages (such as

C++, Pascal, SmallTalk, Actor, and Modula-2), armed with OOP features, were rolled out for programming Windows applications.

Although these early OOP environments did have true object-oriented features, they lacked the capability to easily draw visual objects and manage the interaction with external events. Although much better organized, considerable code still had to be written to get objects to behave as desired. Basically, OOP was hard to learn and hard to use for the average programmer, thus hindering its acceptance.

Filling this void, Microsoft introduced Visual Basic, a visual programming environment based on a beginner's programming language, BASIC (Beginners All-purpose Symbolic Instruction Code). Although Visual Basic lacks pointers and formal OOP language extensions, it implements a number of essential OOP elements. Visual Basic has no doubt been the most popular development tool for Windows programming, clearly stating the importance of the visual side of application development.

With Borland's release of Delphi, you no longer have to decide between visual programming without true OOP features versus OOP without visual programming features. Delphi allows you to use its Object Pascal language in a visual programming environment with pure OOP extensions. This combination is revolutionary, bringing visual programming together with an extremely powerful object-oriented development framework.

Understanding Objects

Thanks to the software industry's marketing machine, the term *object* has lost some of its meaning since it was introduced with object-oriented programming. *Object* is thrown around more loosely now than in the past, with many products putting this newfound buzzword on their boxes, claiming that they're object-oriented when they're perhaps technically only event-driven or object-based.

Being object-based isn't bad—in fact, if you've worked in an object-based programming environment such as Paradox for Windows' ObjectPAL or Visual Basic, you should already be familiar with objects, events, and properties.

What Are Objects?

The definition of an object doesn't have to require using complex programming terminology. Put simply, an object is a thing that you can do things to. In Delphi, like other visual programming environments, objects are items such as buttons, labels, list boxes, fields, and so forth—basically, any item that has been created for use in the application. *Object* is a loosely defined term that shouldn't be taken to define anything too specific. Objects are those items that make up your applications, on whatever scale you want to talk about them. This book might call something on a form as simple as a box an object and later refer to the entire form as an object. A stand-alone accounts receivable module can also be considered an object as well. It's the context surrounding the terms that matters when *object* is used.

Considering the loose definition of *object*, you now might thank the marketers for providing you with what you really needed all along: a term to describe "a thing."

For purposes of clarity throughout this book, consider *object* to refer to an included component as it exists at runtime or after it has been placed on the form.

Creating Objects

Visual programming environments add a new dimension to creating applications by allowing objects to be drawn on-screen before program execution. Without visual programming, the "drawing" process requires writing actual source code to create and further customize these objects. Viewing the coded objects was possible only during program execution. Getting objects to look and behave as needed in this environment quickly becomes a tedious process that requires adjusting program code, then running the program again to finally see the actual results.

Thanks to visual development tools, you now can work with your objects visually, observing immediate on-screen results. The capability to see the object as it will appear at runtime eliminates a mass of manual steps required in a non-visual environment, regardless of whether it's object-oriented. Once an object is placed on a form in a visual programming environment, the object's attributes (size, position, properties, and so forth) are then recorded into code that supports the object as an executable unit at runtime.

Placing objects in Delphi involves a much more intimate relationship between objects and the actual source code. Objects are placed on your form, and code is automatically written for these objects in your source files. This code is eventually compiled, yielding much faster performance than visual environments, which interpret program information at runtime. This feature alone is the main draw for pulling programmers from other visual development environments.

Understanding Properties

Along with the capability to react to events, objects have *properties*. Properties include, among other things, items such as color, height, width, and position. Properties can affect the appearance of an object as well as other nonvisual elements of an object, such as the object's behavior.

To an object, properties are somewhat like local variables in a procedure. For a procedure, local variables belong to the procedure and are used by the procedure for its processing. Properties are directly related to objects in the same manner—they are attributes of objects that describe an object's details.

Changing a local variable within a procedure affects processing by the procedure. Similarly, changing a property of an object affects the object itself. Properties "belong" to objects, but where they differ from procedures is that object properties can be "seen" by external objects (including your code). "Seeing" object properties is the capability to inspect the contents of a specific object property externally. For example, an object of type Human has the following properties: Age, Name, Sex, and Address.

You can affect how a particular object behaves at runtime or design time by manipulating its properties. With the example object of type Human, you can change its address by setting its Address property. You can also query its other properties, such as Age, by inspecting the contents of these individual properties. Jumping ahead a bit and putting this example to Object Pascal code, the following statements can be used to manipulate the object named Human:

```
{Update Human's address property:}
Human.Address := '765 Park Ave'; {Set Human address}

{Set Human's 'CanDrink' property by inspecting Age:}
if Human.Age >= 21
    then Human.CanDrink := true;
    else Human.CanDrink := false;
```

Note

Text between curly braces in Delphi is treated as a comment and is ignored.

Understanding Events

The following sections will familiarize you with Delphi events—specifically, how events interact with objects. If you have experience with another visual or event-driven programming environment, this section helps you become familiar with Delphi's terms and how Delphi uses the "object" vocabulary when dealing with objects and events.

What Is an Event?

Windows applications use event-driven methods to manage interaction between the program and the user. The environment includes user actions and actions of the Windows operating environment itself. Most of the code you'll write in Delphi will be triggered from events generated by the user and by the system. In Delphi, a procedure that's triggered by an event is referred to as an *event handler*.

To understand the dynamics of event-driven programming in Delphi, consider a typical company and its employees. Each employee has a title and a job description defining his or her skills, responsibilities, and role in the company's daily activities. The company interacts with the outside world though a series of events, such as phone calls, mail, Telexes, faxes, electronic bulletin boards, travels, meetings, and so on. Each event is handled by the appropriate employee(s). For example, on the event of Bob's phone ringing, Bob will respond by answering it. Bob doesn't need to answer anyone else's phone, only his. Likewise, other employees don't answer Bob's phone. In this example, Bob is the *event handler* of the ringing event for the phone.

Just like the example company's events, Delphi responds to mouse, keyboard, and system events by invoking the appropriate pieces of logic, or *procedures*. If a procedure isn't associated for a given event, the event is ignored.

To give you a general idea about the life cycle of an event in Delphi, consider the event generated by clicking a button object:

1. The event is generated by the user clicking a button named btnOk.

2. The btnOk object recognizes the action as an event that must be handled (button type objects deal with clicks).

3. Delphi looks for a procedure name matching the name of the object being acted on (btnOk) plus the name of the event (Click). In this example, Delphi would then execute the btnOkClick() procedure.

This logic is encapsulated using the case statement in the following code listing:

```
Case NewEvent Of
    {click mouse button on the btnOk button}
    Case Click:
        btnOkClick();
```

```
        {use Tab key to make Button1 button currently selected component}
        Case Enter:
            btnOkEnter();

        {use Tab key to deselect Button1 button}
        Case Exit:
            Button1Exit();

        Else:
            IgnoreEvent();
End;
```

Event-driven programming is typified by the following code example that uses `Repeat..Until` and `Case` statements:

```
Repeat
    GetNextEvent(NewEvent);
    Case NewEvent OF
        Event1:
            HandleEvent1();

        Event2:
            HandleEvent2();

        Event3:
            HandleEvent3();

        EndApplication:
          Begin
            HandleExit();
            Break;
          End;

        Else:
            IgnoreEvent();
    End;
Until False;
```

The preceding code shows an event-driven application using a loop to obtain events. After the event is obtained, the `Case` statement checks to see whether the event is in the list of events that the application handles. If the event isn't explicitly in the list, it's ignored. The procedures `HandleEvent1`, `HandleEvent2`, and so on are called *event handlers*.

Most of the code you'll write for your Delphi applications will be procedures for handling events. Delphi makes it unnecessary to explicitly code loops for handling events (for example, the `Repeat..Until` block). Delphi also takes care of writing the shell for event-handling procedures, also known as an *event-driven framework*.

Objects and Events

You now know that events are triggered by user- and system-invoked actions. So what does this do for you? In Delphi, you can easily link an event to code by using an *event handler*, which is simply a piece of code you can use to control the user interface (UI) as well as link to your application, or application-specific code. Event handlers are the doorways that allow you to link your code to events generated from within your application.

All objects generally respond to events. Although many basic objects, such as text labels, respond to only a few events, you still have the option of deciding among the following choices:

- *Ignore the event.* Allow the object's default behavior.

- *Trap the event.* Tie into the event handler and tailor, modify, or prevent default behavior.

Modifying default object behavior can be nothing more than than changing the cursor style when the cursor is over a particular object. Modifying behavior can also involve presenting a message to the user when pressing a button and then invoking a major accounting function.

These options aren't made clear to you by any visual development environment. It's up to you to have a clear understanding as to what you (or your users) want the application to do and when. Plan your applications before you begin drawing forms so that you have an idea how many forms your application will have as well as a general idea where processes will be invoked.

From Here...

Becoming very familiar with the Delphi development environment is strongly suggested. The following chapters will help you gain the familiarity:

- Chapter 2, "Understanding the Environment," discusses all the major development tools and options within Delphi.

- For in-depth coverage of Delphi's programming environment, see Chapter 3, "Understanding the Language," which covers the extensions to Pascal that were added with Delphi to create Object Pascal.

- If you're an absolute Delphi expert and need to jump right in, move on to the chapters in Part II, "Components."

Chapter 2
Understanding the Environment

Development environments dictate, to a certain degree, how well you'll be able to produce results. Delphi's environment has been designed with this in mind, from the ground up, giving you a flexible and modern set of tools that you can use to quickly craft applications.

This chapter introduces Delphi's application development environment. Discussed are all of Delphi's major development windows and the purpose that each window serves. Also covered are higher level topics, such as how to use Delphi's environment effectively.

After reading this chapter, you should be comfortable with moving through Delphi's windows, dialog boxes, menus, and other items that at first may appear somewhat confusing. Simple programming examples are presented throughout the chapter to get you quickly familiar with how Windows programs are written in the Delphi environment.

Tip
This is a good chapter to go through while you have Delphi running. A picture is worth a thousand words, but real-time interaction is worth a bit more.

This chapter covers the following topics:

- The key windows in the Delphi environment and the purpose of each
- The fundamentals of working within the Delphi environment
- How to use the Object Inspector to set object properties
- How to edit event-handling procedures
- How Delphi projects are organized and structured
- How to compile and run your Delphi programs

Getting to Know the Delphi Environment

The Delphi development environment, shown slightly adjusted in figure 2.1, consists of four windows managed as a multiwindow single document interface (SDI) application. The main Delphi window controls multiple related windows (Object Inspector, Form window, and Code Editor window). When the main Delphi window is minimized or closed, all the related windows will be told to perform the same action. Delphi's window handling follows the SDI standard.

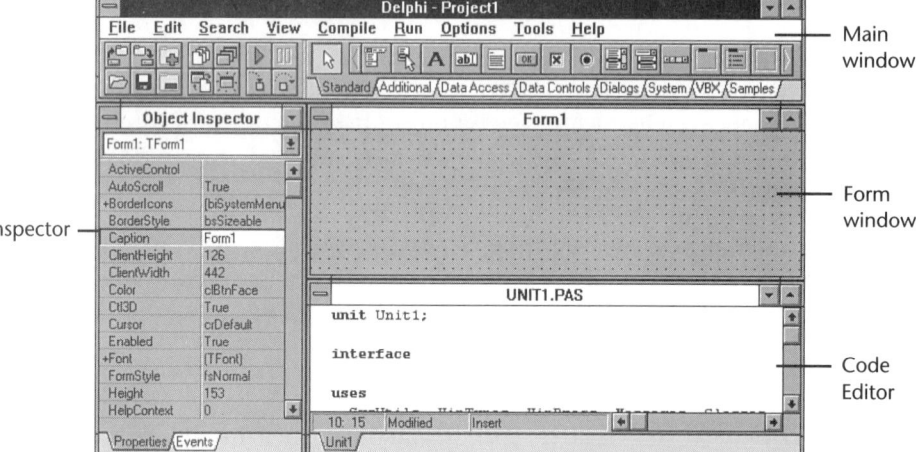

Fig. 2.1
After first loading Delphi, you may want to change the positioning of the three windows to suit your liking.

Multiple document interface (MDI) applications, such as Microsoft Word, consist of a "parent" window, which contains one or more "child" windows. Within the MDI parent window, the child windows are confined to the region of the parent and can't extend beyond the boundaries of the parent window.

Handling single document interface windows is different. SDI applications don't have child windows like those in MDI applications. Instead, SDI applications consist of a set of related or "relative" windows. There's still a window that's designated as the main window, but this window doesn't need to contain any other windows. In fact, the main window can simply consist of a lone menu bar or, in Delphi's case, a menu and a set of tool buttons. For a detailed discussion on the many aspects of MDI and SDI applications and how to create your own using Delphi, refer to Chapter 9, "Creating Applications."

Delphi's SDI window handling may appear somewhat odd at first, with development tools and forms floating all over the place, but it does allow plenty of customizable options. One MDI feature that's missed is the Window menu, which provides quick access to any active window in an application. Delphi's SDI alternative is its Window List dialog, available from the View menu's Window List command or by simply pressing Alt+0.

After an initial contact with Delphi and with some adjustments, you'll soon find yourself moving through the environment quite comfortably.

Delphi consists of four major windows that open when you initially load Delphi:

- *Main window.* The main window is the control center for Delphi development. The main Delphi window contains three distinct elements, which offer unique functionality worth discussing in detail. Contained in the main window are the menu bar, the SpeedBar, and the Component palette.

- *Object Inspector window.* The default location for the Object Inspector window is at the lower left side of Delphi workspace (refer to fig. 2.1). The Object Inspector is a multipage window containing Properties and Events tabbed pages. The Properties page displays the properties available for the currently selected object(s) in the Form window. The Events tab page displays the events that the currently selected object(s) (in the Form window) can respond to.

- *Form window.* This window's title defaults to "Form1" for new projects. The Form window is located on the right side of the workspace above the Code Editor shown in figure 2.1.

    The Form window contains what the user will see and interface with at runtime. When a Delphi application is executed, the Form window and its visual objects become the focal point of the application, or the resulting window presented to the user. An application can consist of many forms, each presented at an appropriate time as designed by the application programmer. All Delphi applications must have at least one form object.

- *Code Editor window.* This window allows you to edit Object Pascal code for your program. In figure 2.1, the window titled UNIT1.PAS is the Code Editor window and shows the window displaying code.

Tip
After loading Delphi, minimize all other non-Delphi windows to move all other applications out of the way, giving you maximum room to work.

Tip
In this book, think of a *form* as a window in development. Once a form is completed, it becomes a Windows window, behaving like any other.

The Code Editor window is a multipage window, allowing you to move between all source files in your project by clicking the appropriate tab. By default, the window contains a single tab for the main unit, UNIT1.PAS. If your project contains multiple "units," the Code Editor will have multiple pages to provide access to the code for these units. Also, if you open the View menu and choose Project Source, a new Code Editor page will be created with source code specific to your overall project. Figure 2.2 shows the Code Editor with multiple pages.

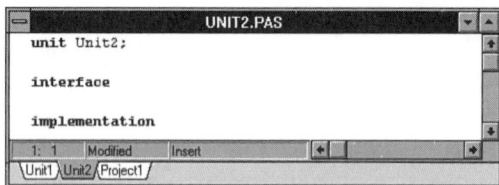

Fig. 2.2
The multipage Code Editor allows you to select and edit any source code file that's part of your project.

Using the Main Window

Delphi's development control functions are accessed by using the main window, shown in figure 2.3.

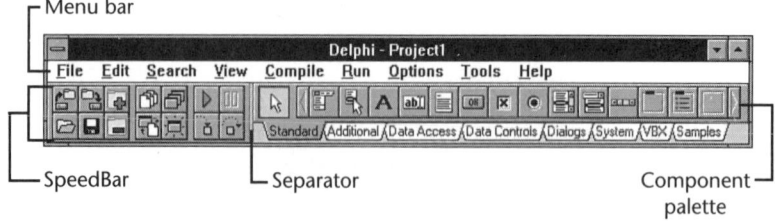

Fig. 2.3
The main Delphi window contains the menu bar, SpeedBar, and Component palette.

Delphi's main window consists of three elements:

- *The menu bar.* The menu bar on the main Delphi window provides menu control for all windows throughout the environment. The menus let you manage the design of your application, manage the Delphi interface windows, configure the Delphi environment, and obtain on-line help, among other things.

- *The SpeedBar.* The SpeedBar appears to the left of the main window separator. The SpeedBar provides quick access to common operations including opening a file, saving a file, cutting and pasting text, selecting and positioning Delphi windows, executing a Delphi program, debugging, and opening and selecting forms and units.

- *The Component palette.* The Component palette, located to the right of the main window separator, allows you to select the necessary tools for your application and place them on your form.

The Menu Bar

Delphi's menu bar is *static*, meaning that it remains the same when moving from window to window within Delphi. The main menu bar allows you to control all aspects of Delphi from a single point, not requiring individual menus for each window in Delphi (this is the SDI). Delphi's menu bar can also be customized somewhat. Delphi allows you to add your own menu choices under the main Tools menu choice. You might want to add one of your frequently used programs—for example, the Windows calculator—to the Tools menu.

The following example shows you how to add an item to the Tools menu:

1. Open the Options menu and choose Tools. The Tool Options dialog appears (see fig. 2.4).

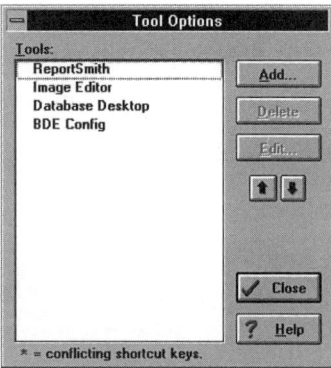

Fig. 2.4
The Tool Options dialog allows you to customize Delphi's Tools menu.

Tip
To set an accelerator key for a menu choice, place an ampersand character (&) before the accelerator character. See Chapter 5, "Using Non-Visual Components," for more information on menu accelerator keys.

2. Clicking the Add button presents the Tool Properties dialog. Figure 2.5 shows this dialog with the Title and Program text boxes filled in with the information for the Windows calculator program (CALC.EXE).

3. Click OK in the Tool Properties dialog to return to the Tool Options dialog, which now shows `Calculator` in the Tools list. Click Close to add the Calculator to the menu.

Fig. 2.5
With the Tool Properties dialog, you can configure individual menu items for the Tools menu.

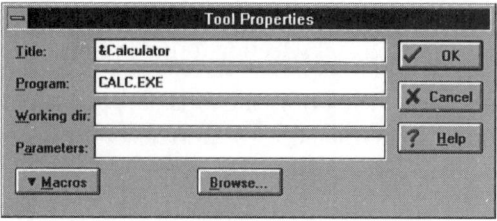

The SpeedBar

The SpeedBar, located to the left of the Component palette, is simply a set of buttons that provide mouse-click access to menu choices. You can also customize the SpeedBar to your liking so that it contains (or doesn't contain) the buttons you want to use. To configure Delphi's SpeedBar, follow these steps:

1. Right-click the SpeedBar. A popup menu appears.

> **Note**
>
> If Delphi's main menu is active (any menu choices are selected), right-clicking won't work. To remove focus from the menu, click an inert region of the SpeedBar (such as a gap between the buttons).

2. Choose the Configure command. The SpeedBar Editor dialog appears (see fig. 2.6).

Fig. 2.6
The SpeedBar Editor dialog allows you to arrange buttons on the SpeedBar to your exact liking.

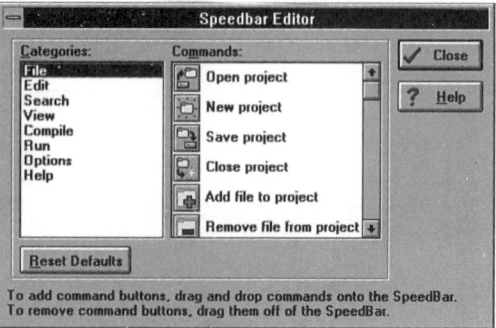

The SpeedBar's command buttons aren't active when the SpeedBar Editor dialog is active. The SpeedBar is now in a state that allows you to actually move its command buttons by dragging and dropping within the SpeedBar.

3. You can add new command buttons to the SpeedBar by dragging from the buttons shown in the SpeedBar Editor dialog and dropping them on the SpeedBar.

   To remove SpeedBar buttons, drag an existing button off the SpeedBar while the SpeedBar Editor dialog is open. Releasing the mouse after the button icon disappears removes the button from the SpeedBar. Existing SpeedBar buttons can also be moved around in this fashion.

   You can reset the SpeedBar to its factory defaults by clicking the Reset Defaults button in the SpeedBar Editor dialog.

The Component Palette

The Component palette is simply a catalog of visual and application objects that you can include in your forms and applications. Delphi arranges its components into eight groups: Standard, Additional, Data Access, Data Controls, Dialogs, System, VBX, and Samples. Each group is presented on a separate tabbed page of the Component palette.

As mentioned in Chapter 1, Delphi is object-oriented. The "meat" of Delphi's object-oriented features lies in its set of components, which are the means by which Delphi allows you to utilize many standard Windows features. Delphi presents these features, packaged as objects, in the form of components. To place a component on your form, you simply drag and drop a component off the Component palette. Once dropped, the component becomes a true object, ready for whatever instruction it was designed to handle.

The Component palette allows you to activate a set of components by clicking the desired page tab. Each page displays a different collection of component icons. Following are the pages of the Component palette and their intended use:

- *Standard.* The Standard page contains the most frequently used Windows-based components, those most common in all Windows programs. Standard page components usually have a one-to-one correspondence to a standard Windows object, thus the name *Standard* page.

- *Additional.* The Additional page contains a slightly more unique set of components that you may not have seen when working with basic Windows applications. A number of components on this page are extremely useful, such as the `MaskEdit` component, which gives you better control over what a user can enter into a field than the standard Edit component. There also are a variety of graphic-oriented visual objects, such as the `Shape` and `Image` components.

Tip
If you place the mouse pointer over individual buttons on the SpeedBar and the Component palette, a hint appears below the pointer to tell you what that button is for.

- *Data Access*. This page provides components that let you connect to and query your data. Chapter 6, "Using Data-Bound Components," focuses on using data-related components.

- *Data Controls*. This page is where the user interface side of data-related components is found. There are a number of components contained that allow you to present data to the user in any Windows way you like. See Chapter 6, "Using Data-Bound Components," for an entire chapter on the components on the Data Access and Data Controls component pages.

- *Dialogs*. On this page you can find a number of utility dialogs for common tasks, such as opening files, setting up the printer, searching text, and so forth.

- *System*. The System page contains visual and non-visual components. On this page is a timer component, drive and file access components, and DDE and OLE components.

- *VBX*. Visual Basic eXtensions (VBXs) are components that follow a format defined by Microsoft for use in Visual Basic. The VBX format has become standard and is supported in a number of development environments, including Delphi. Any VBX that has been imported into Delphi using the Install Components command on the Options menu is available on the VBX page.

- *Samples*. This page contains an assortment of components that are provided primarily to show that external components (VBXs) can be added to the Component palette.

Working with the Component Palette

The Component palette is an extendible tool that you use to bring objects onto your forms. You also can customize the Component palette by adjusting the arrangement of components, adding new components, or deleting existing components.

Since it's customizable, the Component palette can become quite busy and crowded. To give the Component palette maximum area, hide the SpeedBar by using the View menu's Speedbar option.

You also may reduce or expand the area that the Component palette occupies on the main window without entirely doing away with the SpeedBar. To change the size of the Component palette, click and move the separator bar between the SpeedBar and the palette. Figure 2.7 shows a Component palette that has been collapsed a bit. You might want to do this if you want to make more SpeedBar buttons available.

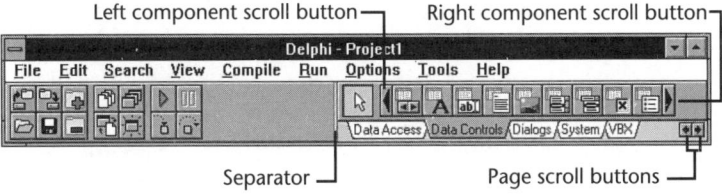

Fig. 2.7
A collapsed palette has additional navigation arrows at its lower right for navigating pages that don't fit on-screen.

Typically, you might actually want to lean toward giving the SpeedBar more room, because when more components exist on a page than can be shown with the current palette's size, left and right component scroll buttons become available (refer to fig. 2.7). Also, page scroll buttons also become available at the lower right of the palette to allow you to scroll to hidden pages of the palette.

Getting Component-Specific Help

Delphi's help system allows you to get specific help on individual components. Delphi's help system contains a significant amount of information that's literally at your fingertips. In many ways, accessing information this way is much more efficient than referring to the appropriate manual.

To retrieve help on a particular component, select the component of interest on the palette and press the F1 key. Help specific to that component's use appears on-screen.

Rearranging the Component Palette

You may feel that the Component palette isn't organized entirely to your liking. Would you prefer having the components arranged in a slightly different manner? If so, follow these steps:

1. Open the Options menu and choose Environment. The Environment Options dialog appears.

2. Select the Palette tab at the bottom of the dialog to see the Palette page (see fig. 2.8).

3. As you move down the Pages list on the left, the Components list on the right shows the available components on that page. In this dialog, you can perform the following functions:

Tip
To go right to the Palette page of the Environment Options dialog, right-click the Component palette and choose Configure from the popup menu.

36 Chapter 2—Understanding the Environment

Fig. 2.8
The Palette page of the Environment Options dialog allows you to rearrange components and tabs in the Component palette.

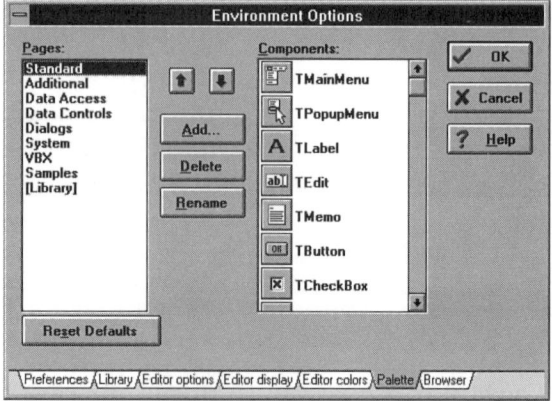

- *Rearrange page or component order.* Click the Pages or Components item to rearrange. Change the visual order of the item by clicking the up- and down-arrow buttons.

- *Add new pages to the Component palette.* Select any page from the list of pages on the left, click the Add button, and then enter the new page name. A new blank page is added to the Pages list. Move components to this page as you want.

> **Note**
>
> You can't add components on the Palette page of the Environment Options dialog. (The following section, "Adding Components to the Palette," explains how to add new components to the palette.) But you can move components from one page to the other.

- *Move components from one page to another.* In the Environment Options dialog, drag and drop the component from the Components list over to the page that you want the component moved in the Pages list.

- *Delete pages or components.* From the appropriate list, select the page or component you want to delete and then click Delete.

> **Note**
>
> To delete entire pages from the Component palette, you must first empty the page of all its components.

Adding Components to the Palette

You can add additional components, such as third-party VBXs, to the Component palette by using the Install Components dialog (see fig. 2.9). To open this dialog, open the Options menu and choose Install Components. In the Install Components dialog, the Installed Units list on the left shows the component units that are already installed in the system. (Notice that this dialog uses the term *units*—a low-level term Delphi uses to describe objects.)

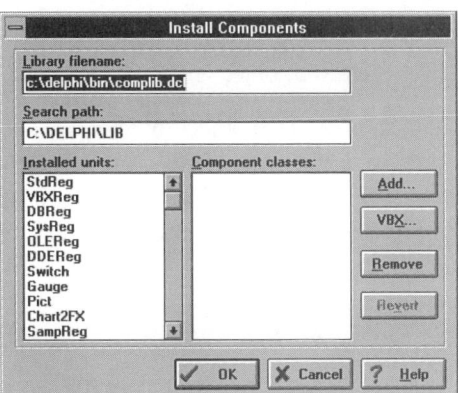

Fig. 2.9
The Install Components dialog allows you to add new components to the Component palette.

> **Caution**
>
> When installing a new component, Delphi must first close any open projects before it can continue with the addition of a new component to the palette. This is necessary since components are compiled before they're inserted into the palette.

Up until now, this chapter has mentioned only a single Component palette. You can have many different palettes, each stored in a separate file. You can create separate Component palettes and load them as you see fit by using the Options menu's Open Library command. Notice the Library Filename text box in the Install Components dialog shown in figure 2.9. This contains the actual library file name of the default palette that ships with Delphi. You can create your own Component palettes and distribute the .DCL files to other members of your group.

The Install Components dialog allows you to specify the actual library file that you want components added to. This is done by specifying the file name and path of the desired component library file.

Using the Object Inspector Window

The Object Inspector is the focal point for working with objects (placed components). The Object Inspector consists of the following elements:

- A combo box allowing selection of the current object

- A Properties page containing fields for the applicable property values of the current (or selected) object(s)

- An Events page containing fields to link program code to built-in events for the current (or selected) object(s)

You can change the current selected object by selecting another object from the combo box at the top of the Object Inspector. You can also change the current object by selecting the desired object in the Form window itself. Depending on your preferences, you may find either method more efficient than the other. Regardless of how objects are selected, you'll see that the Object Inspector contents update with new information each time a new object is selected.

Tip
The list of properties and events on either page of the Object Inspector appears in alphabetical order.

Figure 2.10 shows the Object Inspector displaying the properties of the object named Memo1. Figure 2.11 shows the Object Inspector displaying the Events page for the same memo object. The Events page is your doorway to attaching code to the support events of your objects.

Fig. 2.10
Once an object is selected, the contents of the Object Inspector reflect its properties and events.

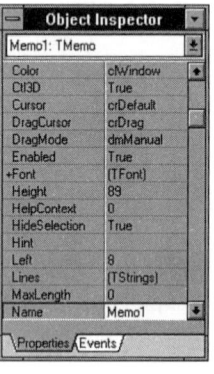

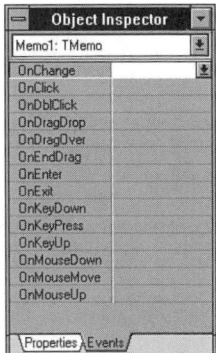

Fig. 2.11
The Events page of the Object Inspector provides access to program code.

Inspecting Properties

A set of properties exists for all components available in Delphi. The form itself also has a set of properties that can change at design or runtime. By looking at the Object Inspector's Properties page, you can inspect an object's predefined properties and default values (refer to fig. 2.10), including the form itself. To examine properties of a form, select the form by using the combo box at the top of the Object Inspector.

The left column of the Properties page contains the names of the predefined properties of the current object, such as Caption and Font for a form or button object. When a new object is selected on a form, the following occurs:

- The Object Inspector is updated to show only the relevant properties of the selected object(s).

- For each property shown in the Object Inspector, current values are automatically updated in the fields of the right column.

You can think of forms and components as customizable entities with factory presets. Default properties are stored with a component as it exists in the Component palette. Once a component is placed on a form, its properties can be changed to suit your particular needs, either at design time or runtime.

Changing a property during *design* time is simply a manual process that involves selecting the desired object, working with the Properties page in the Object Inspector, and changing the desired property value.

Delphi has an object name property, called simply Name, for every object. When a component is placed on a form, Delphi automatically assigns it a unique name (this is even true for "form" objects). The default object name is based on the order that the object was created or placed on the form. For example, placing an `Edit` component on a form results in a name of `Edit1`. Placing a second `Edit` component results in the name of `Edit2`, and so on. It's important to change default object names to better reflect the role of the object in your applications. A button component that sends output to the printer, for example, would be better named `btnPrint` than `Button1`. The name of an object is referenced considerably during program development; giving components meaningful names will save you from much confusion.

Changing properties during *runtime* involves Object Pascal programming statements that assign new property values or modify existing properties while under program control. When the value of a property is changed at runtime, the new property is made active immediately. Changing property values of visual objects at runtime can provide effects such as blinking text, moving percentage bars, spinning wheels, and bouncing balls. For data-bound components, properties are used to link visual data objects to underlying data sources.

Throughout parts II and III of this book are examples of how and why properties can be changed at runtime. Significant functionality can often be implemented by simple property manipulation at runtime, requiring only a single line of code.

Inspecting Events

A default set of events are defined for each component in the Component palette as well as for forms themselves. The response of an object to an event is defined by a specific procedure. For example, if you pressed the A key while an `Edit` object had focus, that object would receive three events: `OnKeyDown`, `OnKeyPress`, and `OnKeyUp`. The default behavior of all these events is to simply process the key following standard Windows guidelines. When you press the letter A, an `Edit` object's default behavior is to add A to the contents of its `Edit` region (or replace selected text according to Windows standards).

Perhaps you wanted to actually trap for the letter A in this `Edit` object and do something, such as beep the user. First, you must select the `Edit` object you want to define this behavior for; then bring up the Events page of the Object Inspector. Double-clicking the `OnKeyPress` event brings up a specific block of event-handler code. Delphi derives the name of the event-handling procedure by combining the name of the object with the name of the event being handled (minus the `On` prefix characters). Delphi uses the following general convention when it creates default event handlers:

```
procedure objectNameEventName(<list of parameters>)
```

where

> *objectName* is the name of the object as set in the Name property
>
> *EventName* is the name of the event from the Object Inspector
>
> *<list of parameters>* is a list of parameters specific to the event named in *EventName*

This way, the functionality of a form or an object is defined by the associated event-handling procedure, based on the object's name and the event being triggered.

When Delphi creates event-handling procedures, it leaves out the first two characters (On) when naming the event-handling procedure. For example, double-clicking an OnKeyPress event in the Object Inspector for the Edit1 object causes the editor to become active with the Edit1KeyPress event-handling procedure. Figure 2.12 shows the Code Editor window maximized with the Edit1KeyPress event handler waiting for you to write programming statements after you've double-clicked the OnKeyPress field in the Object Inspector.

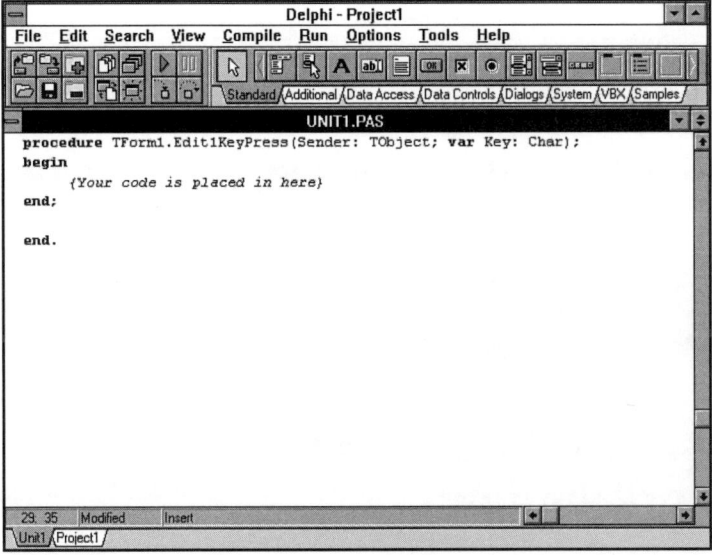

Fig. 2.12
Event-handling procedure names consist of the object name plus the event name.

Notice in figure 2.12 that the TForm1.Edit1KeyPress() procedure seems to be the only piece of code you're dealing with right now. This isn't the case. Notice that the vertical scroll bar in figure 2.12 is more than three-quarters down, showing that there's more code above your procedure. Scrolling up several lines shows additional programming statements (see fig. 2.13). When you move to the Code Editor by double-clicking an event name, Delphi merely positions you at the appropriate location in your source file. When a new event-handling procedure is created by double-clicking a new event, Delphi appends the new code to the end of form's corresponding unit source file.

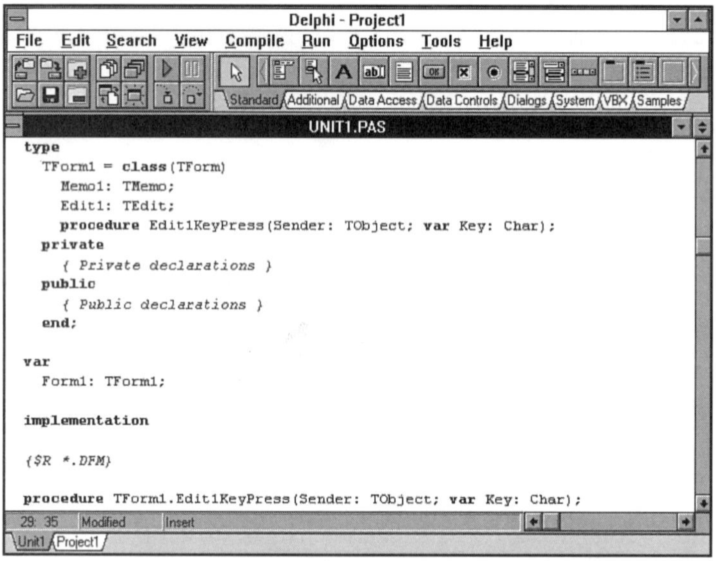

Fig. 2.13
For each form in Delphi, a single source file exists to contain the event-handling procedures.

> **Note**
>
> Don't worry about inadvertently creating unused or unwanted event-handling procedures. When Delphi compiles your program, it will clean up any empty event-handling procedures. This is known as *dead code elimination*.

Using the Form and Code Editor Windows

The Form and Code Editor windows are linked closely with each other. As you learned earlier, the term *unit* is Delphi's name of its actual source code files (.PAS files). Recall that the default title of the Code Editor window is UNIT1.PAS. With this window title, you see Delphi actually referring to a form's source code file as a unit.

The Form window is shown above the Code Editor earlier in this chapter in figure 2.1. The Form window is where all visual and non-visual component objects are placed for use in your application.

When a Code Editor window is active (either when you're working with event-handling procedures or writing free-form code), you have access to a rather powerful set of editing features. The editor is a descendant of Brief, an editor popular among many programmers.

Adding Additional Forms to Your Application

Your Delphi application can contain many different forms, with each providing a specific purpose in your application. For each form that does exist in your application, a corresponding unit file must also exist. You can see this by opening the File menu, choosing New Form, and examining the Code Editor window. After adding a new form to your application, a new unit is also created and made available through the Code Editor. This is exactly how figure 2.2 was produced.

After adding additional forms to your application, you'll soon realize the need for tools in which these forms can be managed. Choosing the View menu's Forms command invokes the View Form dialog (see fig. 2.14).

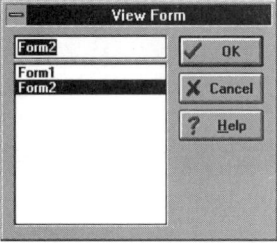

Fig. 2.14
The View Form dialog lets you bring up any form that you want to work with in your application.

Adding Additional Units to Your Application

Contrary to forms, you can have a unit in your application without a corresponding form file. There are a few reasons why you might want to do this:

- To store your application-wide code as opposed to event-handling code specific to a particular form

- To utilize a set of utility procedures that can be used in any application

To add a new unit to your application, open the File menu and choose New Unit. This creates a stand-alone new unit file in your application that's not linked to a form. You now have access to a source file where you can place code that's not specific to any one form and can be shared by all.

After you add new forms to your application, it's good practice to use the File menu's Save File As command and give your form and unit files more meaningful names. Form files are saved with the same root names as your unit .PAS files but have .DFM extensions.

Introducing the Project Manager Window

The Project Manager window, shown in figure 2.15, is a window that allows you to manage your application's form and unit files. By using the Project Manager, you have access to many of the menu and SpeedBar functions to manipulate form and unit files in a single location. See the following sections for more information on the role that the project plays in your application.

Fig. 2.15
The Project Manager allows you to manage your entire application's form and unit files.

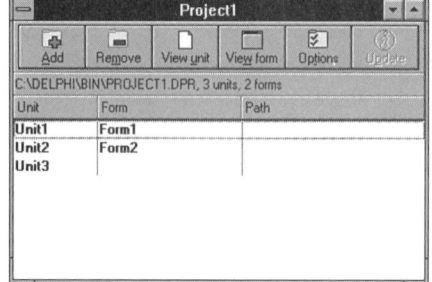

Using the Environment to Build an Application

For your first Delphi application, you'll create a form that contains a button object and an edit object. When you click the button object, the message Hello World will appear in the edit object.

When Delphi is first loaded, it creates a blank project file. You can also create a blank project by opening the File menu and choosing New Project. Creating a new project results in a form window named Form1 (refer to fig. 2.1), a Code Editor window showing UNIT1.PAS, and a project file named PROJECT1.DPR.

As mentioned earlier, the form is where you define the look and feel of your application. The form is also where you place the necessary components needed to implement the functions your application must perform.

From here, building a Delphi application involves the following basic steps:

1. Build the visual interface for your application by selecting the desired components from the Component palette and placing them on your form. If your application consists of six buttons, for example, constructing the visual interface would involve placing, sizing, and aligning six button components on a form.

2. By using the Object Inspector, set the properties of the form and controls to influence their visual appearance and behavior. You might, for example, alter the Caption property of each button to better reflect the function it will perform in your application. A button that causes the application to terminate would much better be labeled Exit than Button6.

3. Attach the necessary Object Pascal code to the components to handle specific mouse, keyboard, system events, and other events.

Placing Objects

You can place an object on a form in several ways. Following are the three most common ways of visually placing an object on a form:

- *Select and click.* Select the desired component on the Component palette by clicking it once. Move to where you want the object placed—in this example, in the upper left corner of the region on the form—and click again.

- *Select, click, and draw.* Using the previous select-and-click technique for placing components results in an object of default size and shape. You may want to place objects using different dimensions than the default size of a particular object. To place a button on a form wider than the default button width, for example, select the Button component from the palette, and then click the form and hold the mouse down. Dragging the mouse shows you a frame that indicates the size and position of the object that will be dropped once you release the left mouse button.

- *Double-click.* Double-clicking a component on the palette causes that component to be placed in the center of the form in the default size.

To begin placing components needed in the first example application, select the `Edit` component from the Standard page on the Component palette and drop it on your form. Then adjust its position and other properties however you see fit.

You can move an object by clicking and dragging it to the new location and releasing the mouse button. You can resize objects by dragging one of the small black sizing blocks (called *handles*) on the side or corners of the object until the object is the size you want.

Add a standard button from the Standard page of the palette. Figure 2.16 shows a form after a button and an edit object are placed.

Fig. 2.16
You can quickly prototype screens using the Form window and Object Inspector.

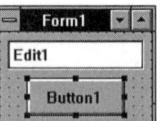

After designing the form shown in figure 2.16, you'll have completed the first basic—but very important—step in developing a real Delphi application. Bring the unit to the front by using the View menu's Toggle Form/Unit command (or by clicking the Toggle Form/Unit SpeedBar button). By looking at the code, you can find quite a few complex lines of code that Delphi has already written for you. Selecting the Run menu's Run command (or by clicking the Run SpeedBar button) will compile and run your application. Since the form doesn't yet contain any additional user-interface or application specific code, the result may be somewhat boring (it doesn't do anything).

Selecting Objects

Each time an object is placed on a form, the new object becomes the current object in the Object Inspector. When designing forms, you can select objects in Delphi in two ways:

- Select the desired object using the combo box at the top of the Object Inspector window.

- Move the mouse to the desired object on the form window and click once.

Also, you may want to select multiple objects that you want to move, align, or even set common properties for. You can select multiple objects in two ways:

- Point at a bare area on the form and draw a box through or around all the objects you want to select.
- Hold the Shift key down and click all objects you want to select.

Once you select multiple objects, you can move them, keeping their relative distances from each other. Perhaps the best aspect of selecting multiple components is that as more objects are selected of different types, only the common properties and events will be shown in the Object Inspector. When you modify a common property for multiple selected objects, all objects will take on the new property once it has been set.

Setting Properties with the Object Inspector

Delphi assigns default names to the properties of the controls you draw. While most of these default values are appropriate, you need to change a few properties for the example. These properties include the button object's Name and Caption properties, the edit object's Caption property, and the Text property of the edit object. Delphi assigns default control names, based on the order you place components on the form. The edit object on the example form is named Edit1 and the button component is named Button1. If you add a second edit object, Delphi will assign Edit2 as the Name property of that edit object by default. Similarly, if you place a second button component, its default Name property will be Button2.

Every component in Delphi has a Name property. As you'll see in later Object Pascal code samples, the Name property plays a vital role in referencing components within your Object Pascal source code. You can change the Name property to better label the button's function for the developer. This property is important when developing, as it will be used in selection lists and as a prefix for event handlers. To change the Name property of the button object in the example, make sure that the Button1 object you placed is the currently selected object.

To change the Name property of the button object from Button1 to btnHello, perform the following steps:

1. Select the button object in the Form window, or select from the combo box at the top of the Object Inspector.
2. Move to the Object Inspector's Properties page.
3. Scroll through the list of object properties until you find the Name property.

Tip
When changing properties of multiple objects, you can save time by selecting the desired objects and working with the Object Inspector's list of shared properties.

4. The field beside the Name property in the Object Inspector is currently set to Button1. Click the field and type **btnHello**. (Be sure not to confuse this step with clicking the object itself on the form.)

The value of the button object's Name property has now been changed to btnHello. As a result, an object named Button1 no longer exists in your form; it now exists as btnHello.

Now select the Edit1 edit object and perform a similar operation to change the control name from Edit1 to editHello. To change these settings, repeat the preceding process.

The edit box has a Text property, which specifies the initial contents of the box when your Delphi application is executed. Display the Properties page and find the Text property. The corresponding setting in the Text field shows the string Edit1. Click the field and erase this string by pressing Backspace or Delete so that this field won't contain a value when you run your application. Notice that when you change properties, they're immediately reflected on the object in your form. When you've deleted the entire string, press Enter.

The button component has the Caption property, which designates the label of the button. To change the current caption from Button1 to Hello, first make the button object current by selecting it. Notice that the contents of the Object Inspector are now associated with the button component. Find Caption in the list of properties in the Object Inspector window. The corresponding setting is Button1. Click the field to the right of the Caption property and type **Hello**. Again, notice that as you type, your actions are reflected on the button component on the form. Press Enter when you finish typing the new caption. Figure 2.17 shows the updated form.

Fig. 2.17
Tailor properties of your objects by using the Object Inspector.

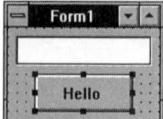

Attaching Code for Events

So far, the example form provides the desired visual appearance but lacks any useful functionality. You can't expect much since you haven't written a single line of code yet. The current handling of events by the edit and button objects is very basic default behavior. Running the application now would allow you to enter text in the edit object and click the button object. Of course, clicking the button doesn't do a thing at this point, and the text isn't used by anything; however, you do see the genesis of what could potentially be an entire business application.

A set of predefined events exists for each component. In the sample application, you want to have the btnHello button component respond to mouse clicks by setting another object's properties.

To attach the necessary event-handling code, double-click the button component on your form. The Code Editor window appears. Your cursor will be placed within the empty procedure btnHelloClick(). Type the following Object Pascal assignment statement inside the begin..end block:

```
editHello.Text := 'Hello World';
```

Assignment statements are how a component's properties are altered during runtime. The assignment statement you typed changes the Text property of the edit box component you named editHello from blank to the string *Hello World*. The general syntax for assigning a new setting to a property of the form and other components objects is

```
objectName.property := newPropertyValue;
```

> **Note**
>
> Properties themselves follow typing rules identical to variable types. For more information on variable typing, refer to Chapter 3, "Understanding the Language."

In the next section, you learn how to compile and run the first sample application.

Managing Delphi Project Files

A *project* is a collection of source files for an entire application. Delphi offers the Project Manager window to allow you to manage which source files (units) and forms are used in your project. You can think of a project as the highest level object in your application, consisting of smaller objects such as forms and actual source unit file objects. Of course, an application can use only form and source files, but this concept will let you migrate to large scales of application development.

To better understand a Delphi project, bring up the Project Manager again by opening the View menu and choosing Project Manager. The Project Manager, shown earlier in figure 2.15, lists the files involved in a Delphi application, or project. There are three types of such files:

- *One project file that contains the main program section.* This section drives the Windows programs created by Delphi. The project file has the extension .DPR and is available through the View menu's Project Source command. The project file is neither a form or unit file, but an overall application file that's run when your application is first loaded.

- *One or more form files (with corresponding unit files).* These files contain the controls drawn on each form. Form files typically have a .DFM extension. You need at least one form in your Delphi applications.

- *Zero or more Object Pascal library unit files (unit files without forms are library unit files).* These are .PAS files that contain libraries of auxiliary and supporting routines that are called by other parts of the application (other modules of the code attached in the forms and controls). You need at least one library unit to implement the code that drives the controls of the main form. Multiple libraries are suitable for large applications. The library units contain the declaration of classes that support the visual form and its controls. These units also contain the implementation for the event-handling procedures that animate the forms.

Saving Your Project

Saving your project files is a practical part of programming in any language, including Delphi. Because a Delphi application project involves multiple files, you have to save each file group separately. Before saving a project file, you must first name and save your form and unit files. See how this works with the sample application.

For a new Delphi project, the default root file name for the form and unit files is UNIT1. To save your form and units with a file name of APP1U, open the File menu and choose Save File As. The Save As dialog appears, with the default file name UNIT1. Here you can specify the root file name that you want to give your form and units. Note that form files have a .DFM extension and unit files have a .PAS extension.

The default file name for the project file is PROJECT1.DPR. To save the project under a new file name, open the File menu and choose Save Project As. The Save Project As dialog appears, allowing you to name your project file whatever you like.

After you specify new file names for your unit and form files, as well as the project source file, you can save subsequent updates by simply choosing the Save File and Save Project commands from the File menu, respectively. If you update the contents of the form and choose to update the project file, Delphi will first prompt you to update the form and any other modules. This is a convenient way to update the project files quickly.

Tip
To automatically save your work before running your application as well as when exiting, set the appropriate Autosave Options in the Environment Options dialog. Access the Environment Options dialog by opening the Options menu and choosing Environment.

> **Caution**
>
> Don't rename or delete form and unit files outside of Delphi. This doesn't update the form and unit file name references stored within the project file. Delphi would then display an error message warning you that some of the project files are missing.
>
> Always update and manage the project files from within Delphi to ensure that the project file is correctly keeping track of the application files.

Opening an Existing Project

When you load Delphi, a new empty project is loaded in memory space. Delphi can work with only one project at a time. To load existing project files, open the File menu and choose Open Project. A file list dialog appears to allow you to select the project file as well as move to different drives and directories. Selecting a new directory causes the file list box to be updated with the .DPR files in the selected directory. Click the desired .DPR file to load its project files. A number of sample projects are in the Demos directory, located under the directory where Delphi has been installed.

> **Note**
>
> By selecting a directory when you load a project file, that directory becomes current. When you subsequently save a form or unit file, you don't need to specify the directory path again, as the project directory will be used as the default.

52 Chapter 2—Understanding the Environment

Listing 2.1 shows the source code for the APP1.DPR project file. Delphi has generated the entire contents in file APP1.DPR.

Listing 2.1 Source Code for the APP1.DPR Project File

```
program App1;

uses
  Forms,
  App1u in 'APP1U.PAS' {Form1};

{$R *.RES}

begin
  Application.CreateForm(TForm1, Form1);
  Application.Run;
end.
```

Listing 2.1 shows that program App1 uses the App1U unit. The App1U unit is linked to the form Form1 whose name appears in the special comment that comes right after the name of the App1U unit. The main section of the program contains a single statement that sends the Run message to the application instance Application.

Listing 2.2 shows the source code for the APP1U.PAS library units. Delphi has generated all the contents of file APP1U.PAS, except the statements that you inserted earlier. The APP1U.PAS library unit declares the class TForm1 that supports the form. The library unit also includes the implementation of the necessary methods of class TForm1.

Listing 2.2 Source Code for the APP1 Unit

```
unit App1u;

interface

uses
  SysUtils, WinTypes, WinProcs, Messages, Classes, Graphics,
  Controls, Forms, Dialogs, StdCtrls;

type
  TForm1 = class(TForm)
    btnHello: TButton;
    editHello: TEdit;
    procedure btnHelloClick(Sender: TObject);
  private
    { Private declarations }
  public
    { Public declarations }
  end;
```

```
var
  Form1: TForm1;

implementation

{$R *.DFM}

procedure TForm1.btnHelloClick(Sender: TObject);
begin
   editHello.Text := 'Hello World';
end;

end.
```

Listing 2.2 declares the class TForm1 to have the data fields editHello and btnHello, which are of component types TEdit and TButton, respectively. The class also declares the method btnHelloClick(), the event handler that responds to clicking the button component. This method has the parameter Sender, which is of the type TObject.

> **Note**
>
> Delphi has extended the syntax of Pascal to use the keyword class in declaring classes. Also, Delphi predefines the class TObject as the parent class for all newly declared classes in Delphi applications. Chapter 3, "Understanding the Language," discusses the extensions to Pascal in more detail.

Running Your Application

From the Run menu choose Run, or press F9 to run your project. Clicking your button at runtime causes the message Hello World to appear in the edit box. Congratulations! You've created your first Windows application in Delphi.

Navigating Delphi

Since Delphi is a multiform SDI application and not a Multiple Document Interface (MDI) application, it doesn't have a Window menu. In essence, each Delphi window (Object Inspector, Form window, Code Editor window, and so on) is an individual application. Delphi has chosen to hide these related forms from the Windows Task Manager (available by pressing Ctrl+Esc), showing only Delphi (the main window) as the running program.

There are a number of options for activating the other Delphi windows:

- Open the View menu and choose Object Inspector to move to the Object Inspector window.

- Clicking the Toggle Form/Unit button on the SpeedBar activates and toggles between the current project's form and unit (source) windows.

- When you have multiple forms and units in your project, you can press Ctrl+F12 or Shift+F12 to see a list of each, respectively. These functions are also available by clicking the Select Unit from List and Select Form from List buttons on the SpeedBar.

Configuring Delphi

Delphi provides a wealth of options for configuring it to your individual needs. The following items are configurable within Delphi:

- *Component palette.* Open the Options menu and choose Environment to view the Environment Options dialog (refer to fig. 2.4). Selecting the Palette tab allows you to arrange the Component palette in any order you like, as explained earlier in this chapter.

    You can also create and load separate Component palettes than the default palette provided within Delphi. Use the Options menu's Open Library and Install Components commands to access dialogs that allow you to build and load customized palettes.

- *General Preferences.* Elements of Delphi's environment—such as the position of windows on the desktop, the last loaded project, form design options, and debugging, compiling, and gallery options—are available on the Preferences page of the Environment Options dialog.

- *The Tools Menu.* You can add commands to the Tools menu by using the Tool Options dialog available when you choose the Options menu's Tools command.

- *The Gallery.* When you find yourself using a form again and again, you can add it to the Gallery, which will allow you to reuse it as a template on later projects.

- *The Code Editor.* Also in the Environment Options dialog are three pages that provide fields allowing customization of the editor's general, display, and color options.

- *Project Options.* A variety of project options—including which forms are auto-created, what icon your application will use, compiler and linker options, and directory options—are available in the Project Options dialog, which you can access through the Options menu's Project command.

- *The Browser.* The Browser is covered extensively in Chapter 11. By using the Browser tab of the Environment Options dialog, you can configure default preferences for the Browser's display of information.

Suggestions for Effective Delphi Development

You may be the best programmer on earth, but without the right tools and environment, a lower caliber programmer with the right tools can be more productive. The following are two items that should allow you to buy yourself increase productivity:

- *Get a proper video subsystem.* If you have a fair performing 486 with ample speed but have only a 14-inch monitor doing plain old VGA or even 800×600 SVGA, your best bet for becoming more productive will be to upgrade your video subsystem. A video board capable of at least a resolution of 1,024×768 pixels and a 17- to 20-inch monitor will change the way you work. You'll have more Delphi desk space to spread out on, allowing you to keep more forms open at once and see more information about your project at a glance.

    If you only have a 14- or 15-inch monitor, a resolution of 800×600 is your best bet.

- *Upgrade your CPU.* Delphi is a compiled environment. Upgrading your CPU will be most useful for decreasing the time you wait for your applications to compile. A faster CPU would also be noticeable at runtime. Understand, however, that at runtime you're spoiled. There simply isn't another product that produces faster Windows database front ends than Delphi.

From Here...

Now would be a good time to spend some more time reviewing Delphi's environment.

- The next chapter, "Understanding the Language," provides a Pascal refresher as well as detailed coverage of the new object-oriented extensions added with Object Pascal.

- If you're an absolute Object Pascal expert and want to learn more about all types of Delphi components, you may want to jump to Part II, "Components."

- For a detailed discussion on working with Delphi forms, refer to Chapter 8, "Creating Forms."

- For a detailed discussion of how to create your own MDI and SDI applications, refer to Chapter 9, "Creating Applications."

- Chapter 10, "Creating Database Applications," shows the results that can be accomplished by using many features of Delphi's environment.

Chapter 3
Understanding the Language

Delphi's programming language is based on Pascal, a language designed by Niklaus Wirth specifically to teach structured programming. This is why many of us were first introduced to Pascal while attending computer-related courses.

Compared to other third-generation languages such as C, Pascal is generally regarded as easier to learn and use. This is due to the English-like structure of the Pascal language. Compared to C, Pascal reads like a book. C and other languages tend to use more arcane code than that used in Pascal. As a result, Pascal code not only reads better, it's easier to write than other compiled languages. This is one major benefit to having Pascal as the underlying development language. Also, applications created with a native compiler result in a single executable file (.EXE). No other front-end development environment today offers this combination.

Another "learning" language is BASIC, which stands for Beginner's All-purpose Symbolic Instruction Code. BASIC has found a home in Microsoft's Visual Basic (VB), a product similar to Delphi but without the same object-oriented features. Although VB is event-driven and has proven suitable for professional Windows development, it had the same basic features for a number of years. Before Delphi, Visual Basic enjoyed years of being the exclusive visual development tool for Windows development.

Delphi's Pascal isn't the same Pascal that you may have used in the past, even if you've used Borland's most recent Pascal version 7. Object Pascal in Pascal 7 is a descendant of Borland's Pascal compiler line that includes powerful object-oriented extensions. Now, Delphi has constructed a new object syntax that's even more powerful than what was supported in Borland Pascal 7. With

Delphi, Borland is continuing its direction in setting the pace for a new Pascal language standard. If you're porting applications compiled in previous versions of Pascal, don't worry. Delphi supports the old object syntax as well as the new.

Borland Pascal has been object-oriented since version 5.5 and has long been regarded as a better object-oriented environment than C++. This high regard is perhaps due to the foundation that Pascal was developed on—as a teaching tool (not to mention that it was developed by the industry's finest compiler team).

This chapter focuses on the following topics:

- The core Pascal language
- Extensions to Pascal, such as open array construction and `Case` statements
- Programmed properties

The Pascal Language

This section covers the core Pascal language as you may have worked with it in the past. Entire books written on the Pascal language go into much more detail than possible in this book. Picking up a good Pascal reference such as *Delphi By Example* or *Turbo Pascal By Example* (both published by Que Corporation) is extremely worthwhile in your quest to become a skilled Delphi programmer. While Delphi does a lot of programming and setup for you, you'll need an understanding of the Pascal language to write your application code.

Delphi provides most of the standard language elements available in many procedural languages. These include the following:

- Pointers and dynamic memory allocation
- A rich set of variable types
- Arrays
- Records
- `if..then..else` statements
- Conditional case branching

- `for`, `while`, and `repeat..until` loops
- Logical comparison operators

Pascal provides an ample amount of language elements to allow you to build your applications in a manner suitable for your needs.

If you are new to or are being reacquainted with Pascal, keep in mind that Pascal is a *strongly typed language*. This means that variables declared as a specific type must be assigned the correct type almost without exception. The compiler will in most cases produce errors if the assigned data is of a type different than that which is declared. The C language, in contrast, is *loosely typed*. A character enclosed in single quotation marks can be assigned to a variable of another type, such as an integer. The compiler will then perform its duties without complaint. The same operation in Pascal, however, will result in a compiler error.

Strong typing requirements are common among compiled languages. By defining variable types at design time, runtime execution is much faster than when using a general-purpose "any type" variable. Although the syntactical requirements may be overwhelming at first, the result is the capability to deliver solid, native-compiled Windows executables and dynamic link libraries (DLLs). Compiled programs are typically the fastest applications possible and make learning Delphi worth the modest learning curve. Delphi's universal appeal is its capability to natively compile programs, which allows you to produce the fastest Windows applications possible.

Data Types

Because Pascal is a strongly typed language, declaring variables requires attention. Procedures, functions, and methods have similar requirements. Typing is a common requirement of language compilers.

Many different data types are available in Delphi. There are seven basic categories:

- Integer
- Real
- Boolean
- Char
- String

- Pointer
- PChar

The name *integer* is typically used to reference, in layman's terms, any ordinal numerical value. Pascal defines several numeric types, the most common being called the integer type. The integer type is 2 bytes long on modern PC hardware. It will stored a signed ordinal value with a range of –32768 to 32767. Other integer types are as follows:

- Shortint, which has a range of –128 to 127. It will store a signed value and is 1 byte long.
- Longint, which has a range of –2,147,483,648 to 2,147,483,647. It will store a signed value and is 4 bytes long.
- Byte, which has a range of 0 to 255. It will store an unsigned value and is 1 byte long.
- Word, which has a range of 0 to 65535. It will store an unsigned value and is 2 bytes long.

Variables declared as *real* data types are non-ordinal and store real numbers. Variables are declared as one of the Pascal real data types when the value must be one of a certain precision, such as 2.221. The standard real data type is 6 bytes long and supports a range of values from $(2.9*10^{39})$ through $(1.7*10^{38})$. Other real types are as follows:

- Single, which has a range of $(1.5*10^{-45})$ through $(3.4*10^{38})$. It's 4 bytes long.
- Double, which has a range of $(5.0*10^{-324})$ through $(1.7*10^{308})$. It's 8 bytes long.
- Extended, which has a range of $(3.4*10^{-4,932})$ through $(1.1*10^{4,932})$. It's 10 bytes long.
- Comp, which has a range of $(-2^{63}+1)$ through $(2^{63}-1)$. It's 8 bytes long.

The Pascal *Boolean* data type typically stores only a signed ordinal value of 1 or 0 and is 1 byte long. The 1 represents true and the 0 represents false. The Pascal Boolean type follows the layman's understanding of true or false but is different in other languages. Windows and C define a Boolean type called BOOL, which is derived from a 2-byte integer. In C, a BOOLean true is considered a non-zero value, and a zero value is considered false. For compatibility, Pascal provides other Boolean types, which are as follows:

- `ByteBool` is 1 byte long. It stores signed values other than 1 or 0.
- `WordBool` is 2 bytes long. It stores signed values other than 1 or 0.
- `LongBool` is 4 byte long. It stores signed values other than 1 or 0.

Sometimes it's hard to know when to use `ByteBool`, `Boolean`, and so on. If a Windows API function returns a `BOOL` value, the value can be stored directly in a `LongBool` because a Windows (or C) `BOOL` is a 2-byte signed integer. `LongBool` is of equal or greater size. An attempt to store a Windows (or C) `BOOL` into a Pascal `Boolean` will result in a data type mismatch. If the value is type cast, the result will be truncation and possibly an incorrect evaluation. The general rule is be cautious when dealing with Boolean variables. Be especially cautious when dealing with Windows API functions or functions in C DLLs that return Boolean values.

Constructs such as `if..then` can evaluate Boolean variables and simplify expressions. Consider the following:

```
var
  li: longint;

begin
  li := 100000000;

  if boolean(li) then
    messagebeep(0);

  if longbool(li) then
    messagebeep(0);
end;
```

The goal of this code is only to determine whether the long integer value stored in `li` is non-zero. A Boolean expression within a `if..then` construct would make this evaluation simple. Because of Pascal's strong type checking, the `longint` variable `li` must be type cast (explained later in this chapter) to one of the Pascal Boolean types in order to compile. This example illustrates a type cast to the incorrect Pascal Boolean type and to the correct Pascal Boolean type. The first `if..then` construct uses a Boolean type cast and evaluates to false even though `li` is non-zero. The reason is that `li` is 4 bytes long and is being cast to a 1-byte data type. This causes the evaluation to be based on a truncated version of `li`. The second `if..then` expression casts `li` as a `LongBool`, which is of the correct length and type. This evaluates to true.

The *char* data type is the same as the integer type byte described earlier but stores an ASCII character representation of its numeric value. Char data types are created by enclosing a single character within single quotation marks or by using the `Chr` function.

The *string* data type is of a dynamic length that's between 1 and 255 positions long. Like an array, the individual characters can be accessed by referencing them by index. The byte in position 0 (only accessible by turning range checking off) stores a numeric value representing the length of the string's current assignment. (Check on-line help under Range Checking for more information.)

The *pointer* data type is a 4-byte (32-bit) selector offset combination that points to a variable of any type. Untyped pointers merely use the word `pointer` in the declaration:

```
var pAnyPoint: pointer
```

The pointer `var pAnyPoint` can point at any variable type.

Pascal also allows variables to be declared as *typed* pointers. The type of variable the pointer points at can be specified explicitly by adding `^datatype`:

```
var pIntegerPoint: ^integer;
```

The pointer `var pIntegerPoint` should point at integer types.

This is important when allocating memory for a pointer variable. An untyped pointer can have memory allocated to it using `GetMem`, which allocates an explicitly specified number of bytes of memory for the pointer. Typed pointers can use functions such as `New()`, which will automatically allocate the correct amount of memory according to the pointer's type. In the preceding example, 2 bytes is allocated because that's the size of an integer.

The *PChar* data type is a pointer to a NULL (not nil) terminated character string. This type exists for compatibility with external functions such as those available in Windows API. Unlike Pascal strings, Windows and C strings don't have a length byte. They instead begin with a 0 byte index and are terminated with a `(#0)`. Pascal RTL string functions depend on the length byte to determine the number of characters stored in a string variable. C functions actually search a character array a single character at a time until a NULL value is encountered to determine the end of the string. Many functions available in the Window API will expect pointers to NULL terminated strings or will fill character buffers and terminate them with a NULL. Use of these functions in Pascal require variables of type PChar. Memory should be allocated to the variable and then used with the desired function. Once the data is retrieved, the data in PChar can be retrieved into a Pascal string variable using the RTL function `StrPas` as defined in the `SysUtils` unit.

Type Compatibility

When working with strongly typed languages, not all variable type assignments are compatible with each other. An obvious example would be the compiler's refusal to assign a string variable to an integer. Other languages, such as C, will let you do this, but this is often the source of obscure bugs. A less obvious example would be assigning a real number to an integer variable, as in the following:

```
var
    intQty:         Integer;
    realPercent:    Real;
Begin
    realPercent := 0.06;
    intQty := realPercent;
End;
```

This example will understandably generate an error, because integers are just that—numbers that store only whole values. This may pose a problem to some programmers who are used to automatic conversions between variable types or environments that don't require types at all. Even simple cases, such as

```
intQty := 1.0;
```

won't be performed. In this example, you're trying to assign 1.0 to the `intQty` integer variable. You know that the equivalent would be

```
intQty := 1;
```

but the compiler won't compile the code because 1.0 isn't an integer—it's truly a real number.

What if you wanted to assign your integer variable to your variable of type real? This is a perfectly acceptable operation since there's no loss in precision. The following line of code is compiled without complaint:

```
intQty := 1;
realPercent := intQty;
```

In general, when going from a type of less precision to a type of higher precision, automatic type conversion will occur.

Typecasting

Automatic type conversion isn't always possible depending on the variable types that are being used. The following code fragment, for example, tries to assign a pointer type to a variable of type `LongInt`:

```
var
  iVal : longint;
  pVal : pointer;
  begin
    iVal := pVal;
    ...
  end;
```

If you actually try to use this code, you won't even get it to compile. The problem lies with the assignment. You simply can't just assign a pointer to a longint type. So what's the problem? A pointer is 32 bits long and so is a longint. Although the sizes are correct, Pascal is very picky about assigning a variable of one type (pointer) to the variable of another type (longint). If the receiving variable is of the same size (or larger) as the passed data, the strong typing can be overcome by *typecasting*. Observe the following modified version of the preceding code fragment:

```
var
  iVal : longint;
  pVal : pointer;
begin
  iVal := LongInt(pVal);
  ...
end;
```

This example will compile. The pointer variable was cast as a longint type, thus allowing you to make the assignment and access its address.

Typecasting, although powerful, should be used cautiously. Incorrect use could return unexpected results, including truncation or even loss of data. You can test a dangerous typecast as follows:

```
var
  bVal : byte;
begin
  bVal := byte(255+1);
end;
```

This example creates a variable of type byte. You try to assign the result of the expression 255+1 to the variable. Without the casting of the result of the expression, the compiler will generate a constant out of range error. At least this example allows you to compile the code, which you may initially think is a good thing—but it isn't. A review of the value of bVal after execution will show that it's zero. This is because the cast is telling the compiler to make the data fit in a single byte. The result of the expression you created is suppose to reside in 2 bytes. This will cause you to lose a significant bit and thus the value changes.

There are two kinds of typecasting, both of which have already been demonstrated:

- Variable typecasts
- Value or results typecasts

The previous example that typecasts the pointer to a `longint` is an example of variable typecasts. The data was a 32-bit pointer. The typecasting of the variable had no effect on the data. It merely changed the recognized type of the variable that the data was stored in.

The most recent example was that of a value typecast. This is where the results of the expression 255+1 were cast into a value of the type `Byte`. This resulted in actual modification of the data.

You'll discover the casting of types is much more powerful than implemented here. From the first time that you cast an object from one type to another, this power will be truly unleashed.

Procedures and Functions

Delphi gives you a strong and sophisticated object model. This way, you can create classes and component classes that can be used to simplify the development process. Delphi's visual environment provides you with an event model in addition to the object model. The event model allows you to attach code and various processes to components and forms according to the firing order of specific events.

Between the two models, the development process is very fast and provides the developer with easy-to-understand processing. This virtually eliminates the old-time procedural design issue of spaghetti code. There may be times, however, when you still want to incorporate some procedural style by breaking large methods or event handlers into smaller, sequentially executed program blocks of functions or procedures. This functionality was available in Pascal and is available in Delphi as well, because Delphi still supports the procedure model.

There are several ways to make a procedure or function available within your main program unit. The simplest way is to define the procedure header and program body at the top of the `implementation` section of the unit. Because it's at the top, the compiler is aware of its existence before any other code has a chance to make a call to it. Observe the following `implementation` section:

```
implementation

{$R *.DFM}

procedure MyProc;
```

```
begin
  MessageDlg('Yes',mtWarning,[mbOk],0);
end;

procedure TForm1.Button1Click(Sender: TObject);
begin
  MyProc;
end;

end.
```

In this example, the code for the OnClick event of a standard button component calls procedure MyProc. The compiler won't complain, as it has already passed over MyProc statements at the top of the implementation section. Try moving the procedure below the OnClick code, as follows:

```
implementation

{$R *.DFM}

procedure TForm1.Button1Click(Sender: TObject);
begin
  MyProc;
end;

procedure MyProc;
begin
  MessageDlg('Yes',mtWarning,[mbOk],0);
end;

end.
```

With this example, the compiler will complain because it's unaware of the existence of MyProc. This problem can be overcome by putting a procedure declaration at the top of the implementation section followed by the keyword forward.

```
implementation

{$R *.DFM}

procedure MyProc; forward;

procedure TForm1.Button1Click(Sender: TObject);
begin
  MyProc;
end;

procedure MyProc;
begin
  MessageDlg('Yes',mtWarning,[mbOk],0);
end;

end.
```

The procedure header is declared, thus the name and parameters expected are visible to any code below it. What changes is that the forward keyword tells the caller to look forward in the code to find the defining statements for execution.

There's yet another way to make the procedure available in your unit. As you may or may not know, anything declared only in the implementation section of a unit is accessible only to that unit. Note that both prior examples made no use of the interface section of the unit. The MyProc procedure is thus local to the unit. If the unit was intended to be placed in the uses clause of another unit, MyProc wouldn't be available. This brings you to third method to include a procedure in a unit. Observe the following:

```
interface
...
procedure MyTest;
implementation
{$R *.DFM}

procedure TForm1.Button1Click(Sender: TObject);
begin
   MyTest;
end;

procedure MyTest;
begin
 MessageDlg('Yes',mtWarning,[mbOk],0);
end;
end.
```

This time, the procedure's declaration is placed in the interface section. This acts as a prototype and makes the function available to the unit or to any units that use the unit.

The visibility of procedures as described in this section apply to functions and procedures.

Program Blocks

Pascal uses a *programming block* structure for setting up groups of related lines of code. A programming block is surrounded by begin and end statements. The following is an example of a programming block within a procedure named CutTheGrass:

```
procedure CutTheGrass;
begin
     { This is a comment }
     { The following logic cuts the grass }
end;
```

Extensions to Pascal

This section looks at the extensions to the Pascal language Borland has provided for Delphi. Some of these extensions enhance the core Pascal language itself, while others make Delphi programming itself much easier. You'll learn about the following topics:

- The Case statement
- Open array construction
- The Result variable in a function
- The return type of a function
- The new object model
- Protecting resources

The following sections present the extensions to the Pascal language by using examples.

The *Case* Statement

Delphi supports the optimization of the Case statement by introducing two modifications in how the statement works:

- Ranges in Case statements must not overrun each other. Here's an example of a Case statement that's no longer permitted:

  ```
  Case MyChar Of
      'A', 'I', 'O', 'U', 'E': Writeln('Vowel');
      'A'..'Z': Writeln('Uppercase character');
  End;
  ```

  This new behavior of the Case statement might affect your programming style if you write Case statements in this manner.

- Ordering the Case constants in collating sequence of the type used, from highest to lowest (sequentially left to right), permits the compiler to optimize the Case statement into jumps rather than calculate the offset every time. Here's an example of a Case statement that yields a set of optimized jumps:

  ```
  Case MyChar Of
      '0'..'9': Writeln('Digit');
      'A'..'Z': Writeln('Uppercase');
      'A'..'z': Writeln('Lowercase');
      Else Writeln('Other characters');
  End;
  ```

Contrast the preceding version with the next one, which requires multiple calculations:

```
Case MyChar Of
    'A'..'Z': Writeln('Uppercase');
    '0'..'9': Writeln('Digit');
    'A'..'z': Writeln('Lowercase');
    Else Writeln('Other characters');
End;
```

Notice that a simple shift in the sequence of a Case label deprives the preceding Case statement from being optimized.

Open Array Construction

Borland Pascal 7 introduced open arrays, which allowed you to develop general-purpose routines that handle static arrays of various sizes. For example, you can declare the function CalcMean() as follows:

```
Function CalcMean(X: Array of Real) : Real;
```

The parameter X is an open array that has the basic type Real. You can use the function CalcMean() to process arrays of different sizes, as shown in the following code fragment:

```
Type
    Array10 = Array [1..10] Of Real;
    Array20 = Array [1..20] Of Real;

Var
    X1 : Array10;
    X2 : Array20;

Function CalcMean(X: Array of Real) : Real;
Begin
    { statements that define the function }
End;

Begin
    GetData(X1);
    GetData(X2);
    Writeln('Mean of array X1 = ', CalcMean(X1));
    Writeln('Mean of array X2 = ', CalcMean(X2));
End.
```

Delphi makes open-array parameters even more useful by allowing you to build an array and to pass it as a parameter. This requires that you enclose a comma-delimited list of values for the array elements in square brackets. Here's a code fragment that uses the CalcMean() function with the new open-array construction feature:

```
Function CalcMean(X: Array of Real) : Real;
Begin
    { statements that define the function }
End;
```

```
Begin
  Writeln('Mean of array 1 = ', CalcMean([1.2, 3.4, 5.6, 7.8]));
  Writeln('Mean of array 2 = ', CalcMean([55.8, 67.6, 41.2, 48.4, ]));
End.
```

A Function's *Result* Variable

Delphi enhances the coding of functions by automatically declaring the local variable Result in each function. This variable has the same data type as the function's result type. The variable Result is an alias to the function's name. Assigning values to the variable Result has the same effect as assigning a value to the function. But what's the advantage of using the variable Result? The answer lies in that you can use the local variable Result to build the function's result without ending up with recursive calls to the same function.

Here's an example of two equivalent forms of the same function:

```
Function Cube(X : Real) : Real;
Begin
    Cube := X * X * X;
End;

Function Cube(X : Real) : Real;
Begin
    Result := X * X * X;
End;
```

Here's another version of function Cube() that uses the local variable Result to obtain the cube number (the long way):

```
Function Cube(X : Real) : Real;
Begin
    Result := X;
    Result := Result * X;
    Result := Result * X
End;
```

The preceding version of function Cube() doesn't involve indefinite recursions.

> **Caution**
>
> The value of variable Result is undefined until you assign it a value. If you're porting Pascal functions to Delphi, be sure to rename your own local variable Result.

A Function's Return Type

Delphi now permits functions to return any type, whether simple or complex, standard or user-defined. The exception to these types include the old Pascal 7.0 object types, and files of type text or file of. Use pointers to objects to handle objects as function results. Here's a simple example of a function that returns a user-defined record type:

```
Type
    Complex = Record
        X : Real;
        Y : Real;
    End;
Function AddComplex(C1, C2 : Complex) : Complex;
Begin
    Result.X := C1.X + C2.X;
    Result.Y := C1.Y + C2.Y
End;
Var
    CN1, CN2, CN3 : Complex;
Begin
    CN1.X := 1.0;
    CN1.Y := 4.0;
    CN2.X := 11.0;
    CN2.Y := 40.0;
    CN3 := AddComplex(CN1, CN2);
    Writeln('CN3 = ', CN3.X, ' +I ', CN3.Y);
End.
```

Notice that function `AddComplex()` returns the record type `Complex`. Also notice that the function uses the predefined local variable `Result` to build the function's result. This example illustrates how the predefined variable `Result` plays an important role in supporting the extended function's result type.

The New Object Model

Turbo Pascal 5.5 introduced static and dynamic object types. Delphi introduces a few changes in the definition of object types. A number of these changes are backward-compatible—you can use them into existing objects. Other changes are exclusive to new-model objects. The compiler offers a new compiler directive, `{$VER70}`, which allows version 7.0 backward compatibility on a unit-by-unit basis. This feature permits you to use both kinds of object types. You declare old-style objects in one unit, declare new-style objects in another unit, and then use both of these units in the same program. You should keep in mind that there are definite distinctions between these objects.

Delphi uses the keyword `class` to declare the new-style objects. The keyword `object` remains reserved for declaring the old-style objects.

The next section presents the changes that are compatible with objects using the version 7.0 and earlier object model.

Protected Parts

Delphi allows object types and classes to declare protected parts, in addition to public and private parts. This feature uses the new directive, `protected`, that operates like its counterparts, `private` and `public`, in that it's reserved only in the type declaration of a class.

Delphi allows access to the protected parts of a class and its ancestor classes through a class declared in the current unit.

Declaring protected parts allows you to combine the features of public and private components. You can conceal the implementation's fine points from the end users as with private components. Unlike private components, however, protected components are still accessible to programmers who want to derive new classes from your classes without the requirement that the derived classes be declared in the same unit. Protected methods are especially advantageous in concealing the implementation of properties.

Default Ancestor

The system unit in Delphi defines an abstract object type called `TObject`. This type is the default ancestor of all instances of the new object types (or classes, if you prefer). Delphi absolves you from having to explicitly declare `TObject` as an ancestor to the derived classes. Thus, the type declaration

```
Type
     TDescendantObject = class
     ...
     End;
```

is in effect a short version of the declaration

```
Type
     TDescendantObject = class(TObject)
     ...
     End;
```

The preceding object hierarchy scheme supports polymorphic behavior in a very convenient way. The class `TObject` includes a fundamental constructor `Create()` and destructor `Destroy()`. The constructor `TObject.Create()` allocates a dynamic instance of the class on the heap and initializes all its fields to zeros. The destructor `TObject.Destroy()` disposes of the memory allocated by `Create()` and destroys the class instance.

Reference Model

Since Delphi creates dynamic instances for all new-style objects, Delphi absolves you from the need to declare separate class and pointer types and explicitly de-referencing class pointers. To understand this feature, first look at a code fragment that uses the old object model:

```
Type
      PDirObject = ^TDirObject;
      TDirObject = object(TObject);
      ThisDirPtr: PDirObject;
        constructor Init;
      End;

Var
      aDirPtr: PDirObject;

Begin
 New(aDirPtr, Init);
      aDirPtr^.ThisDirPtr := getAddress;
End;
```

Delphi's new reference model can simplify the preceding code sample. This reference model automatically de-references object pointer variables:

```
Type
      TDirObject = object(TObject)
      ThisDir: TDirObject;
        constructor Create;
      End;

Var
      aDir: TDirObject;

Begin
      aDir := TDirObject.Create;
      aDir.ThisDir := getAddress;
End;
```

Class Methods

Typically, a *method* is a function or procedure that manipulates an instance of a class or an object type. Delphi permits you to declare methods that manipulate the class itself. Thus, class methods are methods associated with the class type instead of a specific instance. Consequently, you can invoke the class methods without having to construct an instance. The implementation of the class methods should not rely on the runtime states of any fields in the class.

The declaration of a class method requires the reserved word class be placed in front of the method declaration. Here's an example:

```
Type
      TDirObject = class(TObject)
         class function GetCurDir : String;
         constructor Create;
         procedure SelectDrive(Drive : String);
      End;
```

You can call a class method just like a normal method for an instance of that type, but you can also call the method of the type itself:

```
Var
     DirObj : TDirObject;
     DirStr: String;
Begin
     DirStr := TDirObject.GetCurDir;
     Writeln('Current directory is ', DirStr);

     DirObj := TDirObject.Create;
     DirObj.SelectDrive('A:');
     DirStr := DirObj.GetCurDir;
     Writeln('Current directory is ', DirStr);

     DirObj.SelectDrive('B:');
     DirStr := DirObj.GetCurDir;
     Writeln('Current directory is ', DirStr);

     DirObj.SelectDrive('C:');
     DirStr := DirObj.GetCurDir;
     Writeln('Current directory is ', DirStr);
End;
```

Method Pointers

In general, procedural types allow you to pass procedures and functions as arguments to other routines. Delphi also permits you to declare procedural types that are class methods. This way, you can invoke specific methods of particular class instances at runtime. This scheme has the distinct advantage over method pointers in that they permit you to extend a class by empowering some behavior to another class, instead of deriving a new class and overriding methods. Consequently, method pointers assist in reducing the proliferation of a class hierarchy.

Delphi uses method pointers to associate events with particular code in specific locations, such as calling a method of a specific form when the user clicks a list box item. Thus, rather than derive a new class from TListBox and override its click behavior, the programmer connects the existing object to a method of a specific object instance that has the desired behavior.

How does the declaration of a method pointer differ from a procedural type? The only difference between the two declarations is the use of the reserved words of Object after the function or procedure prototype. Here's an example:

```
Type
     ENotify = Procedure(Sender: Tobject) of Object;
```

The preceding code declares the method pointer ENotify, which can be assigned to a field of a class. Here's an example:

```
Type
     TDirObject = class(TObject)
        fOnClick: Enotify;
     end;
```

```
      TDriveObject = class(TObject)
         procedure MyMethod(Sender: TObject);
      End;
Var
      ADirObject: TDirObject;
      ADriveObject: TDriveObject;
Begin
      ADirObject := TDirObject.Create;
      ADriveObject := TDriveObject.Create;
      ADirObject.fOnClick := ADriveObject.MyMethod;
End;
```

Programmed Properties

The components that you draw on a form have properties that determine their visual appearance and behavior. Properties resemble fields but internally encapsulate methods that access (read or write) the value of the property. Properties permit you to control the access of protected fields or create side effects to changing what otherwise look like fields. The following sections discuss various aspects of declaring and using properties.

Property Syntax

Delphi allows you to declare a property field by using the keyword property. Also, the property has a read clause and an optional write clause. These two clauses specify the name of a method that accesses the property. If you use only the read clause, the property is read-only. Here's an example property called MyProperty that uses both the read and write clause:

```
Type
      TMyObject = class(TObject)
         function GetMyProperty : AType;
         procedure SetMyProperty(ANewValue : AType);
         property MyProperty : Atype
         read GetMyProperty write SetMyProperty;
      end;
```

The compiler translates the references to the property into method calls. To set the value of a property, you use an assignment statement:

```
MyObject.MyProperty := MyValue;
```

The compiler translates this statement into

```
MyObject.SetMyProperty(MyValue);
```

Likewise, to retrieve the value of a property, you reference the property, as shown in the statement

```
    MyVariable := MyObject.MyProperty;
```

The compiler translates the preceding statement into the following call to method `GetMyProperty`:

```
    MyVariable := MyObject.GetMyProperty;
```

Fields for Reading and Writing

The read and write clauses of a property may contain the name of class fields to support reading and writing the property. The read clause might yield the value of a class field, for example, while the write clause might set the field. Here's an example:

```
Type
    TDirObject = class(TObject)
        fDirStr : String;
        procedure SetDir(NewDir : String);
        property Dir : String
            read fDirStr write SetDir;
End;

procedure TDirObject.SetDir(NewDir : String);
Begin
    fDirStr := NewDir;
    ChangeDir(NewDir);
End;
```

Indexed Properties

Properties such as fields can be arrays that have multiple values of the same data type and are accessed by an index. Unlike an ordinary array, however, you may not refer to the property as a whole. Instead, you can access only individual elements in the array.

The declaration of an indexed property involves specifying the following information:

- The name of the property
- The name and type of the index
- The type of the elements

Here's an example of a property that resembles an array of long integers:

```
    property Indices[Index : Integer] : LongInt
        read GetIndex write SetIndex;
```

Here's another example of a property that resembles an array of strings:

```
    property Filenames[Index : Integer] : String
        read GetFilename write SetFilename;
```

What about the methods that read and write the array property? The method that reads the property must be a function that has a single parameter with the same name and type as the property index. The read method must return the same type as the elements. Here are examples of read methods for the preceding indexed properties:

```
function GetIndex(Index : Integer): LongInt;

function GetFilename(Index : Integer): String;
```

The function `GetIndex()` returns the `LongInt` value for the given index. Likewise, the function `GetFilename()` yields the `String` value for the argument of parameter `Index`.

The method that writes a value of an indexed property is a procedure that has two parameters. The first parameter has the same signature as the property's index, whereas the second parameter has the same type as the property elements. Here are examples for the previous indexed properties:

```
procedure SetIndex(Index: Integer; const NewValue: LongInt);

procedure SetFilename(Index: Integer; const NewFilename: String);
```

With the read and write methods defined, you can access an indexed property just like elements of an array. Here's an example:

```
property Filename[Index : Integer] : String
    read GetFilename write SetFilename;
    ...

Var
    FileStr : String;

Begin
    Filename[1] := '\AUTOEXEC.BAT';
    FileStr := Filename[1];
End;
```

Delphi supports an interesting feature that allows you to declare an indexed property as the default property. This feature means that you may reference the array using the instance's name (and an index) instead of the name of the indexed property. A class can have only one default property. The declaration of a default indexed property requires adding the directive `default` after an indexed property. Here's an example:

```
Type
    TFileObject = class(TObject)
        property Filename[Index : Integer]: String
            read GetFilename write SetFilename; default;
    End;
```

Accessing the default indexed property requires using an index after the instance's name. Here's an example of accessing the preceding default indexed property:

```
Var
    FileObject: TMyObject;
Begin
    FileObject[1] := 'CONFIG.SYS';
    FileObject[2] := 'AUTOEXEC.BAT';
    FileObject[3] := 'WIN.INI';
    FileObject.Filename[4] := 'SYSTEM.INI';
End;
```

Notice that the last file name assignment explicitly uses the name of the indexed property.

Multiple-Index Properties

Delphi doesn't restrict indexed properties to single-dimensional arrays. You can use indexed properties with multiple dimensions. The corresponding parameters of the read and write methods must still have the same signatures as the indexes of the property and must occur in the same sequence as the indexes. Here's an example of a property that resembles a matrix of reals:

```
property Matrix[Row, Col : Integer] : Real
    read GetMatElem write SetMatElem;
```

The method that reads the Matrix property must be a function that has two parameters with the same names and types as the property index. The read method must return the same type as the elements. Here's an example of read methods for the preceding indexed property:

```
function GetMatElem(Row, Col : Integer): Real;
```

The function GetMatElem() returns the Real value for the given row and column indices.

The method that writes a value of an indexed property is a procedure that has three parameters: the first two parameters have the same signature as the property's indices, whereas the third parameter has the same type as the property elements. Here's an example for the earlier indexed property:

```
procedure SetMatElem(Row, Col : Integer; const NewValue: Real);
```

With the read and write methods defined, you can access an indexed property just like elements of a multidimensional array. Here's an example:

```
Var
    MatElem : Real;
Begin
    Matrix[1] := 123.9;
    MatElem := Matrix[2];
End;
```

Read-Only and Write-Only Properties

Delphi allows you to make a property read-only or write-only by excluding the read or write clause in the property declaration. Here's an example of a read-only property that only uses the read clause:

```
Type
     TFileObject = class(TObject)
     property Filename : String
          read GetFilename;
End;
```

By omitting the method that sets the property, you guarantee that the property is read-only. Trying to write to a read-only property or read a write-only property results in a compiler error.

Object References

Delphi permits the creation of pointers to classes, known as *object references*. By using object references, you can either construct instances of the type assigned to the reference or obtain information about the object type by invoking class methods. Declaring an object reference involves using the reserved word class. Here's an example that creates a reference to the type TObject:

```
Type
     TObjRef = class of TObject;
```

Once you declare a reference, you can assign to it any class assignment compatible with the declared type. This example illustrates the proper use of an object reference:

```
Type
     TObjRef = class of TObject;
     TChildClass = class(TObject)
End;

Var
     AnObjectRef : TObjRef;
     AnObject : TObject;
     AChild : TChildClass;

Begin
     AnObject := TObject.Create;
     AChild := TChildClass.Create;
     AnObjectRef := TObject;
     { statements that illustrate polymorphism }
     ...
     AnObjectRef := TChildClass;
     { statements that illustrate polymorphism }
     ...
End;
```

Runtime Type Information

Often, your application requires object-type information at runtime. The New operator, for example, may need to determine whether a given class is of a given type or one of its descendants. Delphi provides the Boolean operator is to determine whether a class instance is assignment-compatible with a class. Here's an example:

```
If AnObject is TObjectType then
begin
    ...
end;
```

The If statement evaluates the expression and returns true if the instance AnObject is assignment-compatible with classes of type TObjectType or one of its descendants.

Delphi also offers the operator as to assure, at runtime, safe typecasting of objects. Here's an example:

```
Type
    TObjectType1 = class(TObject);
    TObjectType2 = class(TObjectType1);

Var
    Object1 : TObjectType1;
    Object2 : TObjectType2;

Begin
    ...
    Object1 := Object2 as TObjectType1
    ...
End;
```

The assignment statement is equivalent to a typecast, except that using the operator as raises an EInvalidCast exception if Object2 isn't of a compatible class.

Virtual Constructors

Delphi allows new-style objects to have virtual constructors. Although the constructor TObject.Create() itself isn't virtual, many members of VCL class hierarchy have virtual constructors.

Forward Class Declaration

Delphi permits you to make a forward declaration of class to make it accessible to other class declarations before fully defining the first class. This feature greatly resembles the forward declaration a function or a procedure, as described earlier in the "Procedures and Functions" section. Here's an example:

```
Type
    { forward declaration of classes }
    TClass1 = class;
    TClass2 = class;

    TTreeClass = class(TObject)
        fDataNode : TClass1;
        fLinkData : TClass2;
        ...
    End;

    TClass1 = class(TObject)
        fData : String;
        ...
    End;

    TClass2 = class(TObject)
        fIndex : Integer;
        ...
    End;
```

This example has the forward declarations of classes TClass1 and TClass2. The class TTreeClass has fields that are instances of the classes TClass1 and TClass2.

Dynamic Methods

Delphi reintroduces the concept of dynamic method dispatching. Unlike the dynamic methods that are used in the ObjectWindows library (which uses a variant of the virtual directive followed by an integer expression), dynamic methods are declared with the directive dynamic. The compiler assigns its own index (which happens to be a negative number).

Dynamic methods operate just like virtual methods, but instead of an entry in the class's virtual method table, the dynamic method is dispatched by using its index number. The only marked difference between dynamic methods and virtual methods is that dynamic methods are dispatched somewhat more slowly.

Abstract Methods

Delphi supports the formal declaration of abstract methods for virtual or dynamic methods. Previous versions of Borland Pascal, such as version 7.0, allow you to declare a method and call a procedure called Abstract(), which in Delphi raises a runtime error. Delphi now supports the directive abstract, which declares a method as truly abstract. An abstract method doesn't need to be implemented—just declare its heading.

Abstract methods provide a logical template for constructing objects but leaves the implementation of the code up to you. A file I/O object logically would have a FileOpen method, a read method, a write method, and a Close method, among others. Inclusion of the header followed by abstract provides you with the format but leaves it up to you to decide to use the Windows API file I/O, Pascal RTL, or maybe functions in a third-party DLL. Here's an example of an abstract method:

```
Type
    TAbsArrayObject = class
        ...
        procedure Sort; virtual; abstract;
        function BinSearch(Key : String) : Index;
            virtual; abstract;
        function LinSearch(Key : String) : Index;
            virtual; abstract;
    End;
```

The abstract directive is valid only the first time you introduce a method in a class.

Override Directive

In Delphi, virtual methods have two ways of dispatching: VMT-based and dynamic methods that override virtual and dynamic methods. Use the override directive rather than repeat virtual or dynamic. Here's an example:

```
Type
    TClass1 = class
        ...
        procedure Sort; virtual;
    End;

    TClass2 = class(TClass1)
        ...
        procedure Sort; override;
    End;
```

The class TClass2 may declare its own version of method Sort() with either virtual or dynamic, but these keywords lead to different things. Either keyword introduces a different method Sort(), which replaces rather than overrides the inherited method Sort().

Message-Handling Methods

Delphi adds a new and specialized type of dynamic method that's called a *message-handling* method. Message-handling methods have the following distinguishing characteristics:

- They're invariably procedures.

- They're declared with the message directive.

- They take an integer constant as a dynamic index, following the `message` directive.
- They take a single reference parameter.

Delphi supports the actual message dispatching by using the method `Dispatch()`, which is inherited from class `TObject`.

Delphi allows you to create methods that act as message handlers. The processing behind Delphi events is the forwarding of specific Windows messages. All Windows controls and applications communicate through a message dispatch system. If you've done any straight Windows API programming in C or Pascal, you may already be familiar with how this works.

> **Note**
>
> If you aren't familiar with the Windows message dispatch system, don't worry. You need to understand only that Windows sends certain messages to your application, depending on what's happening in the environment. When you run a Delphi program and resize the form, for example, Windows sends a message to the hidden window procedure of your form. Delphi captures the message and, if appropriate, will execute the `OnSize` event.

Because Delphi components provide events, it keeps you (in most cases) from having to worry about capturing the messages. This will change, of course, if you begin creating your own components that directly subclass ancestors of `TComponent`. Direct message processing can become very tricky. It requires an in-depth knowledge of each possible message. It also requires an understanding of the various levels of messages as well as each message's variable message parameters.

Delphi will forward you a specific message, however, if a message handler is created for it. Delphi will also send you a cracked version of the parameters contained within the message. This simplifies the work for you. Once your message-handling method executes its code, the default message handler can then be inherited and continue processing as always. Alternatively, the inherited handling can be ignored, thus the message is thrown out. This allows you to handle all the processing for that message.

An example message handler may be that which captures the `WM_Size` message. Windows sends this message to a sizable window every time it's resized. The form in Delphi doesn't provide an event for this. Instead it provides the `OnResize` event, which fires when a form is minimized, maximized, or restored. Now suppose that you want the form to be sizable but want to limit the width as well as the height to a minimum of 200. One method to do this would be to have Delphi pass to you the WM_Size message. A message handler for WM_Size can be added as a method of the form. The procedure declaration should appear in the type section in the form's class definition, as follows:

```
type
  TForm1 = class(TForm)
  private
    { Private declarations }
    procedure WMSize(Var Message : TWMSize); message WM_Size;
  public
    { Public declarations }
  end;
```

The private section of TForm1's class definition shows the procedure declaration

```
procedure WMSize(Var Message : TWMSize); message WM_Size;
```

The procedure name WMSize was chosen only as a matter of convention. The parameter is a var variable of type TWMSize, which is defined in the messages unit as a record. When the message handler receives the record in the form of the var variable Message, specific fields containing information about the size message are available. A different message would pass a record of its type with a set of fields containing information specific to it.

It would have been possible to use TMessage as the variable type. This is still syntactically correct. You use the type TWMSize because, depending on the message processed, the fields of the Message variable will be different. In the case of TWMSize, the fields made available to you are Width and Height. The message handlers declaration is followed by the keyword message and a constant called WM_Size.

The message keyword is defined specifically for creating message handlers. Any method that makes use of this keyword is dynamic (as opposed to virtual or static). Like any dynamic method, an index into the dynamic method table must be provided. In the example, WM_Size is used. The WM_Size constant is defined with a numeric value in the messages unit. Each message available has a corresponding constant for use as an index defined in the messages unit.

The actual procedure code should be placed within the implementation section of the unit. Observe the following example:

```
procedure TForm1.MSize(Var Message : TWMSize);
begin
  inherited;
  if (Message.Width < 200) then
      self.Width := 200;
  if (Message.Height < 200) then
      self.Height := 200;
end;
```

The limiting of the form's width and height properties was chosen for the processing in the example. The method begins with a call to the `inherited` method. The `inherited` keyword doesn't require declaration of an ancestor (or default) method. This denotes a special use of the `inherited` keyword within message handlers.

> **Note**
>
> Delphi provides default handling for all messages. A particular component may capture some of these messages and process accordingly. When you write a message handler, it could potentially inhibit the default handling—thus, `inherited` should be called.

The added processing contains two `if..then` constructs. The first checks the `Width` field of the passed `Message` variable. If it's less than 200, the `Width` property of the form is set to 200. The second checks the `Height` field of the `Message` variable. If it's less than 200, the `Height` property of the form is set to 200. This processing limits the width and height of the form each to 200.

The example also demonstrates the use of the `inherited` statement and how to access the fields within the passed message parameter.

From Here...

The Delphi language is based on Borland Pascal. An understanding of the core Pascal language is a preliminary for the more low-level Delphi programming issues. The extensions Delphi provides to the Pascal language and use of the visual environment stem from the information provided in this chapter and into some chapters that follow:

- Chapter 7, "Customizing and Reusing Components," makes use of most of the language extensions discussed in this chapter and their application in component writing.

- Chapter 14, "Handling Errors," discusses Delphi's implementation of exception handling and methods of including exception handling in your code.

- Chapter 15, "Using Delphi's Debugging Features," provides you with methods and techniques for finding errors in your program.

Part II

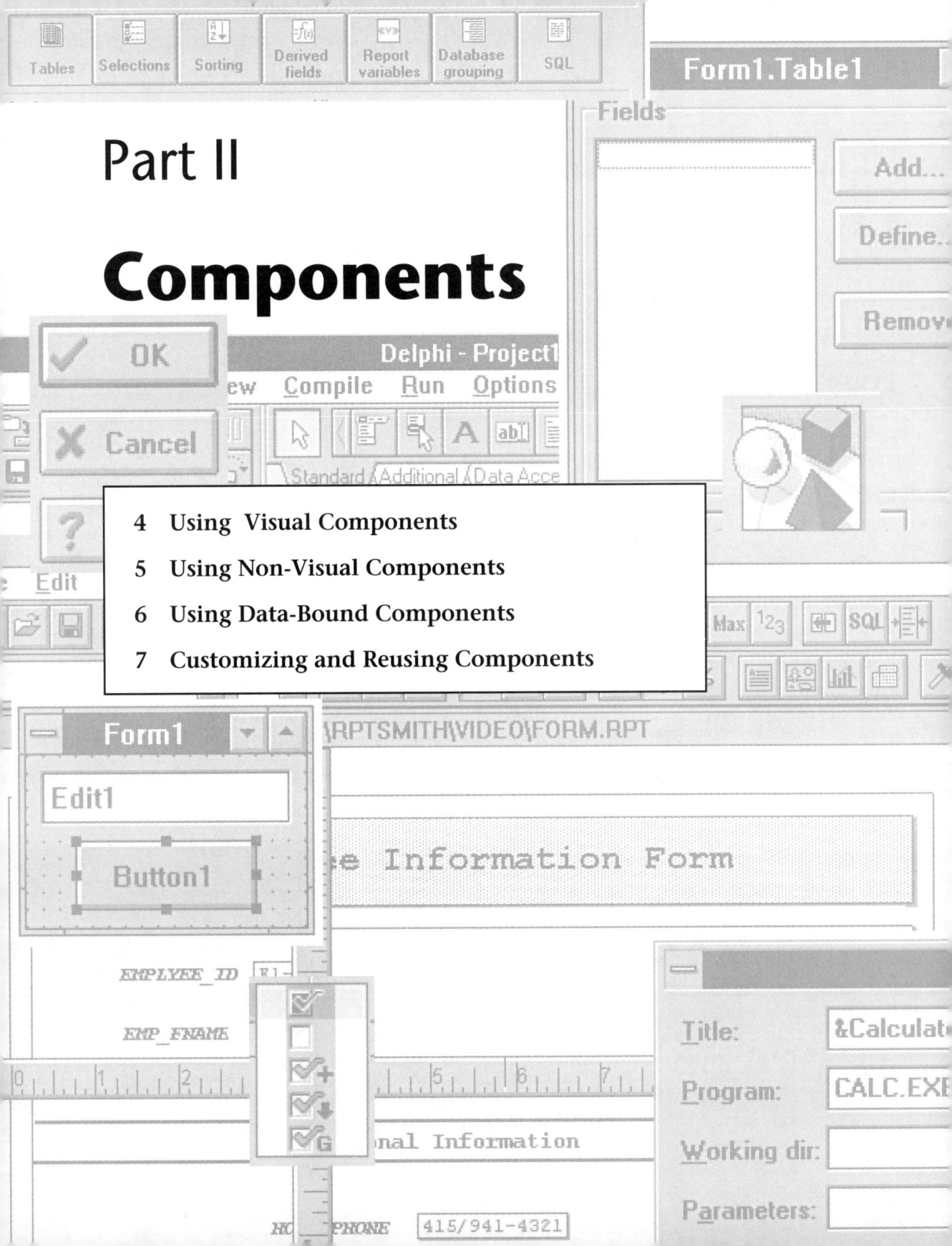

Components

- 4 Using Visual Components
- 5 Using Non-Visual Components
- 6 Using Data-Bound Components
- 7 Customizing and Reusing Components

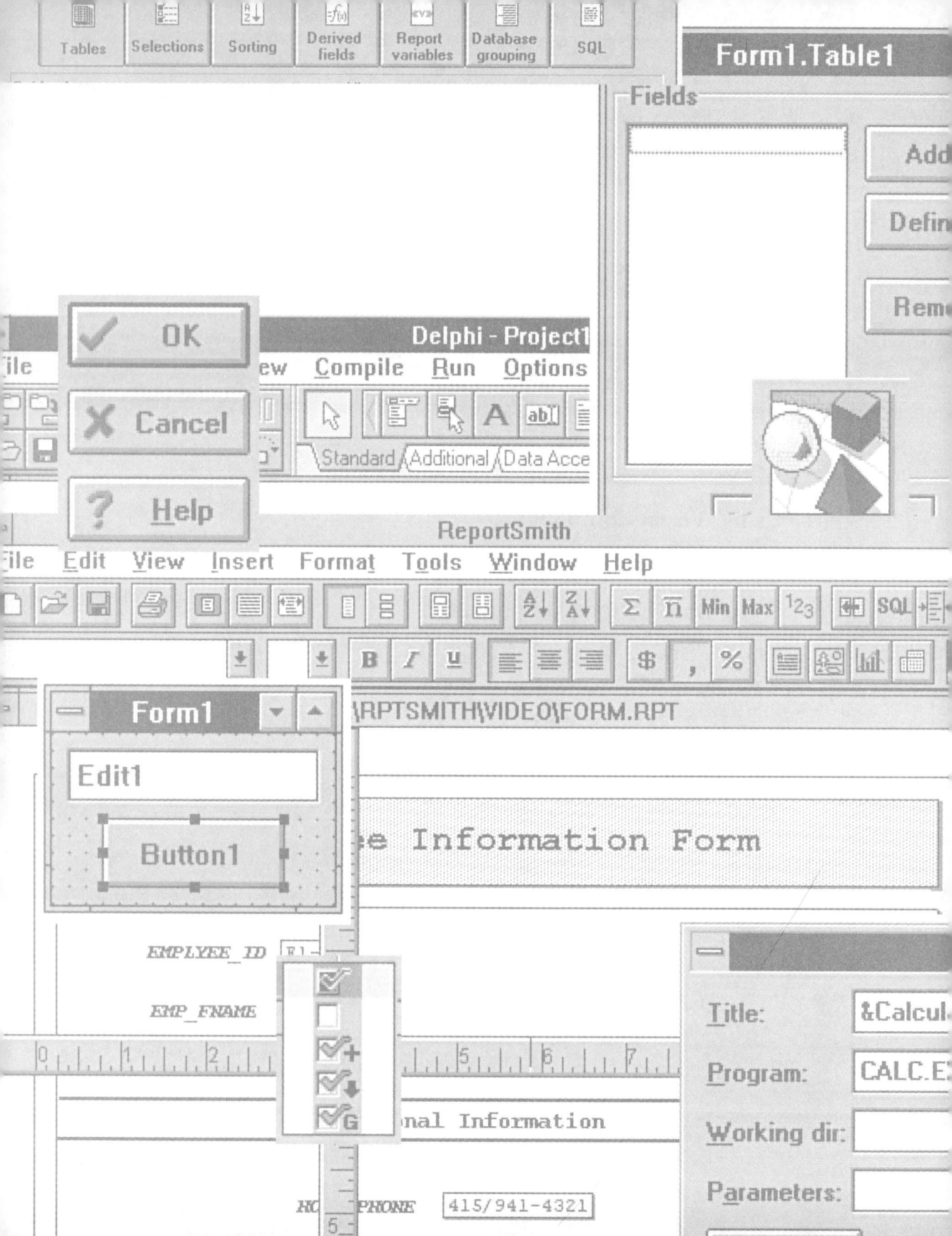

Chapter 4
Using Visual Components

This chapter shows you how to use Delphi's visual components for building your application's user interface. Visual components are WYSIWYG (what you see is what you get) when working in the form designer. Visual components are contained on a number of different pages of the Component palette.

In this chapter, you learn about:

- Text components, including labels, list boxes, and memo components
- String grid components
- Buttons and check boxes
- Components that group other components together
- Scrolling components
- Graphical components, such as images, shapes, and bevels
- File- and directory-access components
- Multimedia and OLE components
- VBX controls

Text-Related Components

The following sections deal with components that display text in various formats. Most of the components are used as means for data input. Use of a component depends on what you're trying to accomplish with your application. You should have a clear idea of how to use each component after reading each section.

Label Components

Labels are useful for identifying other objects in your application. Typically, you'll want to put labels next to objects such as memos and groups of check boxes or radio buttons. Labels can help with navigation and can also provide information for the user, other than the label's name itself.

> **Note**
>
> To create a functional link between a label and another object in your application, use the `FocusControl` property. This is accomplished by ensuring that the `Caption` property makes use of hot keys. When a user presses that hot key, the focus will move to the object that's associated with that label.

WordWrap and *AutoSize* Properties

The `WordWrap` and `AutoSize` properties are helpful when customizing the label component. Set `WordWrap` to true, and Delphi will automatically word wrap the label's caption. The `AutoSize` property is true by default. This may annoy you if you constantly need to have labels that occupy more than one "line" of space. Most programmers will have in mind the size of the label they want to place on the form. Initially, you can drag the outline to any size, but the moment you change the caption, the label will autosize to one line. If this is the case, the easiest solution is to set `AutoSize` to false before adjusting the caption. Enter the caption for the label and then resize it, if you want. Setting `AutoSize` back to true now will produce the desired effect; the label will grow in a downward direction as you add text to the caption.

OnClick Event and Focus Control

The `OnClick` event for a label is useful for helping the user with navigation. Even though you may have set the `FocusControl` property of a label to correspond with an object, that doesn't mean that a mouse click will also set focus on that object. However, this desired functionality can be achieved with one short line of code:

```
(sender as tLabel).focusControl.setFocus;
```

It's possible (and usually a good idea) to centralize your code for events, minimizing overall coding time. You could use the code in this example for all label objects in your application, as long as their `FocusControl` properties are set up correctly. This would take care of all mouse clicks on all labels in the application. Note that this code example won't work if a label object's `FocusControl` property is blank.

Edit, MaskEdit, and Memo Components

These three components are used to get text input from the user and to display text. The main differences between them are that the memo component allows multiple lines of input, while the other two components allow only one line of input; and the maskEdit component masks input, while the edit component doesn't. All have similar properties; in this section you'll go through the common ones first and then look at out the unique properties later.

The *Autoselect* Property

Autoselect is an interesting property. Those of you who have lost data just by pressing a key, especially those who had this occur in an application that didn't support the Undo feature, will appreciate this one. When moving around in Windows applications, sometimes the text you arrive on is automatically highlighted (selected). As soon as you press a key, that text is replaced with the key you just pressed. To minimize user errors, you may want to set this property to false for applications that require data entry using edit or memo objects. This will cause any existing text not to be selected on arrival to that object.

The *PasswordChar* Property

The PasswordChar property is used to hide the text that's being entered. The property name suggests, rightly so, that it be used when password entry is required. To provide an additional level of security, you could use this property to mask a user name. The value #0 is the default; it means that all characters appear as typed. Any other character will appear when text is entered via this object.

The *ReadOnly* Property

The ReadOnly property controls editing access to an object's value. You can set this property to false or true at runtime to allow and disallow editing access to that object. If an object's ReadOnly property is set to true, the user will still be allowed to move to the object and highlight any text for copying to the Windows Clipboard.

The *MaxLength* Property

To limit the number of characters entered into these objects, use the MaxLength property. If you're storing data that someone is entering, this property is useful because the user will know immediately what the limits are.

A Unique Property for the MaskEdit Component

The maskEdit component has an additional property that makes it stand out from the edit component. This property, `EditMask`, is used to mask (filter) characters being entered from the keyboard while on this object. Another common reference to this type of functionality is *picture*. The mask, or picture, defines which characters will be accepted and which ones won't. This is extremely useful for formatting character input. Click the ellipsis button in this property to open the Input Mask editor. This editor provides some sample masks, plus an area where you can quickly design and test a new mask. You can also choose which character, if any, to display in place of a blank. The default is the underscore character, which may not be pleasing to certain people. Consult the Delphi manuals or on-line help for the syntax of edit masks.

Unique Properties for the Memo Component

It's important to note the difference between the `Align` and `Alignment` properties for the memo object in figure 4.1. `Alignment` refers to text alignment, inside the object. `Align` refers to how the object is aligned on the form. The `Alignment` property for the memo object in the example is set to `taCenter`. The same object also has its `Align` property set to `alBottom`.

Fig. 4.1
Different uses for the edit and memo components. The memo object shows word wrapping with centered text.

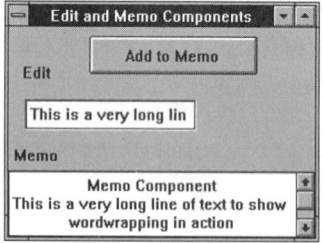

The `WordWrap` property allows you to control word wrapping within a memo object. Chances are that you'll want to have a vertical scrollbar also. Note the vertical scrollbar for the memo object in figure 4.1. You can use the `ScrollBars` property to set up scrollbars for the memo component, but note that having a horizontal scrollbar will effectively disable word wrapping. It's also much easier to see lengthy text in a memo object that has only a vertical scrollbar, not a horizontal *and* a vertical. The default value for the `ScrollBars` property is `ssNone`, meaning no scrollbars showing.

All the text entered via the memo object can be accessed from the `Text` property, but the `Lines` property offers some additional advantages. The text strings accessed through the `Lines` property are actually stored in a `TStrings` object. The `TStrings` object itself has properties and methods that make accessibility to the stored text very easy. The following sample code, taken from figure 4.1, shows how you can add lines to a memo field by using the `Lines` property and methods associated with the `TStrings` object.

```
procedure TForm1.AddButtonClick(Sender: TObject);
begin
  memo1.lines.add(edit1.text);
end;
```

The value that's in the edit object will be inserted into the memo object.

Tip
This code also will work on the list box object, except that you must change `memo1` to the name of the list box object, `list1`.

List Box Components

List box components present a list of items for selection. Sometimes you'll need to show a very large list of items in your application. The list box supports the standard-looking scrollbar for this type of requirement.

List box items can be added and removed dynamically, making them useful for displayed data that isn't constant. This component has a variety of properties that control how it appears. You may also opt to sort the items in a list box.

Depending on how they're placed on the form, list boxes can take up a lot of space. The combo box component (described next) is sometimes a better choice for listing items, where space is a factor. Take into account also if you want to show a certain number of items at the same time or all the time, or if you need to see only the item that's selected from the list.

Combo Box Components

Combo boxes, short for *combination boxes*, are similar to list box components in that they display lists of items. Combo boxes, however, take up less space and show only one item in the list at a time. This item is the default item or the item selected by the user. Many Windows programs use the combo box when showing disk drives available. Coincidentally, Delphi provides a component to do this for you automatically. It's called the *drive box component* and will be discussed later in this chapter.

The following code example shows how to initialize the combo box text with the first item, in the list of items, if the text is blank. This is like providing the user with a default value.

```
procedure TForm1.ComboBox1Enter(Sender: TObject);
begin
  if ComboBox1.text = '' then
    ComboBox1.text := ComboBox1.items.strings[1];
end;
```

The initialization in the code example takes place when the user physically arrives on that object. You can have this code elsewhere in an application for the purpose of initializing the text without the requirement of arriving on the object.

String Grid Components

A string grid component is just that—a grid of strings. String grid components can be used to simulate anything that's laid out in a grid, such as spreadsheets or the button pad on a touch-tone phone. You access these grid squares through the `Cells` property, which is a two-dimensional array of strings, one string per cell. The `Cells` property is set at runtime.

You can "fix" rows and columns of cells so that the user can't select them. This is useful for displaying column and/or row titles that you don't want to change. The values in the `FixedCols` and `FixedRows` properties determine the number of fixed columns and rows. You set the number of rows and columns to display in the grid in the `RowCount` and `ColCount` properties. The size of each cell is adjusted by setting desired values for the `DefaultColWidth` and `DefaultRowHeight` properties.

There are many set members for the `Options` property. (Think of set members as specific aspects of a particular property. Each set member of a property has specific, defined values.) Of particular interest are `goEditing` and `goTabs`, which are relevant for data entry via a string grid. Including `goEditing` in the set will allow data entry at runtime. Including `goTabs` will allow the user to use the Tab and Shift+Tab keys to navigate the string grid. These two are by no means the most important, and you'll want to explore all the set members to understand the different ways to configure a string grid. Check out the on-line help for more information on this property.

Button and Check Box Components

Button and check box components are common to many existing Windows applications. They present information to the user in a visual sense, much like an indicator light on your car's dashboard. The components are sometimes used to mimic an actual paper form that has check boxes or areas you color in with a pen or pencil.

Button Components

Buttons are typically used in dialog boxes. You've seen the familiar OK-Cancel pair in many Windows applications. You don't have to design a dialog box just to use the button component, however. Button components can be placed anywhere in your application to provide any type of functionality you want at the "touch of a button." You may also have seen applications that show hints as the mouse cursor passes over the button, or as the mouse button is pressed but not released. Either function is easily added to your application with a few lines of code.

BitBtn (Graphic Button) Components

Bit buttons are very similar to button components, except that they allow you to place a *glyph*, or small picture, on the button along with text. The glyph will usually provide a pictorial example of the button's functionality. Delphi provides a standard set of buttons from which you can draw during design of your applications. These Kinds of buttons (Kinds being the property that specifies the kind of button) are the "standard" e, Yes, No, Cancel, and more.

You can use these buttons to quickly design dialog boxes with built-in returning functionality. This is accomplished by setting the ModalResult property to match the function of the button—for example, a ModalResult of mrOK and a button Kind of bkOk.

Speed Button Components

Speed button components are provided for easy design of toolbars. Speed buttons have only a glyph and no caption. You can have more than one glyph on a speed button and even change the glyph at runtime.

You can use speed buttons to simulate radio buttons, for use on a toolbar. Setting the GroupIndex property to a value other than 0 will accomplish this. It's easy to see how you can have multiple groups of speed buttons on a toolbar using this property.

Also note that setting the AllowAllUp property to true using the GroupIndex property will allow all the buttons to be in the "up" state at the same time, as opposed to one of the buttons always being in the "down" state.

Speed buttons can also perform the functions of button and bit button components.

Radio Button Components

Radio button components are useful for displaying data in a visual context and for visual data entry. Radio button components, when grouped together, are useful for displaying a list of choices that the user can select from. The key concept for a group of radio button objects is that only one can be selected at any point in time, just like the buttons on an old car radio. You may designate one of the radio buttons, at design time or runtime, to be the default. This way you can assist the user in selection, or visually show that a selection was made or an action has occurred.

Figure 4.2 shows an example use of the radio button component to elicit a color selection from the user. Notice the box surrounding this group of radio buttons. The purpose of this box is revealed later in the "Grouping Components" section.

Fig. 4.2
Selection of a color implemented with radio button components. The use of the BitBtn components here suggest that this form is a dialog box.

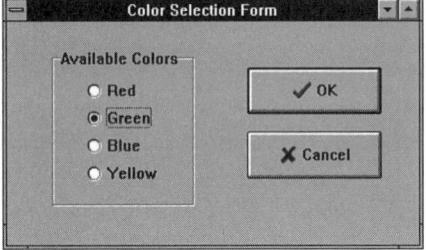

Check Box Components

Check box components are similar to radio button components in that they display data visually. Unlike radio buttons, however, check boxes aren't "aware" of the state of other check boxes. This means that multiple check box objects are independent of each other.

The check box component, however, has one additional state available. It can appear checked, unchecked, or grayed. The grayed state can be used to show a "maybe" or "not available (N/A)" answer, as opposed to a yes (checked) or no (unchecked) answer.

Check boxes are normally used in a situation where you need to get a yes or no (and possibly maybe) answer in your application. Figure 4.3 shows two possible uses for check box components. One of the examples makes use of the grayed state, and the other uses only the checked and unchecked states. You can see how the grayed state (maybe-type answer) wouldn't apply to the top-most check box.

Fig. 4.3
Context-sensitive uses of the check box component.

Grouping Components

You can use all the components in the following sections to group other components together. They are also useful for providing borders and areas on your form that appear strikingly different from other areas.

Usually, you'll group components together that have common functionality. If you need to have more than one group of radio buttons on a particular form, for example, you'll have to use either of these two objects to logically separate the groups. Otherwise, Delphi will assume that only one of all the radio button objects can be selected at any point in time. Also, each object you place within a group box or panel is a child of that object. When you move the container object, all objects in that container will move also.

Group Box Components

Group boxes have a caption that you can use to assign a title to the group of objects contained in it. Figure 4.2 shows the use of a group box, with the caption `Available Colors`.

Group boxes aren't limited to containing one type of component. Note that having too many components in a group box may lead to confusion, when the original idea was to prevent that very situation. The idea is to use group boxes to make your application easy to use.

Panel Components

Panels have captions also, but the caption can be situated in various places. Panels are well suited to be customized into status regions or toolbars. You can code the capability to pass hints and help messages to a status region. Toolbars are also common in Windows applications. You can have multiple panel objects, such as toolbars, displayed at the same time.

Sometimes you'll want to simply associate a group of objects together by drawing a box around them. This is a simple yet functional use of these controls. The sex panel in figure 4.3 shows how radio buttons are grouped together using the panel component. If the dialog box in figure 4.3 had other radio buttons, they would act independently of the radio buttons in the sex panel.

Tab Set Components

By itself, the tab set is simply a group of related items. When you couple the tab set component with the notebook component (covered later), you can achieve a space-saving, friendly interface to a large amount of information. For example, a system configuration dialog box that has many options can be implemented in such a manner that it isn't overbearing. You would categorize configuration elements in the dialog box, and then split them up onto separate notebook pages and use the tab set object to navigate the pages.

The Tabs property, which is a TStrings instance, contains the list of strings that compose the entire tab set. How the strings are organized is up to your imagination. When the Style property is set to tsOwnerDraw (the default), the tabs themselves will automatically size to the text contained in them. You can use glyphs on the tabs, but this requires extra programming control to work properly. You also have control over the colors of the selected and unselected tabs. These are set through the SelectedColor and UnselectedColor properties. A small scrollbar will automatically appear if more tabs are present than can fit in the allotted space.

Notebook Components

As mentioned in the preceding section, the notebook component is very useful when used with the tab set component. A notebook component is similar to multiple group box components, with the restriction that you can view only one "page" of the notebook at a time. All objects placed on a notebook page are children of that notebook object.

Other than the use mentioned in the preceding section, you can use a notebook component to provide a context-sensitive area in an application. This area would display a certain set of objects, depending on user interaction.

The Pages property contains a list of page names. Be flexible with page names because you won't have to reference them by their names when coding. Instead, you can use the PageIndex property, which is an integer, to set the active page. If you synchronize tab set strings with page name strings, you won't have to worry about which page name corresponds to which index number. You can do this at runtime by setting the Tabs property of a tab set to the Pages property of a notebook object. This way, you can create as many pages as you want at design time and not have to worry about resynchronizing the tabs themselves.

Scrolling Components

The two components in the following sections are examples of widely used Windows interface objects. Scrollbars are common to a large number of Windows applications. You also can use scroll box components to implement a scrolling area on your form and save a great deal of space.

Scrollbar Components

Scrollbar components are good for providing an interface to anything that needs to be changed and can be quantified somehow with a whole number. Control of the scrollbar is well thought out in Delphi, with a variety of properties to control its behavior. If you had a hardware link to a variable speed motor on a PC, the scrollbar would lend itself perfectly to controlling the speed of the motor. The following code example shows how to constantly display the position of the scrollbar:

```
procedure TForm1.ScrollBar1Change(Sender: TObject);
    var s: string[4];
begin
    str(scrollBar1.position, s);
    scrollBarPosition.caption := 'Position: ' + s;
end;
```

This code also could be attached to the `OnScroll` event instead, producing the same results.

The `Position` property tells you where the scrollbar is at a point in time. The value in this property is an integer value. You can manipulate this property through code at runtime if you need to dynamically change the position of the scrollbar.

Scroll Box Components

Scroll box components act much like group box components, only with a little bit of added functionality. It's no wonder, since both components are derived from the `TWinControl` object. Scroll boxes are useful for providing an area in an application that's scrollable and doesn't affect other areas of the application. This can save space on a form by showing only what usually needs to be shown, with other objects accessible simply by scrolling.

The easiest way to design a scrolling area is to maximize the scroll box and then place all the desired components. When you're finished with the layout of this area, size the scroll box appropriately, and the scrollbars will appear automatically. The `Position` property, which is nested under the `HorzScrollBar` and `VertScrollBar` properties, can be set at design time to show a default area of the scroll box. Conversely, you could set this property at runtime, depending on user input.

Graphical Components

Graphical components are used for displaying shapes and objects, and displaying data in a visual form. Some of these components are quite simple, while others are more complex. Each, however, is suited toward particular tasks, which will make themselves evident as you read each section.

Image Components

Use an image component to place a picture on a form. The image file, named under the `Picture` property, can be a bit map (.BMP), an icon (.ICO), or a metafile (.WFM).

You should note a few things about placing images on a form. The settings of the `Stretch` and `AutoSize` properties will have a noticeable effect on the image. If you want your image to appear at its original size, be sure to set `AutoSize` to true before you load the image. If you already have an image on the form, changing `AutoSize` from false to true will size the image to its original dimensions. `Stretch` set to true will allow you to resize the image manually; when you do this, the image will stretch or shrink to match the size of the object.

Tip
A paintbox component can't show its boundaries. To fix that, place the component inside a group box object. Align the paintbox's borders with the group box's borders to put a border around the paintbox.

Paintbox Components

Paintbox components provide a way to draw graphics in a limited area on the form. Drawing in the paintbox is accomplished by modifying the `Canvas` property, which is available only at runtime. Figure 4.4 shows a form with a paintbox.

Fig. 4.4
Sketching is done on the `Canvas` property of the paintbox component.

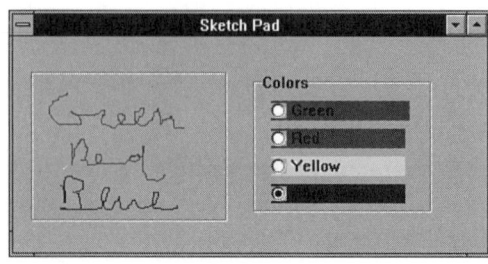

The following code, in the `TForm1.ColorRadioButtonsClick` method, sets the color of the pen.

```
procedure TForm1.PaintBox1MouseDown(Sender: TObject; Button:
  TMouseButton; Shift: TShiftState; X, Y: Integer);
begin
  isDown := true;
  paintbox1.canvas.moveto(x,y);
end;

procedure TForm1.PaintBox1MouseUp(Sender: TObject; Button:
  TMouseButton; Shift: TShiftState; X, Y: Integer);
begin
  isDown := false;
end;

procedure TForm1.PaintBox1MouseMove(Sender: TObject; Shift:
  TShiftState; X,Y: Integer);
begin
  if isDown then paintbox1.canvas.lineto(x,y);
end;

procedure TForm1.ColorRadioButtonsClick(Sender: TObject);
begin
  paintbox1.canvas.pen.color := (sender as TRadioButton).color;
end;
```

This is an example of how to minimize coding through clever configuration of object properties. The remainder of the code example is methods that show how the actual drawing capability is implemented.

Shape Components

The shape component is very basic in nature. Its uses, however, are limited only by your imagination. You can use shapes to add style to your application.

The color of the shape and the shape's outline are set with the nested properties of the Pen and Brush properties. The nested Style property has some interesting settings. You should play around with them to get a feel for how the shape component can be configured. The on-line help provides detailed explanations of these properties.

Bevel Components

Bevels are good for making areas of your form appear raised or lowered. You can place groups of buttons or check boxes inside the bevel, making them appear related because of the bevel border around them. For example, the sex panel shown earlier in figure 4.3 is beveled.

You can configure the bevel's border appearance by setting the Shape property. The border can actually be set as a single line, vertical or horizontal. You could use this type of configuration to underline or separate objects from each other, or to designate areas on your form to make it more user-friendly. The Style property controls the appearance of the border itself, which can be raised or lowered.

Outline Components

Outlines are useful for showing hierarchical data, such as a directory tree. The outline component in Delphi is highly configurable, appearing as basic or complex as you want. In addition to the displayed text, you can associate data with an outline item. The Add function, as defined for the outline component in the on-line help, documents how to do this. You can also configure how to display branches of the outline.

The outline consists of strings, accessed through the Lines and Items properties. The Lines property is a TStrings instance, and all outline items can be entered through Delphi's string list editor. When you enter items in the string list editor, place a space before an item to designate that item as being one level down in the tree. Generally, the number of spaces before the actual text is the number of levels down in the tree the text will appear. Once you leave the string editor and re-enter, you'll notice that any leading spaces are replaced with tabs.

> **Note**
>
> You can't use the Tab key in place of a space when entering items in the string editor.

The OutlineStyle property is used to configure the type of outline desired. Through this property you control how expandable and collapsible branches appear, whether to draw connecting lines, and whether to display symbols next to the items. If you intend to show glyphs in the outline, you can use the Picture property to indicate what will show. The appearance of the glyphs depends on the setting in the OutLineStyle property.

Various information is available at runtime. You can extract an index, which is an integer representation of the current position in the outline. The name of the items as well as the complete path name are also available. Figure 4.5 shows the name, index, and full path information on an outline item.

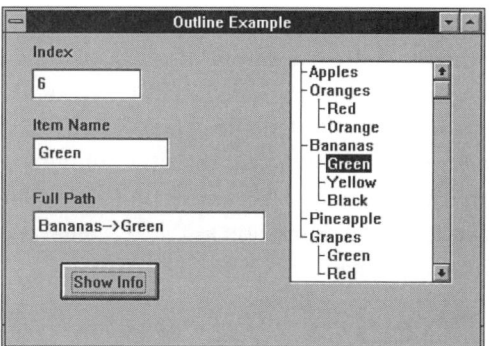

Fig. 4.5
Green is the current item in this figure, but you need the full path of the item to determine exactly where you are. In this example, "Green" is also an item under Grapes.

The following code, attached to btnShowInfo in figure 4.5, shows how to obtain various information from an outline object.

```
procedure TForm1.btnShowInfoClick(Sender: TObject);
var o: toutlineNode;

begin
  edtItemName.text := outLine1.items[outline1.selectedItem].text;
  edtFullPath.text :=
outLine1.items[outline1.selectedItem].fullPath;
  edtIndex.text := intToStr(outLine1.selectedItem);
end;
```

Color Grid Components

The color grid component provides an interface to controlling foreground and background colors. You could add this in a dialog and provide the dialog as a way for a person to customize the colors of your application. This would make the application more personal, and people will be happier looking at the colors they like most.

You can set the foreground and the background color with the color grid. The ForegroundColor and BackgroundColor properties contain the color that's selected. You can directly assign the values in these properties to another object's color properties to adjust the color of any object, including fonts contained in objects.

Draw Grid Components

The string grid component was actually derived from the draw grid component. This means that the draw grid component is a more general-purpose grid object. You can place drawings along with text in the draw grid. The functionality of the draw grid is similar to that of the string grid in that you use it to display data in a grid format. Each cell is accessible as in the string grid, and you can allow or disallow selection of multiple cells at a time.

Header Components

The header component is more of a graphical component than a text-related component, event though text is displayed in it. This component can provide an adjustable title bar or table header. The default value of its `AllowResize` property is true, meaning that a user can resize the columns with the mouse. You can disable this by setting the `AllowResize` property to false. The `Enabled` property also performs the same function as the `AllowResize` property.

File and Directory Access Components

The components covered in this section are used for different file- and directory-related activities. If you need more functionality than the open and save dialog components provide, you can use these controls in your forms to design a custom dialog for your specific purposes. The controls are easy to use and robust with functionality.

> **Note**
> For all the components in the following sections, scrollbars will appear automatically if there's not enough room to display all the information.

FileListBox Components

The fileListBox component provides a list-type interface in a directory. The default setting is to show all files in the directory.

Tip
Use the ; character to separate masks when specifying multiples masks.

The `Mask` property is used to provide filters, or masks. By using standard DOS wild-card conventions in this property, you can show only the files you want, such as .EXE or .TXT files.

The file name selected by the user is accessed via the `FileName` property. Use the `Directory` property to specify the directory—local or network—that you would like to show all files for.

Tip
Set the `ShowGlyphs` property to true to show a glyph next to the file name.

The `FileType` property contains a set of attributes that specify which files to show in the list box. You can use this property to show all types of files, such as system or hidden files. The default setting for this property is to show only normal files. Of particular interest here is the set member ftDirectory. Including this member in the set for the FileType property causes directories to be displayed along with the file names. One drawback to this is that you can't browse through the directory structure by clicking a directory name, as you can with most Windows directory browsers. Be careful when using this feature so as not to confuse your users. If you need this type of functionality, use the directoryListBox component.

You can configure the fileListBox component to allow selection of multiple files. Each item in the list box is accessed via the Items property, which is a TStrings instance. By using the Selected property, you can manually determine the individual files that were selected and process them accordingly.

The following example code shows how to extract the file names and store them in a list box. Also, as long as the count of items isn't 0, the Text property will be set to the first item in the list.

```
procedure TForm1.btnTransferClick(Sender: TObject);
var x:integer;
begin
  for x:= 0 to fileListBox1.Items.Count - 1 do
    if fileListBox1.Selected[x] then
      filesComboBox.Items.Add(fileListBox1.Items[x]);

  if filesComboBox.items.count <> 0 then
    filesComboBox.text := filesComboBox.items[0];
end;
```

DirectoryListBox Components

This component is used to select a directory much in the way that a fileListBox component is used. The value of the Directory property holds the current directory name along with the drive letter. The Drive property contains the current drive only.

If you're short on space on your form, you can configure this component to display information in more than one column. Figure 4.6 shows how the directoryListBox appears at runtime when the Columns property is set to 2. As you can see, the component takes up less vertical space but more horizontal space in this type of configuration. Delphi will split up the available vertical space into equal parts (columns), so take care that you provide enough room for displaying longer directory names.

Tip

Change to a different drive and directory at the same time by entering a new value in the Directory property only. The Drive property will resync on its own.

Fig. 4.6
The fileListBox and directory ListBox objects are linked together, so when you choose a new directory in the directory ListBox object, the contents of the fileListBox object are updated.

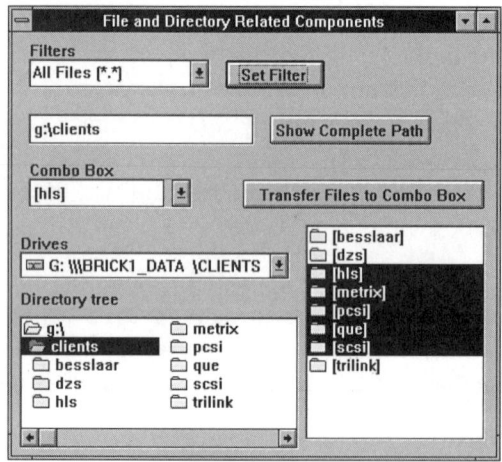

DriveComboBox Components

The driveComboBox component provides a combo-box type interface to all drives available on your system. As with the two previous components, the Drive property contains the current drive letter as a string. You have a choice of displaying the drives in upper- or lowercase, which is done through the TextCase property.

> **Note**
> You should provide exception-handling logic for the exception that occurs when a user selects a drive that isn't available, such as a floppy drive.

FilterComboBox Components

This component provides a way to screen out certain files using the standard DOS wild cards. All filters you intend to provide are entered as strings in the Filter property. When you're entering filters into the Filter property, you need to provide a pair of strings. The first member of the pair is a text description of the filter, such as Executable Files. The second member is the actual filter, such as *.EXE. To provide multiple string pairs, separate each pair with the ¦ (vertical bar) character. You can provide multiple filters in a pair by separating the filters with the ; (semicolon) character. You need to separate the members of the pair with the ¦ character also.

The following example code sets the Filter property of a filterComboBox2 at runtime with multiple filters. The string pairs and separators have been broken out to illustrate the assignment syntax more clearly.

```
filterComboBox2.filter := 'All Files (*.*)|*.*' +
                          '|' +
                          'Executable (*.exe)|*.exe' +
                          '|' +
                          'Pascal Source (*.pas)|*.pas';
```

Multimedia and OLE Components

These two components are in a class by themselves. With them, you can easily develop a multimedia application or an application that acts as an OLE client or an OLE server. Both components are easily configured to produce the desired results.

Media Player Components

The media player component is quite useful when dealing with media files. You tell it which file to play, and it will play that file, regardless of the type. You can, however, turn off the auto media type detection of the media player by setting the `DeviceType` property. The name of the file you want to play is entered in the `FileName` property.

You have a good deal of control over the buttons on the media player. Besides deciding which ones are enabled, you can also control the color display and how they function in relation to each other. The `ColoredButtons` and `EnabledButtons` properties have several nested properties each related to a particular button's appearance and accessibility. The `AutoEnabled` property, when set to true, will automatically enable and disable buttons depending on the state of other buttons.

> **Note**
>
> `AutoEnable` overrides `EnabledButtons` settings. If you need to control button enabling and disabling, you can query the `Mode` property to determine the current mode (play, recording, and so on) of the media player.

The `Wait` and `Notify` properties are used to gain additional control and information about the events that are occurring. When `Wait` is set to true, the media player object won't return control to the application until the next media control method finishes executing. When `Notify` is set to true, the next media control method that completes will cause an `OnNotify` event to occur. Also, the `NotifyValue` property will be set to the appropriate constant (see the on-line help for constant values). You may need to use `Notify` and `Wait` if you're expecting the next control method to take up a good amount of time.

Errors are more likely to occur when using the media player due to the additional dependence on hardware devices and drivers. It's important to have thorough exception-handling logic to prevent your application from crashing.

OLE Container Components

The OLE container component is used whenever you need to interface with an object that's external to Delphi, such as a Paradox table, a Word document, or a spreadsheet. This object's native application must support OLE for this to work. This type of functionality can provide inexperienced users with easy routes to other applications and the objects they control, allowing on-the-fly changes of objects external to Delphi.

Delphi provides a list of applications that support OLE, shown after clicking the ellipsis in the `ObjClass` property. You simply need to select an application here and, if necessary, fill in the `ObjDoc` and `ObjItem` properties. Displaying the object as an icon is a great space-saver, since you may not want to display the entire object in your application. Consult the OLE documentation for the applications you want to use to determine the values for these properties.

Common Component Properties

The properties in this section are some of the common properties for all the components discussed in this chapter. Not all of the components have these properties, but most do. Rather than mention them over and over again under each component's section, these properties are covered here for simplicity.

Popup Menus

You can link popup menus to a label via the `PopupMenu` property. The popup menu will appear when the user right-clicks the label. You can design a popup menu that offers customization of the label on the fly. The same menu could also offer help for the object that the label is attached to, if any.

The *TabStop* Property

The Tab key is used to navigate the objects in your application. Setting an object's `TabStop` property to true will ensure eventual arrival on that object when the Tab key is used.

Applications that require data entry sometimes have optional regions or sections that don't have to be complete for the entire data-entry session to be viewed as complete. In an order-entry application for a pet supply store, for example, you might have a field that shows personal information about the customer and whether the customer has pets. This information may be requested by the marketing department, but certain sales associates may choose not to provide (or forget to ask the customer for) this information. You could use the TabStop property, set to false, to aid the user entering orders so that the order is entered quickly, avoiding the places where personal information is entered. This way, the user doesn't have to travel to and from objects for which no values will be entered.

Visual Basic Controls

Visual Basic programmers looking for a new application builder will be happy to discover that Delphi can accept Visual Basic controls. Delphi provides an interface to adding these controls to its component library. This interface is also used to add any custom controls that you want. However, only Visual Basic controls that support the Visual Basic 1.0 specifications can be added to the component library. You can find more information on VBX controls in Chapter 7, "Customizing and Reusing Components."

Adding Visual Basic Controls

A Visual Basic control is added through the Install Components dialog box, accessible from the Options menu. You can choose to specify a different name for the control, along with the choice of where to place the control on Delphi's Component palette. Each time you add a control, Delphi will rebuild its component library. Delphi ships with only a few Visual Basic controls, leaving room on the Component palette for any you might want to add.

Using Delphi's Visual Basic Controls

If you use Visual Basic controls in your application, it's important to note that these controls won't be linked to the application's executable file. You must ensure that all necessary VBX files are available to your application; if you distribute your application, you must also provide the VBX files. If any VBX files are missing, your application won't run.

BiSwitch

The BiSwitch control's basic functionality is equivalent to a radio button's functionality. The difference is obvious, the BiSwitch being a pictorial representation of a toggle switch. You can set the default position of the switch by adjusting the pOn property. You can locate the string value in the Caption property at different positions in relation to the switch itself. This is configurable through the TextPosition property. The OnOff and OnOn events occur when the switch is moved to the on and off positions.

BiPict

The BiPict control is similar to Delphi's image control. You specify the image to be displayed in the Picture property. The dialog that opens displays the list of default styles. You can stretch the image by setting the StretchBlt property to true. Now, when you resize the control with the mouse, the image will resize to match the dimensions of the control.

BiGauge

Delphi provides a sample gauge much like the Visual Basic BiGauge control. As with Delphi's sample gauge, you can configure the type of the gauge as well as the foreground and background colors. Unless you're absolutely in love with the BiGauge, you'll want to stick with Delphi's sample gauge for simplicity and to avoid the overhead of having a Visual Basic object in your application.

TKChart

The TKChart control is a chart or graph object. A variety of properties control how the chart appears. You can adjust the font as well as the location of the axis titles. Adjusting the space between the data is accomplished by setting the xGapStyle and zGapStyle properties. The value in the Chart property determines the format in which the data is displayed. There are quite a few choices here, and experimentation is the easiest way to determine your needs.

From Here...

You should be familiar with all the components available in Delphi. The following chapters will help you accomplish this task:

- The next chapter, "Using Non-Visual Components," deals with other components you'll most likely want to use in your applications.

- Chapter 6, "Using Data-Bound Components," is a must-read if you intend to develop database applications with Delphi.

- Chapter 8, "Creating Forms," goes into detail about how to create effective, easy-to-use forms with the various components.

Chapter 5

Using Non-Visual Components

Chapter 4, "Using Visual Components," covers the components that are presented to the user in the same way they're displayed at design time. Delphi has another set of components, called *non-visual components*, that by themselves don't do anything—they're invisibly embedded on your form at runtime. For the most part, when working with non-visual components you'll be writing code to use and invoke the component's features. Some non-visual components have interactive setup features, such as the menu and query components, but you'll always end up writing code to support them. Query components and other data-bound components are discussed in Chapter 6, "Using Data-Bound Components."

In this chapter, you'll learn how to:

- Create menus
- Control menu items at runtime
- Use timer and DDE components
- Create standard Windows dialogs

This chapter is dedicated to all non-visual components except data-bound components, which are covered in Chapter 6.

Creating Menus

The menu component is one of a handful of components that has a built-in interactive designer. When working with the menu component, you can invoke the Menu Designer.

The Menu Designer allows you to create menus at design time and examine your menu structure as you go. Menus appear exactly as designed, providing an immediate view of how the menu will look in the application you're building. The Menu Designer is so easy to use, you can jump right in and create a pull-down menu right now. (Popup menus are created in a similar manner, so there's no need to go over them specifically.)

After you create a pull-down menu, you'll learn how to fine-tune menus in general.

Using the Menu Designer

Now, you can create a sample pull-down menu to see how easily and efficiently you can design menus. First, go through the steps for creating a menu. To create a menu, you first need to place a menu object on the form. Click the Main Menu button on the SpeedBar and then place the object on the form using the mouse. At this point, there are two ways to jump right into menu construction:

- Move to the Object Inspector. The menu object you just placed will be automatically selected, as long as you haven't moved off that object. Now click the item's property and then the ellipsis (the button with the three dots).

- Double-click the menu object you just placed on the form.

You're now in the Menu Designer and parked on the first menu item that's yet to be defined. At this point, enter a top-level menu item and press Enter. A top-level menu item is the name of the menu as it appears on the menu bar. For example, in Delphi's main window, some top-level menu items are File, Edit, and Search.

You'll now be at the first menu item under the item you just entered. Continue entering menu items under the top-level menu item until you're done. Now, move to the next top-level menu item and continue adding menu items as necessary until your menu is complete.

The Menu Designer window contains a popup SpeedMenu that provides quick access to the most frequently used Menu Designer commands and access to menu template options (see fig. 5.1). To display the SpeedMenu, either right-click in the Menu Designer window or press Alt+F10 when the cursor is in the Menu Designer window.

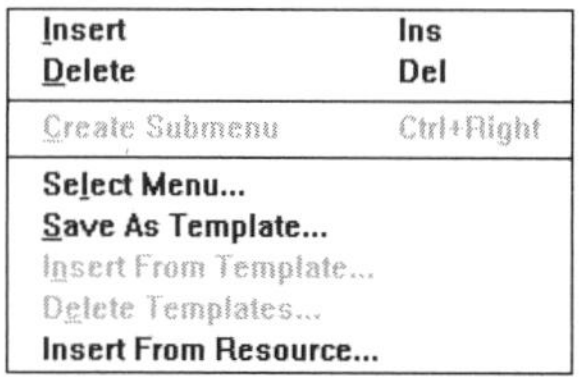

Fig. 5.1
The SpeedMenu provides quick access to frequently used functions.

Once you have your menu in place, you'll want to connect some code to complete the task. The `OnClick` event is the only event related to menu items. This event occurs when you click a menu item or when you use the shortcut or accelerator keys associated with that menu item. To design an event-handling procedure for the `OnClick` event, simply double-click the menu item while in the Menu Designer; if you're on the form, single-click a menu item. A source code window will appear where you can add the desired code related to this event. You can also double-click any menu item to get to the existing event-handling procedure. Alternately, you can double-click the procedure name shown in the Events page of the Object Inspector.

That's all there is to creating a menu in Delphi. The process is very streamlined and efficient. In case you didn't notice, every menu item you created is actually an object itself. You can access all these objects through the Object Inspector. The following sections discuss some methods and techniques relating to menu construction.

Providing Menu Names and Captions

During menu design, you're actually providing the captions for the menu item objects, not the names. The text in the `Caption` property is the text a user sees. A default `Name` will be assigned based on the caption you've entered. If you have a decent-sized menu, it's likely you'll need to adjust the default names assigned by Delphi to distinguish between menu items. At any point during the menu design process, you can move back to the form to see the results. You can also browse through the menu via mouse or keyboard commands.

Including Separator Bars

You can add separator bars by using the hyphen (-) character for the caption. There's no need to enter a name for the separator unless you plan to reference it from within your application. Separator bars are useful for visually grouping related menu selections together. This gives your application a user-friendly feel.

Adding Accelerator and Shortcut Keys

You'll want to integrate accelerator and shortcut keys in your menus for your application to behave in a standard Windows-like manner. Individual menu items typically have accelerator keys and shortcut keys assigned to them to help the user with navigation of the menu.

An *accelerator key* is simply an underlined letter in a menu item that can be used in conjunction with the Alt key to invoke that menu item. An example of this is the W in the common Window menu that's standard on most MDI applications. A *shortcut key* is usually a Ctrl+*key* combination that provides direct access to that menu choice without having to actually go through the menu. Shortcut keys are usually assigned to menu items that are used frequently.

You assign an accelerator key to a menu item through that menu item's Caption property. When entering the caption, put the ampersand (&) character immediately before the letter that you want to designate as the accelerator key. For example, **&Close** will appear in the menu as simply Close. Pressing C when the menu bar is active (or Alt+C when the menu bar is inactive) will immediately select the Close menu choice.

You can assign a shortcut key to a menu by setting the ShortCut property. The drop-down list for this property shows all available key combinations. The shortcut key you assign will appear next to that menu item's Caption property.

You may have shortcut keys *and* accelerator keys assigned to menu items. Figure 5.2 shows an example of a menu with shortcut and accelerator keys.

Fig. 5.2
Menu accelerators and shortcut keys increase the usability of a menu.

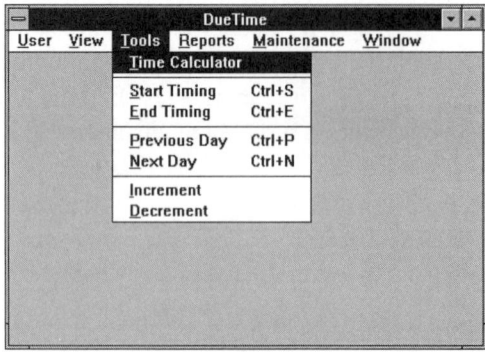

Creating Submenus (Nested Menus)

Menu branches can also be nested or *hung* as submenus off higher level menu items (see fig. 5.3). This functionality is extremely desirable, since a large list of top-level menu items can be confusing. You can use submenus to resolve this problem by grouping menu items of related functionality together and placing them in a submenu under a main menu choice. Since the menu items that "pull down" are usually grouped by functionality, you can easily relate a submenu to a top-level menu item.

Tip
Too many submenu levels can be just as confusing as one long list of menu items, so plan your menu structure well.

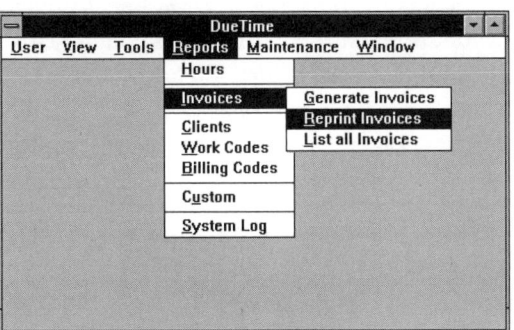

Fig. 5.3
Nested menus make the overall menu structure more usable and concise.

To create submenus off of a menu item, press Ctrl+right arrow; you'll be placed on the first menu item in a new submenu. You can now enter more menu items and even create additional submenus, if you want.

Dragging and Moving Menu Items

The Menu Designer supports relocation of menu items via the familiar drag-and-drop operation. While you're dragging a menu item, the cursor changes shape to indicate whether you can release the menu item at the current location. If you can't place the menu item at the current position, you'll see a circle with a line through it. If you can, the mouse cursor will appear as an arrow with a outlined box next to it. The Menu Designer also allows you to move menu items into and out of submenus. In a pull-down menu, for example, you can drag a top-level menu item into a submenu, and all the menu items (if any) contained under the dragged menu item will appear as a submenu off the dragged menu item in its new location.

Including Menu Hints

Hint is a very useful property that allows you to provide more detailed information about a menu item than simply its name alone. When a menu item is highlighted, a hint can appear in a status bar at the bottom of the form.

Hints allow users to get a one-line description of what a menu choice will do before they actually initiate the menu choice. When looking for a particular menu choice, users may go through several menu choices before deciding on the choice they want to invoke. You can show complete descriptions of a menu item's functionality, making your application more informative and user-friendly.

To add hint text to a menu item, enter the text that will appear as a hint in the Hint property of that menu item. You'll need to perform a few more steps for these hints to show up at runtime. The on-line documentation has a good example of how to link these menu hints into your application. To get to this information, click on the Hint property for any menu item in the Object Inspector, and then press F1. You may have to dig around a bit to get what you need because there are a few examples of how to do this.

Controlling Menu Items at Runtime

While some Windows applications use the same menu structure throughout a program session, other applications may require manipulating the menus dynamically at runtime. For example, your application may need to disable certain menu items at certain points in the application. This is how menus are made context-sensitive. You may also want to "check" certain menu items to indicate that they have been selected. Also, you may want to hide certain commands to dynamically create a short version of a menu. You can do all this by manipulating the properties of menu items at runtime.

Disabling Menu Items at Runtime

You can disable a menu item at design time and also during runtime by setting the Enabled property to false. This disables the associated menu item and displays it in gray.

You can also examine the Enabled property to determine the state of menu items at runtime. This is useful for preventing access to particular menu items. In this manner, you can provide menus that are context-sensitive—that is, sensitive to a user's location in the application. You can also disable menu items to secure certain users from accessing them by programatically linking user security rights to the menu. This way, the menu will change based on the level of security for a particular user. Of course, user security is something you'll have to implement yourself.

Toggling Menu Items at Runtime

A menu item can also act as an option that users can toggle. The Checked property is useful here for showing (with a check mark) that the user has selected a certain menu item (see fig. 5.4). When using a group of menu items in this manner, you can use the Checked property to determine which menu items are now selected by examining the property at runtime. A common use of this is seen in MDI applications, under the Window menu. You'll usually see a list of windows currently open, with a check mark next to the one that you're working in.

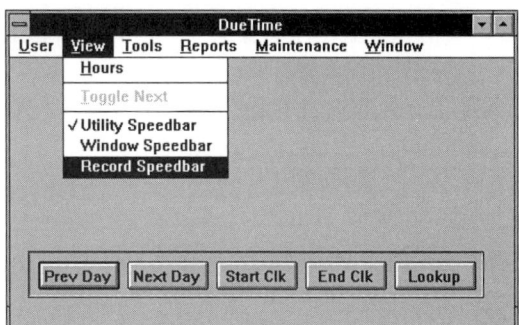

Fig. 5.4
You can indicate checked and disabled menu items to enhance the functionality of a menu.

Hiding Menu Items at Runtime

Some applications offer two versions of a menu: one that's aimed at the novice user, and another aimed at the experienced user. You can implement multiversion menus (advanced and novice) by hiding the menu items that are no longer needed by the experienced user or that the novice user has chosen not to see.

The Visible property allows you to show or hide individual menu items. If you hide a menu item, any submenus contained under the hidden menu item will also become invisible and inaccessible.

Using the Timer Component

Timer objects are independent objects that can initiate processing at specific intervals during program execution. Timers are a rather simple Windows-related component and are extremely useful when initiating logic independent of Windows and application events.

The `Timer` object triggers a single event—the `OnTimer` event. This event occurs every *x* milliseconds, *x* being the value in the `Interval` property of the timer. Here are some examples of uses for `Timer` objects:

- Flashing a text or picture object on-screen to remind a user to perform an action or that an action has occurred

- Simulating clocks and timers, showing the results visually

- Checking for certain system events or situations and taking action depending on the outcome

The following code example shows a simple use for the `Timer` object. In this example, you're simply increasing the `Progress` property of a gauge to show elapsed time visually. The following code is attached to the `OnTimer` event of the `Timer` object:

```
if pieGauge.Progress = 100 then
  pieGauge.Progress := 0
else
  pieGauge.Progress := pieGauge.Progress + 1;
```

If the `Interval` property of the `Timer` object is set to 100, the preceding code will execute every 1/10th of a second, and you'll see the results visually in the gauge object. The Stop/Start button stops and restarts the timer by alternately setting the `Enabled` property to true and false. This is accomplished via the following code, which is attached to the `OnClick` event of the `StopStartButton` object:

```
procedure TForm1.StopStartButtonClick(Sender: TObject);
begin
  if StopStartButton.Caption = 'Stop' then
    StopStartButton.Caption := 'Start'
  else
    StopStartButton.Caption := 'Stop';
  timer.Enabled := not timer.Enabled;
end;
```

You may also disable a timer by setting the `Interval` property to a negative value or to zero. If you have the example applications, you'll see this happen if you set the scroll bar to 0 and then click the Change Interval button. The maximum value of a the timer's `Interval` property is 32767.

Using DDE Components

Dynamic data exchange (DDE) allows you to send data to and receive data from other applications. Both applications must support DDE for this to work.

DDE also allows you to send commands and macros to other applications. In this manner, you can control other applications through DDE:

- *DDE conversation.* The DDE link between two applications. To have this conversation, you must have a DDE client and a DDE server.
- *DDE client.* The application that requests data from the DDE server.
- *DDE server.* Conversely, the application that updates the DDE client(s) with data.

You may create DDE clients and DDE servers with Delphi. You may also create an application that's both a DDE client and a DDE server.

DDE Client Conversation

The DDE client conversation component (`DDEClientConv`) is used to set up a DDE client in your application. You link the DDE client conversation component to a DDE client item component, which is the object that holds the data that's exchanged.

The two values for the `ConnectMode` property determine how the link to the DDE server is established. The `DDEService` and `DDETopic` properties hold the name of the DDE server application and the topic that the conversation is about. A sample application could be PDOXWIN, with the topic ORDERS.DB. The `FormatChars` property is used to screen unwanted characters such as line feeds and carriage returns. The `ServiceApplication` property should contain the full path plus the name of the executable file that's the DDE server application.

DDE Client Item

The DDE client item is the pathway for the data that's to be exchanged. As mentioned earlier, you link the DDE client item object to the DDE client conversation object.

The `DDEConv` property holds the name of the DDE client conversation object. The `DDEItem` property contains the item of the conversation, the "data." The value of this property depends entirely on the DDE server application you're linked to. Most importantly, the `Value` property holds the actual data that's exchanged.

Again, the type of data held here depends on the linked DDE server application. The `OnChange` event is useful for assigning the data just received to another object, like a combo box object or an edit object. The following sample code shows how this is done:

```
procedure TDDEServer1.Edit1Change(Sender: TObject);
begin
  DDEServerItem1.value := Edit1.Text;
end;
```

This code is attached to the OnChange event of an edit component. When the value in the edit box changes, the Value property of the DDEServerItem1 object will also change to match it.

DDE Server Conversation

The DDE server conversation object, combined with the DDE server item object, allows you to add DDE server capability to your application. DDE servers update DDE clients with data, or items of the conversation.

The only event associated with a DDE server conversation, OnExecuteMacro, is used to control what happens when DDE clients send macros to the server. You can use macros to control the DDE server application.

DDE Server Item

The DDE server item object is linked to the DDE server conversation object through the ServerConv property. All data being exchanged passes through this object to the DDE clients. The Value property contains the latest value of the exchanged data. The OnChange event is used to take specific actions depending on the current and previous values of the data.

Creating Dialogs

Windows supports a set of common dialogs that are used to open files, save files, select fonts, select and configure colors, and select and configure printers. Delphi supports these dialogs by implementing classes for them and offering controls that represent instances of the common dialog classes. Delphi supports the following dialogs:

Open	Print
Save	Printer Setup
Font	Find
Color	Replace

Open and Save Dialog Components

The Open and Save dialogs are covered at the same time since they have matching functionality.

Don't read too much into the component names—these components won't automatically open and save files for you. You can, however, use these dialogs to elicit a file selection from the user (see fig. 5.5). You then can do whatever you want with the file name that's returned. This chapter covers the more useful properties to gain an understanding of how to control these two dialogs.

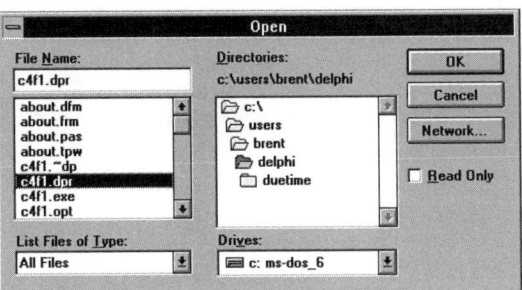

Fig. 5.5
You can easily link the standard Windows Open dialog into your application.

Providing a Default Extension

The `DefaultExt` property provides added functionality in that the user won't have to add the extension to the file name. This property designates up to three characters for the file extension (don't include the dot character).

The value of this property is added to the file name that's entered in the File Name text box when the file extension isn't present. The `DefaultExt` property is ignored if the file extension is included along with the file name. To avoid the automatic addition of a file extension (when an extension isn't required), simply leave this property blank.

Designating File Edit Region Interface Styles

The `FileEditStyle` property determines whether the Open dialog contains an edit or combo box control in which you type a file name. Setting the `FileEditStyle` property to `fsComboBox` permits you to designate which file names appear in the combo box. See how to use the `HistoryList` property relating to this property later in the "Using File Name History Lists" section.

Using the *FileName* Property

The `FileName` property designates the default file name to appear in the File Name text box when your application executes the Open dialog. When you click OK to confirm your selection, the dialog assigns the selected file name to the `FileName` property.

Specifying File Masks

A *file mask* or *file filter* is a file name that typically includes wild-card characters, such as *.FRM and *.PAS. You can use a mask to present to the user only the appropriate file types, since only the files that match the selected file filter in the list box will be shown. Also, the dialog displays the selected file filter in the File Name text box.

The Filter property specifies the file masks accessible to the user to decide which files to display in the list box, which is located directly under the File Name text box of the dialog.

The file filter itself is a string that consists of one or more pairs of strings. Each pair of strings is considered one filter. The string pairs are delimited by the bar character. Each string pair contains a string that describes the filter and a string that contains one or more valid file-name filters. In the case of multiple filters, you need to delimit them using the semicolon character. Here's an example that provides multiple filters for a dialog:

```
MyOpenDialog.Filter := 'Batch files (*.BAT, *.PIF)|' +
                       '*.BAT;*.PIF|' +
                       'Executables (*.EXE)|*.EXE|' +
                       'Initialization files (*.INI)|*.INI|' +
                       'Pascal files (*.PAS)|*.PAS';
```

Using the *FilterIndex* Property

The FilterIndex property is used to designate a default filter index number, in the case of multiple filters. You can use this to give users a hint as to which type of file they should select or which type of file the application is expecting.

Using File Name History Lists

You can use this property to save the user a good deal of time if the application requires frequent file selection. The HistoryList property holds the file names that are shown in the File Name drop-down combo box. The HistoryList property requires that the FileEditStyle property to be set to fsComboBox. You may use the HistoryList property to support a history list of the preceding file names opened with the Open dialog. Use a TStrings instance to maintain the list of strings and to assign this instance to the HistoryList property. Here's an example that shows how to implement the common history list feature:

```
procedure TForm1.Open2Click(Sender: TObject);
begin
  MyOpenDlg.FileEditStyle := fsComboBox;
  if MyOpenDlg.Execute then
    MyOpenDlg.HistoryList.Insert(0, MyOpenDlg.FileName);
end;
```

This example simply adds the selected file name to the `HistoryList` property, which is itself a list of strings. The user has to click OK for this to occur.

> **Note**
>
> `FileEditStyle` doesn't need to be set each time. It's shown here only to reiterate the connection between the two properties.

Using the *Options* Property

The `Options` property contains a variety of values that you can use to fine-tune the behavior of this dialog. This property has too many values to cover here, so if you need some added functionality that you can't get with the other properties, check out the on-line help for the set members of the `Options` property. Pressing F1 while parked on the set member will bring you to the correct area in the help.

Color Dialog Component

The Color dialog permits you to elicit a color selection and optionally to configure custom colors. You can use this dialog to provide an interface for a user to select one or more colors, and then use those colors to custom configure how an application appears.

The Color dialog also has some of the same properties as the Open and Save dialogs. This component doesn't have many properties, so this chapter covers just the two you'll most likely use. The remainder of the set members are covered adequately in the on-line help.

The *Color* Property

The `Color` property is the color that's selected when the dialog opens. This color will be outlined with a dotted line, distinguishing it from the other unselected colors. The color that's selected by the user is also returned here.

Color Dialog Options

Through the `Options` property, you can control a user's access to the custom color configuration. You may configure this property to open the dialog fully, which allows access to color configuration, or disable the button that expands the dialog.

Font Dialog Component

The Font dialog permits the user to choose a font and set that font's attributes (see fig. 5.6). The following sections discuss the more useful properties and methods for the Font dialog.

Fig. 5.6
The standard Windows Font dialog can be easily accessed from your application.

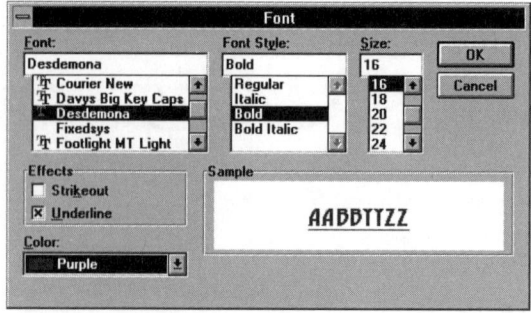

Selecting and Configuring Fonts
The values of the Font property determine which font appears in the dialog when it's open. You can use this property to supply a suggested default font to the user, along with style and size information. The font that the user selects is also returned here, along with all related information, such as style, size, and color.

Using Font Dialog Options
You can fine-tune the behavior of the Font dialog by using the Options property. Through this property you can control specifically what aspects of the font the user has access to. For example, setting the fdTrueTypeOnly set member to true will result in the dialog showing only TrueType fonts. The other set members are covered in the on-line help.

Using the *OnApply* Event
The OnApply event occurs when you click the Apply button in the Font dialog. The Font dialog shows the Apply button only when the calling form (your application) has an OnApply event handler. The Apply button lets you immediately apply the font that's selected in any manner you choose.

Print and Print Setup Dialog Components
You can use the Print dialog component to present an interface to report or file printing. This is a useful component to add to an application; because some users tend to freak out if they don't have a hard copy of something, the common dialog access capability will likely pacify them. Also, the common Print Setup dialog is available through this dialog, so you don't have to supply the Print Setup dialog separately (see fig. 5.7). The Print Setup dialog is used to configure the output and to choose a different printer.

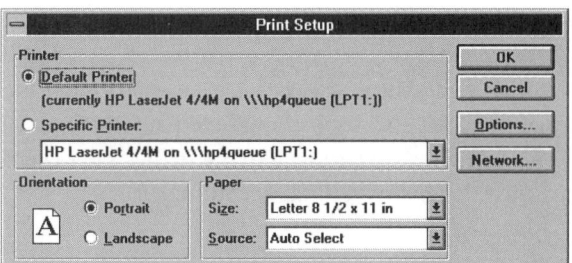

Fig. 5.7
The standard Windows Print Setup dialog is easily accessed from your application.

Various properties of these components can be set to provide additional information or guidance to the user of your application. The MaxPage property specifies the highest page number you can enter while selecting a range of pages to print. The MinPage property specifies the lowest page number you can enter while selecting a range of pages to print. To support these two features, the value for the PrintRange property must be PageNum and the Options property must include the set member poPageNums.

Find and Replace Dialog Components

Delphi supports the modeless Find and Replace dialogs. These two dialogs are extremely useful for searching for and replacing text. An end user will find them invaluable to the application if frequent access to this type of functionality is required. The two dialogs are similar, so this chapter covers their properties all at once to make things easy.

Specifying the Text to Find

The FindText property stores the search text that appears in the Find What text box of the Find dialog. You can assign text dynamically according to the user's current context, to help them out. This type of functionality is seen in most of today's word processors.

Using the *OnFind* Event

The OnFind event occurs when you click the Find Next button in the Find dialog. At this point, you'll use the text in the Find What text box, which is the value to search for.

Specifying the Replacement Text

The Replace dialog has the ReplaceText property, in addition to the property used in the Find dialog. The ReplaceText property stores the replacement text that appears in the Replace With text box of the Replace dialog. You can offer a suggestion to the user by dynamically altering this property at runtime or by entering a value at design time.

Using the *OnReplace* Event

The Replace dialog also has the `OnReplace` event handler, in addition to the event handler in the Find dialog. The `OnReplace` event occurs when the user clicks the Replace or Replace All button in the Replace dialog. At this point, you'll have in hand a Find string and a Replace string. Your event-handling code would now process the two strings accordingly.

From Here…

This chapter has covered some extremely useful components, and you may be itching to start building an application. The following chapters will help you on your way:

- Chapter 6, "Using Data-Bound Components," is a must-read if you intend to develop database applications with Delphi.

- Chapter 8, "Creating Forms," goes into detail about how to create effective, easy-to-use forms with the various components.

Chapter 6

Using Data-Bound Components

One of the most important features of Delphi—or any other front-end database development tool—is its capability to provide access to your data. By using the Borland Database Engine (BDE, and also known as IDAPI), Delphi provides direct access to many types of local and remote server databases.

Without the BDE and Delphi's built-in data accessing components, you would have to rely exclusively on third-party vendors to provide tool kits to access your local and remote data.

The BDE is the *middleware*, or "glue," that provides transparent access independent of the target data format being accessed. You, the programmer, do not have to worry about how exactly you connect to your data once the BDE has properly been configured. A key to this connectivity is accomplished using the BDE and its *alias* feature, which is described later in this chapter. Once the BDE is configured for your development and production environments, accessing data in Delphi becomes almost trivial. Regardless of the type of data you're accessing, the up-front setup and programming is essentially the same. This results in the seamless capability to access data in a variety of formats simultaneously within a single application. For example, your application can access data on a Sybase server for one function while retrieving data from an Oracle server in another.

It's a good idea to examine the shipping Delphi database demos to see how they were built. The database demo projects are stored in their own subdirectories in the \DEMOS\DB directory, which is located in the directory where you installed Delphi. Open Delphi's File menu, choose Open Project, and examine the included demos. You should first have a general feel for what type of data access is available through Delphi before reading this chapter.

In this chapter, you

- Learn about database aliases and how they're used to access your data with flexibility
- Create a simple table browser
- Learn how `Table`, `Query`, `DataSource`, and visual data control components are linked to present your data
- Learn how to use the `Query` component with the Visual Query Builder
- See an example of a one-to-many table relationship
- Learn about the many different visual data control components

Using Aliases

Simply put, an alias is a name given to a database. Aliases are used as "nicknames" when referring to the link with a remote server database. In their simplest form, aliases can be used to name local databases (those that are on your C drive or LAN).

Aliases are very useful when used to reference local data. Suppose that you have a collection of related tables (a database) on your LAN in your G:\CLIENTS\TRACKING\DATA directory. Wouldn't it be nice to refer to this long path name with a simple and concise name, such as TrackingData? Aliases allow you to do just that. Setting up a TrackingData alias in the BDE allows you to refer to the data in the G:\CLIENTS\TRACKING\DATA by a simple (and more intuitive) reference.

In addition to being much easier to refer to throughout your program instead of using explicit paths, aliases also provide additional flexibility. For example, the following options are available when using database aliases:

- The capability to separate source code from your data
- The capability to test your application using a different set of data by simply changing an alias reference
- The capability to easily move your application from a local to a client/server database

Although aliases do allow you to migrate your application to client/server without changing a single line of code, there are often many architectural considerations that arise from doing this. Client/server databases are designed to be accessed differently than local databases on a network. An awareness of the finer points of client/server versus local data access will help you develop a local database application that can easily be migrated to client/server.

Aliases and Local Data

When you installed Delphi, it created an alias that points to a demo database named DBDEMOS. The Delphi demo database contains sample Paradox and dBASE files used in the sample projects that are also included in Delphi. If you installed Delphi on your C drive with the default paths, the location of the DBDEMOS database is C:\DELPHI\DEMOS\DATA. Figure 6.1 shows the BDE Configuration Utility running with the DBDEMOS alias selected.

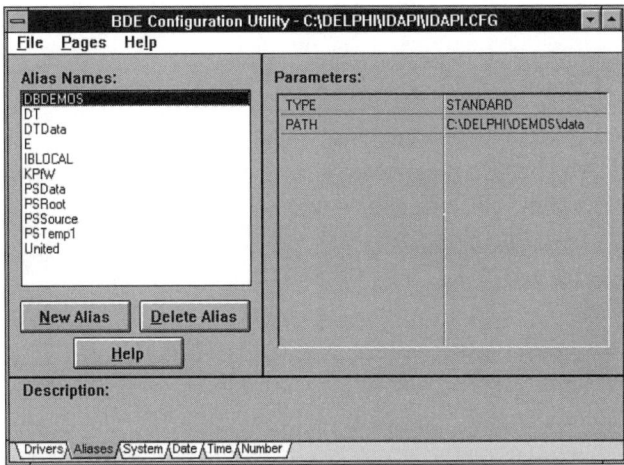

Fig. 6.1
You can maintain your aliases by using the BDE Configuration Utility.

> **Note**
>
> The BDE Configuration Utility isn't the only place where you can set up aliases. Another alias configuration dialog is available by opening the File menu and choosing Aliases in the Database Desktop. See Chapter 12, "Using the Database Desktop," for more information.

Tip
Although you can access local data without using aliases, using aliases is highly recommended because it provides portability when moving your data from one location to another (or even from a local to a server database).

Alias names are stored in database configuration files, which have .CFG extensions. If you selected the default paths when installing Delphi, your default configuration file is stored in C:\IDAPI as IDAPI.CFG.

The BDE Configuration Utility allows you to store many different aliases in different configuration files, with each file saved using a different file name with .CFG extension. Since you may be managing multiple configuration files in your environment, the BDE Configuration Utility allows you to merge configuration data from one .CFG file into another. This is accomplished by using the File menu's Merge command and specifying the configuration file to be merged into the currently opened configuration file.

> **Note**
>
> The default BDE configuration file location is stored in your WIN.INI file, which is located in your Windows directory. See the [IDAPI] section for the exact name and path of your configuration file. If the BDE is configured properly, the default configuration file is also shown in the title of the BDE Configuration Utility.

By using the BDE Configuration Utility, you can add, delete, and configure your aliases. The BDE Configuration Utility is installed in the same program group where Delphi was installed.

Aliases and Client/Server Data

Aliases are even more useful when accessing remote database servers. With database servers, you must perform complex sign-on and attachment procedures every time you want to communicate with a remote database. By using a database alias, you need to get this right only the first time; thereafter, you rely on the BDE to properly connect to the database referred to with your alias.

You use the BDE Configuration Utility to configure an alias that's used to connect to a database server. Even if you don't have access to a database server, you can simulate a client/server environment by using the InterBase Local Server, which was installed when you installed Delphi.

The following steps show you how to configure an alias that references an InterBase Local Server database:

1. Load the BDE Configuration Utility from the Delphi program group.

2. Go to the Aliases page (refer to fig. 6.1) and click the New Alias button. The Add New Alias dialog appears.

3. Enter **IBExamples** in the New Alias Name text box.

4. Open the Alias Type drop-down list and select INTRBASE.

> **Note**
>
> If INTRBASE doesn't appear, the InterBase drivers haven't been installed. You must first go back to the Delphi installation program and install the InterBase drivers.

The Add New Alias dialog should look like figure 6.2.

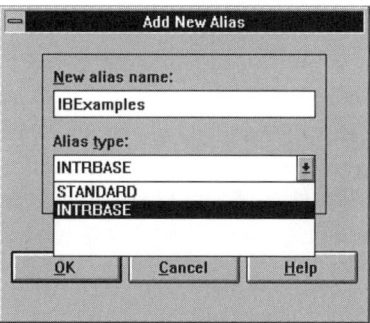

Fig. 6.2
Only BDE server drivers that have been installed appear in the Alias Type drop-down list.

5. Click OK. You're brought back to the BDE Configuration Utility window.

6. A new alias titled IBExamples is created and added to the Alias Names list. Select this alias to display the parameters available for it.

7. In the Parameters list, enter **C:/IBLocal/Examples/Employee.GDB** for the SERVER NAME setting. If the InterBase local server has been installed in a different directory, adjust this parameter accordingly.

8. Specify the user name that your DBA has given you in the USER NAME field. The InterBase local server allows default access by a user named sysdba with a password of masterkey. At this time you specify only the user name. Later, when actually connecting to the database, you're prompted for a password for the user connecting.

9. Configure remaining parameters as you want. The result should look similar to figure 6.3.

Fig. 6.3
The BDE Configuration Utility adjusts the Parameters list, depending on the type of alias being configured.

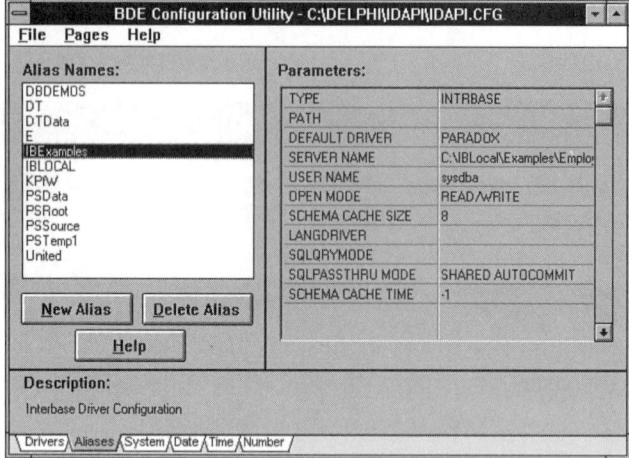

Notice in figure 6.3 that there are additional parameters that haven't been discussed. These parameters are specific to the InterBase Local Server. If you were using another BDE driver, such as a Sybase server driver, the parameters would be somewhat different.

Using Non-Visual Data Components

In Chapter 5, "Using Non-Visual Components," a special group of components—including menu, timer, DDE, and dialog components—are discussed. These components handle tasks and functions that require behind-the-scenes work for them to perform correctly and provide their intended functionality. Non-visual components often have complex processing structures that are hidden from programmers. To get a PopupMenu object to display, for example, you simply tell it to Execute. You don't particularly care about how the PopupMenu component shows the menu, just that it does indeed do it.

The same applies to non-visual database components. (Non-visual *database* components were purposely left out of Chapter 5 and placed in this chapter so that there could be a complete chapter on database access using Delphi.) Database components are extremely complex under the hood because they encapsulate many features of the BDE. While some would like to know how a Paradox table is opened and a record locked, you don't need to know exactly how in order to deliver database applications. In fact, detailed knowledge isn't required, since database components provide access to a very well-thought-out database engine, the BDE. Let the BDE worry about connecting to your data so that you're free to concentrate on your application.

A variety of visual and non-visual components allow you to produce full-featured Windows database applications. Visual database components can't perform without properly configured non-visual database components. This is why this section discusses non-visual database components before moving on to visual components.

In the following sections, you learn how to create a simple table-browsing application in Delphi. This application allows you to navigate records in the Customer table that's in your IBExamples database.

Using Tables

A *table* is a single data file that's a member of a database. Table components, along with Query components, are the primary components used when connecting your application to data.

Drop a Table component on your form and take a look at its properties in the Object Inspector. Using the Object Inspector, perform the following steps to connect the Table object to your actual database table:

1. Go to the Name property and give the Table object a descriptive name, such as tblCustomer.

2. Whether you're accessing a single table on your C drive or a remote table on a server database, you must always specify a database name. The DatabaseName property drop-down list displays a list of aliases that have been defined. Select the IBExamples alias that you defined earlier.

3. After setting the DatabaseName property, drop down the list for the TableName property and select the CUSTOMER table.

If this is the first time that you've accessed the IBExamples alias during this Delphi session, you will be prompted with the dialog shown in figure 6.4.

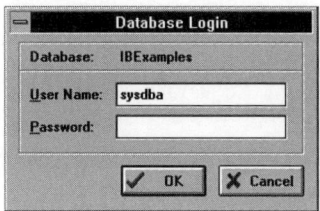

Fig. 6.4
The BDE automatically presents the Database Login dialog for password-protected databases.

Your `Table` component is now configured to provide transparent access to your local InterBase Customer table. The `Table` component alone doesn't show the user anything—it only provides the connection to your data. What you need to do now is add a visual component to show that you've indeed connected to the Customer table.

Going Visual with the *DataSource* Component

You now have a `Table` component sitting patiently on your form, waiting for you to give it a role or something to talk to. The contents of the Object Inspector aren't that interesting even after you configure your table. The form itself isn't much more interesting, especially if you run your application now, which would display a blank window. What you need to do is see that your data is indeed attached to the database and table you specified in the Object Inspector.

Before you can see the actual table data, you must add another component that provides the final link between your `Table` component and a visual component. You can't directly link a visual database component, such as a `DBGrid`, to your existing `Table` component. Visual components require connection to `DataSource` objects. You must first add a `DataSource` component that allows you to complete the chain. All visual data components interface with a `DataSource`. A `DataSource` component can funnel data in from a variety of sources, including tables, queries, and stored procedures. Perform the following steps to add a `DataSource` component to your example form:

1. Add a `DataSource` component to your form. Use the Object Inspector to give it a name, such as `dSrcCustomer`.

Once placed, the `DataSource` object can't do anything since it's not yet referencing any other objects, and no other objects are currently referencing it. A `DataSource` object provides the interface to the data for visual data access objects. So, to finish the job, you must hook the `dSrcCustomer` `DataSource` object to an object that's actually connected to data, such as the `tblCustomer` table object that you placed previously.

2. Select `tblCustomer` from the DataSet drop-down list.

You're now ready to connect your `Table`-`DataSource` object relation to a visual object. Finish the Table Browser application by going to the Data Controls page on the Component palette and adding a `DBGrid` object to your form. A `DBGrid` offers a generic presentation of the data that it's connected to. In this example, connect the `DBGrid` to the `dSrcCustomer` `DataSource` object. Later, the "Querying Data" section discusses how to connect a `DBGrid` to a `Query` component.

Perform the following to connect a visual database grid object (a `DBGrid` component) to the `dSrcCustomer` component:

1. Place a `DBGrid` component on your form and name it `dbgCustomer`. (Don't worry about sizing right now because you haven't defined the fields.)

2. Go back to the `tblCustomer` object and change the `Active` property from false to true using the Object Inspector. This makes the table active and linked to live data. This has the `DBGrid` show the actual data at design time. The Customer Table Browser form window now looks something like that shown in figure 6.5. Setting a `Table` object's `Active` property to false allows development of your application without requiring you to be connected to the actual database.

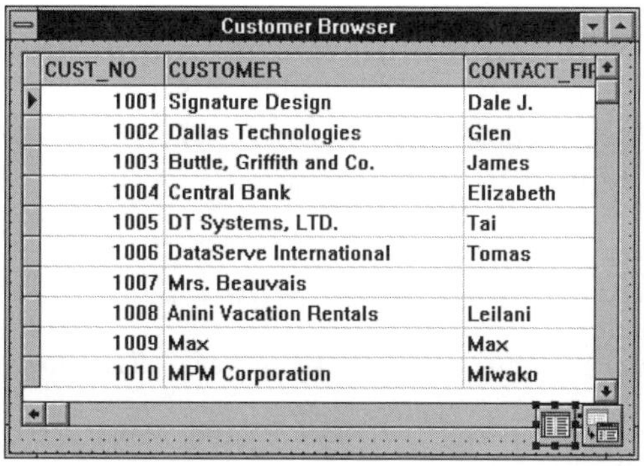

Fig. 6.5
Visual database components require a `DataSource` and something to "feed" the `DataSource`, such as a `Table` or `Query` object.

3. Run the application. If your server database has a password, the Database Login dialog appears (refer to fig. 6.4). Entering the password allows the application to run, showing the underlying Customer table.

So how many lines of Object Pascal code have you written to produce this high-speed table browser? None! Not bad for just pointing and clicking the mouse around a bit.

Querying Data

If you want to see every single record in the Customer table, the Customer Table Browser is fine. What if you only want to see certain types of customers or those customers in a specified range? How do you narrow the view of the Customer table? You can do this by redirecting the `DataSource` object to point to a Query object. By having a Query object provide the interface to the BDE instead of a Table object, you can specify whatever selection criteria you like for the customer table.

Using SQL Off the Cuff

Queries are based on SQL statements, which provide a variety of operations for querying your data. Queries contain an SQL property, which is of type TString. TStrings allow multiple strings to be contained as a single object, which means that many lines of SQL code can be contained in a Query component's SQL property.

By manipulating a Query object's SQL property, you can write SQL to extract the data in any way you desire. For example, the SQL syntax to ask for all customers with a customer number of 1010 or greater is

```
select * from Customer where Customer.Cust_No >= 1010
```

By simply setting the SQL property equal to this one line of SQL code, you can add substantial functionality to the Customer Table Browser. Without changing the current form, perform the following:

1. Add a Query component to the form from the Data Access page of the Component palette and name it qryCustomer.

2. Specify the IBExamples alias as the DatabaseName property for the Query.

3. Select the SQL property for the Query, and click the ellipsis button to display the String List Editor dialog.

4. Entering the SQL code from the previous example into the String List Editor results in the dialog shown in figure 6.6.

5. Clicking OK stores the SQL code as a TString in the Query object's SQL property.

Fig. 6.6
You can enter raw SQL code directly for a Query component using the String List Editor dialog.

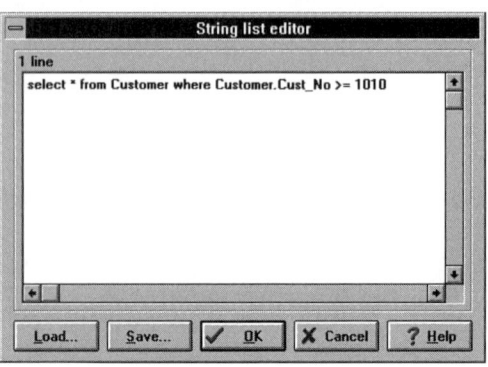

> **Note**
>
> Changing an SQL TString while a Query object's Active property is set to true causes the Active property to automatically be set to false. To see the results of the new query, you must set Active back to true.

6. At this point, you have a stand-alone Query object that's not being used anywhere yet. You must redirect your dSrcCustomer DataSource object to point at the Query object you just placed instead of the existing tblCustomer Table object. Change the dSrcCustomer object's DataSet property to qryCustomer, the name of the new Query component. This causes the Query object to be the source of the data instead of the Table object.

7. Set the qryCustomer Query object's Active property to true. The DBGrid object now shows only those records in the Customer table that have a Cust_No field value of 1010 or higher.

To take the Customer Table Browser a step further, add two radio buttons labeled Table and Query to toggle between the two data sets at runtime. Name these buttons rBtnTable and rBtnQuery, respectively. You can do this by redirecting your dSrcCustomer DataSource object's DataSet property to toggle between the Table and Query objects at runtime. Once the radio buttons are placed on the form, you can add code to each button's OnClick event to control the data that's shown in the DBGrid object. The following event handlers for the Table and Query radio buttons cause the DataSource object to point to the Table object or the Query object, depending on which radio button the user selects:

```
procedure TfrmCustomer.rBtnTableClick(Sender: TObject);
begin
     dSrcCustomer.DataSet := tblCustomer;
end;

procedure TfromCustomer.rBtnQueryClick(Sender: TObject);
begin
     dSrcCustomer.DataSet := qryCustomer;
end;
```

Running the form with these two radio buttons allows the user to select the desired view. Figure 6.7 shows the form with the added querying feature.

Fig. 6.7
You can deliver substantial functionality by writing few (but proper) lines of code.

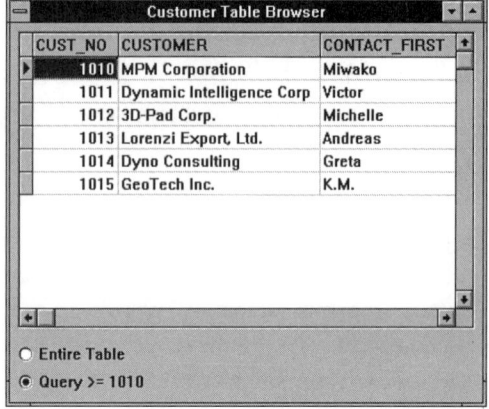

Doing Power SQL with the Visual Query Builder

Delphi provides a powerful utility that allows you to visually build SQL syntax without having to be an SQL master. In fact, with the Visual Query Builder (the VQB), you may never need to know SQL or even look at the generated SQL code.

To access the Visual Query Builder, follow these steps:

1. Select the Query object on your form.

2. Right-click anywhere in the client area of your form to open the popup menu.

3. Choose Query Builder. The VQB loads and then presents the Add Table dialog (see fig. 6.8).

> **Note**
>
> It's common when right-clicking for the popup menu to appear right under your mouse pointer. Since the popup menu is triggered when you press the right mouse button, the popup actually receives an event and thinks that you selected a menu choice (you did). Be aware that this may happen because you may invoke an undesirable operation. To get around this, right-click, hold, and then see where the menu pops up before releasing the right mouse button.

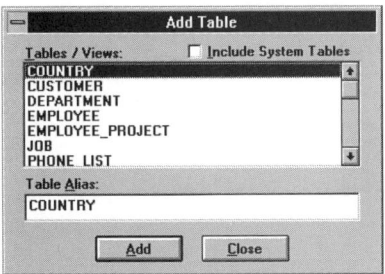

Fig. 6.8
When designing a new query, the Visual Query Builder first prompts you for the table(s) to include in your query.

Once in the Visual Query Builder, you can easily construct complex SQL queries by using the VQB's set of visual tools. In the IBExamples database, there's a Customer table as well as a Country table. A COUNTRY field exists in the Customer table that provides a link to the Country table. Suppose that you want to know how many customers are in each country stored in the Country table. To find this out, you need to perform a multitable join between the Country and Customer tables. In this scenario, the Country table is referred to as the *master* and the Customer table the *detail*. Follow these steps to build the query using the Visual Query Builder:

1. Add the Country and Customer tables to the query by using the Add Table dialog. (The Add Table dialog is available at any time by clicking the VQB's Table SpeedBar button.)

2. Maximize the VQB window and stretch the Customer table window down until its COUNTRY field is showing.

3. Link the Country table to the Customer table by clicking the Country table's COUNTRY field and dragging that field to the Customer table's COUNTRY field. Releasing the mouse button connects the tables, which is shown with a line joining the table windows.

    You now must specify which fields you want to include in the query result. This is done by dragging the desired fields from their table windows and dropping them into the query result area.

4. Drag the Country table's COUNTRY field into the query result area (the lower half of the VQB; see fig. 6.9).

Fig. 6.9
The Visual Query Builder virtually eliminates the need for you to know SQL.

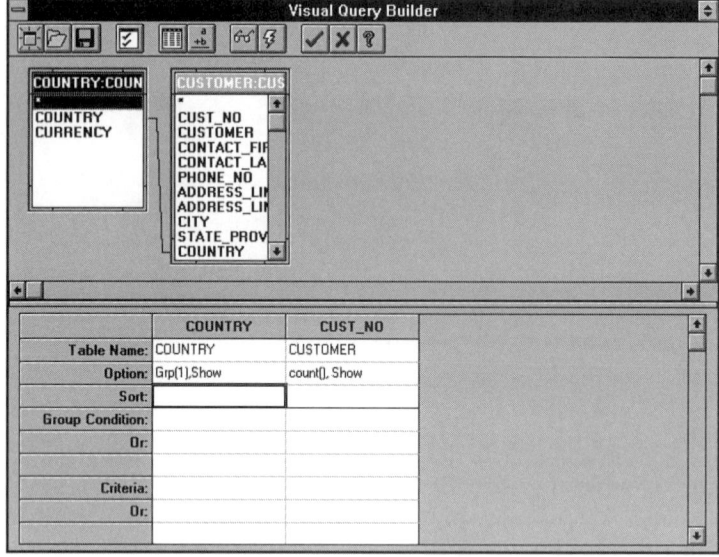

5. In the VQB's query result area, right-click the COUNTRY field's Option field. In the popup menu that appears, select the <u>G</u>roup menu choice.

6. Drag the Customer table's Cust_No field into the query result area.

7. In the VQB's query result area, right-click the Cust_No field's Option field. In the popup menu that appears, select the <u>C</u>ount menu choice. This will count all occurrences of the Cust_No field for each COUNTRY.

Once the fields are in the query result area, you can specify how they'll be grouped and sorted, as well as the criteria that's involved. Figure 6.9 shows your query in the Visual Query Builder set up to count how many customers exist in each country in the Country table.

Clicking the Visual Query Builder's Run SpeedBar button runs the query and produces a temporary Result Window, where you can browse the results (see fig. 6.10).

Selecting and double-clicking the line joining two tables displays the Join dialog (see fig. 6.11). By using the Join dialog, you can link detail records logically. For example, you can ask for a list counting all customers that don't belong to a particular country by linking with the not-equal operator (<>).

A variety of other options available within the Visual Query Builder allow you to build complex queries. You can define fields that are the result of an

Querying Data   **141**

expression involving functions and even multiple fields (field1 + field2). Clicking the VQB's Expression SpeedBar button presents the Expression dialog, which provides additional options for specifying result fields in your queries (see fig. 6.12).

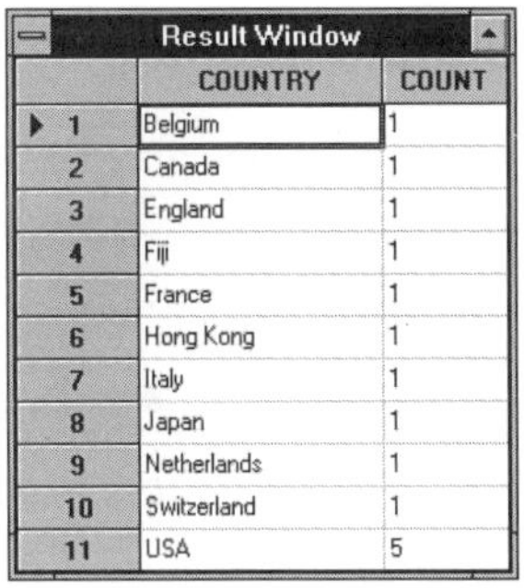

Fig. 6.10
You can test the results of your queries without leaving the Visual Query Designer.

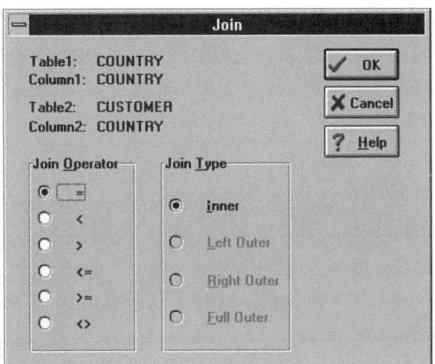

Fig. 6.11
The Join dialog provides a variety of options that allow you to define how your query tables are linked.

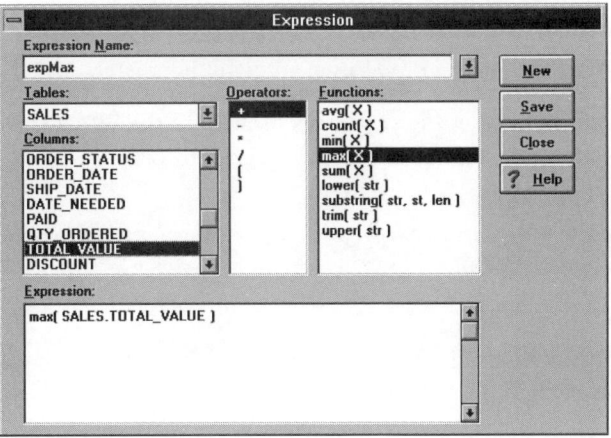

Fig. 6.12
Within the Visual Query Builder, the Expression dialog provides an interface that allows calculated fields to be treated as data within your queries.

You can examine the expression field shown in figure 6.12 by comparing its results with another field. The expression field shown calculates the maximum value of the TOTAL_VALUE field from the Sales table, which is now added and linked to the Customer table. Dragging the Sales TOTAL_VALUE field into the query result area and selecting the Sum option value provides a comparison of total sales versus simply the largest sale. To verify the result, you need to compare these two values by simply clicking the Run SpeedBar button, which produces the Result Window (see fig. 6.13). As you see, the SUM column values are greater than or equal to the EXPMAX values, thus validating the logic.

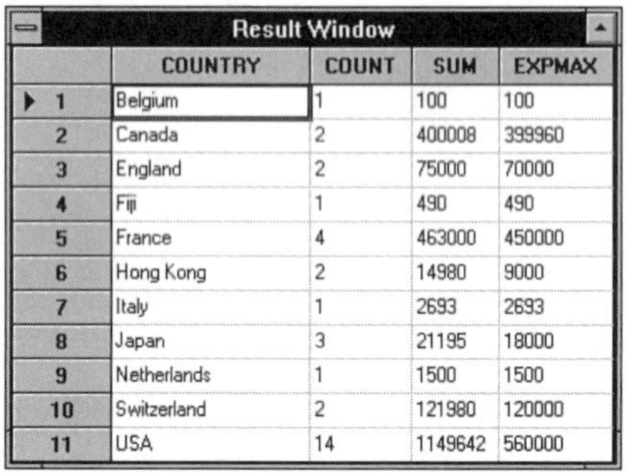

Fig. 6.13
While in the Visual Query Builder, you can inspect the design and results of your queries.

	COUNTRY	COUNT	SUM	EXPMAX
1	Belgium	1	100	100
2	Canada	2	400008	399960
3	England	2	75000	70000
4	Fiji	1	490	490
5	France	4	463000	450000
6	Hong Kong	2	14980	9000
7	Italy	1	2693	2693
8	Japan	3	21195	18000
9	Netherlands	1	1500	1500
10	Switzerland	2	121980	120000
11	USA	14	1149642	560000

Saving and Loading Visual Query Files

Clicking OK in the Visual Query Builder causes the VQB to close and store the actual query in the current Query object's SQL property. Before clicking OK and after spending any length of time in the Visual Query Builder, you should save your work to a file by clicking the VQB's SaveAs SpeedBar button. This SpeedBar button invokes a Save Query dialog, which allows you to save the query with a .QRY extension. (Saved query files are stored as ASCII and can be examined with a file editor.) Once you save your query file, you'll be able to retrieve the query in the Visual Query Builder later.

You might think that getting your work back up in the Visual Query Builder should be automatic, but it's not. When you want to return to the VQB and modify your query, follow these steps:

> **Note**
> These steps assume that you've saved your query file before you shut down the Visual Query Builder. Unless you save your query files, you won't be able to load your previous work.

1. Select the Query object that contains your query.

2. Right-click and select the Query Builder menu choice from the popup menu. The Databases dialog appears (see fig. 6.14).

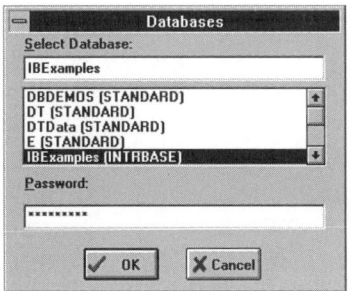

Fig. 6.14
The Databases dialog appears when you're returning to the Visual Query Builder on an existing Query object.

3. Select your query's original database from the scroll box in the middle of the Databases dialog.

4. Enter the database password, if any, in the Password text box and click OK.

5. The Visual Query Builder appears with the Add Table dialog open (refer to fig. 6.8). Click the Close button from within the Add Table dialog. You're then brought to the VQB with a blank VQB workspace.

6. Click the VQB Open SpeedBar button to retrieve the query file you saved. Your original query will load and you may make any changes you want.

Be sure to save the changes to your .QRY file so that you can return to the Visual Query Builder in the future and make visual changes to your query.

Controlling *DataSource* Objects at Runtime

So now that you can build high-power queries, how do you apply this control at runtime? The answer is simple: Just like you handle a basic visual property, such as Color, you can handle a Query's SQL property or a DataSource component's DataSet property in the same manner at runtime.

Recall from the previous examples that your Customer Table Browser form has a tblCustomer object that's accessed by the dSrcCustomer DataSource object. dSrcCustomer also accesses the qryCustomer object, depending on which radio button the user selects. Suppose that you want to add another Query object to your form that produces an entirely different set of fields than those in tblCustomer and qryCustomer. Recall that the dSrcCustomer DataSource object feeds the `dbgCustomer` DBGrid visual object with data. What would happen if you had the `DataSource` object feed your `DBGrid` object with a completely different set of data, like that in the previous example? Well, the `DBGrid` object doesn't really care what it gets, it simply presents the data on-screen.

You can test `DBGrid` handling by adding a new `Query` object and radio button. This radio button performs the same functions as the existing `rBtnTable` and `rBtnQuery` buttons, but feeds the `DBGrid` object data a completely different format. Adding this functionality to your form and running it produces the form shown in figure 6.15.

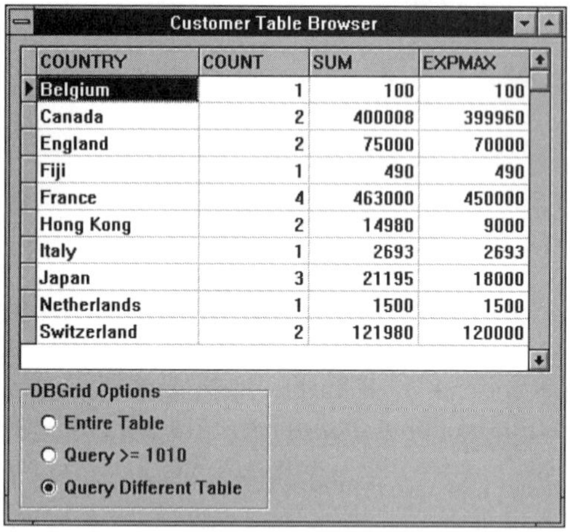

Fig. 6.15
The `DBGrid` object can handle being "fed" data from completely different sources.

COUNTRY	COUNT	SUM	EXPMAX
Belgium	1	100	100
Canada	2	400008	399960
England	2	75000	70000
Fiji	1	490	490
France	4	463000	450000
Hong Kong	2	14980	9000
Italy	1	2693	2693
Japan	3	21195	18000
Netherlands	1	1500	1500
Switzerland	2	121980	120000

DBGrid Options
- Entire Table
- Query >= 1010
- Query Different Table

The `DBGrid` object is entirely dynamic and doesn't care at all how or what data is being passed to it. `DBGrid` knows only that it's receiving data, and its job is to display it and handle the user interface. This is how many of the visual data components behave.

Understanding One-to-Many Relationships

Delphi doesn't include a specific one-to-many design tool but allows you to do it yourself by working with the `MasterSource` and `MasterFields` properties of `Table` and `Query` objects.

When creating one-to-many views of data tables, you must first determine which `Table` object is the detail in the one-to-many or master-detail relationship. You must also know what field in the master table is used to link to the detail records.

Once you identify and create a `Table` object that references your detail records, select the detail `Table` object on your form. Looking at the Properties page in the Object Inspector, you see two fields: `MasterSource` and `MasterFields`. To create a master-detail relationship, you must have both tables existing on your form. From the detail `Table` object, choose the name of the master `Table` object from the `MasterSource` property drop-down list. Once this is done, you can click the ellipsis button of the `MasterFields` property to display the Field Link Designer dialog (see fig. 6.16).

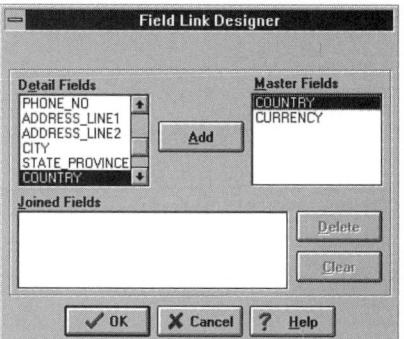

Fig. 6.16
Defining a master-detail table relationship is done by using the Field Link Designer dialog.

After you successfully link your detail table to your master table, you can now visually inspect the relationship using visual Data Controls objects, such as a `DBGrid` component for the detail and a `DBEdit` component for the master. Figure 6.17 shows the Country-to-Customer relationship using two `DBGrid` objects.

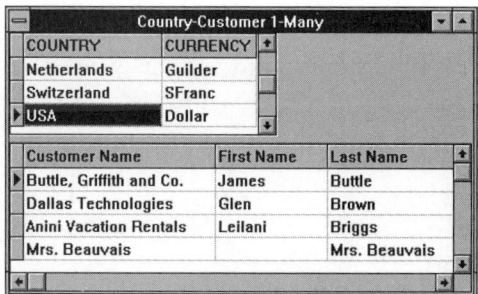

Fig. 6.17
One-to-many relationships are built without writing a single line of code.

Using Other Non-Visual Components

You covered the non-visual database components necessary for database development earlier in this chapter. A few remaining components are somewhat different but can be extremely useful for putting the finishing touches on your database applications.

Databases

At first glance, most new Delphi users think that the Database component is a crucial piece necessary for building your database applications. Logically, a programmer knows that a database contains tables; therefore, you must need a Database object on your forms when you access tables.

The quick answer to whether a Database component is necessary is that it's not. You can create robust Windows-compatible database applications without even using the Database component. What the Database component does for you is allow your programs to have explicit—as opposed to implicit—control over connections to your databases.

You may have seen various password dialogs, such as the one in figure 6.4, appear while working within Delphi and when running the examples in this chapter. These password dialogs are presented automatically, controlled by Delphi as it receives requests to connect to different databases. The problem is that you may want your program to manage passwords to some degree, not requiring the user to enter a password for every single database your program is connecting to.

Perhaps you have a system-controlled database that you want the program to automatically connect to and supply a hidden password. You may have several databases of this type within your organization and don't want to require the user to enter 50 different passwords. Typically, users require a single password, and the program handles the lower-level database passwords.

Explicit database password handling is performed using the Database component. The Database component allows you to embed password information within it, as well as turn off the password login prompt entirely by setting its LoginPrompt property to false.

Stored Procedure Control

The StoredProc component provides a programming interface for stored procedures on your database server. To set up a StoredProc component that links to the InterBase example database, follow these steps:

1. Drop a `StoredProc` component on your form.

2. In the Object Inspector, select IBExamples for the `DatabaseName` property.

3. Open the `StoredProcName` property drop-down list and select ORG_CHART.

4. Drop a `DataSource` component on your form and set its `DataSet` property to the `StoredProc` object's name.

The ORG_CHART stored procedure's output is data. Verify this by placing a `DBGrid` object on your form and linking it to the `DataSource` object that's linked to the `StoredProc` object. You can examine input and output fields of stored procedures by following these steps:

1. Select the `StoredProc` object that's now on your form.

2. Go to the Object Inspector and select the `Params` property.

3. Click the ellipsis button to open the dialog shown in figure 6.18.

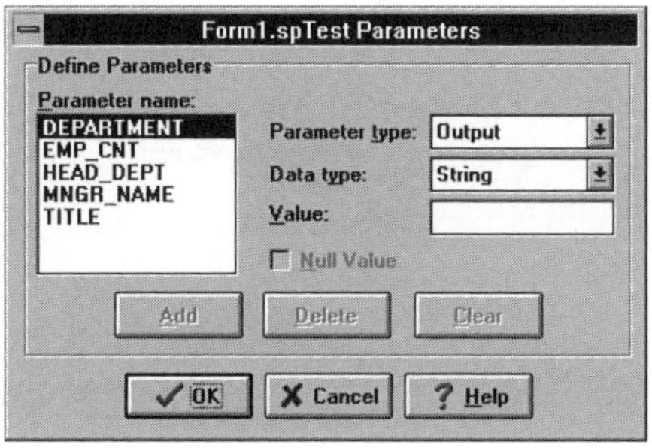

Fig. 6.18
You can examine input and output parameters of a `StoredProc` object by way of this dialog.

Stored procedures can perform a wide variety of operations and don't have to return data. This section's `StoredProc` example used the InterBase local server's ORG_CHART example, which does return data. You can write stored procedures that don't return data but would perform some sort of operation on the database server. In these cases, you often need to specify parameters before running the stored procedure. Set stored procedure parameters using the `Params` property.

Batch Move of Data

The Database Desktop (DBD), discussed in Chapter 12, "Using the Database Desktop," is a tool that lets you perform high-level operations with your data. Of interest for this section is the Database Desktop's copy table facility, available by choosing the DBD Utilities menu's Copy command. The DBD copy facility allows you to copy data from one type of data format to another. The same holds true when copying from one type of database server to another, such as from Sybase to InterBase.

The `BatchMove` component is a high-level component that allows you to perform functions from the Database Desktop's utilities menu. These functions include Add, Copy, and Subtract. Like the Utilities functions within the DBD, the `BatchMove` component allows you to move data from one database server to another or from a server to a local database and vice versa.

When moving data in batches and depending on the setting of the `Mode` property, the following can result in a `BatchMove` execution:

- *Key violations*. If a table is added to another with the `Mode` set to `batAppend` or `batAppendUpdate`, and source records exist with the same primary key values as those on the target table, the new records are not added to the target table. A table name can be specified in the `KeyViolTableName` property that stores the key violation records that weren't added to the target table.

- *Changed records*. If `Mode` is set to `batUpdate`, records that would have been key violations when `Mode` was `batAppend` now cause target records to be updated with the incoming source data. All updated records can be stored as they existed before the update by specifying a table in the `ChangedTableName` property in the `BatchMove` object.

- *Problem records*. If a record makes it past a key-violation check but is kicked out for a different reason (such as field validation), that record is stored in a Problems table. The Problems table is specified in the `ProblemTableName` property.

Reports

Delphi ships with ReportSmith, a powerful reporting tool integrated within the Delphi programming environment. By using the `Report` component, you can specify a number of report options that are passed to ReportSmith when the report executes.

For more information on the `Report` component, see Chapter 13, "Reporting with ReportSmith."

Using Visual Data Components

Now that you're comfortable with connecting Table and Query components to DataSources and, in turn, to visual database objects, it's time to discuss the other useful visual data-aware components. Visual data components send and receive data from DataSource objects at runtime (and design time, in some cases). As the name suggests, visual data components mirror much of the functionality provided by components on the Standard page of the Component palette. Not only do many visual data components look the same as standard components, they're configured and behave in a very similar manner. Their events and properties are very similar, and of course, the data-aware components have events that allow logic to be triggered for certain database-related processing.

> **Note**
>
> Database Control components that have standard component counterparts are those whose names match standard component names minus the DB naming prefix.

DBGrid

The DBGrid component was used in all the previous examples to show data for all fields in the underlying table. There are many times when you might need to show only a few fields in the underlying table. This, and other field type control, is available using Delphi's Fields Editor. To invoke the Fields Editor, follow these steps:

1. Select a DataSet component (Table, Query, or StoredProc) on your form.

2. Right-click and choose Fields Editor from the popup menu. The Fields Editor window appears (see fig. 6.19).

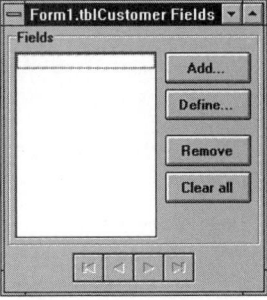

Fig. 6.19
Use the Fields Editor to access field level control for a DBGrid object.

150   Chapter 6—Using Data-Bound Components

3. Click the Add button to open the Add Fields dialog.

4. Select only those fields that you want to include in the resulting set of data. Figure 6.20 shows the Add Fields dialog with four fields selected.

Fig. 6.20
Use the Fields Editor's Add Fields dialog to specify the fields you want to include in the resulting data.

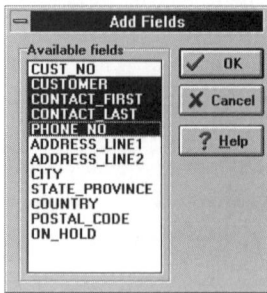

5. Click OK. Fields that were selected now appear in the Fields Editor.

Now, the good part—take a look at the objects available in the Object Inspector. Find the `DataSet` object that you just used the Fields Editor for. Notice that field objects are now available for which a variety of properties and events are available. The Fields Editor is the key to getting field-level control of `DBGrid` objects.

DBNavigator

The `DBNavigator` component is an example of a component that participates in sending and receiving data from `DataSource` objects. A `DBNavigator` is a small group of buttons that are associated with a single `DataSource`. By using `DBNavigator`, you can quickly add push-button data navigation capabilities by simply assigning the `DataSource` property of the `DBNavigator` component at design or runtime.

DBText

The `DBText` component reads data from its assigned field in its `DataSource` and simply displays it. This is useful when you always want to show certain single-record information as read-only.

DBEdit

The `DBEdit` component provides an editable field linked to a data field. To connect, you simply supply the Object Inspector, the `DataSource`, and `DataField` names.

DBMemo

The DBMemo component simply provides a visual presentation of a memo field from a database. Regardless of the way the back-end database implements its memo feature, the DBMemo component provides consistent functionality.

DBImage

In the same manner that the DBMemo component provides access to a database memo field, the DBImage component presents graphic information on-screen independent of how the image is actually stored in the data table.

Database List Components

These components are used primarily for data collection, as opposed to data presentation. All database item list components deliver their data through their TString property, which is of object type TString. Since TString is an object, it supports a number of methods that can be used to configure item lists at runtime.

DBListBox

A DBListBox component is used to write data into a database field, not to display existing data or to provide a lookup of data contained in another table. For these functions, consider using a DBLookupList or DBComboBox component.

It's possible, however, to read data into a DBListBox component's TString property and populate the choices when loading the form.

DBComboBox

A DBComboBox component behaves very much like a DBListBox in that it primarily sends data to a DataSource field.

DBCheckBox

A DBCheckBox component is useful when you have a list of items for which you want to allow the user to select multiple items.

DBRadioGroup

You can use a DBRadioGroup component to present the user with multiple choices but allow only a single choice to be selected.

Database Lookup Components

Database lookup components provide the capability to present data from one source for selection and post it to a field in a different table. The two lookup components are very similar in nature, differing only in the way they interface with the user.

DBLookupList

The DBLookupList component can show multiple items on-screen all the time. This component behaves like the List component found on the Standard page.

DBLookupCombo

The DBLookupCombo component provides a drop-down list for selection of a lookup value.

From Here...

This chapter briefly discussed the many involved topics and components required when building a database application. Now that you're more familiar with the possibilities and requirements, consider the following for more information:

- Chapter 12, "Using the Database Desktop," shows that database components alone aren't the best way to manage and maintain your data files. This is done using the Database Desktop, an interactive end-user application that allows you to work with your data visually.

- Chapter 13, "Reporting with ReportSmith," shows how to tie Delphi's Report component to reports written with Delphi's reporting tool, ReportSmith.

- Chapter 16, "Delivering Your Application," discusses a number of issues concerning the BDE at runtime, specifically which files are required when distributing your application.

Chapter 7
Customizing and Reusing Components

Up to now, you've developed a good foundation for creating applications in Delphi. Now it's time to encapsulate this knowledge and apply it toward enhancement of the overall development environment. In Delphi, this is done by extending the functionality of base classes and existing components. This process involves forming them into time-saving, reusable visual entities known as *components* and *custom components*.

In this chapter, you'll learn about:

- Component libraries
- Component writing
- Generic installation of components
- Component resources
- How to modify your first component
- How to test the component
- VBX controls

Introducing Component Libraries

For many years, developers have been grouping together their related functions and procedures into files called *procedure libraries*. Libraries are "black box" collections of code that save developers from time-intensive re-engineering of code and data. Beyond procedure libraries, they encapsulated their code and data into reusable containers. They grouped these containers, called *classes*, together into class libraries. Following the object-oriented paradigm, they use inheritance and *polymorphism* to extend the functionality of each class. Instantiation from these classes results in completely self-contained entities called *objects*. Polymorphism provides the capability to redefine methods that originate in the parent class and thus affect the behavior of the current (descending) class as well as any new classes derived from the current class.

Components use the Visual Components Library (VCL) as a base—thus, they are built on various levels of predefined classes. These classes are written following a certain syntax that allows Delphi to recognize them as components. These components are grouped together according to relation, and then compiled into a dynamic component library (DCL) file. Many details and a lot of theory are behind the creation of components. All this theory and constructive implementation results in what the Delphi applications developers use every day (and possibly take for granted) in the form of components. This implementation is demonstrated as they click bit maps on the Component palette and drop fully functional objects onto a form.

Details of DCL Files

The components that ship with Delphi are stored in the COMPLIB.DCL file. Optionally, you can use other DCL files that contain another set of components or merely just the components you work with on a regular basis. Delphi lets you add components and remove them from DCL files at the unit level (or file level, which is discussed later). The DCL file in use is recompiled automatically each time a unit containing a component(s) is added or removed. The most recent version of the DCL is saved to a file with the same name and a .BAK extension. This occurs with each recompilation.

COMPLIB.DCL is stored in the \DELPHI\BIN directory on initial installation. This file can actually be placed in another directory—locally or on a network drive.

If Delphi can't find COMPLIB.DCL when Delphi is started, you'll receive the error dialog shown in figure 7.1, followed by the default Delphi error dialog shown in figure 7.2. This error dialog will also reflect the path and file name of the DCL file according to the current configuration. Note that Delphi will still load but won't display the Component palette.

Introducing Component Libraries **155**

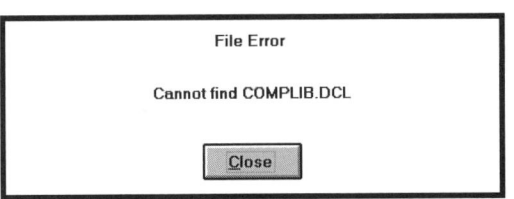

Fig. 7.1
The first error dialog displayed when COMPLIB isn't found.

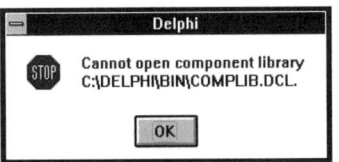

Fig. 7.2
The second error dialog displayed when COMPLIB isn't found.

Delphi stores the path to the DCL file and its name in the DELPHI.INI file, which is created in the \WINDOWS directory on installation of the product. DELPHI.INI is Delphi's initialization file in Windows standard INI file format. The [library] section in DELPHI.INI contains an entry called ComponentLibrary, which specifies the path and the name of the DCL file to use. Note that only one DCL file can be specified at a given time.

How to Manipulate DCL Files

Delphi allows flexibility in the use of component libraries:

- You can use DCL files other than COMPLIB.DCL.

- You can create DCL files from existing DCL files, starting with the contents of all the initial DCL's components.

- You can configure Delphi to reflect only select components within a DCL file on the Component palette.

- You can configure Delphi to reflect multiple palette pages with custom captions for related groups of controls.

- You can modify DCL files to remove any desired components at the unit level.

- You can add custom components to COMPLIB.DCL or to your own DCL file (covered later in this chapter).

First, you need to do some DCL file manipulation. This chapter assumes that COMPLIB.DCL is the DCL file now in use. Before you begin, however, make a backup of COMPLIB.DCL onto a floppy or other protected media.

To give a better ideal of what Delphi does behind the scenes, perform the following steps (which need to be performed only once for the exercises in this chapter):

1. From the Options menu, select Environment. The Environment Options dialog appears.

2. In the Compiling section of the Preferences page, select the Show Compiler Progress check box, as shown in figure 7.3.

3. Click OK to save your change.

Fig. 7.3
Configure Delphi to show the progress of compilations from the Preferences page of the Environment Options dialog.

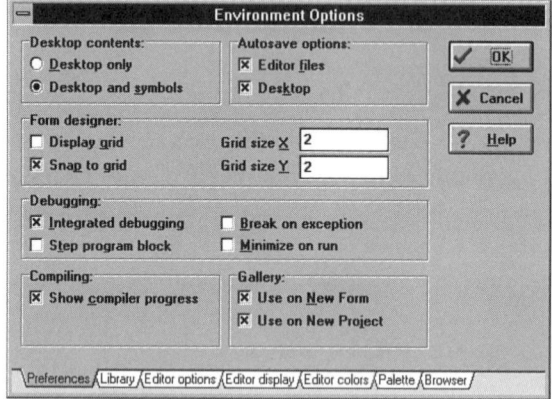

This setting will force Delphi to display a dialog that tracks progress of compilation and will reflect the name of the main program file being compiled. Because the DCL as well as the components on it require compilation, the resulting dialog will provide information that may help you with any troubleshooting. This chapter also points out some information that the Compiling dialog displays as a visual aid.

Now you will create a new DCL file based on the default COMPLIB.DCL. The resulting file will contain all the components now available from COMPLIB.DCL and will be called CUSTLIB.DCL. It will be used through the remainder of this chapter. Follow these steps:

1. Start Delphi (if it isn't already running) and close any open or default projects.

2. From the Options menu, select Install Components. The Install Components dialog appears (see fig. 7.4).

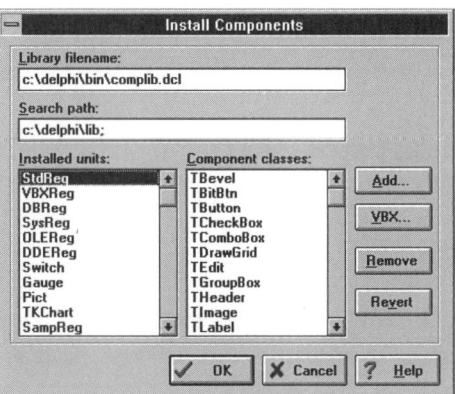

Fig. 7.4
The Install Components dialog shows installed units and the classes it contains.

3. The Library Filename text box reflects the current library's path and file name. The current file name should be COMPLIB.DCL. Change COMPLIB.DCL to **CUSTLIB.DCL**.

Delphi is designed to use library files with the extension .DCL. The Library Filename text box will allow you to change the extension of the specified file to an extension other than DCL. Delphi will change the extension you specify *back* to .DCL when the library file is recompiled.

4. Click OK. Delphi will compile the new DCL file.

The Compiling dialog appears (see fig. 7.5). Notice that the Project field reflects that the file being compiled is CUSTLIB.DPR.

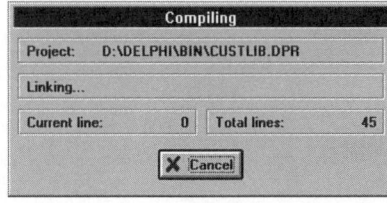

Fig. 7.5
The Compiling dialog displays the current progress of compilation.

CUSTLIB.DPR is a Delphi-generated project source file for the library being created. By default, this file is deleted after compilation but can be retained by selecting the Save Library Source Code check box on the Library page of

158 Chapter 7—Customizing and Reusing Components

the Environment Options dialog. You may want to retain this file for a manual edit of the project or to open later with a text editor just to see what's going on behind the scenes.

After the compilation, open the Options menu and choose Install Components again to bring up the Install Components dialog. Notice that the Library Filename text box now shows CUSTLIB.DCL. CUSTLIB.DCL is now created and currently active.

Customizing the Components on the Palette
CUSTLIB.DCL is intended to be a customized version of COMPLIB.DCL. This scenario is set up to have Delphi reflect only the controls in CUSTLIB that are used on a regular basis on the Component palette.

Assume that you don't want any Samples components or VBX components to appear on the Component palette and want these pages removed from the palette. You also want to combine the Standard page with the Additional page. The following exercises will show how to remove components and pages from the Component palette, move components between palette pages, and add blank pages to the Component palette. First, follow these steps to remove components and pages:

1. Right-click the Component palette and select Configure from the SpeedMenu. The Environment Options dialog will appear with the Palette page already selected.

2. Highlight Samples in the Pages list box. This will cause the Components list box to show all the components on the Samples page (see fig. 7.6).

Fig. 7.6
Select the Samples page to show its components in the Tools list box.

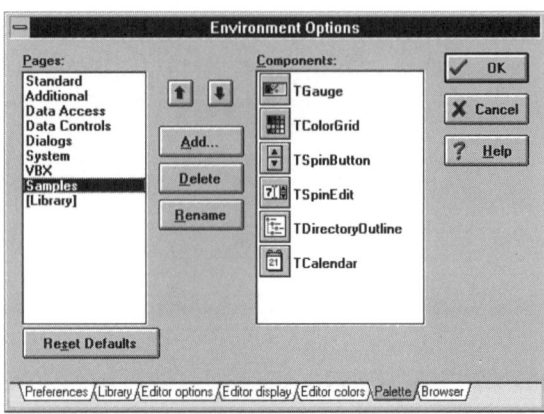

3. Highlight the first component in the Tools list box, and then click the Delete button as many times as necessary to remove all the components.

> **Note**
>
> Selecting OK at this point would result in an empty Samples page on the Component palette. Don't click OK yet—you aren't done.

4. In the Pages list box, click the Samples page and then click the Delete button. This removes the Samples page from the Pages list box and thus from the Component palette.

5. Repeat steps 1 through 4 for the VBX page.

Keep the Environment Options dialog open for the next exercise, which shows how to move components from one page of the Component palette to another. Follow these steps:

1. To move the components from the Additional page to the Standard page, select the Additional page in the Pages list box.

2. Drag the topmost component in the Components list box over the Standard page entry of the Pages list box. Notice that the cursor changes from the standard cursor to a standard Windows drag cursor.

3. Release the mouse button. Notice that the component you just dragged is no longer visible in the Components list box.

4. Repeat steps 1 through 3 until all components for the Additional page are gone from the Components list box.

5. Reselect the Additional page in the Pages list box and then click Delete to remove the page.

This next exercise demonstrates how to rename a page on the Component palette. Follow these steps:

1. Select the Standard entry in the Pages list box. Notice that all the controls previously in the Additional page are now located in the Components list box for the Standard page.

2. Select the Standard entry in the Pages list box. Click the Rename button. The Rename Page dialog appears.

160 Chapter 7—Customizing and Reusing Components

   3. In the Page Name text box, type **Main**. Click OK.

   4. Click OK twice to close the Rename Page and Environment Options dialogs.

If all steps were successful, the Component palette should now contain a Main palette page, which should contain all the components that were previously on the Standard and Additional pages. The Standard, Additional, VBX, and Sample pages should all be completely removed from the Component palette (see fig. 7.7).

Fig. 7.7
Your Component palette should look like this now.

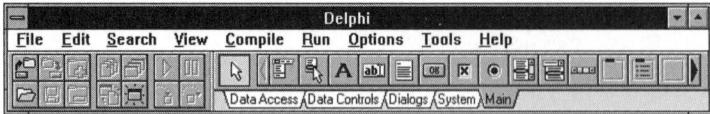

Reopen the Environment Options dialog. To add a new blank page to the Component palette, follow these steps:

   1. Click any entry in the Pages list box and then click the Add button. The Add Page dialog appears (see fig. 7.8).

   2. Type **Custom** in the Page Name text box.

   3. Click OK in the Add Page dialog. This results in an empty page that you will add components to later. Then click OK in the Environment Options dialog.

Fig. 7.8
The Add Page dialog allows you to name a page on the Component palette.

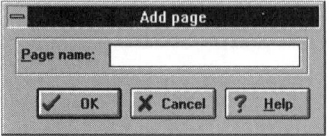

After completing the last exercise, you may have expected the Compiling dialog to appear to update the current configuration of the DCL file. This wasn't the case because the Component palette's configuration isn't built into the DCL file. In fact, when you removed all those components from the Samples and VBX pages, they weren't removed from the DCL file at all, nor was the Custom page added to the DCL file.

The Component palette configuration is stored in Delphi's initialization file (DELPHI.INI). Each time a new DCL file is opened, Delphi adds a section to the DELPHI.INI file. The section that's created starts with the word Palette followed by a period and the name of the DCL file with its DCL extension. Following the section name is an entry for each page on the Component palette. Assigned to each entry is a list of component class names to display on that page.

Because it's possible to open any one DCL file, Delphi stores the arrangement of the components in the DELPHI.INI file. You may have configured Delphi to reflect only four components out of a DCL file that contains 10. If the DCL file was closed and then later reopened, it would open up according to the stored configuration instead of the default. The default is to show all the components in the DCL file. If you look at the DELPHI.INI file now, you would see two sections for COMPLIB and for CUSTLIB, as follows:

```
[Palette.COMPLIB.DCL]

Standard=TMainMenu;TPopupMenu;TLabel;TEdit;TMemo;TButton;TCheckBox;
TRadioButton;TListBox;TComboBox;TScrollBar;TGroupBox;TPanel;TScrollBox;

...

[Palette.CUSTLIB.DCL]

Main=TMainMenu;TPopupMenu;TLabel;TEdit;TMemo;TButton;TCheckBox;
TRadioButton;TListBox;TComboBox;TScrollBar;TGroupBox;TPanel;
TScrollBox;TSpeedButton;TTabSet;TNotebook;TOutline;TStringGrid;
TDrawGrid;TPaintBox;TShape;TBevel;THeader;TMediaPlayer;TMasData

...
```

Removing Components from the DCL

So if removing a component from the Component palette doesn't actually remove it from the DCL file, how is removal accomplished? You may want to remove select components to save disk space. After all, they're already available in COMPLIB.DCL.

To answer this, first review the hierarchy of a DCL file. You can see a good first-level example of this by again viewing the Install Components dialog (see fig. 7.9).

Notice that the Install Components dialog has a list box labeled Installed Units. This list box contains an entry representing each unit from which the current DCL file is composed. If an entry is highlighted, the neighboring Component Classes list box displays all the component classes defined in that unit. When a DCL file is created, the compiler will compile into it various files with a .DCU extension. DCU files are compiled source files. Source files have the .PAS extension. The default DCU files are configured to be stored in the \DELPHI\LIB directory.

Fig. 7.9

The Install Components dialog reflects installed units and components each unit contains.

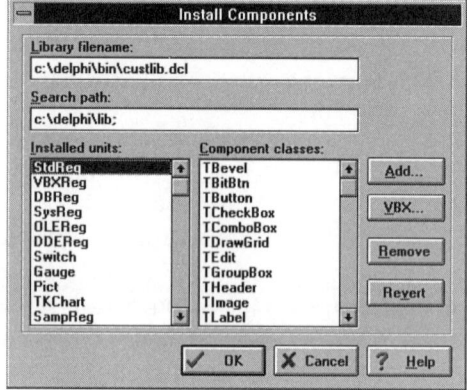

Delphi allows only the removal of complete units from the DCL file, because one unit may contain multiple components. In most cases, therefore, you're forced to remove groups of related components contained within a single unit.

As part of an exercise, you'll now remove the Samples and VBX components from CUSTLIB.DCL by removing the units that contain them. You've already removed them from the Component palette. (If you're concerned about removing these units from the current DCL file, don't be. You can add them back just as the exercises show later in the section "Performing a Generic Install of Components.") Follow these steps:

1. Open the Options menu and choose Install Components to bring up the Install Components dialog.

2. From the Installed Units list box, highlight the entry called SampReg and then click the Remove button.

3. Repeat step 2 for the Installed Units entries TKChart, Pict, Gauge, and Switch.

4. Click OK.

This time you'll see the Compiling dialog, and the DCL file will be regenerated without the units that were removed and without their defined components.

Later, this chapter discusses creating your own components by changing existing components, and how to include the components in the DCL file along with Component palette bit maps.

What DCL Files Are Made Of

A DCL file is a Windows dynamic link library (DLL) with a special interior and file extension. The DCL extension means Dynamic Component Library. When the developer drops a component onto a form, code is generated that instantiates an instance of the selected component's class. A study of the form's Type section will show this behavior. Follow these steps:

1. From the File menu, choose New Project to open a blank form.

2. From the Component palette, select the Main page. (You created this page earlier in the "Customizing the Components on the Palette" section.)

3. Click the Button component and then click the form.

4. Go to the Type section of the form's unit in the Code Editor.

Notice that a Button1 member has been added to the form's definition, and that it's of type TButton. TButton is a component class that's subclassed from many layers of class definitions deep within the Visual Components Library (VCL).

Adding this member results in the creation of the Button object within the class definition of the actual form. When the form is created, an instance of the TButton type will appear on the form. Creating an object instance of a component class is what's meant by instantiation of a component.

It's important to know that the DCU file is not only compiled into the DCL but is also compiled into any executables using a component that the DCU contains. It's necessary for the DCL to have the DCU compiled to give the component design-time behavior. This is proven in that the component can paint itself at design time. It's necessary for the application using the component to compile in the DCU so that the component will have runtime behavior.

Delphi will add the DCU file to the uses clause of the application you're creating. At compile time, each component's DCU file is compiled into the resulting executable. This is what allows Delphi programmers to distribute their applications without having to ship separate component-dependent modules.

Introducing Component Writing

Delphi component writing is different than Delphi application development in that the process isn't a visual one. Point-and-click development isn't an option here. This can be intimidating, but understand that some developers would have it no other way. Because Delphi is primarily a visual development environment, configuration and project management provisions aren't as intuitively available for component writing. Delphi's Integrated Development Environment (IDE) provides a Project Manager (available from the Tools menu) as well as a component expert (available on the File menu). Up to this point, you may have ignored these items or not even known that they exist. This section makes use of both.

The development process of components in Delphi is quite different than that of application development and requires a deeper understanding of the Visual Components Library (VCL) and the overall IDE. For this reason, this chapter touches on only the more important issues of the customization and modification of components. It's also for this reason that component writing is considered an advanced topic in Delphi programming. Entire books could be written on this topic alone. In fact, Borland provides a very complete reference to the topic in the *Component Writers Guide*, which ships with the product.

> **Note**
>
> The creation of custom property editor isn't discussed at all. Discussion of the creation of custom property editors is one or two steps beyond the level of what this chapter covers.

Component modification is by far the simplest method of component writing and possibly the most useful. The term *component modification* can be misleading. In a literal sense, it could be misunderstood as modifying the source code of an original component, recompiling it, and then giving it a new name. This scenario doesn't follow the standard object-oriented paradigm, however, and is in fact *not* what's meant to be understood.

Because a new variable type can be created from an existing type, a new class can be created from an existing class through subclassing. The new class takes a descendant role in the initial classes hierarchy. Available to the new class are the members of the parenting class and of all the ancestor classes. Component writing demonstrates an awesome truth to this object theory, as you'll soon see.

How to Set Up a Project with the Component Expert

Whether you're modifying an existing component or creating a new component, you should first perform these steps as an example exercise:

1. With Delphi running, close any currently open projects by opening the File menu and choosing Close.

2. Open the File menu again and choose New Project, which will open a new project.

3. Again from the File menu, choose New Component. The Component Expert dialog appears (see fig. 7.10).

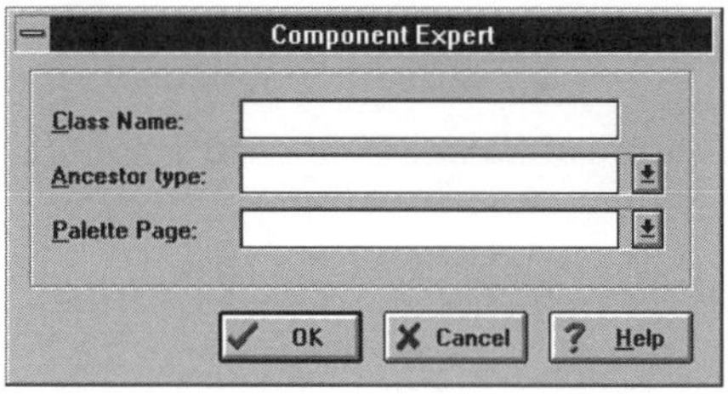

Fig. 7.10
The Component Expert dialog begins the component-writing task.

4. In the Class Name text box, enter a descriptive name for your component's class. The first character should be the letter T. (Use **TCloseButton** for this example.)

> **Note**
>
> Using a T as the first character is a matter of convention. Although not required by Delphi, the convention should be used to maintain consistency with the classes currently defined in Delphi. TMyFirstCtrl is a generic example class name, although it isn't very descriptive. TCloseButton is a descriptive name that gives you a better idea of what the control might do.

5. In the Ancestor Type combo box, enter the name of the existing class from which you want your control to inherited all the properties and methods. (Use **TButton** for this example.)

> **Note**
>
> To modify an existing component class, you need to select the type of component that you want to modify. TButton is an example of a commonly modified component.
>
> To create your own custom control, you'll usually select an existing control, such as TButton. TCustomControl, TGraphicControl, or TComponent could also
>
> *(continues)*

> (continued)
>
> be selected, depending on your needs. These three classes provide the basic methods, properties, and events of most every component type available.
>
> To really start from scratch, one of the more abstract methods could be used, such as TPersistence. This likely would require much more work re-creating functionality already available from TComponent and its descendants.

6. In the Palette Page combo box, enter the page of the Component palette on which the new component's *bit map* (the image on the Component palette that visually represents the component) should be displayed. (Use **Custom** for this example.)

> **Note**
>
> If the entry doesn't exist on the Component palette, the page will be created when the new component is installed. You created the page in an earlier exercise.

7. Click OK.

8. Open the File menu and choose Save File As. Enter **CUSTCOMP.PAS** in the Save File dialog's text box. Click OK.

9. Open the View menu and choose Project Manager. The Project Manager appears (see fig. 7.11). Click the Add SpeedBar button. The Add to Project dialog appears.

10. Enter **CUSTCOMP.PAS** in the text box, and then click OK. CUSTCOMP.PAS is now added to the Project Manager.

The SpeedBar buttons Add and Remove simply add or remove a unit from the current project. The View Unit SpeedBar button will result in the display of the code of the currently selected unit. The View Form SpeedBar button will be enabled only if the unit comprises a form. Selecting it will result in the display of the form.

> **Note**
>
> Although a project was open before the current unit was opened, the unit doesn't automatically become part of that project. Component units must be explicitly added to the project in order to be compiled as part of that project.

Introducing Component Writing

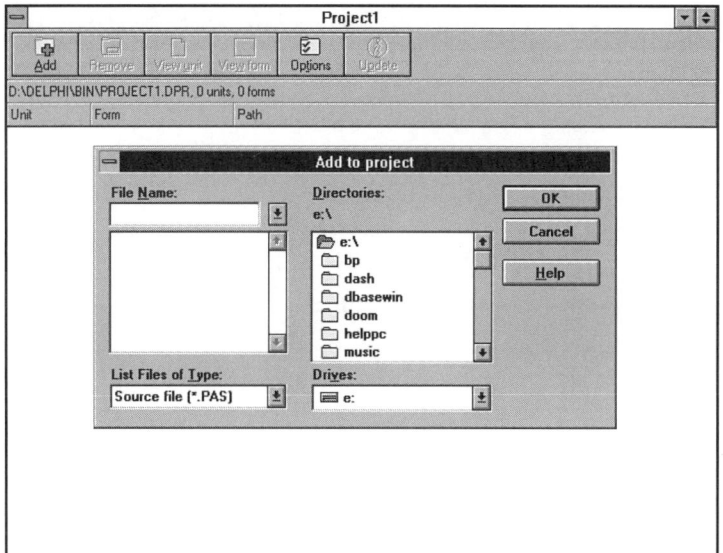

Fig. 7.11
The Add to Project dialog appears when you click the Add SpeedBar button.

11. Select UNIT1.PAS (which was part of the new project by default). It's displayed in the box below the SpeedBar. Click the Remove SpeedBar button to remove the unit.

> **Note**
>
> The unit that opens with the project (UNIT1.PAS by default) instantiates a form within the project and isn't needed for component creation. It therefore should be removed as in step 11.

12. Close the Project Manager and view the code composing CUSTCOMP.PAS.

Code the Component Expert Generates

The source code generated by the Component Expert into CUSTCOMP.PAS should appear as shown in listing 7.1. This code displays an empty skeleton that results from subclassing a component using the Component Expert.

Listing 7.1 A Code Template for Your Component

```
1 unit Custcomp;

2 interface
```

(continues)

168 Chapter 7—Customizing and Reusing Components

Listing 7.1 Continued

```
 3 uses
 4    SysUtils, WinTypes, WinProcs, Messages, Classes, Graphics,
 5    Controls, Forms, Dialogs, StdCtrls;

 6 type
 7   TCloseButton = class(TButton)
 8   private
 9     { Private declarations }
10   protected
11     { Protected declarations }
12   public
13     { Public declarations }
14   published
15     { Published declarations }
16   end;

17 procedure Register;

18 implementation
19 procedure Register;
20 begin
21   RegisterComponents('Custom', [TCloseButton]);
22 end;

23 end.
```

> **Note**
>
> The lines are numbered in listing 7.1 because individual lines will be specifically referred to in the following discussions. These numbers don't actually appear in the code itself.

Notice line 7. The name you entered into the Class Name text box of the Component Expert dialog appears in the unit `type` section. Assigned to it is `class(TButton)`. This statement means give `TCloseButton` all the members of `TButton`, properties and methods included. The `type` section only provides `TCloseButton` with a definition. Here you have subclassed `TButton`'s definition.

Source Sections for the Component's Declarations

Lines 8, 10, 12, and 14 in listing 7.1 are areas within `TCloseButton`'s definition into which you can add or overwrite functionality. These sections effect the visibility of members within the current unit and within any programs that might make use of the current unit. These areas are defined as follows:

- `private` This directive acts the same as `Public` but only within its unit. Members under this directive aren't accessible outside of the unit. This allows you to hide implementation details.

- **protected** This directive acts as `Private` but allows members to be accessible outside of the unit if they're descendants of the component.

- **published** This directive acts as `public` but results in the generation of runtime type information for its members. Editable properties visible to the Object Inspector are defined under `published`. Published members make up the design-time interface of your component.

- **public** This directive allows members to be generally accessible to all areas. It defines the runtime interface by making properties available that aren't necessarily appropriate for the design-time interface.

Component Registration

Line 17 in listing 7.1 is the declaration within the `interface` section that defines the `Register` procedure. The `Register` procedure is defined beginning on line 19 in the `implementation` section. This procedure has one statement, as follows:

```
RegisterComponents('Custom', [TCloseButton]);
```

The `RegisterComponents()` function tells Delphi what components to add to the component library (DCL). The first parameter, `Custom`, specifies on which page of the Component palette the component should appear. If the specified page doesn't exist, Delphi will create it. The second parameter, `TCloseButton`, is the name of the component. The name is placed within an open array.

If the component's unit defines several components, still only one `Register` procedure is necessary. Only one `RegisterComponents` statement is necessary if all the components defined in the unit are to be placed on a single page.

If your unit defined multiple components,

`TCloseButton`	To be placed on the Custom page
`TMinMaxButton`	To be placed on the Custom page
`TSlidePanel`	To be placed on the Cust2 page

the `Register` procedure would contain the following two statements:

```
RegisterComponents('Custom', [TCloseButton, TMinMaxButton]);
RegisterComponents('Cust2', [TSlidePanel]);
```

Registration is a very important process and must be performed for your components to be recognized. The `Register` procedure is called indirectly via `RegisterModule` from within the DPR file.

170 Chapter 7—Customizing and Reusing Components

If you recall from earlier in this chapter, the generated source files for component libraries have a .DPR extension. Once a component is written and ready to install, Delphi recompiles the DCL from the generated DPR file. An examination of the DPR will show that the component's unit name is listed in the uses clause of the DPR file. The main program body will contain a `RegisterModule` call for each unit specified for installation into the component library.

Performing a Generic Install of Components

Your first component defines a new class called `TCloseButton`, subclassed from `TButton`. At this point, `TCloseButton` does nothing different than `TButton`. This exercise is to show only how to install a new component. `TCloseButton` is stored in CUSTCOMP.PAS.

To install the `TCloseButton` component into the current component library (CUSTLIB.DCL), you must install the CUSTCOMP.PAS unit. Follow these steps:

1. With Delphi running, invoke the Environment Options dialog (open the Options menu and choose Environment). From the Library page, select the Save Library Source Code check box and then click OK (see fig. 7.12).

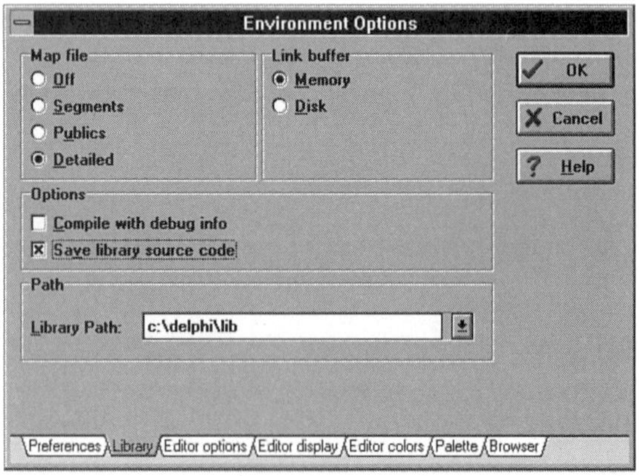

Fig. 7.12
The Environment Options dialog's Library page with the Save Library Source Code check box checked.

2. Compile CUSTCOMP.PAS (you can press F9 or use the Compile menu's Build All command).

3. Invoke the Install Components dialog (open the Options menu and choose Install Components).

4. Bring up the Add Module dialog by clicking the Add button (see fig. 7.13).

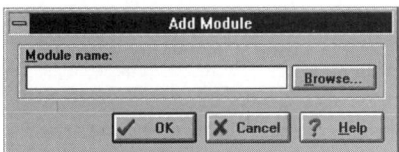

Fig. 7.13
The Add Module dialog provides an entry for specifying the path and unit (PAS) file containing the component(s).

5. Type the path and `CUSTCOMP.PAS` into the Module Name text box. If the path is unknown, use the Browse button to make the selection from the resulting File Open dialog and click OK.

6. Click OK to close the Install Components dialog.

The Compiling dialog will appear as it did after you removed the units from CUSTLIB.DCL earlier. Again, notice that the Project field shows that the file being compiled is CUSTLIB.DPR. With the Save Library Source Code check box selected in the Environment Options check box, CUSTLIB.DPR will be retained.

It's worth pausing to view the contents of this file. The file is in text format and can be opened with any text editor such as Notepad. Note the `uses` clause for inclusion of CUSTCOMP. Note the main program body for the `RegisterModule` statement that references the CUSTCOMP module and `CustComp.Register` procedure.

Now take a look at the Component palette. Notice that `CloseButton` is now a component on the Custom page, as reflected in the hint. (A *hint* is a text description for a control that appears when you place the mouse pointer over that control.) But where's the `T` from `TCloseButton`? Delphi assumes that you named your component class according to the convention of starting each class name with a T. Delphi will hide the T if it's the first character of the class name, and thus display only `CloseButton`. This behavior is for readability purposes.

Using Component Resources

A complete component is created from a combination of four files with the following extensions:

Extension	Description
.PAS	Source file
.DCR	Dynamic Component Resource file
.HLP	Compiled Windows help file
.KWF	Keyword file

Of these files, only the PAS file is necessary to create a component. When the component is compiled, another file is generated with the same name as the PAS file but with a .DCU extension. The DCU file is important, as it's compiled into the DCL file as well as into the EXE file of any applications that uses the component.

The DCR and Design-Time Bit Map

The DCR file is a compiled Windows resource file (Windows resource files typically have the .RES file extension). In Delphi, resource files that contain bit maps to use on the Component palette should be named with a .DCR extension, which stands for *dynamic component resource*. The DCR file should be placed in the same directory as the PAS file and/or DCU file that contains the associated component. When the component is installed, the data in the DCR file is compiled into the current component library (DCL file) along with the DCU. It isn't compiled into the EXE of applications using the component. This is only a design-time resource.

When creating DCR files, it's important to know that the DCR file must have the same name as the unit that the component is defined in. DCR files can actually contain multiple bit-map resources. Each bit map should have the same name as the class name given to the associated component.

If, for example, the unit you create is called CUSTCOMP.PAS and contains two components, TCloseButton and TConfirmButton, the DCR file should be called CUSTCOMP.DCR. The bit maps inside should be named TCloseButton and TComfirmButton.

DCR files can be created with the Image editor available from the Tools menu or from any Windows resource editor such as Borland's Resource Workshop.

Custom Help Files for Components

HLP files are binary files in a format that the Windows help system can interpret. HLP files, optionally included as part of a component, provide the user with context-sensitive information about each property and event.

HLP files are produced using the Windows help compiler, which is included with Delphi. The HLP file should be stored in the directory containing the DCU file. The Windows help compiler generates an HLP file based on the source file(s) specified in a HPJ file. An HPJ file is a text format project file that specifies various options about how to compile your help source files. The HPJ file also specifies the source file(s) to include in the project. The source files for HLP files have an .RTF extension (RTF stands for *Rich Text Format*). RTF is just another Windows file format but is important in that it's the format expected by the Windows help compiler.

RTF files can be generated by using a word processor (usually Microsoft Word) or a third-party help file generator such as ForeHelp, which is available from Borland International.

For more information about the creation of Windows help files, check the CHW.HLP file, which is distributed with Delphi. This help file contains complete information on this topic. To access this file, click the Creating Windows Help icon in the Delphi program group.

Keywords and the KWD File

The last file type to discuss is a keyword file, which has a .KWD extension. Delphi merges the KWD file into Delphi's master search index. The KWD file provides Delphi with the information necessary to search for a specific topic related to the item currently selected in the Object Inspector. The keyword file should be located in the directory containing the DCU file.

> **Note**
>
> The topic of the creation of Windows help files and keyword files is beyond the scope of this chapter and therefore isn't covered beyond the information already discussed.

Modifying Your First Component

Now it's time to modify your first component. At this point in the chapter, you should have the following:

Chapter 7—Customizing and Reusing Components

- An active component library called CUSTLIB.DCL
- A Component palette page called Custom
- A unit source file called CUSTCOMP.PAS and a compiled version called CUSTCOMP.DCU
- A custom component called TCloseButton on the Component palette's Custom page

Although you created a component called TCloseButton and have installed it onto the Component palette, this component has no functionality beyond the component from which it descends. Your first goal is to provide more functionality to TCloseButton.

Add the following right after the keyword protected in TCloseButton's type definition in the CUSTCOMP.PAS file:

```
Procedure Click; Override;
```

In the implementation section of the unit, insert the following procedure after line 22 of listing 7.1:

```
procedure TCloseButton.Click;
Begin
  inherited Click;
  (Owner as TForm).Close;
End;
```

The resulting modified unit should appear as follows:

```
unit Custcomp;

interface

uses
  SysUtils, WinTypes, WinProcs, Messages, Classes, Graphics,
  Controls, Forms, StdCtrls;

type
  TCloseButton = class(TButton)
  private
    { Private declarations }
  protected
    { Protected declarations }
    Procedure Click; Override;
  public
    { Public declarations }
  published
    { Published declarations }
  end;

procedure Register;
```

```
implementation

procedure Register;
begin
  RegisterComponents('Custom', [TCloseButton]);
end;

procedure TCloseButton.Click;
Begin
  inherited Click;
  (Owner as TForm).Close;
end;

end.
```

The unit at this point could be recompiled into CUSTCOMP.DCL and implemented into an application. If the user clicks the TCloseButton of the application, the application's form would close.

This is a very simple extension of TButton. TCloseButton contains all the functionality of TButton but with a twist of automatically closing the form. Although only a subtle enhancement, it stills saves the applications programmer time from recoding a close into the OnClick event of a standard TButton for every program using a close button.

Overriding Standard Methods

A review of the written code reveals a statement added to the Protected section of TCloseButton's type:

```
Procedure Click; Override;
```

You gave TCloseButton functionality by overriding the standard Click method with your own. Each existing component contains a group of standard dynamic methods that are passed down the hierarchy chain of classes that ultimately compose each existing component. By overriding the click method, polymorphism is achieved and your new functionality is implemented.

In the case of TCloseButton, the ancestral hierarchy appears as follows:

- TCloseButton is a descendant of TButton.

- TButton is a descendant of TButtonControl.

- TButtonControl is a descendant of TWinControl.

- TWinControl is a descendant of TControl.

- TControl is a descendant of TComponent.

- TComponent is a descendant of even more abstract classes.

176 Chapter 7—Customizing and Reusing Components

The original click method is defined in CONTROLS.PAS, which is located in the \DELPHI\SOURCE\VCL directory. It's a protected member of TControl. To find additional methods that can be overwritten, you can examine CONTROLS.PAS as well as the other PAS files in the \DELPHI\SOURCE\VCL directory.

Alternatively, Delphi comes with a Browser utility, which is accessible from the View menu. Using the Browser is much more convenient than using a text editor and performing text searches on PAS files. The Browser is a visual utility that lets you step through the object hierarchies, units, and global symbols of your application (see fig. 7.14). Consult the on-line help documentation for more information on how to use the Browser. Chapter 11, "Using the Browser," also discusses how to use this utility.

Fig. 7.14
The Browser displays the object hierarchies of a loaded compiled program.

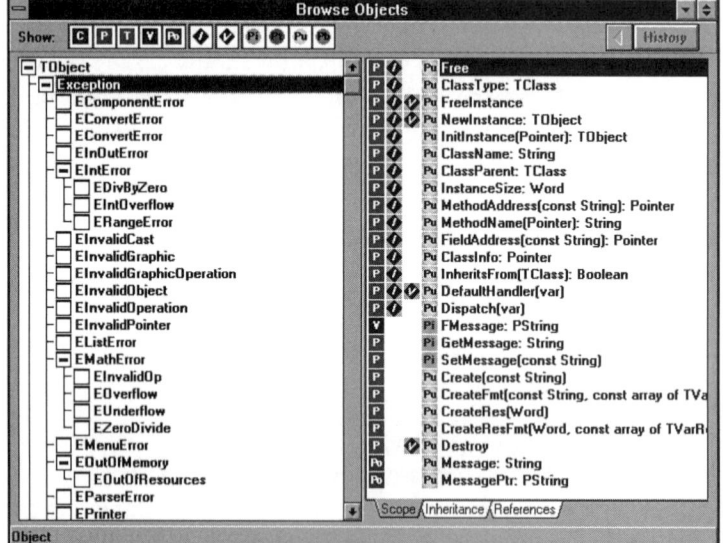

Inheriting Default Behavior

The original click method defined in TControl's definition checks to see whether the applications developer has assigned any code to the OnClick event of the button. If code was assigned, the code is executed.

Although you chose to override this method, you still want the default handling for the OnClick method to occur. This was accomplished by including the statement inherited Click; in the new click procedure.

The inherited statement results in the inclusion of the original method's click behavior. It knows which method to include because you specified inherited with the method name Click following it. The inherited statement is very powerful and should be the first statement in the overridden method, as it was in your click method. This ensures that your new functionality doesn't interfere with the default click method behavior. The power of the inherited statement is its capability to call and execute the original method defined in the parent class definition, and then return and execute the statements in the current method.

The final statement in your new click method is (Owner as TForm).Close. The form is the owner of all components as the application is the owner of the form. Using (Owner as TForm) ensures that the correct close method is executed.

Adding Properties or Events

Now you can add even more functionality to TCloseButton by including a new event. As you may or may not know, the click event doesn't actually fire until the button is released. You'll add a new event to TCloseButton in the next section.

Adding Object Fields

You'll now add a new event to TCloseButton that fires immediately following the execution of any code attached to the OnClick event. This event is to be named OnClickRelease. You accomplish this with several additions to CUSTCOMP.PAS, starting with the private section of TCloseButton's definition. It should look like this:

```
private
  { Private declarations }
  FOnClickRelease : TNotifyEvent;
```

This adds a new private member or object field called FOnClickRelease. *Object fields* are used to implement an event property's read and write behavior. Object fields are pointers to the component user's code assigned to the associated events. Object fields shouldn't be accessed directly and should always be declared as private. Instead, the associated property should be used for access. Object fields should be of the same type as the event property and, by convention, have the same name preceded by the letter F.

Adding and Overriding Methods

You'll now add a new method called Click to the component's class definition. The parent class, TButton, also contains a Click method and is overridden in the following statements. This is done because you want to add your own code to execute when the Click method gets called, or you may want to change entirely what the parent (TButton) Click method does.

The `protected` section should be modified to appear as follows:

```
protected
  { Protected declarations }
  Procedure Click; Override;
  procedure ClickRelease; dynamic;
```

Here, the `ClickRelease` method is added to the `protected` section of the object's definition, thus encapsulated and recognizable within the unit and to any descendent classes. The `ClickRelease` method will be responsible for executing any code assigned to the new `OnClickRelease` event. The first declaration overrides the standard `Click` method. The second declaration declares a new method called `ClickRelease`.

Making Custom Properties Available to the Object Inspector

For a component's properties to be visible and modifiable in the Object Inspector at design time, the properties must be declared as published. For this example, the `published` section should be modified to appear as follows:

```
published
  { Published declarations }
  property OnClickRelease: TNotifyEvent read FOnClickRelease write
        FOnClickRelease;
```

Properties are recognized by the inclusion of the property keyword. In this example, your property is `OnClickRelease` and is defined in the `published` section. Properties defined in the `published` section are available at design time and are automatically made available in the Object Inspector.

Firing a Custom Event

The earlier section "Adding and Overriding Methods" showed how to declare a method in the component's class definition and override its ancestor method. The following is the actual content of the overriding method.

The `Click` method should appear as follows:

```
procedure TCloseButton.Click;
Begin
  inherited Click;
  ClickRelease;
  (Owner as TForm).Close;
End;
```

Although you declared the `ClickRelease` method in `TCloseButton`'s definition, the method still requires a means to be fired. The logical place to call the method is in the initial click method after the `inherited` behavior is complete. The `inherited` behavior is responsible for executing any code associated with the `OnClick` event. Once this is complete, the `ClickRelease` method can then be called. Then the form's close method is executed.

The actual `ClickRelease` method should be added to the `implementation` section as follows:

```
procedure TCloseButton.ClickRelease;
Begin
  if assigned(FOnClickRelease) then FOnClickRelease(self);
End;
```

This method simply checks to see whether `FOnClickRelease` is pointing at a valid method. This means it's checking to see whether code has been assigned by the component user to the `OnClickRelease` event. If it has, it's executed.

Changing Property Defaults

Suppose that you want to modify the default value of an existing property. Assume that the default font is System and is 10 points in size. The default width of `TCloseButton` is only 89, which is too small to display the entire caption clearly. A width of 115 would make a much clearer display.

> **Note**
>
> The default caption of a component is that of the class name. If the class name is preceded by the letter T, it isn't included in the caption.
>
> The class name is followed by a number that represents the numerical order of the instance that the control was dropped. The first instance of `TCloseButton` will have the caption `CloseButton1`. The second instance will have the caption `CloseButton2`.

Changing the Default Values

You can change the default value of a component's property to a new default value. Changing the default font size of a button so that a long caption will fit is an example of when new default values should be established. You can correct this cosmetic flaw by changing the default value assigned to the width property. Each component being a descendent of `TComponent` has a constructor method called `create`. When you're creating properties from scratch, they're automatically assigned the following default values based on their data type if a default isn't assigned. In most cases, default values should be assigned to the properties of your component. If you choose not to, the following is what you can expect:

Data Type	Default Value
Numeric	0
Boolean	False
Pointer	nil
String	Empty (the length bit set to zero)

As you may have noticed in the original TButton component, the Width property doesn't have a value of zero on initial drop. This means that the programmer of TButton (someone at Borland) has assigned a new default width that appears to the component user as the literal default. In most cases, this assignment takes place in the constructor method of the component. It could be a constant value or even a calculation. Sometimes the assignments are made in other methods that execute after the constructor. CreateParams is an example of a method that's executed before the Create method and that's a member of other components such as TPanel and TEdit. Sometimes it's necessary to trace through the maze of a component's ancestor code to determine the exact method in which the default value of a property is initialized. In most cases, the assignments of the new default values can be made by overriding the parent Create method and making the new assignment.

You may think that changing the default value of a property is just a matter of adding a new published Width property and assigning it a default value or even directly writing to the assumed existing FWidth object field. This won't work. Although the FWidth object field does exist somewhere back in the hierarchy of objects, it's declared in the private section of the component's definition and thus isn't available.

Overriding the Constructor

The default value of the Width property is changed by overwriting the constructor where the initial assignment takes place. The new constructor, also called Create, will inherit from the original Create method, thus executing the code in the original Create, and then assign the new default value to the already existing Width property.

The constructor is declared public, so it has complete visibility and can be executed by the application using the component. Modify TCloseButton's definition so that the public section appears as follows:

Modifying Your First Component

```
public
  { Public declarations }
  constructor Create(AOwner: TComponent); override;
```

Next, the new overriding constructor must be created. Add the following to the implementation section of CUSTCOMP.PAS:

```
constructor TCloseButton.Create(AOwner: TComponent);
begin
  inherited Create(AOwner);
  Width := 115;
end;
```

This new Create method inherits all the functionality of the original Create method. It then assigns a new value to the Width property. The Width property is accessible because it was initially declared as published. Similarly, these steps may be implemented to change the defaults of any inherited properties.

Determining Design Time vs. Runtime

As a component writer, sometimes you may want to determine whether a component is now being used at design time. An example may be the display of a copyright message at design time. Similar functionality is commonly added by VBX writers to the VBX controls that they distribute. You'll add this functionality to TCloseButton.

The message will be displayed using the Windows API function MessageBox. MessageBox isn't a Delphi function but is contained within one of the Windows core files. It's made available to Delphi users by inclusion of the WINPROCS unit in the unit's uses clause.

You'll implement this example by overriding yet another method—CreateWnd. The CreateWnd method is declared in the protected section of the TWinControls definition. Since TCloseButton is a descendant of TWinControl and is declared as protected, the CreateWnd method is available to be overridden.

Add the following to the protected section of TCloseButton's type definition:

```
procedure CreateWnd; override;
```

Add the following procedure to the implementation section of CUSTCOMP:

```
procedure TCloseButton.CreateWnd;
begin
  inherited CreateWnd;
  if csDesigning in ComponentState then
    MessageBox(0,'TCloseButton Copyright 01/01/95 by John
              Doe','Note',mb_Ok);
end;
```

What the `CreateWnd` method does isn't important for this example. What's important is when it is executed. This method is fired on creation of the actual component. If your `MessageBox` statement isn't conditional, it would be executed at several different times including at runtime of the application using the component. The goal, however, is to display the message only during design time. This is accomplished by making execution of the `MessageBox` statement conditional. The condition depends on `csDesigning` being assigned to the `ComponentState` property.

The `ComponentState` property is initially declared in the `Classes` unit and is inherited from `TComponent`. The value of the `ComponentState` property is checked against `csDesigning`. All the options are `csLoading`, `csReading`, `csWriting`, and again `csDesigning`. These are nothing more than items in a set called `TComponentState`. The property `ComponentState` is of type `TComponentState`. The `ComponentState` property reads and writes the object field called `FComponentState`. `FComponentState` is (of course) also of type `TComponentState`. Note that the `if` statement is using traditional `set` syntax for checking the value using `in`.

But why override another method? Wouldn't this be just as effective if added to the constructor? The answer is no. The `ComponentState` property won't get set for `csDesigning` until after the constructor is called. The choice of overriding the `CreateWnd` method as opposed to another came from `CreateWnd` being fired consistently and very soon after the constructor.

Testing the Component

Now it's time to test your new component. Do a visual check for syntax errors and misspellings. Press Ctrl+F9. The Compiling dialog will appear. If any errors occur, they will be highlighted on the offending line. Correct any errors. On successful compilation, click OK in the Compiling dialog.

If you started this chapter from the beginning and followed all the steps, the CUSTLIB.DCL file will be the currently active component library. Also, a version of CUSTCOMP has already been installed into CUSTLIB. If you were now to go directly through the installation process and try to reinstall the completed version of CUSTCOMP, you would receive an error on installation (see fig. 7.15).

This error is automatic protection from installing multiple units of the same name, which would cause errors. This is also a form of overwrite protection.

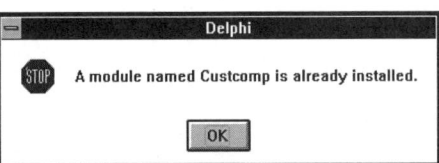

Fig. 7.15
This dialog results from a failed reinstall of CUSTLIB.

You can overcome this error in two ways. First, you can follow the steps described earlier for removing a unit from a DCL file. Once CUSTCOMP is removed, CUSTLIB will recompile without including CUSTCOMP. Then the latest version of CUSTCOMP could be installed. Alternatively, you can open the Options menu and choose Rebuild Library to recompile the DCL using the most current component DCU files. This method is faster because the DCL is compiled only once but requires that the DCU be previously installed.

If the unit you're adding to the DCL is being installed for the first time, follow the steps described earlier in the section "Performing a Generic Install of Components" for adding a unit to a DCL file.

At this point, CUSTCOMP has been installed and CUSTLIB recompiled. Before you actually test the component, you should save the current project and open a new one as follows:

1. Go ahead and save the project by opening the File menu and choosing Save Project.

2. Now open the File menu and choose New Project. A new project and blank form appears.

3. Click the Custom page of the Component palette. The earlier created bit map should be visible.

4. Move the mouse cursor over the bit map and let it sit there for 2 or 3 seconds. The hint should display CloseButton.

5. Click the CloseButton bit map and drop it on the form. The copyright message should appear, as in figure 7.16. Click OK on the message box.

Fig. 7.16
The copyright displays when you drop TCloseButton on the form.

184 Chapter 7—Customizing and Reusing Components

6. Click the Events tab of the Object Inspector. Double-click in the space next to the `OnClickRelease` event. The Code Editor will move to the front, if it isn't already there.

7. Modify the `CloseButton1ClickRelease` method to appear as follows:

    ```
    procedure TForm1.CloseButton1ClickRelease(Sender: TObject);
    begin
      MessageBox(0,'Success: OnClickRelease','Note',mb_Ok);
    end;
    ```

8. From the Object Inspector, double-click the space next to the `OnClick` event. The editor will again move to the front if it isn't already there.

9. Modify the `CloseButton1Click` method to appear as follows:

    ```
    procedure TForm1.CloseButton1Click(Sender: TObject);
    begin
      MessageBox(0,'Success: OnClick','Note',mb_Ok);
    end;
    ```

10. Save the project and the applications unit. Press F9 to compile and run.

11. When the application comes up, click the control icon.

    The message in the `OnClick` method should appear, displaying `Success: OnClick` followed by the message in the `OnClickRelease` method displaying `Success: OnClickRelease`. Close the application.

This base component can be used as a guide for modifying any existing component. Much functionality available for component writers has been demonstrated in these few lines of code.

This information should provide a jump start to component writing and prompt many questions. The topic of component writing is very large, and this chapter has only skimmed the surface. Be aware that Delphi ships with a complete component writer's guide and has much more in-depth information included in the on-line help.

Using VBX Controls

The remaining content of this chapter is dedicated to using components that are based on VBX controls. *VBX controls* are Visual Basic (VB) controls. Like Delphi, VB also makes use of visual controls that are selected from a palette and dropped onto a form. These controls are similar to components, as they require a true compiler to generate and act as visual tools within the development environment in which they're used. The only drawback to the use of

VBX controls is that the VBX file must be distributed with the application using the control. For Delphi programmers, this means the VBX must be available at runtime and design time.

VBX controls were initially created for use with Microsoft's Visual Basic. VB is a visual programming environment similar to Delphi but lacks a true compiler. Add-on controls in VB are made available from VBX files. VBX files are dynamic link libraries that were written following a specific and now standard format and saved with a .VBX extension. A VBX file may contain a single control or multiple controls.

It didn't take long for other products to find a way to implement these time-saving controls. Products such as Delphi, C++, dBASE for Windows, and others all can make VBX controls available for the user's applications.

Using VBX Controls in Delphi

Delphi supports any VB 1.0 compatible versions of VBX controls. VBX compatibility in general extends to 3.0, but Delphi can't make use of these.

> **Note**
>
> You might consider this a major limitation of Delphi. Keep in mind that the majority of VBX controls that exist and that are now being written are 1.0 compatible. This means Delphi can actually access the majority of the controls in the current VBX market. It's possible that future versions of Delphi will support 2.x or above VBX controls.

Delphi ships with four VBX controls, which are stored in files of similar names with a VBX extension:

- `TBiSwitch` Stored in SWITCH.VBX
- `TBiGauge`   Stored in GAUGE.VBX
- `TBiPict`   Stored in PICT.VBX
- `TTkChart`   Stored in TKCHART.VBX

A default installation of Delphi will place these VBX files in directory \DELPHI\BIN. Each VBX has a compiled Delphi component wrapper file of the same name with a DCU extension. Each VBX also has a resource file of the same name with a DCR extension. These files are stored in the \DELPHI\LIB directory by default.

VBX controls other than those shipped with Delphi can be used as well. They must be VB 1.0 compatible; otherwise, Delphi will generate an error. To use these VBX controls, you first must install them. The installation is similar to the installation of a Delphi component. Once the VBX is installed, it's available to you from the Component palette just as any other component is.

Components based on VBX controls can be manipulated just like regular components. The default values of properties can be changed, methods can be overwritten, events can be added, and a Component palette bit map can even be included. The primary difference is that you must distribute the VBX file along with the application. Once the VBX-based component is installed, everything you've learned in this chapter can be implemented in very much the same way. With VBXs, however, making all the changes you want isn't always possible. VBX controls, being almost entirely self-contained, don't always make all the methods and data available. This limitation is inflicted on the user by the VBX programmer and will vary between controls.

Installing VBX Controls

If you've followed the exercises as given in this chapter, CUSTLIB.DCL is the current component library in use. As you may recall, the steps earlier in the section "Removing Components from the DCL" included the removal of the VBX page of the Component palette. All the controls on the VBX page were removed from the DCL file as well. These VBX components are, of course, installed automatically during Delphi installation. The removal of the VBX components was in preparation for this section of the chapter.

Begin by reinstalling the TBiSwitch VBX control:

1. Bring up the Install Components dialog by opening the Options menu and choosing Install Components.

2. Click the VBX button. An open file dialog will appear.

3. If necessary, switch to the \DELPHI\BIN directory. Select SWITCH.VBX and click OK.

   Delphi brings up the Install VBX dialog (see fig. 7.17).

   > **Note**
   >
   > The first text box in this dialog, VBX File Name, specifies the name of the VBX file as selected. This text box is read only. The second text box, Unit File Name, specifies the path and file name of the PAS file to generate. By convention, this PAS file should have the same name as the VBX that's associated with it.

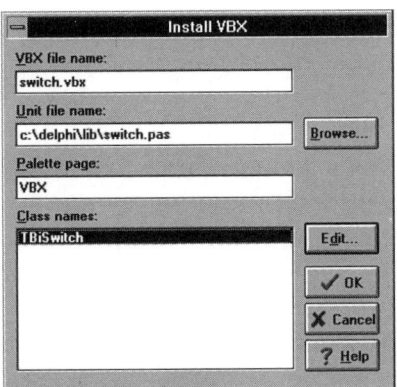

Fig. 7.17
In the Install VBX dialog, enter the name of the VBX file, a path to generate the wrapper PAS file, the palette page on which to install, and the classes contained within the file.

4. Change the path in the Unit File Name text box to \DELPHI\LIB\ followed by the name of the PAS file. (The purpose of this PAS file will be explained shortly.)

5. The Palette Page text box specifies the palette page on which to install the component. Enter **VBX**.

> **Note**
> Since the VBX page doesn't exist yet, Delphi will create it on installation of the VBX-based component.

The Class Names list box lists the names of all the controls available within the VBX. Like a standard Delphi component, VBX files may contain more than one control. In the case of SWITCH.VBX, it contains only one control with the default name TBiSwitch.

6. Click the text TBiSwitch in the Class Names list box to highlight it. Now click the Edit button.

7. When the Edit Class Name dialog appears, enter **TSwitch** and click OK.

8. Click OK in the Install VBX dialog.

   The Installed Units list box in the Install Components dialog will now reflect the SWITCH unit, and the Component Classes list box will state not available.

9. Click OK in the Install Components dialog. The Compiling dialog will appear, and then the new component and VBX page will be created.

These simple installation steps can be followed for adding any compatible VBX control to the Component palette.

Using the VBX Wrapper

Installation of a VBX control forces a recompilation of the DCL file. This may be surprising. You may have expected a simple reference to the VBX in the [Palette.DCLFileName] section of DELPHI.INI, but this isn't the case. So if a VBX comes precompiled, the DCL is already compiled, and the VBX can't be compiled into the DCL or into the user's application, then why would the DCL have to be recompiled at all?

You may have noticed when installing SWITCH.VBX that a file called SWITCH.DCU and a file called SWITCH.DCR already existed in the \DELPHI\LIB directory. The DCU and DCR files were distributed with Delphi. If these were deleted or never installed, they were re-created when the VBX was reinstalled in the previous steps. If you were to check \DELPHI\LIB again, a third file—SWITCH.PAS—would be present as well.

When a VBX is installed, several events happen behind the scenes:

- A DCR file is generated to hold the bit map extracted from the VBX for use on the Component palette.

- A PAS file that acts as a wrapper is generated and compiled into a DCU of the same name.

- The DCL file is recompiled to include the DCU and DCR containing the bit map.

- Delphi updates the appropriate sections of the DELPHI.INI file.

The unfamiliar event should be the generation of the PAS file. The DCU is created from the PAS file. Just like with a regular Delphi component, the DCU is compiled into the DCL. The DCU must remain available as it's compiled into any EXEs that make use of the VBX that the DCU references.

Once compiled, the PAS file (in your case, SWITCH.PAS) acts as a *wrapper* or interface for communication between Delphi and the VBX, and between the application using the VBX and the VBX itself.

Since a VBX can come from almost anywhere, Delphi obviously can't ship with the details and source code of every compatible VBX in existence. Sometimes the only programmer-level information about the data and methods in a VBX control will be contained in the PAS file that Delphi generates for you. This file deserves at least a brief examination.

You can open SWITCH.PAS—and any PAS file—with any text editor such as Notepad. It won't take long for you to notice that the file is laid out very similarly to the CUSTCOMP custom component unit created earlier in this chapter.

SWITCH.PAS opens with a header stating which VBX the file was generated from (in this case, SWITCH.PAS). This is followed by the unit name and the `interface` section. The `uses` clause deserves note because it references a file called VBXCtrl. This unit contains additional code that makes the VBX available to Delphi and any applications using the VBX. Also deserving note is the line

```
TSwitch = class(TVBXControl)
```

`TSwitch`, a descendant of `TVBXControl`, is the name you specified during installation of the VBX. `TVBXControl` is the class from which all VBX components are subclassed. The remainder of the `type` section should by now be quite familiar. The object fields are in the `protected` section, the constructor is public and overridden, and most of the properties are published.

The rest of the `interface` section merely contains the required declaration to the `Register` procedure, as described earlier in the section "Component Registration."

The `implementation` section is another story. Likely the only thing familiar to you is the unit's `Register` procedure and the overridden constructor. Elsewhere within the `implementation` section are methods and statements that may make little or no sense. Some of these statements are generated in assembly language and exist only to help Delphi or the application using the VBX communicate with the VBX; they're really nothing you need to be concerned about.

From Here...

Being able to create Delphi components demands a good understanding of the core Pascal language. Beyond this, you need a general understanding of the typical behaviors of components; an understanding of exception handling, which will provide your components with robustness; and knowledge of debugging techniques, which will help you with overall troubleshooting. These topics are covered in the following chapters:

- Chapter 3, "Understanding the Language," discusses the primary language elements.

- Chapter 4, "Using Visual Components," discusses the use of visual components in your application.

- Chapter 5, "Using Non-Visual Components," discusses the use of non-visual components in your application.

- Chapter 6, "Using Data-Bound Components," discusses the use of data-bound components in your applications.

- Chapter 11, "Using the Browser," explains how to use the utility that allows you to study a hierarchy of the relation of classes in your components.

- Chapter 14, "Handling Errors," discusses error handling and the use of exceptions in Delphi.

- Chapter 15, "Using Delphi's Debugging Features," discusses various methods for debugging your applications.

Part III

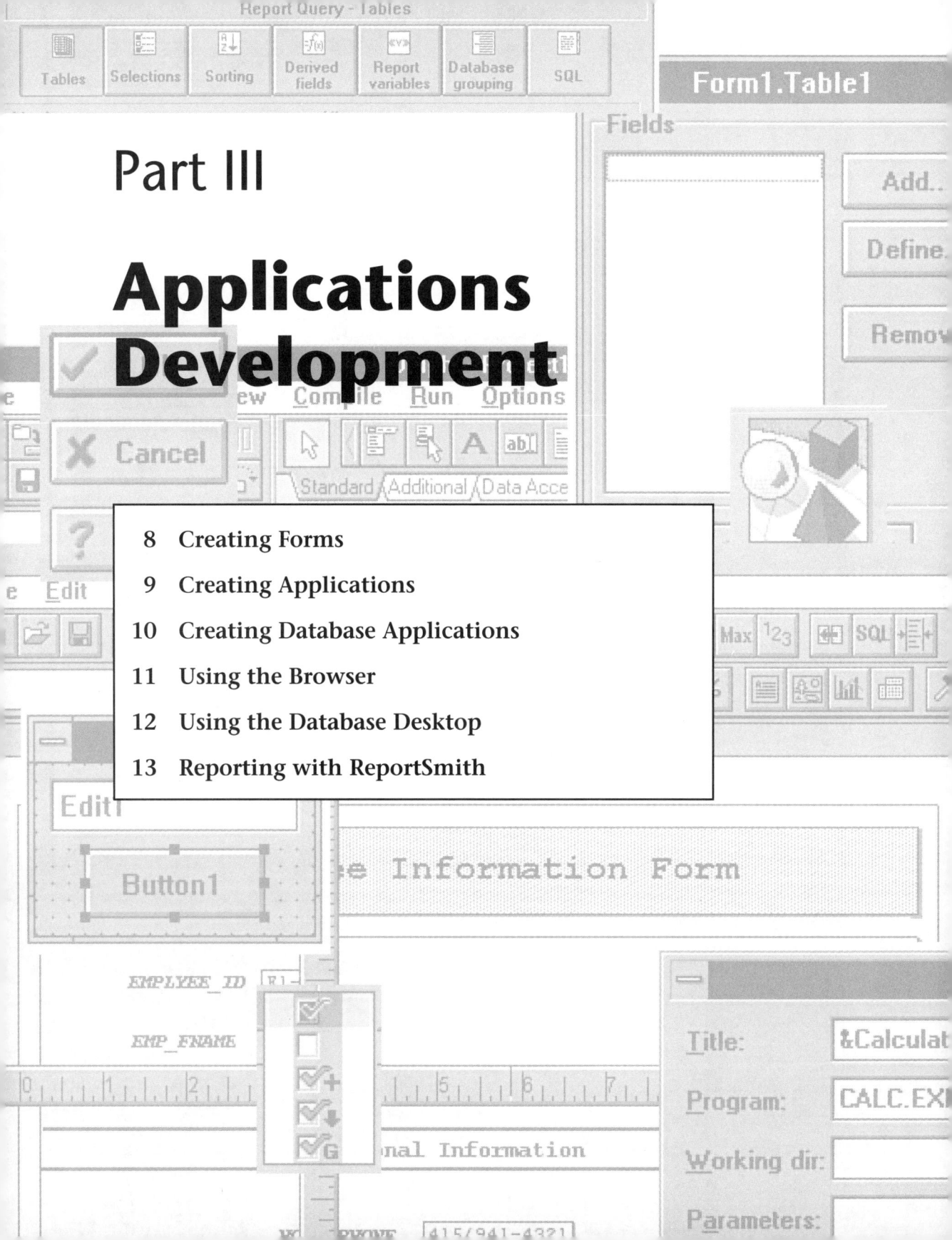

Applications Development

- 8 Creating Forms
- 9 Creating Applications
- 10 Creating Database Applications
- 11 Using the Browser
- 12 Using the Database Desktop
- 13 Reporting with ReportSmith

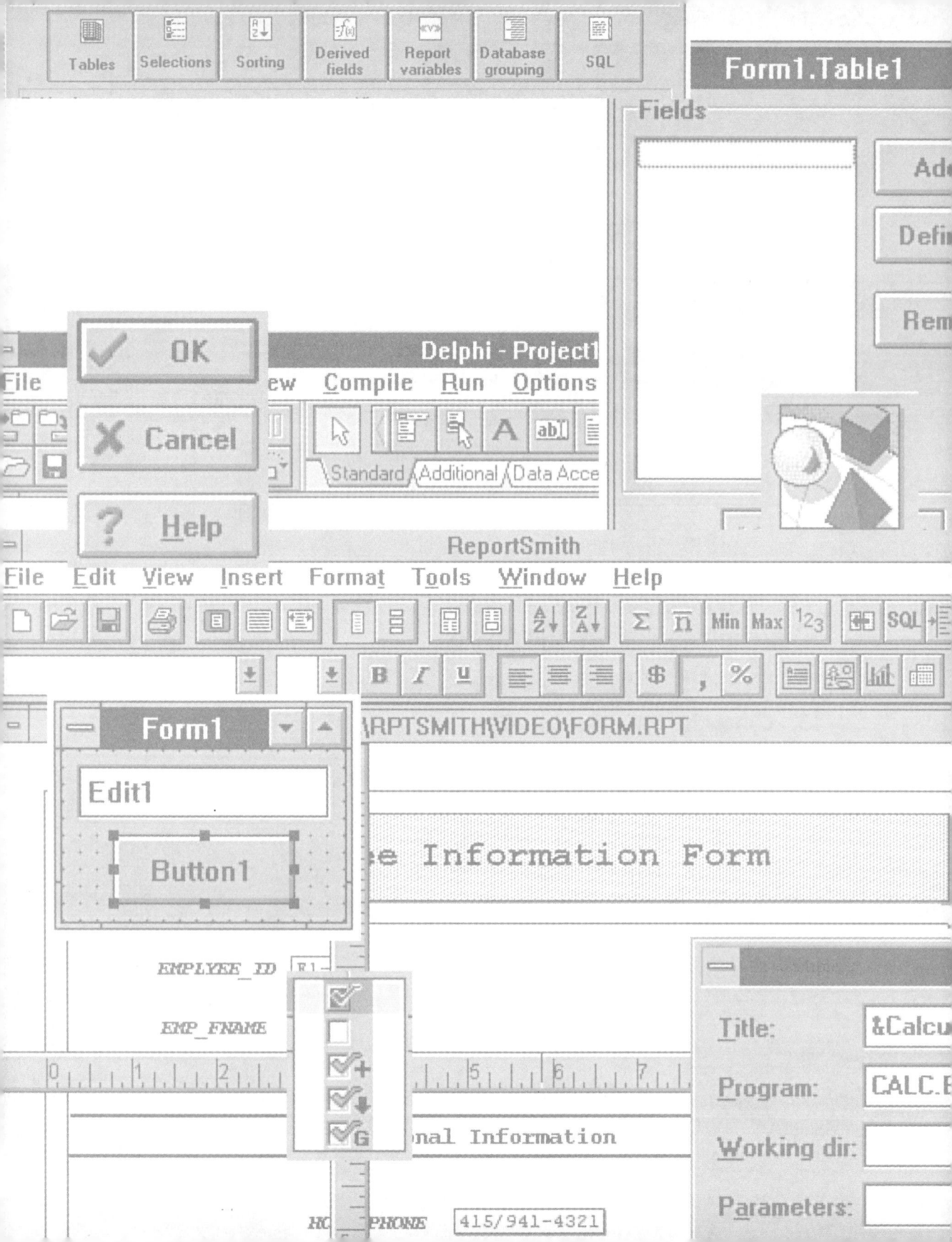

Chapter 8
Creating Forms

Developing applications in Delphi is a matter of designing forms, adding components to the forms, and placing code behind the components. Forms are the basic building blocks on which your application is built. Forms are so basic to Delphi that Delphi creates a new blank form for you whenever you start the program. Because forms are so important, this entire chapter is devoted to them.

In this chapter, you learn how to:

- Create forms
- Modify form properties with the Object Inspector
- Modify form properties with code
- Create applications that use multiple forms
- Use and create form templates

Setting Form Properties

Forms can take on a number of different properties at design time or runtime. These properties determine how the form is physically displayed and behaves. Form properties are set at design time with the Object Inspector (see fig. 8.1). During runtime, most of these same properties can be set with code.

Delphi makes it very easy to apply or hide a number of properties on a form. Although it's a good idea to experiment with these properties, be conservative when setting them for a real application. One of the benefits of Microsoft

Windows is that most Windows programs behave in a similar fashion. Once a user has been trained with one Windows program, the user can at least take a stab at using any other Windows program. Keep this in mind when designing your programs. Users are lost when they open a program that's missing a control menu on the main form. In general, the properties that Delphi uses as defaults are fine for most forms, although you need to change them a bit for dialogs. If you're not sure what style to use, find a window in another Windows program that's similar to what you're creating and mimic its behavior, look, and functionality.

Fig. 8.1
Set a form's properties with the Object Inspector.

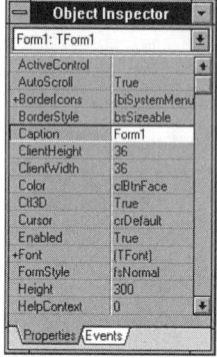

The following sections explain each of the important form properties.

> **Note**
>
> Many of these properties aren't necessary in the sense that you could easily program a form with the same functionality these properties exhibit. But it's nice to be able to set form properties from the Object Inspector without having to write a single line of code.

ActiveControl

The `ActiveControl` property determines which control on your form has the focus when the form is initially opened. For example, in a client-tracking system, you might want to set the `Active Control` property to the `TDBEdit` component associated with the client number.

AutoScroll

Like many form properties, the AutoScroll property isn't really necessary—you can easily program its behavior yourself. But, as with much of Delphi, the existence of this property makes your job easier.

You use this property with resizable windows. When AutoScroll is set to true and a user resizes the form in such a way that a component would be cut off, the form automatically displays scroll bars. Figure 8.2 shows a resizable form that has scroll bars. Scroll bars are also automatically displayed if the user moves a child window off the main window in an MDI application.

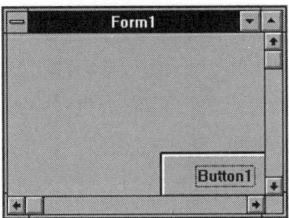

Fig. 8.2
Delphi forms can automatically provide scroll bars.

Border Icons

Most windows programs have three very familiar icons on the top of each window: the control box icon on the left and the Minimize and Maximize icons on the right. The BorderIcons property of the form lets you decide which of these icons is displayed when your form is run. For regular forms, you should leave all these icons on. Only in special situations should you turn off the control box; users expect it to be there and become confused when it's missing. The Object Inspector is an example of a window with a control box and a Minimize icon but no Maximize icon.

> **Note**
>
> The BorderIcons property is a nested property. To set the individual icons within this property, click the + that appears to the left of BorderIcons in the Object Inspector. The + turns into a -, and the individual icons are displayed as properties (see fig. 8.3).

196 Chapter 8—Creating Forms

Fig. 8.3
Some of the form's properties are nested properties.

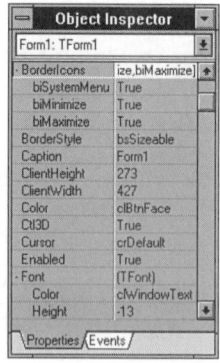

Since dialogs don't normally have Minimize and Maximize icons, the `biMinimize` and `biMaximize` settings don't have any effect on dialogs. Forms that have no border at all have no room for border icons and therefore the `BorderIcons` property is ignored.

You can add or remove border icons from a form at runtime. For example, the following code removes the control icon from a form:

```
Form1.BorderIcons:=Form1.BorderIcons-[biSystemMenu];
```

Border Styles

Each form you design has one of four possible border styles. Figure 8.4 shows a simple Delphi program with four buttons. Each button changes the border style of the form to the name of the button.

Fig. 8.4
Delphi programs can have one of four possible border styles.

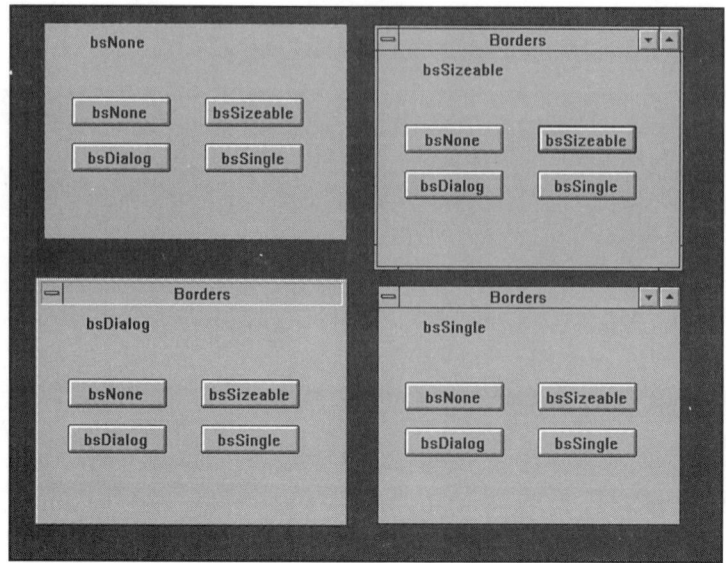

Normally you select a border style while designing a form. To do this, click anywhere on a form and select `BorderStyle` in the Object Inspector. A drop-down list is available with the four border styles.

You also can set the `BorderStyle` property at runtime. Use code similar to the following to accomplish this:

```
procedure Form1.Button1Click(Sender: TObject);
begin
Form1.BorderStyle:=bsNone;
end;
```

You should use `bsSizeable` for most of the forms you create. This gives the form a double-line border, allowing the user to resize the form at runtime. When running, the form behaves just like any other Windows program. By default, a `bsSizeable` form includes a control box, title bar, and Minimize and Maximize icons.

Use the `bsSingle` border style for forms that you want to behave like windows but that can't be resized by the user at runtime. This makes sense on forms where resizing the window makes the window unusable. For example, figure 8.5 shows a calculator program. If users could resize the window, they would succeed in hiding some of the calculator buttons.

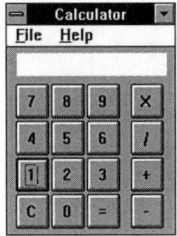

Fig. 8.5
Some forms shouldn't be resizable.

By default, a `bsSingle` form includes a control icon, title bar, and Minimize and Maximize icons. In most cases, you should remove the Maximize icon from `bsSingle` forms, but leave the Minimize and control icons (as fig. 8.5 shows). Delphi automatically matches the control menu to the border icons. In this case, the control menu has Restore, Size, and Maximize disabled, but Minimize is enabled.

`bsDialog` is the second most popular border style. Use `bsDialog` on windows that are meant to appear as dialogs. Dialogs contain a control icon and a title bar but don't have Minimize or Maximize icons.

Normally you shouldn't use the bsNone border style. This style displays a window with no control, Minimize, or Maximize icon and no title bar. You can use this border style to simulate a screen saver, to flash warning messages, or to show full-screen bit maps.

ClientHeight and *ClientWidth*

The ClientHeight and ClientWidth properties determine the size of the usable area of a form measured in pixels. A common programming task is to create a form that's longer than the physical dimensions of the screen. This often happens with preprinted medical forms that require a lot of information. In this case, the Height property of the form is set to a value that lets the form be reasonably displayed on the physical screen. ClientHeight, on the other hand, is set to a much larger value, large enough to fit the entire medical form. If the AutoScroll property is set to true, the programmer and the user can scroll the form up and down to see the hidden parts. The ClientWidth and Width properties can be used in the same way to create a very wide form.

Color

A form's Color property sets the background color of a form. The Object Inspector provides a drop-down list with quite a number of predefined colors. You can also create you own colors by double-clicking the current color property. Although you may want to choose some wild colors for games, be conservative with real-life applications.

As rule of thumb, select clWindow as the color for most of your forms. Choosing this color uses the color set up by the user through the Windows Control Panel.

To see a flashy demo of form colors, create a new blank form and drop a TTimer component on it. Set the Interval property of the timer to 100 and add the following code to the timer's OnTimer event:

```
procedure TForm1.Timer1Timer(Sender: TObject);
begin
  form1.color:=trunc($02ffffff*random);
end;
```

Run the form. The form quickly flashes a dizzying variety of random colors.

Ctl3D

The Ctl3D property can't give a form a 3-D appearance, but it changes the color of the form to gray and can give a 3-D appearance to any components on the form. Many components in the VCL have Ctl3D and ParentCtl3D properties. If a component's `ParentCtl3D` property is set to true, that component uses the `Ctl3D` property of its parent. In most situations, `ParentCtl3D` should be set to true so that you can change the appearance of every component on a form just by changing the form's `Ctl3D` property.

When `Ctl3D` is set to `True` for a component, that component is drawn with alternating gray, white, and black borders. The effect makes the component either pop out or sink in. When `Ctl3D` is set to false for a component, that component is drawn with a flat black border. The move today is toward the more interesting looking 3-D components. The components in form 2 in figure 8.6 have `Ctl3D` enabled, while the components in form 3 have `Ctl3D` disabled.

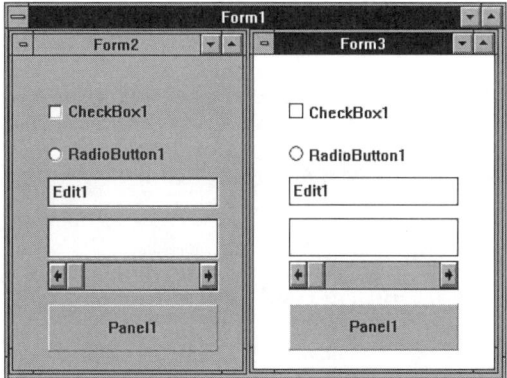

Fig. 8.6
Setting Ctl3d at the form level changes the appearance of all the controls on a form.

Cursor

A form's `Cursor` property lets you select the shape of the cursor when it's over your form. Usually this property is set to `crDefault` and changed only at runtime. The most common reason to change the cursor shape is when you're beginning a process that requires the user to wait. In this case, the cursor should be changed to an hourglass. Use code similar to the following:

    Form1.Cursor:=crHourGlass;

To list all the cursor shapes that Delphi supports along with pictures of each cursor, look up Cursor Property in Delphi's on-line help.

Enabled

A form's `Enabled` property lets you enable or disable a form. A disabled form doesn't respond to events such as mouse clicks, timer events, or keystrokes. Use this property during runtime when you don't want the user to interact with a particular window.

Font

The form's Font property has almost no effect on the form itself. After all, a form has no text on it (the title bar isn't affected by the Font property). This property is important, however. Many components have a ParentFont property. With the ParentFont property set to true, a component's font uses the properties of the parent's font. By setting the ParentFont property to true for all of a form's components, you can just change the form's Font property and effectively change the font properties of all the components.

To be consistent with other Windows applications, you should select the System font in 10-point bold. (This is usually the same as MS Sans Serif.) On machines where the user has configured the system font to a different font, choosing System lets your program use the user-configured font. The Font property is a nested property, so click its + sign in the Object Inspector to set the font's Color, Height, Name, Size, and Style.

> **Note**
>
> You can put text directly on a form without a TLabel component by using code such as the following:
>
> ```
> TForm1.Canvas.TextOut(10,10,'Hi Mom');
> ```
>
> This text is displayed in the font specified in the form's Font property.

FormStyle

Windows programs use a number of different methodologies when displaying more than one form. The most common of these is *Multi Document Interface* (MDI). In this methodology, one form is the main window, and all child windows remain within the confines of the main window. A common example of this is found in most word processors. Word processors usually have a main form used to display a menu, toolbar, and status bar; child windows are used to display each document being edited. The TextEdit demo project that comes with Delphi is an example of an MDI program (see fig. 8.7).

To create an MDI program, set the FormStyle property of your master form to fsMDIForm. Set the FormStyle property of all other forms in the project to fsMDIChild. For modal dialogs in your project, you may want to set the FormStyle property to fsNormal. This allows the dialogs to exist outside the physical dimensions of the main form, which is reasonable for modal dialogs. With MDI programs, you should include a Window menu with choices such as Arrange, Tile, and Cascade to be consistent with other MDI programs.

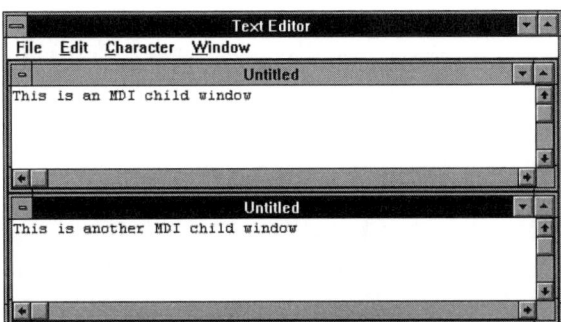

Fig. 8.7
The TextEdit demo program is an MDI program; the document windows always remain within the text editor window.

> **Caution**
>
> A form with its `FormStyle` set to `fsMDIChild` causes an exception if the main form isn't an `fsMDIForm`.

Another methodology is *Single Document Interface* (SDI). In this methodology, each form exists as a independent window. Delphi itself is a SDI application. The main form contains the menu bar, SpeedBar, and Component palette. Other windows, such as the Form, Object Inspector, and Code Editor windows, are completely independent of the physical confines of the main form and can be moved around the screen. To create an SDI style application, set the `FormStyle` property of each form in a project to `fsNormal`.

Delphi provides one other `FormStyle` known as `fsStayOnTop`. When this property is set for a form, the form stays on top of other forms in the same application that don't have this property. Even with this property, other applications can still cover your program.

> **Caution**
>
> Don't set the `FormStyle` property of your main form to `fsStayOnTop`. If you do, child windows aren't usable because they're hidden behind the main form.

HelpContext

One of the features of Microsoft Windows that makes it user-friendly is that most Windows programs contain context-sensitive help. Your applications should also contain context-sensitive help. When you create a help system, each form in your application should be a separate topic within the help system. Place the topic number for a given form in the form's `HelpContext` property. When the form receives a help event, the help system is invoked and the specified topic is displayed. See the description of the KeyPreview property later to see how the form's HelpContext can be used for all the components on a form. If your application doesn't provide help, set the HelpContext property to 0.

HorzScrollBar and VertScrollBar

The HorzScrollBar and VertScrollBar properties of a form let you manually control a form's scroll bars. Most of the time you should just set the AutoScroll property of the form to true and let the scroll bars be handled automatically. To display a scroll bar manually, you must set the scroll bar's nested Visible property to true and set the nested Range property to a number larger than the ClientHeight or ClientWidth. To do this at runtime, use code similar to the following:

```
Form1.HorzScrollBar.Visible:=true;
Form1.HorzScrollBar.Range:=Form1.ClientWidth+1;
```

Icon

The form's Icon property lets you specify the icon that's displayed when your application is minimized. See the section "Setting Up Icons" in Chapter 16, "Delivering Your Application," for more information on this property.

KeyPreview

When the KeyPreview property is set to true, certain key events (OnKeyDown, OnKeyUp, and OnKeyPress) are first sent to the form and then sent to the component with the focus. With the KeyPreview property set to false, the key events are sent only to the component with the focus.

This property saves you from having to write a lot of redundant code to process certain keystrokes. For example, if you want to provide help for a form but don't want to provide help for every component on the form, set the KeyPreview property to true. When the user presses F1, the form's help system takes over.

Another example is a form that functions as a calculator with buttons for numbers 0 through 9. While clicking the buttons works just fine, users may want to type the digits. When a digit is typed, a single line of code can call the OnClick event of the associated button. The problem is that whichever button has focus normally picks up the key event. With the form's KeyPreview property set to false, you need to place the single line of code in the key event of every single component on the form that can have focus. With KeyPreview set to true, the single line of code can simply be attached to the KeyPress event of the form.

Left and Top

The `Left` and `Top` properties of the form determine the position of the form when it's opened. The `Left` and `Top` properties are measured in pixels. You can either type numbers directly into these properties in the Object Inspector or move your form with the mouse. When you move your form during design time, Delphi automatically updates the `Left` and `Top` properties. See the *"Position"* section later in this chapter to learn how to have the form automatically centered on-screen at runtime.

Menu

When building simple applications, your forms probably contain only one `MainMenu` component. With a more complex application, your form may contain more than one menu. Use the `Menu` property of the form to specify which `MainMenu` component is displayed. When you drop the first `MainMenu` component on a form, Delphi automatically sets the form's `Menu` property to that component. When more than one menu is present, use the drop-down list of the `Menu` property to select the proper component.

Name

The `Form` component, like all Delphi components, has a `Name` property. When you first create a form, the `Name` property is set to `Form1`. Since your code may reference this name quite often, it's a good idea to change the name to something more descriptive before you write any code. Delphi automatically changes references to the form's `Name` property in code it generates, such as

```
Application.CreateForm(TBordersss, NewFormName);
```

But Delphi can't fix references in your custom code. The following line of code fails when you change the form's name late in the development process:

```
Form1.Color:=clWindow;
```

Because of this, giving the form a reasonable descriptive name is the first thing you should do to each form.

PixelsPerInch and Scaled

By setting a form's `PixelsPerInch` property to a value other than the default and setting the `Scaled` property to true, you can effectively magnify or decrease the size of your form. This is useful when designing a form at one screen resolution but using the application at another screen resolution. When you increase the `PixelsPerInch` property, your form appears smaller. When you decrease the `PixelsPerInch` property, your form appears bigger. If your form contains `TImage` components, be sure to set the `Stretch` property of these components to true so that they're scaled when the form is scaled. To change the magnification of a form at runtime, use the `ScaleBy` procedure.

> **Note**
>
> If you're going to change the `PixelsperInch` property to a larger number, consider using TrueType fonts. TrueType fonts scale better than bit-mapped fonts such as MS Sans Serif.

PopUpMenu

One aspect of many Windows programs that Borland can take credit for inventing is the right mouse click displaying a SpeedMenu or property inspector. Nowadays, when using many Windows programs, if you're unsure of the functionality of an object—be it a component or a paragraph in a word processor—you just right-click the object to get a menu specific to that object. Your programs should have this very user-friendly feature.

To create a SpeedMenu for your form, drop a `TPopUpMenu` component on the form. Set the form's `PopUpMenu` property to the name of the `TPopUpMenu` component. When the user right-clicks the form, your popup menu is displayed.

Position

While you can specify the exact position and size of your form during design, Delphi provides the `Position` property to automatically place your form at runtime. The following table shows each possible value for the `Position` property.

Value	Description
`poDesigned`	The form is displayed at runtime in the same position and size as it's displayed during design. The size of the form is determined from the form's `Height` and `Width` properties, while the position of the form is determined from the form's `Left` and `Top` properties. This is the default value of the `Position` property.
`poDefault`	The size and position of your form are automatically chosen at runtime. The form usually aligns to the right and toward the bottom of the screen.
`poDefaultPosOnly`	The position of your form is automatically chosen at runtime. The size of the form is determined by the form's `Height` and `Width` properties.

Value	Description
poDefaultSizeOnly	The size of your form is automatically determined at runtime. The position of the form is determined by the form's Left and Top properties.
poScreenCenter	The size of your form is determined from the form's Height and Width properties, but the form is centered on the user's screen. This is a very useful property value, and you should experiment with it to see whether it suits the needs of your applications.

Visible

When you create a multiform application, there are usually forms that you don't want visible until some action occurs. If your program includes an about box, for example, the about box isn't shown to the user until the user opens the Help menu and chooses About. To control whether a form is visible at runtime, you set its Visible property. By default, all forms have their Visible property set to false.

The Visible property doesn't affect the main form of your program—it's visible regardless of the setting in the Visible property. Use the Show command to turn the Visible property on during runtime, as follows:

```
About.Show;
```

WindowMenu

Most MDI applications have a menu called Window. Under this menu are choices such as Arrange All and Cascade, plus a list of all child windows. When the user selects a child window from the menu, that window gains the focus. Delphi automates the functionality of the child window list with the WindowMenu property. Simply set a form's WindowMenu property to a TMenuItem component that exists in a menu. The child window list is added to that TMenuItem component.

WindowState

The WindowState property controls whether a window is minimized, maximized, or normal. It's often convenient to start an application in the maximized state so that the user can see all the information on the main form. To do this, set the form's WindowState property to wsMaximized. You can also set the WindowState property to wsNormal or wsMinimized.

Creating Projects with Multiple Forms

Almost every Delphi application you write should have more than one form. Even the simplest application can use a second form to display an about box. You need to know a few programming concepts when working with more than one form.

Creating a Form with an About Box

Creating a two-form application—a master form and an about box—shows some important multiform programming techniques. Create a new project in Delphi and add a TButton component to the blank form. To create a second form, open the File menu and choose New Form. If the Browse Gallery dialog appears, select the Blank Form template; if it doesn't appear, a blank form is automatically created for you. The object here is to get the button on the first form to display the second form. You may add some labels and other components to the second form to make it appear like an about box.

Double-click the Button control on Form1. Delphi displays UNIT1.PAS in the Code Editor window. Add the following code to the Click method of the button:

```
procedure TForm1.Button1Click(Sender: TObject);
begin
  Form2.show;
end;
```

If you immediately try to run this application, Delphi complains that Form2 is an unknown identifier. This is because Form1 and Form2 are in separate units and the compiler is unaware of the identifiers in other units unless those units are added to the uses clause. Add Unit2 to the uses clause of UNIT1.PAS. You can find the uses clause at the beginning of UNIT1.PAS; press Ctrl+Home and you see

```
uses
  SysUtils, WinTypes, WinProcs, Messages, Classes, Graphics,
  Controls, Forms, Dialogs, StdCtrls, Unit2;
```

Now you can run the program; the button should display Form2 (see fig. 8.8).

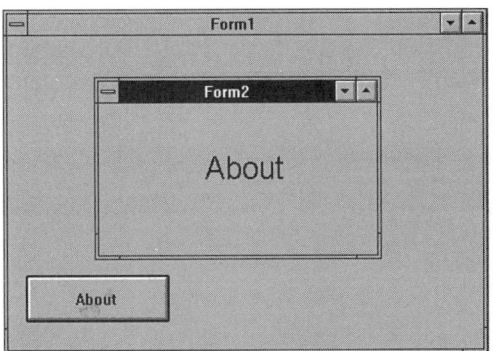

Fig. 8.8
It's easy to have one form open another form.

To make the second form into a more realistic about box, the second form must become a modal dialog. In design mode, set the second form's BorderStyle property to bsDialog. Add a button to the second form and set the button's ModalResult property to mrOK. Also give the button a caption of OK. The application is about ready to go, but the second form must still be made modal. This isn't done through a property—instead, it's done with the ShowModal command. Change the code in the first form's button to read as follows:

    Form2.ShowModal;

Now when you click the button on the first form, the second form is displayed in a modal fashion. The users can't interact with the first form until the second form is closed with the control icon or the OK button.

Tip
When designing forms, the form you're trying to work with is often completely covered by other forms. Press Shift+F12 to bring up the View Form dialog, which lets you pick the form by name.

Using Autocreate Forms

In the preceding section, the second form is automatically created when the application is started. The form remains hidden, so the user can't see it until the Show command is used. While the form is hidden, it's still using precious Windows resources. In larger applications, you may not want all the forms created automatically when the application is loaded.

To specify which forms are automatically created, open the Options menu and choose Project. Delphi displays the Project Options dialog (see fig. 8.9). Click the Forms tab if it's not already the current tab.

The Project Options dialog shown in figure 8.9 is for the TextEdit demo project that ships with Delphi. In the Main Form text box, the name of the main form is entered. The main form is the form that's automatically opened and given the focus when the application is started. For MDI applications, the main form must be the form with the `FormStyle` property set to `fsMDIForm`.

Fig. 8.9
You can decide which forms are automatically created.

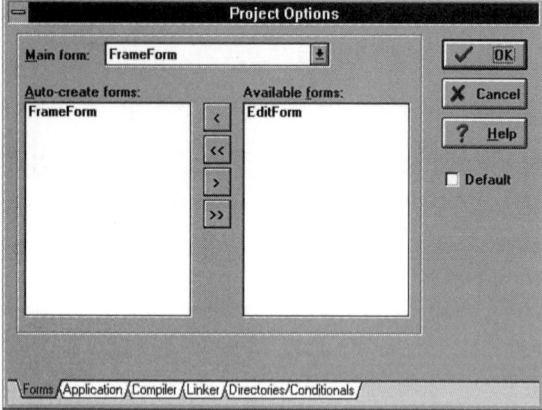

In the Auto-Create Forms list box, Delphi lists the forms that are automatically created at startup. By default, all the forms in a project are in this column. If you don't want a form to be automatically created, use the arrow buttons to move forms to the Available Forms list box.

When a form isn't automatically created, you can't use just the `Show` method to display the form. The following code is used in the TextEdit demo project to display the second form:

```
var
  EditForm: TEditForm;
begin
  EditForm := TEditForm.Create(Self);
  EditForm.Open(OpenFileDialog.Filename);
  EditForm.Visible := True;
end;
```

Note that when you use the `Create` method to create a form, you must set the form's `Visible` property to true after the form is open.

Using the Project Manager

As the number of forms in your project increases, it can become a headache to track the forms and their associated units. Fortunately, Delphi provides the Project Manager to deal with these headaches.

To open the Project Manager, open the View menu and choose Project Manager. The Project Manager window appears (see fig. 8.10).

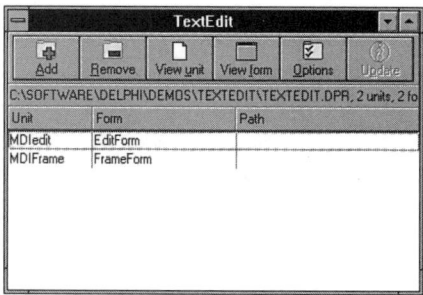

Fig. 8.10
Delphi's Project Manager lets you track the forms in a project.

The main section of the Project Manager lists the units and their associated forms and paths. Not every unit has to have an associated form. Paths aren't displayed for units in the same directory as the project. You can double-click any of the listed units or forms, and Delphi brings up the editor for that object. Use the Project Manager as a quick directory or map of your project.

The Project Manager speedbar has buttons for adding and removing objects and viewing objects. The Options speedbar button opens the Project Options dialog (described earlier). If you edit the project source code while the Project Manager is open, click the Update speedbar button to refresh the object list.

Using Form Templates

As you saw in the earlier example, it's a simple process to make an about box. But it still takes some work. The design philosophy behind Delphi is reusable components, so it only makes sense that forms themselves can be reusable components. Delphi ships with a number of useful templates already created for you, such as an about box.

Configuring Delphi to Use Form Templates

Before you can use a form template, you need to configure Delphi to let you do so. Open the Options menu and choose Environment. Delphi displays the Environment Options dialog (see fig. 8.11). Click the Preferences tab if it's not already the current tab.

Fig. 8.11
Be sure to turn on the Gallery options.

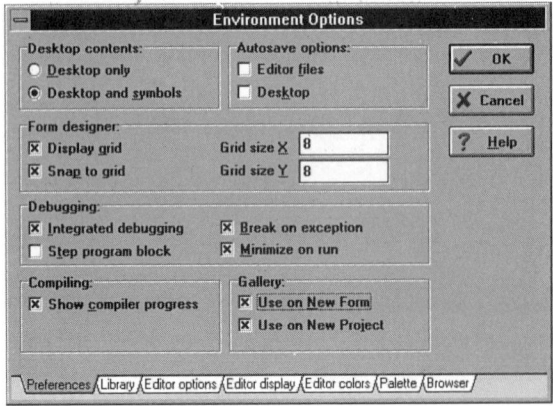

Delphi keeps form templates in what is known as a *gallery*. The template options are set in the Gallery section of the Preferences tab. Mark the Use on New Form check box if you want the gallery displayed when you add a new form to an existing project. Even if you don't plan on using the gallery, go ahead and mark this option because the gallery includes a blank form template.

Using Default Templates

When you create a new project, Delphi creates a new blank form for you (unless you use the project gallery). If you want to use a form template, you should go ahead and delete the blank form (open the File menu and choose Remove File). Delphi displays the Remove From Project dialog with the blank form highlighted (see fig. 8.12).

Fig. 8.12
Use the Remove From Project dialog to remove the blank form that Delphi starts you with.

Click OK, and Delphi removes the blank form from the project. Now, open the File menu and choose New Form. Delphi displays the Browse Gallery dialog (see fig. 8.13).

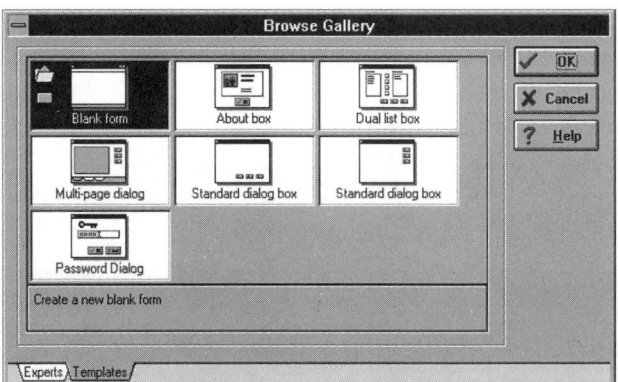

Fig. 8.13
Creating forms is a breeze with form templates.

Select the appropriate template from the gallery and click OK. A new form that's already set up with components and functionality is added to your project. If you choose the About Box template, a premade about box is added to your project. It's up to you to supply your application title and company name to the about box.

Saving Your Own Templates

Of course, the templates that ship with Delphi are useful, but you can expand the gallery's functionality by creating your own templates. To do this, create a form, right-click the form to display its SpeedMenu, and choose Save As Template. Delphi displays the Save Form Template dialog (see fig. 8.14).

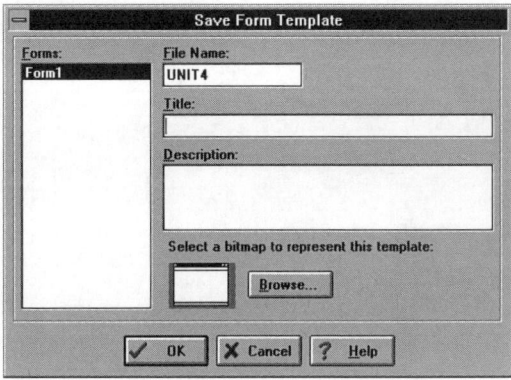

Fig. 8.14
Delphi lets you create you own form templates.

In the Forms list box, select the form you want to create a template from. In the File Name text box, enter a file name for the form and unit. The template is stored in the \DELPHI\GALLERY directory, so the file name you provide can't already exist in that directory. In the Title text box, enter the text that

Tip

To create an icon for your template, press Alt+Print Screen while browsing the gallery to copy the screen image to the Clipboard. In Microsoft Paintbrush, open the Edit menu and choose Paste. Crop a single icon, copy it to the Clipboard, create a new file, and copy from the Clipboard. Modify the bit map and save it.

you want to appear under the icon in the gallery. In the Description section, enter a longer description of you template. The description is displayed in the status panel while browsing the gallery. To specify an icon to represent your template, click the Browse button and select a .BMP file. When you've completed the Save Form Template dialog, click OK. Delphi creates a .DFM and a .PAS file in the GALLERY subdirectory and adds the template to the Browse Gallery dialog.

> **Note**
>
> The form and unit files of each object in the gallery are stored in \DELPHI\GALLERY directory by default. To change this directory, you must edit the DELPHI.INI file located in your Windows directory. Edit the `BaseDir` variable in the Gallery section.

Setting Gallery Options

Once you've built a number of your own form templates, you may want to remove from the gallery the templates that shipped with Delphi. Delphi provides a dialog for managing your templates. Open the Options menu and choose Gallery. The Gallery Options dialog appears (see fig. 8.15). If the Form Templates tab isn't the current tab, click it.

Fig. 8.15
Use the Gallery Options dialog to manage your templates.

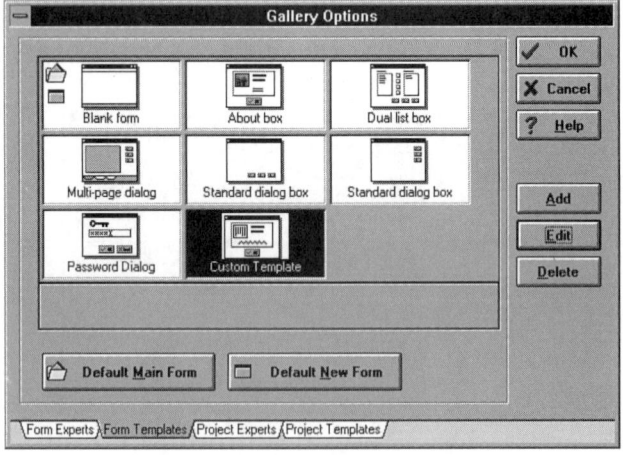

Use this dialog to delete any templates that you don't want to appear in the gallery. Don't worry—when you delete a template, it's not physically removed from the hard disk; it's just not displayed in the gallery. You can always add a template back into the gallery at a later date.

To change the title and description of a template, click the Edit button. The Edit Template Info dialog appears (see fig. 8.16). This dialog has the same fields that were used when the template was created, so you can modify the title, description, and bit map.

Fig. 8.16
Delphi lets you edit the title and description of existing templates.

Normally when you create a new project, Delphi starts you off with a new blank form, but it doesn't have to. In fact, you can choose any form template to be the form automatically added to a new blank project. Select the form template you want, and click the Default Main Form button in the Gallery Options dialog. Delphi puts a modified open file icon next to the selected form template. The next time you start a new project, the selected form is automatically added to your project.

Likewise, when you add a form to a project, it doesn't have to be a blank form. Select the form template you use most often and click the Default New Form button. Delphi puts the form icon next to the selected form template. The next time you add a new form to a project, your selected template is the default.

Using Form Experts

While form templates are very useful, they're really just saved forms presented with a user-friendly interface. Form experts, on the other hand, contain intelligence that creates complicated forms on the fly from information you provide. To use a form expert, make sure that you have the Gallery option turned on as described earlier in the section "Configuring Delphi to Use Form Templates." Add a new form to your project by opening the File menu and choosing New Form. The Browse Gallery dialog appears. Click the Experts tab. Delphi displays the available experts (see fig. 8.17). Double-click the expert you're interested in, and the first dialog of the expert appears (see fig. 8.18).

Fig. 8.17
Use experts to help you create complex forms.

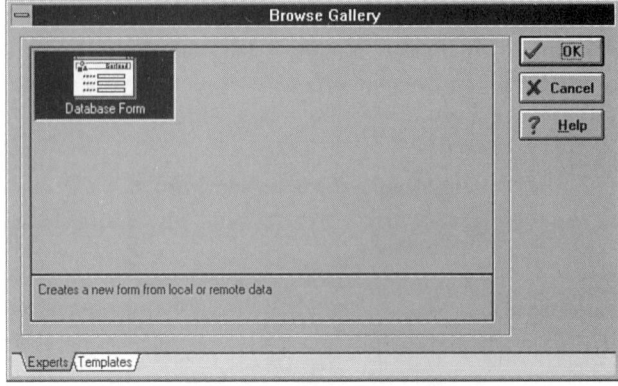

Fig. 8.18
Experts lead you through form design with questions.

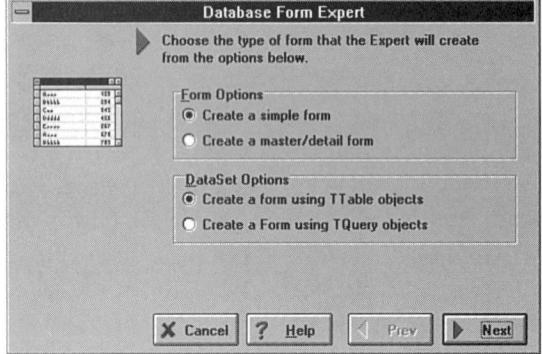

Each expert is a series of dialogs that ask you questions about the form being designed. For a one-to-many form, for example, the expert asks for the name of the master and detail tables. As you answer each question, click the Next button to go to the next screen. If you need to review you answers, click the Prev button to back up a screen.

Experts are modal, so you must finish with an expert or cancel before getting back to Delphi. When you've completed all the forms of the expert, click the Create button. Delphi creates the complex form for you. You're then free to use Delphi to modify the form the expert created.

From Here...

You can find more information about forms in the following chapters:

- Chapter 4, "Using Visual Components," describes the visual components you can place on forms.

- Chapter 5, "Using Non-Visual Components," shows how to use non-visual components such as common dialogs in your forms.

- Chapter 10, "Creating Database Applications," contains more information on MDI and SDI applications.

- Chapter 16, "Delivering Your Application," describes how to assign icons to your form.

Chapter 9
Creating Applications

In Chapter 8, "Creating Forms," you learned about the various form and window types that are available in Delphi and how they're used to build single-form applications. While a form alone can certainly be considered an application, applications typically consist of more than one form.

When developing a multiform Windows application, you can choose from primarily two routes for your overall application interface:

- Multiple Document Interface (MDI)
- Single Document Interface (SDI)

Each interface style provides unique features on how the application is presented to the user. MDI applications have been thought of as "proper" Windows style, but recently, SDI applications are becoming more popular. Both interface styles are discussed in detail in this chapter.

In this chapter, you will:

- Learn the basics of setting up an MDI application
- Design code to control MDI applications
- Learn about MDI-related properties and methods
- Develop an example MDI application
- Gain an understanding of how SDI applications are built and handled
- Cover techniques useful for managing SDI applications

MDI Applications

Delphi allows you to create Windows applications that support the Multiple Document Interface (MDI) standard. Examples of MDI applications are the Windows Program Manager, File Manager, Microsoft Word, and most Windows text editors that support loading multiple files at once. This section's focus is on creating MDI-compliant applications.

MDI-compliant applications have an MDI *parent window* with a client area that displays an MDI *child window* (or *children*). MDI child windows are confined to the client area, meaning that child windows can't extend outside the parent window's border. MDI child windows can be minimized, maximized, or sized to fit anywhere within the client area. Typical MDI capabilities include tiling and cascading MDI child windows, as well as arranging the icons of minimized child windows. The MDI parent window contains the application's master menu, used to manipulate the MDI child windows, which don't have menus.

Setting Up MDI Parent and Child Forms

MDI applications consist of two or more forms. A single-form MDI application is contradictory and should be developed as a SDI application. All MDI applications must have a parent window with at least a single MDI child window. To implement this relationship in Delphi, you need to manage at least two individual form files in your project.

The easiest way to create an MDI application is to use Delphi's own MDI Application project template (described in detail in the "Application Templates" section later in this chapter). The sections immediately following will show you how to build an MDI application from the ground up and do not use the MDI Application project template.

Parent and MDI Child Form Project Units

Chapter 2, "Understanding the Environment," discusses how applications or projects are created and managed. A project is simply a collection of related forms and units that, when working together, produce an application.

The following steps show you how to quickly set up an MDI application from the ground up that contains MDI parent and child windows. Detailed coverage of individual elements, such as a form's FormStyle property, is provided in the sections following these steps.

1. Start with a new project by opening the File menu and choosing New Project.

MDI Applications   **219**

If you have the Gallery option on for new projects, the Browse Gallery dialog appears (see fig. 9.1).

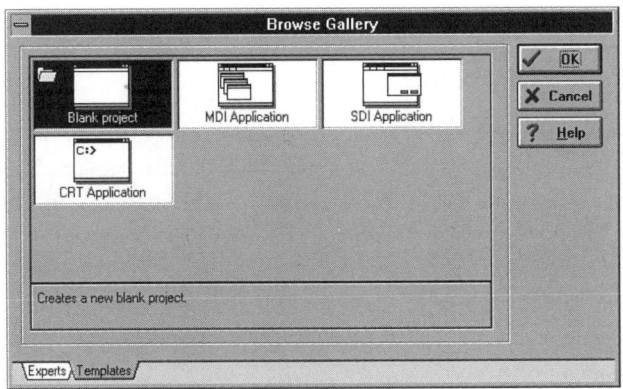

Fig. 9.1
The Browse Gallery dialog for projects appears when the Gallery option in the Environment Options dialog is active for projects.

2. In the Browse Gallery dialog, select the Blank Project template and click OK.

3. Make the default form an MDI parent form by setting its FormStyle property to fsMDIForm.

4. Give the MDI parent form a name of frmMDIParent.

5. Add another form that will be used for MDI children by opening the File menu and choosing New Form. This causes a new form and unit to be added to your project.

    If you have the Gallery option on for new forms, you're prompted with a different Browse Gallery dialog (see fig. 9.2).

Tip
Giving your form objects, unit files, and project files meaningful names makes them easier to work with and to document.

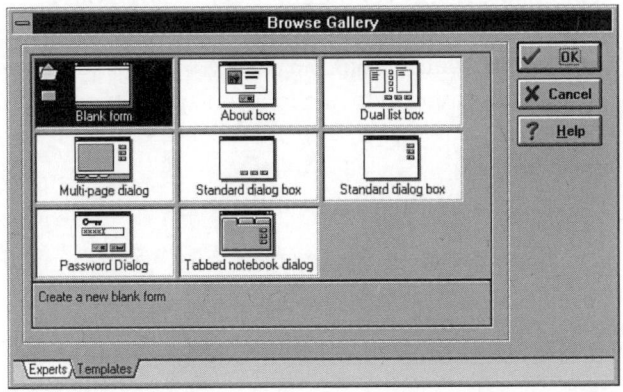

Fig. 9.2
The Browse Gallery dialog for forms appears when the Environment Options dialog's Gallery option is active for forms.

6. In the Browse Gallery dialog, select the Blank Form template and click OK.

7. In the Object Inspector, give your form a name and caption. The name is used as the basis for the form's class name, and the caption is the text that's placed in the title bar.

8. If you're creating a new MDI child, set the FormStyle property to fsMDIChild. If you're creating a new MDI parent, set FormStyle to fsMDIParent. (See the following section, "MDI Parent and Child Window Types," for more details on MDI window types and the FormStyle property.)

Once this is done, a new unit appears in the Project Manager. Bring the Project Manager on-screen by opening the View menu and choosing Project Manager. Figure 9.3 shows the Project Manager window with two form types defined. Note the term *form types*. In MDI terms, a form's type indicates whether it's an MDI parent or child, fsMDIParent or fsMDIChild.

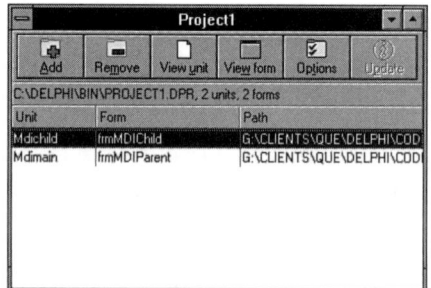

Fig. 9.3
A project may contain many forms, but only two types are needed for an MDI application.

At runtime, multiple instances of these new form classes can be created and are limited only by system resources. The term *classes* is used here, since when adding a new form to a project, you are essentially subclassing the basic form class, TForm. This is shown by the following piece of code from a unit's type declaration:

```
type
     TfrmChild = class(TForm)
```

See Chapter 3, "Understanding The Language," for more information on object classes.

MDI Parent and Child Window Types

The forms that were presented in Chapter 8, "Creating Forms," were limited to normal and dialog form types. When producing MDI applications, you can use two additional types to identify the MDI parent and child windows.

> **Note**
>
> The `FormStyle` property specifies the style of a form. See the later section "Setting a Form's Type" to learn how to change a form's type.

Referencing MDI Child Windows

Quite a few techniques and concepts can be used in MDI application development. Many properties and methods allow you to control MDI child windows within your application. The following example of an imaginary company illustrates several techniques for controlling MDI child windows.

Suppose that you have a user request from Bob, the head of the user department at a company called XYZ. Bob has just requested that a function be added to XYZ's Bonus Calculation system to allow creation of additional bonus calculation windows within the application. Bob explains that a New option on the Window menu is necessary so that he can calculate his bonus multiple times, receiving a bonus amount for each additional window he creates. After failing to persuade Bob that this isn't the most ethical way to increase one's compensation, you reluctantly agree to implement Bob's new feature.

You determine that you'll simply add a new menu choice to the system that allows the creation of a new MDI child window by creating another instance (instantiating) of the child window form.

To complete the task, use the following procedure, which is linked to your MDI parent window's Window, New menu choice:

```
procedure TfrmMDIParent.menuNewClick(Sender: TObject);
var
    frmChildTemp: TfrmMDIChild;

begin
    { Create a new instance of the MDI child window form }
    frmChildTemp := TfrmMDIChild.Create;
end;
```

> **Note**
>
> You need to enter only the body of these procedures, since Delphi automatically writes the procedure's structure when linking code to an object using the Object Inspector. See Chapter 5, "Using Non-Visual Components," for more information on creating and linking code to menus.

In this procedure, the `var` statement declares a form object named `frmChildTemp`, which is of the `TfrmMDIChild` class. This is also the same syntax by which new variables are defined. The object type `TfrmMDIChild` is available from the MDI child unit that you added to the project in step 5 in the preceding section. Attached to the child unit is a form named `frmMDIChild`, which contains the definition for the `TfrmMDIChild` class.

This example highlights how child windows (which are essentially objects) are created by using a handle of the same object type as that of the actual window's class. Additional properties and methods can be used to control MDI applications. These properties are discussed in the following sections along with this concept of creating new MDI child windows.

Using Useful Properties for MDI Window Management

The highest window class, `TForm`, includes a number of properties that support MDI parent and child windows. You can use these properties to affect the behavior of all child forms in your MDI application. Since forms are used as the basis of the user interface, changing overall form-handling properties often has a major effect on interface functionality.

Using Read- and Runtime-Only Properties

A number of MDI parent window properties that are read- and runtime-only aren't available in the Object Inspector at design time because these properties aren't applicable during actual form design. The read- and runtime-only properties are:

- `MDIChildCount`   An integer value containing the number of open MDI child windows.

- `ActiveMDIChild`   A `TForm` value that can be used as a handle to manipulate the active MDI child window.

- `MDIChildren`   An integer-indexed array of `TForm` containing MDI child window handles in the order the child windows were created.

Setting a Form's Type

As discussed earlier, two types of forms are required in MDI applications—one for the parent form and one for the child form. The forms from Chapter 8, "Creating Forms," use FormStyle property values of fsNormal or fsDialog only.

FormStyle values of fsMDIForm and fsMDIChild play the key role in the relationship of parent and child MDI windows. To specify an MDI parent window, set the FormStyle property to fsMDIForm. Child MDI windows, on the other hand, must have their FormStyle property set to fsMDIChild.

All MDI applications consist of a parent form having a FormStyle property value of fsMDIForm, which identifies the parent MDI form. The parent MDI form must also be referenced in the application's CreateForm method, which Delphi handles automatically. The FormStyle property is set at design time in the majority of the cases but can also be set at runtime.

> **Note**
>
> Changing a child window's FormStyle property from fsMDIChild to fsNormal allows that window to be brought outside the parent MDI window, as it's no longer a child window. This can be done at design time or runtime.

Controlling Form Visibility

The Visible property determines whether a visual object is to be shown (or hidden) at runtime. Typically, MDI parent forms are not hidden. It's also somewhat odd to consider hiding child forms, and most likely the reason is that this is simply not allowed in a Delphi MDI application.

Incorporating MDI Window Methods

This section looks at the additional methods of class TForm that work with MDI windows. Along with the Create method used in the previous example, a number of additional methods are useful when putting together MDI applications.

> **Note**
>
> MDI methods are recognized only by MDI parent windows or those with a FormStyle property value of fsMDIForm.

Creating MDI Child Windows

The following example creates and shows an MDI child window:

```
procedure TfrmMDIParent.menuNewClick(Sender: TObject);
var
    frmChildTemp: TfrmMDIChild;

begin
    frmChildTemp := TfrmMDIChild.Create(Self);
    frmChildTemp.Caption := IntToStr(MDIChildCount);
end;
```

Figure 9.4 shows an MDI parent form after the preceding code has been issued three times by opening the Window menu and choosing New three times.

Fig. 9.4
New MDI child forms are created at the upper left of the client area by default.

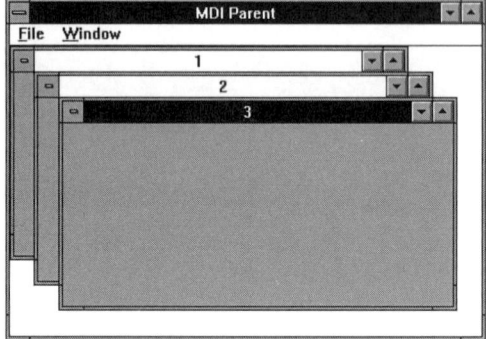

Arranging Icons

The ArrangeIcons method organizes the icons of minimized MDI child windows so that they're evenly spaced along the bottom of the parent MDI window. The ArrangeIcons method must be sent only to MDI parent windows (those having a FormStyle property value of fsMDIForm).

The ArrangeIcons method is typically linked to your MDI application's Arrange Icons command on the Window menu (if you have one). Following is an example showing the ArrangeIcons method:

```
procedure TfrmMDIParent.menuArrangeIconsClick(Sender: TObject);
begin
    TfrmMDIParent.ArrangeIcons;
end;
```

Alternatively, you can abbreviate the ArrangeIcons syntax by using a more object-oriented syntax:

```
procedure TfrmMDIParent.menuArrangeIconsClick(Sender: TObject);
begin
    ArrangeIcons;
end;
```

Abbreviations of this type apply to all MDI methods as well as for all properties belonging to the procedure class.

Add this code to your form and then create and minimize some MDI child windows. Shuffle their arrangement on the MDI parent window. Choosing the Window menu's Arrange Icons command causes the MDI child window icons to be arranged as shown in figure 9.5.

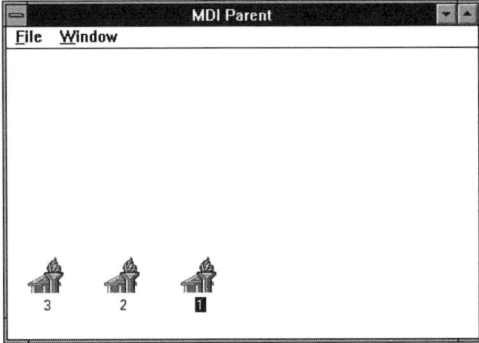

Fig. 9.5
Icons are lined up neatly along the bottom of the MDI client area after the ArrangeIcons method is issued.

You may wonder why you have to bother issuing an ArrangeIcons method, since virtually all MDI applications provide support for arranging icons and tiling and cascading their child windows. There is indeed an easier way, which involves using what Delphi calls an *application template*. Application templates are simply prebuilt prototypes that you can reuse over and over. Application templates are covered later in the "Application Templates" section.

Cascading MDI Windows

The Cascade method arranges the child windows so that they overlap each other. A cascaded set of windows shows title bars of as many windows that fit on-screen, allowing the user to easily choose one of the available MDI child windows.

The following is an example of how the Cascade method is used:

```
procedure TfrmMDIParent.menuCascadeClick(Sender: TObject);
begin
     Cascade;
end;
```

Figure 9.4 shows how an MDI parent form with child windows might look after it receives a Cascade method.

> **Note**
>
> When MDI child windows are first created (using the Window menu's New command), they're placed in a cascaded arrangement within the parent.

Closing the Current Child Window

The Close method closes an MDI child or parent window. The Close method isn't actually an MDI method but can be used to provide additional control of your child MDI windows. The following is an example on how the Close method is used to close the current MDI child window through the File menu's Close command:

```
procedure TfrmMDIParent.menuFileCloseClick(Sender: TObject);
begin
     ActiveMDIChild.Close;
end;
```

Because the Close method isn't an MDI method, in the previous example substituting the line

```
ActiveMDIChild.Close;
```

with only

```
Close;
```

closes the MDI parent window—not what the user expects when hooked up with the File menu's Close command. This happens since the single Close statement is issued within the context of TfrmMDIParent, or the parent MDI form. This situation is more applicable to closing the entire application, or MDI parent window.

Selecting the Next MDI Child

The Next method makes the next MDI child window in the MDI parent window sequence the active MDI child form. The Next method treats the list of MDI child windows as a circular list. For example, if you send the Next method to the MDI parent window and the currently selected MDI child window is the last MDI child window out of at least two, the Next method causes the first MDI child window in the list to be made active.

The following example illustrates use of the Next method:

```
procedure TfrmMDIParent.menuNextClick(Sender: TObject);
begin
    Next;
end;
```

Selecting the Previous MDI Child

The Previous method behaves similarly to the Next method but selects child windows in the opposite direction. Like the Next method, the Previous method also treats the list of MDI child windows as a circular list. If the Previous method is issued when the first MDI child is active, the last MDI child becomes active.

Tiling MDI Children

The Tile method sizes the MDI child windows so that they don't overlap each other. The client area of the MDI parent window is divided into different regions, each with an MDI child window contained. The following is an example using the Tile method:

```
procedure TfrmMDIParent.TileMenuClick(Sender: TObject);
begin
     Tile;
end;
```

Issuing the Tile method on the parent form shown in figure 9.4 results in figure 9.6.

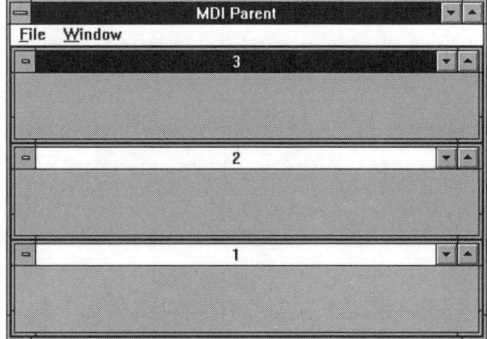

Fig. 9.6
Tiling shows as much of each child window as possible within the parent's client area.

By default, windows are tiled horizontally. To control whether an MDI parent's child forms are tiled vertically or horizontally, the parent's TileMode property is set to either tbVertical or tbHorizontal. The following is the previous code example tiling MDI child windows vertically:

```
procedure TfrmMDIParent.TileMenuClick(Sender: TObject);
begin
     TileMode := tbVertical;
     Tile;
end;
```

SDI Applications

Tip
You can pack a lot of "application" into a single-window SDI form by using the TabSet and TabbedNotebook components. The BDE Configuration Utility is a good example of how a tabbed technique is used.

The Single Document Interface (SDI) name implies that SDI applications consist of only a single window. While this is certainly true for many SDI applications, such as the Windows PIF Editor and the BDE Configuration Utility, SDI applications most often consist of multiple windows. In fact, unless an SDI application has multiple windows, it's usually regarded as a simple program and not a full-blown SDI application.

Multiwindow SDI applications can behave very much like MDI applications but require more programming depending on the complexity with which the application must manage its SDI windows. Examples of complex SDI applications are Borland's own Delphi, as well as Microsoft's Visual Basic. Each product allows multiple windows that aren't confined to the client area of a parent MDI window. SDI applications typically have a window designated as the *master window*, sometimes consisting of only a menu bar.

When an SDI master window is closed, minimized, or maximized, the master window first performs the necessary operations on its related windows or family members. Before Delphi's master SDI window is minimized, for example, Delphi minimizes its family of windows first. You can think of this as a parent putting children to bed. Before the parent can go to bed, all the children must be attended to and put to bed.

Multiwindow SDI applications pose some concern when "MDI-like" behavior is desired of them. An example is support for the master window's menu throughout the application, even when focus is on other forms. For example, a master window might contain a File menu that you want to make available to your family of SDI windows. In an MDI application, the parent menu is always available; this doesn't require any effort to program because it's simply a matter of defining the parent's menu. In an SDI application, the default menu is simply the current SDI window's menu. If there isn't a menu on the current SDI window (as with the Object Inspector), by default, pressing Alt+F to request the File menu does not have any effect. Additional code must be written to have the master SDI window process the requested menu choice.

Controlling SDI Family Windows

SDI window families are controlled much like their MDI counterparts. Just like MDI, the key is getting a handle on the SDI window. This doesn't mean that controlling SDI windows is as easy as with MDI—it's not. With SDI, no specific properties (such as ActiveMDIChild) are available to help you with window management. To get around this, you must perform your own window management.

If you want to provide SDI functionality in the same way that a program such as Delphi presents itself to the user, you must identify windows as being either the master or a family member. Family member windows behave as normal windows, allowing the user to open, minimize, maximize, and close them at will. However, when a user performs any of these operations on the master window, you may want to dispatch control requests to your family members as well—for example, closing the member windows before closing the actual master window. The result is an interface similar to an MDI application but with more flexibility. The cost is additional programming.

The key to controlling SDI windows is to maintain the form-handle variables for the SDI windows that must be controlled. Assume that you have the following global definition in your main `var` statement:

```
var
    frmNormal: TForm;
```

With this variable, you can open and control an individual SDI window. Take a look at what the procedure for Delphi's own View, Object Inspector menu command might look like. Instead of `frmNormal`, assume that `frmOI` is the name of the global form variable.

```
procedure TfrmDelphi.menuObjInspectorOpenClick(Sender: TObject);
begin
     frmOI := TfrmOI.Create(Self);
     frmOI.Show;
end;
```

You may have noticed that Delphi hides the Object Inspector just before it runs your programs. To do this, all program logic must do is simply reference the global variable associated with the handle of the Object Inspector window:

```
frmOI.Hide;
```

Also, all the objects contained in `frmOI`, the Object Inspector form, can be controlled by using the `frmOI` variable.

Manipulating Master SDI Window Objects

When you work with Delphi, you expect Delphi's main menu bar to be available by the simple menu accelerator keys that have been defined for each menu. When in the Form Designer, you can press Alt+F to access the File menu. What's the big deal—shouldn't this always happen? Actually, no. The Form Designer itself is a separate window of `FormStyle fsNormal`. As you can see, it doesn't have a menu bar, so unless it actually processes an Alt+F key combination, you shouldn't expect Alt+F to do anything. Fortunately,

Delphi's family member windows are aware that there is a master window that must be reported to. If member windows receive a key sequence they don't understand, the key is passed to the master window for processing.

Manipulation of master SDI window objects by SDI family members is achieved by performing the following:

- A master SDI window typically creates and handles SDI family member windows at runtime. To do this, you must include a reference to the member window's unit in the master window's interface-uses area. This reference must be in place for both MDI and SDI window control of child and member windows, respectively. An example interface uses section, which is at the header of a unit file, might look like the following:

```
interface

uses
  SysUtils, WinTypes, WinProcs, Messages, Classes, Graphics,
  Controls, Forms, Dialogs, Menus, MDIChild, StdCtrls,
  ExtCtrls;
```

- A member SDI window that requires access to a master form's objects, such as the menu, must include a reference to the master window's unit file. This reference, in the implementation uses section, simply references the unit file name of the SDI family member window's form.

- To globalize control of key events at the form level first, set the member form's KeyPreview property to true. This allows the current form to have first access to a key event before the object itself (the object that initially received the key event). This saves coding a key-event handler for every object on your form that can receive focus. Once this is done, routing Alt+F to access the master form's File menu can be done in a single block of code in one of the form's OnKey event handlers.

Because you have the following line defined in the SDI member window's unit, you can access the frmMDIParent form object directly:

```
implementation

uses
     MDIMain;
```

Proper handling of SDI family member windows by the master window is a matter of proper programming at the master-form level. When a menu is requested via the mouse, the window it's associated with becomes current. Once a menu choice has been selected, your application logic gains control and can manipulate the SDI member windows as needed, such as hiding SDI members during certain processing.

If one of your SDI member forms is a floating speedbar, you might want to link buttons of the SDI member window to objects such as menu items in your SDI master form. Your SDI member form, frmSDI, has a button named btnTile. When frmSDI's btnTile button is clicked, you want the master SDI window's menuTile TMenuItem object to receive a click message (or method).

```
procedure TfrmSDI.btnTileClick(Sender: TObject);
begin
    frmMDIParent.menuTile.Click;
end;
```

Why not simply call the SDI master form's code that's linked to the OnClick event of the Tile menu choice? You can, and the following code fragment produces the same results:

```
procedure TfrmSDI.btnTileClick(Sender: TObject);
begin
    frmMDIParent.menuTileClick(Self);
end;
```

A discussion over which one is better borders on the topic of "programming religion," but the first case is more object-oriented. The actual procedure name that handles the OnClick event may not be named as you see it here. If this is the case, you can make sure that simply sending a Click method out to the object gets the job done. If you want to execute the procedure directly, you have to verify the name because the event handler for the object in question could be named anything at all.

Application Templates

A basic skeleton structure of MDI and SDI applications is available by creating a new application using one of the included Delphi application templates. Application templates come complete with a set of components—visual and non-visual—configured to provide you with a starting point for developing your application. After an application is created using an MDI or SDI template, what remains is much of the application code as opposed to creating the framework over again.

Telling Delphi to Use Application Templates

To be presented with an application template option when creating a new project, you must first do the following:

1. Save and close the current project.

2. Open the Options menu and choose Environment to display the Environment Options dialog (see fig. 9.7).

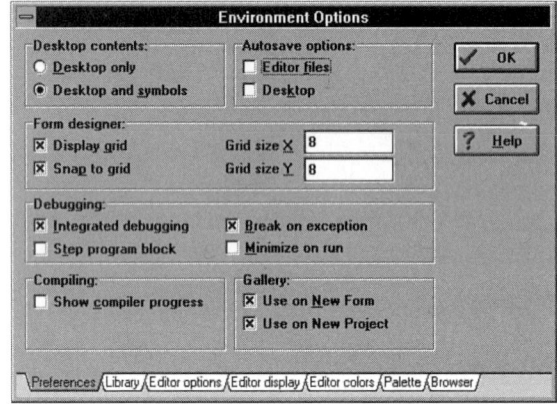

Fig. 9.7
You must use the Environment Options dialog to tell Delphi to present the application gallery.

3. Select the Preferences page.

4. In the Gallery section, select the Use on New Form check box.

> **Note**
> Delphi refers to a collection of application templates as a *gallery*.

Using Application Templates

Performing the steps to configure the gallery in the previous section and choosing the File menu's New command brings up the Browse Gallery dialog (see fig. 9.8).

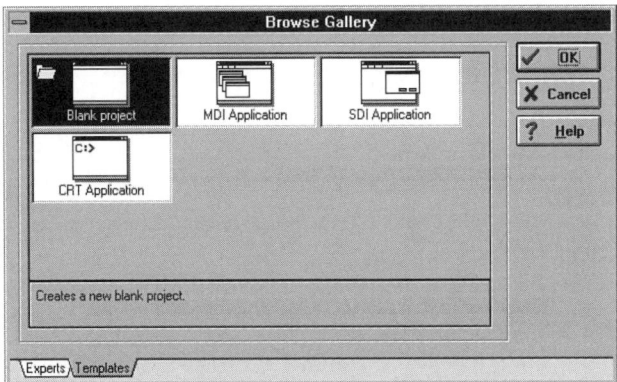

Fig. 9.8
This dialog is presented for new projects when the Gallery setting Use on New Project is checked in the Environment Options dialog.

Notice the four templates in the gallery:

- *Blank Project.* Selecting this option is the same as not using an application template at all.

- *MDI Application.* Selecting this option creates two forms and three units. A number of objects are placed on your main form to handle common MDI functions, such as the Window menu.

- *SDI Application.* Selecting this option creates a single form and unit, also with a number of objects placed on the form. The default objects for an SDI application template are a menu, a `SaveDialog` object, and an `OpenDialog` object.

- *CRT Application.* This template is used to provide a simple means by which you can output text to your program window. This is in the style of original and older Pascal programming techniques for DOS and Windows.

> **Note**
>
> You may find that the included application templates aren't quite what you need for repeated use. The templates may have the basic structure, but you often find yourself changing a menu or removing some of the added components. You can get around this by adjusting the template (or creating a new template) and saving your work as a template. You can add templates to the gallery by right-clicking the form or by using the Edit menu's Save As Template command.

Advanced Coding Issues

In this chapter, you've learned about two types of application structures for handling multiple windows: MDI and SDI. Moving out from a single-form application mentality requires extra preparation on the part of the programmer. With multiple forms and units all over the place, you need to make sure that your application is using shared pieces of code so that you can maintain your work easily.

Where to Put the Code

As you're coding your application, you might notice that your logic begins to repeat itself in many objects of your application's forms. This is rather undesirable if the required functionality of the repeated logic has to be consistent throughout the entire application. Changing one piece of repeated logic in one form without changing it throughout all related forms produces an inconsistency in the application's interface. Even if you managed to change all the individual parts in your application, this approach lends itself to error and difficult maintenance.

There are a number of places where you can write code:

- Attached to the object that's using it
- Attached to the form containing the object using it
- In a separate unit

There are no hard-and-fast rules for where code must go; the situation for which you're programming must be taken into consideration. When deciding where your code should go, ask yourself the following questions:

- Is it code I want associated only with this type of object? If so, will any other object need access to the code?
- Is it code I want associated only with this form? This is essentially the same question as the previous, but many consider forms and other objects, such as buttons, to be distinctly different. They are, in fact, not that much different. As mentioned earlier, however, forms can trap key events for processing before individual objects receive the key events.
- Is it application-specific type code where the code isn't necessarily linked to a specific object?

Depending on your needs, code can be written in any combination of the following areas:

- As a new method specific to an object
- Global form-level code
- Application-specific code stored in a stand-alone unit

Shared Procedures

You can easily reference procedures in other units of your application by simply appending to the uses clause of your form's unit file. An example uses statement is

```
uses
     WinTypes, WinProcs, SysUtils, Classes, Graphics, Forms,
     Controls, Menus, StdCtrls, Dialogs;
```

This uses statement contains references to libraries needed to support basic processing, the form types selected, and the components being used on the form. To add a reference to another unit, you simply append your unit file name to the uses list:

```
uses
     WinTypes, WinProcs, SysUtils, Classes, Graphics, Forms,
     Controls, Menus, StdCtrls, Dialogs, MDI;
```

Remember that units don't need to have forms attached. Using the File menu's New Unit command causes a new unit to be added to your project without an attached form. This is where you want to place your application-specific or business-rules logic.

Shared Event Handlers

When setting up default event-handling code in your application, you may find yourself duplicating blocks of code for each new event handler. One way to resolve this issue is to use shared procedures, which are called inside each individual event handler. There is a better way, one that's achieved by sharing event handlers themselves, thus eliminating the need for indirect routing of logic.

An example that calls for this need is if you wanted to provide special support for the right-click event on all your button objects. Rather than set up individual event handlers for each button, you use a common event handler that handles right-clicks for all your button objects.

From Here...

You can find more information about the topics discussed in this chapter in the following chapters:

- Chapter 4, "Using Visual Components," discusses what objects can be placed on your forms now that you know how to control them.

- Chapter 5, "Using Non-Visual Components," shows how to use non-visual objects, such as menu objects, to control the user interface.

- Chapter 8, "Creating Forms," discusses the finer points of normal and dialog forms.

Chapter 10
Creating Database Applications

Creating a database application with Delphi is as easy as creating any other kind of Delphi application. Delphi gives you all the tools you need to create powerful database applications—programs that can access many kinds of databases across a wide variety of platforms. Just place a few database-related components on a form, set their properties, and presto! You have a working database application. If you know how to add a few lines of SQL or Object Pascal code, you can create even more robust database programs.

This chapter teaches you everything that you need to know to start writing database applications you'll be proud of. By the time you finish this chapter, you'll be able to:

- Create and manipulate data on forms using Delphi's data-aware components

- Write and execute SQL instructions in two different ways: by setting component properties and by executing SQL statements programmatically

- Display data from multiple tables on the same data grid, synchronizing the display so that changing data displayed in one data grid also changes the data shown in other grids

- Filter the information displayed on grids so that only desired columns are displayed

- Customize the formatting of data displays with a tool called the DataSet Designer

- Calculate the contents of fields in real time by using the DataSet Designer

To help you learn all these things, this chapter provides four sample projects that demonstrate various features and capabilities of Delphi database programs. Each project creates an individual application, but each application builds on previous projects. The four projects presented in this chapter are as follows:

- DATAGRID.DPR, a simple program that displays database data inside a grid in a window and lets the user view and edit the data. This program introduces the DataSet Designer—a tool for customizing fields in tables and queries and controlling the way they behave—and introduces some of the most fundamental principles of database design.

- SQLEDIT.DPR, an application that creates an SQL editor. This project is a two-pronged introduction to SQL. First, you write some SQL to build the project; then you learn more about SQL by running it. When you finish the SQLEdit project, you have an editor that you can use to type SQL statements and then try them out. As soon as you finish writing an SQL instruction, you can execute an SQL statement in real time at the click of a button.

- DATAFORM.DPR, an application that creates a form for viewing and editing database data.

- LINEITEM.DPR, another data-form application with a number of powerful added features, including outer joins, calculated fields, and field formatting.

By the time you finish this chapter, you'll know how to write several different kinds of database applications using Delphi. As a special bonus, the exercises that you'll complete provide you with several projects you can use as frameworks for your own Delphi database applications.

Understanding Delphi Database Basics

You create a Delphi database using Delphi's object-oriented components, in the much same way that you create any other Delphi application. To create a database application, you place components on a form and then set their properties—either programmatically or by selecting and filling in fields in the Object Inspector window.

You'll see in this chapter that Delphi database applications are very versatile. With Delphi, you can create and manipulate tables and data by using the familiar Delphi components, Pascal source code, and even SQL (Structured Query Language), the standard language for developing large-scale database operations.

A database application built with Delphi can create and access database data by itself or with the help of many different kinds of other database programs. Delphi database applications can work with Paradox, dBASE, and InterBase for Windows, as well as ODBC-aware database packages such as FoxPro and Access. If you own the Enterprise edition of Delphi, you can also connect to remote database servers from vendors including Oracle, Sybase, and Informix, as well as to InterBase remote databases.

Once you've configured a Delphi application for client-server operations, users of your database application can run it in the same way they run any Delphi database application, without paying any attention to the fact that they're communicating with a remote server.

The Borland Database Engine

When you create a Delphi database application, it accesses desktop database applications and remote database servers through a component called the *Borland Database Engine* (BDE). You don't have to know anything about the BDE to write Delphi database applications, and the users of your applications don't have to know anything about the BDE to run them. The BDE is installed automatically when you install Delphi, and it runs behind the scenes from then on.

Once the BDE is up and running, you can create Delphi database applications that access data from database tables stored on a local disk drive or, if you have the Enterprise edition, from remote database servers on a network. The Enterprise edition comes with a software package called SQL Links for Windows that can be used to access and manipulate SQL data stored in InterBase, Informix, ORACLE, Sybase, and Microsoft SQL Server databases. SQL Links for Windows provides drivers that lets Delphi users access networked SQL databases as well in exactly the same way they access local (Paradox and dBASE) databases. For more details, see the Borland SQL Links for Windows manual that comes with Delphi.

> **Note**
>
> Because database management can get incredibly complicated, Delphi has many features that add extra robustness to database applications. Delphi provides many database-related components, properties, and events that can create surprisingly sophisticated Delphi database applications without writing any code at all. Occasionally, though, you may find that some database operations require some coding, and Delphi lets you incorporate Pascal code and SQL queries into your database applications.

Components, Controls, and Classes

Delphi database applications work just like other kinds of Delphi applications, but they use some additional components, controls, and classes. Components, controls, and classes have similar names in all Delphi applications, so explanations of how they work can get confusing. In database applications, the names of these three kinds of objects can get even more confusing because database programs have more kinds of objects to keep track of.

To help you keep everything sorted out, this chapter uses a consistent set of conventions to refer to the different kinds of components, controls, and classes found in Delphi database applications. Here's an overview of the naming conventions used in this chapter:

- In database applications, just as in other kinds of Delphi applications, components are those little icons that you select from the Component palette and then copy onto a form to implement functionalities in your programs. In this chapter, names of components are preceded with a T; for example, Delphi database applications use components with names such as TTable, TDataGrid, and TDataSource.

- You can use many Delphi components to create Windows controls—that is, interactive controls that work just like ordinary dialog controls. When you use a Delphi component to create a Windows control, the control you create has the same name as the component that created it, minus the component's preceding T. For instance, a control created by the TDBEdit component is a DBEdit control; a control created by the TDBNavigator component is a DBNavigator control; and so on.

- When you run a Delphi application, each component used in the program accesses an Object Pascal class that has the same name as the component. Because Object Pascal classes have the same names as their corresponding components, this chapter uses the convention of preceding the name of every component-related class with a T (programmers might notice that this is the same way component-related classes are referred to in Delphi source files). In this chapter, the Object Pascal class accessed by a TTable component is the TTable class, the class accessed by a TDataSource component is the TDataSource class, and so on.

- Delphi has a special category of database components called *data-control components*, which are accessed from the Data Control page of the Component palette. They're called data control components because they create controls that look just like ordinary dialog controls but have data-aware features that make them especially useful in database applications. In this chapter, as noted earlier, a control created by a component is referred to by the same name as the component that created it, minus the component's preceding T. This convention applies to data-control appointments as well as to other kinds of components used in Delphi. Thus, the TDBEdit component is a data-control component that creates a DBEdit control, and so on. (Another characteristic of data-control components is that their names contain the letters DB. Thus, data-control components have names such as TDBEdit, TDBNavigator, and so on.)

- Every Delphi component is associated with a set of methods and a set of properties. When you select a component on a form, the properties associated with a component are listed in the Object Inspector window associated with the component. These properties often refer to other components and often have the same names as the components they refer to. In this chapter, properties that have the same names as components are specifically referred to as properties.

The Database Component Pages

As noted in Chapter 6, "Using Data-Bound Components," the Delphi database components are provided on two Component palette pages: the Data Access page and the Data Controls page. The Data Access page, shown in figure 10.1, contains—as you might expect—components for accessing database data. The TTable and TQuery components and a number of other data-access components are accessible from the Data Access page. (The TQuery component is a component used for writing and executing SQL commands, as you'll see in one of the exercises presented in this chapter.)

242   Chapter 10—Creating Database Applications

Fig. 10.1
This is the Data Access page.

Fig. 10.2
This is the Data Controls page.

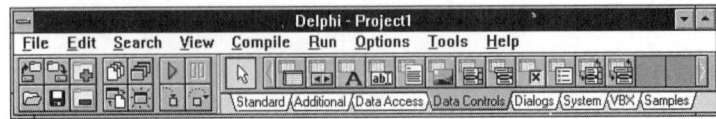

Database Components

A Delphi database application—like any other Delphi application—is usually created from a design form that contains at least three database components:

- A data-access component, such as TTable or TQuery, that connects your application with a database table. The data-access component shown in figure 10.3 is a TTable component.

- A TDataSource component, which makes information stored in the database table available to the application.

- One or more data-control components, such as TDBEdit, TDBGrid, and TDBNavigator. The user of your application enters, manipulates, or browses through data using the data-control components that you supply. The data-control component shown in figure 10.3 is a TDBGrid component. The TDBGrid component creates a DBGrid control, which displays information from the table in a grid so that it can be viewed and edited.

Fig. 10.3
You need three components to create a Delphi database application.

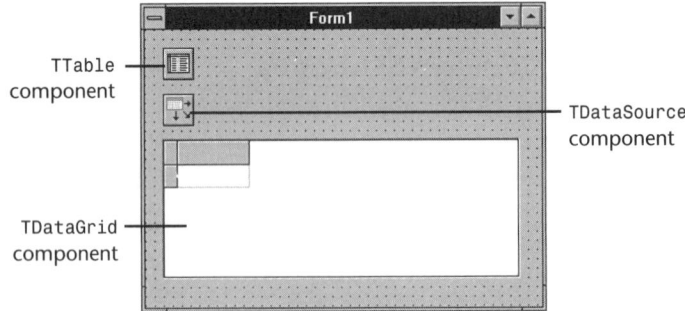

Non-Visual Components

As noted in Chapter 6, "Using Data-Bound Components," some database components—such as TTable and TDataSource shown in figure 10.3—are non-visual components. Non-visual components are ones that the user of your application can't see at runtime. The TTable and TDataSource components are non-visual because their job isn't to interface with the user of your application but to interface your application with the BDE.

The job of the TDataSource component is not to interface with the user, but to link a data-access component such as a TTable or a TQuery to data-control components such as TDBGrid, TDBEdit, or TDBNavigator components.

Data-control components, on the other hand, are always visual; they have to be because they provide the user with a visible interface to database data. Data-control components can include not only data grids, edit controls, and navigation controls, but also other kinds of controls such as labels, list and combo boxes, check boxes, and buttons.

When you place a TDataSource component on a form and link it with a TTable component and one or more data-control components, the user of your application can view, edit, or manipulate database data using the data-control components you've provided.

The *TField* Component

One important component that usually works behind the scenes is the TField component, which is an object-oriented encapsulation of a column in a database table. It contains properties describing the column's data type, current value, display format, edit format, and other attributes. When you retrieve a table from a database using a TTable or TQuery component, each column in that table has an individual TField component.

You can do a lot of database programming without being aware of TField components because Delphi's default behavior is to generate a TField component for every column in a table each time the table is activated by a TTable or TQuery component. The TField components that Delphi generates for a particular table at runtime are based on the underlying physical structure of the table.

Because Delphi generates TField components dynamically, the TField objects that describe the columns change whenever the underlying structure of the table changes. If, for example, a column is dropped from a table that your Delphi application accesses, there will be no information about that column in the table's `TField` component the next time a user starts your application. That means your application may wind up trying to access a column that holds unrecognized data or no longer exists. That can, of course, mean big trouble for your application.

You can prevent this kind of disaster by creating a static list of `TField` components for each table your application uses. Then Delphi uses your static components rather than dynamically generate a set of default `TField` components for every table that's activated.

Once you create a set of static `TField` components for each table in your application, those components will be the `TField` objects Delphi uses to access your tables, even if their underlying structures change. Of course, you still won't be able to retrieve information from a column that no longer exists, but at least Delphi will notice the error and throw an exception rather than cluelessly try to obtain data from a missing column. (For details on Delphi's exception-handling features, see Chapter 14, "Handling Errors.")

To help you roll your own static `TField` components, Delphi provides a special tool called the DataSet Designer. You can also use the DataSet Designer to limit the number of columns displayed in a data grid and to control how those columns are displayed. Later in this chapter, you learn more about the DataSet Designer and get a chance to use it in some example programs.

The *TDataSet* Class

Along with its non-visible components, Delphi also makes use of some database-related OOP classes that the user of your applications will never see. One such class is the `TDataSet` class, an abstract class normally hidden from the creator of an application as well as the user. The `TTable` and `TQuery` classes are descended from the `TDataSet` class through an intermediate class, `TDataSet`.

> **Note**
>
> The `TDataSet` class, as you might guess from its name, is an Object Pascal class that your application accesses when you place a `TDataSet` component on a form. In this respect, Delphi's database classes are just like other component-related Object Pascal classes used in Delphi—they access Object Pascal objects and have the same names as their corresponding Object Pascal classes. For more information about components, Object Pascal classes, and how they are related, see the *Component Writer's Guide* that comes with Delphi.

The *TDataSource* Component

The TDataSource component is an essential part of a Delphi database application. Every design form that contains one or more data-control components that the user can interact with must also contain at least one TDataSource component.

The job of the TDataSource component is to act as a conduit between a TTable or TQuery component and one or more data-control components. TDataSource is essential to the operation of a database because data-access components can't communicate directly with data-control components. When a data-control component needs to access a data-access component, the two components must communicate through a TDataSource component.

To access the same table from multiple forms, place a separate TDataSource component on each form. Each TDataSource component can access the table, which can be placed on any form.

Creating a Customized DataGrid Application

Now that you know something about how Delphi database applications work, it's time to create your first Delphi database project. You'll start with the DataGrid project, a simple application that displays database records in a grid inside a window. When you create the DataGrid application, you use the DataSet Designer to limit the number of columns the data grid displays and customize some of the other features of your application.

When you finish your application, the user can scroll through the data displayed in the grid and can insert, update, delete, and add data to the columns of data that the grid displays.

As you create the DataGrid project, you'll review some of the basic database-creation procedures you learned in Chapter 6, "Using Data-Bound Components." This time, though, you're laying the groundwork for more advanced operations that are presented in later examples in this chapter.

Designing a Customized DataGrid Application

As you learned in Chapter 8, "Creating Forms," the first step in creating a Delphi project is to create a *design form*, usually referred to simply as a *form*. The second step is to place some components on your form. Then you can start getting fancier, as you'll see in the example project presented in this section.

To create the first project in this chapter, you start by placing a `TTable` component on a form. `TTable`, as you may recall, is a component that connects an application to a specified table. When you place a `TTable` component on a form and then connect it through `TDataSource` to other components that display data—such as text boxes, buttons, and data grids—the user of your application can establish a connection to a database and can then create, view, and edit database data.

If the `ReadOnly` property of a `TDBGrid` component is set to false—its default setting—the user can also insert, add, or delete database data using the interactive controls you provide.

Creating a DataGrid Project Step by Step

In the following exercise, you design a form by placing a `TTable` component on the form and then connecting your table to a data-control component (in this exercise, a `TDBGrid` component).

To create your DataGrid application, follow these steps:

1. Select the `TTable` icon from the Component palette's Data Access page and place a `TTable` component on a design form.

2. In the Object Inspector window, set your `TTable` component's `DatabaseName` property to `DBDEMOS`. `DBDEMOS` is an alias that the BDE sets up automatically when you run the Delphi installer. This alias is a shortcut for the path name of the sample databases that ship with Delphi.

When the `DBDEMOS` alias is set up, Delphi can find the sample databases supplied by Borland without requiring you to type their path names, so you can tell Delphi where they are without really knowing where they are yourself. If you installed Delphi on your C drive using the installer's default settings, the sample database are in C:\DELPHI\DEMOS\DATABASE.

3. In the Object Inspector window, select the list box next to the `TableName` property and choose the sample database table named CUSTOMER.DB. CUSTOMER.DB is the name of one of the tables in the sample database files supplied with Delphi. It provides information about the customers of a fictional maritime and salvage company named MAST.

Again, you don't have to know where the CUSTOMER.DB table is stored to select it for the `TableName` property. However, if Delphi is installed on

Creating a Customized DataGrid Application

your C drive using the installer's default settings, the default path name of the CUSTOMER.DB table is C:\DELPHI\DEMOS\DATABASE\CUSTOMER.DB. The other database tables used in this chapter are stored in the same directory.

4. Double-click the list box next to the Active property to set the Active property of your TTable component to true. That action activates the CUSTOMER.DB table.

5. Place a TDataSource component just below the TTable component on your design form.

6. To connect your TDataSource component to your TTable component, make sure the TDataSource component is selected and then open the list box next to the DataSet property in the Object Inspector window. From the list box, choose Table1—the default name of the TTable component on your design form.

7. On the Data Controls page, select the TDBGrid component, and place a DBGrid control on your design form. Your form now resembles the design form shown earlier in figure 10.3.

8. Make sure the TDBGrid component on your form is selected. Then, in the Object Inspector window, select the list box next to the DataSource property. When the list box appears, set your grid component's DataSource property to DataSource1—the name of the TDataSource component you created in the previous exercise.

Notice that data from Table1 appears inside the data-grid component on your form (see fig. 10.4).

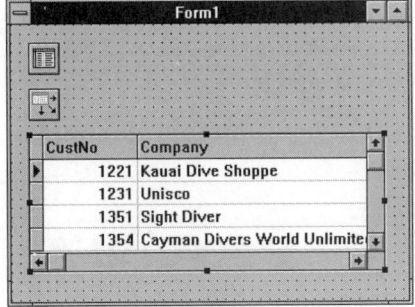

Fig. 10.4
When you set the TDBGrid component's DataSource property to DataSource1, Delphi fills the component with database data.

Testing Your Application

Although your application isn't finished yet, you can execute it at this point to see how it's working. First, save your project in its current form by choosing Sa&ve Project or Sa&ve Project As from the Delphi &File menu. Save your project files as DBGRID.PAS and DATAGRID.DPR in whatever directory you like. Execute your application by choosing &Run from the &Run menu. When your program starts, it displays a window similar to the one shown in figure 10.5.

Fig. 10.5
If you run the DataGrid application now, this is what you see.

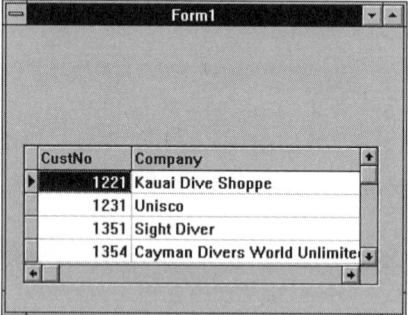

When your program is running, select a field and edit the text in the field by typing something different. If the AutoEdit property of your data grid is set to true—its default setting—you can use standard Windows editing commands to edit the information inside the grid you've created. By using menu commands, the keyboard, or the mouse, you can add, insert, update, or delete data but only a whole field or record at a time. You can also use the scroll bars below and alongside your grid to scroll the data in the table you're accessing.

If everything works correctly, you've now completed the basic framework of the DataGrid project. In the next exercise, you'll add extra features that make the application more useful and more interesting.

You can now quit the DataGrid application-in-progress by double-clicking its control box.

Improving the DataGrid Application

The DataGrid application you just created is a nice introduction to Delphi database programming, but it isn't a very sophisticated database application. In the next exercise, you'll get a chance to make some major improvements in the DataGrid application. In subsequent exercises, you'll keep building on what you've learned as you create more and more ambitious and impressive applications.

Using the Customization Popup Menu and the DataSet Designer

You can modify the appearance and contents of a Delphi DBGrid control in several ways. Two popular methods are to use the customization popup menu and the DataSet Designer.

The customization popup menu (see fig. 10.6) is a menu that pops up when you left-click a `TTable` or `TQuery` component. You can use the customization popup menu to control the display of the components on a form. With the customization popup menu, you can align components, move components forward or backward in relation to other components, and save components as templates so that you can use them later in other forms.

The DataSet Designer is a Delphi tool that lets you make more substantial changes in `TField` components. With the DataSet Designer, you can limit the number of columns displayed in a data grid and control how those columns are displayed. You can also use the DataSet Designer to specify the names of fields shown on a form; specify the names of components shown on a form; and specify the kinds of data displayed in a field.

Using the Customization Popup Menu

The customization popup menu, shown in figure 10.6, isn't designed solely for the `TDBGrid` component. You can display the same menu by right-clicking other data-control and data-access components such as the `TTable` and `TDataSource` components.

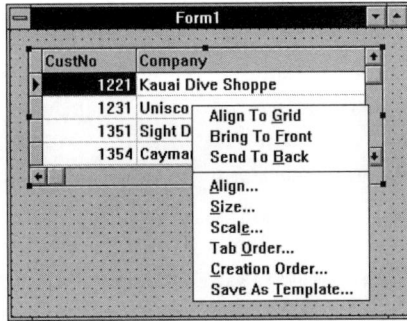

Fig. 10.6
When you right-click a `TDBGrid` component, Delphi opens the customization popup menu. The same trick works with other data-control and data-access components such as TTable TDataSource.

To use the customization popup menu, right-click a DBGrid control that has been placed on a form. The customization popup menu then appears.

250 Chapter 10—Creating Database Applications

By choosing items from the customization popup menu, you can control the display of the components on a form in various ways. For example, you can align components, move components forward or backward in relation to other components, and save components as templates so that you can use them later in other forms.

Using the DataSet Designer

With the DataSet Designer, you can control several characteristics of TField components. For example, you can limit the number of columns shown in a data grid; define field names, component names, and fields; and control how columns in a data grid are displayed.

To activate the DataSet Designer, you double-click a TTable or TQuery component. When the DataSet Designer opens, its title bar provides information about the form on which it appears. Figure 10.7 shows the DataSet Designer.

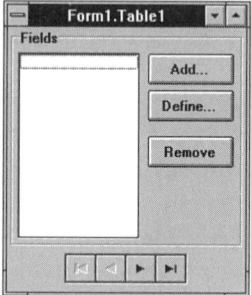

Fig. 10.7
You can customize TField components with the DataSet Designer.

Tip
Creating static TField objects is a good programming practice because it lets you control the way your application retrieves data from tables.

You can also use the DataSet Designer to create static TField objects that describe the fields in database tables. The alternative is to let Delphi create your application's TField objects dynamically. That practice is less safe, however, because it can result in attempts to retrieve data from columns that have been modified or no longer exist. For more information on this topic, see "The *TField* Component" section earlier in this chapter.

What You Can Do with the DataSet Designer

A TField component, as you may recall, is a component that stores display-related information about a database column or field. For example, a TField component has properties that determine whether a column is displayed in a data grid, the position in the data grid in which the column is displayed, and the formatting rules that are used to display the information in the column.

When you connect a TDataSet component (usually a TTable or TQuery component) to a database table and set the Active property of the TDataSet component to true, Delphi dynamically generates a TField component for each column in the database table.

Alternatively, you can use static TField components in your application and set their properties yourself, which is the recommended programming practice. The Delphi tool that lets you do this is the DataSet Designer.

You can do other useful things with the DataSet Designer. For example, you can equip a table with temporary fields used for display purposes only, and you can calculate the values of fields at runtime rather than retrieve their values verbatim from a table. You'll get a chance to do both jobs with the DataSet Designer before you finish this chapter.

Modifying a DataGrid Step by Step

In the following exercise, you use the DataSet Designer to modify your application's TDBGrid component. As you work through the exercise, you reformat your TDBGrid component to display just two columns and change the order in which the columns are displayed.

To work through the exercise, follow these steps:

1. On the design form you created in the previous exercise, double-click the TTable component. Delphi displays the DataSet Designer window shown earlier in figure 10.7.

   Notice that the Fields list box in the DataSet Designer window is empty. That's because all the fields in the CUSTOMER.DB table are dynamic fields, and dynamic fields aren't listed in the DataSet Designer. When you add a field to the Fields list box, it becomes a static field. From then on, Delphi generates an exception whenever an attempt to access the field is unsuccessful.

2. To add a field to the Fields list box, click the Add button. Delphi displays the Add Fields dialog (see fig. 10.8).

3. Select Company from the Available Fields list box and then click OK. The Add Fields dialog closes, and the word Company appears in the DataSet Designer's Fields list box.

Tip
To select multiple fields, Ctrl+click or Shift+click just as you can in the Windows File Manager.

Fig. 10.8
To add a field, select the field in the DataSet Designer's list box and click OK.

4. Click Add again in the DataSet Designer to display the Add Fields dialog.

5. Select the CustNo item from the Available Fields list box and click OK. The Add Fields dialog closes, and CustNo appears with the name of the Company field in the DataSet Designer's Fields list box (see fig. 10.9).

Fig. 10.9
You can add static fields to a TField component with the DataSet Designer.

> **Note**
>
> Because Delphi supports drag and drop in its list boxes, you can easily change the order of fields displayed in a data grid by moving the names of the fields around in the Fields list box. In figure 10.9, for example, the CustNo item is the second item shown in the Fields list box, making it the second column displayed in the data grid that's being designed. In figure 10.10, the CustNo field has been dragged to the top of the Fields list box, and thus appears in the left column of the data grid being designed (see fig. 10.11).

Improving the DataGrid Application   253

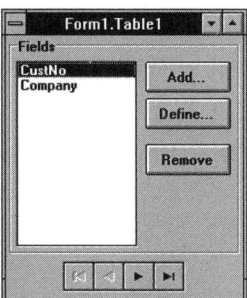

Fig. 10.10
To change the order of fields shown in a data grid, use drag and drop to rearrange the field names in the Fields list box.

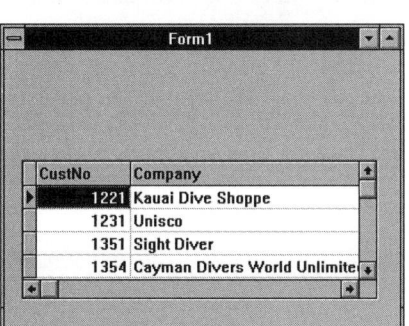

Fig. 10.11
You can rearrange the order of fields displayed in a data grid by using the DataSet Designer.

6. Save your work, and then close the DataSet Designer window by double-clicking its control box.

7. Select the TDBGrid component on your form and widen the grid until you can see the end of the Company field. Notice that the data grid's horizontal scroll bar disappears when you do that because now only two fields are in the grid: CustNo and Company. The form you are designing then looks like the form shown in figure 10.11.

8. Execute your application by choosing the Run command from the Run menu. The program's main window should resemble the one shown in figure 10.11.

When the DataGrid program starts, check out how it works. Use the TDBGrid component to navigate to the next record, the previous record, the first record, and the last record. Then edit a record or two. By the time you're done, you'll see how easy it is to display and edit records using the TDBGrid component.

As neat as that may be, `TDBGrid` doesn't provide tools that are important in many data-entry operations—for example, tools for inserting records, deleting records, or posting or correcting editing changes. For that you need a control with the capabilities of the `TDBNavigator` component, which is introduced in the "Using the *TDBNavigator* Component" section later in this chapter.

Using SQL in Delphi Databases

Queries are an essential part of database management. Most large relational database systems, such as those manufactured by Oracle, Informix, and Sybase, execute queries using SQL.

Delphi is compatible with large database systems that use SQL, so it should come as no surprise that Delphi speaks SQL too. In fact, for developers interested in accessing large databases, SQL support is one of the most important features of Delphi.

In this section, you learn how expand your DataGrid application into a slightly more sophisticated project named Query. Query is a simple application that executes queries written in SQL.

> **Note**
>
> This section introduces you to enough SQL so you can understand the examples presented in this chapter. But this chapter is far from a complete course in using SQL. SQL is a fairly complex language that takes some time (and practice) to master. Many good books about SQL are available. In fact, the SQL tutorials that come with some relational database management systems, such as the Informix RDBMS, aren't bad. So if you need to learn SQL to interface Delphi with a client-server RDBMS system, you might find the information you need in some good books about SQL you may already have lying around.

Getting Started with SQL

One of the most important statements in SQL is the `SELECT` statement. SQL programs use the `SELECT` statement to retrieve information from database fields. For example, the statement

```
SELECT CustNo, Name FROM Customer
```

retrieves the `CustNo` and `Name` fields from the Customer database. As you can see, though, `SELECT` doesn't say where the information it retrieves should be placed. When you use the SELECT command in a Delphi application, you can place the data you select in a data-control component, such as TDBGrid or TDBEdit. You'll learn how to do that in the next exercise in this chapter.

> **Note**
>
> SQL isn't case-sensitive, but for the sake of readability, your SQL statements should at least be case-consistent. One common convention is to capitalize SQL keywords and lowercase all other kinds of words, which is the convention followed in this book.

SQL, like DOS, recognizes the asterisk as a wild-card character. Thus, the statement

```
SELECT * FROM Customer
```

means, "Select all fields from the Customer database." Again, you must provide a place to put the fields once they're retrieved.

Writing SQL Queries

You can write and execute SQL queries in Delphi applications in many ways. One method is to set the SQL property of a TQuery component to the text of an SQL command. Then, when you execute your application, Delphi executes your query. If you connect your TQuery component through a TDataSet component to a data-access component, the results of the query are displayed in the data-viewing component that's linked to the TQuery component.

Another way to write an SQL statement for a TQuery component is to include SQL statements in the Pascal units (blocks of executable Pascal code) that Delphi creates for your project.

In the next two exercises, you learn how to place SQL queries in Delphi applications using both methods.

To execute an SQL query using the SQL property of the TQuery object, follow these steps:

1. Place a TQuery component on your DataGrid application's design form. By default, Delphi names the new component Query1.

2. Set the DatabaseName property in TQuery's Object Inspector window to DBDEMOS.

3. Double-click TQuery's SQL property in the Object Inspector window. Delphi then displays the String List Editor dialog (see fig. 10.12).

Fig. 10.12
With the String List Editor, you can write and execute SQL commands.

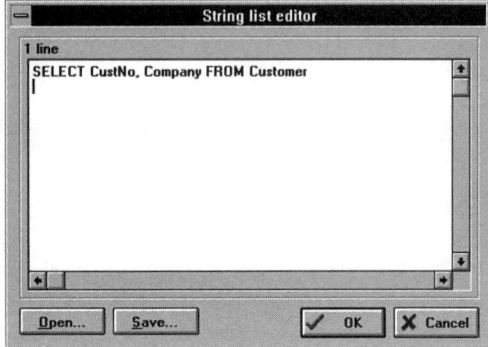

4. In the String List Editor dialog, enter the following SELECT statement:

    `SELECT CustNo, Company FROM Customer`

5. Click OK to close the String List Editor dialog.

6. Place a second TDataSource component on your design form. Delphi names this component TDataSource2.

7. In the Object Inspector window, set the TDataSource2 component's DataSet property to Query1.

8. Select the TDBGrid component.

9. In the Object Inspector window, change the DataSource property of the TDBGrid component to DataSource2 (the name of the TDataSource component that you linked to your TQuery component in step 6). When you make this change, notice that the contents of the TDBGrid component don't change. That's because the SQL line

    `SELECT CustNo, Company FROM Customer`

    produces the same screen display as selecting the CustNo and Company fields using the DataSet Designer and then placing the results in a TDBGrid component.

10. Execute your DataGrid application by opening the Run menu and choosing Run. As figure 10.13 shows, the application produces the same display you saw when you completed the previous example.

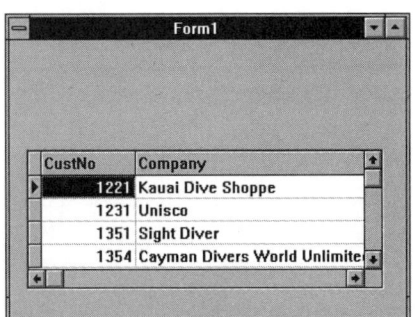

Fig. 10.13
This is still the DataGrid application's screen display.

Using the *TDBNavigator* Component

To help users of your applications navigate through the records in a database, Delphi provides a component called TDBNavigator. This component creates a control called DBNavigator, which is a tape recorder-style control that can scroll to and display the following:

- The next record in a database
- The previous record in a database
- The first record in a database
- The last record in a database

The TDBNavigator component can also

- Place a record in editing mode so that it can be edited
- Take a record out of editing mode so that it can't be edited
- Insert a record into a database
- Remove a record from a database
- Post an editing change (changes aren't incorporated into the database until they're posted)
- Cancel an editing change that hasn't yet been posted
- Refresh the data shown in a data-access component

Those are a lot of jobs for one component to do, but the TDBNavigator does them all—it's quite a versatile component.

258 Chapter 10—Creating Database Applications

By connecting the TDBNavigator component to a data grid, you can create a DBNavigator control that can be used to move through the data in the table one record at a time and to display multiple fields in a record simultaneously. Alternatively, you can connect a single DBNavigator control to several single-field display components, such as DBEdit controls. Your DBNavigator control can then display each field in a record inside separate data-viewing or data-editing controls.

The TDBNavigator component is as easy to use as it is versatile. In fact, it takes just three steps to add a DBNavigator control to the DataGrid application that you've been working on in this chapter:

1. Place a TDBNavigator component on your form. (The TDBNavigator component is the tape-recorder style bar shown at the top of the form.)

2. Arrange the other components on your form as shown in figure 10.14.

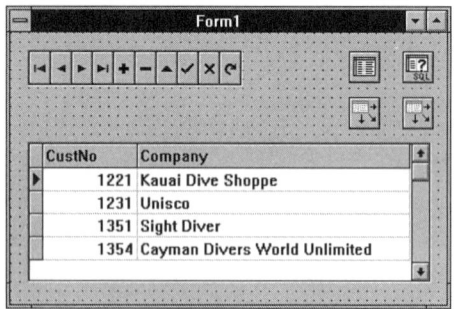

Fig. 10.14
This form creates a window that contains a working DBNavigator control.

3. In the Object Inspector window, set the TDBNavigator's DataSource property to DataSource1—the default name of the TDataSource component bound to your application's TTable component.

When you've equipped your application with a DBNavigator control, try it out. Navigate through the Customer table, edit some records, insert and delete some records, post some changes, and refresh your data display. Then, if you like, you can save your application one final time. You won't be needing it any more in this chapter.

In the next exercise, you'll create an all-new database application: an SQL interpreter that you can use to write SQL statements and execute them in real time.

Designing an SQL Editor

Once you know how Delphi handles SQL queries and how the TDBNavigator component works, you can start developing more ambitious database applications. In the next exercise, you'll build a project named SQLEdit, which creates an interactive SQL editor. By building and running the SQL editor, you can learn a lot about how Delphi uses SQL. When you've built your SQL editor, you can practice SQL by writing commands and watching Delphi execute them at the click of a button.

Building an SQL Editor Step by Step

To create and build the SQLEDIT.DPR program, follow these steps:

1. Open a new design form.

2. Move to the Standard page of the Component palette.

3. Place a standard TMemo component on your form. A TMemo is a component in which you can type text. Each line of text is stored in memory as a string. In the SQLEdit application, your TMemo component serves as a simple but serviceable interactive text editor in which you can type SQL commands.

4. Place two standard TButton components on your design form.

5. In the Object Inspector window, set the Text properties of these two buttons to Execute and Clear. When you finish your application, you invoke SQL commands by typing them in the memo component and then clicking the Execute button. The program then executes your SQL command. To clear the memo box, click the Clear button.

6. Arrange the three controls you've placed on the form as shown in figure 10.15.

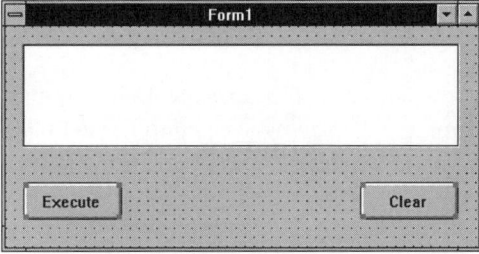

Fig. 10.15
When you place these three controls on your design form, you're on your way to creating an SQL editor.

260 Chapter 10—Creating Database Applications

Adding Data-Access Controls

When you've equipped your application with a TMemo component and two TButton components, you can add database connectivity to your project by following these steps:

1. Move to the Data Access page of the Component palette, and place TQuery and TDataSource components on your form.

2. Move to the palette's Data Controls page, and place a TDBGrid component on your form.

3. Rearrange the components on your design form into an arrangement similar to the one shown in figure 10.16.

Fig. 10.16
When your form looks like this, your SQL editor is almost ready to use.

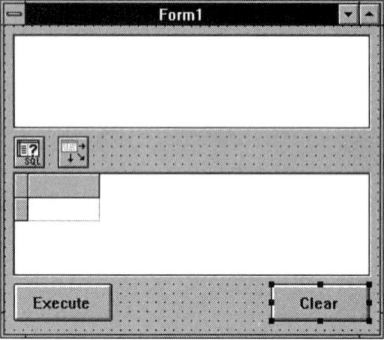

4. Select the TQuery component you placed on your form in step 1.

5. In the Object Inspector window, set the DatabaseName property to DBDEMOS.

6. Select the TDBGrid component.

7. In the Object Inspector window, set the TDBGrid component's DataSource property to DataSource1—the default name of the TDataSource component you placed on your form in step 1.

8. Double-click the button labeled Execute. Delphi responds by opening the Code Editor and displaying a function named TForm1.Button1Click. That's the function your application executes when the user clicks the Execute button.

9. When the Delphi Code Editor opens, type the following lines of SQL code (as shown in fig. 10.17):

    ```
    Query1.Close;
    Query1.SQL.Clear;
    Query1.SQL.ADD(Memo1.Text);
    Query1.Open;
    ```

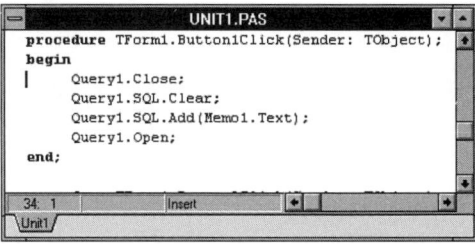

Fig. 10.17
Type the code that executes your query between the words begin and end in your source file.

Executing Queries

The first line of code,

    Query1.Close;

closes your application's TQuery component so that you can change its contents. It's always safe to execute the Close command to close a query. If the query is already closed, the command does nothing. The second line,

    Query1.SQL.Clear;

removes any old SQL text that the query may contain. The next SQL statement,

    Query1.SQL.Add(Memo1.Text);

copies any text that has been entered in your application's TMemo component into the TQuery component. Finally, the statement

    Query1.Open;

reopens the TQuery component. Your application then executes the SQL code that has been copied into the TQuery component. If the query retrieves database data, the retrieved information is displayed in the data grid on your design form.

Clearing Queries

When the user clicks the Clear button, your application clears any text that's displayed its data grid.

To set up the data-clearing part of your application, follow these steps:

1. Double-click the Clear button. Delphi opens the Code Editor and displays the TForm1.Button2Click function. This is the function that your application executes when the user clicks the button labeled Execute.

2. In the Code Editor, type these three lines of code (see fig. 10.18):

    ```
    Query1.Close;
    Query1.SQL.Clear;
    Query1.ExecSQL;
    ```

Fig. 10.18
This code clears the memo control.

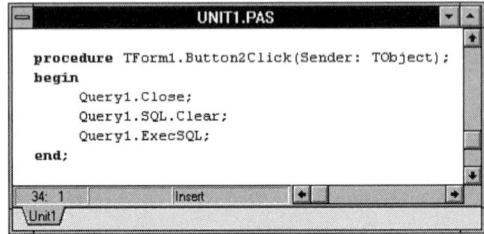

The first line of code,

```
Query1.Close;
```

closes the TQuery component so that its contents can be changed. The second line,

```
Query1.SQL.Clear;
```

clears all text from the TMemo component. The third line,

```
Query1.ExecSQL;
```

reopens the TQuery component. When a TQuery component has no SQL instruction to execute, you should close it by calling the ExecSQL method instead of calling the Open method. Open returns an error if the TQuery component being opened has no SQL method to call.

When you execute the ExecSQL method, your application clears all text from its data grid.

When you've finished the preceding exercise, you may want to save your project by choosing Save Project or Save Project As from the Delphi File menu. Then execute your program by choosing Run from the Run menu.

Writing and Executing SQL Commands

When you execute the SQLEdit application, the program displays a window that contains a memo control, a data grid, and two buttons. To write and execute an SQL command, type it in the memo control and click the Execute button. Your application then executes your SQL command.

> **Note**
>
> For the sake of simplicity, the SQLEdit application doesn't contain any special code for exception handling. To learn about Delphi's exception-handling features, see Chapter 14, "Handling Errors."

Creating a Data-Entry Form

Sometimes, the more complex a Delphi application seems to be, the easier it actually is to develop. In this section, you get a chance to develop an impressive application (named DataForm) that's very easy to create.

You don't have to write any SQL queries to create the DataForm project; you merely set the properties of some DBEdit controls that display and manipulate database data. When you've finished setting the properties of your application's DBEdit controls, Delphi automatically writes and executes all the SQL queries that are required to store, display, and modify the appropriate data.

When you finish the DataForm project, it displays database information in DBEdit controls.

The DataForm application creates a data-entry form. A data-entry form is, of course, a form used to enter and edit data. The form you create in the next exercise displays information from the CUSTOMER.DB table in the DBDEMOS sample database.

Rather than display data records in a data grid, the DataForm project places each field retrieved from a database in a separate one-line edit control—a format that most data-entry engineers like better than grid-style controls.

Using the *TDBEdit* Component

A DBEdit control, as explained in Chapter 6, "Using Data-Bound Components," is a special data-aware version of the ordinary Edit control that appears on the Standard page of the Component palette.

The difference between a DBEdit control and a standard Edit control is that the TDBEdit component used to create DBEdit controls has two extra properties: DataSource and DataField.

To use the TDBEdit component, you place the name of a TDataSource component in the TDBEdit component's DataSource property. Then you place the name of a database field in the TDBEdit component's DataField property.

When a TDBEdit component is connected to a TDataSource component and a database field, it automatically displays the data field that it's linked to. When the information in the field changes, the text inside the DBEdit control changes automatically.

Creating a Form for the DataForm Project

To develop the DataForm project, follow these steps:

1. Open a new design form.

2. Place the following components on the form:

    - A TTable component

    - A TDataSource component

    - Five standard TLabel components (it isn't necessary to use the data-aware TDBLabel components provided on the Data Controls page of the Component palette; it's more efficient to use ordinary TLabel components from the Standard page).

    - Four TDBEdit components

    - A TDBNavigator component

Setting Component Properties

When you've placed all the necessary components on your application's form, set their properties by following these steps:

1. Select the TTable component.

2. In the Object Inspector window, set the DatabaseName property to DBDEMOS.

Creating a Data-Entry Form

3. Set the TableName property to CUSTOMER.DB.

4. Set the Active property to true.

5. Select the TDataSource component.

6. In the Object Inspector window, set the TDataSource component's DataSet property to Table1—the default name of the table you placed on your form in the previous exercise.

7. Select the TDBNavigator component.

8. In the Object Inspector window, set the TDBNavigator component's DataSource property to DataSource1—the default name of the TDataSource component that appears at the top of the design form.

9. Select the TDBEdit component labeled Customer Number.

10. In the Object Inspector window, set the DataSource property to DataSource1 and the DataField property to CustNo.

11. Select the TDBEdit component labeled Name.

12. In the Object Inspector window, set the DataSource property to DataSource1 and the DataField property to Company.

13. Select the TDBEdit component labeled City.

14. In the Object Inspector window, set the DataSource property to DataSource1 and the DataField property to City.

15. Select the TDBEdit component labeled Country.

16. In the Object Inspector window, set the DataSource property to DataSource1 and the DataField property to Country.

When you complete these steps, arrange your design form to look like the one shown in figure 10.19.

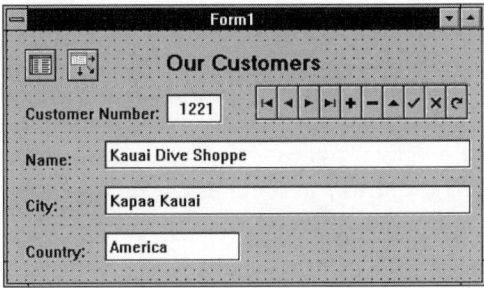

Fig. 10.19
When the DATAFORM.DPR design form looks like this, the DataForm application is ready to run.

266 Chapter 10—Creating Database Applications

If you'd like to save the DataForm project, choose Sa*v*e Project or Sav*e* Project As from the Delphi *F*ile menu.

Execute your application by choosing *R*un from the *R*un menu. When the DataForm application starts, it displays a window like the one in figure 10.20.

Fig. 10.20
When you execute the DataForm application, this is the display you see.

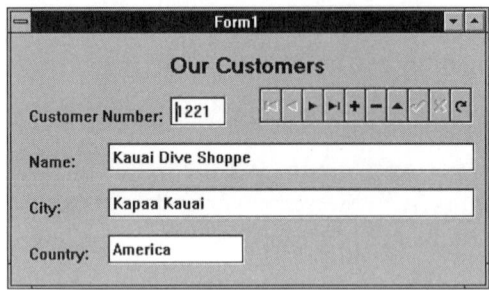

When the DataForm application starts, use the DBNavigator control to navigate through the customer numbers in the Customer database. When data appears in the Customer Number text box and the three other DBEdit controls, notice that you can edit it using standard Windows menu, mouse, and keyboard controls.

Creating the LineItem Application

If your application hasn't all been put together yet, it will be by the time you finish the next exercise. In this exercise—the last one in this chapter—you'll create a database application that demonstrates how to:

- Execute SQL instructions programmatically
- Display data from multiple tables on the same data grid
- Customize the display of fields with the DataSet Designer
- Calculate the contents of fields at runtime

Figure 10.21 shows what the screen display of the LineItem application will look like when you finish creating the program and then execute it. The application displays a data-entry form named the Customer Invoice Form. When you run the program, you can scroll through records in the DBDEMOS database by clicking the arrows in the DBNavigator control, and you can display and edit information from three different database tables using the DBEdit and DBNavigator controls.

To use the Customer Invoice Form displayed by the LineItem application, scroll through a database named CUSTOMER.DB by clicking the arrows in the DBNavigator control at the top of the form. As you scroll through the CUSTOMER database, customer information stored in the database appears inside the DBEdit controls at the top of the invoice form.

As the information shown in the DBEdit controls changes, the data in the two tables below the DBEdit controls also changes, in synchronization with the changes in the DBEdit controls.

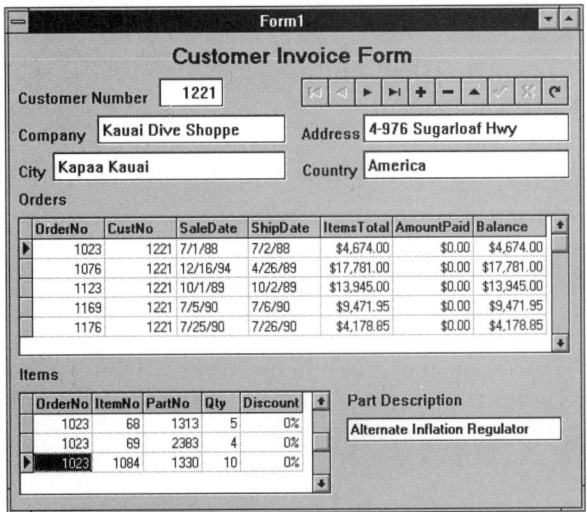

Fig. 10.21
The LineItem application is a world-class data-entry and data-viewing form.

When you execute the LineItem application, the table labeled Orders in the middle of the form displays information from a database table named ORDERS.DB. The ORDERS.DB table, one of the sample database tables shipped with Delphi, stores information about orders that have been shipped to customers whose names appear in the CUSTOMER.DB table.

The lower data grid at the bottom of the LineItem form, labeled Items, displays information from another sample database table named ITEMS.DB. The ITEMS table contains information on the contents of orders shipped to customers. The LineItem application uses information stored in the ITEMS.DB table to list the items that make up each merchandise order shipped to each customer.

Each time the name of a new customer appears in the Name text box, the Orders data grid shows the latest information about orders that have been shipped to the specified customer. Only orders that have been shipped to that one customer appear; orders that have been shipped to other customers are filtered out.

Each time the information in the Orders grid changes, the data in the Items grid also changes to show exactly what items were included in that order. The data in the Items grid comes from a table named ITEMS.DB, which stores information about items that are available to ship to customers.

When you understand how this all works, you can see what a sophisticated database application the LineItem program is. It combines data from three different tables using what database programmers call *outer joins* (operations that combine data in different tables), and it displays matching information from all three tables in real time.

And that isn't all the program does. It also calculates the value shown in one field, and it displays the calculated values in real time.

In the Orders grid in the middle of the form, the Balance field is a calculated field. It subtracts any figures in the AmountPaid field from the figures in the ItemsTotal field and displays the results.

Finally, the Discount field in the Items grid on the Customer Invoice Form is user formatted to display percentage values. (You learn how to create user-formatted fields in the next exercise.)

Designing the LineItem Form Step by Step

To start building the LineItem project, follow these steps:

1. By using the procedures you followed in earlier examples, place the following components on a design form:

    - Eight standard TLabel components
    - Five TDBEdit components
    - One TDBNavigator component
    - Two TDBGrid components
    - Three TTable components
    - Three TDataSource components

2. Group the components on your form into the arrangement shown in figure 10.22.

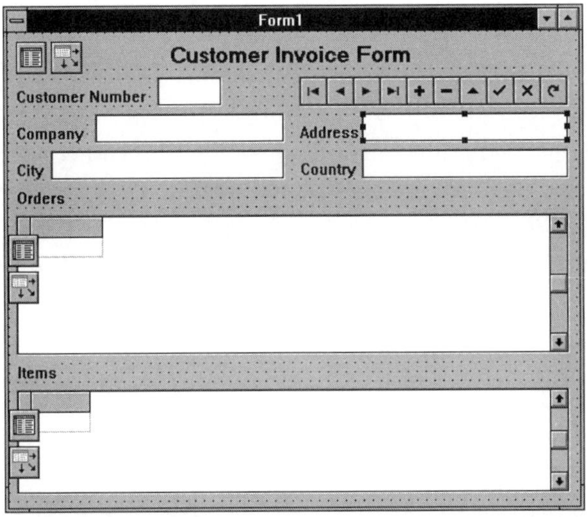

Fig. 10.22
These are the components it takes to create the LineItem application.

3. Select the TTable component in the upper left corner of your form (the component named Table1). Set the table's DatabaseName property to DBDEMOS, and connect the table to the CUSTOMER.DB table by setting its TableName property to CUSTOMER.DB. Then set the Active property of the Table1 component to true.

4. Connect the TDataSource component in the upper left corner of your form (named DataSource1) to the Table1 component by setting its DataSet property to Table1.

5. Connect the TDBNavigator component in the upper right corner to DataSource1 by setting its DataSource property to DataSource1.

6. Connect the four TDBEdit components on your form to the Company, City, Addr1, and Country fields of TTable1 by setting their DataSource property to DataSource1 and setting their DataField properties to the appropriate fields in the CUSTOMER.DB table.

7. Select the TTable component in the left center portion of your design form (the TTable component named Table2). Set the table's DatabaseName component to DBDEMOS. Then set Table2's TableName property to ORDERS.DB, and set the Active property of the Table2 component to true.

Tip
To make the typefaces on your data grids match those shown in figure 10.22, set the Font property to MS Sans Serif, 8 point regular, and the TitleFont property to MS Sans Serif, 8 point bold.

8. Set the DataSource property of the TDataSource component in the middle of your form (named DataSource2) to the Table2 component.

9. Connect the TDataGrid component labeled Orders in the center of your form to DataSource2 by setting the grid component's DataSource property to DataSource2. Notice that information about customers' orders then appears inside the data grid component.

10. Select the TTable component in the bottom left corner of your design form (the TTable component named Table3). Set its DatabaseName property to DBDEMOS. Then set Table3's TableName property to ITEMS.DB, DatabaseName property to DBDEMOS, and Active property to true.

11. Connect the TDataSource component in the bottom left corner of your form (DataSource3) to Table3.

12. Connect the TDataGrid component labeled Items to DataSource3. Data should now appear in all the data controls on your form (see fig. 10.23).

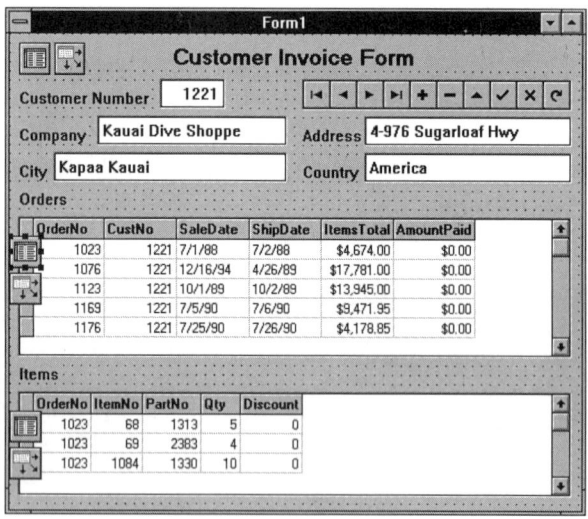

Fig. 10.23
When all the data control components on the Customer Invoice Form are connected to TDataSource components, data appears inside all the data controls.

13. Save the LineItem application in its current stage of development and execute it to see if you've done everything right so far.

Customizing Fields with the DataSet Designer

To make the LineItem application do everything it's supposed to, you have to add some controls to the Customer Invoice Form and customize some others.

You'll do most of this work with Delphi's DataSet Designer. First, to tweak some of the fields shown in the Orders grid and to edit the order in which the fields are displayed, follow these steps:

1. Double-click the TTable component in the left center portion of your form (the component named Table2). The DataSet Designer appears.

2. In the DataSet Designer window, click the Define button.

3. Delphi displays the Define Field dialog. Define a CurrencyField named Balance by selecting the CurrencyField item in the Field Type list and typing **Balance** in the Field Name text box. Delphi automatically fills in what it considers an appropriate component name (see fig. 10.24). (You can change the component name to something you like better if you want, but for this exercise accept Delphi's default name, Table2Balance).

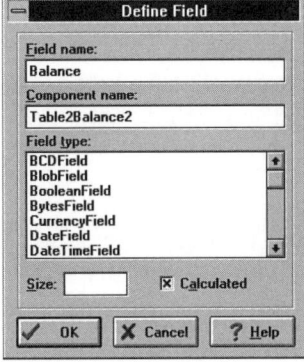

Fig. 10.24
When you type a field name, Delphi assigns a default component name.

4. Make sure the Calculated check box at the bottom of the dialog is selected.

5. Click OK to close the Define Field dialog. When the DataSet Designer window reappears, notice that Balance now appears in the Fields list box.

6. Open the Add Fields dialog by clicking the DataSet Designer's Add button.

7. From the Available Fields list box, Ctrl+click these database fields: OrderNo, CustNo, SaleDate, ShipDate, ItemsTotal, AmountPaid, and Balance.

8. Click OK to close the Add Fields dialog. Notice that the fields you selected in step 8 now appear in the Fields list box.

9. By dragging and dropping, arrange the items in the Fields list box in the order shown in figure 10.25.

Fig. 10.25
Drag and drop the items in the Fields list box to arrange them into this order.

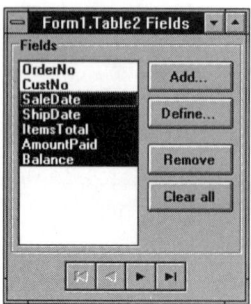

10. Close the DataSet Designer window by clicking its control box.

Merging Information from Two Tables

Now it's time to join the ORDERS.DB table to the CUSTOMERS.DB table so that their data can be merged and their displays synchronized. To merge information from the ORDERS and CUSTOMERS tables, follow these steps:

1. In the `Table2` component's Object Inspector window, set the `MasterSource` property to `DataSource1` and then double-click the ellipsis button next to the `MasterFields` property. Delphi opens the Field Link Designer dialog (see fig. 10.26). The Field Link Designer, as you might guess from its name, is a Delphi tool you can use to link database fields.

Fig. 10.26
With the Field Link Designer, you can combine information from different database tables.

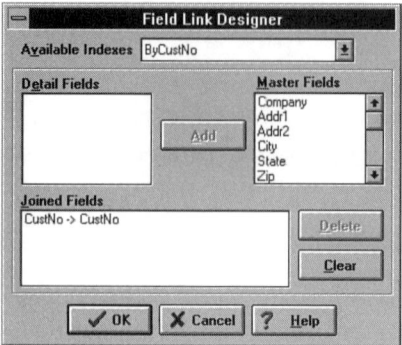

2. From the Field Link Designer dialog, select ByCustNo from the Available Indexes drop-down list. Notice that the name of the `CustNo` field then appears in the Detail Fields list box.

3. To link the `CustNo` field in the CUSTOMER database to the `CustNo` field in the ORDERS database, select CustNo in both the Detail Fields list box and the Master Fields list box, and then click the Add button. Delphi responds by placing this message in the Joined Field list box:

   ```
   CustNo -> CustNo
   ```

   This message means that Delphi has joined the Orders grid with the Customers table in such a way that the contents of the Orders grid changes each time a new customer number is selected in the CUSTOMERS database.

   The Field Link Designer dialog should now look like the one shown earlier in figure 10.26.

4. Click OK to close the Field Link Designer dialog.

5. To link the Items grid at the bottom of the Customer Invoice Form to the Orders grid in the middle of the form, select the `Table2` component in the center left portion of the form, and set the table's `MasterSource` property to `DataSource1`. Then, using the same procedures you followed in steps 1 through 3, set `Table2`'s `MasterFields` component to the `CustNo` field of the CUSTOMER.DB table (`Table1`).

6. Save your work up to this point.

7. Execute the LineItem application in its current state.

Notice that when you navigate through names of customers by clicking arrows in the application's DBNavigator control, the information in the Orders table changes to show orders shipped to the specified customer. Also notice the small arrow to the left of the OrderNo field on the Orders grid. When you move that arrow up and down to point to different records in the Orders grid, the contents of the Items grid at the bottom of the form change to show the items that were shipped to the specified customer in the order to which the arrow is pointing.

Reformatting Database Fields

Notice that the Items grid on the Customer Invoice Form has a field labeled Discount. Discounts are usually expressed as percentage, but the Discount field isn't formatted to display numbers followed by a percent sign. You can easily fix that by customizing the display format of the Discount field. To display the Discount field in the Items table as a percentage figure, follow these steps:

1. Open the DataSet Designer and select the Discount field.

2. Notice that the information in the Object Inspector window changes to display the properties of the Discount field. In the Object Inspector window, set the `DisplayFormat` property to

    `0.##%`

    As soon as the `DisplayFormat` property in the Object Inspector window loses focus, notice that Delphi reformats the data in the Discount field into a percentage format.

3. Save your files if you like, and then run the LineItem application.

Calculating Values of Fields

In the next exercise, you add an important feature to the LineItem application: the capability to display fields that aren't supplied by a database table but are dynamically calculated at runtime. In the exercise, you customize the Balance field of the ORDERS table. When you complete this exercise, your application will calculate and display each customer's current balance in the Balance field at runtime.

To equip your application with this kind of data-calculation capability, follow these steps:

1. Double-click the `Table2` component at the left center of your form to display the DataSet Designer.

2. In the DataSet Designer window, click the Define button. Delphi displays the Define Field dialog.

3. Define a calculated CurrencyField named `Balance`.

4. Click OK to close the Define Field dialog.

5. When the DataSet Designer window reappears, click the Add button. Delphi displays the Add Fields dialog.

6. Select the following fields in the Available fields list box: OrderNo, CustNo, SaleDate, ShipDate, ItemsTotal, and AmountPaid. Then click OK.

7. When the DataSet Designer window reappears, rearrange the fields in the Fields list box in the order shown in figure 10.27.

Creating the LineItem Application   **275**

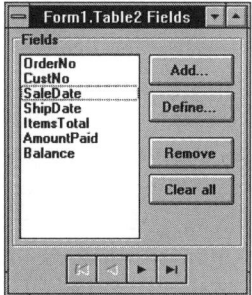

Fig. 10.27
Arrange the fields in the Orders table by dragging and dropping their names in the Fields list box.

8. Close the DataSet Designer by clicking its control box.

9. Double-click the `Table2` component (the `TTable` component in the left center portion of the Customer Invoice Form). Delphi opens the DataSet Designer.

10. In the Object Inspector window, click the Events tab.

11. Double-click the `OnCalcFields` event. The Code Editor opens at a procedure named `TForm1.Table2CalcFields`.

12. Type the following Pascal statement between the `begin` and `end` delimiters (see fig. 1.28):

    ```
    Table2Balance.Value :=
        Table1ItemsTotal.Value - Table2AmountPaid.Value;
    ```

When you implement the preceding statement as part of a table's `OnCalcFields` event, Delphi executes the procedure each time information in the specified table changes. The statement you have written then sets the value of the Balance field in `Table2` to the difference between the ItemsTotal field and the AmountPaid field in the same table (see fig. 10.28).

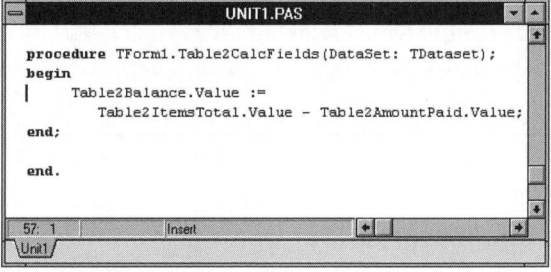

Fig. 10.28
This code calculates the value of the Balance field in the Orders table.

Linking a Table to a DBEdit Control

The LineItem application is almost finished, but it's missing one important ingredient. At this stage of your application's development, the Customer Invoice Form provides a wealth of information about orders that have been shipped to various customers. It also shows a lot of information about those orders and about the payments customers have made. It even tells you the part numbers of items you have shipped to your customers in each order. Unfortunately, it doesn't translate part numbers into part descriptions, so unless you know the part number of every item you sell, you can't tell from the Customer Invoice Form what items of merchandise you have shipped to your customers in each order. In the final exercise of this chapter, you correct that flaw.

In the sample database tables that come with Delphi, there's a two-field table—named PARTS.DB—that simply lists the part number of every item in the ITEMS table and describes the part that's listed. To add the names of parts to your Customer Invoice Form, you merely have to obtain the description of each part from the PARTS table. Then you have to add the part description to your invoice from.

There are many ways to combine data from different tables and display it. The following steps use a simple technique that doesn't require any SQL commands:

1. Use the DataSet Designer to reduce the widths of the fields. Make each field just five or six characters wide to narrow the width of the Items table.

2. Move the narrowed Items grid to the left and place five components to the right of the grid: a standard TLabel component, a TDBEdit component, a TTable component, and a TDataSource component. Set the caption of the TLabel component to read Part Description.

3. Use the techniques you learned in the previous exercises to link the new TTable component (Table4) to the sample PARTS.DB table and connect the new TDataSource component (DataSource4) to Table4.

4. Set the DataSource property of the new TDBEdit component to DataSource4, and set the TDBEdit component's DataField property to Description.

5. Set Table4's Active property to true. Text then appears inside the new TDBEdit component (see fig. 10.29).

Creating the LineItem Application **277**

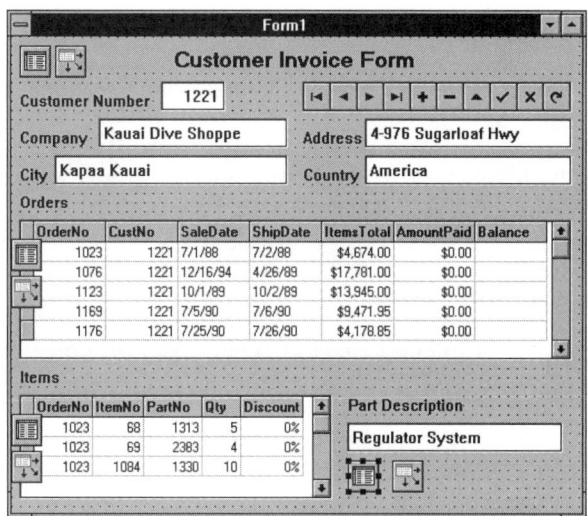

Fig. 10.29
Narrow the width of the Items grid and place some new components next to it.

6. The LineItem application is now finished. Execute it and you'll see a screen display like the one shown in figure 10.30. Notice that when you move the arrow next to the Items grid up and down, the Part Description text box displays the description of the part next to the arrow.

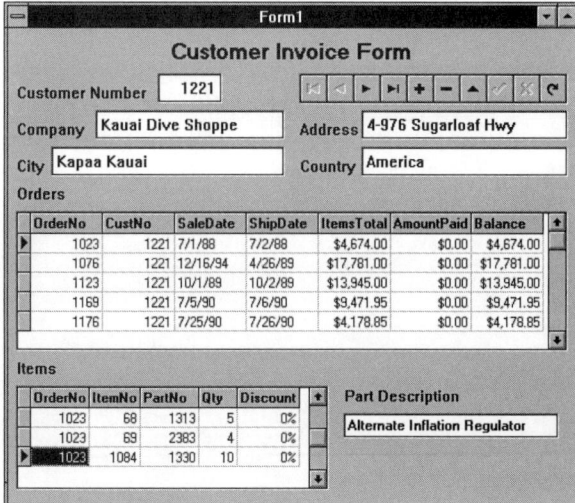

Fig. 10.30
The LineItem application displays this screen when you execute it.

From Here...

For more information about Delphi's database-related features and capabilities, refer to the following chapters:

- Chapter 5, "Using Non-Visual Components," is a closer examination of components that don't create visible controls.

- Chapter 6, "Using Data-Bound Components," examines data control components in more detail.

- Chapter 12, "Using the Database Desktop," shows how to use Delphi's Database Desktop tool to create, edit, and modify database tables.

- Chapter 13, "Reporting with ReportSmith," shows how to design and create printed reports of database data.

Chapter 11

Using the Browser

Delphi's Browser is a tool that helps you explore the wealth of features linked into your program without having to read thousands of lines of source code. The Browser lets you visually explore object hierarchies, list all symbol references, and list the units your program references. Figure 11.1 shows the Browser's display for a form.

> **Note**
>
> From the Browser's standpoint, a *symbol* can be just about anything, including objects, units, procedures, functions, global variables, and more. The Browser's speedbar contains filter icons that let you limit the types of symbols displayed.

As you can see in figure 11.1, the Browser is mainly made of two sections: on the left is the Inspector pane, and on the right is the Details pane. These panes display the symbols that are referenced in your program. The Browser's SpeedMenu controls the content of the Inspector pane, which can display objects, units, and globals. The Details pane always displays symbols related to the symbol selected in the Inspector pane. The three tabs at the bottom of the Details pane—Scope, Inheritance, and Reference—control the content of the pane.

In this chapter, you learn how to:

- Compile with Debug
- Set filters
- Use the Browser's SpeedMenu
- Navigate the Browser
- Configure the Browser

Fig. 11.1
Delphi's Browse Objects window lets you visually explore object hierarchies, symbol references, and units.

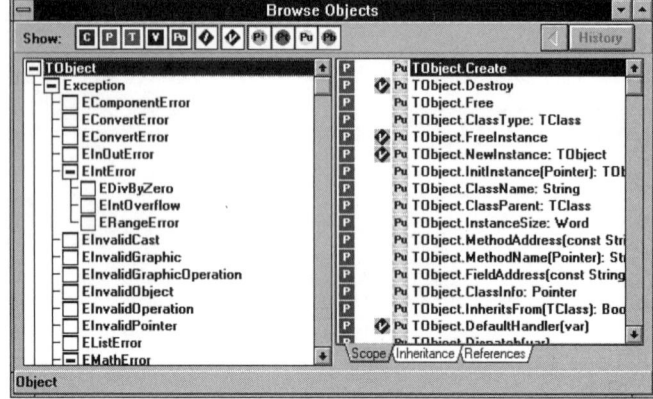

Compiling with Debug

Create a new Delphi project. Then open the View menu and choose Browser. You can't do it; the Browser command is grayed out and unavailable. A couple of things need to happen before you can use the Browser. First, your project must be compiled with debug information. By default, debug information is included, so compile the project by pressing Ctrl+F9. Now the Browser menu choice should be available.

To configure Delphi to include the debug information, open the Options menu and choose Project. Delphi displays the Project Options dialog. Select the Compiler tab to see the options shown in figure 11.2.

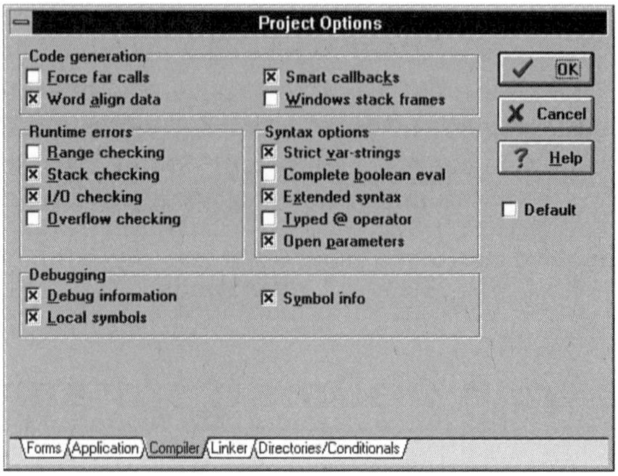

Fig. 11.2
Use the Compiler options in the Project Options dialog to include debug information.

In the Debugging section, turn on Debug Information, Local Symbols, and Symbol Info. This gives the Browser all the information it needs to display symbols. For more information on these options, see Chapter 15, "Using Delphi's Debugging Features."

Tip
The options you set in this dialog affect only the current project. To make these options the default for future projects, click the Default check box.

Using the Browser Window

The Browser is Delphi's way of providing the developer with a visual display of the objects, units, and symbols that make up a program. Even an empty form has a wealth of objects linked to it. The Browser provides you with a way of exploring these objects and can teach you about the very nature of OOP and Delphi.

Filters

The Browser displays *symbols*, which can be anything from variable declarations, to names of functions, to instances of objects. Because Delphi programs contain so many symbols, the Browser display can be unreadable when all the information is displayed. The Browser allows you to turn on and off filters that narrow the number of symbols displayed.

The filter icons are arranged in four independent groups. The first group identifies the symbol as a Constant, Function/Procedure, Type, Variable, or Property. A symbol can be any of these types, but it can't be more than one. The second and third groups each have only one icon: Inherited and Virtual, respectively. The fourth group identifies how a symbol is declared: Private, Protected, Public, or Published. A symbol can be declared in only one of these sections.

You can turn the filters on and off by clicking one of the 11 icons at the top of the Browse Objects window (see fig. 11.3). All the filters are turned off by default, meaning that they don't filter anything. When you turn a filter on, its icon changes appearance to look like a button, and the symbol lists are filtered.

The Constants Filter

The Constants filter lets you hide or reveal the display of constants. *Constants* are identifiers that can't change value during the life of a program. For example, virtual key codes are declared as constants. Figure 11.4 shows the

282 Chapter 11—Using the Browser

Browser with the constants declared in the WinTypes unit. All type filters are turned on except the Constants filter (that is, the Functions, Types, Variables, and Properties filters are turned on).

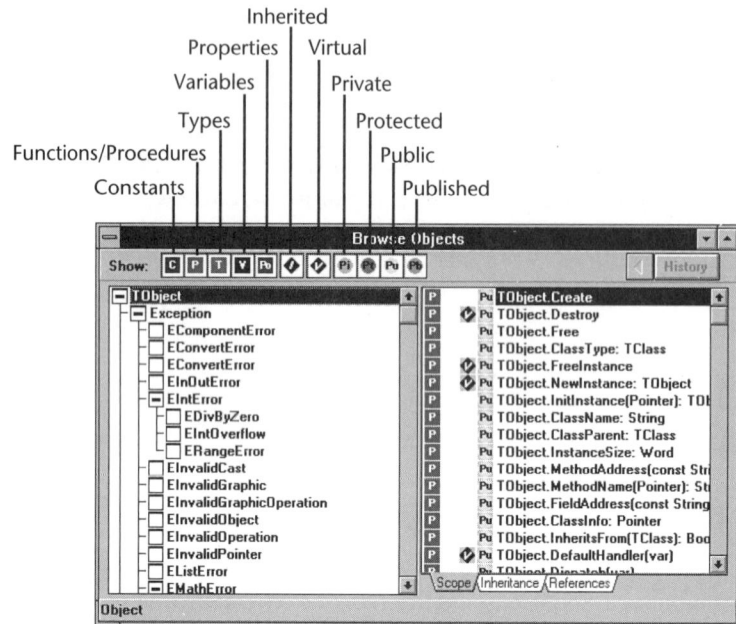

Fig. 11.3
Use the Compiler options in the Project Options dialog to include debug information.

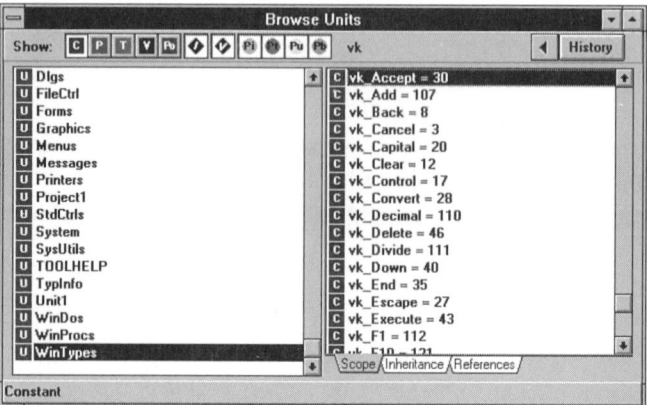

Fig. 11.4
Use the Browse Units window to display the constants declared within a unit.

The Functions/Procedures Filter

A *function* is a named block of code that returns a value; a *procedure* is a named block of code that doesn't return a value. By turning on all the type filters except the Functions/Procedures filter (that is, turning on the Constants, Types, Variables, and Properties filters), you can display the functions and procedures that are either declared or inherited by an object, as in figure 11.5.

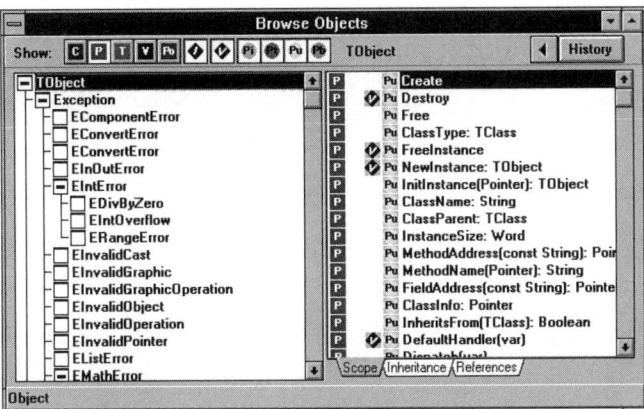

Fig. 11.5
You can view Functions/Procedures in the Browser.

You can use the Browser as a quick reference to the functions and procedures available for any type of object. For example, consider the shell code that Delphi provides for a button click method:

```
procedure TForm1.Button1Click(Sender: TObject);
begin

end;
```

As you can see, a Sender variable of type TObject is passed into the procedure. Often you write code that casts the Sender variable to a particular type and then references the properties and methods associated with that type. Sometimes, however, you need to write generic code that works with just the TObject type. To do so, you need to know what functions and procedures are defined for the TObject type. Figure 11.5 shows the Browser being used to list the functions and procedures associated with the TObject type.

The Types Filter

In Delphi, as in most programming languages, every variable has a "type." Common types are integer or TBitButton. The type of a variable determines the values the variable can contain and the operations that can be performed on the variable. In Delphi, you can use the predefined variable Types, or declare your own variable Types. Figure 11.6 shows the types that are declared within the Buttons unit.

Fig. 11.6
Use the Browser to display variable Types declared within a unit.

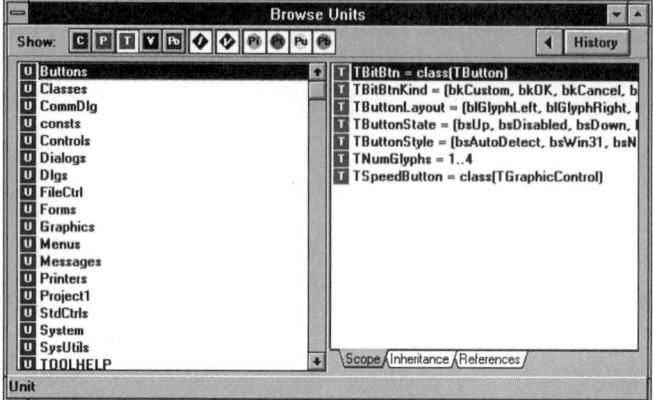

The Variables Filter

A *variable* is a symbolic name given to an area of memory. The name is referenced by programs to change the value of the memory location. The Browser shows variables that an object can reference. For example, figure 11.7 shows the variables declared in the TComponent object.

Fig. 11.7
Use the Browser to display the variables that an object can reference.

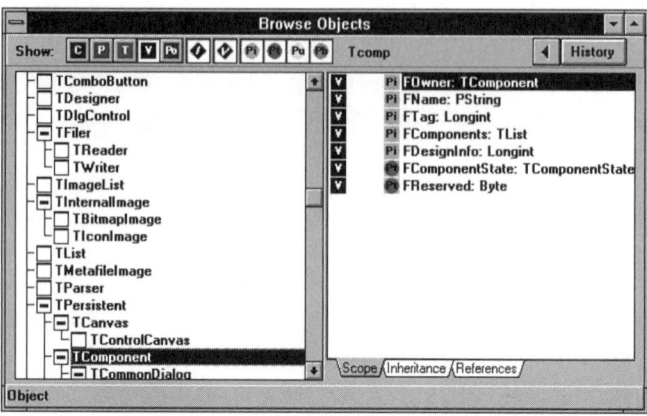

The Properties Filter

When designing Delphi forms, you have no doubt used the Object Inspector to set the properties of objects. But the Object Inspector shows only properties of an object that are published. You can use the Browser to see all the properties of a symbol. Figure 11.8 shows the properties of a button. Notice that certain properties such as `Color` appear in the Object Inspector, while other properties such as `Align` don't appear in the Object Inspector.

Tip
It's useful to turn off only one of the first five filters to display a particular kind of symbol, such as the Properties filter.

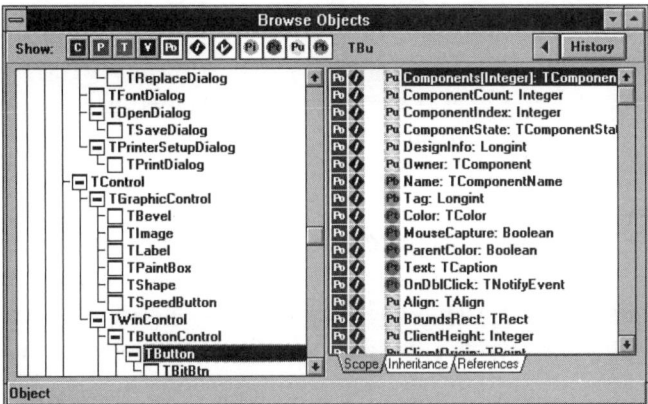

Fig. 11.8
The Browser shows properties of an object.

The Inherited Filter

Inheritance is one of the major features of OOP. With inheritance, you can create your own objects by inheriting many features of an existing object. In Delphi, all objects are descendants of the `TObject` type. With the Inherited filter turned off, you can see which symbols are inherited. With the Inherited filter turned on, you can see which symbols are created within an object. Figure 11.9 shows that the procedure `SetFocus` is inherited from `TWinControl`, while the procedure `TButton.Click` isn't inherited.

Fig. 11.9
The Browser showing inheritance.

The Virtual Filter

Polymorphism is another important aspect of OOP programming. *Polymorphism* is a method's capability to perform different actions, depending on the type of object that called the method. For example, `Cat.noise()` would cause a meow, while `Dog.noise()` would cause a bark. In Delphi, polymorphism is implemented through virtual methods. The address of a virtual method isn't determined at compile time but is looked up at runtime. When an object declares a method as virtual, it means descendants of that object can override the method.

The Virtual filter lets you use the Browser to either filter out or display virtual methods. Figure 11.9 shows that `TButton.Click` is virtual while `TButton.CNCommand` isn't virtual.

The Private Filter

Most objects have inner workings that shouldn't be accessible to users. To hide fields, methods, and functions from users, the fields, methods, and functions are declared private. Only code located in the same unit has access to private functions. By turning off the Private filter, you can view symbols in Browser that are declared private. Figure 11.9 shows that `TButton.SetDefault` is private.

The Protected Filter

Some components have parts that must be protected from the user but still be available to descendants of the component. These parts are declared protected. By turning off the Protected filter, you can view symbols in the Browser that are declared protected. Figure 11.9 shows that `TButton.CreateWnd` is protected.

The Public Filter

Public parts of a component have no special restrictions. Code that has access to a component can call that component's public methods and access that component's public properties. Turning off the Public filter allows you to view symbols in the Browser that are declared public. Figure 11.9 shows that `TButton.Create` is public.

The Published Filter

The published parts of a component are available not only to code that accesses a component, but also on Delphi's Object Inspector. Turn off the Published filter to view symbols in the Browser that are declared published. Figure 11.10 shows that `TButton.Caption` is a published property.

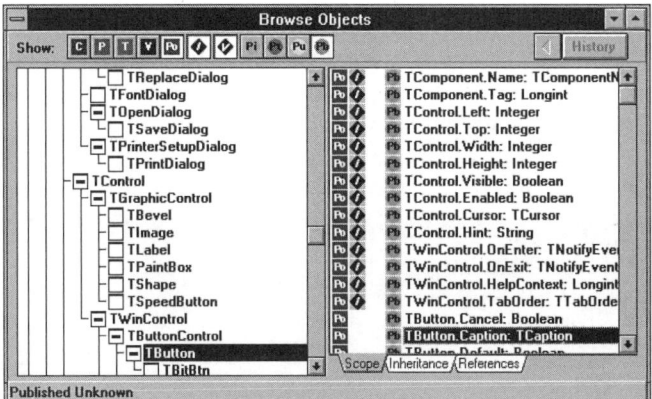

Fig. 11.10
The Browser shows published properties.

The Browser's SpeedMenu

Like all the windows in Delphi, the Browser provides a SpeedMenu that gives you quick access to options. Simply right-click in the Browser window or press Alt+F10, and the SpeedMenu in figure 11.11 appears.

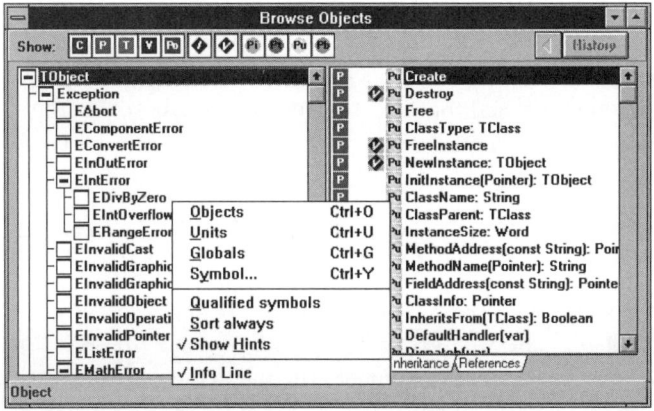

Fig. 11.11
You can configure the Browser on the fly with its SpeedMenu.

The Objects Command

The first choice on the Browser's SpeedMenu is Objects, which causes the Browser to display the Object Tree in the Inspector pane (refer to fig. 11.1). Most of the time this display is static and doesn't change as you add standard components to your program. This is because Delphi links the code for all the standard components by default. You can use this feature to create standard components on the fly during runtime.

The Units Command

A Delphi *unit* is a single disk file of source code. Units are used to break large sections of code into manageable modules. To view the units that are linked to your program, choose Units from the Browser's SpeedMenu. The Browser displays the units in the Inspector pane, as shown in figure 11.12.

Fig. 11.12
Use the Browser to display the units linked to a program.

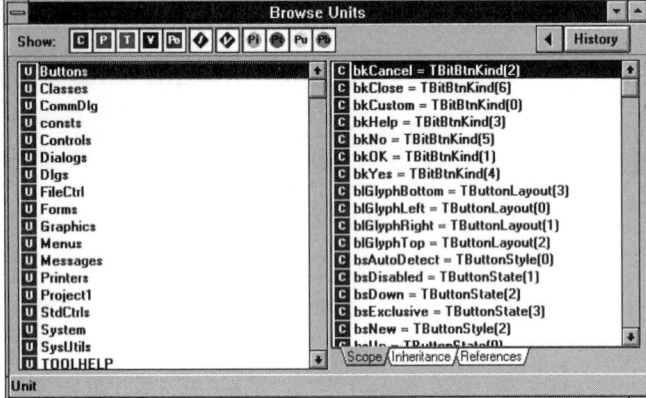

As you can see, Delphi links a rich set of units into your program by default. If you need to access functions in a unit that isn't linked to your program by default, you must add that unit to your uses clause. For example, to play a .WAV sound file, you must add a MMSystem unit to your uses clause, as follows:

```
uses
    SysUtils, WinTypes, WinProcs, Messages, Classes, Graphics,
    Controls, Forms, Dialogs, StdCtrls, MMSystem;
```

MMSystem is a unit that passes function calls between Delphi and MMSYSTEM.DLL, the Microsoft Windows Multimedia API. To actually play the .WAV file, create a button and add the following code to its OnClick method:

```
procedure TForm1.Button1Click(Sender: TObject);
begin
  sndPlaySound('C:\windows\ding.wav',0);
end;
```

Run the form and click the button you created; your machine dings. Bring up the Browser, open the SpeedMenu, and choose Units. Notice the units list contains the MMSystem unit. While displaying the units, the Details pane can provide useful information. For example, figure 11.13 shows the Browser with the MMSystem unit selected. The Details pane shows all the function calls and procedure calls in the unit. Your program has access to all these functions and procedures.

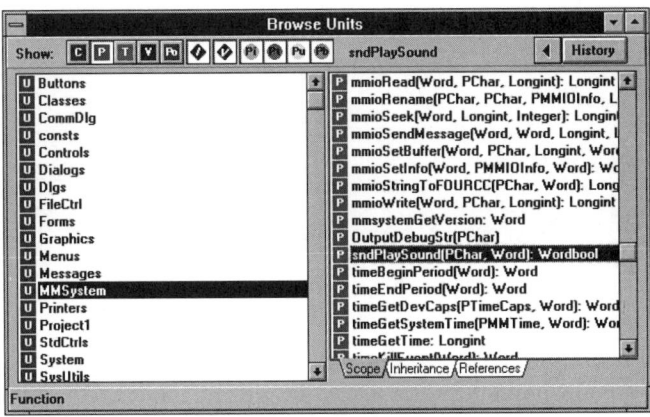

Fig. 11.13
You can make several multimedia calls, including sndPlaySound.

Each standard unit linked to your system is precompiled. The units exist as .DCU (Delphi Compiled Unit) files in your \DELPHI\BIN directory. Check out a listing of the units in that directory. If you find one that you're unfamiliar with, add the unit to your uses clause and recompile your program. Then use the Browser to explore the unit and see what it contains.

When you create a new form in Delphi and compile it, Delphi creates two units: Project1 and Unit1. These two units appear as tabs on the Code Editor window and are compiled to PROJECT1.DCU and UNIT1.DCU in the current directory. These two units also appear in the units listing in the Browser's Inspector pane. This is very useful for examining the symbols that are directly accessed by your program.

The Globals Command

Global symbols are symbols that have scope in more than one function. Symbols are made global when they are declared in the Interface section of a unit. They're available for use in any function, procedure, or method. To see the global symbols available for use in your program, open the Browser's SpeedMenu and choose Globals. The Browser displays a list of global symbols and information about each symbol's type or parameters. For a new form, the Browser display looks like the Browse Globals window shown in figure 11.14.

Fig. 11.14
The Browse Globals window shows global symbols.

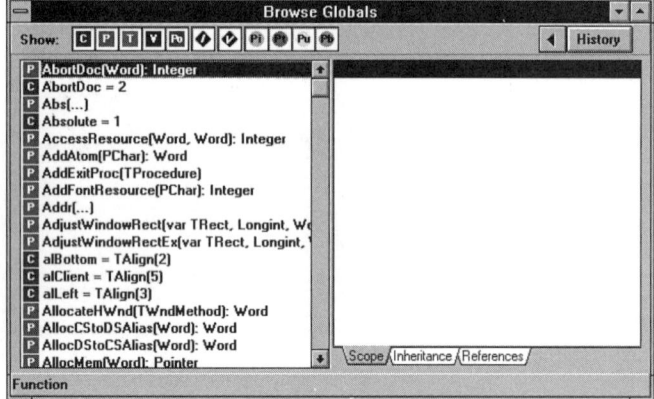

Consider the following code example, which is for a form with two buttons and a label. The first button, Increment, increases the value displayed in the label. The second button, Decrement, decreases the value displayed in the label.

```
unit Globalu;

interface
uses
  SysUtils, WinTypes, WinProcs, Messages, Classes, Graphics,
  Controls, Forms, Dialogs, StdCtrls;

type
  TForm1 = class(TForm)
    Increment: TButton;
    Decrement: TButton;
    Label1: TLabel;
    procedure IncrementClick(Sender: TObject);
    procedure DecrementClick(Sender: TObject);
    procedure FormCreate(Sender: TObject);
  private
    { Private declarations }
  public
    { Public declarations }
  end;

var
  Form1: TForm1;
  Value: integer;

implementation

{$R *.DFM}

procedure TForm1.IncrementClick(Sender: TObject);
begin
  inc(value);
```

```
  Label1.Caption:=inttostr(Value);
end;

procedure TForm1.DecrementClick(Sender: TObject);
begin
dec(Value);
Label1.caption:=inttostr(Value);
end;

procedure TForm1.FormCreate(Sender: TObject);
begin
  Value:=0;
  Label1.caption:=inttostr(Value);
end;

end.
```

The preceding code uses the global variable Value to store the value that's now being displayed by the label. The Browser shows this global symbol in figure 11.15.

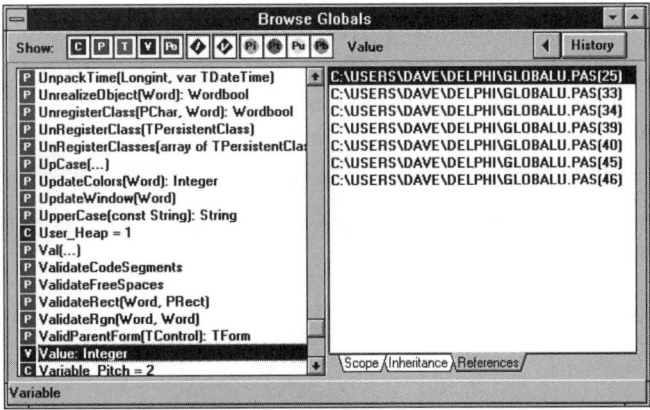

Fig. 11.15
Use the Browser to show a global symbol from custom code.

> **Note**
>
> In real use, the Value variable shouldn't be declared as a global because it isn't being accessed outside the form. The preceding code should be modified so that the variable declaration comes within the form class declaration. To do this, move the existing Value declaration to the private section, as follows:
>
> ```
> private
>    { Private declarations }
>      Value: integer;
> ```
>
> In this case, Value isn't global and therefore doesn't appear in the Browser's global symbol listing.

Chapter 11—Using the Browser

The Symbol Command

As you can see, the Browser display is rather crowded with information in its default display. Using filters can help narrow the display, but sometimes a single symbol needs investigation. To find and display a single symbol, open the Browser's SpeedMenu and choose Symbol. The Browser displays the Browse Symbol dialog shown in figure 11.16.

Fig. 11.16
You can use the Symbol command to search for a single symbol within the Browser.

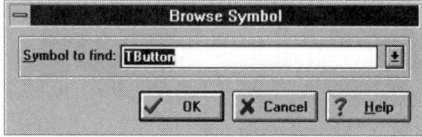

After you type or select the symbol that you want to search for, click OK. The Browser displays that symbol—and only that symbol—in the Inspector pane (see fig. 11.17). The Browse Symbol dialog keeps a history list of past symbols that you've searched for. To cycle through each of your previous searches, press ↓ or ↑. To see a list of past searches, click the drop-down arrow in the dialog. Note that the searches aren't case-sensitive, so don't worry about matching the exact case of the symbol name.

Fig. 11.17
The symbol search works only in the Inspector pane.

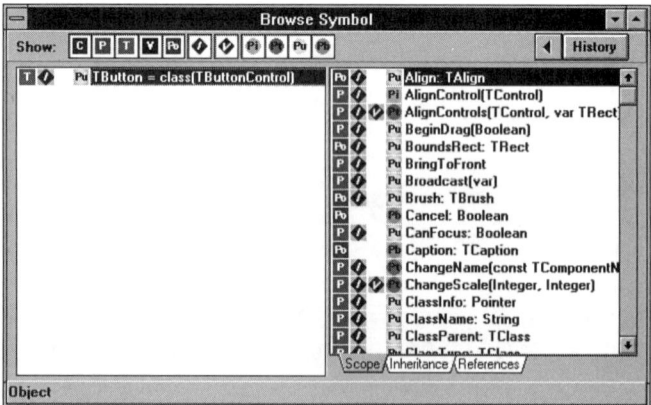

The symbol search works only in the Inspector pane. Even if you click the Details pane first, the symbol search still searches the Inspector pane. The symbol search can search on either Objects, Units, or Globals according to the current view in the Inspector pane.

The Qualified Symbols Command

Qualified Symbols—one of the Browser SpeedMenu's choices—affects the display of the Inspector and Details panes, but only when symbols are displayed. You can toggle Qualified Symbols off (refer to fig. 11.11) or on (see fig. 11.18).

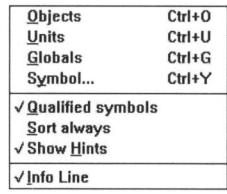

Fig. 11.18
Toggle the Qualified Symbols menu choice on to get more information about each symbol.

It has no effect on the Object Tree, Units, Globals, Inheritance, or References screens. With Qualified Symbols turned off, symbols are displayed with just their name, type, and parameters. With Qualified Symbols turned on, symbols are displayed with all the previously listed information, plus the base class in which the symbol was declared (see fig. 11.19).

Fig. 11.19
The Browser showing the base class in which a symbol is declared.

In figure 11.19, TControl is the qualified part, while SetVisible is the symbol. Turn on Qualified Symbols to help you find the source code that implements a given symbol. If, for example, you're interested in how the Visible property of a BitButton is set, bring up the Browser, find TBitBtn in the Object Tree, and find SetVisible in the Details pane. Turn on Qualified Symbols, and the Browser displays the screen shown in figure 11.19. Qualified Symbols shows you quickly that the SetVisible procedure is declared in the TControl object.

294 Chapter 11—Using the Browser

Without the Qualified Symbols option, you would have had to check the source code for the TButton, TButtonControl, and TWinControl objects, only to find that SetVisible is inherited in all these objects from TControl.

The Sort Always Command

Like Qualified Symbols, Sort Always is a toggle menu choice that can be turned off (refer to fig. 11.11) or on (see fig. 11.20).

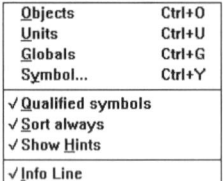

Fig. 11.20
Toggle the Sort Always menu choice on to display symbols in alphabetical order.

With Sort Always turned off, the Browser doesn't sort the symbols, but instead displays them in the order they're declared within the source code. In figure 11.21, for example, the source code to STDCTRLS.PAS is shown in the Code Editor and the symbols from that unit are shown in the Browser. As you can see, the variables are declared and displayed in the same order.

Fig. 11.21
The Browser can show symbols in declarative order.

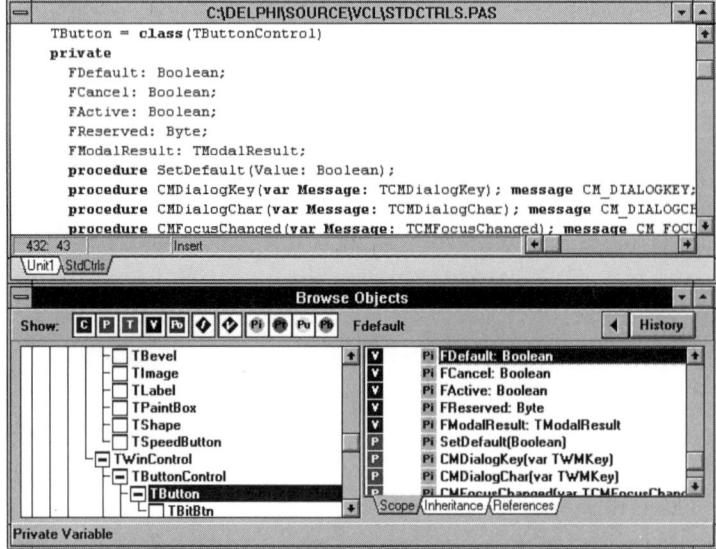

With Sort Always turned on, the Browser displays the symbols in alphabetical order. The Browser doesn't sort the qualified name of the symbol, so the Qualified Symbols command has no effect on the sort order. Sort Always has no effect on the Object Tree, Units, Globals, Inheritance, and References screens.

The Show Hints Command

The Show Hints SpeedMenu choice also is a toggle. With Show Hints turned on, the Browser displays the name of each filter button if the mouse pointer lingers over that button (see fig. 11.22).

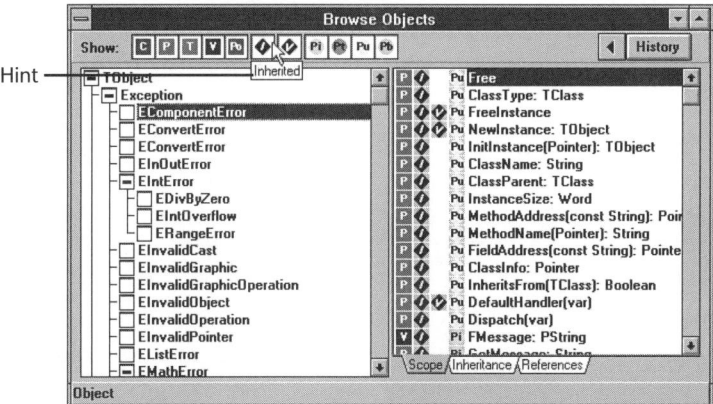

Fig. 11.22
Help hints are available for filter buttons.

If filter hints bother you, you can turn them off by toggling Show Hints. Most of the time the hints are a convenient reference and should remain turned on.

The Info Line Command

The fact that the Browser displays objects, variable functions, and procedures on the same screen can be mystifying. At first glance, it's often hard to discern what type of symbol you're viewing. The Info line in the bottom-left corner of the Browser window helps avoid some of the mystery by displaying a written version of the symbol type. In figure 11.23, for example, a public virtual inherited procedure is selected and the Info line displays an appropriate message.

Fig. 11.23
The Info line shows you what kind of symbol is selected.

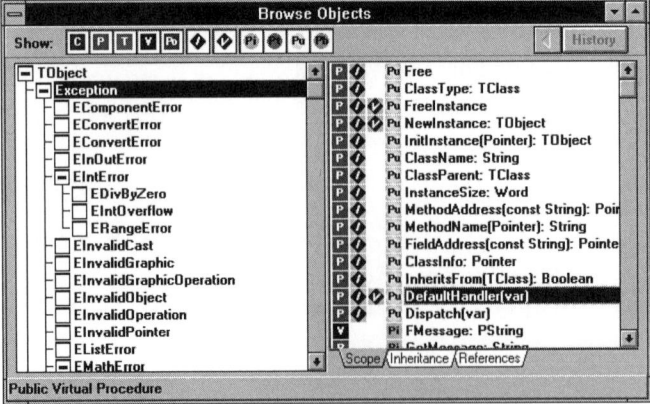

If you don't want the Info line displayed, toggle it off by using the Info Line command on the SpeedMenu. By doing this, you gain enough space to display one more line of symbols. Usually it's best to leave the Info line turned on, however.

The Previous Button

As you drill down through symbols, investigating a particular line of inheritance, you may eventually reach a dead end. To step back one level and view the symbol you were previously viewing, click the Previous button. The Previous button is the button with the left-pointing triangle, next to the History button near the top right corner of the Browser window. You can step back through as many levels as the Browser has recorded.

The History Button

The Browser keeps a history list of each symbol you investigate. If you need to reselect a symbol, click the History button in the upper-right corner of the Browser window. The Browser displays the Object Browser History dialog (see fig. 11.24). Select the symbol that you're interested in and click OK. The Browser finds and selects that symbol.

The Scope Tab

When you select the Scope tab on the Details pane, you see the symbols associated with the symbol selected in the Inspector pane. If you select TButton in the Inspector pane, for example, the symbols within the scope of the TButton are displayed in the Details pane (see fig. 11.25).

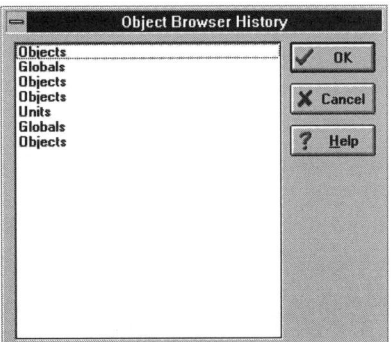

Fig. 11.24
Use the History button to display a list of the symbols you've browsed.

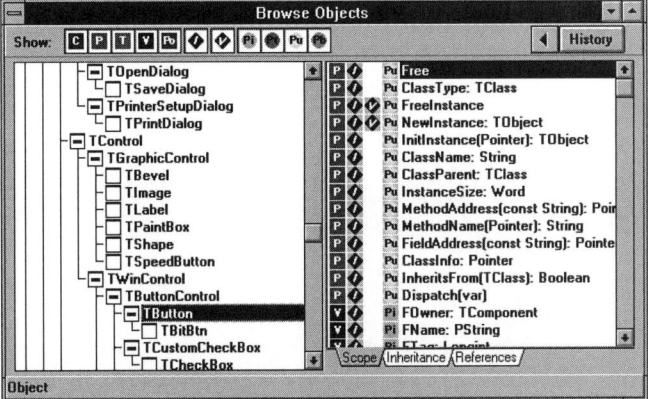

Fig. 11.25
The symbols within the scope of the TButton object.

Each symbol has as many as four icons next to it. The following is a brief description of each icon:

- The first icon represents the type of the symbol.

- The second icon is present only if the symbol is inherited from a parent.

- The third icon is present only if the symbol is a virtual symbol.

- The fourth icon tells you in what section of the source code the symbol is declared: Private, Protected, Public, or Published.

For more information on each icon's meaning, see the "Filters" section earlier in this chapter.

The Inheritance Tab

Select the Inheritance tab on the Details pane to see the object tree associated with the symbol selected in the Inspector pane. To see the object tree associated with the TControl symbol, for example, select TControl in the Inspector pane and click the Inheritance tab. The Browser shows the parent of TControl as well as its children (see fig. 11.26).

Fig. 11.26
The Browser can show the inheritance of a symbol.

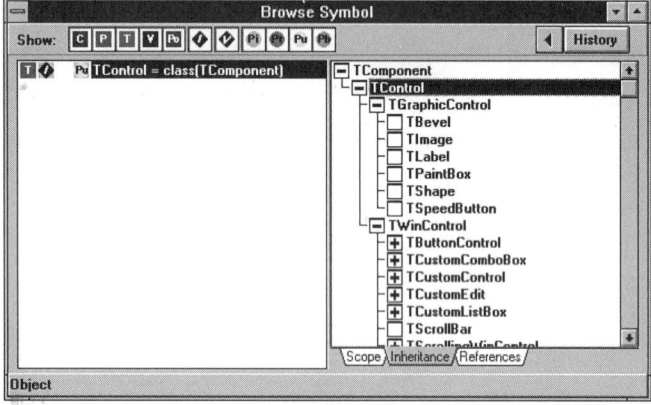

The References Tab

Tip
Double-click a reference, and the Browser brings the associated source code in the Code Editor.

Every symbol you display in the Browser is declared somewhere in the source code. Select the References tab on the Details pane to display a listing of source code references to the symbol selected in the Inspector pane. Figure 11.27 shows that UNIT1.PAS makes five references to TButton. The Browser displays the complete path to the source code file. This is convenient in large projects that have code in many directories. Each number in parentheses indicates the line number of the code that refers to the symbol.

Fig. 11.27
Source code references to the TButton symbol.

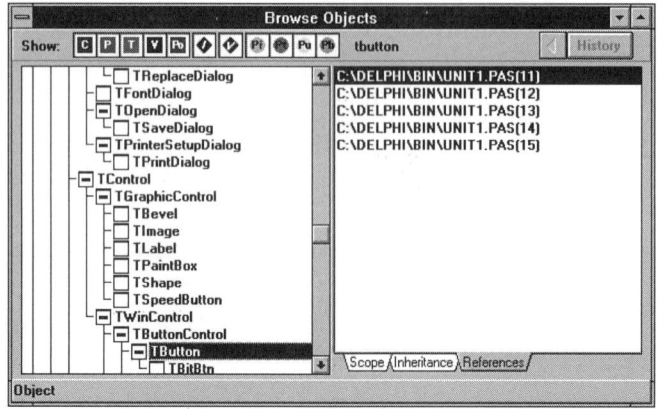

Navigating the Browser

The Browser has several features, which aren't readily apparent, that make it a useful tool. The Browser does incremental searching, has a number of keyboard shortcuts, and allows you to adjust the size of its window panes.

Typing to Find a Symbol

Although you can find a symbol by choosing Symbol from the SpeedMenu, that symbol is displayed without its parents. But here is an easy way to find a symbol that doesn't orphan the symbol:

  1. Select the pane with the symbol you're looking for by clicking that pane.

  2. Just start typing the name of the symbol at any time while the Browser is active.

As you type each character of the symbol's name, the Browser does an incremental search. The characters you type are displayed in the area to the right of the filter buttons. For example, if you want to find the TShape object in the object tree, click the object tree pane and type **TShape**. As you type, the Browser closes in on the TShape symbol (see fig. 11.28).

Tip
If the symbol for which you're looking isn't unique, press Ctrl+N and the Browser finds the next symbol that begins with the characters you typed.

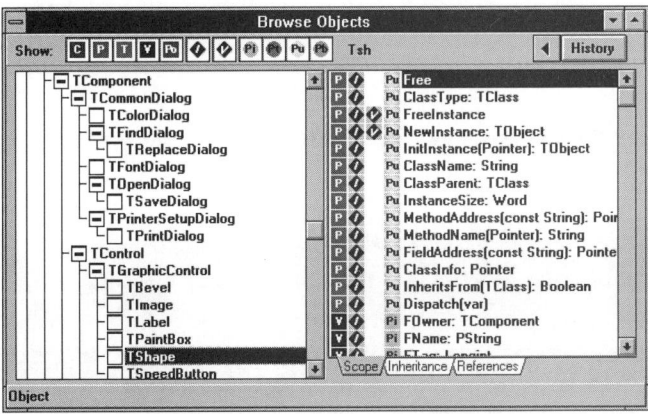

Fig. 11.28
You can find a symbol in the Browser just by typing its name.

Using the Enter Key

The Browser reacts to the Enter key differently depending on the current pane. In the Inspector pane, pressing Enter moves the symbols in the Details pane into the Inspector pane. The Details pane is updated with the details of the new symbol selected in the Inspector pane. You can think of this as *drilling down* into a symbol. For example, find TButton on the Inspector pane and press Enter. The Browser moves symbols associated with the TButton symbol into the Inspector pane (see fig. 11.29). Because FOwner is the first symbol declared in TButton (if the Functions/Procedures filter is turned on), FOwner becomes the current symbol. Because FOwner is a TComponent type, the symbols in TComponent are displayed in the Details pane. This pane shows the exact symbols that are displayed when you select TComponent from the Object Tree in the Inspector window.

Fig. 11.29
TButton has a TComponent symbol that has its own symbols.

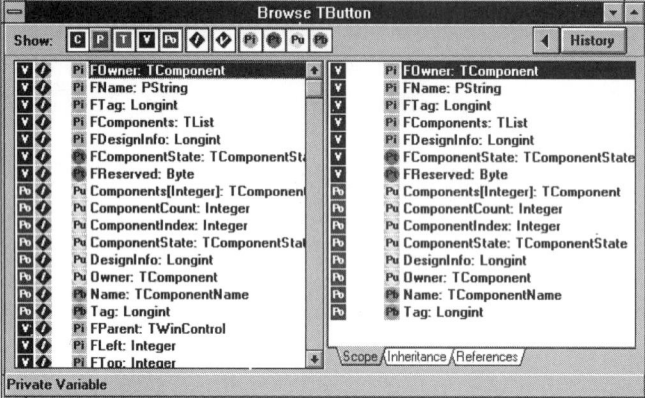

On the Details pane with the References tab selected, pressing Enter forces the Browser to find the declaration of the selected symbol in the source code. The Code Editor is given focus and the declaration line is highlighted. This works only for source code in the current project. Because many symbols displayed by the Browser are symbols from the VCL libraries, pressing Enter on most symbols doesn't have any effect.

Using Keyboard Shortcuts

You can use the keys in table 11.1 to navigate the Browser.

Table 11.1	Keys Used to Navigate the Browser
Key	Description
↑	Moves the highlight up one symbol. If you're in the Inspector pane, the Details pane is updated to reflect the new symbol.
↓	Moves the highlight down one symbol. If you're in the Inspector pane, the Details pane is updated to reflect the new symbol.

Key	Description
Ctrl+↑	Scrolls the current pane down one line without selecting a different symbol.
Ctrl+↓	Scrolls the current pane up one line without selecting a different symbol.
Ctrl+Page Up	The first visible symbol in the current pane becomes the selected symbol.
Ctrl+Page Down	The last visible symbol in the current pane becomes the selected symbol.
Home	Selects the first symbol in the current pane. If that symbol is off the screen, the pane is scrolled appropriately.
End	Selects the last symbol in the current pane. If that symbol is off the screen, the pane is scrolled appropriately.
+	In the Inspector screen with the Object Tree displayed, pressing + expands the Object Tree associated with the current symbol.
–	In the Inspector screen with the Object Tree displayed, pressing – collapses the Object Tree associated with the current symbol.
*	When you expand an Object Tree with the + key, the tree expands only one level. If that level has expanded trees, those trees are displayed—but collapsed trees on that level aren't expanded. To expand all the levels and sublevels of an Object Tree, press *.
Page Up	Selects the symbol that's one visual page above the currently selected symbol. The pane is scrolled appropriately to display the new symbol.
Page Down	Selects the symbol that's one visual page below the currently selected symbol. The pane is scrolled appropriately to display the new symbol.
Tab	Moves control between the Inspector pane and the Details pane.

While using these navigation techniques, Delphi keeps the code window in sync with selected symbols, when possible. This happens in the Inspector and Details panes, but only when those panes display variables (in other words, it doesn't work with the Object Tree or units displays). For example, create a new project and view the Project Manager. Add the VCL buttons' source code to the project with the Project Viewer. If you did a complete installation of Delphi, the source code should be in the \DELPHI\SOURCE\VCL directory

302 Chapter 11—Using the Browser

name and should be named BUTTONS.PAS. From the Compile menu, choose Build All (you can't just do a compile because BUTTONS.PAS hasn't been changed). View the Browser and arrange the Browse Objects window and Code Editor window so that they're both visible (see fig. 11.30).

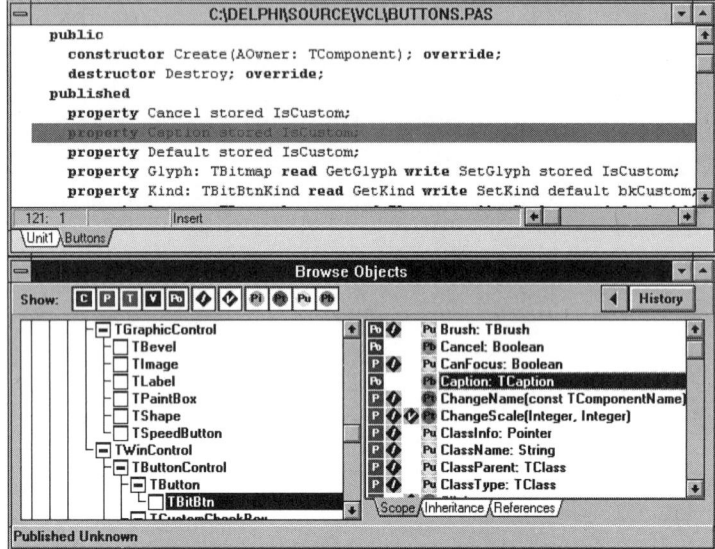

Fig. 11.30
The Browser can show the source code where symbols are declared.

Select TBitBtn from the Object Tree in the Inspector pane. The Browser displays the symbols associated with TBitBtn in the Details pane. Select the first symbol in the Details pane and then navigate through the list with the arrow keys. When you get to a symbol such as Caption, the Browser finds and highlights Caption's declaration in the source code.

Adjusting the Browser Panes

The Browse Objects window includes the Inspector pane on the left and the Details pane on the right. By default, these two panes are of equal size—each taking up about half of the Browser window. If symbols are too long to be displayed in one of the panes, you can increase the display size by maximizing the Browse Objects window. If the symbols are still too large, you can change the size of the panes. To do so, position the mouse pointer in the tall, thin divider that separates the two panes. Your mouse pointer should change to a double I-beam with arrows. Hold down the mouse button and move the divider left or right, depending on which pane you want to enlarge. Figure 11.31 shows a pane resizing in progress.

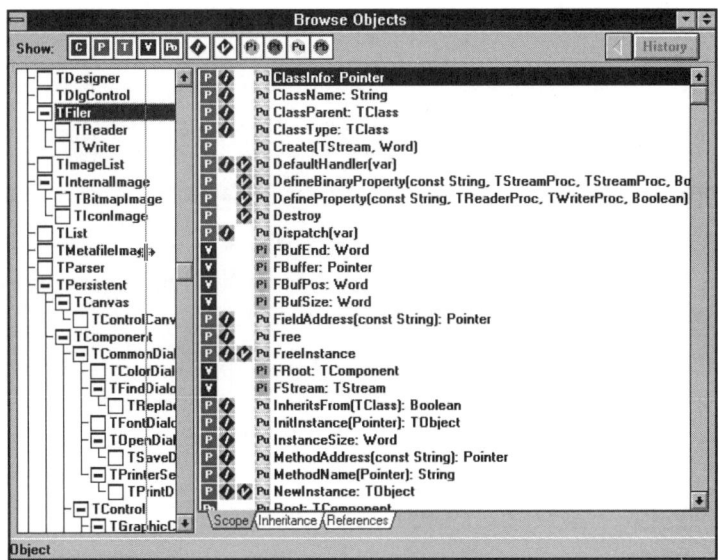

Fig. 11.31
You can resize the Inspector and Details panes by moving the divider that separates the two panes.

Configuring the Browser

Not only does Delphi allow you to change the functionality of the Browser on the fly with its filter buttons and SpeedMenu, Delphi also allows you to configure the Browser's default state.

To configure the Browser, open the Options menu and choose Environment; the Environment Options dialog appears. Select the Browser tab to see the Browser options (see fig. 11.32).

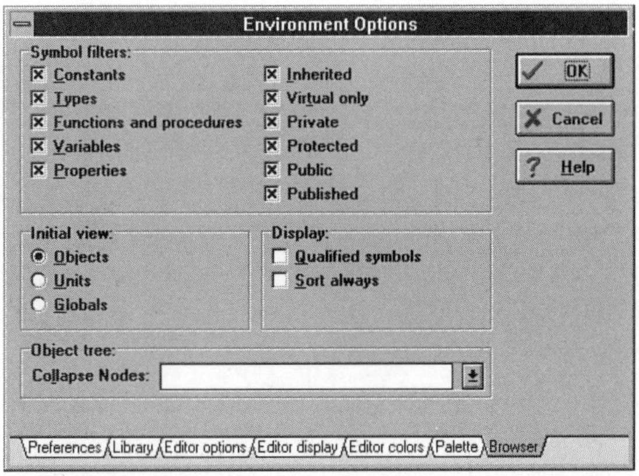

Fig. 11.32
Use the Browser tab in the Environment Options dialog to set Browser defaults.

Delphi ships with all the symbol filters checked. This is a little confusing, but when a symbol filter is checked in the Environment Options dialog, the same filter is disabled in the Browser window. With all the filters disabled, the Browser displays all the symbols within a program, regardless of type. If you prefer to view a smaller set of symbols, deselect the symbol filters corresponding to the symbols that you don't want to see displayed.

This configuration setting affects the status of the Browser only when it's first displayed. You can always turn a filter back on by clicking a filter button in the Browser window.

The Browser supports three initial views: Objects, Units, and Globals (refer to fig. 11.32). While using the Browser, you can switch between these views by using the SpeedMenu. Select a view in the Initial View section of the Environment Options dialog to specify which view the Browser shows each time it's invoked. Figure 11.31 shows the Browser configured to view objects when the Objects radio button is selected.

The Display section lets you configure how the Browser displays symbols. If you turn on the Qualified Symbols check box, the Browser displays the symbol's name and its qualified identifier—for example, the Browser displays, along with other symbols, `TObject.Free`. With the option turned off, the Browser just displays `Free`. The qualified part, `TObject`, tells you the base unit in which the symbol is declared.

The Display option also includes Sort Always, which tells the Browser how to sort the symbol display. With this option turned on, the Browser sorts symbols in alphabetical order by symbol name. With this option turned off, the Browser doesn't sort the symbols at all, but instead displays the symbols in the order in which they're declared in the source code.

By default, the Browser shows the Object Tree fully expanded, which is probably more information than you want. To have the Browser automatically collapse certain Object Tree nodes, type the name of that node in the Collapse Nodes text box (refer to fig. 11.32). If you don't want to view the expanded tree of the `Exception` object, for example, type **Exception** in the Collapse Nodes text box. When you next invoke the Browser, `Exception` is collapsed (see fig. 11.33). You can always expand the `Exception` tree while using the Browser by clicking `Exception`'s + icon.

To have the Browser collapse more than one tree, type a list of objects, separated by semicolons, in the Collapse Nodes text box. For example, if you type **Exception;TFiler** in the Collapse Nodes text box, the Browser collapses the

`Exception` and `TFiler` trees. Because the `Exception` tree is rather large and you don't normally need to explore it, you should type **Exception** in the Collapse Nodes text box.

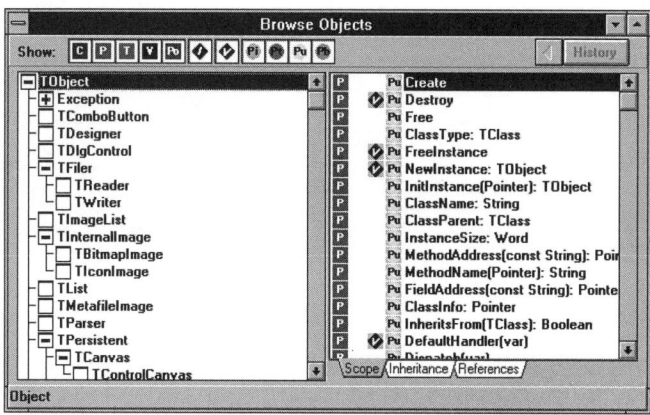

Fig. 11.33
The Exception tree collapsed.

> **Caution**
> When typing in the Collapse Nodes text box, don't include a space after the semicolon (;). If you do, the Browser ignores the entire field.

When you're done configuring the Browser, click OK. The Environment Options are saved.

From Here...

The Browser is a very powerful tool for exploring your programs and the symbols that are automatically linked into them. Read the following chapters for more information on programming:

- Chapter 3, "Understanding the Language"
- Chapter 4, "Using Visual Components"
- Chapter 5, "Using Non-Visual Components"
- Chapter 6, "Using Data-Bound Components"
- Chapter 7, "Customizing and Reusing Components"

Chapter 12
Using the Database Desktop

Delphi takes the art of Windows programming out of the realm of gurus and puts it in the hands of the average programmer. Delphi was designed from the ground up to be a database client, and yet it's not bogged down with an end-user database interface. Instead, Delphi ships with another Borland product, the Database Desktop (DBD).

The DBD is like a mini-version of Paradox or dBASE for Windows. It provides you with a method of creating, viewing, editing, restructuring, indexing, sorting, querying, and manipulating tables. Figure 12.1 shows the DBD with a Paradox table in Edit mode.

In this chapter, you learn how to:

- Create Paradox, dBASE, and SQL tables
- Restructure tables
- Adjust the visual appearance of tables
- Edit tables
- Create and perform queries
- Create SQL statements
- Add, copy, delete, empty, rename, sort, and subtract tables

Fig. 12.1
Use the Database Desktop to manipulate tables.

Understanding the DBD Screen

With the DBD you can open and maintain tables, queries, and SQL files. To start the DBD, simply double-click the Database Desktop icon in your Delphi program group. The DBD starts with the opening screen shown in figure 12.2.

Fig. 12.2
This DBD window is your interface to tables, queries, and SQL files.

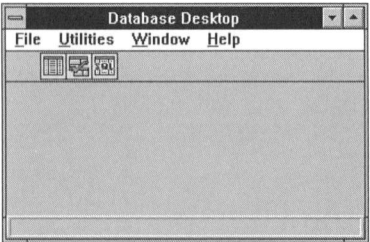

The DBD is an MDI (Multi-Document Interface) program. This means that each item you open is placed in a child window, but the child windows always exist within the DBD's parent window. You can have tables, queries, and SQL files all open and active at the same time. The DBD's menus and toolbar automatically change to correspond to the currently selected object. Figure 12.3 shows a crowded DBD screen with the SQL Editor as its current item.

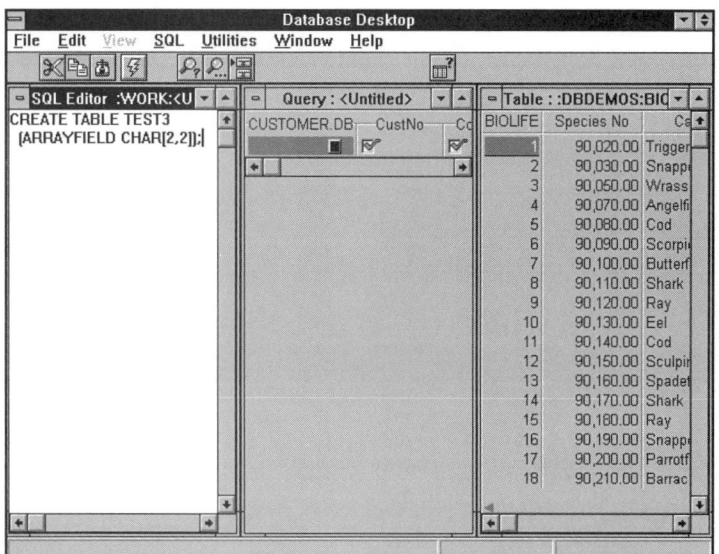

Fig. 12.3
Tables, queries, and SQL files can all be open at the same time in the DBD.

Creating a Table

Creating tables is a topic that has been covered in multivolume books. This section just covers the basics, concentrating on building a Paradox table because Paradox tables are rich in field types and referential features. Many concepts covered here apply to all databases, no matter what type.

Starting a New Table

To create a new table, open the File menu, choose New, and then choose Table. Alternatively, you can right-click the Open Table icon and choose New from its SpeedMenu. The DBD displays the Table Type dialog.

Click the drop-down list button to see a list of possible table types (see fig. 12.4). By default, you should at least have Paradox and dBASE table types in the list. Use the Database Engine Configuration program to set up other table types. Select the appropriate table type and click OK.

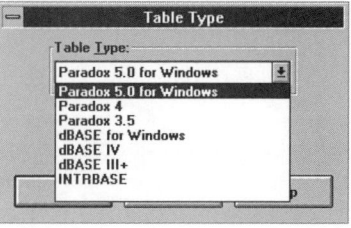

Fig. 12.4
The DBD lets you select the type of table you're creating.

Working with Paradox Tables

Next, the DBD displays the Create Paradox 5.0 for Windows (or the appropriate version of Paradox) Table dialog (see fig. 12.5). This is a modal dialog, so you can't use other the DBD features until you click OK or Cancel.

Fig. 12.5
The DBD lets you create Paradox tables.

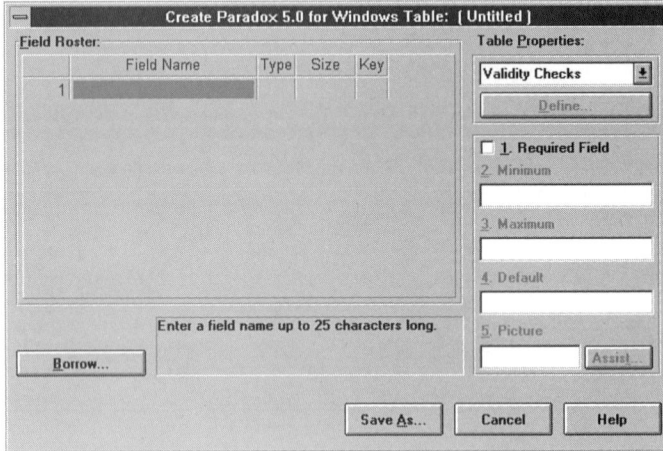

Using the Field Roster

The Field Roster section of the Create Table dialog is where you list the names and sizes of the fields for the new table. Paradox allows field names of up to 25 characters long. You can use most alphabetic characters and spaces in the name, but it's a good idea to use only A through Z and numbers in the field names since some SQL servers don't allow special characters. Paradox doesn't allow duplicate field names. You can use upper- and lowercase characters in field names, but case can't be used to make a field name unique.

> **Caution**
>
> Although you're allowed to use spaces in a field name, don't. Most SQL servers don't support spaces in field names, and spaces can cause syntax problems when you're composing SQL queries.

Use the Type and Size columns to specify the data type of each field. For a list of available field types, right-click or press the space bar with the highlight in the Type column.

Each data type has an associated symbol that's displayed in the Type column. Paradox supports the data types listed in table 12.1. As the table shows, some data types have sizes, while others don't. For those that don't, Paradox has a built-in size. For example, numbers take up to 8 bytes. Although the DBD lets you create fields with complex data types such as memos and graphics, you can't edit these fields with the DBD.

Table 12.1 Paradox Field Types

Symbol	Size	Type	Comments
A	1 to 255	Alpha	Regular text and numbers
N		Number	Floating-point numbers
$		Money	Same as number but formatted for currency
S		Short	2-byte integer
I		Long Integer	4-byte integer
#	0 to 32	BCD	Binary Coded Decimal
D		Date	Jan. 1, 9999 B.C., to Dec. 31, 9999 A.D.
T		Time	Milliseconds since midnight
@		Timestamp	Combination of Date and Time
M	1 to 240	Memo	Very large amounts of text
F	0 to 240	Formatted Memo	Memo with formatting
G	0 to 240	Graphic	Pictures
O	0 to 240	OLE	Object linking and embedding
L		Logical	True/False
+		Autoincrement	Long Integer that automatically increments
B		Binary	BLOBS stored in an .MB file
Y	1 to 255	Bytes	Binary data stored in a .DB file

Paradox tables store data in two files: .DB and .MB. The .DB file stores most of a table's field types, such as alphas, numbers, dates, and so on. The .MB file stores parts of large fields, such as memos. For this field type, the Size column determines how much of the field is stored in the .DB; the rest is stored in the .MB file. For this reason, the Size column doesn't in any way limit the amount of data that can go in a memo field. Delphi handles multiple file problems automatically, so you don't need to worry about the data being split between files.

Paradox tables support primary and secondary indexes. Primary indexes are created by placing an asterisk (*) in the Key column. More than one field can be part of the primary index, but the fields must be consecutive and must start with the first field in the table. Paradox insists that each record in a keyed table must have a unique key. Add an autoincrement field if your data is going to have duplicates in the primary key. For example, if you create a table to hold the addresses of your friends, you might key the [First_Name] and [Last_Name] fields. But there's always a chance that you could have two friends with the exact same name. Adding an autoincrement field as the third field and keying it allows you to enter both of your friends' names.

Setting Validity Checks

Paradox tables support a number of table properties. These properties are *data-validation rules* that are applied to new data as it's entered into the table. Both the DBD and Delphi support these rules.

Validity checks are *field-level data rules*. To set validity checks for a field, select the field and then select Validity Check from the Table Properties drop-down list.

Select the Required Field check box when you want to insist that a field not be left blank. Use the Minimum and Maximum text boxes to limit the valid range of a particular field. Use the Default text box to supply a default value. Use the Picture text box to supply a field mask that field data is checked against. For example, a picture of ###-##-#### can be used for data validation on Social Security number fields. (For more information on pictures, click the Assist button.) Figure 12.6 shows a field with a number of validity checks set up.

Creating a Table   **313**

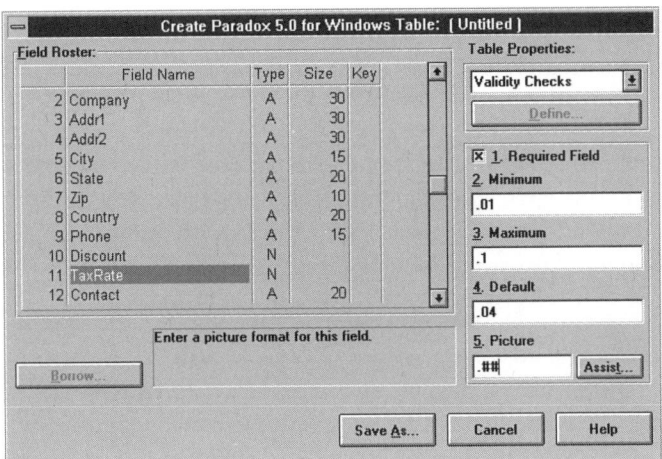

Fig. 12.6
The DBD lets you set up field-level rules for Paradox tables.

Specifying a Lookup Table

Paradox tables support a feature that lets you specify a list of valid values for a field in another table. This second table is known as the *lookup table*. To specify a lookup table, open the Table Properties drop-down list and select Table Lookup. Click the Define button, and the DBD displays the Table Lookup dialog (see fig. 12.7).

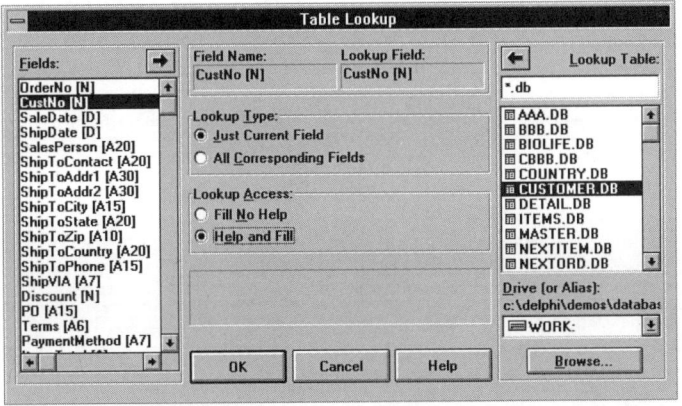

Fig. 12.7
Paradox lookup tables allow you to limit the valid entries of a field to the entries listed in another table.

On the left side of the dialog, select the field that you want to attach a lookup table to. On the right side of the dialog, select the lookup table. The first field of the lookup table must be of the same type as the field it is being attached to.

The Lookup Type section lets you specify how data is retrieved from the lookup table. If you specify All Corresponding Fields, the record is updated with all the fields from the lookup table that have the same names as fields in the current table. If you specify Just Current Field, only the lookup field is affected by the lookup data. The value of the Lookup Type section affects only users of interactive Paradox. As a Delphi developer, you can use the TDBLookupList and TDBLookupCombo components and some code to provide All Corresponding Fields functionality to your users.

The Lookup Access section lets you specify if the user has the right to see the data in the lookup table. Specify Help and Fill to allow the user to peruse the lookup table and select an appropriate value. Choose Fill No Help, and the lookup table is used only to validate the lookup field. The value of the Lookup Access section affects only users of interactive Paradox. As a Delphi developer, you can use the TDBLookupList and TDBLookupCombo components to provide help and fill functionality to your users.

Specifying Secondary Indexes

Secondary indexes are used on Paradox tables to speed searches and queries and to change the order in which the records are viewed. In the Create Table dialog, open the Table Properties drop-down list and select Secondary Indexes. Click the Define button to create a new index, or click the Modify button to modify an existing index. The DBD displays the Define Secondary Index dialog (see fig. 12.8).

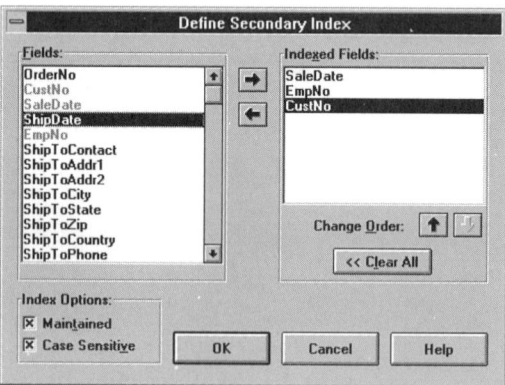

Fig. 12.8
Paradox tables support secondary indexes.

In the Fields list, select the field(s) you want to base the index on and click the right-pointing arrow button. You can rearrange the order of the selected fields in the Indexed Fields list by clicking the up- and down-arrow buttons.

In the Index Options section, always make sure that the Maintained check box is selected. This tells the database engine to update the index whenever changes are made to data in the main table. Select the Case Sensitive option if you want a case-sensitive index sort.

When you've completed the dialog, click OK. If the secondary index is based on a single field and is case-sensitive, the DBD gives the secondary index the same name as the field it's based on. Otherwise, the DBD asks you to supply a name.

Tip
Within Delphi, use the IndexName property of a TTable object to specify the order that the records are displayed in.

Ensuring Referential Integrity

Paradox tables support a feature know as *referential integrity* that enforces relationships between tables. For example, referential integrity can be set up between the Orders and Customer tables. This ensures that every order is associated with a customer, and a customer record can't be deleted if that customer has orders.

In the Create Table dialog, open the Table Properties drop-down list and select Referential Integrity. Click the Define button to create a new setting, or click the Modify button to modify an existing setting. The DBD displays the Referential Integrity dialog (see fig. 12.9).

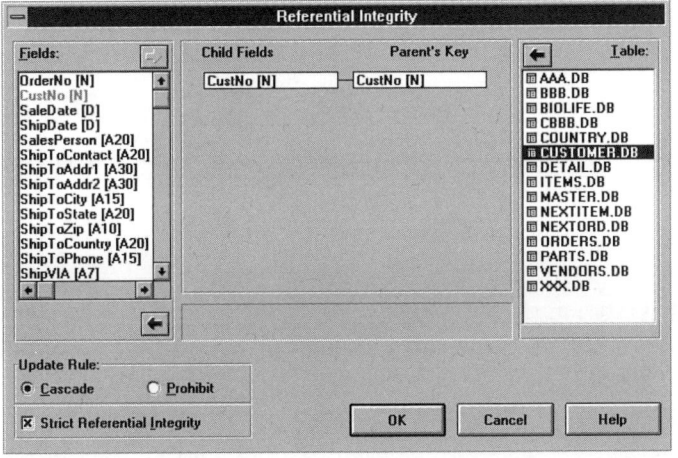

Fig. 12.9
Paradox tables support referential integrity.

On the right side of the dialog is the list of parent tables. Select a parent table, and the fields that make up the primary key of the parent table are listed under Parent's Key. Select the linking fields for the current table from the left side of the dialog. Linking fields must have the same data type as the field they're being linked to in the parent table. You don't have to specify a linking field for every field in the parent table.

316 Chapter 12—Using the Database Desktop

Select Cascade in the Update Rule section if you want changes made to linking fields in the parent table to be made automatically to the linking fields in the child table. Select Prohibit if you don't want to allow linking fields in the parent table to be edited when associated records are in the child table. Select Strict Referential Integrity to prevent earlier versions of Paradox from breaking the referential integrity rules.

When you've completed the Referential Integrity dialog, click OK. The DBD asks you to supply a name for the referential integrity setting. Supply a name and click OK.

Setting Passwords

Paradox tables support data encryption through a password system. A master password is used to protect all rights to a table. Secondary passwords are used for limited access to a table.

In the Create Table dialog, open the Table Properties drop-down list and select Password Security. Click the Define button; the DBD displays the Password Security dialog (see fig. 12.10).

Fig. 12.10
Paradox tables support password security.

Enter a password in the Master Password text box and the Verify Master Password text box. The two passwords must match for you to continue. If a password already exists, you can change it by clicking the Change button or remove it by clicking the Delete button. To specify secondary passwords with limited table access, click the Auxiliary Passwords button. The DBD displays the Auxiliary Passwords dialog (see fig. 12.11).

> **Note**
> If you're modifying an existing table, you need to know the master password before you can modify or delete it.

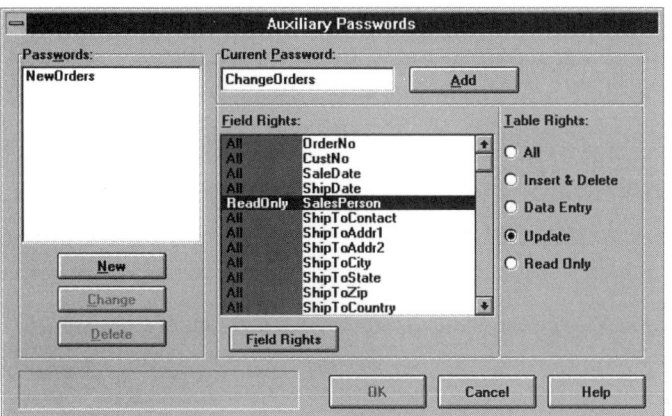

Fig. 12.11
Auxiliary passwords allow limited table access.

As figure 12.11 shows, you can create passwords and assign access rights to those passwords on a field-by-field basis. When you complete this dialog, click OK. The Password Security dialog reappears; click OK in this dialog as well. When you actually save the table you're building, it's encrypted. All software that accesses the table—be it the DBD, Delphi, or Paradox—must supply a password.

Specifying a Table Language

Paradox tables support a number of table languages. A table's table language determines the available character set and the order in which sorts are done. The DBD defaults new tables to the LANGDRIVER that's set up in the Database Engine Configuration program. To specify a different table language, open the Table Properties drop-down list and select Table Language. Click the Define button, and the DBD displays the Table Language dialog. Select the appropriate Language (see fig. 12.12) and click OK.

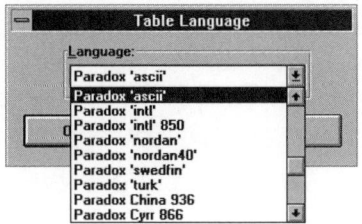

Fig. 12.12
Paradox tables support different language drivers.

318 Chapter 12—Using the Database Desktop

Listing Dependent Tables

When you set up a referential integrity link between tables, you establish a relationship between a parent and child table. You can always see to which tables a child is linked from the referential integrity information. To see what tables a parent is linked to, pull down the Table Properties list in the Create Table dialog and select Dependent Tables. In figure 12.13, the list of child tables has only one entry, ORDERS.DB. This list is only for reference and can't be changed.

Fig. 12.13
The Database Desktop can list associated tables.

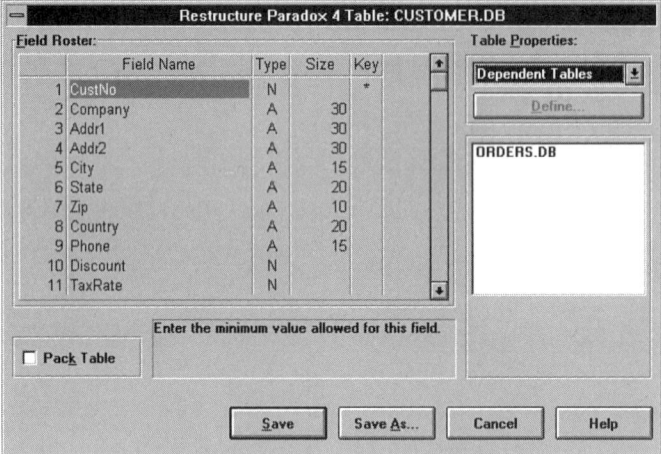

Borrowing Table Structures

You don't have to create tables from the ground up; the DBD lets you borrow field rosters from other tables. To do this, the current field roster must be completely blank. Click the Borrow button in the Create Table dialog; the DBD displays the Borrow Table Structure dialog (see fig. 12.14).

Select the table that you're interested in. It doesn't have to be in the same directory, but it must be a Paradox table. By default, the DBD borrows only the field names and types. Select the appropriate check boxes in the Options section to borrow other table properties. When you've completed the dialog, click OK; the current field roster is populated with the borrowed information.

Naming the New Table

With the Create Table dialog completed, click the Save As button. The DBD displays the Save Table As dialog (see fig. 12.15).

Give the new table an appropriate name. If you want, you can select the Display Table check box, which causes the DBD to display the table as soon as it's created. Click OK. The DBD creates the new empty table.

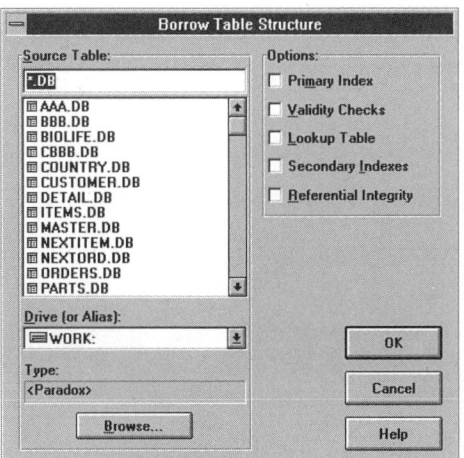

Fig. 12.14
The DBD lets you borrow fields from other tables.

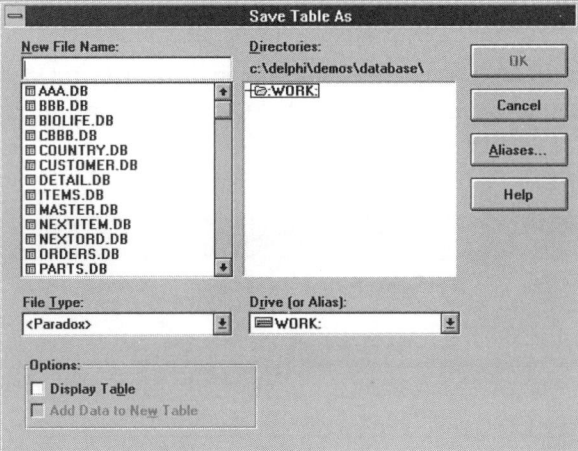

Fig. 12.15
The DBD lets you choose the directory to save the new table in.

Working with dBASE Tables

Creating dBASE tables is much like creating a Paradox table. The following sections highlight some of the differences.

To create a dBASE table, open the File menu, choose New, and then choose Table. The DBD displays the Table Type dialog. Select dBASE for Windows and click OK. The DBD displays the Create dBASE for Windows Table dialog (see fig. 12.16).

Fig. 12.16
The DBD helps you create dBASE tables.

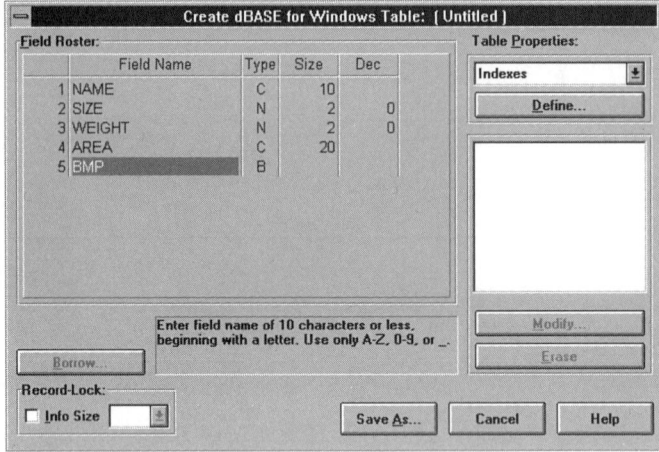

Using the Field Roster

The dBASE field roster is very similar to the Paradox field roster. dBASE field names must be in all capital letters, spaces aren't allowed, and field-name length is limited to 10 characters. Each field name must be unique. Table 12.2 shows the valid field types.

Table 12.2	dBASE Field Types			
Symbol	Size	Decimal Point	Type	Comments
C	1 to 254		Character	Regular text and numbers
F	1 to 20	0 to 18, and <= Size to 2	Float	Floating point numbers
N	1 to 20	0 to 18, and <= Size to 2	Number	Binary Coded Decimal
D			Date	8-byte date field
L			Logical	True/False
M			Memo	Very large amounts of text
O			OLE	Object linking and embedding
B			Binary	BLOBS

Creating Indexes

dBASE tables support indexes. To create an index, pull down the Table Properties list and select Indexes. Click the Define button. The DBD displays the Define Index dialog (see fig. 12.17).

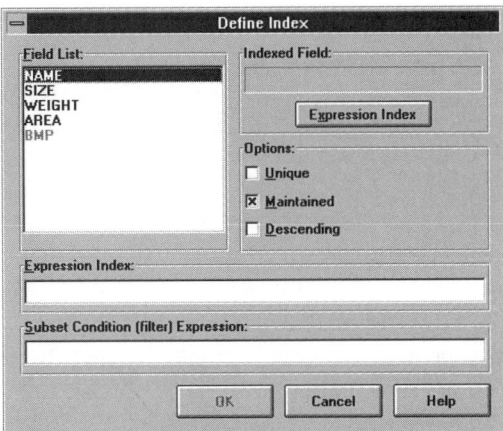

Fig. 12.17
dBASE tables have a number of indexing options.

From the Field List, select the field you want to base the index on. If you want to base the index on more than one field, click the Expression Index button. In the Expression Index text box, enter an expression such as **WEIGHT+SIZE**.

To have the index based only on unique values, select the Unique check box in the Options section. To have the index sorted in descending order, select the Descending check box. To have the index automatically maintained after record updates, select the Maintained check box.

dBASE indexes support filtering. When displaying a table based on a filtered index, only a subset of the data is shown. To create a filtered index, enter an expression into the Subset Condition (Filter) Expression text box. For example, to view only those customers who live in Hawaii, type **STATE=HI**.

When you've completed the Define Index dialog, click OK. The DBD asks you to supply a name for the index. Enter a name and click OK. The new index is added to the index list.

Locking Records

dBASE tables support record locking, but it must be enabled while creating or restructuring the table. Record locking is implemented through an extra field in the table that holds the locking information. The field can be from 8 to 24 bytes long. The first 2 bytes indicate if the record has been changed; the next 6 bytes indicate the time and date the record was locked. The final and optional 16 bytes indicate the name of the user who locked the record. To enable record locking, select the check box in the Record-Lock section and select a size from the Info Size drop-down list in the Create Table dialog.

Working with InterBase Tables

The process of creating InterBase tables is very similar to the process of creating Paradox and dBASE tables. The following sections highlight some of the differences.

To create an InterBase table, open the File menu, choose New, and then choose Table. The DBD displays the Table Type dialog. Select InterBase and click OK. The DBD displays the Create INTRBASE Table dialog (see fig. 12.18).

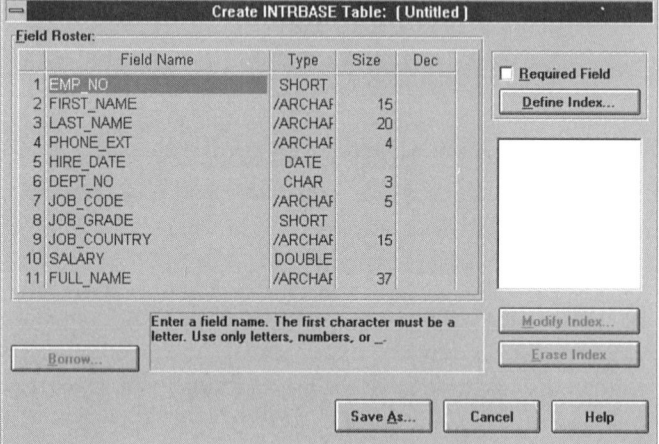

Fig. 12.18
You can create InterBase tables with the DBD.

Using the Field Roster

InterBase field names can be up to 31 characters long, aren't case sensitive, must be unique, and can't start with numbers. Certain reserved words such as DATE can't be used as field names. InterBase supports the field types listed in table 12.3.

Table 12.3 InterBase Field Types

Name	Size	Comments
SHORT		16-bit integer
LONG		32-bit integer

Name	Size	Comments
FLOAT		7 digits of precision
DOUBLE		15 digits of precision
CHAR	1 to 32767	Fixed-length strings
VARCHAR	1 to 32767	Variable-length strings
DATE		January 1, 100, to December 11, 5941
BLOB		Binary Large Object
ARRAY		The DBD can't create this field type

Creating Indexes

To define InterBase indexes, click the Define Index button. The DBD displays the Define Index dialog (see fig. 12.19).

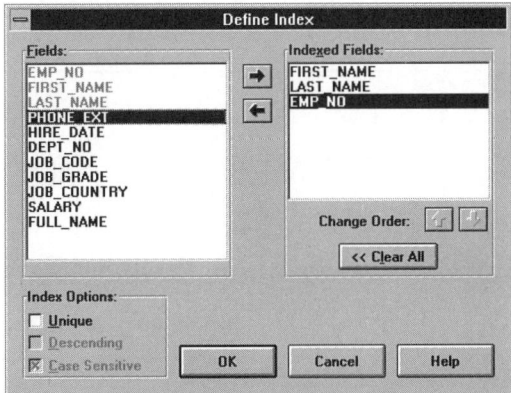

Fig. 12.19
The DBD lets you define InterBase indexes.

Select field(s) from the Fields list on the left side of the dialog and click the right-pointing arrow button. You can reorder selected fields in the Indexed Fields list by clicking the up- and down-arrow buttons. To make an index unique, select the Unique check box in the Index Options section. To have the index sorted in reverse order, select the Descending check box. To make the index case sensitive, select the Case Sensitive check box. When you've completed the dialog, click OK. The DBD asks you to name the index and then adds that name to the index list.

Naming the New Table

When you've completed the Create INTRBASE Table dialog, click the Save As button. The DBD displays the same Save Table As dialog as it does for Paradox (refer to fig. 12.15), but in this case, you must select an InterBase alias. Give the new table a name and click OK. The DBD sends the necessary SQL commands to the InterBase server to create the table.

Restructuring Tables

Once you create a table with the DBD, its structure isn't set in stone. You can begin the restructuring process in a number of ways:

- While viewing the table, open the Table menu and choose Restructure Table.

- While viewing the table, click the Restructure icon on the toolbar.

- Open the Tools menu, choose Utilities, and then choose Restructure. The DBD displays the Select File dialog. Select the table you want to restructure.

> **Caution**
>
> Because table restructures must completely rewrite a table's data, they require an exclusive lock. DBD automatically places the required lock for you. Nobody else can use a table during the restructure process.

The Restructure dialogs for Paradox and dBASE tables are the same as the Create Table dialogs with the addition of the Pack Table check box (see fig. 12.20).

When records are deleted from Paradox and dBASE tables, the disk space the record occupied isn't recovered but is marked as unused. Although the space can be used by new records, you can recover disk space by selecting the Pack Table option.

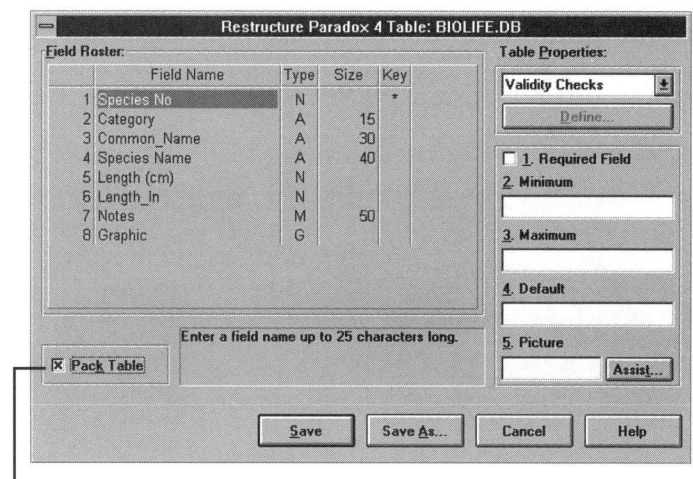

Fig. 12.20
The DBD allows you to restructure existing tables.

The Pac**k** Table check box

Viewing a Table

When developing and debugging applications, it's often necessary to quickly view the data your application is working with. Often, a bug is caused by an unexpected value in a table. While you can quickly write Delphi programs that let you view tables, it's easier to use the DBD.

Opening a Table

You can open a table in the DBD in two ways:

- Open the File menu, choose Open, and then choose Table.
- Click the Open Table icon on the toolbar.

In either case, the DBD displays the Open Table dialog (see fig. 12.21).

If you know the name of the table you want to open, enter the name in the File Name text box. If the table is located in a different directory, use the directory tree to navigate to the proper directory. If the table is in a parent directory, select the root drive from the Drive (or Alias) combo box. If an alias is associated with the database, select the alias in the Drive (or Alias) combo box. If you're working with an SQL table, you must select an alias. If an alias

326 Chapter 12—Using the Database Desktop

hasn't already been set up, click the Aliases button to display the Alias Manager dialog. Once you've found the table you're interested in, click OK. If you're opening an SQL table or an encrypted table, the DBD asks for a password.

Fig. 12.21
The DBD's Open Table dialog lets you browse your machine and SQL servers to select a table.

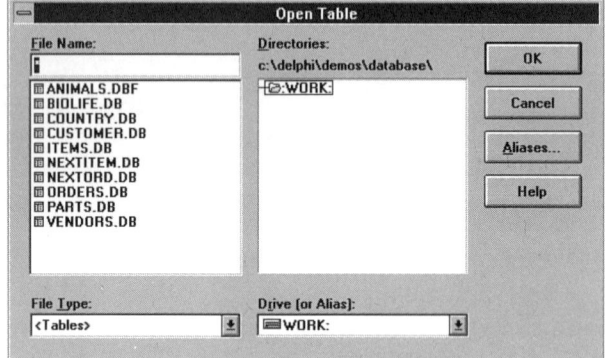

Once you're viewing a table, the DBD updates the menu, toolbar, and status bar with table-specific information. If you're viewing a non-SQL table, record updates are displayed as they're posted from other sessions. To see records update in an SQL table, press Ctrl+F3.

To close a table, double-click its close box or open the File menu and choose Close. If the table is in Edit mode, the DBD posts any pending record changes, goes back into View mode, and then closes the table.

Adjusting Table Properties

The DBD allows you to adjust a number of the visible properties of a table. For example, you can adjust the size of rows and columns. These adjustments don't in any way affect how the data is stored on disk and don't affect your Delphi programs. Use these adjustments simply to improve your view of the data.

Resizing Columns

You can resize the columns in the DBD table grid. Position the mouse pointer over a column divider on the first visible record in the table grid. When the mouse pointer is positioned properly, the pointer becomes a double-headed arrow. Press down the mouse button and drag the column divider to its new position. As you drag, a vertical gray line appears on the table grid to indicate the new column size. Figure 12.22 shows a table with a number of columns that have been resized and a column that's in the process of being resized. If you make a text column smaller than the text being displayed, the text is truncated. If you make a numeric column smaller than the numbers being displayed, the numbers are displayed as a series of asterisks.

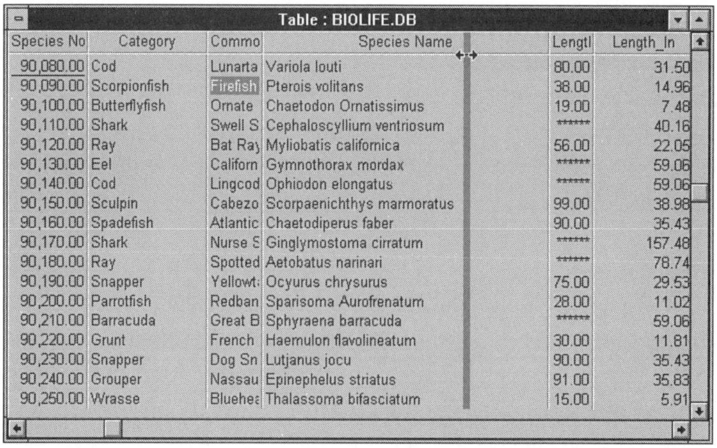

Fig. 12.22
You can resize table columns in the DBD.

Resizing Rows

You also can resize rows in the DBD table grid. Put the mouse pointer over the record divider on the first visible record in the first visible row in the grid. Normally, the field in this position is underlined to remind you of its functionality. When the mouse pointer is positioned properly, the pointer becomes a double-headed arrow. Click the mouse and drag the row divider to its new position. As you drag, a horizontal gray line appears on the table grid to indicate the new row size (see fig. 12.23).

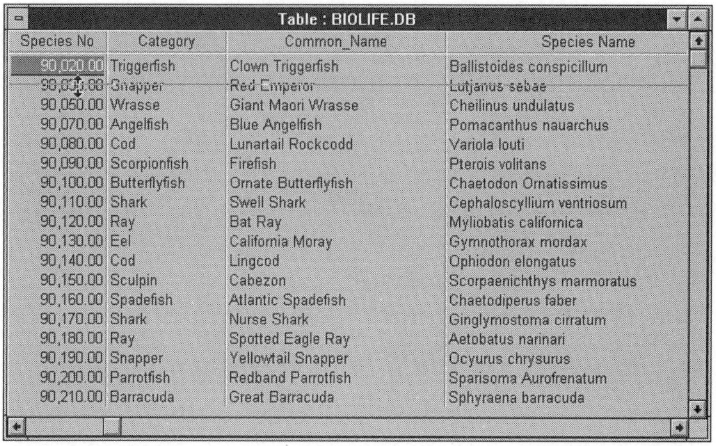

Fig. 12.23
You can resize table rows in the DBD.

> **Note**
>
> Be careful not to make your rows too small. The DBD chops off field data extending beyond the row boundary, thus making the rows unreadable in some cases.

Resizing the Table Header

The table header above the first row of a table contains the table name and field names. Put the mouse pointer on the horizontal line just under the table name. Now you can resize the Table Header as if you were resizing a row, as described in the preceding section.

Moving a Column

You can reorder the columns in the DBD table grid with respect to each other. You can move the Common_Name column, for example, so that it's next to the Record Number column. Put the mouse pointer in the heading of the column to be moved. When the pointer is properly positioned, it changes into a mailbox icon (see fig. 12.24).

> **Note**
>
> Moving columns in the DBD has absolutely no effect on how the table is actually stored on disk. Moving columns is simply a cosmetic change.

Fig. 12.24
Click and drag a column header to move the column.

Hold down the mouse button; the column separators on either side of the selected column are highlighted to indicate the column is ready to be moved. Drag the column to its new position. As you do so, a single vertical gray bar shows the column's new position. If you drag the column off the edge of the grid, the grid is scrolled to reveal other columns. When the column is positioned correctly, release the mouse button, and the DBD displays the column in its new position.

> **Note**
>
> Some databases have a record number column that can't be moved. It must remain as the far left column.

Rotating Columns

You can quickly get an uninteresting column out of the way by rotating it. Rotating makes the current column the last column of the table. Select the column to be rotated by clicking any data value and pressing Ctrl+R. The selected column is sent to the far right side of the table.

Using the Scroll Lock

As you use the scroll bars to move left and right in a table, columns of data are scrolled off the display. This can make it difficult to associate a particular cell with its record number or key fields. The scroll-lock feature of the DBD lets you lock certain columns so that they're never scrolled off the visible display.

To access the scroll-lock feature, view a table and scroll all the way to the left so that the Record Number column is showing. In the lower left corner of the screen is the scroll lock, a small left-pointing triangle. The mouse pointer changes to a double-headed arrow when it's positioned over the scroll lock. To set the scroll lock, drag it to a new column (see fig. 12.25).

When the scroll lock is positioned correctly, release the mouse button. The scroll lock appears as two inward-facing triangles positioned around the locked column. In figure 12.26, the lock is placed between the Category and Common_Name fields. As the table is scrolled to the right, the Record Number, Species No, and Category columns remain fixed, while the other columns are scrolled into view.

Fig. 12.25
Setting the scroll lock keeps columns from being scrolled off the display.

Fig. 12.26
Important columns remain fixed while other columns scroll.

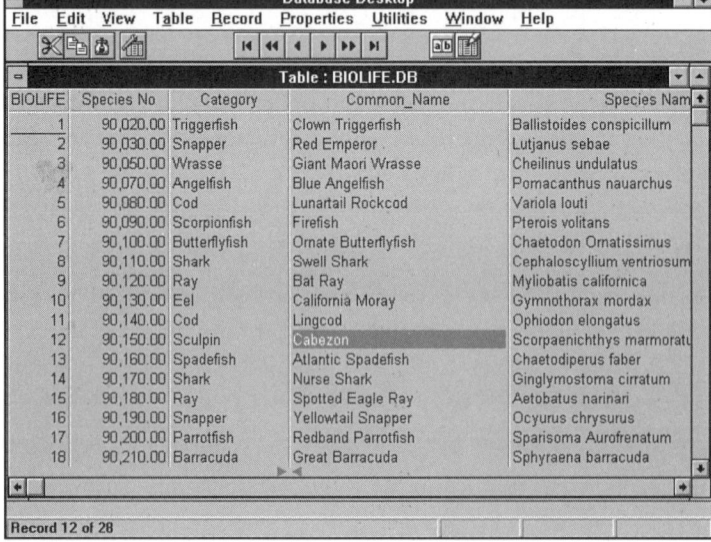

Saving Table Properties

All the table properties discussed so far can be saved with a table. The next time the table is viewed, those saved properties are automatically applied to it. Saving, restoring, and deleting table properties is accomplished through the Properties menu. If you don't save the properties, they're lost when the table is closed.

To save table properties, open the Properties menu and choose Save. The DBD creates a file with the same name as the table but with a .TV? extension (TV stands for *table view*). For Paradox, the extension is just .TV; for dBASE, it's .TVF; and for SQL tables, it's .TVS. For SQL tables, the .TVS file is stored in your private directory; for other tables, the .TV? file is stored in the same directory as the table. The next time the table is opened, the DBD applies the properties found in the .TV file to the table.

> **Note**
>
> The DBD uses your private directory to store a number of temporary files and other files that only you should have access to. To set your private directory, open the File menu and choose Private Directory. Type a directory name in the Private Directory dialog and click OK.

If you change the properties of a table and decide you don't like the changes, you can undo your changes. Open the Properties menu and choose Restore. If the table has an associated .TV? file, the properties in the file are applied to the table. If no .TV? file exists, the DBD applies a default set of properties to the table.

If you open a table that already has properties applied to it that you don't like, you can delete the table's properties. Open the Properties menu and choose Delete. If no .TV? file exists, the Delete menu choice is grayed out. If properties do exist, the DBD asks you to confirm the deletion. The DBD deletes the associated .TV? file and displays the table with default properties.

When you close a table, the DBD checks to see whether you've changed the table's properties. If you have, it asks whether you want to save the property changes. Most of the time you should answer no to this question, because most property changes are either inadvertent or are needed only temporarily.

Navigating a Table

Although the DBD doesn't provide a feature for interactive searching or filtering of data, it does offer a number of table-navigation features.

In the DBD, the normal set of navigation keys work as you expect them to. Arrow keys take you in the direction of the arrow. The Tab key takes you to the next field, while Shift+Tab takes you to the previous field. Page Up and Page Down take you up or down one set of records. Home takes you to the first field in a record, whereas End takes you to the last field in a record.

332   Chapter 12—Using the Database Desktop

Ctrl+Home takes you to the first field of the first record, and Ctrl+End takes you to the last field of the last record.

You can also navigate records with the Record menu and its associated shortcut keys (see fig. 12.27).

Fig. 12.27
You can use the shortcut keys on the Record menu to navigate a table.

Record	
First	Ctrl+F11
Last	Ctrl+F12
Next	F12
Previous	F11
Next Set	Shift+F12
Previous Set	Shift+F11
Insert	Ins
Delete	Ctrl+Del
Lock	F5
Cancel Changes	Alt+Bksp
Post/Keep Locked	Ctrl+F5
Lookup Help	Ctrl+Space
Move Help	Ctrl+Shift+Space

The DBD toolbar contains a VCR-type control panel as an alternative way of navigating a table. Figure 12.28 shows the VCR controls. The first button takes you to the first record. The second button takes you up one screen of records. The third button takes you to the previous record. The fourth button takes you to the next record, and the fifth button takes you to the next screen of record. The final button takes you to the last record.

Fig. 12.28
The VCR control panel lets you surf a table.

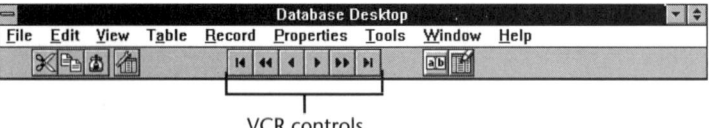

VCR controls

There's still one more way to navigate a table. The DBD displays tables with a scroll bar on the right side of the screen if there are records that aren't displayed. Use the scroll bar like any other scroll bar to move up and down in the table.

Editing a Table

The DBD allows you to do more than just view a table—you can also edit the data in the table. The DBD takes care of the locking, referential integrity, and SQL commits for you.

Using Edit Mode

Before you can make any changes to table data, you must first put the table in Edit mode. Open the <u>V</u>iew menu and choose <u>E</u>dit Data. Alternatively, you can press F9 or click the Edit Data icon on the toolbar. The second field in the status bar displays the message Edit.

Edit mode is table specific. If you have more than one table open in the DBD, only the current table is put into Edit mode. With the table in Edit mode, you are free to navigate around the table, making changes. When you first make a change to a record, the DBD does any multiuser housekeeping that needs to be done. If you're editing a multiuser Paradox table, for example, the DBD places the appropriate table- and record-level locks.

> **Note**
>
> It's a good idea to leave Edit mode and return to View mode as soon as you're done making changes. This ensures that you hold table-level locks for the least amount of time and helps you avoid mistakes such as inadvertently deleting records. To return to View mode, click the Edit Data icon again, press F9, or open the <u>V</u>iew menu and select <u>V</u>iew Data.

Using Field View Mode

When you arrive on a field using any of the navigation techniques discussed earlier, the DBD selects the contents of the entire field. DBD editing works like any other Windows editing, so when you type a letter, the selected region is replaced with that letter. To avoid replacing an entire field, you need to go into Field View mode. The DBD requires you to use Field View mode on certain field types, such as numbers with more decimals than are displayed. Use any of the following methods to enter Field View mode:

- Press F2.
- Click the Field View button on the toolbar.
- Open the <u>V</u>iew menu and select <u>F</u>ield View.
- Click the selected field. The insertion point is placed where you click.

> **Note**
>
> You don't have to be in Edit mode to enter Field View mode. Use Field View mode when not in Edit mode to see the contents of wide fields.

334 Chapter 12—Using the Database Desktop

Tip
While in Field View mode, use the normal Windows editing techniques to change the value of the field.

Once in Field View mode, the navigation keys take on a different, more localized meaning. The left-arrow key moves the insertion point left within the field, while the right-arrow key moves the insertion point right within the field. Home takes you to the beginning of the field, and End takes you to the end of the field. Keys such as up arrow and Page Up don't change meaning. In fact, they take you out of Field View and off the current record.

To exit Field View mode, use any of the techniques to get into Field View mode again. You can also leave Field View mode by pressing Tab or using a record-navigation command.

Some databases allow rules to be applied at the field level. These rules limit the valid entries that may be placed in a field. If a value that you place in a field violates one of these rules, the DBD refuses to post the new value and displays a warning message in the lower right corner of the screen (see fig. 12.29).

The DBD doesn't allow editing of complex field types such as memos and graphics. To edit these fields, you need to write a Delphi program or buy a complete database package such as Paradox or dBASE for Windows.

Fig. 12.29
The status bar displays a warning message when a field-level rule is broken.

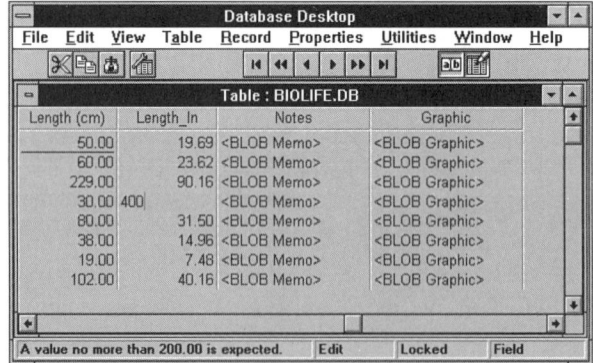

Undoing Changes

While editing a record, the DBD provides a limited undo feature. You can undo changes to a record using any of the following methods:

- Press Alt+Backspace.
- Open the Edit menu and choose Undo.
- Open the Record menu and choose Cancel Changes.

The DBD undoes changes to the entire record, not just individual fields.

> **Caution**
>
> Undo works only before a record is written to disk. If you leave or post a record for any reason, your changes can't be undone. See "Posting Records" later for more information on how records are posted.

Inserting Records

The DBD supports a number of ways of inserting a new record into a table:

- Press the Insert key.
- Open the Record menu and choose Insert.
- Move beyond the end of a table in Edit mode.

No matter which method you choose, the DBD inserts a new blank record at the location of the cursor. If you leave the new record without making any changes to it, the DBD deletes the blank record.

Deleting Records

The DBD supports two ways of deleting records from a table:

- Press the Ctrl+Delete key.
- Open the Record menu and select Delete.

The DBD deletes the current record from the table. If you need to delete many records from a table, consider opening the Utilities menu and choosing Empty, or using a delete query.

Certain databases have table-level rules that can prevent you from deleting records. For example, a Paradox database can include a one-to-many relationship between two tables. That relationship can be set up in such a way as to prohibit deletions of records from the master table if dependent records are in the detail table. In this case, the DBD doesn't delete the master record and displays a warning message in the status bar (see fig. 12.30).

> **Caution**
>
> Be careful—the DBD doesn't ask for confirmation when deleting records and can't recover a record once it's deleted.

Fig. 12.30
The DBD displays a warning message in the status bar when you try to break a table-level rule.

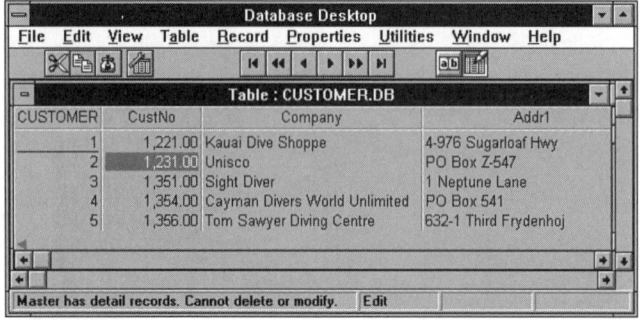

Locking Records

In a multiuser environment, problems can occur when two or more users try to edit the same record. To avoid these problems, the DBD automatically locks a record when you begin editing for Paradox and dBASE tables.

For SQL tables, you can manually lock records by selecting a record and pressing F5 or opening the Record menu and choosing Lock. The DBD tries to lock the current record and displays a success or failure message in the status bar. To manually unlock a record, press Shift+F5 or open the Record menu and choose Unlock.

Posting Records

As you make changes to a record, those changes are kept in memory until the record is posted. You can use any of the following techniques to post a record:

- Leave the record using one of the record navigation techniques.

- Unlock the record by opening the Record menu and choosing Unlock or by pressing Shift+F5.

- Post the record while keeping it locked by opening the Record menu and choosing Post/Keep Locked or by pressing Ctrl+F5.

Records are also automatically posted if you go into View mode or if you close the table or the DBD. No matter which method you use, the DBD tries to post the changes to the underlying table. The DBD treats each record edit as a transaction and automatically commits each transaction during record posting.

Many databases have rules that are enforced on the record level to ensure data integrity. Paradox, for example, doesn't allow records with duplicate primary keys. If you try to post a record that violates a record-level rule, the DBD doesn't post the record and displays an error message on the status bar (see fig. 12.31). You must correct the error before posting the record.

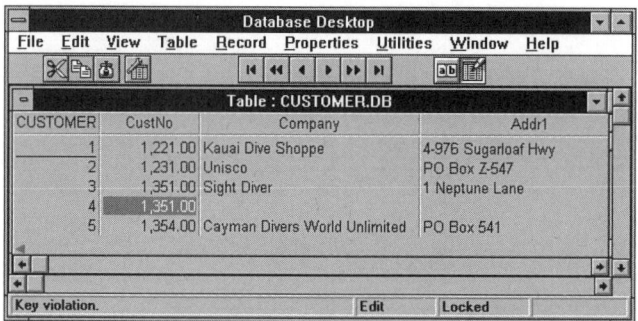

Fig. 12.31
DBD enforces record-level rules.

> **Note**
>
> If you can't figure out how to fix a record that doesn't post, open the Edit menu and choose Undo. You lose your record changes, but at least you can leave the record.

Performing Queries

Not only does the DBD allow you to create, view, and edit tables, it also allows you to ask questions of the data. Like many topics in this chapter, queries are a subject that entire books have been written about. This discussion just covers the basis. For more information, see Que's *Using Paradox 5 for Windows*, Special Edition; *Killer Paradox 5 for Windows*; *Using dBASE 5 for Windows*, Special Edition; and *Killer dBASE 5 for Windows*.

Using QBE

The DBD uses QBE (Query By Example) to ask questions of data. Although the concept is the same as the Delphi's Visual Query Builder, the DBD has a different user interface and is limited in its capabilities.

To begin a query, open the File menu, choose New, and then choose QBE Query. Alternatively, you can right-click the Query toolbar icon and choose New. The DBD displays the normal Select File dialog. Select the table(s) you want to query and click OK. The DBD displays the Query window (see fig. 12.32).

Fig. 12.32
The DBD lets you ask questions of your data with Query By Example.

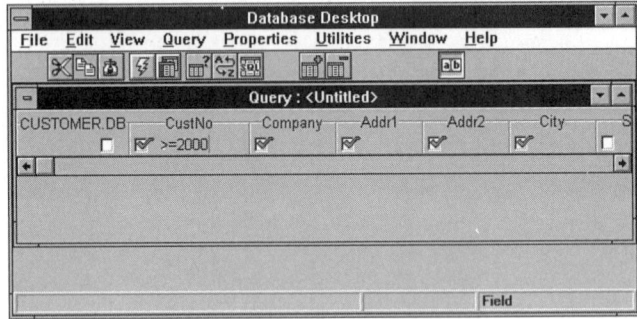

In general, queries are started by selecting the tables to be queried. Next, check marks are used to determine which fields are included in the ANSWER table. Conditions are applied to the query to narrow the scope of the question. Examples can be used in the conditions and to link tables together. When a query is all set, you can run it by pressing F8, clicking the Run Query toolbar icon, or opening the View menu and choosing Run Query. The DBD processes the query and displays the results in the ANSWER table.

Setting ANSWER Table Properties

You can set certain properties for the ANSWER table before you begin a query. Click the Answer Table Properties icon on the toolbar, or open the Properties menu and choose Answer Table. The Answer Table Properties dialog appears (see fig. 12.33). This dialog lets you name the ANSWER table and decide whether it should be a Paradox or dBASE table. If you're querying SQL tables, the ANSWER table is still either a Paradox or dBASE table.

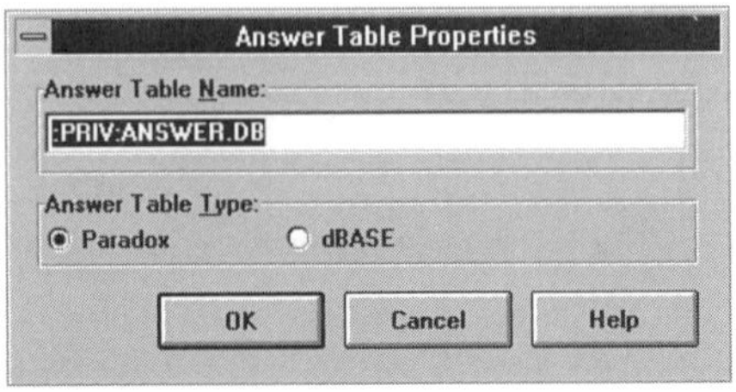

Fig. 12.33
The DBD lets you name and select a type for the ANSWER table.

Using Check Marks

To specify which fields are to be included in the ANSWER table, you check-mark those fields. Click the small white box in a field you're interested in. The DBD displays the drop-down list shown in figure 12.34.

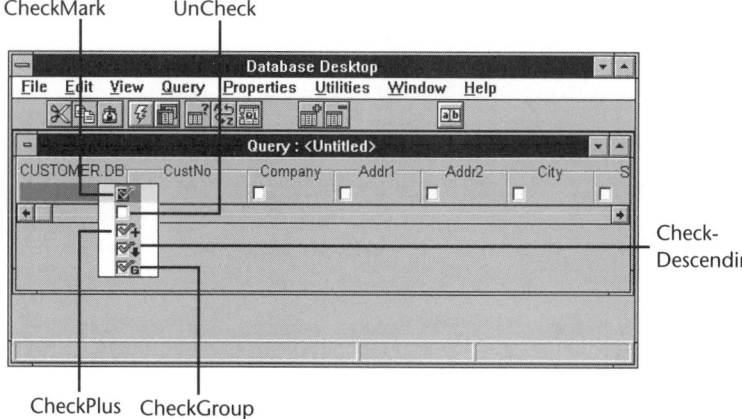

Fig. 12.34
Check marks in QBE queries determine which fields are included in the answer.

The first item in the check mark list is the regular CheckMark. Select the CheckMark for each field you want to include in the ANSWER table. The CheckMark tells the DBD not to include any duplicate records in the output. It also causes the ANSWER table to be sorted in ascending order.

For example, start a new query on the Customer table. Place a regular CheckMark in the Company field, and then press F8 or click the lightning bolt icon on the toolbar. The DBD performs the query and displays the resulting ANSWER table (see fig. 12.35). Notice that no duplicate companies are in the ANSWER table and that the ANSWER table is sorted.

Tip
If you place a check mark in the far left field, that check is applied to all the fields. Any existing check marks in the fields are overwritten.

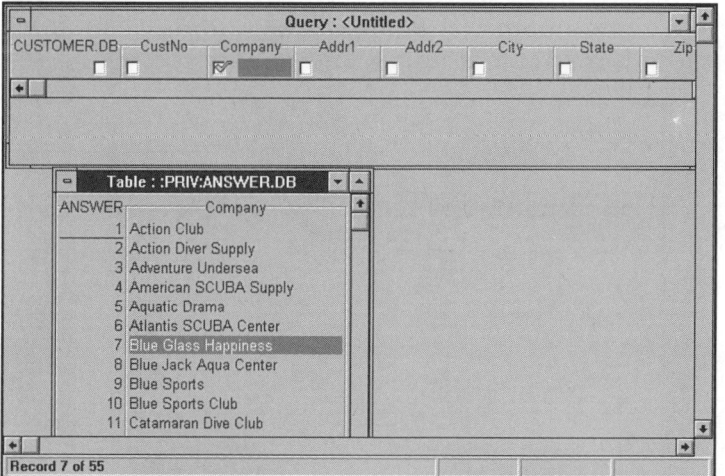

Fig. 12.35
A CheckMark query can get a single column from a table.

340 Chapter 12—Using the Database Desktop

If you do want duplicate records in the ANSWER table, use the CheckPlus, the third item in the check mark list. CheckPlus still causes a field to be included in the ANSWER table, but it tells the DBD not to remove duplicates. You need to include only a single CheckPlus in a query to keep all the duplicate records. CheckPlus also tells the DBD not to sort the ANSWER table.

CheckDescending is the fourth item in the check mark list. Like the regular CheckMark, CheckDescending doesn't allow duplicate records in the ANSWER table. Unlike CheckMark, however, CheckDescending tells the DBD to sort the ANSWER table in descending order.

Unlike the other check marks, CheckGroup, the last item in the check mark list, doesn't include the field in the ANSWER table. CheckGroup is used only in set queries and specifies a field to group by.

Applying Conditions

Normally when you create a query, you don't want all the records from the table you're querying to appear in the ANSWER table. Instead, a set of conditions that asks a question of the data is applied to the query. To apply a condition in a DBD query, enter a statement in a field. If you want the ANSWER table to list customers who live in Hawaii, for example, enter **HI** in the State field.

To place two conditions on a field that are logically ANDed together, separate the conditions with a comma. For example, to limit the answer to just those customers who placed orders in January 1995, enter **>=1/1/95, <2/1/95** in the SaleDate field.

You can also logically OR conditions in a field by using the keyword OR. For example, if you want a list of customers from Hawaii or California, type **HI OR CA** in the State field. To perform an OR query on conditions in more that one field, pose the conditions on multiple query rows (see fig. 12.36). This query gets a list of customers who are either from HI or have a CustNo greater than 1500. Internally, the DBD performs each row of a query separately and adds the resulting answers together.

Fig. 12.36
The DBD supports multiple-row queries.

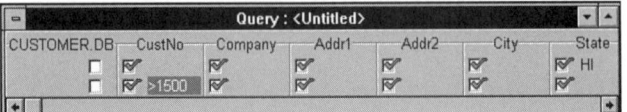

Using Wild Cards

The DBD supports wild cards in query conditions. Use two periods as a wild card for any group of characters—for example, type **T..** in the Company field. The DBD returns all the companies whose names begin with the letter T.

The wild card for a single character is @. For example, if you type **9@768** in the Zip field, the ANSWER table includes records with ZIP codes such as 96768 and 97768.

Using Operators

Conditions can include a number of operators. Use the LIKE operator to do a *fuzzy search*. The ANSWER table includes exact matches and matches that are similar.

Use the NOT query to specify the records you don't want in the ANSWER table. To get a list of customers who aren't from Hawaii, for example, enter **NOT HI** in the State field.

Use the BLANK operator to include records that have a field that doesn't contain a value. For example, to get a list of customers who haven't paid their bills, enter **BLANK** in the AmountPaid field.

Use the TODAY operator as a replacement for entering the current date into a condition.

Use the AS operator to specify the name of a field in the ANSWER table. For example, if you wanted the Addr1 field to be called Address1 in the answer, enter **AS Address1** in the Addr1 field of the query image.

Use the CALC operator to perform calculations within a query. For example, if you wanted to see what your receivables are if you increased everyone's bill by 10 percent, enter **_a, CALC _a*1.1 as AmountDue** in the Amount Due field. (Note that _a is an example element, which is explained later in the "Using Example Elements" section.)

You can combine the CALC operator with the COUNT or SUM operators. CALC COUNT tells the DBD to count the occurrences of a field's value within the answer. COUNT SUM tells the DBD to sum the values in a field. In either case, the results are included as a field in the ANSWER table.

Use the CHANGETO operator to change the value of a field. For example, if you decide to go ahead with the 10 percent rate increase, enter **'_a, CHANGETO _a*1.1'** in the AmountDue field.

> **Note**
>
> You can't use check marks with CHANGETO queries.

Performing Action Queries

DBD queries can do more than just answer questions—they can also add or delete records from a table. If you click and hold the mouse in the first column of a query, the DBD displays a drop-down list of keywords (see fig. 12.37).

Fig. 12.37
DBD queries can perform data operations.

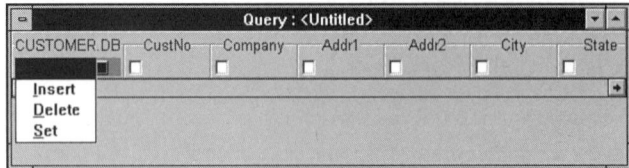

Choose the Insert keyword from the list to add records to a table. Often, insert queries are performed with multitable queries to add records from one table into another. You also can use insert queries to insert particular records into a table. For example, choose Insert from the list and enter field values in each field where you would normally enter query conditions. When you perform the query, the DBD inserts a new record into the table.

> **Note**
>
> You can't use check marks with insert queries.

Delete queries are just the opposite of insert queries—they remove data from the table. Choose Delete from the drop-down list and supply query conditions. If you want to remove all old customers from a table, for example, enter <1/1/90 in the LastInvoiceDate field.

> **Caution**
>
> Be sure to supply some query conditions when doing a Delete query. Otherwise, the DBD empties your entire table without confirmation.

When the DBD executes a delete query, it puts the deleted records in a table called DELETED in your private directory (see fig. 12.38). If after reviewing the records you decide that you didn't want them deleted, add the DELETED table to the original table. DELETED is overwritten the next time you do a delete query and is erased when you exit DBD.

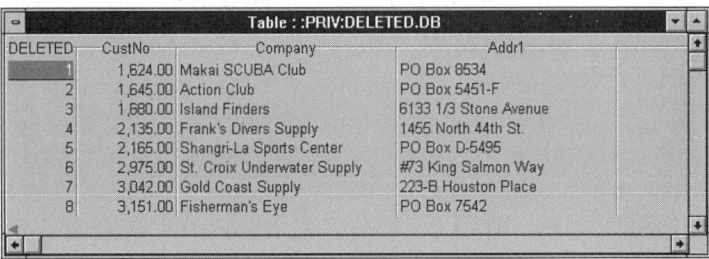

Fig. 12.38
The DBD puts deleted records in a table named DELETED.

Set queries don't insert or delete records—they define a group of records as a set. Once a set query is defined, comparisons to other sets can be made using the Only, No, Every, and Exactly operators. Set queries are often quite difficult to set up. Sometimes it's easier to perform a small simple query to get a group or groups of records and then perform subsequent queries on the ANSWER table.

Using Example Elements

An *example element* is a variable that takes on the value of the field data it represents while a query is running. Example elements are especially useful in CHANGETO and CALC queries but are also used for joining tables together. To place an example element, click the appropriate field, press F5, and enter the name of the example element. Alternatively, you can just enter an example element's name if you begin by typing the underscore character. Figure 12.39 shows a query designed to calculate the grand total of each order. The items Total and Tax are example elements.

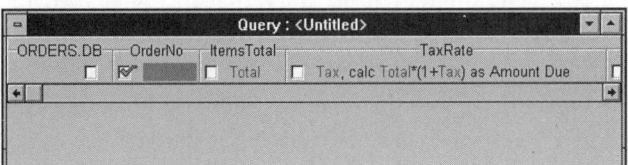

Fig. 12.39
Total and Tax are example elements used to calculate an amount due.

When this query is run, the DBD looks at each record in the Orders table. From each record it assigns the value of the ItemsTotal field to the Total example and the value from the TaxRate field to the Tax example. It then has enough information to do the calculation that follows the CALC operator. Note that the `calc Total*(1+Tax) as Amount Due` part of the query isn't really specific to the Tax field and can be moved to any other field in the query.

Performing Multitable Joins

The DBD lets you perform queries on more than one table at a time. To include another table in a query, open the Query menu and choose Add Table, or click the Add Table icon on the toolbar. To remove a table that's already in a query, open the Query menu and choose Remove Table, or click the Remove Table icon. The DBD even lets you perform joins between local tables and SQL tables.

To query on two tables, the tables must be joined. This is done by placing an example element of the same name in similar fields of each query image. To do so, click the Join Tables icon on the toolbar, click the linking field in the master table, and then click the linking field in the detail table. The DBD places the example elements for you (see fig. 12.40).

Fig. 12.40
The DBD lets you do queries on more than one table at a time.

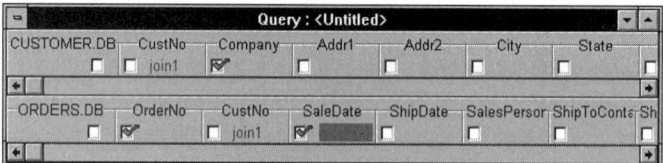

The tables are now joined by the CustNo field and you can put check marks in either table. For example, the ANSWER table resulting from the query in figure 12.40 includes the Company field from the Customer table and the OrderNo and SaleDate fields from the Orders table.

In this example, if a customer has no order, that customer's record isn't included in the ANSWER table. This is known as an *inner join query*. In an *outer join query*, customers are included whether they have an associated order or not. To perform an outer join query, enter ! next to the customer's example element in the CUSTOMER.DB query image (see fig. 12.41).

Performing Queries   **345**

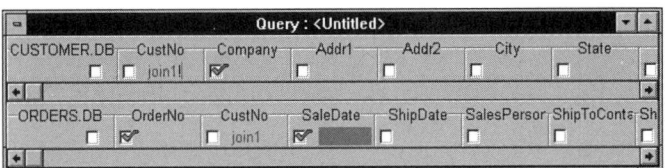

Fig. 12.41
The ! next to the join1 example element in the CUSTOMER.DB query image signifies an outer join.

Performing an ANSWER Table Sort

The DBD lets you specify the fields the ANSWER table is to be sorted on. Click the Sort Answer Table icon on the toolbar, or open the Properties menu and choose Answer Sort. The DBD displays the Sort Answer dialog (see fig. 12.42). Select the fields that the answer is to be sorted on and click OK.

> **Note**
> The Sort Answer dialog works only with CheckPlus queries.

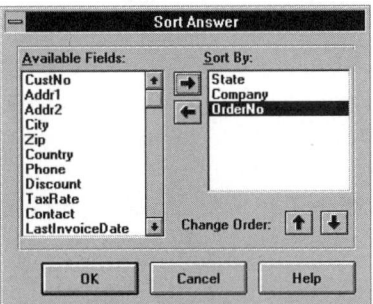

Fig. 12.42
The DBD lets you specify what fields to sort the answer on.

Setting Execution Options

You can set a number of options that control how DBD performs a query. Open the Query menu and choose Execution Options. DBD displays the Query Option dialog (see fig. 12.43).

When you're querying tables in a multiuser environment, it's possible that another user can make a data change while your query is executing. The Table Update Handling section lets you specify how the DBD handles this situation. Select Restart Query on Changes to tell the DBD to completely restart your query if another user changes a table during query execution. Select Lock All Tables To Prevent Changes to prevent other users from making changes during query execution. Select Ignore Source Changes to tell

346   Chapter 12—Using the Database Desktop

the DBD to do a *dirty query*. This means that if the table you are querying is changed while the query takes place, the query doesn't restart. The results of a dirty query may not be perfect, but this is the fastest query method, and it places the least amount of table locks.

Fig. 12.43
You can control how DBD performs a query through the Query Options dialog.

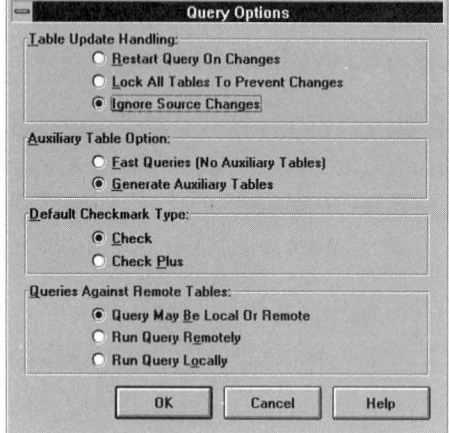

When you perform INSERT, DELETE, and CHANGETO queries, the DBD creates auxiliary tables with the results of the query. During a DELETE query, for example, the DBD creates a DELETED table with all the records that were removed from the main table. If you don't need these auxiliary tables, select Fast Queries (No Auxiliary Tables) in the Auxiliary Table Option section.

When you click a field's white box and don't drag the mouse, the DBD supplies the default check mark. Choose the default check mark type you prefer in the Default Checkmark Type section.

When you query against an SQL table, the DBD can bring records across and perform the query locally, or it can tell the SQL server to perform the query. Use the Queries Against Remote Tables options to tell DBD where remote queries should be performed.

Saving Queries

After you set up a complicated query, you may want to save the query for later use. When you try to close the Query window, the DBD prompts you for the name of your query. You can also save a query by opening the File menu and choosing Save. The DBD saves the query as a text file with a .QBE extension. You can edit the text file with any editor, but it's usually easier to use the DBD's visual QBE environment. To open a saved query, open the File menu, choose Open, and then choose QBE Query. Alternatively, you can click the Open Query icon on the toolbar.

Using SQL Scripts

The DBD table-editing and querying features are powerful, but they can't do everything. For example, you can't interactively create an InterBase table with an array field type. To help out in these situations, the DBD provides SQL scripts, which are sent directly to your SQL server. You can send any valid SQL command.

Creating an SQL Script

Open the File menu, choose New, and then choose SQL Statement. The DBD displays the SQL Editor (see fig. 12.44).

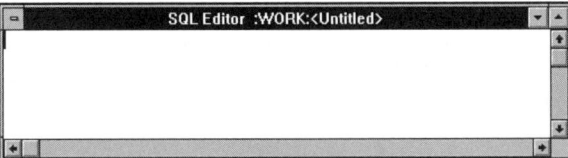

Fig. 12.44
You can send SQL commands directly to your server.

The easiest way to connect to an SQL server is to use an alias that has already been configured for SQL use. Open the SQL menu and choose Select Alias, or click the Select Alias icon on the toolbar. The Select Alias dialog appears. Pick the appropriate alias and click OK. Now SQL commands that you type are sent to the server associated with that alias.

Type a valid SQL command in the SQL Editor window. Figure 12.45, for example, shows an SQL command that creates a table with an array field type.

Fig. 12.45
You can create InterBase tables with array type fields.

After you finish typing your SQL statements, click the Run SQL icon or press F8. The DBD tries to send your SQL statements to the SQL server. If you aren't yet connected to a database, the DBD displays the Database Information dialog (see fig. 12.46). Fill in the appropriate fields and click OK.

Fig. 12.46
The DBD helps get you connected to an SQL database.

While the DBD waits for information from the SQL server, the pointer changes to an hourglass with the letters SQL. If any errors are returned from the server, the DBD displays an error message dialog. If no errors occur, focus is returned to the SQL Editor window.

If your SQL statements perform a query that returns data, the DBD places that data into an ANSWER table (see fig. 12.47).

Fig. 12.47
SQL statements can return a table.

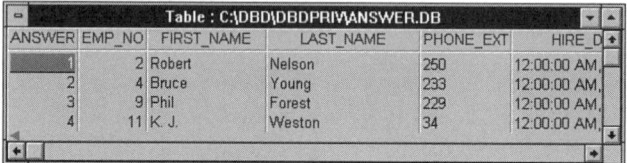

Saving Your SQL Statements

If you want to save an SQL file for later use, open the File menu and choose Save. Supply a name for the SQL file. The DBD saves the file with an .SQL extension. The file is a text file that can be edited with any text editor. To open an existing SQL file, open the File menu, choose Open, and then choose SQL Statement. Alternatively, you can click the SQL icon on the toolbar.

Using DBD Tools

The DBD provides a number of utilities that let you quickly perform operations such as adding or subtracting tables. To access these utilities, open the Utilities menu (see fig. 12.48).

Add

The Add utility lets you add the contents of one table to another table. The tables must have similar field structures. Database rules such as no duplicate keys are still enforced.

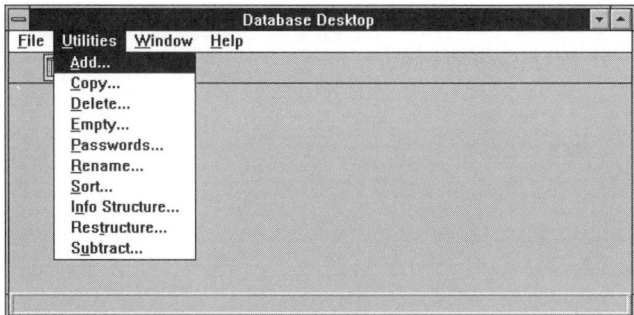

Fig. 12.48
The DBD has many table utilities.

To add two table together, open the Utilities menu and choose Add. The Add dialog appears (see fig. 12.49).

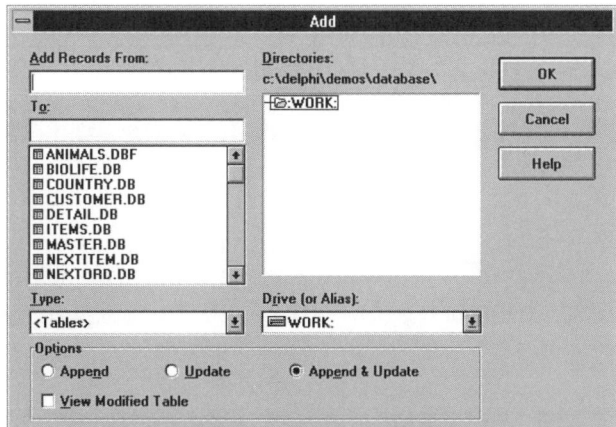

Fig. 12.49
The DBD lets you add tables together.

Enter the name of the source table in the Add Records From text box and the name of the destination table in the To text box. If you want the new records to be appended to the destination table, select Append in the Options section at the bottom of the dialog. Records with duplicate primary keys are thrown out. To have the DBD find records with matching keys in the destination table and then update the non-key fields from the source table, select Update. To perform both functions, select Append & Update.

Copy

The Copy utility lets you copy a table, including its indexes, validity checks, and table view settings. To copy a table, open the Utilities menu and choose Copy. The Copy dialog appears (see fig. 12.50).

350 Chapter 12—Using the Database Desktop

Fig. 12.50
The DBD makes it easy to copy tables.

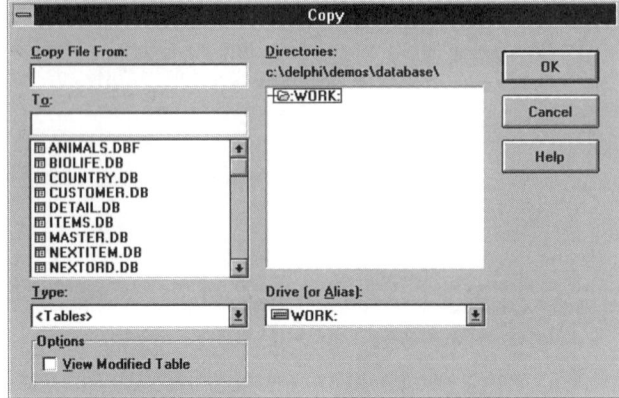

Type the name of the source table in the Copy File From text box and the name of the destination table in the To text box. You can also copy other objects such as .QBE and .SQL files by selecting a different file type from the Type drop-down list. By selecting an SQL table as the source table and a Paradox table as the destination table, you can create a local copy of an SQL table.

Delete

To remove a table or file from your computer, use the Delete utility. Open the Utilities menu and choose Delete. The Delete dialog appears (see fig. 12.51).

Fig. 12.51
It's also easy to get rid of tables.

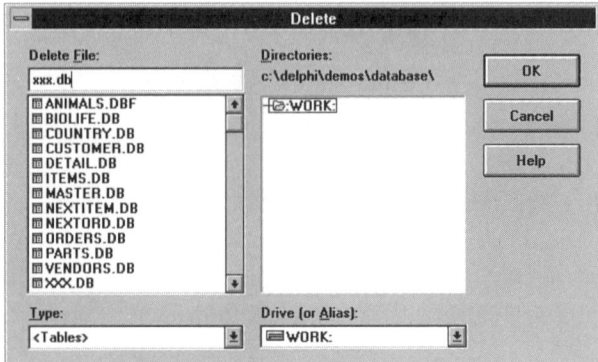

Use the Type drop-down list to specify the type of file to be deleted. Type the name of the file in the Delete File text box. When you click OK, the DBD confirms the deletion and then deletes the select file.

Empty

To remove all the records from a table, use the Empty utility. To empty a table, open the Utilities menu and choose Empty. The Empty dialog appears (see fig. 12.52).

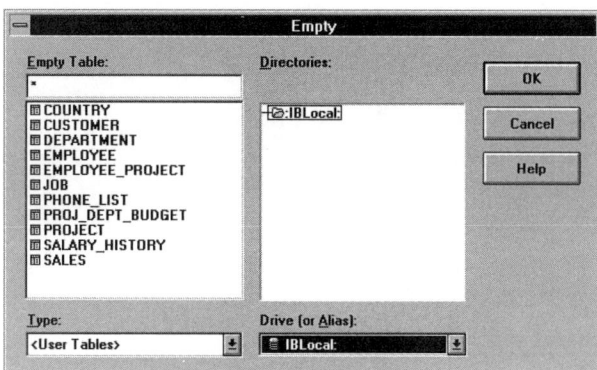

Fig. 12.52
The DBD lets you empty tables.

Enter the name of the table to be emptied in the Empty Table text box and click OK. The DBD confirms the action and then removes all the records from the table.

Passwords

The DBD can keep a list of passwords in memory so that it doesn't have to ask you for a password every time a table is opened. To maintain this list, open the Utilities menu and choose Passwords. The Enter Password(s) dialog appears (see fig. 12.53).

Fig. 12.53
The DBD keeps a list of passwords in memory.

Enter a password and click the Add button to add it to the memory list. The next time the DBD needs a password for some activity, it will first try to use the passwords in memory before asking you for a password. Enter a password and click the Remove button to remove it from the memory list. Click the Remove All button to revoke all current passwords.

Rename

The DBD makes it easy to rename tables. This is often done after a query to prevent the ANSWER table from being overwritten by subsequent queries. To rename a table, open the Utilities menu and choose Rename. The Rename dialog appears (see fig. 12.54).

Fig. 12.54
The DBD lets you rename files.

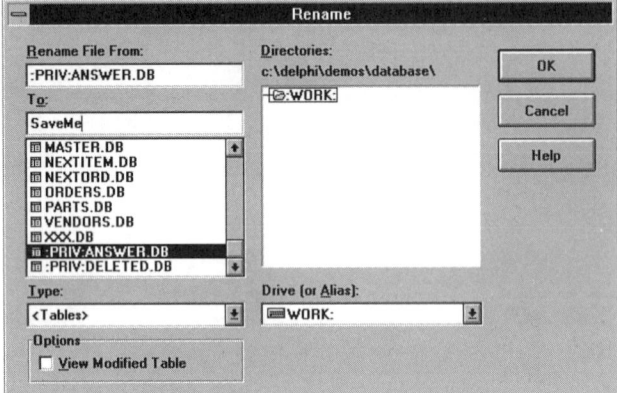

Select the type of file you're renaming from the Type drop-down list. Enter the name of the source file in the Rename File From text box, and enter the new name of the file in the To text box.

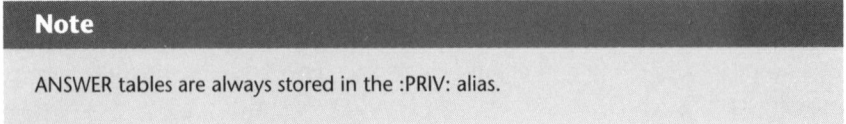

ANSWER tables are always stored in the :PRIV: alias.

Sort

The DBD lets you easily sort tables. If the source table is a keyed table, it's sorted to a new name. To sort a table, open the Utilities menu and choose Sort. The Sort Table dialog appears (see fig. 12.55).

Select either the New Table or Same Table radio button to specify the destination of the sort. Choose the fields on which the sort is to be applied from the Fields list. Change the order of the sort fields by clicking the up- and down-arrow buttons. Click the Sort Direction button for each sort field to toggle between ascending and descending order. When you click OK, the DBD asks you for the new table name, if necessary.

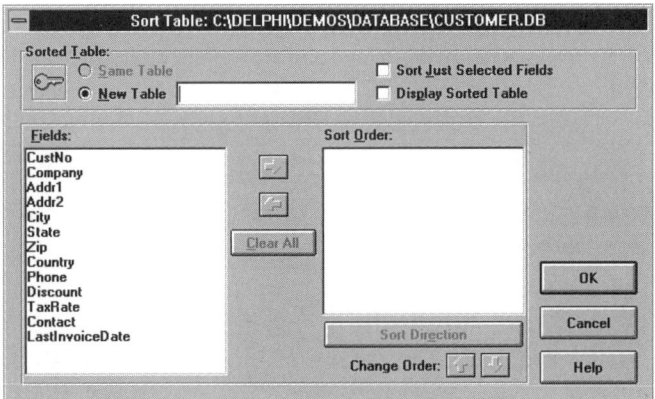

Fig. 12.55
The DBD has built-in table-sorting functions.

Info Structure

The DBD lets you see the structure of a table without having to go into the Restructure dialog. To do this, open the Utilities menu and choose Info Structure. The DBD displays the normal Select File dialog. Select a table and click OK. The DBD displays the Structure Information dialog (see fig. 12.56).

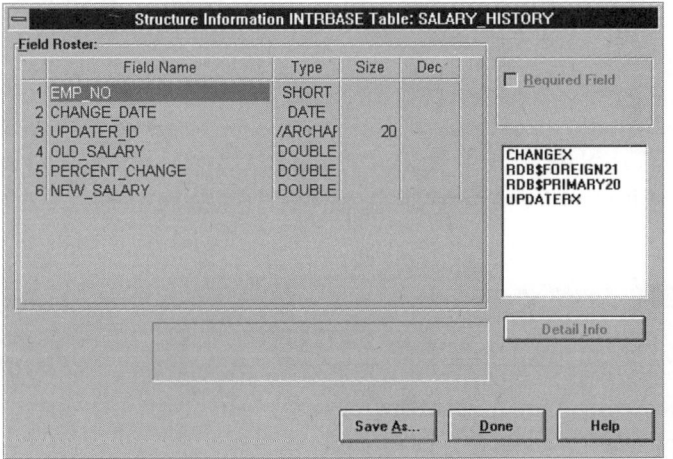

Fig. 12.56
The DBD lets you easily view the structure of a table.

If you want to save the structure as a table for later reference and printing, click the Save As button. The DBD prompts you for the name of the new table.

Subtract

The DBD includes a feature that lets you subtract one table from another. The tables must have a similar field structure. If the tables you're subtracting are keyed, only the key fields have to match for records to be removed. If the tables are unkeyed, all the fields must match for a record to be removed.

To subtract tables, open the Utilities menu and choose Subtract. The Subtract dialog appears (see fig. 12.57).

Fig. 12.57
The DBD lets you subtract one table from another.

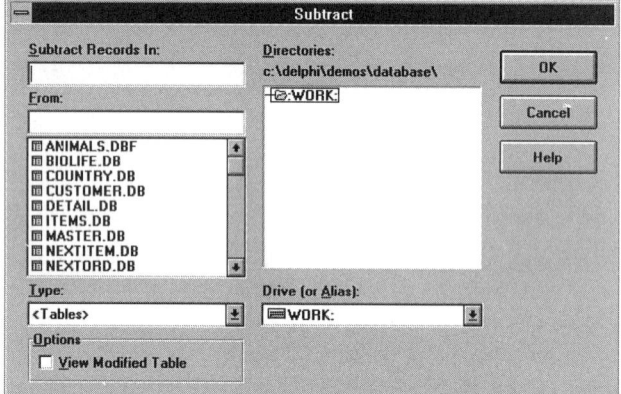

Enter the name of the table with the source records in the Subtract Records In text box. Enter the name of the table that's going to have records removed in the From text box, and then click OK. The DBD asks you to confirm the subtraction with a warning message.

From Here...

For more information, refer to these chapters:

- Chapter 6, "Using Data-Bound Components," tells you how to use all the DBD data in a Delphi application.

- Chapter 13, "Reporting with ReportSmith," describes how to print all the data that you use the DBD to manipulate.

- Chapter 14, "Handling Errors," shows you what to do when your Delphi application encounters table-level and field-level rules.

Chapter 13

Reporting with ReportSmith

One of the major components of any application is the capability to print. Printing can involve anything from simple screen printing or text output to complex statistical analysis reports. The report generator for the Delphi environment is ReportSmith, a stand-alone report engine that Borland sells for usage with all its products, as well as for use in reporting against various other database products and SQL servers.

The beauty of ReportSmith is twofold:

- It allows you to create reports against any data without knowing complex SQL command structures, yet it offers the power of SQL data filtering and an advanced macro language.

- ReportSmith allows you to design and produce reports using "live data"; other programs, on the other hand, show only were the data is to go.

As you'll see, the reports and graphs you design on-screen show the actual data of the database, meaning that any alterations you make to the reports are instantaneously reflected exactly as the hard copy will appear.

Because ReportSmith is an entirely separate program to Delphi, this chapter presents a simple introduction of it. This chapter examines the following topics:

- How to start ReportSmith
- The ReportSmith environment
- How to create a report

- Types of reports
- How to connect to a data source
- How to manipulate data
- How to change the appearance of your report

Starting ReportSmith

The first thing you'll do with ReportSmith is start the program. You can start ReportSmith in three ways:

- From Program Manager, double-click ReportSmith's icon.
- Open the File menu and choose Run. Type `c:\delphi\bin\delphi.exe` in the Command Line text box.
- Double-click the TReport component in the form window.

When you load ReportSmith, the first thing you see is the dialog in figure 13.1. This dialog allows you to open a pre-existing report. If you don't want to open a report but would prefer designing a new report, simply click Cancel. This dialog is automatically displayed whenever you start ReportSmith and is identical to the one you would receive by clicking the Open icon on ReportSmith's toolbar or by using the File menu's Open command.

Fig. 13.1
To create a new report, simply select Cancel.

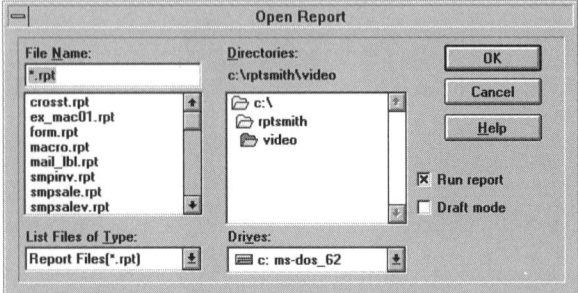

> **Note**
>
> If you don't want the Open Report dialog to appear each time you start ReportSmith, use the Tools menu's Options command and set the program startup options to New Report or None.

Understanding the ReportSmith Environment

Because ReportSmith is a program designed to give you, the user, a great deal of flexibility and control over how your data is presented, you must look at a great number of controls on the interface. These interface controls are generally divided into five areas: the menu bar, the toolbar, the ribbon, the report window, and the rulers (see fig. 13.2). Table 13.1 describes these items, as well as the report window's title bar.

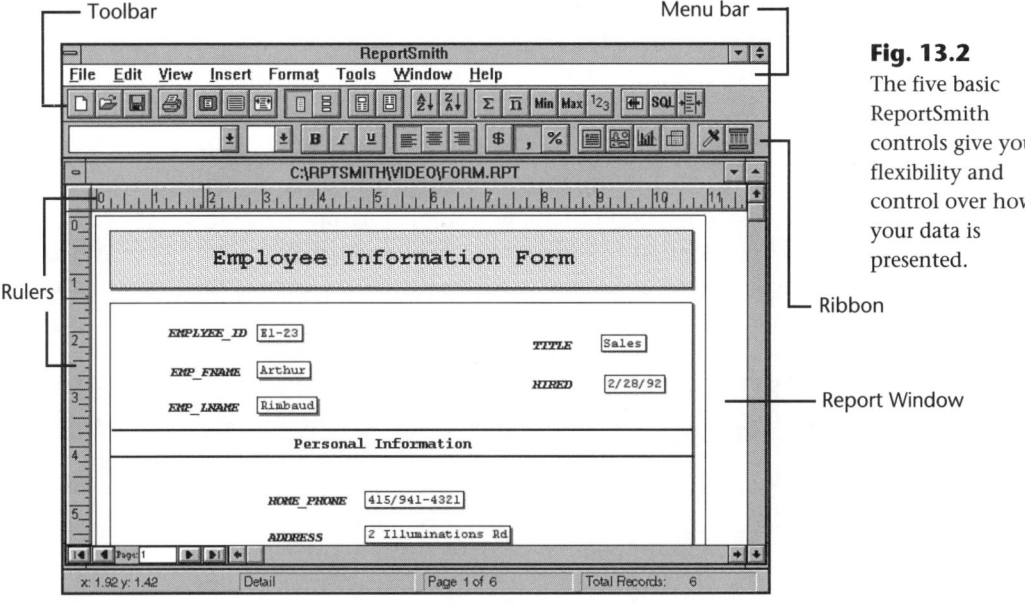

Fig. 13.2
The five basic ReportSmith controls give you flexibility and control over how your data is presented.

Table 13.1 ReportSmith's Interface Features

Control	Description
Menu bar	Contains all the commands and functions that allow you to control the output and functionality of ReportSmith.
Toolbar	The top row of buttons that allow you to control the more common user functions of the system. These buttons include such things as New Report, Open, Save, Sort, and Print.
Ribbon	Allows the user to control the placement of various report objects such as text, graphs, and graphics. It also allows you to perform standard text formatting such as boldfacing, underlining, and alignment.

(continues)

358   Chapter 13—Reporting with ReportSmith

Table 13.1 Continued	
Control	**Description**
Report window	Contains an individual report that you're working with. ReportSmith allows you to use multiple reports at a time, each in a separate window. You can toggle between different report windows via the Window menu.
Title Bar	Displays the file name and path of the report that's currently active. A report that's new and yet to be named will have a default name of Report1. The title bar also has the standard Windows control menu and Minimize and Maximize buttons.
Rulers	The horizontal and vertical rulers that you can move around the report to help with aligning objects.

The Toolbar

The toolbar contains icons representing most of the common functions that you'll need to perform in the process of designing a report (see fig. 13.3). These functions all correspond to a menu option and simply serve as a way to speed development time. You can control the display of the toolbar though the View menu's Toolbar command.

Fig. 13.3
To find out the function of a button on the toolbar or ribbon, simply put the mouse pointer on it, and the status bar will display a description.

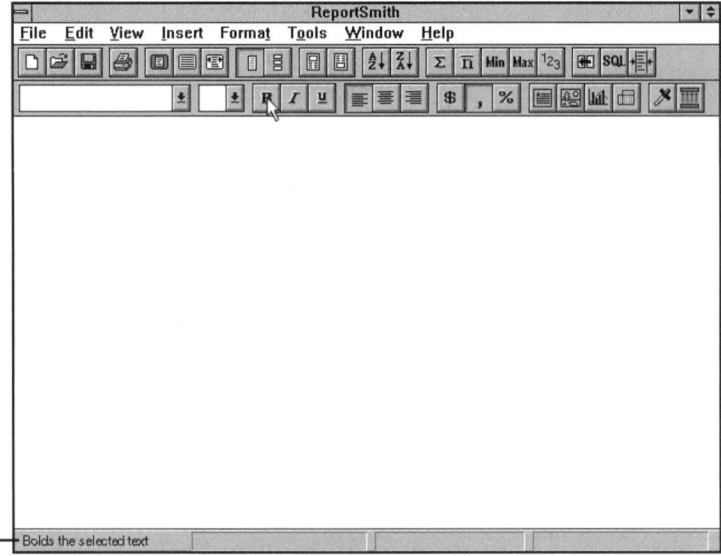

Toolbar button description

The Ribbon

The ribbon allows you to easily apply formatting attributes to text (refer to fig. 13.2). It also gives you quick access to the different display objects, such as graphs or crosstabs, that you might want to add to your reports. Also, there are buttons representing more advanced features such as styles. These functions all correspond to a menu option and simply serve as a method for speeding your development time.

Tip
You can toggle the display of the ribbon though the View menu's Ribbon command.

The Report Window

The report window is the canvas where you design and display your report. In this way, the window serves as the representation of the hard-copy output. There's no limit to the number of report windows that you can have open on the desktop at once, other than a practical limit placed on the quantity by your system resources.

Rulers

The report window is simply a container and has no real functionality beyond that, with the exception of the rulers. These rulers, as figure 13.4 shows, provide you with a powerful tool for measuring and aligning information in the report. To adjust the position of the rulers, click at the intersection of the horizontal and vertical rule and drag them into position. Notice that both rulers move in conjunction with each other.

Tip
You can toggle the display of the rulers from the View menu.

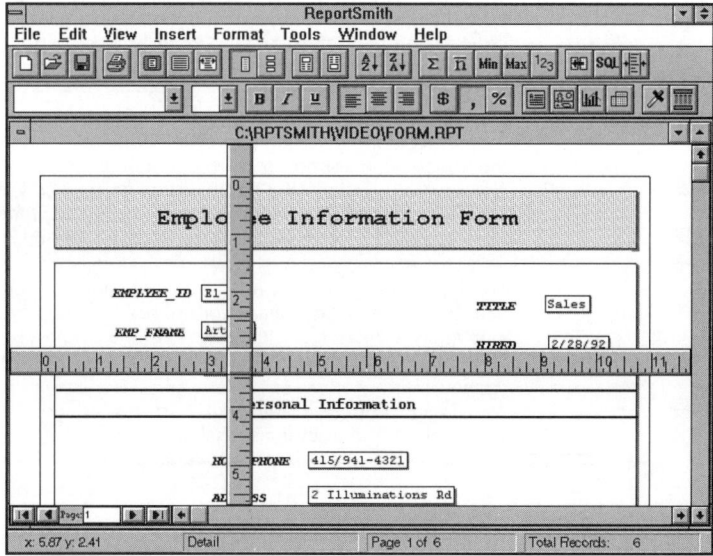

Fig. 13.4
The rulers help you align objects on your report.

Creating Reports

The first thing that you need to do when creating a report is to define the report. The following sections describe how you can do this.

Choosing the Report Type

You can create a new report by opening the File menu and choosing New, or by clicking the New Report toolbar button. ReportSmith displays the Create a New Report dialog (see fig. 13.5).

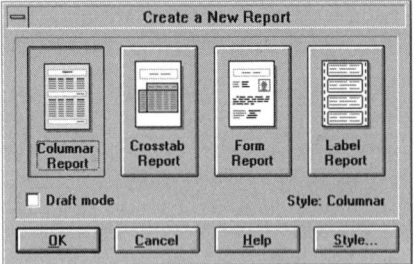

Fig. 13.5
ReportSmith supports four basic report types: columnar, crosstab, form, and label.

In this dialog, notice that you have four report types to choose from:

Report Type	Description
Columnar Report	The classical listing type of report, this report type is great for displaying large volumes of information in a grouped fashion, possibly with subtotals. Figure 13.6 shows an example of this report type.
Crosstab Report	In a crosstab report, summary information is presented in spreadsheet format, giving the reader instant access to the report's totals in a simple format. Crosstab reports aren't just summary versions of a columnar report—in fact, they are attached to the header or footer of existing columnar reports. Figure 13.7 shows an example of this report type.
Form Report	This type of report is used when presenting information in a fashion where a individual record needs to be displayed in a highly formatted fashion, such as in the employee information form in figure 13.8.
Label Report	As the name implies, a label report format is designed specifically to print out mailing labels (see fig. 13.9).

Creating Reports **361**

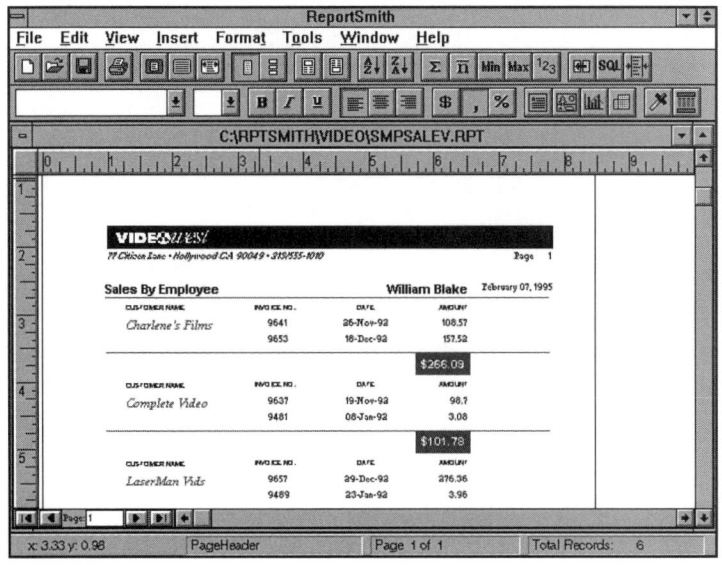

Fig. 13.6
Columnar reports are great for displaying a large number of detail records in a listing format.

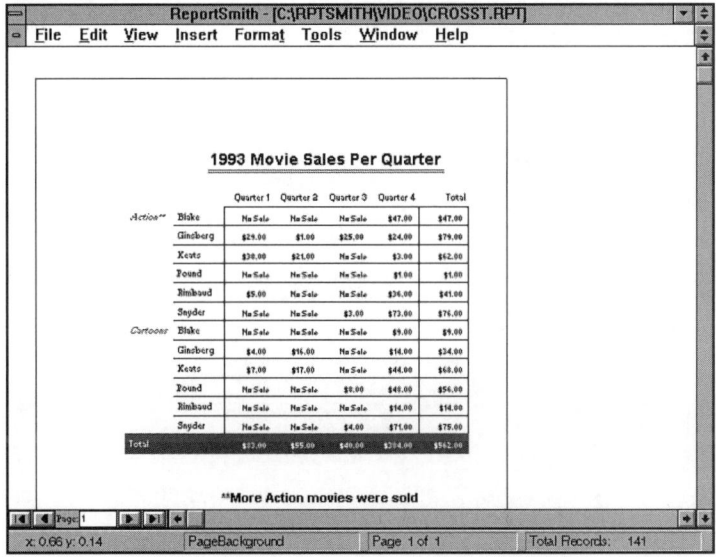

Fig. 13.7
Crosstab reports summarize columnar data.

Fig. 13.8
Form reports are commonly used to print data sheets.

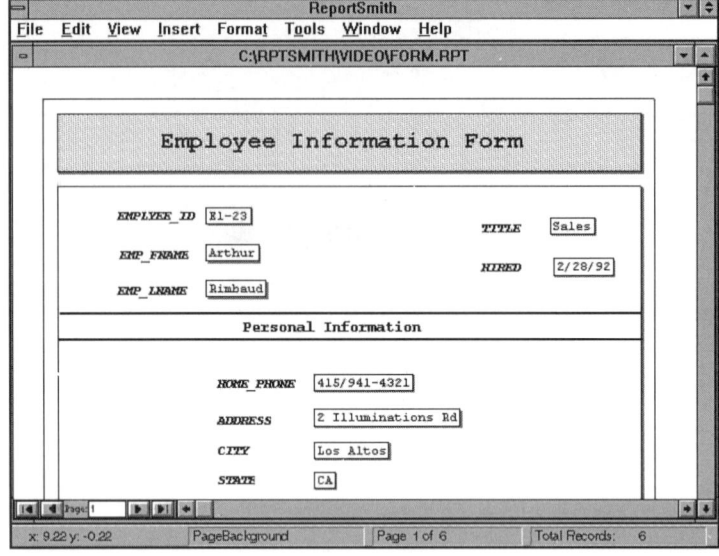

Fig. 13.9
ReportSmith makes it easy to print mailing labels.

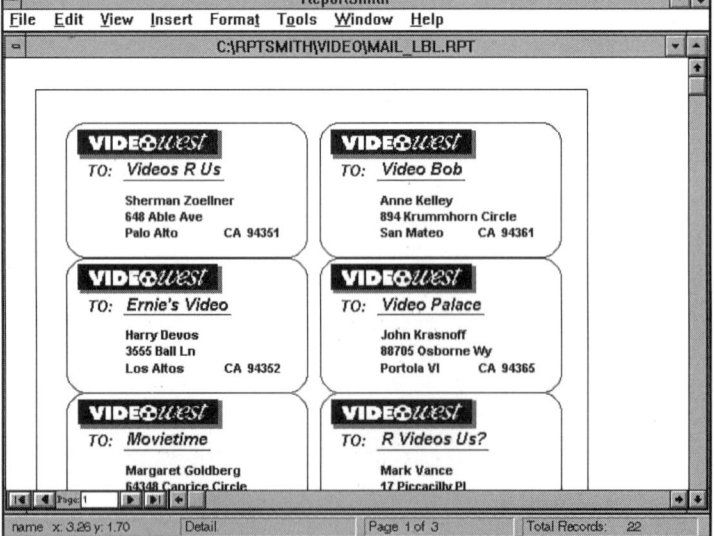

Applying Report Styles

Once you choose which of the report types best fits your needs, ReportSmith allows you to choose a basic predefined appearance set, called a *style*, to apply to the report. The currently selected default style appears next to the word Style: in the Create a New Report dialog (refer to fig. 13.5). To access the palette of appearance sets from the Create a New Report dialog, click the Style button.

The resulting New Report Style dialog has three sections (see fig. 13.10). The top left corner of the dialog lists predefined styles you can select. The currently highlighted style's appearance is reflected in the area to the right labeled Sample. You can define custom styles as well; these are displayed, if defined, in the bottom left section of the dialog. If you select a custom style, the effect of the style would appear in the Sample box as with the predefined styles.

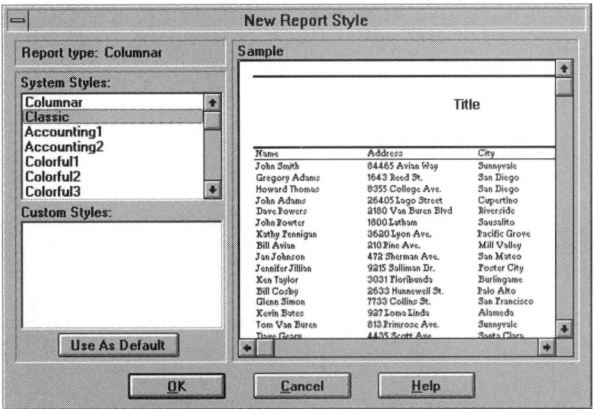

Fig. 13.10
You can quickly create highly formatted reports using the New Report Style dialog.

Note

Each report type has a default style that's applied to all new reports until you change that style for the individual report. You can set this default behavior by selecting a style and clicking the Use As Default button.

After you select a report style and click OK, you're returned to the Create a New Report dialog. The dialog reflects the selected style by the Style: indicator. To complete the definition of the report type and style, click OK to continue.

Generating a Report Query

Once you define the type of report you want and the style set you want applied to the report, you're asked for the *report query*. This simply means that you have to define the data to be presented in the report. This report query will be run each time you load or run the report to obtain the date to display. To do this, you have to answer the following questions:

Chapter 13—Reporting with ReportSmith

- Which data tables are you reporting against?
- What type of tables are they and where are they?
- What are the relationships between the tables?
- Which records do you want to see?
- Which fields do you want to see?
- Do you want the report sorted?

The Report Query dialog walks you through these questions, using a series of buttons found at the top of the dialog (see fig. 13.11). These buttons will be grayed out when not relevant but otherwise can be accessed in any order desired. The buttons are as follows:

Button	Description
Tables	Allows you to add and delete tables in the data model. In doing so, you define the links between the tables and the columns of the tables displayed in the report.
Selections	Allows you to define which records in the tables will be displayed in the report. This is done by using English-language sentences rather than SQL statements.
Sorting	Lets you define or change the manner in which the report will be sorted.
Derived Fields	Lets you define or erase calculated fields in the report. This is done either with SQL commands or by using ReportSmith's own macro language.
Report Variables	Defines runtime level variables in the report. This allows you to alter the appearance of the report each time it's run.
Database Grouping	Allows you to group and select the data before it's displayed on the report.
SQL	Allows you to do two things. First, you can view the SQL code generated by your responses to the other facets of this dialog. Second, if you're familiar with the SQL language, you can enter some, none, or all of your data model definition here.

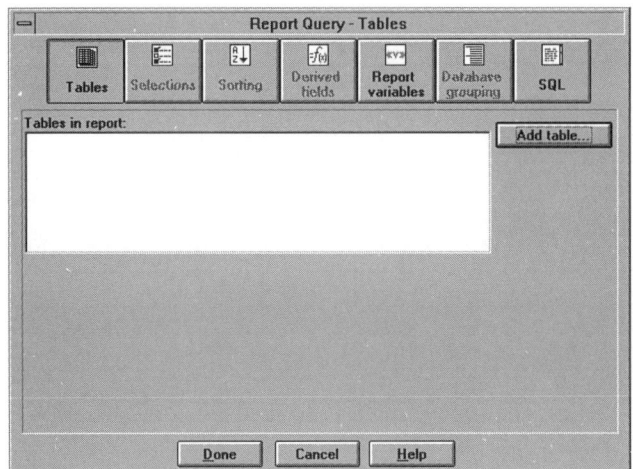

Fig. 13.11
You can define the report table setup by using the Report Query dialog or though direct SQL statements.

> **Note**
> The Report Query dialog automatically appears when you're defining a new report. However, sometimes you'll want to edit these settings after the initial definition of the report is complete. You can do this by opening the Tools menu and choosing Report Query. Then you can change any Report Query setting you want in this dialog.

Defining Tables

Before you can do anything else with the Report Query dialog, you must define the tables that you'll be reporting against. This is done with the Tables option. You'll begin by adding a table.

Adding Tables. To add one or more tables to the report query data model, follow these steps:

1. Click the Tables button.

2. On the right side of the dialog, click Add Table. The Select Table To Be Added dialog appears (see fig. 13.12).

Fig. 13.12
Use the Select Table To Be Added dialog to add tables to the data model.

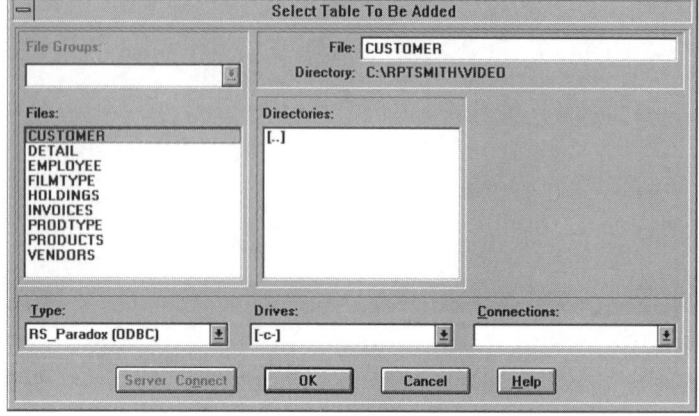

3. Select the type of table you want to access from the Type drop-down list in the bottom left corner. The dialog dynamically changes depending on whether you're accessing local or client/server data. (The rest of this discussion assumes local data—Paradox or dBASE, for example.)

4. Define the drive, path, and file name of the table you want to add to the model.

5. Choose OK. You return to the Report Query dialog, where the table you selected is now displayed in the Tables in Report list (see fig. 13.13). You'll also see new sections in the dialog—for linking tables and for assigning aliases. Also notice that the four buttons that were previously grayed out are now available.

Fig. 13.13
Once you add multiple tables to the report query, you have to define links using the Add New Link button.

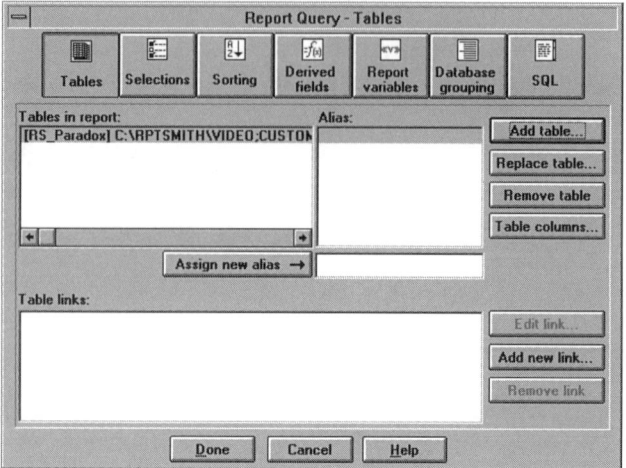

6. If you need to use multiple tables in the report, repeat steps 2 through 5 for each table to be added.

The preceding steps allow you to add the tables required in your data model, thus providing the data you need to report on. You can also delete and edit this set of tables in similar ways by using the Replace Table and Remove Table buttons in the Report Query dialog.

Adding New Links. Once all the tables you require are added to the model, you must define the relationships between the tables. You can do so with the Add New Link button on the bottom right of the Report Query dialog. The dialog in figure 13.14 shows that a data model has been defined that contains two tables: a customer table and a invoice table. These tables have an obvious relationship, but you must manually define that relationship as follows:

1. Click the Add New Link button. The Create New Table Link dialog appears (see fig. 13.14).

2. At the top of the dialog you define the tables that you'll link. Select the name of one of the tables on the left and the other on the right. In the example, notice that Customer is selected on the left and Invoices is selected on the right.

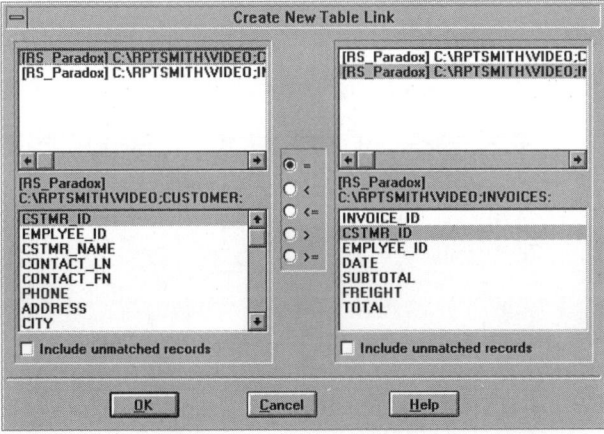

Fig. 13.14
You must define each relationship separately, which may mean performing the linkage steps several times for multiple tables with multiple links.

3. At the bottom of the dialog select the corresponding fields in the tables. In figure 13.14, both tables have a field called CSTMR_ID, and thus that field has been selected as a link.

4. Between the lists relating the tables is a group of relationship operators—the =, <, <=, >, and >= symbols. The equals (=) symbol is the default relationship between the fields, but you can alter this by selecting the appropriate radio button to accommodate your needs.

5. When you've completed the relationship, choose OK to return to the Report Query dialog.

6. If you have multiple tables, you have to repeat the preceding steps for each link needed.

The preceding process enables you to link the tables in your data model, thus providing accurate matching of their records. You can also delete and edit these links in similar ways by using the Edit Link and Remove Link buttons.

Selecting Fields. When you design a report, not only do you need to control the tables that appear, but on a more detailed level you need to control the fields of those tables that appear. For example, you're printing mailing labels for your customers but don't want to have the labels show their customer number. To accomplish this, you need to eliminate the customer number from the report. ReportSmith lets you control this aspect of the report by adjusting what it calls the *table columns*. Follow these steps:

1. In the Report Query dialog, select the table that you want to restrict columns for. Then click the Tables Columns button to display the Table Columns dialog (see fig. 13.15).

Fig. 13.15
Often in reports, you want to see only particular pieces of information per record. To control this, use the Table Columns dialog.

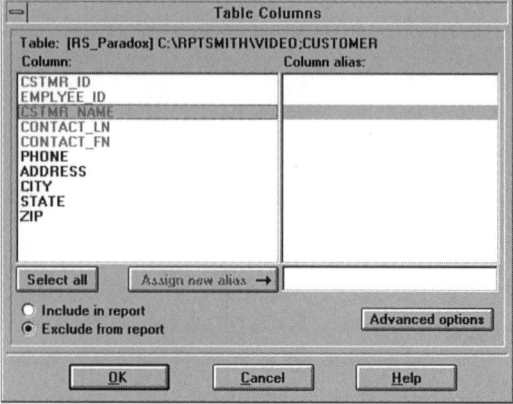

> **Note**
>
> If you don't specifically select the table columns that you want to view in a report, ReportSmith automatically assumes that you want to see them all.

2. In the Column list on the left of the Table Columns dialog, you see all the fields in the table you selected. You can now select the fields that you want to see in the report. This is accomplished with standard Windows selection commands:

   - To select a single field, simply highlight it and then select either Exclude in Report or Include in Report at the bottom of the dialog before selecting OK.

   - To select multiple continuous fields, select the first in the set and then Shift+click the last field in the set. This will highlight all the fields between the first and the last. Then choose either Exclude in Report or Include in Report.

   - To select multiple fields that aren't listed in order, Ctrl+click each one. This way, you can select a number of fields without regard to their location relative to each other. As with other selection methods, choose Exclude in Report or Include in Report.

   - If you want to include or exclude all fields in the table, choose Select All and then choose Exclude in Report or Include in Report.

   - To change the status of an individual field from Exclude in Report to Include in Report or from Include to Exclude, simply double-click the name of the field in the Column list.

3. To accept the Exclude/Include selections you've made, choose OK and return to the Report Query dialog.

> **Note**
>
> If you neglect to exclude columns from your report query here, you still can delete columns while designing the report. To do so, simply select a column and press Delete. Such deletion, however, removes the columns from the display only, not from the Report Query.

370 Chapter 13—Reporting with ReportSmith

The process detailed here will allow you to set the column selection for your report. In addition to this initial setup, you can access the Table Columns dialog as required to edit the selections you've made, thus accommodating the changing requirements of your report.

Choosing a Sort Order

In addition to the definition of tables to be included in the report, the Report Query dialog allows you to define how the selected data will appear when presented. Sorting, however, can greatly affect this appearance. Sorting allows you to control the order in which the data is displayed. For instance, a telephone book is generally sorted by Last Name, and within Last Name by First Name. An aging report might be sorted by Customer Name or Number.

Your reports can be sorted in three ways: ascending, descending, or not sorted at all. The Report Query dialog puts this power in your hands (see fig. 13.16). The Sorting version of the Report Query dialog can be accessed either through the Sorting button in the Report Query dialog or by opening the Tools menu and choosing Sorting.

Fig. 13.16
Use the Report Query dialog to adjust the sort order of the report from ascending to descending to no sorting.

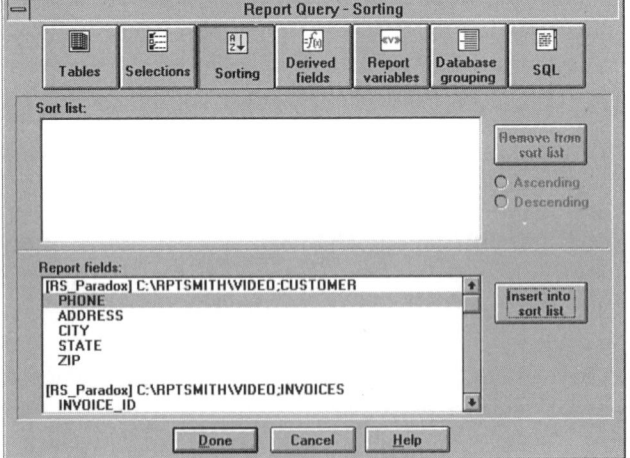

As you can see, the Report Query dialog shown in figure 13.16 has two distinct sections. The top section contains the current sort order of the report; the bottom section lists the available fields that you can sort the report on. To change the sort order of a report, you must build a sort statement in the top section by using the fields at the bottom in conjunction with the Ascending and Descending radio buttons on the right side of the top section. It works like this:

1. Select a field from the Report Fields list and either double-click it or click the Insert into Sort List button to add the field to the Sort List. The Report Fields list now shows the field with an asterisk (*) in front of it to indicate it has been used in the sort order.

2. With the new sort statement is highlighted, select either Ascending or Descending from the radio buttons to the right. (The default is Ascending.) When you do this, the list changes to reflect your choice (see fig. 13.17).

3. If you want to add more fields to the sort order, simply repeat steps 1 and 2. The order in which you add them to the Sort List is the priority they will be sorted in. (For instance, if you put Customer Last Name first in the sort order and then add First Name, the result will be a listing by Last Name with ties sorted by First Name, like a phone book.)

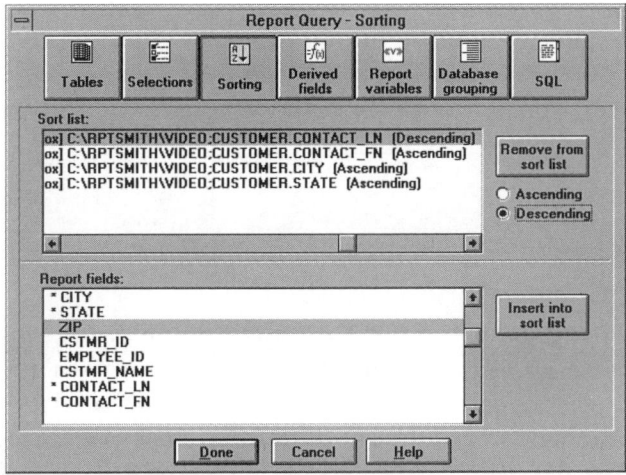

Fig. 13.17
When you add fields to the sort list, they indicate the order in which your report will be sorted.

Removing a Field from the Sort List. If you want to remove a field from the sort list, you can do so in two ways:

- Highlight the field in the Sort List and then click the Remove from Sort List button.

- Double-click a field name in the Report Fields list that has been marked with an asterisk to remove it from the Sort List.

Inserting a Field in the Middle of the List. When you're adding sort fields to the sort list, it's naïve to believe that you'll always be adding them in order. To alleviate this problem, ReportSmith has allowed you to add a field to the middle of the sort order. To do so, simply drag a field from the Report Fields list to the Sort List. As you do this, the mouse pointer changes from an arrow to a hand holding a record to an insertion pointer (see fig. 13.18). Position the insertion pointer in the Sort List where you want the new field, and release the mouse button. The new field is inserted into the sort order.

Fig. 13.18
The insertion pointer indicates that you can insert fields in the Sort List rather than simply append the current list.

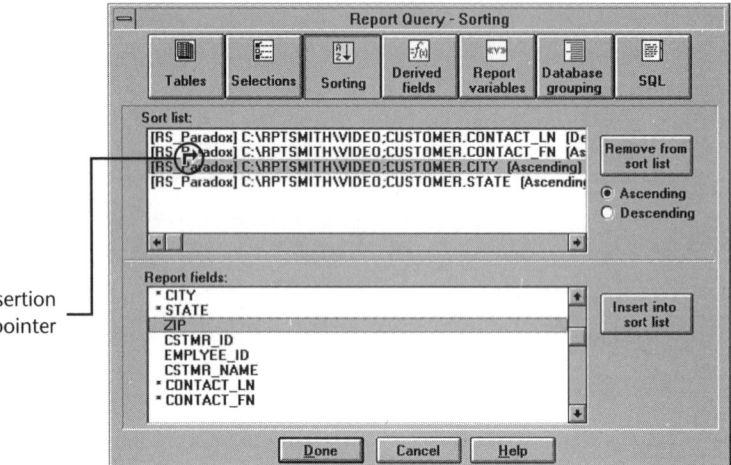

Insertion pointer

Changing the Order of the Sort List. You could remove fields from the Sort List and then read them to the list to change the order that they appear in. This wouldn't be much fun, however. Instead, ReportSmith allows you to click and drag fields around the Sort List, so you can very easily alter the sort of the report.

When you complete the process of selecting your tables, linking them, choosing which fields to display, and specifying how to sort the records, click the Done button. ReportSmith then determines the SQL statement needed to create the report you've requested (see fig. 13.19). Then it will execute this request, displaying the starting point for your report, as requested (see fig. 13.20).

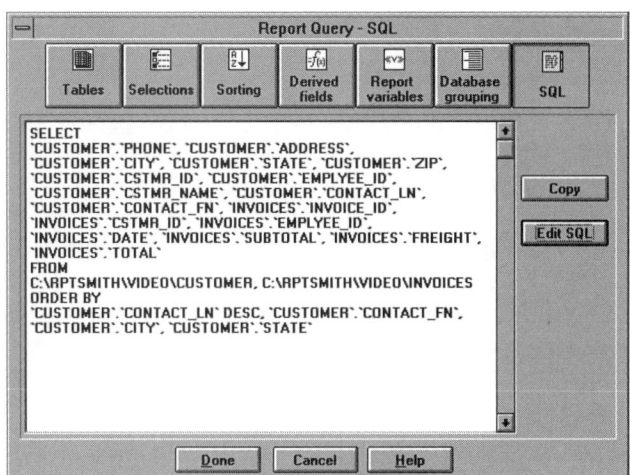

Fig. 13.19
ReportSmith translates all your Report Query dialog answers into an SQL statement before execution.

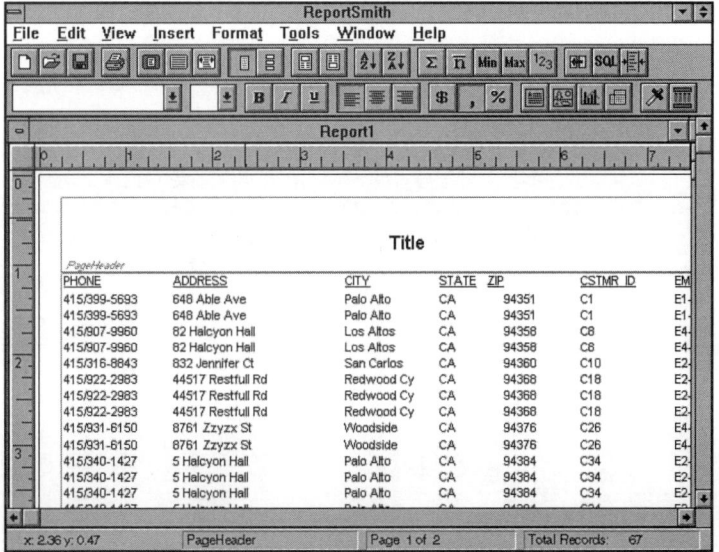

Fig. 13.20
Once ReportSmith executes your SQL statement, it returns to you a beginning point for your report.

This isn't an end, but just a beginning, for now you must format your report to look how you need it to look.

Formatting Your Report

Once the basics of the report have been defined, what you're left with is a very drab listing of information. If the information is all you're after, this would be fine. But more often than not, you want to make the information easy to read for those that need to use it. This requires formatting.

Formatting can take many forms, from changing fonts to sorting, grouping, and summarizing information. Formatting can include the addition of graphics, crosstab summaries, or even graphing data. The following sections discuss how to use some of these features with your reports.

Making It Fit

When you first view your report in the report window, you'll see that it looks like figure 13.20. This looks pretty good; however, if you use the horizontal scroll bars at the bottom of the screen, you'll see that you have a problem—you have too much information to fit on the paper (see fig. 13.21).

Fig. 13.21
Often you'll be faced with the dilemma of how to get your report to fit onto the page.

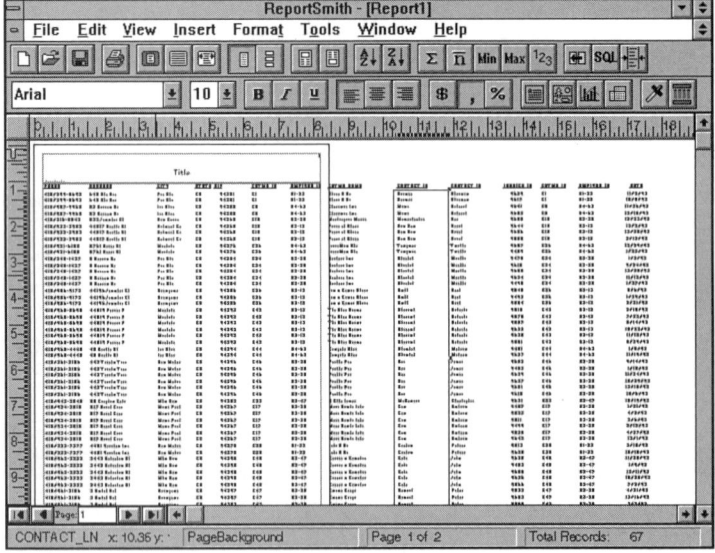

This problem is common, however, as it's hard to estimate the results of your table column selections on a report. You can fix it, though. Try these techniques:

- Open the Report Query dialog and redefine the column selections for the report. However, with this method you're still guessing at the effect of your data model on the final report. It would be better if you could work visually with the report to adjust this.

- Use the Best Fit toolbar icon to set the width of the columns to the best-fit size. The result of this may not fully resolve the situation (see fig. 13.22). In this case, you must explore other options.

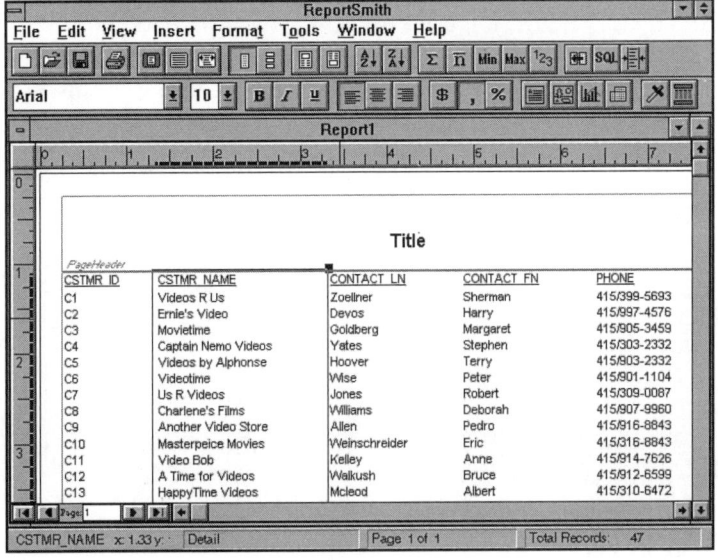

Fig. 13.22
The Best Fit feature can help you make your data fit on the page.

- Use the Format menu's Column Width command to manually adjust the size of individual columns. This is sometimes a good way to get the appropriate column sizes. However, be careful that you don't make the columns too narrow for your data to be displayed.

  In figure 13.22, notice a black square attached to the column selected. If you click and drag this black square, you'll see that you can adjust the column width with the mouse alone.

- You might try to adjust the font size of the report, but this normally won't give the effect you need without making the report too small to read. (Changing font sizes is discussed in a later section.)

376   Chapter 13—Reporting with ReportSmith

- Normally, if you have too much information for the page, you'll find you need to reduce the information to be put on the page. For the example, select the Phone Number and the extra Customer Number fields since you really don't need them, and press Delete to remove them from the report. (Remember, this won't remove them from the data model, only from the report page.)

By using these techniques, you'll be able to make your report fit on the page, as shown in figure 13.23. This is important, because the formatting you're about to do is of no use if it can't be printed on the report.

Fig. 13.23
With a little effort, you can make the report data fit on your page.

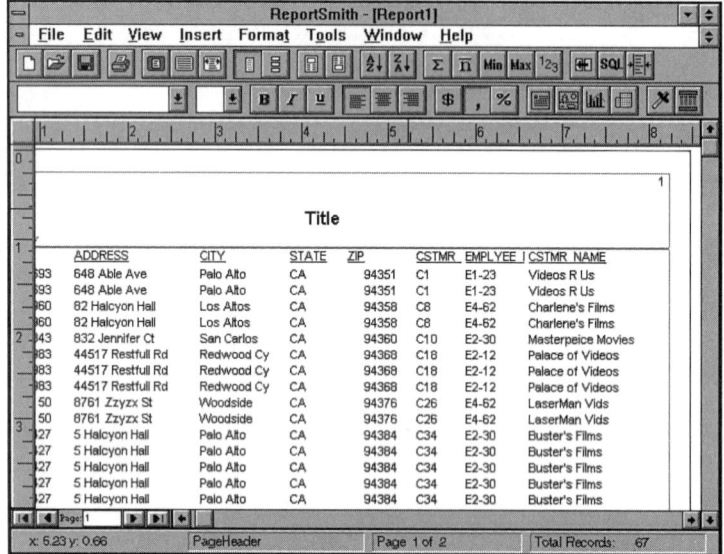

Reordering the Columns

As you're working on the format of your report, you may discover that you want to change the horizontal order of your fields. You can easily do so by using the mouse. Follow these steps:

1. Highlight the column you want to move.

2. Click the column with the mouse and drag it toward the location where you want to leave it. When you get it there (indicated by a light blue line between pre-existing columns), release the mouse button. ReportSmith automatically moves the column for you.

Changing the Text

One of the next things that you'll want to do to your report is change the appearance of your text. This can include changing the wording, the font, or even the alignment of the text. To do this is easy as punch.

Selecting Text

First, you need to select the text you want to change (as in fig. 13.24). You have three basic approaches:

- Click a text item you want to change. This area could be a label, a column, or a column header. When you click, the item will be highlighted.

- Ctrl+click to select multiple items. These areas can be labels, columns, column headers, or any combination of these. When you finish, the items you selected will be highlighted.

- Click the first item in a list, and then Shift+click the last desired item to select a continuous set of items. These areas can be labels, columns, column headers, or any combination of these. When you finish, the items you selected will be highlighted.

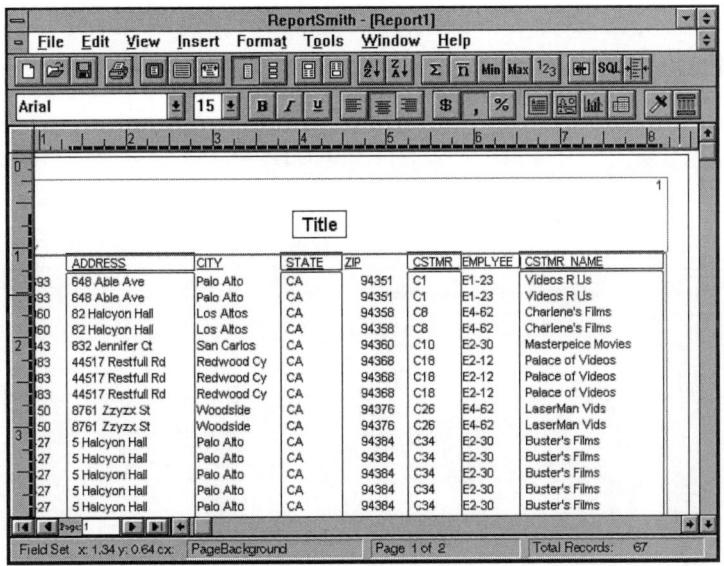

Fig. 13.24
Use the mouse with the Ctrl or Shift key to select the text you want to change.

Changing Fonts and Attributes

Once the text to be changed is highlighted, you can change the font of that text, if you want. You can do so by using the font drop-down list on the ribbon. You can also set the size of the font with the font size drop-down list.

If you prefer, you can get more control over the font by using the Forma<u>t</u> menu's <u>C</u>haracter command (see fig. 13.25). This dialog allows control over formatting such as font color and strikethrough that aren't available elsewhere.

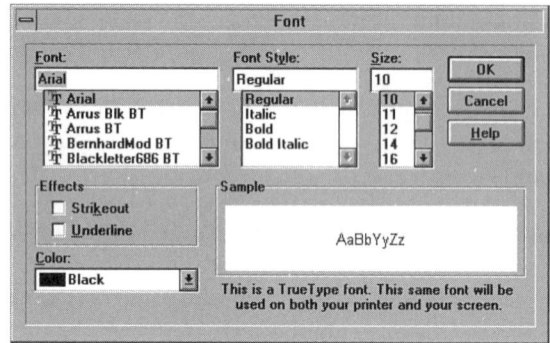

Fig. 13.25
For sophisticated font manipulation with a preview feature, the Font dialog is a great tool.

Once you've made all your formatting changes, you're left with a partially formatted report (see fig. 13.26). As you can see, you have work left to do to it, but it's coming along nicely.

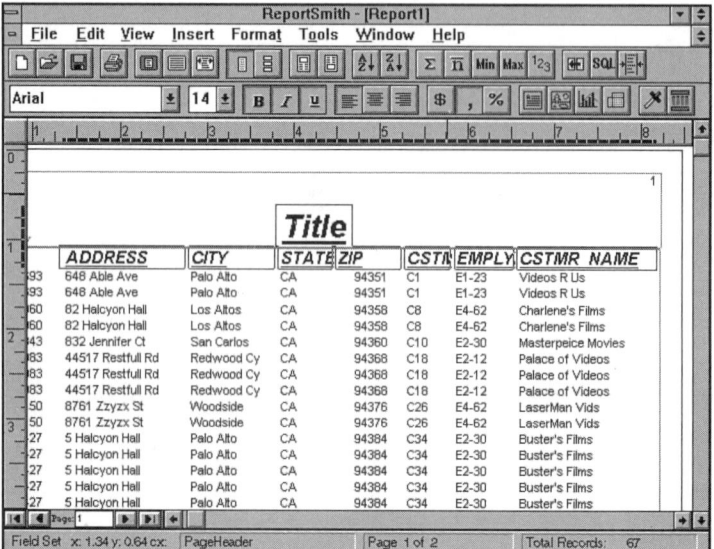

Fig. 13.26
You can change the appearance of the report a great deal with simple text formatting.

Changing and Adding Text

The next thing you might want to change about the format of the text is the actual words used in that text. This is accomplished by selecting (as described earlier) and then clicking the text once more to place the cursor on that object and allow you to edit it. In figure 13.27, you can see the text changed in this sample report.

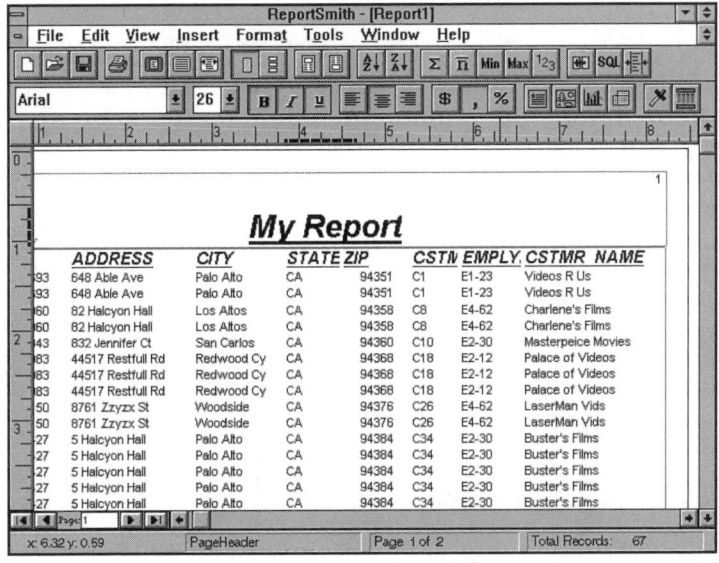

Fig. 13.27
Changing the actual text of labels can often make them more descriptive or useful to the reader of the report.

You also may need to add text to a report. This text can be used for titles, notes, headers, footers, and so on. To do this, follow these simple steps:

1. Select the Text Addition tool from the ribbon.

2. Position the cursor where you want to see the text appear. (Don't be too concerned with this, because you'll be able to move the text by selecting and dragging it into position.)

3. Click to position the text cursor on the report. Type your desired text.

4. If the text needs to be moved, move it by clicking and dragging it.

Adding a Graphic

If you want to add some spice to your report by including a graphic, you can do so very easily with the following steps:

1. Click the Graphic Addition tool (with the tree on it), or open the Insert menu and choose Picture. The Picture dialog appears.

380 Chapter 13—Reporting with ReportSmith

2. Use the file browser to select you favorite .GIF, .PCX, .TIF, .BMP, or .DIB graphic file.

3. Choose OK.

4. When you return to the report, simply position the mouse pointer where you want to see the graphic placed and click. The graphic is added to the report, as in figure 13.28.

5. If you need to move or resize the graphic, select and drag it, or grab its handles to adjust its size.

Fig. 13.28
A graphic and new text have been added to this report.

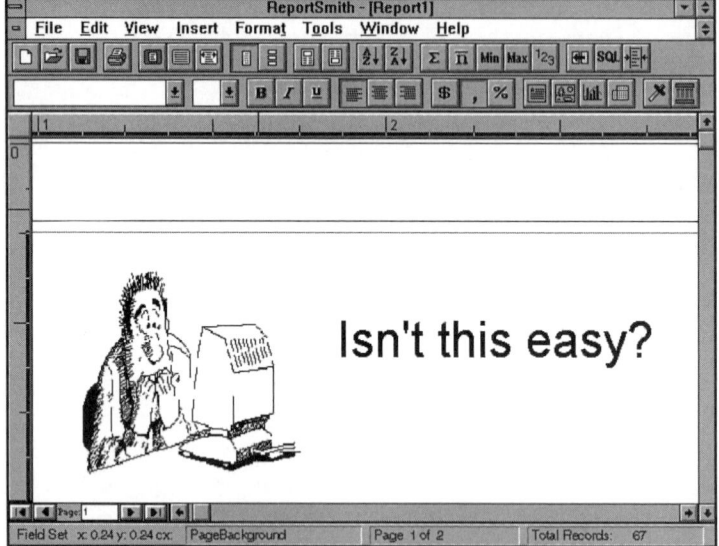

Grouping Information

Your report is very nice, but you have no real way of seeing the information broken down per company. This is where *grouping* comes in. If you want to see the companies broken down into separate areas of the report, add a grouping mark based on a field that's unique to the company, such as Company ID. Follow these steps:

1. Select the column to be grouped (like in fig. 13.29, where the Cstmr Name field is selected).

Formatting Your Report **381**

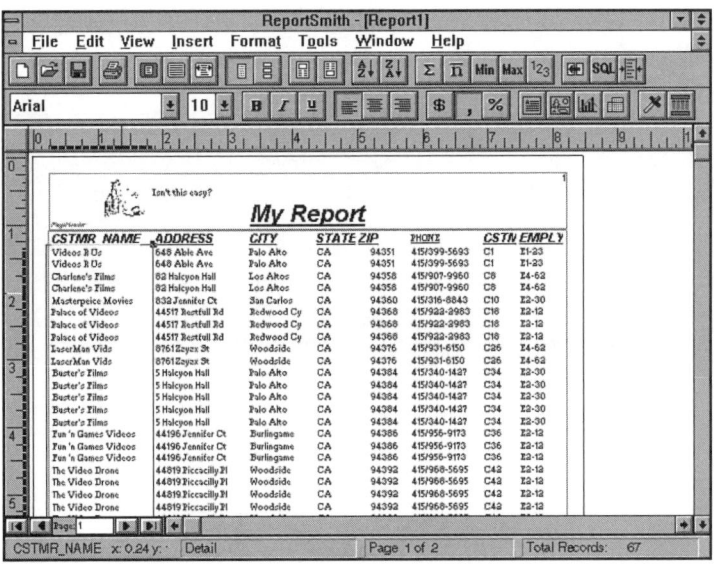

Fig. 13.29
Group your reports based on unique data such as a customer number or employee ID.

2. If you want to place a header on the group, use the Group with Header button on the toolbar. The result will look like figure 13.30.

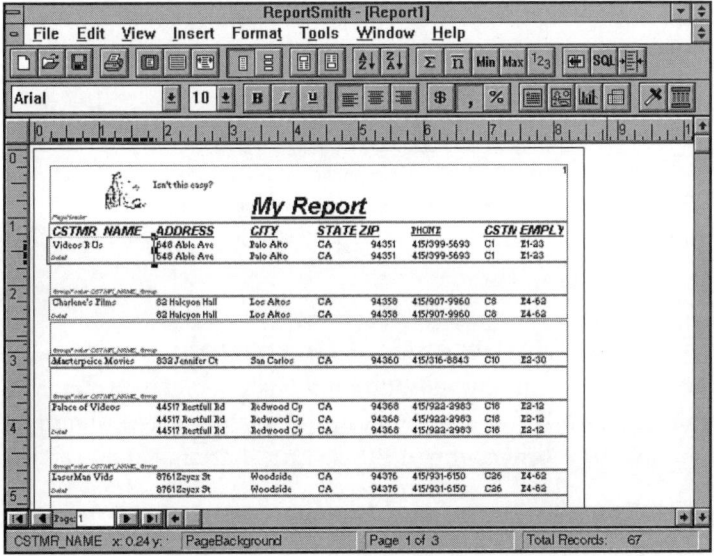

Fig. 13.30
Group headers are great tools to let readers know what they're about to read. This can be used to contain the basic header information of a record set, where more detail will follow next.

382 Chapter 13—Reporting with ReportSmith

3. If you want to place a group footer on the group, use the Group with Footer option on the toolbar. This footer can be seen in figure 13.31.

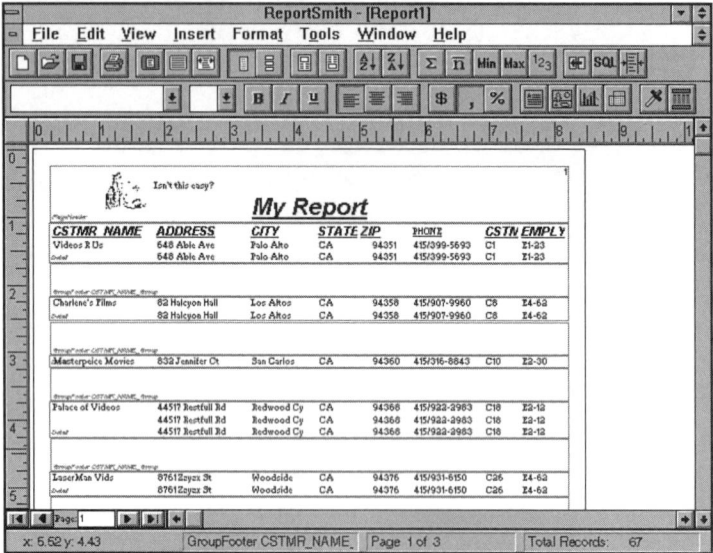

Fig. 13.31
Footers are the most common place to provide summary data.

When you group, ReportSmith does the hard work for you. All you're left to do is fill in the contents of the footer or header.

> **Note**
>
> The header and footer grouping features aren't mutually exclusive. You can have both a header and a footer for the group—simply select the column and then click the Group with Header and Group with Footer icons.

Performing Mathematical Operations

ReportSmith automatically adds the appropriate summary data to your report without much work from you. You can add totals, averages, minimums, maximums, and record counts at the click of a button. Follow these steps:

1. Highlight a column or set of columns to be summarized.

2. On the toolbar, click the Sum button for totals and subtotals, Averages button for averages, Min button for minimum values, Max button for maximum values, and Count button for record counts. ReportSmith then places summary data in the report footer and subtotal type data in the grouping footers.

Changing the Sort Order

Here's a really simple question: How you change the sort order of the report without having to access the report query? Highlight a field and use the sort icons on the toolbar. ReportSmith will sort the report based on the selected field and your selection of either Ascending or Descending.

From Here...

You can find more information about applications and their delivery in the following chapters:

- Chapter 9, "Creating Applications," tells you what you need to do to create an application.

- Chapter 10, "Creating Database Applications," teaches you everything that you need to know to start writing database applications you'll be proud of.

- Chapter 16, "Delivering Your Application," shows you how to put the application together for shipment to your users.

Part IV

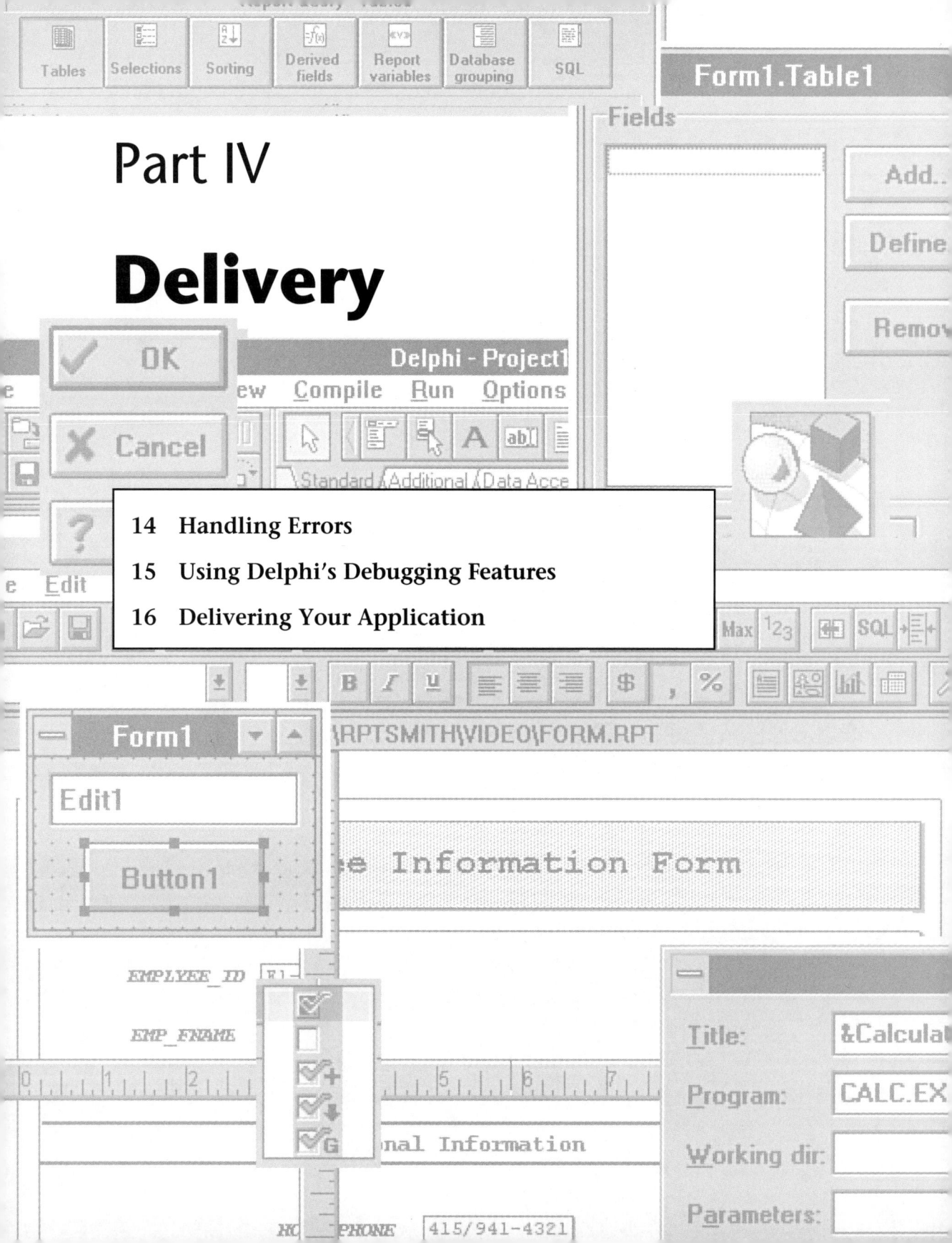

Delivery

14 Handling Errors

15 Using Delphi's Debugging Features

16 Delivering Your Application

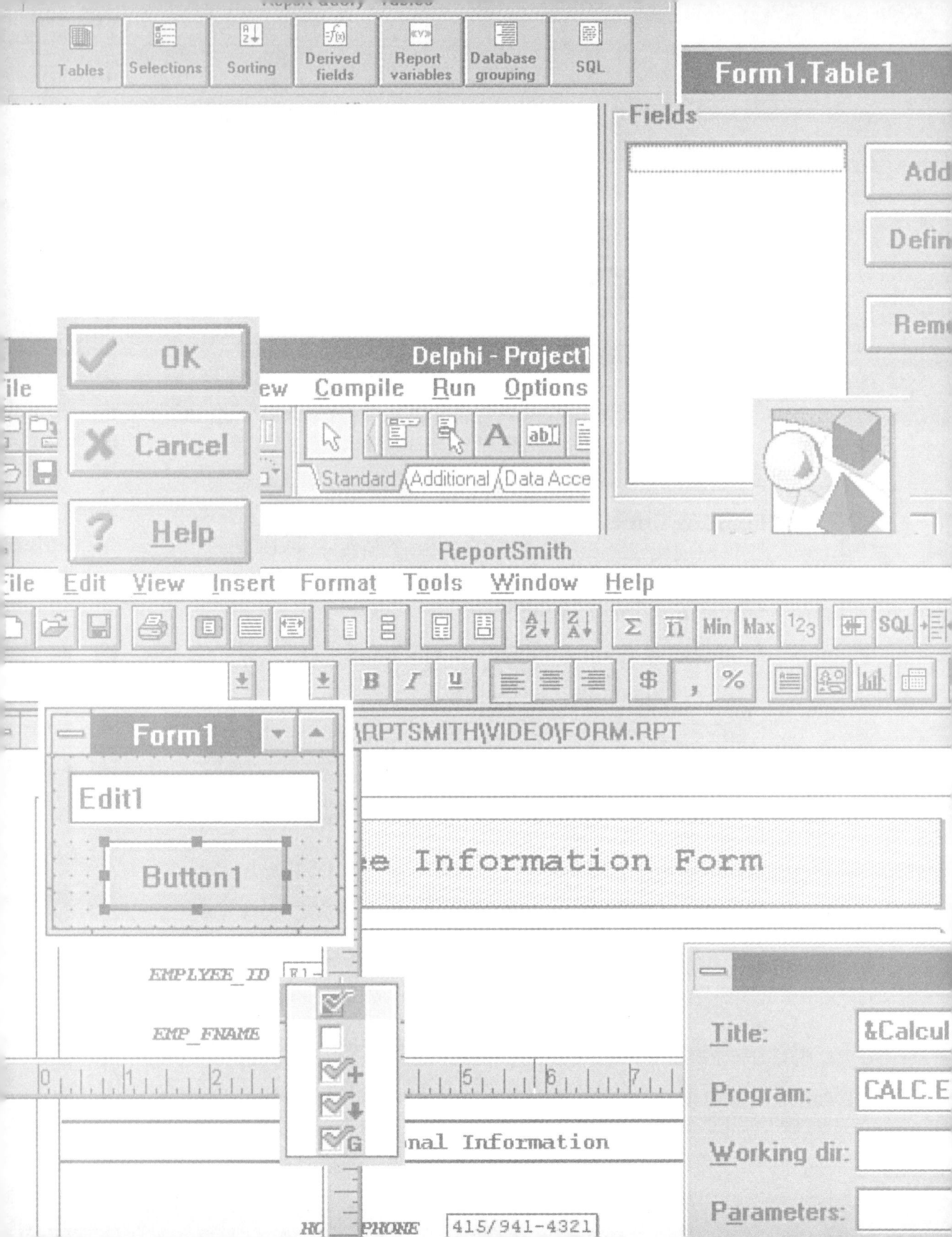

Chapter 14
Handling Errors

A primary part of the development cycle of any application is dealing with errors. Programming 101 will teach you that even though you may be able to compile a program, the program's code probably isn't error-free.

Already you may be familiar with the most common type of errors, which are those that occur at compile time. You can avoid compile-time errors by paying careful attention to the data types used for variables and to the particular syntax for any language elements you include in your code.

Other types of errors include logic errors and runtime errors. Logic errors are frequent in interactive applications. They are typically a result of the programmer of the application not taking into account all the possible variable actions the user of the application may take. The results of these errors may be anything from the display of runtime error dialogs to the complete lockup or crash of an entire system. You can avoid logic errors by carefully planning the design of your application. Assume nothing and provide handling for any perceivable action the user may take when using your program.

Runtime errors are those errors that occur when the program is actually running and, thus, are a result of not completely handling all conceivable variants in processing. Perhaps the best way to avoid runtime errors is through correct implementation of any one of several methods of error handling.

Delphi provides a mechanism for handling runtime errors, whatever the source of them may be. Delphi treats these errors as *exceptions*. Delphi also allows you to create your own types of exceptions and provides a special syntax that you can use to *raise* (or execute) them.

This chapter concerns itself primarily with those errors that may occur at runtime as a result of logic errors, math errors, memory errors, or even hardware errors.

In this chapter, you learn:

- How exceptions behave and are used
- How to program with exceptions
- About exceptions as object classes on a Delphi form, their optional constructors, and their properties
- How to create new exceptions
- How to prevent errors

This chapter also provides an example scenario of creating a new exception class and its implementation.

Chapter 15, "Using Delphi's Debugging Features," explains how to use some of Delphi's powerful tools to find errors that are seemingly impossible to find.

Understanding Exceptions

Handling runtime errors is a rather frustrating part of programming, especially when a programming language offers limited error checking. This limitation fosters defensive programming techniques. Many languages, such as Ada, C++, and even BASIC, support exception handling. Delphi offers an extension to its language for exception handling. Exception handling allows the program to trap the errors, report and/or correct the error, and continue running or even terminate the application.

What Are Exceptions?

Exceptions are a change in processing conditions that cause an application to stop processing so that a special routine designed to handle certain errors can be executed. In Delphi, exceptions come in the form of objects. When an application is running, the operating system, Windows, the hardware, or even a Delphi component can at any time raise an exception. The application is notified that an exception has occurred and can either be handled by that application or let a default handler take effect. Exceptions can occur as a result of low memory, memory overwrite, a failed attempt to write to a device, an invalid value assigned to a component's property, or even as the result of a calculation.

The capability to capture exceptions as Delphi provides empowers you to avoid defensive programming techniques that require frequent error checking. This frequent error checking is an additional overhead. Moreover, it makes it harder to follow the statements that implement the basic algorithms contained within a program. Consequently, you can separate the statements that support the normal program execution from those statements that execute when an exception occurs. In this case, the program execution jumps to the exception-handling block that either resolves the error and then resumes normal program execution, or executes some termination statements before exiting. Thus, exceptions enable you to introduce more effective error-resolution code that permits your program to recover from the errors.

When Are Exceptions Raised?

An application raises an exception when a standard runtime error occurs or when the application or a component used in the application explicitly raises an exception. The exception stays raised until it's handled. Typically, a program doesn't concern itself about the circumstances that raised the exception. Instead, the program handles exceptions no matter how they're raised.

Exception-Handling Syntax

Delphi applications handle exceptions using a special programming construct. An application can specify a block of statements to execute and define how to respond to any exceptions raised within that construct. There are two kinds of exception-handling constructs: `try..except` and `try..finally`.

Exceptions and the Runtime Library

It's very convenient to set up exception handlers for any exception conditions that may result from use of statements in the runtime library (RTL) without rewriting any code you may have already written in Delphi or are possibly porting from Pascal.

The code for your main applications—or any unit used by these applications—contains the `Excepts` unit in its `uses` clause. The RTL automatically transforms most conditions that would otherwise create a runtime error into exceptions. By default, the RTL handles exceptions by displaying an error message and then terminating the application. Consequently, you won't experience a lot of difference from the typical way for handling errors in most cases.

Programming with Exceptions

Delphi applications have built-in default exception handling that may be sufficient in some cases. The built-in handling consists of the display of a default message and is sometimes followed by immediate termination of the application. Because exceptions can result in the almost immediate termination of an application, the processing and handling of exceptions should be included in your program code.

This programmatic handling should be used to preserve data, close files, release memory, or do any cleanup operations the application would normally require before termination. An example of the cleanup operations that should be performed when an exception occurs is in an application that works with volatile data. Volatile data is information that's loaded into memory and exists only in memory. If an exception occurs that terminates the application, the data would be lost. Especially in the case of table manipulation, lack of exception handling could result in the corruption of volatile data and can make even persistent data (data that has been written to disk) more volatile as well. The programmatic inclusion of exception handling may also be necessary as the default errors displayed may not be sufficient for the users of the application to troubleshoot. To strengthen your applications and avoid such problems, the exceptions should be programmatically handled.

Setting Up *try* Blocks

To make Delphi applications use the exception-handling features, you need to place the normally executed code in a `try` block. There are two kinds of `try` blocks: `try..finally` and `try..except`. Which `try` block you should use depends on how the statements within the block are to execute.

In the case of blocks that merely terminate safely when an exception occurs, use `try..finally`. The `try..finally` block executes its `finally` statements whether or not an exception occurs. The `finally` statements should be normal tasks in logical order, such as closing open tables, releasing DOS-level file variables, and releasing allocated memory.

> **Note**
>
> It doesn't actually resolve the exception. If the `try..finally` isn't nested within a `try..except`, the exception will be raised to the default handler.

By contrast, the try..except block executes its except statements only if an exception occurs. The try..except block actually handles the exception or specified exception, releasing it in the process. Unlike finally statements, except statements should be those that provide special handling in case of an exception. These statements may also include tasks such as closing open tables, releasing DOS-level file variables, and releasing allocated memory.

Handling Exceptions in the IDE

When an exception occurs while running a program through the Integrated Development Environment (IDE), Delphi will by default handle the exception and display the offending line in the program's source file. This feature, although generally powerful, will inhibit you from accurately testing your exception-handling routines and statements. To see the results of the exception-handling statements for your applications and for the examples in this chapter, this feature can be turned off as follows:

1. Select Environment from the Options menu. The Environment Options dialog appears (see fig. 14.1).

2. With the Preferences page selected, deselect the Break on Exception check box in the Debugging section.

3. Click OK. The dialog will close, and Delphi will write the setting to the BreakOnExceptions entry under the debugging section of the DELPHI.INI file.

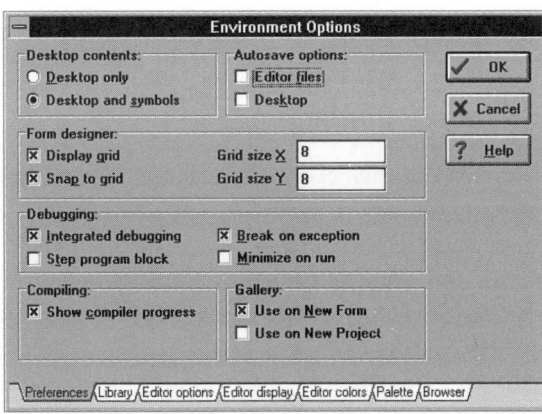

Fig. 14.1
The Environment Options dialog shows the Preferences page with an option for displaying the Compiler Progress dialog on compilation.

It may seem strange that you should perform the preceding steps. The Break On Exception setting is on by default as a safety net. Most programmers using Delphi will encounter exceptions while programming before they ever learn to include exception handling in their own code. Having this setting on by default protects those users who don't initially include exception handling.

Terminating on Exceptions

In the cases when you can't recover from certain kinds of runtime errors, your applications still may need to execute termination code. Among typical examples is file input/output (I/O) operations or the release of allocated memory. Delphi's exception-handling language extensions give you a way to execute code whether or not an exception occurs. The exception is then passed to the actual exception handler. Delphi provides a construct for this type of processing—the `try..finally` block.

The general syntax for the `try..finally` block is

```
try
    statement1;
    statement2;
...
finally
    statement1;
...
end;
```

The statements following the opening `try` are the possible triggers for the exception. The statements following the `finally` statements are executed regardless of an exception. In the event of an exception, the statements following `finally` are immediately executed. A closing `end` statement terminates the `try..finally` block.

Look at the case of the buffered file I/O exceptions. Typically, you open a file, perform I/O operations, and then close the file buffer. The program may raise an exception either when opening the file fails or when performing a file I/O operation fails. In both cases, you need to close the file buffer to release the buffer area in memory. Here's a code fragment that shows how the `try..finally` block closes the file, whether or not an exception occurs:

```
Var
    BinFile : File;
Begin
    System.Assign(BinFile, 'DATA.BIN');
    Reset(BinFile);
    try
        { File I/O statements }
```

```
      finally
          System.Close(BinFile);
      End;
  End;
```

The `System.Close()` statement executes in any case. If the program raises no exceptions, the `System.Close()` statement is executed after the file I/O statements finish. If the program raises a file I/O exception, the execution jumps to the statements in the `finally` section of the `try` block—in this case, `System.Close()`, which will close the file and release the file variable. This is an example cleanup operation involved in handling the runtime error and a textbook example of when a `try..finally` block should be used.

> **Note**
>
> `Assign` and `Close` are RTL functions as well as component methods. `Assign` and `Close` are prefixed with `System.` so that the compiler knows to call the function from the `System` unit instead of that method of the form or a component.

How to Handle Exceptions

In the case when you can recover from an exception, the statements in the except section of the `try..except` block need to clear the error condition. This isn't accomplished by a call to a magic error-clearing function but by the mere execution of the statements following the word `except`.

The general syntax for the `try..except` block is

```
try
  Statement 1;
  Statement 2;
  ...
except
  on Exception1 do Statement;
  on Exception2 do Statement;
  ...
  else
     Statement1;
end;
```

The statements following the opening `try` are the possible triggers for the exception. The `except` statement begins the execution of the special error-handling statements that are executed only if an exception occurs. The `on..do` statements that follow the `except` keyword are used to trap for a specific type of exception. The `else` clause represents the default error handler clause for the `on..do` statements. The statements following the `else` keyword will be executed only if the particular type of exception isn't handled by the `on..do` statements following the `except` keyword.

Here's an example of a basic try..except block:

```
type
  TRealPtr = ^Real; {Create a new type that's a pointer to a Real.}
var
  prVal : TRealPtr;
begin
  GetMem(prVal,sizeof(Real)); {Allocate memory to prVal.}
  prVal^ := 0;
  try
    prVal^ := (10 / prVal^);
    {... more calculations using prVal.}
    FreeMem(prVal,sizeof(Real));   {Free memory when all
                                    calculations are complete.}
    {... other statements to execute}
  except
    FreeMem(prVal,sizeof(Real));
  end; {End try..except.}
end; {End Proc.}
```

This example creates a variable called prVal that's simply a pointer to a real. Pointer variables require the allocation of global memory using functions such as GetMem before assignment. The prVal variable is de-referenced and assigned a zero value.

The statement following the try keyword attempts to perform an illegal floating-point math operation that results in an EZeroDivide exception. Because of this exception, execution drops to the first statement following except, which releases the memory allocated to the pointer variable. If the operation was legal, more calculations would have been performed before the variable was released.

Using the *on..do* Construct

This next example takes advantage of the on..do and else statements:

```
var
  rVal, rInVal : Real; { Create a variable of type Real.}
begin
  try {Begin try..except block.}
    rVal := (10 / rInVal); {Assign the result of 10 divided by
                             rInVal to rVal.}
    { ... other statements to execute}
  except
    on EZeroDivide do
      MessageDlg('EZeroDivide',mtWarning ,[mbOk],0);
    on EOutOfMemory do
      MessageDlg('EOutOfMemory',mtWarning ,[mbOk],0);
    else
      MessageDlg('Exception Unknown',mtWarning ,[mbOk],0);
  end; {End try..except.}
end; {End Proc.}
```

> **Note**
>
> This example makes use of the on..do statements. Each on..do has the potential to execute a single MessageDlg statement (see the on-line help under Message Dialogs for a description of the MessageDlg function). The on..do statement supports the use of begin..end, which are reserved words that group a series of statements together into a compound statement. If you were to try to execute multiple statements following an on..do without using begin..end, you would receive an END Expected compiler error. A format example of using begin..end to group on..do statements is
>
> ```
> on EDiskFull do
> begin
>   Statement 1;
>   Statement 2;
> end;
> ```

This time you simply create a variable called rVal of type real. The first statement following the try statement divides 10 by an unknown input value stored in rInVal and assigns the result to rVal. Next, other statements that aren't shown are executed. If an exception occurs in the calculation or from any of the other statements, program flow jumps to the first statement following the except keyword. In this example, you don't know what's stored in rInVal. If the value is zero, the exception EZeroDivide will occur and a message is displayed. This is because you've explicitly specified EZeroDivide in your on..do statement.

You also check for EOutOfMemory that isn't likely to occur in this example, thus its message is never executed. What if another exception occurs? Remove the On EZeroDivide do MessageDlg() lines and assign a zero value to rInVal. Now EZeroDivide isn't explicitly handled. The on EOutOfMemory line obviously won't catch the exception, so the program will drop down to the first statement following the else keyword. This executes a generic message stating that the exception is unknown.

Almost anytime groups of statements are embedded between try and except, there's potential for more than one type of exception. You should carefully match the on..do statements to the likeliest exception types to occur. A method that performs a handful of math calculations may use on..do to check for EZeroDivide as well as EUnderFlow, EOverFlow, and EInvalidOp. An exception such as EFileNotFound isn't likely to occur within such a block of statements.

The inclusion of EFileNotFound in this example would be redundant overcoding. Exceptions may occur, however, that you may not have taken into account, such as EPageFault. An EPageFault exception will occur if Windows' memory manager can't correctly use the swap file. Unexpected exceptions should be handled by the else statements. By convention, the else statement should be used only to execute a generic exception procedure for unexpected exceptions or to raise the current exception to another exception level. If the else is left out, the exception will automatically be raised—if not trapped by—the on..do statements.

Nesting *try* Blocks

Sometimes you may want to execute a statement or group of statements whether or not an exception occurs. You already know that the try..finally block is perfect for this. The problem is that try..finally doesn't actually handle the exception.

Delphi allows you to nest try..finally blocks within try..except blocks. This allows you to execute the finally statements unconditionally, yet still allows the execution of any special except statements in the actual event of an exception.

An example of nesting a try..finally within a try..except block is as follows:

```
var
  pVal : pointer;
begin
  try
    try
      New(pVal);
      WriteLn(LongInt(pVal^));
    finally
      Dispose(pVal);
    end;
  except
    on EGPFault do
      MessageDlg('De referenced invalid pointer',mtWarning
                 ,[mbOk],0);
    else
      MessageDlg('Exception Unknown',mtWarning ,[mbOk],0);
  end;
end; {End Proc.}
```

This example creates a pointer called pVal. Memory is then allocated to the pointer using New. When you're done with a pointer, the allocated memory should be released whether or not an exception occurs. This makes the Dispose statement a primary candidate for a finally statement. Following the `try..try`, the pointer is de-referenced without having ever been assigned. This operation results in an `EGPFault` exception. The `finally` statement (in this example, `Dispose`) is executed. Because `try..finallys` don't actually handle the exception, the `except` statements are then automatically executed. The `except` statements (in this example) execute an `on EGPFault do` followed by a message if `EGPFault` is the actual exception. If it isn't, the `else` statement executes, displaying a different message.

You could position a `try..finally` block on the outside of a `try..except` block as follows:

```
var
  pVar : pointer;
begin
try
    New(pVar);
  try
    WriteLn(LongInt(pVar^));
  except
    on EFault do
      GlobalErrorHandler;
    else
      raise
  end;
   MessageBeep(0);
  finally
   Dispose(pVar);
  end;
```

This example chooses to execute a user-defined global error-handling function called `GlobalErrorHandler` if the exception is one that's very serious, such as an `EFault` or an exception descending from `EFault`. The global handler might write some volatile data, shut down some files, and terminate the program. If the exception isn't `EFault`, it's raised. If the exception is raised, it executes the next level of `except` or `finally` statements it encounters. In your case, it executes the `Dispose` statement in the `finally` section. The `MessageBeep` statement is ignored. Because `finally` doesn't actually handle the exception, it continues its search for another level of `finally` or `except` statements to execute. This process continues until the exception is actually handled.

If there are no more except statements, the exception will be handled in Delphi's default exception handler. If an exception didn't occur in this example, the `MessageBeep` statement would execute as well as the `finally` statements. If the `MessageBeep` statement itself were to cause an exception, the finally statements would still execute and the exception would seek handling.

Raising Exceptions

Raising exceptions introduces you to a new keyword called `raise`. The Delphi language offers `raise` as an addition to the exception syntax. When certain types of invalid processing occur, you may receive an exception.

Some exceptions may be raised to you from the hardware. Some may be raised from the RTL. Some may be raised from the system (Windows) or even from a particular component. The `raise` keyword identifies the particular instance of an exception and passes upward to the first `try` block encountered. If the `try` block is a `try..finally` block, the finally statements execute. If the `try` block is a `try..except` block, the exception is flagged as handled and the except statements are executed. It doesn't matter if the exception comes from the RTL, a component, or even a module you wrote yourself; exceptions are raised the same way using the `raise` keyword.

Some of the examples shown earlier in this chapter make use of the `raise` keyword. In these examples, the exception was initially raised from a lower level, either from the code of a particular component, the RTL, and so on. The `raise` syntax you've seen so far is for use in the actual processing of an already raised exception. The `raise` keyword embedded within the except statements of a `try..except` block merely captures the particular exception instance and passes it up to the next level of exception processing or `try..except` block. If there isn't another level of `try..except` processing, the exception is handled by Delphi's default handler, which displays an instance- specific message and destroys the exception object.

Although this explains how to raise exceptions that have already occurred, it doesn't explain how the exceptions were raised to begin with. Exceptions are raised by using an alternative syntax to the `raise` keyword used in the `try..except` block. If you were to create your own component, you may want to define a custom exception that's to occur when the user assigns an invalid value to a property of the component. This requires at a minimum the creation of an exception class. When the code in the component chooses to raise the exception, an instance of the class is created. The syntax is as follows:

```
raise TMyException.Create(constant message: string);
```

`TMyException` is the new hypothetical exception class you created directly from the base exception type. `Create` is the constructor method for your class and is passed a message describing the exception. The preceding `raise` keyword captures the `TMyException` instance and the exception is raised. A user of your component could then use a `try` block to process your raised exception and then raise it further if desired or use `try..except` to handle the exception.

You may have expected a := (colon equals) assignment operator to follow the word raise. This isn't necessary because raise uses its own special syntax. Don't try to figure out why, just accept it. More information on this topic and all the information on exception handling is available in Chapter 7 of the *Delphi User's Guide*, which ships with the product.

You may think that this information isn't important if you don't plan to venture into the realms of component writing. This information can be used, however, to define your own exceptions within your programs as well.

Understanding Exceptions as Object Classes

You may have noticed several object-oriented terms used for describing exceptions throughout this chapter. As you may or may not have expected, all exceptions defined in the Delphi language are object classes. The base object class for all VCL-defined exception classes is Exception. It's this type that acts as the default handler for all exceptions.

> **Note**
>
> Initially, the naming convention of this object class may appear odd, as it isn't preceded by the letter T. This is because the Exception object class defines a different naming convention. The Exception object class and any of its descendants should be named descriptively preceded by the letter E. ERangeError and EGPFault are examples of these. The preceding E isn't required but should be used for quick identification and to maintain consistency with the VCL.

The Exception object class is an immediate descendant of TObject, which is the base or parent of all other object classes in Delphi. Because Exception descends from TObject directly, the class definition of Exception is actually very simple. It's defined in the SysUtils unit as follows:

```
Exception = class(TObject)
  private
    FMessage: PString;
    function GetMessage: string;
    procedure SetMessage(const Value: string);
  public
    constructor Create(const Msg: string);
    constructor CreateFmt(const Msg: string;
                         const Args: array of const);
    constructor CreateRes(Ident: Word);
    constructor CreateResFmt(Ident: Word;
                            const Args: array of const);
```

```
        destructor Destroy; override;
        property Message: string read GetMessage write SetMessage;
        property MessagePtr: PString read FMessage;
    end;
```

The Exception object class begins with FMessage declared in its private section. The FMessage object field is a pointer to a given message string. Since the FMessage object field can't be accessed directly, it's indirectly accessible by the GetMessage and SetMessage methods. Since GetMessage and SetMessage are declared as private, they're accessible only by members within the object class or by descending classes within the SysUtils unit.

Defining the Exception Object's Default Constructors

The public section of the Exception object class defines several constructors and a single destructor. The destructor should never be explicitly called, as it's called automatically when the exception is handled (and thus isn't discussed in the following list). The constructors are

- Create(const Msg: string)

- CreateFmt(const Msg: string; const Args: array of const)

- CreateRes(Ident: Word)

- CreateResFmt(Ident: Word; const Args: array of const)

The constructor to use depends on the desired format of the message and the source of the message.

The Create constructor is the most commonly used and will be used within this chapter. The Create constructor accepts a single parameter of type string. The string should be a descriptive or otherwise meaningful string representing the exception or exception class.

The CreateFmt constructor is like the Create constructor, except that it allows special formatting of a message. The first parameter is the message that's of type string. The second parameter specifies an open array of constant values. The contents of these constant values are inserted at the location specified by the format specifiers embedded within the string in parameter one. For example, the resulting message of

```
        MyException.CreateFmt('Exception %s. %f exceeds MaxRate',
                                        ['ETaxRate',20.75]);
```

will format as

```
        Exception ETaxRate. 20.75 exceeds MaxRate
```

The following table lists the supported format specifiers for the `CreateFmt` constructor.

Specifier	Description
%s	String
%d	Signed decimal
%f	Floating point
%e	Scientific
%g	Floating point terminated at precision
%n	Number (same as %f but specifies thousands separator)
%m	Money (format depends on the currency specifier set up in the international section of the Windows Control Panel)
%p	Pointer that formats into an *XXXX:YYYY* value

The `CreateRes` constructor allows the loading of a string resource for use as the exception message. As you may or may not know, executable programs created with Delphi contain various default string resources. Resource strings can be added as well. Each group of related strings is loaded into memory on call into logically identified groups. Each group is referred to as a *string table*. Each string in a string table has a unique sequential identifier.

If you've ever done any Windows API programming in Pascal or C, you may be familiar with the `LoadString` Windows API function. The resource ID value required in the second parameter of `LoadString` is the same as that required by the `CreateRes` constructor. See the Windows API `LoadString` function description in Delphi's on-line help to obtain a better understanding of string resources and resource IDs.

The `CreateResFmt` constructor behaves as a combination of `CreateFmt` and `CreateRes` constructors. The first parameter specifies the ID of the string resource to load. The second parameter specifies an open array of constant values and behaves just as the second parameter of `CreateFmt`. The format specifiers must be embedded within the string resource and are the same as those in `CreateFmt`.

Using Properties of the *Exception* Object Class

The two remaining declarations in the public section of an exception's object class are properties. The first property, called message, reads and writes to the FMessage object field using the GetMessage and SetMessage methods. These methods are within scope of the message property, and the message property is within scope of your application. It's the message property that provides instance-specific access to the FMessage object field. The second property is MessagePtr, which is read only and is a pointer to the string containing the message.

In most cases, you won't knowingly use these two properties. They're there for use with the special syntax for receiving instance-specific messages from raised exceptions. Any custom properties added to your own exception object classes can be used when processing raised exceptions. An example of this will be demonstrated in the "Defining New Exceptions" section later in this chapter.

Descending Object Classes from *Exception*

A closer review of the SysUtils unit source would reveal several immediately descending classes of the Exception object class, as follows:

```
EOutOfMemory = class(Exception)
EInOutError = class(Exception)
EIntError = class(Exception);
EMathError = class(Exception);
EInvalidPointer = class(Exception);
EInvalidCast = class(Exception);
EConvertError = class(Exception);
EProcessorException = class(Exception);
```

These aren't the only exceptions that you may encounter when using Delphi. In fact, these are the only ones in the SysUtils unit that are immediate descendants of TException. The SysUtils unit defines several other exceptions that are descendants of the preceding exceptions. EMathError, for example, is an immediate descendant of Exception. The EMathError object class appears as

```
EMathError = class(Exception)
```

The SysUtils unit defines several more exceptions, as follows:

```
EInvalidOp = class(EMathError);
EZeroDivide = class(EMathError);
EOverflow = class(EMathError);
EUnderflow = class(EMathError);
```

Notice that each of these is a descendant from EMathError.

Handling Exceptions on the Class Level

Because no new members are added to these object classes, you may question why they aren't simply made to descend directly from the Exception class. The reason is that Delphi's exception syntax allows exception handling on the class level. Look at the following example:

```
var
  iVal : integer; {Create integer variable.}
begin
  iVal := 0; {Assign zero to variable.}
  try {Begins outer try..except block.}
    try {Begins inner try..except block.}
      iVal := 10 DIV iVal; {This line will cause the exception.}
    except {The inner except statements execute first.}
      on EIntError do {if EIntError or descent of then:}
      raise; {Raise the exception to the next level of handling.}
    else {Wasn't EIntError so display unknown error message.}
      MessageDlg('UnKnown Exception',mtWarning,[mbOk],0);
    end; {End inner try..except block.}
  except {Begins outer try..except, except statements. }
    on EDivByZero do {}
        MessageDlg('EDivByZero',mtWarning,[mbOk],0);
    else
        MessageDlg('UnKnown EIntError Exception',mtWarning,[mbOk],0);
  end;
end;
```

This example is the first in this chapter that takes advantage of nested try..except blocks. As you may have guessed, this is perfectly legal and, if used with the raise statement, adds the flexibility of multiple levels of exception processing. The offending statement is one that divides a signed ordinal value by zero and will raise an exception.

The inner except statements are the first to execute. The exception is evaluated by the on..do construct. If the exception is EIntError or a descendant of EIntError, the exception is raised. If it's another exception type, the else statement is executed, which displays a message stating that the exception is unknown. Because the example will cause an EIntError exception, it's a given that the exception will be raised. The outer except statements then execute. The on..do construct of the outer except evaluates for the more specific EDivByZero exception. If the exception is EDivByZero, a message is displayed. If it isn't, the else statements execute. The else statement in this example displays a message stating that the specific EIntError message is unknown.

Once you understand this example, it won't take long for you to realize the benefits of processing exceptions on the class level.

Using Members of the Exception Instance

The programmer of a specific exception class will instantiate an instance of the exception at the time that the exception is raised. As discussed earlier, an exception descending from the Exception object class may be executed with any one of a number of default constructors. The things that the constructors have in common are they all have one or more parameters that allow the programmer of the new object class to specify as a default message string. As you've learned so far in the chapter, the only time that the string would be used is if you let Delphi handle the exception for you.

You otherwise haven't seen anything that would allow you to access the message in the raised exception. Delphi's special exception syntax has a way to do just that. In fact, it will allow you to access any public members of a raised exception. Examine the following:

```
begin
try
  ScrollBar1.Max := (1-2);
except
  on E: EInvalidOperation do
       MessageDlg(E.Message,mtWarning,[mbOk],0);
end;
```

This example tries to assign a scrollbar's Max property the illegal results of a calculation. This forces the scrollbar component to raise an EInvalidOperation exception. The except statements of the try..except block evaluate the exception using the on..do construct. If the exception is EInvalidOperation, the message Scrollbar property out of range would be displayed. But wait—you displayed the message dialog, but nowhere did you create that message. A closer look at the on..do construct in this example will reveal a modification of the construct's syntax. An E: is placed in front of EInvalidOperation to create an instance-specific variable of the EInvalidOperation exception. Once this is created, the public properties are accessible until the except statements are completely executed and the exception instance destroyed.

> **Note**
>
> Don't destroy the exception instance (E in this example), as the handling of the exception destroys it automatically.

Exception Object Summary

The explanations provided in this discussion should have shown you that the topic of exceptions and exception processing has a little more substance than just some high-level automation. Since the Exception class descends directly from TObject, the hierarchy of the various exceptions should be easy to interpret. Now that the syntax and hierarchy have been explained (and maybe even understood), it's time to define your own exception object class. You'll even raise an exception instance of your own.

Defining New Exceptions

You can define a new exception by declaring a new exception class. This class is a descendant of the Exception base class or of a descending exception class. The new exception class should either provide more specific information about an existing error, or support a brand new category of error conditions.

The creation of a custom exception object class begins in the type section of a unit's interface section:

```
interface
type
  ECustomException = class(Exception)
  ...
  ...
  end;
```

Because exceptions are just like any other object classes, members can be added, constructors overridden, and property defaults changed:

```
type
  ECustomException = class(Exception)
  public
    CustomProperty: Integer;
    constructor Create(const Msg: string);
  end;
```

By using this example exception, you may raise the exception as follows:

```
if ErrorCondition then
    raise ECustomException.Create('A Custom Exception has occurred');
```

This example simply checks a hypothetical Boolean variable called ErrorCondition. If it evaluates to true, the exception is raised. The raise keyword is used, followed by the exception type, a period, and the constructor (Create in this example). The constructor is passed a constant string describing the exception condition.

The exception object classes that you create will likely linger in the deepest levels of your application's code. This will allow many levels that the exception could be raised to. You may choose to define all your custom exceptions in a separate unit (which is recommended) and add the unit's name to the uses clause of any applications using the exceptions. This is a matter of design and varies depending on implementation.

The higher-level code that the exceptions are raised to can choose to capture the raised exception by using try blocks. The handling for custom exceptions is just like the handling for the ones already created for you in Delphi. If the exception isn't handled, it will be raised all the way up to Delphi's default handler and result in an error.

A more in-depth example of creating custom exceptions is demonstrated in the code of a custom component described in the next section.

A Healthy Example of Creating New Exceptions

Suppose that you're creating a front end for a data-entry application. The data-entry screen will have a custom component descending from TEdit that contains a validation method. An entry into the edit control (determined by the validation method) should raise an exception if the entered data doesn't meet the validation requirements.

Because a validation method is just that—a method—it can be called from any of the component's events. The most likely place (in this example) would be when the OnExit event fires. If the method call is embedded within try blocks, the user can execute any finally statements, handle the exception, store an ErrorNumber representing the exception, and continue with various processing depending on what the value of the error number is.

Processing may involve moving the cursor, truncating the data, changing the case of the data, or any other type of processing desired. No matter how the entry is deemed illegal, a message describing the offense will be made available for display.

You'll use the preceding scenario in your efforts to learn how to create your own exceptions. The custom edit component will be called TValidateEdit. The method added to this custom component will be a procedure called ValidateData.

The scenario provides rationale for the creation of a new class of exceptions. The new exception class will descend directly from the `Exception` object class. It will override the `Exception` constructor and add a new member, called `ErrorNumber`, as follows:

```
EValidationError = class(Exception)
  public
    ErrorNumber: Integer;
    constructor Create(const Msg: string ; ErrorNum: Integer);
  end;
```

The new exception object class adds a `public` member that stores an error number. When the exception is raised, the user can trap the exception using the `on..do` construct and store the error number to a local variable.

Remember that the handling of an exception destroys the exception instance. This error number allows you to carry an ID of the occurred exception out of the `try..except` block and still gives you a way to determine the error in later processing.

The constructor in this example is overridden and appears as follows:

```
constructor EValidationError.Create(Msg: string;
                                    ErrorNum: Integer);
begin
  inherited Create(Msg);
  ErrorNumber := ErrorNum;
end;
```

The new `Create` constructor simply adds a second parameter that's an integer type. The integer will represent an error number of the executed exception. The inherited `Create` is called and passed the message describing the exception. Then the `ErrorNumber` member is assigned the passed error number from the `ErrorNum` parameter.

The `EValidationError` exception will act as an ancestor to its descending exception object classes that are declared as follows:

```
ERequiresEntry = class(EValidationError);
EMustBeLower = class(EValidationError);
EMustBeUpper = class(EValidationError);
```

The `EValidationError` class and its descending object classes must be declared in the `type` section of a unit's interface section and, for this example, may appear as follows:

```
type
  TValidateEdit = class(TEdit)
  public
    procedure ValidateData; virtual;
  end;
```

```
EValidationError = class(Exception)
public
  ErrorNumber: Integer;
  constructor Create(const Msg: string ; ErrorNum:Integer);
end;

ERequiresEntry  = class(EValidationError);
EMustBeLower    = class(EValidationError);
EMustBeUpper    = class(EValidationError);
```

The constructor procedure for `EValidationError` is placed, of course, in the implementation section of the component's unit. The `TValidateEdit` component would have its new `ValidateData` method placed in the implementation section of the component's unit as well. The actual validation method may appear as follows:

```
Procedure TValidateEdit.ValidateData;
const
  CRequiresEntry = 1;
  CMustBeLower = 2;
  CMustBeUpper = 3;

begin
  if Length(Self.Text) < 1 then
    raise ERequiresEntry.Create(
      'This field requires an entry',CRequiresEntry);
  if not MyIsLowerRoutine then
    raise EMustBeLower.Create(
      'This field requires an all lowercase entry',
        CMustBeLower);
  if not MyIsUpperRoutine then
    raise EMustBeUpper.Create(
      'This field requires an all uppercase entry',
        CMustBeUpper);
end;
```

The validation method `ValidateData` in the preceding code defines three constants representing the specific descending classes of `EValidationError`. The body of the method contains only three `if..then` constructs. The first uses the `Length` function to determine whether `TValidateEdit`'s text property contains any data. If not, the `ERequiresEntry` exception is raised. The `Create` method is passed the defining message and the constant representing the error number of the exception. The second `if..then` construct executes a hypothetical Boolean method called `MyIsLowerRoutine` that validates the case of the data. This `Create` method is passed the message and constant error number parameters. The third `if..then` construct mirrors the second but is concerned with the data being uppercase.

When creating new exception object classes, it may initially be difficult to determine when to add additional members, override the constructor, and so on. This is because multiple perspectives are required and the developer must be able to think out those perspectives simultaneously. The first perspective is from the point of view of the creation of the new exception class and the raising of an instance of the class. This perspective has already been demonstrated in the creation of your EValidationError object classes. The other perspective is of how the exception would be handled or processed by the try blocks or even Delphi's default handler. This perspective was demonstrated in the opening examples of this chapter.

Now that you've seen both sides of the coin, you'll put your custom edit component to use and handle the exceptions it may raise. Because you created the EValidationError object classes yourself, implementing them will help reinforce your understanding of both perspectives.

> **Note**
>
> If you plan to actually implement the following examples, the TValidateEdit component previously described must be actually created and installed into the current component library. As it sits in the preceding examples, the implementation of the MyIsLower and MyIsUpper methods are excluded. These would need to be constructed to complete the component.
>
> If you aren't familiar with the creation and modification of custom components, you should review Chapter 7, "Customizing and Reusing Components." The following samples are to assist in explanation. If component writing, creation, and installation are new to you, just using the following for reference is suggested.

To simplify the initial scenario of a data-entry screen, you'll place only two controls on it for use in the following examples. Open a new project and place two TValidateEdit components on the form. By default, the first instance will be named ValidateEdit1 and the second ValidateEdit2.

> **Note**
>
> Because the OnExit event fires only when a component loses focus within the application, a second component must be on the form. When the second component receives focus, the OnExit event of the first component will fire. The second component can be any windowed component. A second instance of TValidateEdit was chosen for simplicity.

Add the following code to the `OnExit` event of the first instance of `TValidateEdit`:

```
ValidateEdit1.ValidateData;
```

Now run the program. When the form comes up, remove all text from the control, and then press Tab. The `OnExit` event will fire, thus executing the `ValidateData` method. Since no data is in the text property, the `ERequiredEntry` exception will fire. Because this example made no attempt to handle the raised exception, the default handler kicks in and should display a message dialog containing the error provided when you called the exception's `Create` constructor within the component's code.

Now modify the `OnExit` code to appear as follows:

```
begin
try
  ValidateEdit1.ValidateData;
except
  on ERequiresEntry do
    MessageDlg('ERequiresEntry',mtWarning,[mbOk],0);
  on EMustBeLower do
    MessageDlg('EMustBeLower',mtWarning,[mbOk],0);
  on EMustBeUpper do
    MessageDlg('EMustBeUpper',mtWarning,[mbOk],0);
  else
    MessageDlg('Unknown exception',mtWarning,[mbOk],0);
end;
```

Here, the exception is handled on the specific exception level. If you failed to enter data into `TValidateEdit`, the `ValidateData` method will raise an `ERequiresEntry` exception and will display a message dialog stating so. Each `on..do` construct evaluates the exceptions that descend directly from `EValidationError`. The exception could be trapped by using a single `on..do` construct that checks for `EValidationError`, as in the following example:

```
try
  ValidateEdit1.ValidateData;
except
  on EValidationError do
    MessageDlg('EValidationError',mtWarning,[mbOk],0);
  else
    MessageDlg('Unknown exception',mtWarning,[mbOk],0);
end;
```

This example handles the exception on the class level, but doesn't provide any information about which specific exception occurred. You can, however, modify the `on..do` construct to return an instance variable and then place the message contents of the specific exception instance into the message dialog. This at least will allow you to display an exception specific message to the user, as in the following example:

```
on E:EValidationError do
    MessageDlg(E.Message,mtWarning,[mbOk],0);
```

This is fine if your handling is only to display a message. But what if you want to handle the exception at the class level of `EValidationError`, continue processing, and then manipulate the component depending on the specific exception instance? If you recall, your custom `EValidationError` object class has an additional member added. This member, called `ErrorNumber`, contains an exception-specific code. Look at the following example:

```
const
  CRequiresEntry = 1;
  CMustBeLower = 2;
  CMustBeUpper = 3;
var
 iExceptionID: integer;
begin
 iExceptionID := 0;
 try
   ValidateEdit1.ValidateData;
 except
   on E:EValidationError do
       iExceptionID := E.ErrorNumber
   else
       raise;
 end;
 {statements for further processing here.}
 if iExceptionID > 0 then
 begin
  case iExceptionID of
    CRequiresEntry :
        MessageDlg('ERequiresEntry',mtWarning,[mbOk],0);
    CMustBeLower :
        MessageDlg('EMustBeLower',mtWarning,[mbOk],0);
    CMustBeUpper :
        MessageDlg('EMustBeUpper',mtWarning,[mbOk],0);
  end; {End case.}
 end; {End if.}
end; {End proc.}
```

Initially, the preceding code may seem like overkill for the exception types that it handles. It does, however, demonstrate some powerful alternatives in the way exceptions are handled, as well as how to access and process data that's specific to the exception instance.

For readability, the error codes are defined in the form of constants—for example, `CRequiresEntry = 1`. A local variable called `iExceptionID` is created and is initialized to zero. This variable will store the error number of the instance of the exception. The `ValidateData` method is called within the `try..except` block. If you failed to enter data, an `ERequiresEntry` exception is raised from the component. The `except` statements then execute.

The on..do construct evaluates the exception instance to determine whether it's an Evaluation error or descending object class. If it is, the exception instance is stored to variable E. The local variable iExceptionID is assigned the instance-specific value of E.ErrorNumber. If another unknown exception occurs, the else statements would execute, which simply raise the exception to the next level of processing.

After the exception is handled, the instance variable E is destroyed. Further statements in the event's code then execute. Once executed, an if..then construct checks the value of your local iExceptionID variable to see whether an exception occurred. If an exception occurred, iExceptionID will contain a value greater than zero that will cause the following case..of construct to execute. Using the earlier defined constants, iExceptionID is evaluated. The evaluation determines which instance-specific exception occurred previously. The appropriate message is then displayed accordingly.

Preventing Errors

Preventing errors in a given application is a responsibility that lies in the developer's lap. The best cure for errors in a program is to prevent errors from occurring in the first place.

Tip
By far the cleanest way to prevent errors is to use special constructs that are designed to capture and handle exceptions, as discussed in the preceding sections.

Error handling is another design element that must be considered when creating any application. The better you get to know the language that you use, the better you'll know what type of errors can occur in a given form of processing.

Depending on the language you use, various degrees of error handling are available. Some companies provide integrated development environments with configuration options that will automatically catch overflow errors and range errors if turned on. Borland Pascal and Delphi are examples of this type of environment. These languages also provide compiler directives that allow these settings to be turned on or off programmatically. (A list of Delphi's compiler directives is available in the on-line help under Compiler Directives.)

Another form of error prevention is the evaluation of return values. A Delphi function such as Assigned() will return a Boolean true value if a given method pointer isn't nil. This process of error checking is very delicate and usually requires a lot of extra code that in many cases will never be used and can appear quite cryptic.

From Here...

Be sure and take the time to implement what you've learned into all your Delphi applications. You may find other chapters useful to enhance what you've learned in this chapter:

- See Chapter 7, "Customizing and Reusing Components," for information on the creation of custom components, as this is where custom exception classes will really come in handy.

- See Chapter 9, "Creating Applications," for information on application development, as this is where your knowledge of exception handling will come into play.

- See Chapter 11, "Using the Browser," so you can learn how to use the Browser to display the Exception class hierarchy.

- See Chapter 15, "Using Delphi's Debugging Features," to learn about Delphi's debugging features and other ways to trap program errors.

Chapter 15
Using Delphi's Debugging Features

As a Windows user, you've most certainly been the unwilling recipient of a message similar to figure 15.1. Now that you're writing Windows programs, the shoe's on the other foot—you can now be the *cause* of these wonderful messages. But don't worry. Although Delphi can't completely stop you from causing errors, it sure helps you fix them.

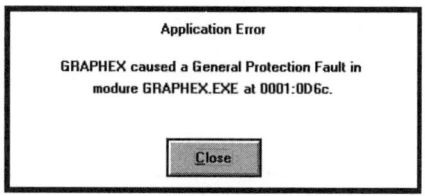

Fig. 15.1
Finally, a GPF caused by you!

If you've already started using Delphi, you're no doubt impressed with it so far. But no matter how good a programming product is, how rich the language, how fast the compiler, or how much time is saved because of reusable objects, you still have to write code, and that code will have *bugs*. The best products in the world are completely crippled if programmers aren't given the proper tools to track down and fix bugs.

Like the rest of Delphi, the integrated debugging features are a pleasure to use. Delphi has all the features that low-level programmers have come to expect in a professional debugger, yet these features can be used without a master's degree in programming. Take the time to learn most of the debugging features, and you'll save yourself a lot of time and frustration in the future.

One aspect of Delphi that makes programming easy is that all the code from a form is kept within one Pascal file. This makes reviewing your code and working with global variables quite easy. Other products break code into little chunks that are stored with each object, making it difficult to get an overall feel for the underlying code.

This chapter uses the GraphEx project. If you did a complete installation of Delphi, this project exists in your C:\DELPHI\DEMOS\DOC\GRAPHEX directory. You'll get more out of this chapter by referring to this project while reading.

> **Note**
>
> This chapter introduces bugs into the project, so you may want to make a copy of GraphEx before starting. When you're done with this chapter, restore GraphEx from your copy so that you can use the bug-free version.

In this chapter, you learn how to:

- Identify three different kinds of bugs: syntax errors, runtime errors, and logic errors
- Configure and use the built-in debugger
- Use debugging tools such as the Watch List window and the Debug menu
- Use other tools that aren't integrated into Delphi, such as WinSight and WinSpector

Understanding Delphi Bugs

You really need to worry about only three types of errors or bugs when writing Delphi programs: syntax errors, which are often typos; runtime errors, which are any errors that occur while a program is running; and logic errors, which happen when a program doesn't do what you expect or does what you don't expect it to do.

Syntax Errors

Syntax errors are usually typos that occur while typing program code. They also occur when you don't know the exact syntax of a Pascal statement. You can't run your program until all the syntax errors have been removed.

The good news is that when a syntax error occurs, Delphi gives you a reasonable error message (usually) and leaves the insertion point in your code where Delphi thinks the problem is.

Letting Delphi Do the Work

Pascal in general—and Object Pascal in particular—is one of the most syntactically demanding languages around. While some other languages are forgiving, Delphi insists that your code be perfect. The upside of this is that your code is compiled very, very quickly. The downside, of course, is that you have to type everything exactly. Luckily, Delphi handles a lot of the syntactically challenging coding for you. For example, consider the following code from the beginning of the GraphEx project:

```
unit GraphWin;

interface

uses
  SysUtils, WinTypes, WinProcs, Messages, Classes, Graphics,
  Controls, Forms, StdCtrls, Buttons, ColorGrd, Menus, Printers,
  ClipBrd, Dialogs, ExtCtrls;

type
  TDrawingTool = (dtLine, dtRectangle, dtEllipse, dtRoundRect);
  TForm1 = class(TForm)
ToolBar: TPanel;
    Panel1: TPanel;
    LineButton: TSpeedButton;
    RectangleButton: TSpeedButton;
...
    ScrollBox1: TScrollBox;
    Image: TImage;
    procedure FormMouseDown(Sender: TObject; Button: TMouseButton;
      Shift: TShiftState; X, Y: Integer);
...
```

The unit definition, typing, and procedure definitions take up the first 87 lines of GRAPHWIN.PAS. If you had to type all this yourself, you'd be fixing syntax errors all day. Fortunately, all this code is automatically created by Delphi, thus ensuring that it's syntactically correct. When the author of this program added the TPanel object named Panel1 to the form, for example, Delphi automatically added the Panel1: TPanel line of code. While you could type this part yourself, don't bother—it's not worth it.

Configuring Delphi to Find Syntax Errors

Like everything else in Delphi, the compiler is configurable. To configure the compiler, open the Options menu and select Project. Delphi displays the

Chapter 15—Using Delphi's Debugging Features

Project Options dialog. Select the Compiler tab to see the compiler options (see fig. 15.2).

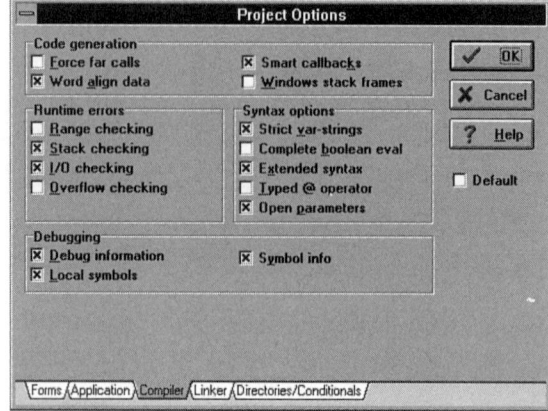

Fig. 15.2
You can configure how strict Delphi is when it checks the syntax of your code.

The Syntax options let you tell Delphi what type of syntax checking to do:

- *Strict Var-strings*. This option tells the compiler to compare the type of string being passed to a procedure or function with the formal parameter declared for that function. With this option on, the compiler generates a syntax error if you try to pass a string type variable to a function with a different string type variable declared in that function's formal parameter list. For example, the following code causes a syntax error if this option is turned on:

    ```
    procedure test(var s:String);
    begin
      s:='xxxxx';
    end;

    procedure TForm1.Button1Click(Sender: TObject);
    var
      s:string[3];
    begin
    test(s);
    end;
    ```

    You should always leave this option on to help ensure that you don't overwrite memory that may not be declared for a string parameter.

- *Complete Boolean Eval*. This option tells the compiler to generate code in such a way that at runtime Boolean expressions are completely evaluated. With this option off, the compiler generates code that can "short circuit" Boolean expressions when the results are known early in the expression evaluation. In most cases, you should leave this option off, as it generates faster code. This option doesn't affect how the compiler checks for syntax errors.

- *Extended Syntax*. This option tells the compiler to use a set of extended Pascal syntax rules. This option lets you use a function as a statement; the results of the function are ignored. More importantly, this option also allows you to use PChar type strings. As PChar strings are used extensively when making Windows API calls, you should always leave this option on.

- *Typed @ Operator*. This option tells the compiler to return a pointer of a type similar to the operand of the @. For example, a byte variable would return a byte pointer. With this option turned off, the compiler always returns an untyped pointer. You should leave this option off so you can avoid writing code that deals with incompatible pointer types.

- *Open Parameters*. This option tells the compiler to consider any string passed to a function an open string or PChar within that function, regardless of the type of string declared as a formal parameter. You should turn this option on, as it makes your programs slightly safer.

Finding Common Syntax Errors

If you're coming from another programming language (especially a fourth generation language), there are two simple syntax problems that might haunt you at first. The first problem involves using the assignment operator. The second problem involves using the statement terminator ; correctly.

If you haven't done so already, open the GraphEx demo project. Click the paintbrush icon to make it the current object and then click the Events tab in the Object Inspector. Double-click the OnClick method; Delphi displays the Code Editor window with the cursor at the OnClick method. Remove a : and a ; from code so that it reads as follows:

```
procedure TForm1.BrushButtonClick(Sender: TObject);
begin
  BrushBar.Visible = BrushButton.Down;
end
```

420 Chapter 15—Using Delphi's Debugging Features

You can tell Delphi to check the syntax of your code in two ways. The first way is to open the Compile menu and choose Syntax Check. Delphi compiles each unit in your project, stopping when it finds an error. The second way is to open the Compile menu and choose Compile (or press Ctrl+F9). This method is sometimes better than the first method because it causes Delphi not only to compile your project, but also to link it. If your program has no syntax errors, clicking the Run button after a compile launches your program instantly because the executable already exists. If a syntax error is found while using either method, Delphi responds by placing an error message in the Code Editor's status bar and leaving the insertion point in the Code Editor at the cause of the error, as shown in figure 15.3.

Fig. 15.3
Assignments in Pascal are made with :=, not =.

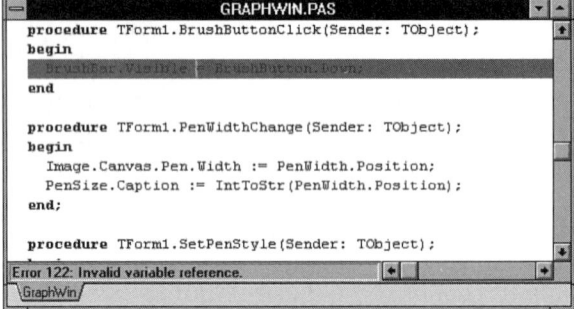

> **Note**
> Delphi allows you to configure the Code Editor with one of four keystroke mappings: Internal, Classic, Brief, and Epsilon. The keystrokes referred to in this chapter correspond to the Internal mapping. If you're using a different mapping, look up your keystrokes in the menus, on-line help, or in the manuals.

Tip
Typing a few lines of code and pressing Ctrl+F9 is an easier way to track down syntax errors. When you have enough code to do a runtime test, press F9 to run your program.

The Delphi compiler can't tell whether the code is supposed to make an assignment or compare two values, so it complains about an illegal variable reference. Thus, although syntax errors are often simple typos, the compiler's error messages may be a bit misleading. Before digging too deep into your code because of a misleading error message, be sure to check your code for obvious typos.

Click OK. Delphi clears the error message and leaves the Code Editor's insertion point right where the error was found. In this case, the insertion point is just before the =, so go ahead and type the missing :. Then press Ctrl+F9 again to find the next error. This time, Delphi displays the message shown in figure 15.4.

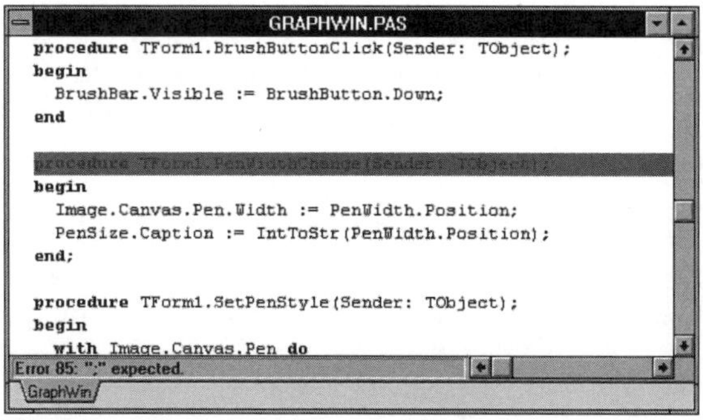

Understanding Delphi Bugs   **421**

Fig. 15.4
Pascal statements must end with a semicolon (;).

This time, Delphi's error message is right on the mark and tells you what to do. Simply add a ; after the end keyword and press Ctrl+F9 again. Delphi compiles the whole program without any errors.

Finding the Source of a Syntax Error

In the previous two examples, Delphi can place the insertion point in the code at the exact point where the problem exists. Sometimes, though, Delphi doesn't do as well. Consider, for example, the following code fragment that's intended to sort an array.

```
procedure TForm1.Button1Click(Sender: TObject);
var
   x,y,z:byte;
begin
  for x:= 1 to 4 do
    for y:=x to 5 do
      if face[y]>face[x] then begin
        z:=face[x];
        face[x]:=face[y];
        face[y]:=z;
      end;
    end; {end of inner loop}
end;
```

The code has a syntax error, and Delphi complains with the message in figure 15.5.

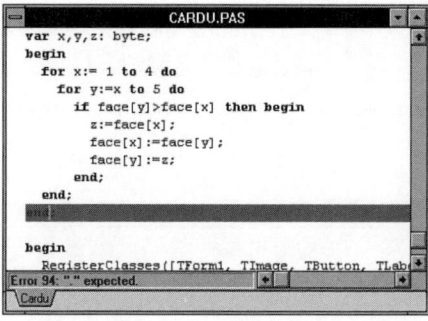

Fig. 15.5
Syntax errors can be misleading.

Delphi places the insertion point between the last end and the last ;. A quick look at the code should show that, in fact, the code can't possibly be missing a . at this point. That indicates the end of the unit, which isn't true. You know there's an error—however, you really don't know where it is.

One technique that can save you a lot of time (and a lot of thinking) is to narrow the scope of the problem. This is done by commenting out as much code as possible until the error goes away. Once it's gone, you can uncomment code one line at a time until you find the offending statement.

Tip
As you cycle between editing, compiling, and running your code, be sure to save often. If Windows happens to crash, you'll lose all the changes you made between your last save and the crash.

In the preceding code sample, if the entire inner for loop is commented out, the problem goes away. If just the code that's within the inner for loop is commented out, the problem returns. This shows that the problem must be with the for loop declaration itself. Indeed, this is the problem, as the inner for loop is missing the begin keyword. When Delphi tried to compile the code, it matched up every begin with an end, and therefore expected a period after the last end.

Use Help to Avoid Syntax Errors

One way to avoid typos is to avoid typing. If, for example, you want to call the MessageDlg function, rather than type the call, look it up in Delphi's online help (see fig. 15.6). You can copy examples for most functions straight from the help system and paste them into your code.

Fig. 15.6
By copying code from Delphi's help system, you can avoid typos.

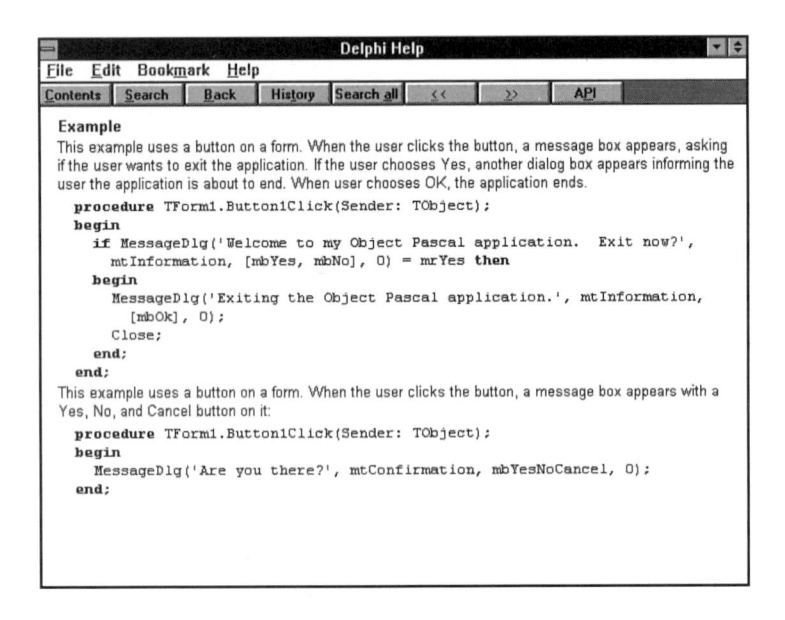

```
                        Delphi Help
File  Edit  Bookmark  Help
Contents  Search  Back  History  Search all  <<  >>  API

Example
This example uses a button on a form. When the user clicks the button, a message box appears, asking
if the user wants to exit the application. If the user chooses Yes, another dialog box appears informing the
user the application is about to end. When user chooses OK, the application ends.
    procedure TForm1.Button1Click(Sender: TObject);
    begin
        if MessageDlg('Welcome to my Object Pascal application.  Exit now?',
           mtInformation, [mbYes, mbNo], 0) = mrYes then
        begin
            MessageDlg('Exiting the Object Pascal application.', mtInformation,
               [mbOk], 0);
            Close;
        end;
    end;
This example uses a button on a form. When the user clicks the button, a message box appears with a
Yes, No, and Cancel button on it:
    procedure TForm1.Button1Click(Sender: TObject);
    begin
        MessageDlg('Are you there?', mtConfirmation, mbYesNoCancel, 0);
    end;
```

Runtime Errors

Runtime errors occur when your code is syntactically correct and can be compiled, but an error happens during runtime. For example, consider the following code from the GraphEx demo:

> **Caution**
>
> The following code has a runtime error. The results of this runtime error vary from machine to machine, but be aware that this code may hang your machine.

```
procedure TForm1.FormCreate(Sender: TObject);
var
  Bitmap: TBitmap;
begin
  {Bitmap := TBitmap.Create;}
  Bitmap.Width := 200;
  Bitmap.Height := 200;
  Image.Picture.Graphic := Bitmap;
end;
```

Line 5 of this code has been purposely commented out to cause an error. While this code passes the syntax check and compiles just fine, it doesn't work. When the code runs, it tries to access an unassigned variable and causes the error shown in figure 15.7.

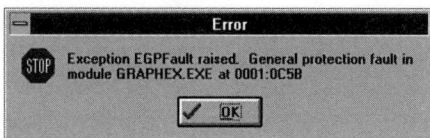

Fig. 15.7
A runtime error can halt execution.

The results of this error are even worse if the program is launched from the Windows Program Manager instead of Delphi. Figure 15.8 shows the Windows error message in this case.

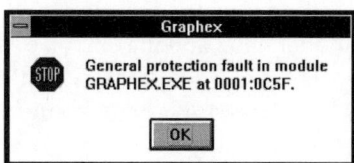

Fig. 15.8
Programs with a runtime error can cause a Windows GPF error.

Delphi has a number of tools to help you track down and eliminate runtime errors. The first is subtle and you may have already seen it if you tried to run the code. If Delphi can recover from the runtime error, it places the insertion point in the Code Editor at the point of the offensive command. In this example, Delphi left the insertion point on the Width line (see fig. 15.9).

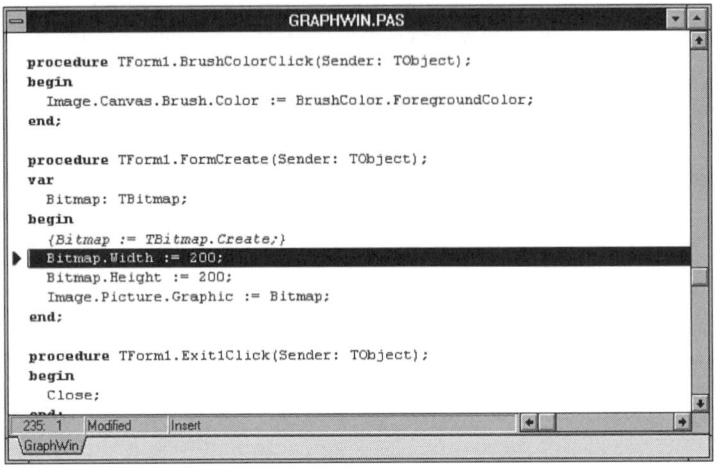

Fig. 15.9
Delphi leaves the cursor at the problem after an error.

```
procedure TForm1.BrushColorClick(Sender: TObject);
begin
    Image.Canvas.Brush.Color := BrushColor.ForegroundColor;
end;

procedure TForm1.FormCreate(Sender: TObject);
var
    Bitmap: TBitmap;
begin
    {Bitmap := TBitmap.Create;}
▶   Bitmap.Width := 200;
    Bitmap.Height := 200;
    Image.Picture.Graphic := Bitmap;
end;

procedure TForm1.Exit1Click(Sender: TObject);
begin
    Close;
```

The placement of the insertion point should give you a clue as to what causes the problem. In this case, since the Bitmap variable never got created, the assignment to its Width property failed. If you can't figure out the problem, read on—Delphi has lots of tools to help you.

Logic Errors

Even after you have your program really running so that it never crashes, it may not work the way you want it to. Certain logic errors present themselves to you quite readily. If, for example, you have a calculator form in which the addition button actually does subtraction, you know that you've got a logic error to take care of. In this case, the solution might be simple—make the addition button call the addition function. In other cases, the logic error may happen only once in a hundred times and may involve the interaction of many variables and procedures. These kind of bugs are the hardest to detect and fix. And it's while tracking down these kind of bugs that you really appreciate Delphi's wealth of debugging tools.

Using the Debugger

Delphi creates compiled executable programs. Because of this, your programs run very fast—way too fast for you to be able see code as it's executed. Delphi has a number of built-in tools that let you slow down execution of your program and interrogate the program's status at any time.

Configuring the Debugger

Before you can use the Delphi's debugging tools, you must tell the compiler to generate special information necessary for the tools to function. To configure the debugger, open the Options menu and choose Project to display the Project Options dialog. Select the Compiler tab. Delphi displays the compiler options page, as shown in figure 15.10.

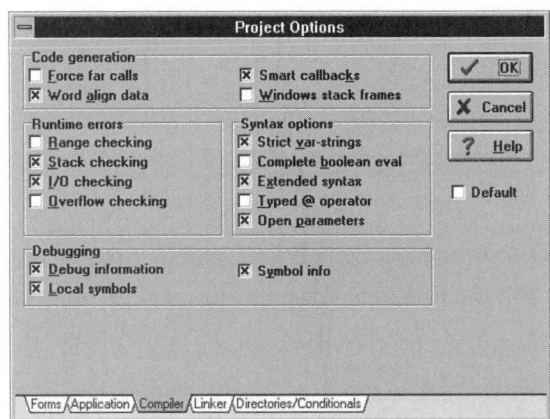

Fig. 15.10
Use the Compiler page of the Project Options dialog to include debugging information in your project.

The Debugging options let you tell the compiler what kind of debugging information it should generate:

- *Debug Information.* This option tells the compiler to generate debug information while it's compiling. This information, stored in the project's .DCU file, is basically a map that correlates the line number of each statement in your code and the corresponding position of the compiled object code in the executable. Always leave this option on during development so that you can use Delphi's debugging features.

- *Local Symbols.* This option tells the compiler to create a list of variables used in your program and store that list in the project's .DCU file. The list maps each variable name with its memory location in the generated executable. If this list is available to the debugger, it allows you to interrogate the value of a variable and even change the value during runtime. Always leave this option on during development, because it adds powerful features to the debugger.

- *Symbol Info.* This option tells the compiler to add to the list of variables stored for the debugger information about how the variables are declared and where they're referenced. You should leave this option on during development.

> **Note**
>
> Storing the debug information slows the compiler down a little and causes the compiler to use a bit more memory. If you run into a memory limit while compiling a program, first try unloading other programs. If that doesn't help, you can try turning off the debug options.

There's another debugger option that you should know about on the Linker page of the Project Options dialog (see fig. 15.11). The Include TDW Debug Info option tells the compiler to store debug information directly within the executable. This information is in addition to the information stored in the DCU. Use this option only if you're going to be using Borland's Turbo Debugger or a third-party debugger, because Delphi's internal debugger makes no use of this information. (For more information on the Turbo Debugger, see the "Turbo Debugger" section later in this chapter.)

Fig. 15.11
Use the Include TDW Debug Info option on the Project Options dialog's Linker page if you use Turbo Debugger.

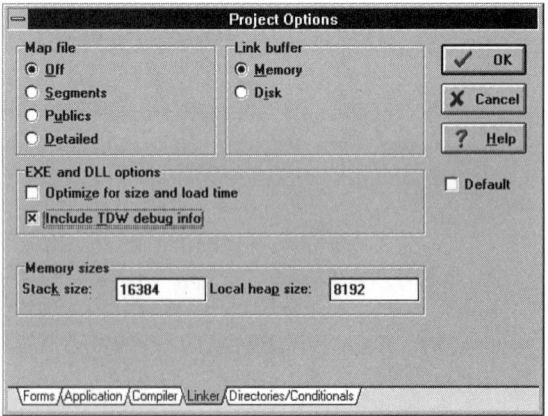

> **Note**
>
> The Include TDW Debug Info option's debug information takes up space in the compiled EXE. Be sure to compile your programs *without* this option when you go to deliver your final product.

Using Breakpoints

Breakpoints are places in your code where you want execution to stop so that you can investigate the status of the program and hopefully figure out what's going wrong. When you set a breakpoint in your code, Delphi runs the code up until that point and then halts execution and displays the code. You can't directly interact with your program until you tell Delphi to start running your program again.

You can set breakpoints in Delphi in a number of ways:

- In the Code Editor, click in the left margin of the line where you want a breakpoint to be inserted. Delphi displays a small stop sign in the margin and highlights the line of code (see fig. 15.12). This is the easiest way and the method you should use most of the time.

- With the cursor on the line where you want a breakpoint, press F5.

- With the cursor on the line where you want a breakpoint, select Toggle Brea<u>k</u>point from the SpeedMenu.

- View the Breakpoint List window by opening the <u>V</u>iew menu and choosing B<u>r</u>eakpoints. Then choose <u>A</u>dd Breakpoint from the Breakpoint List window's SpeedMenu.

Tip
To set breakpoints even if your program is already running, switch to the Code Editor or Breakpoint List window using the normal Windows controls, such as Alt+Tab, and set your breakpoints.

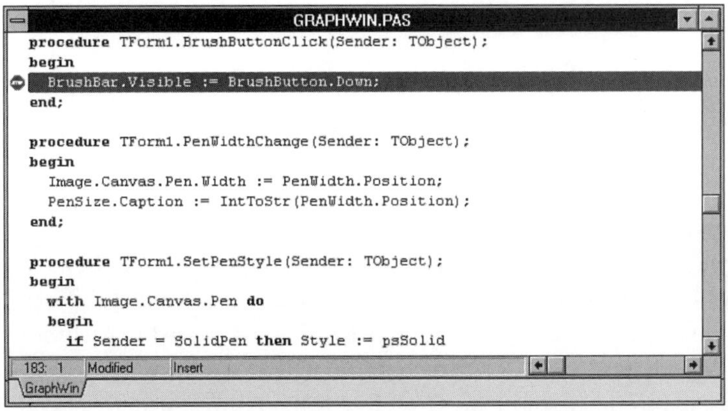

Fig. 15.12
Delphi automatically enters debugging mode when execution reaches a breakpoint.

Note
You can place breakpoints only on lines of code with valid statements. Delphi doesn't allow a breakpoint on a comment.

428 Chapter 15—Using Delphi's Debugging Features

With a breakpoint set, press F9 or click the Run button on the toolbar. Delphi recompiles your program and runs it until it reaches the breakpoint. Since the breakpoint set in figure 15.12 doesn't occur until you click the paintbrush icon, you're free to use the program as though it had been launched from the Windows Program Manager. Normally, you would use this time to initiate the events that cause a runtime or logic error. Click the paintbrush icon, and your cursor immediately changes to a stop sign (see fig. 15.13). At this point, you can use Delphi's debugging features to evaluate variables or step through code as explained later in this chapter. To just get the program running again, press F9.

Fig. 15.13
Delphi shows the stop sign cursor while debugging.

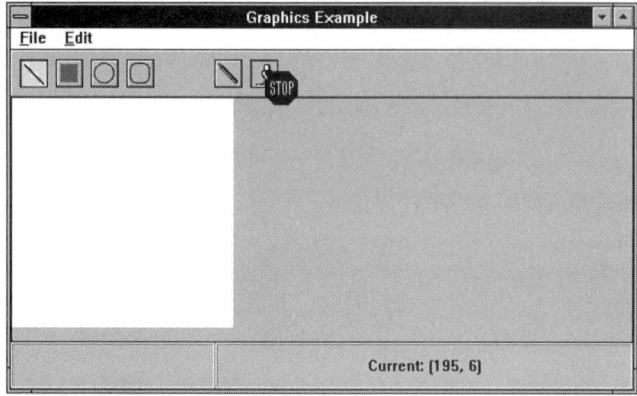

You can use any of the preceding methods in reverse to remove an existing breakpoint. To remove all the breakpoints at once, select Delete All Breakpoints from the Breakpoint List window's SpeedMenu.

The Breakpoint List Window

The Breakpoint List window adds a lot of functionality to your breakpoints (see fig. 15.14). The list displays the file name and line number of each breakpoint as well as any conditions or pass counts related to each breakpoint, as explained later. It can be brought up while editing your code or during a debugging session. To view the Breakpoint List window, open the View menu and choose Breakpoints.

Fig. 15.14
The Breakpoint List window allows you to manipulate breakpoints.

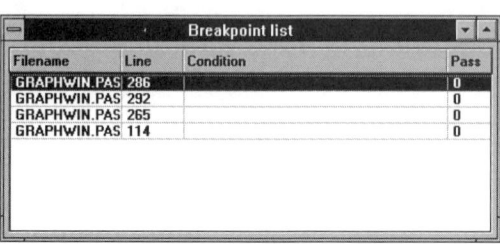

If you have a breakpoint set but don't need that breakpoint all the time, you can temporarily disable it. This is useful when a breakpoint is in a loop and the program keeps stopping on every iteration of the loop. To disable a breakpoint, click that breakpoint in the Breakpoint List window and select Disable Breakpoint from the SpeedMenu. The breakpoint remains on the list but is grayed out in the dialog and in the Code Editor window. To enable the breakpoint, select Enable Breakpoint from the SpeedMenu. To enable or disable all your breakpoints at once, select Enable All Breakpoints or Disable All Breakpoints from the SpeedMenu.

The Breakpoint List window allows you to quickly jump to the code where the breakpoint is located. Just select a breakpoint and choose View Source from the SpeedMenu. Delphi positions the insertion point at beginning of the line of code with the breakpoint. If you want the Code Editor to actually gain focus so that you can immediately begin editing, choose Edit Source from the SpeedMenu.

Breakpoint Pass Count

Often, problems in your programs don't happen on the very first iteration of an event. In this case, the debugging process can be slowed considerably if your breakpoint keeps getting called before the problem happens. To speed things up, Delphi allows you to set a breakpoint that triggers only after a set number of passes. For example, set a breakpoint on the button click of the rectangle tool in the GraphEx demo. View the Breakpoint List window and highlight the new breakpoint. Choose Edit Breakpoint from the SpeedMenu; Delphi displays the Edit Breakpoint dialog (see fig. 15.15).

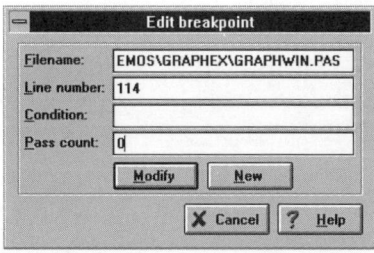

Fig. 15.15
Delphi allows you to modify breakpoint settings.

Set the Pass Count to 5 and press Enter. Run the program and click the rectangle icon 5 times. On the fifth mouse click, Delphi enters debugging mode. By default, this kind of breakpoint is called only once. If you want the breakpoint called again during program execution, you can bring up the Edit Breakpoint dialog again and change the Pass Count value. If you change the Pass Count to 0, the breakpoint is called every time program execution reaches it.

Conditional Breakpoints

Tip
You can place almost any valid Pascal expression into the Condition text box that doesn't call a function. The expression must evaluate to true or non-zero for the breakpoint to be invoked.

Some bugs occur only when certain conditions are met within your program. For these bugs, Delphi provides conditional breakpoints that are called only when a preset condition is met. Assume that the GraphEx program has a bug that happens only while drawing in the GraphEx program with the ellipse tool. Place a breakpoint on line 130 of GRAPHWIN.PAS (this is the first line of code in the TForm1.DrawShape procedure) and bring up the Edit Breakpoint dialog. Type **DrawingTool=dtEllipse** into the Condition text box and press Enter. Run the program and draw a rectangle; nothing happens. Now try to draw a ellipse; Delphi enters debugging mode.

Since Delphi checks the condition every time the breakpoint is reached, the breakpoint can be invoked again. Press F9 to continue running the program. If you draw another ellipse, the breakpoint is called again.

Temporary Breakpoints

If you want to invoke the debugger at a certain line of code just once, you don't actually need to set a breakpoint. Place the cursor on that line of code and press F4 or open the Run menu and choose Run to Cursor. Delphi compiles your program if necessary and runs your program until code execution reaches the line of code with the cursor.

You can also have Delphi go right into debug mode before it executes any of your code. While in the Code Editor, press F8 or open the Run menu and choose Step Over (explained in detail later). Delphi compiles your program, if necessary, and brings up the debugger at the begin keyword (see fig. 15.16).

Fig. 15.16
While in the Code Editor, press F8 to begin debugging at the first line of code.

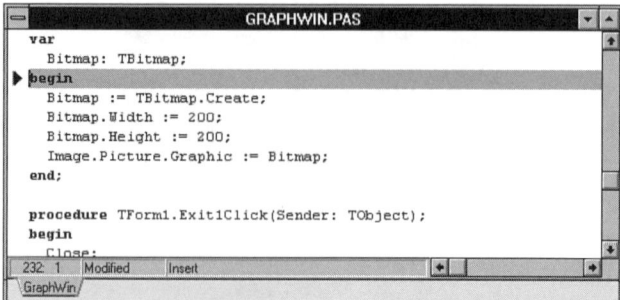

Letting Your Program Run

Once a breakpoint is invoked, your program is stopped and Delphi is in debug mode. You can't interact with the program until you start it up again. Delphi provides a number of useful ways to restart your program.

Run

The simplest way to get your program running again is to simply press F9 or open the Run menu and choose Run. Your program runs normally at full speed as though a breakpoint had never been encountered.

Step Into

Once a breakpoint has occurred, Delphi lets you step through your code one line at a time. At each line of code you can watch the results of the code, evaluate variables, and generally get an idea of what the code is doing. There are three ways to step into your code:

- Press F7.
- Open the Run menu and choose Trace Into.
- Click the Trace Into button on the speedbar.

No matter which method you use, Delphi executes the current line of code and moves the insertion point to the next line of code to be executed. Figure 15.17 shows this process.

Tip
If you're going to single-step through a couple lines of code, in general it's fastest to step through them by pressing the F7 key.

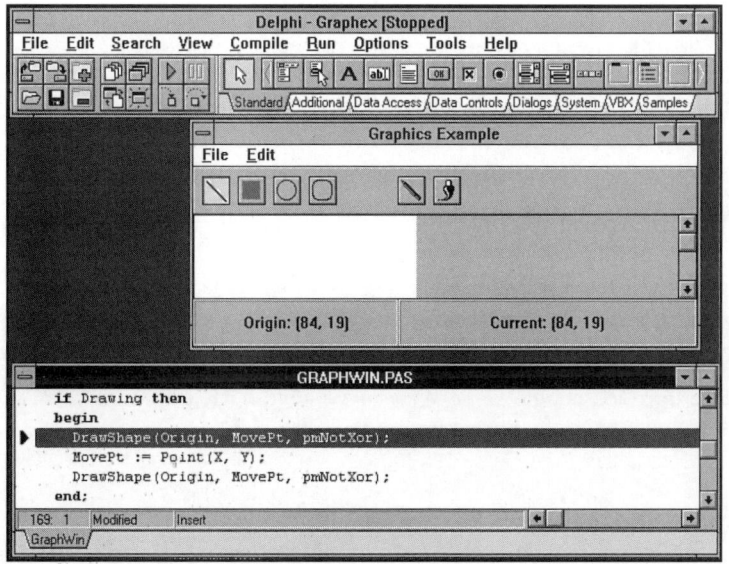

Fig. 15.17
Delphi highlights the next line to be executed.

Notice in figure 15.17 the placement and sizing of the Code Editor window and the GraphEx window. They're placed in such a way that they don't overlap. This is because Delphi has to redraw the program window after each line of code is executed. If the Code Editor window overlaps the program window, Delphi must also redraw the Code Editor window, which slows things down.

This single-stepping is known as Trace Into because Delphi *traces into* a function, if it can. If, for example, the next available line calls the DrawShape function, as in figure 15.17, Delphi calls this function and leaves the cursor on the first line of code within the function. If the function doesn't have debug information available, Delphi executes the function but doesn't trace into it and leaves the cursor at the next line of code to be executed.

Step Over

Sometimes you don't need to—and don't want to—trace into a function. Often you're sure that a given function is bug free and not related to problems you're tracking down. In this case, Delphi lets you *step over* a function call or line of code. In figure 15.17, for example, if the DrawShape function isn't involved in a bug, you don't want to have to step through all 15 lines of its code. You can step over code in three ways:

- Press F8.

- Open the Run menu and select Step Over.

- Click the Step Over button on the speedbar.

When you step over code, that code is still executed. Stepping over a line of code that doesn't contain a function call is exactly the same as stepping into the same line of code. The only difference occurs when you step over or into a line of code with a function call to a function with debug information available.

> **Note**
>
> Don't step over or into two many lines of code. If you don't need to see what happens at each line, put the cursor on the next line you're interested in and press F4. Delphi runs your program until it reaches the cursor.

Taking Advantage of Debugger Tools

Just starting and stopping program execution is limited in its usefulness. To really find the bugs, Delphi provides a number of tools—such as the Watch List window and Evaluate/Modify dialog—that let you investigate and change the state of your program and its variables while debugging.

The Watch List Window

The Watch List window allows you to view the contents of a variable during program execution. As you step through your code, the Watch List window is updated dynamically so that you can see the effect of each line of code on your variables.

To view the Watch List window while editing code or at runtime, open the View menu and choose Watches. Figure 15.18 shows the Watch List window open at runtime.

Fig. 15.18
The Watch List window shows a variable's values during runtime.

As you can see, the Watch List window can display any type of variable. Figure 15.18 shows a button, Boolean, and point are all displayed, each in their proper format.

The Watch List window can show only meaningful values for variables while those variables are in scope. For example, the Watch List window indicates `Process not available` when your program isn't running. In figure 15.18, the variable x isn't within the scope of the function at the breakpoint, so the Watch List window shows `Unknown identifier`.

Adding Variables to the Watch List Window

When the Watch List window is initially displayed, the variable list is empty. You can add a variable to the Watch List window in a number of ways:

- In the Code Editor, highlight a variable and press Ctrl+F5. Delphi brings up the Watch Properties dialog with the name of the variable in the Expression combo box (see fig. 15.19). Press Enter, and the variable is added to the Watch List window.

Fig. 15.19
Use the Watch Properties dialog to configure watch variables.

- In the Code Editor, highlight a variable and select Add Watch at Cursor from the SpeedMenu.

- Open the Run menu and choose Add Watch. The Watch Properties dialog appears, but unlike the preceding methods you must type the name of a variable.

- Choose Add Watch or Edit Watch from the Watch List window's SpeedMenu.

- Press Ctrl+A while the Watch List window has focus.

Using the Watch Properties Dialog
Within the Watch Properties dialog you have a number of options. In the Expression combo box, type the name of a variable or select a variable from the drop-down list. (Delphi remembers the name of each variable you watch and adds it to the drop-down list for later use.)

Delphi does a good job of determining the type of variable you're watching and displays it in an appropriate format. If you want to see the variable in another format, choose one of the radio buttons in the Watch Properties dialog. Delphi provides the following formats: Character, String, Decimal Integer, Hex Integer, Ordinal, Pointer, Record, Default, and Memory Dump. Most of the time, the Default setting should give you what you need. For floating-point numbers, you can specify the number digits to be displayed by typing that number in the Digits text box.

You can view an entire array by typing the array name in the Expression combo box. The Watch List window displays a comma-separated list of array values. To see a particular array element, type the array name with its index in the Expression combo box—for example, `TextArray[3]`. If you want to see a range of values from an array, type the array name with the index of the first value in the Expression combo box, and then type the number of array elements you want to see in the Repeat Count text box. If, for example, you type `TextArray[2]` in the Expression combo box and 2 in the Repeat Count text box, the Watch List window displays elements 2 and 3.

If you have an expression that you want to leave in the Watch List window but don't need to have evaluated, deselect the Enabled check box in the Watch Properties dialog. The Watch List window grays out that expression.

Simplifying Operations with the Watch List Window's SpeedMenu
The Watch List window has a SpeedMenu to simplify its operations. The following options are on the Watch List window's SpeedMenu:

- *Edit Watch.* This menu choice brings up the Watch Properties dialog and lets you modify the properties of the current watch variable.

- *Add Watch.* This menu choice brings up the Watch Properties dialog with a blank expression.

- *Delete Watch.* If you have too many watch variables displayed in the Watch List window, the display can become confusing. Use this menu choice to remove unneeded watch variables from the window. You can easily add the variables back to the Watch List window later. You can also select a watch variable and then press Delete to remove a watch variable.

- *Enable/Disable Watch.* By default, your watch variables are enabled, meaning that they're evaluated at each breakpoint. A disabled watch variable is grayed out and never evaluated. Use these menu choices to toggle a variable between the enabled and disabled states.

- *Enable/Disable All Watches.* These menu choices allow you to quickly enable or disable all watch variables. This is useful if you want to concentrate on one variable. Just disable all watches and then individually enable the watch variable you're interested in.

- *Delete All Watches.* This menu choice removes all watch variables from the Watch List window. The Watch List window isn't closed, though, so you can still add other watch variables.

The Evaluate/Modify Dialog

Besides just viewing variables with the Watch List window, Delphi allows you to quickly view and modify the value of any single variable. This is useful when you want to inspect a variable once but don't want to bother adding it to the Watch List window. This is also useful when debugging a situation that occurs only under strange circumstances. By changing the value of variables on the fly, you can easily simulate the strange circumstances.

To invoke the Evaluate/Modify dialog, run your program to a breakpoint. Put the Code Editor window's insertion point in the variable you're interested in, and then do one of the following:

- Press Ctrl+F7. The Evaluate/Modify dialog appears (see fig. 15.20).

- Choose Evaluate/Modify from the Run menu.

- Select Evaluate/Modify from the Code Editor's SpeedMenu.

Fig. 15.20
The Evaluate/Modify dialog lets you inspect variables on the fly.

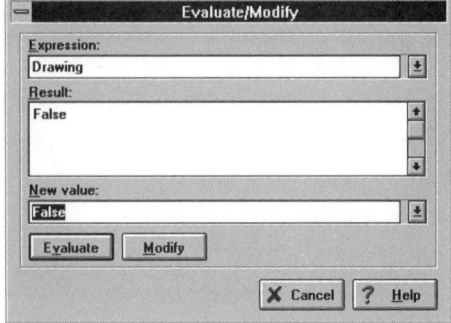

Delphi brings up the Evaluate/Modify dialog with the variable that was at the cursor in the Expression combo box. The Result list box and the New Value combo box should contain the value of the variable.

Tip
You can use the Evaluate/Modify dialog as a quick calculator. Just type an expression, such as at **6*7**, and click the Evaluate button.

You can type any legal Pascal expression in the Expression combo box as long as that expression doesn't contain any function calls. Of course, variable scoping rules still apply, so you can use only variables that are within the scope of the current breakpoint. Click the Evaluate button, and the results of the expression are displayed in the Result box. If the expression contains a single variable that can be modified, the results are also shown in the New Value combo box.

Most of the time the Result box displays the information in a manner you can read, but Delphi also allows you to format the results of your expression. This is done by appending a comma and a format string to the end of the expression. Table 15.1 lists the valid format strings.

Table 15.1	Expression Formatting Strings	
Character	**Type**	**Results**
H or X	Integer	Displays the results in hexadecimal format.
C	Char, String	In addition to normal characters, displays special characters for low-order ASCII characters.
D	Integer	Display results in decimal form.
Fn	Floating point	Displays a floating point number with *n* significant digits.

Character	Type	Results
nM	All	Displays a memory dump of *n* bytes starting at the location of the variable. This format string can be combined with other format strings.
P	Pointer	Display a pointer's value and information about the pointer.
R	Structure, union	By default, displays a comma-separated list of structure field values. This format string displays the field's names and values.
S	Char, String	Displays low-order ASCII characters as C escape sequences.

If you specify an unrecognizable format string, the Result box is left blank.

To modify the content of a variable, type a value in the New Value combo box and click the Modify button. Delphi tries to assign the new value to the variable and displays the results in the Result list box. If the new value can't be assigned to the variable, the Result box displays an error message.

The Call Stack Window

When debugging complex programs with many nested functions, especially recursive routines, it's quite difficult to remember exactly what routines were called to get to a particular point in a program. The Call Stack window eases this burden by providing a list of called routines (see fig. 15.21). To display the Call Stack window, open the View menu and choose Call Stack.

Tip
You can use the Evaluate/Modify dialog as a quick hexadecimal converter. To convert 44 decimal to hex, type **44,H** in the Expression combo box. To convert 2C from hex to decimal, type **$2C,D**.

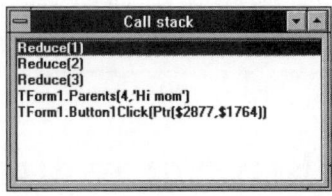

Fig. 15.21
The Call Stack window shows the function call history.

The top item in the Call Stack window is the current function. The item below the first function is the function that called the first function, and so on.

The Call Stack window displays not only the names of the functions, but the parameters that were passed to them. This saves you from having to set up those variables in the Watch List window or the Evaluate/Modify dialog.

The Call Stack window is linked to the Code Editor. Double-clicking a function in the Call Stack window moves the insertion point in the Code Editor to the last line that was executed in that function. You can also press Ctrl+I or choose View Source from the Call Stack window's SpeedMenu to get the same functionality. To have the Code Editor window gain focus at a given function, select that function and select Edit Source from the Call Stack window's SpeedMenu.

Pause and Reset

So far this chapter has covered most of the items in Delphi's Run menu, with two important exceptions: Program Pause and Program Reset.

Normally, you use breakpoints to invoke the debugger while your program is running. You can invoke the debugger even if your program doesn't have any breakpoints, however. Use the normal Windows control features to make Delphi your active window. Open the Run menu and choose Program Pause. Your program stops just as if a breakpoint had been encountered. You can use any other debugging features at this point.

Sometimes while stepping through a program, you may realize that you've stepped too far into your code. To start the debugging process again, you don't need to close down your program and run it again. Instead, choose Program Reset from Delphi's Run menu. This causes your program to run again from the beginning.

> **Caution**
>
> While Delphi does its best to release your program's resources when you choose Program Reset, such as memory and open files, sometimes it can't close every Windows resource. If you're running low on Windows resources, you may have to close your program and run it again rather than do a Program Reset.

Knowing When *Not* to Use Delphi's Debugging Tools

There are times when using Delphi's debugging features that these features actually interfere with the debugging process. With all things in nature, it's impossible to observe something without changing it. This is true of the debugger as well. It causes subtle changes to your program's environment by using memory, changing timing, and stealing focus. If these changes affect your bug, then you may have to use old-fashioned techniques to debug your program.

One technique is to have your program display messages. These messages can be as simple as `Go to line 135` or include the values of variables. In Delphi, an easy way to implement messaging is to place a blank edit field on your form. In your program, just add code similar to the following:

```
Edit1.Text:="Entered Main Procedure";
```

The edit field displays your message when the line of code is executed.

Using Other Borland Tools

In addition to Delphi's integrated debugging features, Borland produces a number of other tools that may help you track down bugs.

Turbo Debugger

The Turbo Debugger is a third-generation language debugger that ships with Borland languages such as C, C++, and Pascal. At the time of this writing, the Turbo Debugger had not been completely updated to support Delphi programs, but a new version is expected soon. The screen shots in this chapter are from a previous version. The Turbo Debugger is a large product in and of itself and too much to completely cover in this book. A few highlights are presented here to point out the available tools.

To load Turbo Debugger, double-click its icon in Windows Program Manager. You should notice something strange right away—Turbo Debugger runs in character mode (see fig. 15.22). Don't worry, it's a real Windows program—it just uses a character-based interface. Because Turbo Debugger is a special program meant to take control of another program, you can't use the normal Windows task-switching functions such as Alt+Tab.

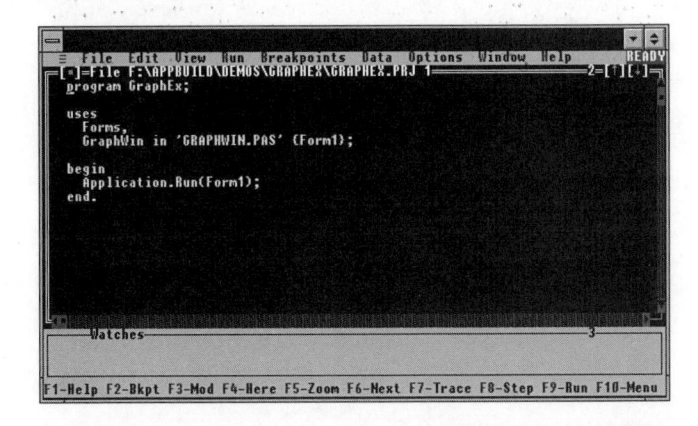

Fig. 15.22
You can use Borland's Turbo Debugger to debug Delphi programs.

Open the File menu and choose Open. Type or select the name of the program you want to debug and click OK. Turbo Debugger loads your program and highlights the first available line of code.

You're already familiar with some of the keystrokes necessary to control the debugger. For example, F8 is Step Into and F7 is Step Over, just like in Delphi's integrated debugging environment.

Since Turbo Debugger doesn't understand the debug information in your .DCU files, you must tell Delphi to link the debug information right into the executable before using Turbo Debugger. Open Delphi's Options menu, choose Project, and then select the Linker tab in the Project Options dialog. Select the Include TDW Debug Info check box (see fig. 15.23). When you recompile your program, the executable includes symbolic debugger information.

Fig. 15.23
You must include debug info in the EXE to use Turbo Debugger.

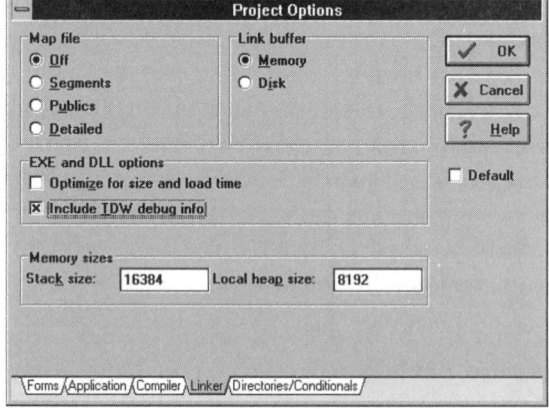

Although Turbo Debugger shares features with the integrated debugger, it has many unique features of its own. Since it's designed for use with lower-level languages, it gives you much greater control over low-level hardware information. You have complete access to the CPU's registers and flags as well as system memory. You can follow far pointers to memory locations and examine their contents directly. Unlike Delphi's integrated debugger, Turbo Debugger can trace into code even if the source code isn't available. In this case, the CPU pane is shown with the assembly language instructions, as shown in figure 15.24.

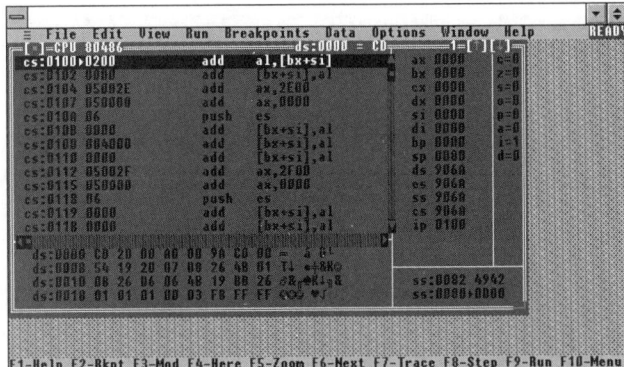

Fig. 15.24
Turbo Debugger can trace programs without source code.

Turbo Debugger supports a number of Windows-specific features. It tracks Windows messages, lets you view your program's local heap as well as the global heap, and supports the capability to view a complete list of the units making up your program, including DLLs.

Another important aspect of Turbo Debugger is its capability to be run remotely. You can configure Turbo Debugger to control another machine connected by a serial link or via a network that supports NetBIOS. In this mode, one machine displays the debugger screen and the other machine displays the program being debugged. This allows you to step through the code on one screen and watch the results on another. There's no screen flash because the debugger doesn't need to switch video modes or redraw overlapping windows. Also, the memory used on the program machine is reduced, thus making less of an impact on the program.

WinSight

A Windows program is a set of objects sending and receiving messages. WinSight is a debugging tool that lets you graphically view these objects and track the messages. To start WinSight, double-click the WinSight icon in Program Manager's Delphi group. Figure 15.25 shows WinSight tracking the GraphEx program.

WinSight has many important features that are beyond the scope of this book. Be sure to look through the menus and on-line help to get a handle on its use.

Fig. 15.25
WinSight lets you spy on the inner workings of Windows.

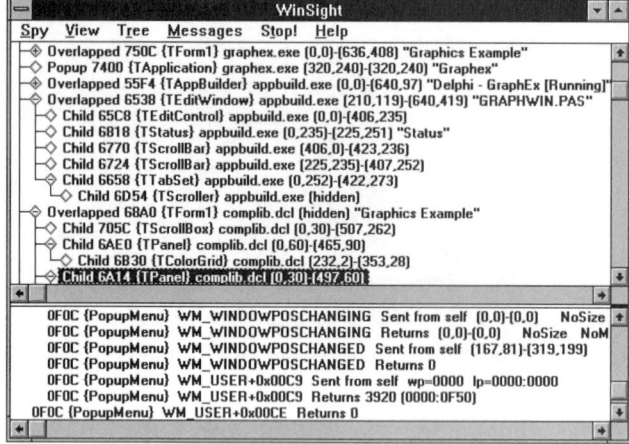

You definitely don't want to watch all the messages that go between windows. There are just too many of them, and the interesting information gets buried among them. Instead, open WinSight's Messages menu and choose Selected Windows. Now select the objects you're interested in by Shift+clicking them in the window tree panel (the top panel). Any messages going to the selected objects are displayed in the message trace panel. If you only want to track certain classes of messages, open the Messages menu and choose Options. Use the check boxes as in figure 15.26 to filter the messages.

Fig. 15.26
WinSight lets you filter out messages you aren't interested in.

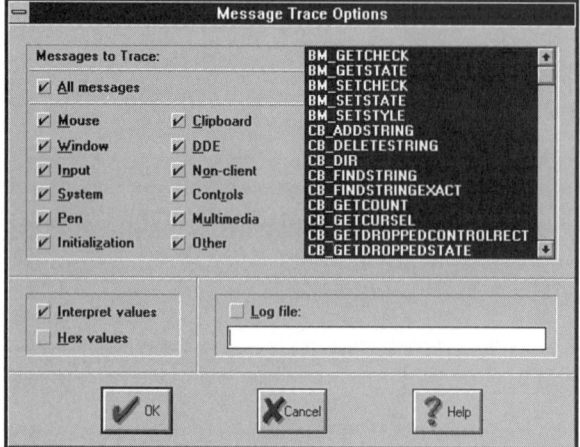

One more notable feature of WinSight is its capability to display detailed information on an object. Double-click an object in the window tree panel; WinSight displays the WinSight Detail window (see fig. 15.27).

Using Other Borland Tools   **443**

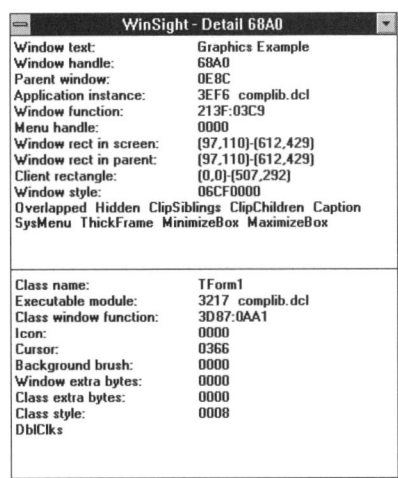

Fig. 15.27
You can use WinSight to display detailed object information.

WinSpector

WinSpector is a tool used to help track down the causes of Unrecoverable Application Errors (UAE) and General Protection Fault (GPF) errors. When one of these errors occurs, WinSpector wakes up and logs system information.

To load WinSpector, double-click the WinSpector icon in Program Manager's Delphi group. WinSpector runs but immediately minimizes itself so that you don't see it.

To set WinSpector options, use the normal Windows features to switch to the WinSpector program. Click the Set Prefs button to display the configuration window.

When a UAE occurs, WinSpector wakes up and asks you to type a comment explaining the circumstances of the problem (see fig. 15.28). WinSpector then logs what information it can and minimizes itself again.

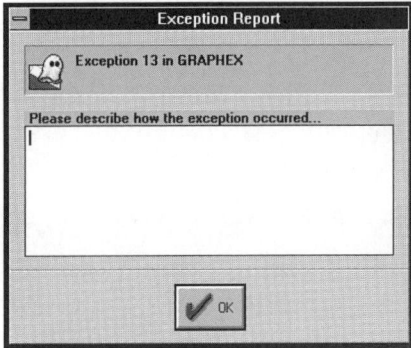

Fig. 15.28
WinSpector allows you to record UAE circumstances.

444 Chapter 15—Using Delphi's Debugging Features

To see the WinSpector log, switch to the WinSpector window and click the View Log button. WinSpector displays a screen of information similar to figure 15.29.

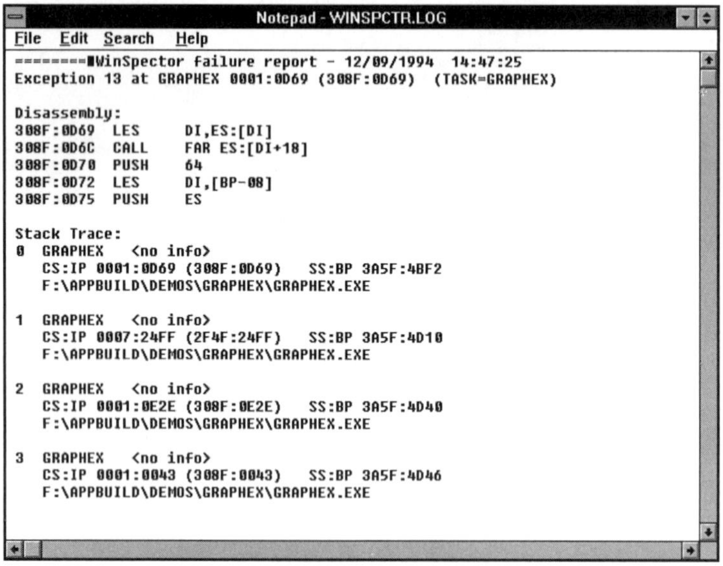

Fig. 15.29
The WinSpector log shows your system status at the time of an exception.

```
========WinSpector failure report - 12/09/1994  14:47:25
Exception 13 at GRAPHEX 0001:0D69 (308F:0D69)   (TASK=GRAPHEX)

Disassembly:
308F:0D69   LES    DI,ES:[DI]
308F:0D6C   CALL   FAR ES:[DI+18]
308F:0D70   PUSH   64
308F:0D72   LES    DI,[BP-08]
308F:0D75   PUSH   ES

Stack Trace:
0  GRAPHEX    <no info>
   CS:IP  0001:0D69 (308F:0D69)    SS:BP 3A5F:4BF2
   F:\APPBUILD\DEMOS\GRAPHEX\GRAPHEX.EXE

1  GRAPHEX    <no info>
   CS:IP  0007:24FF (2F4F:24FF)    SS:BP 3A5F:4D10
   F:\APPBUILD\DEMOS\GRAPHEX\GRAPHEX.EXE

2  GRAPHEX    <no info>
   CS:IP  0001:0E2E (308F:0E2E)    SS:BP 3A5F:4D40
   F:\APPBUILD\DEMOS\GRAPHEX\GRAPHEX.EXE

3  GRAPHEX    <no info>
   CS:IP  0001:0043 (308F:0043)    SS:BP 3A5F:4D46
   F:\APPBUILD\DEMOS\GRAPHEX\GRAPHEX.EXE
```

From Here...

Delphi doesn't skimp on its debugging tools. For the most part, the integrated debugging tools should cover of your needs. Be sure to *test! test! test!* your program before you give it out to users. Keep in mind also that the programmer who works on a particular program is the worst person to test the program.

To continue to sharpen your debugging and programming skills, refer to the following chapters:

- Chapter 3, "Understanding the Language." Knowing the basics is vitally important for writing a robust program.

- Chapter 7, "Customizing and Reusing Components." A good way to avoid debugging is to use components that have already been debugged.

- Chapter 11, "Using the Browser." This is another debugging tool that should make life easier.

Chapter 16

Delivering Your Application

Once you've created a Delphi application, you have to deliver that application. The delivery process involves packaging the application along with any support files and databases and getting it ready for installation. The good news is that Delphi applications are easy to deliver. You can deliver standalone utilities as simple .EXE files with no additional runtime programs or DLLs. Database applications and applications that do reporting require a few more files, as this chapter explains.

> **Note**
>
> Be sure to check your licensing agreements before doing any installation so that you don't illegally copy software.

In this chapter, you learn how to deliver

- A simple application
- An application with VBXs
- An application with on-line help
- An application with database access
- An application with ReportSmith reports

Delivering Simple EXEs

Delphi provides the easiest way known to write Windows programs. Many programmers use Delphi to write simple utilities that can be shipped as a single .EXE file. Figure 16.1 shows a very simple calculator created with Delphi.

Fig. 16.1
You can ship a simple utility as a single EXE.

To deliver this calculator program to the end user, all you need to do is compile the program and ship the EXE. To compile the program, open the Compile menu and choose Build All. Delphi compiles the program and creates an .EXE file with the same name as your project—in this case, CALC.EXE. While CALC.EXE is truly a working program and can be delivered as is, the following sections explain some of the items that need attention before delivering your application.

Configuring the Linker

Before delivering a Delphi application, make sure that the EXE doesn't contain debug information. Debug information includes, among other things, a map of variable names and locations and a map to source code lines. This information takes up extra disk space and could help a hacker decompile your executable.

To make sure that the executable doesn't contain debug information, open the Options menu and choose Project. In the Project Objects dialog, select the Linker tab (see fig. 16.2).

Make sure that the Debug Info in EXE check box isn't selected. Click OK and recompile your project if the check box was originally selected. If you did include debug information in your .EXE file, you should notice the size of the EXE reduce after you recompile.

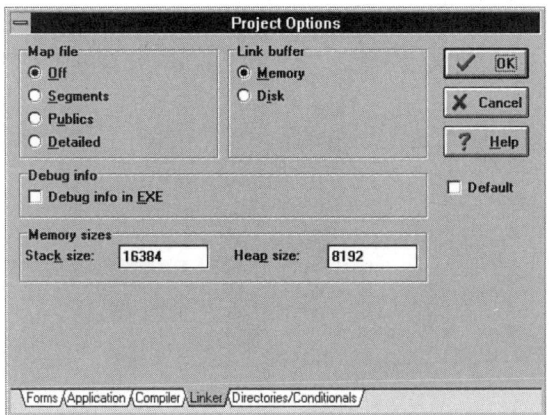

Fig. 16.2
You don't want to include debug information in your final EXE.

> **Note**
>
> You don't normally need to include debug information during development—Delphi's integrated debugging features don't use this information. It's used only by Turbo Debugger. For more information on debugging, see Chapter 15, "Using Delphi's Debugging Features."

Setting Up Icons

Most Windows programs, including programs created with Delphi, contain public resources that the operating system uses. Icons are one such resource. Delphi programs contain at least two icons: one that's displayed when your program is minimized and one that's displayed by the Windows Program Manager. If you don't specifically set up icons for your program, Delphi uses the default Delphi icon (see fig. 16.3).

To set up the icon that's displayed when your application is minimized, view the Object Inspector for your program's main form. Select the Icon property and click the ellipsis button. Delphi displays the Picture Editor dialog. Figure 16.4 shows the Picture Editor with a homemade generic icon loaded.

Click the Load button, and Delphi displays the normal Open dialog. Search your hard disk for the appropriate .ICO file. Once you've selected an icon, click OK. Recompile and run your program. Now when you minimize your program, the icon you selected is displayed.

448 Chapter 16—Delivering Your Application

Fig. 16.3
Delphi assigns this icon to your program if you don't supply one.

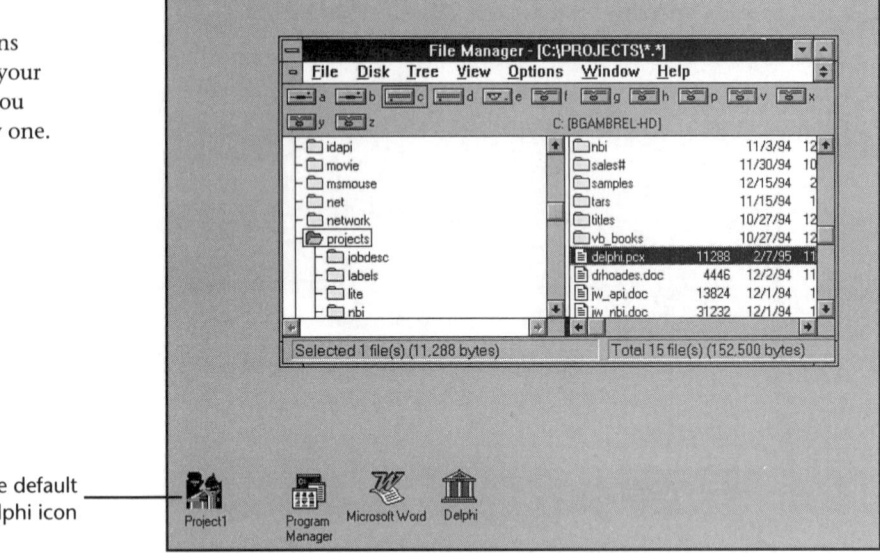

The default Delphi icon

Fig. 16.4
Delphi lets you select an icon to display when your program is minimized.

To set up the icon that represents your program in the Windows Program Manager, open the Options menu and select Project. In the Project Options dialog, select the Application tab (see fig. 16.5).

> **Note**
>
> The Help File text box shown in figure 16.5 is discussed later in this chapter.

Click the Load Icon button, and Delphi displays the Application Icon dialog (see fig. 16.6). Use this dialog to select the appropriate icon. Often you use the same icon for the application as used for the minimized form.

Delivering Simple EXEs **449**

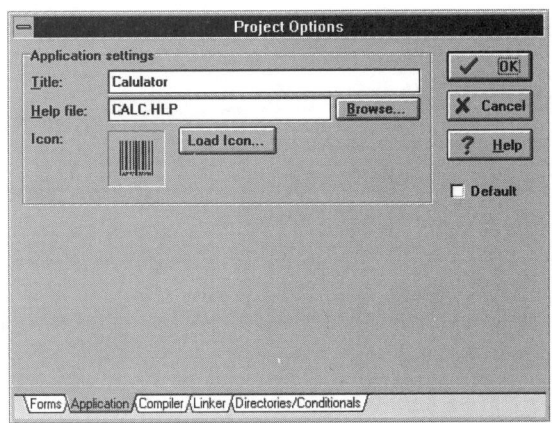

Fig. 16.5
Delphi lets you specify a Program Manager icon.

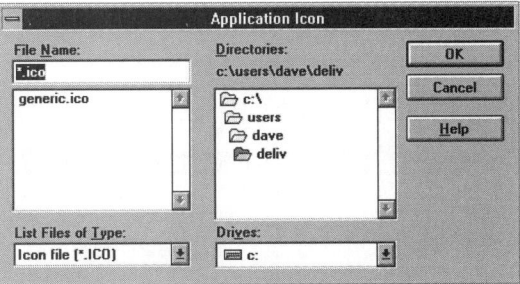

Fig. 16.6
Use this dialog to search your hard disk for an application icon.

When you recompile your program, the icons are included in the .EXE file. You don't have to include separate .ICO files when you deliver your program.

Creating Your Own Icon

There are two ways to get an icon: borrow one that has already been made or create your own.

Icons exist as stand-alone .ICO files, or they exist within .EXE and .DLL files. If you plan on borrowing an icon, search your hard disk for .ICO files—you should find a few. Many bulletin boards these days have large collections of icons you can download and use royalty-free.

If you can't find an appropriate icon for your application, create your own. To do so, you need an icon editor. If you want to stick with a Borland tool, Borland's Resource Workshop has an icon editor (see fig. 16.7). If you're a Norton Desktop for Windows user, you can use the Norton Icon Editor (see fig. 16.8).

Fig. 16.7
If you don't already have an icon, use Borland's Resource Workshop to create one.

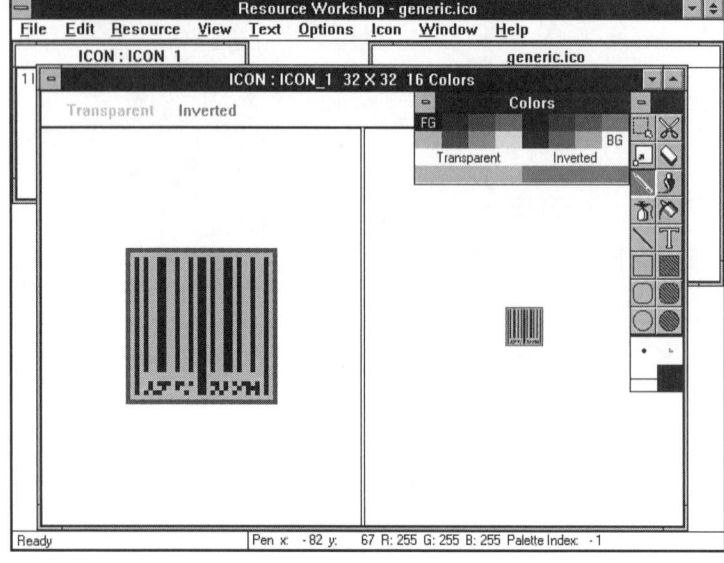

Fig. 16.8
The Norton Icon Editor is another tool you can use to create icons.

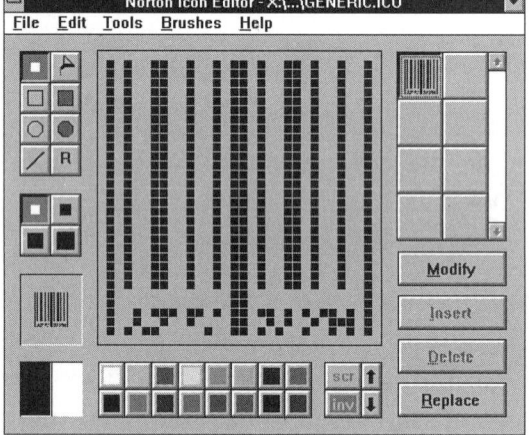

Both programs allow you to extract icons from EXEs and DLLs, create new icons, and write icons to .ICO files.

Hooking Up Your Icon

Once you've copied your program to a user's machine, you need to create an icon to launch the program from the Windows Program Manager. Open Program Manager's File menu and choose New. In the New Program Object dialog, choose Program Group if you want to create a new window on the Program Manager screen for your program, or Program Item if you just want to add an icon for your program to an existing group.

If you choose Program Group, Windows asks for the name of the group and creates the group. After creating a group, repeat the process and choose Program Item.

When you choose Program Item, Windows displays the Program Item Properties dialog (see fig. 16.9).

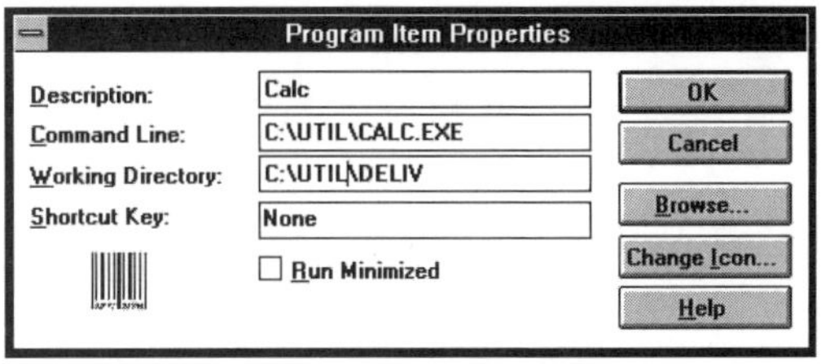

Fig. 16.9
Be sure to hook your program up to Program Manager.

Click the Browse button and use the Browse dialog to select your program. When you select a program from the Browse dialog, Windows automatically fills in the Command Line text box for you. Type the name that you want to appear below the Program Manager icon in the Description text box. In the Working Directory text box, type the name of the directory that you want to be the default directory for your program. If all your database references use aliases to reference tables, the Working Directory value may not matter. To be safe, though, set the working directory to the same directory that the EXE is located in. If you want, you can specify a shortcut key in the Shortcut Key text box. When you click OK, Windows adds your program's icon to the current group. If that isn't the correct group, just drag the icon to the correct one. When you double-click the icon, your program should run.

Including Help Files with Your Program

A complete Windows program should include standard Windows help. When you deliver your application, you should include one or more .HLP files. There are a number of places to store these files and a number of ways to retrieve them.

> **Note**
>
> Creating help files in Delphi uses a process that's the same in most Windows programming environments. In a nutshell, you create a document in a word processor with special formatting and then use a help compiler to turn the document into a true help file. Delphi's built-in on-line help has a complete discussion on creating help files. To find it, press F1 at any point in Delphi to invoke the help system. Open the File menu, choose Open, and then select the CWH.HLP help file, which should be in the \DELPHI\BIN directory.

In the calculator example, a simple help file called CALC.HLP exists to help the users. If the user presses F1 at any time while using the calculator, the calculator help is displayed.

To specify the default help file for an application, open the Options menu and select Project. In the Project Options dialog, select the Application page tab (refer to fig. 16.5). Type the name of your help file in the Help File text box and click OK. Many of the components you place on forms have a HelpContext property. Supply this property with the topic number associated with the help topic that explains each object. When the user presses F1, a context-sensitive help screen appears.

Problems can occur if the Windows help system can't find the appropriate help file. If you don't supply a path to the help file, Windows searches the current directory, the Windows directory, and the path for the help file. For small in-house installations, you can consider placing the help file in the Windows directory or in the path. For larger installations, place the help file in the working directory. As long as your startup icon in Program Manager specifies the correct working directory and your code doesn't change the working directory, this method should work.

To offer the most flexibility, consider using a completely specified path and file name to your help file that's set during runtime. Use the following line of code to set the help file at runtime:

```
Application.HelpFile := 'C:\UTIL\CALC.HLP';
```

You can use this code at any point in your application, but most of the time you should just add it to your main form's OnCreate event. During your installation process, you may want to allow the user to specify the directories where files are located. Use the TIniFile object to record these directories in an .INI file. For example, use the following code during installation to store the name of a directory where a help file is located:

```
uses
  SysUtils, WinTypes, WinProcs, Messages, Classes, Graphics,
  Controls, Forms, Dialogs, StdCtrls, IniFiles;
...
var
  IniFile: TIniFile;
begin
  IniFile:= TIniFile.Create('CALC.INI');
  IniFile.WriteString('Configuration', 'HelpFile',
    'C:\UTIL\CALC.HLP');
  IniFile.Free;
end;
```

During runtime, use the following code to read the name of the help file:

```
procedure TForm1.FormCreate(Sender: TObject);
var
  IniFile: TIniFile;
begin
  IniFile:= TIniFile.Create('CALC.INI');
  Application.HelpFile:=IniFile.ReadString('Configuration',
    'HelpFile', '');
  IniFile.Free;
end;
```

Delivering VBXs

Unlike most components, .VBX files aren't included directly in the EXE. Because of this, you need to be aware of how Delphi tries to locate .VBX files at runtime so that you can install them in an appropriate directory.

When Delphi needs to load a VBX, it starts by looking for the VBX in the current directory. If it isn't found there, Delphi checks the Windows directory and then the path. If the VBX still isn't found, your program causes a GPF when it runs.

Tip
You don't need to worry about VBRUN###.DLL, which is required in other environments. This file isn't needed during Delphi development nor is it needed by a delivered application.

For small in-house programs, you may want to install .VBX files in the Windows directory. For most systems, the best place to put the .VBX files is in the working directory. As long as the icon that launches your program from Program Manager is configured with the correct working directory, you should have no problems.

Delivering Database Applications

Delphi applications that talk to databases do so through the *Borland Database Engine,* sometimes called IDAPI. You must install the BDE on any machine that will use your Delphi programs to access databases.

Installing the BDE

The installation of the BDE uses the same process you used when you installed Delphi. From the Windows Program Manager, open the File menu and choose Run. Enter A:\SETUP.EXE (or the appropriate drive) and click OK. Delphi displays the Delphi Installation dialog (see fig. 16.10).

Fig. 16.10
If your application accesses databases, you'll need to install the BDE on your users' machines.

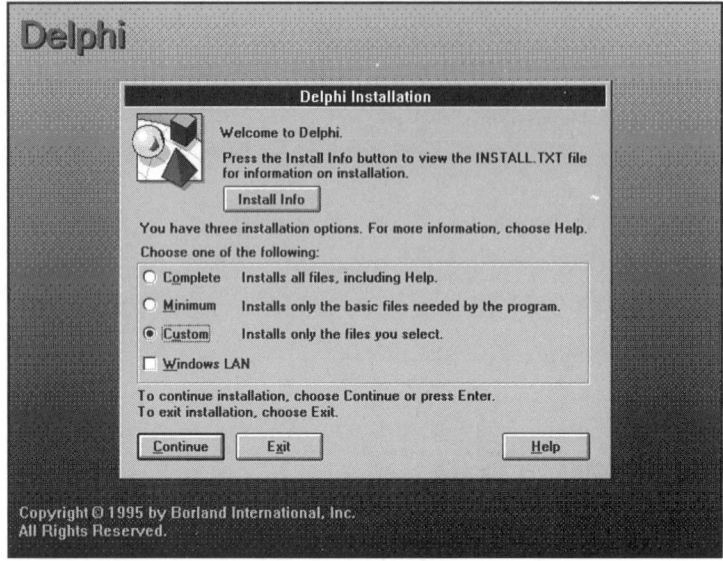

Select the Custom radio button and then click the Continue button. Delphi displays the Customize Installation dialog (see fig. 16.11).

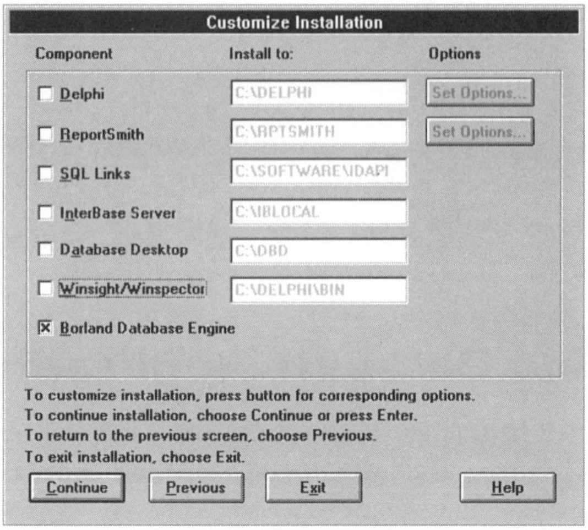

Fig. 16.11
Since users' machines don't need all of Delphi, select only Borland Database Engine.

To install the BDE, deselect all the check boxes except Borland Database Engine. (If your program also accesses SQL data, you can select the SQL Links check box.) Click the Continue button; the Borland Database Engine Location Settings dialog appears (see fig. 16.12).

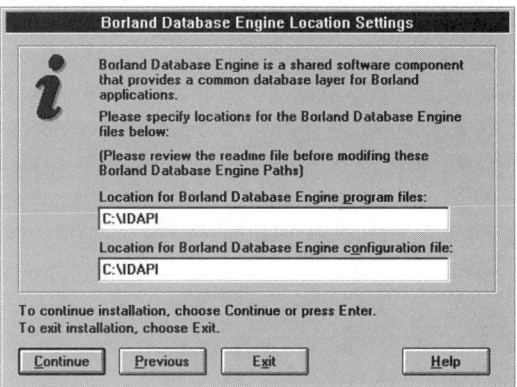

Fig. 16.12
Select a spot for the BDE files.

Because the BDE is shared between Borland programs, select a directory that's common to other Borland database programs, such as Paradox and dBASE. Click the Continue button, and the BDE is installed on the machine.

If it's impossible for you to use your Delphi disks to install the BDE, you can install it manually. Copy all the files from the BDE directory on your machine to a directory on the user's machine. Add the following section to the end of the user's WIN.INI file:

```
[IDAPI]
DLLPATH=C:\DELPHI\IDAPI
CONFIGFILE01=C:\DELPHI\IDAPI\IDAPI.CFG
```

Also, you should set up a Program Manager icon to launch the IDAPICFG.EXE program. This program lets you configure certain aspects of the BDE.

Installing SQL Links

Installing SQL links follows the same process as installing the BDE. Use your Delphi installation disks and select a customized installation with SQL links. Choose the SQL link that your program accesses. When you choose to install an SQL link, the installation program automatically installs the BDE. Depending on which SQL link you install, the installation program prompts you for specific information. For example, the Informix link needs a location for its message file. Each link that you select causes one or more extra DLLs to be copied to the BDE directory. The Oracle link, for example, uses ORA7WIN.DLL. For some SQL links you need to add the directory with the vendor-specific DLLs to your path statement.

Adjusting Parameters to Use Paradox

If your Delphi program is using a Paradox database, you don't need to install any SQL links. You do need to adjust at least one parameter in the BDE configuration, however. Start the BDE Configuration Utility by clicking its icon in the Delphi Program Manager group. The program displays a tabbed window (see fig. 16.13).

Fig. 16.13
Use the BDE Configuration Utility to configure information specific to each database type.

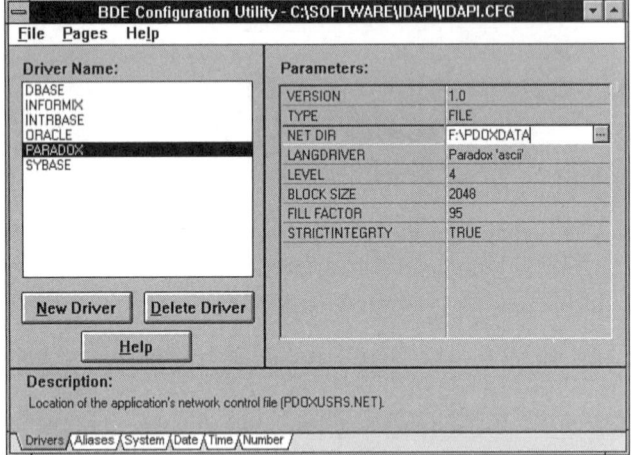

For a program that accesses Paradox data on a network or more than one Windows session, you must configure the NET DIR parameter. In this directory, a file called PDOXUSRS.NET is created. This file contains a list of current Paradox users. For any network sharing Paradox data, there should be only one PDOXUSRS.NET file.

Using ReportSmith Runtime

Most database programs include a way to print data. With Delphi programs, the easiest way to do this is with ReportSmith (see Chapter 13, "Reporting with ReportSmith"). While you use interactive ReportSmith during development to design reports, you don't install the interactive version on your users' machines. Instead, Delphi ships with a runtime version of ReportSmith. It doesn't allow new reports to be designed, but existing reports can be printed.

When you create a report with ReportSmith, you create an .RPT file. This file isn't included in your .EXE file. Like other external files, you need to make sure that ReportSmith can find the .RPT file at runtime. This is done with the ReportDir and ReportName properties of the TReport component. You can use the techniques discussed earlier in the "Including Help Files with Your Program" section to find the .RPT files at runtime.

As with the other parts of Delphi, the easiest way to install the runtime version of ReportSmith is to do so from the Delphi installation disks. On the Customize Installation dialog shown in figure 16.11, select the ReportSmith check box and click the Set Options button. The ReportSmith Installation Options dialog appears (see fig. 16.14).

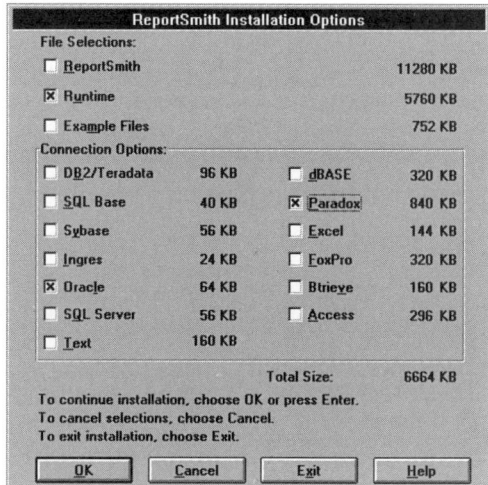

Fig. 16.14
Use this dialog to configure the ReportSmith runtime options.

Under File Selections, select only the Runtime check box. In the Connections Options section, select the check boxes that correspond to the database type that your program reports on.

The installation program installs ReportSmith runtime in the \RS_RUN directory. One thing that the installation program doesn't do that's absolutely necessary is add the \RS_RUN directory to the path. You need to manually do this on the user's machine, or Delphi can't launch ReportSmith at runtime.

If you can't use the Delphi installation disk, create a directory on the user's machine and copy all the files from the \RS_RUN directory. Be sure to add this new directory to the user's path.

From Here...

You can find more information about applications and their delivery in the following chapters:

- Chapter 9, "Creating Applications," tells you what you need to do to create an application.

- Chapter 10, "Creating Database Applications," teaches you everything that you need to know to start writing database applications you'll be proud of.

- Chapter 13, "Reporting with ReportSmith," shows you how to print data from within your applications.

Appendixes

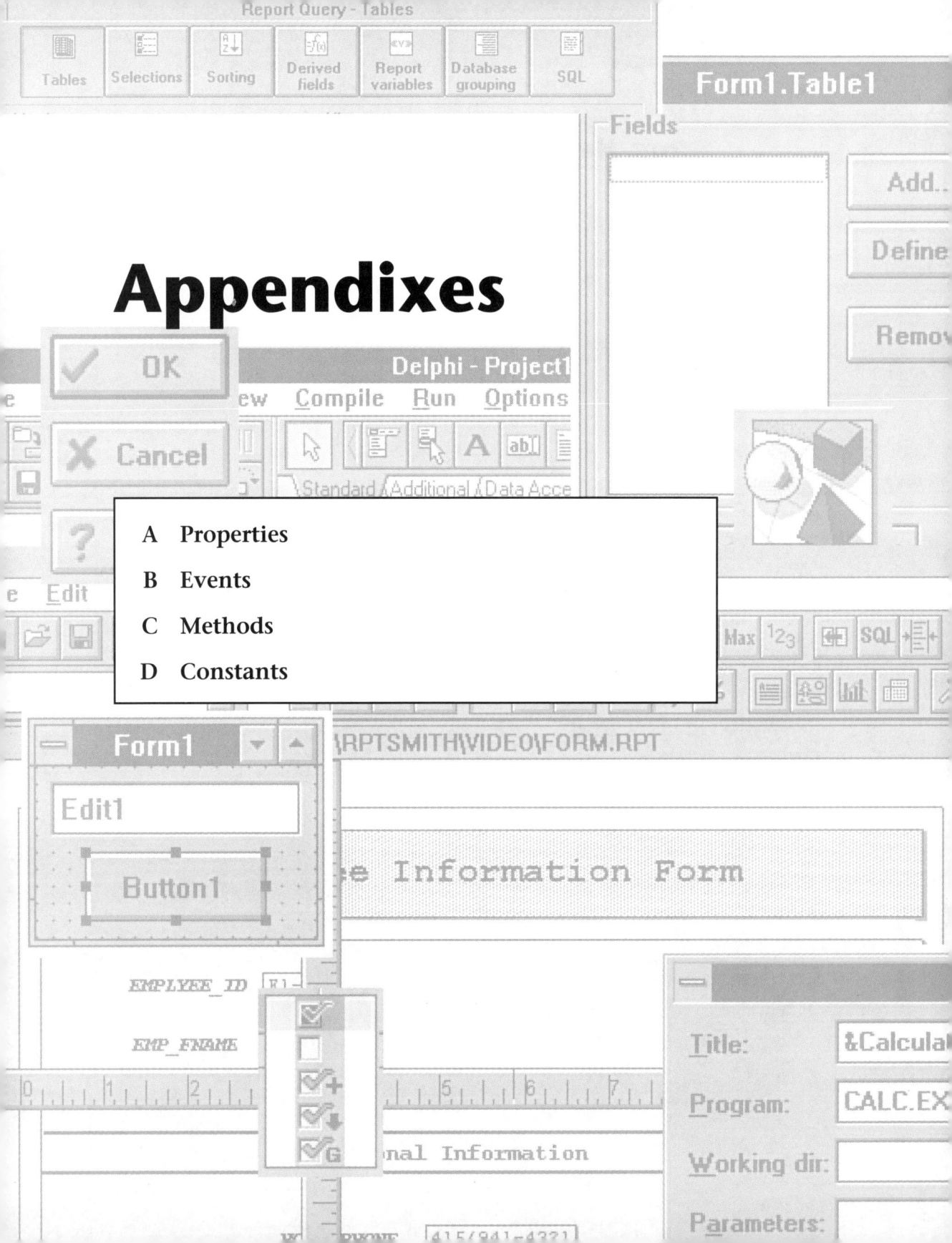

- A Properties
- B Events
- C Methods
- D Constants

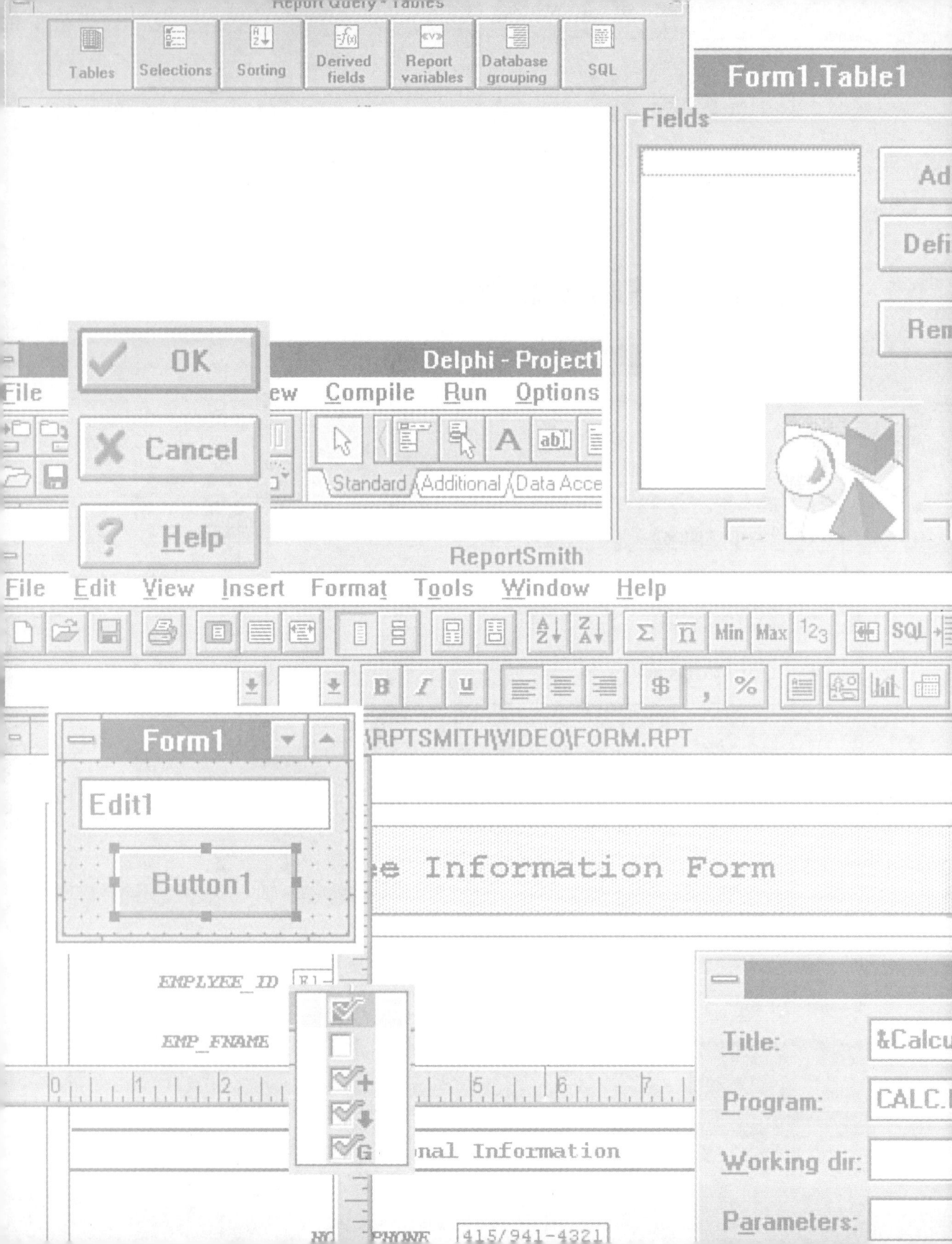

Appendix A
Properties

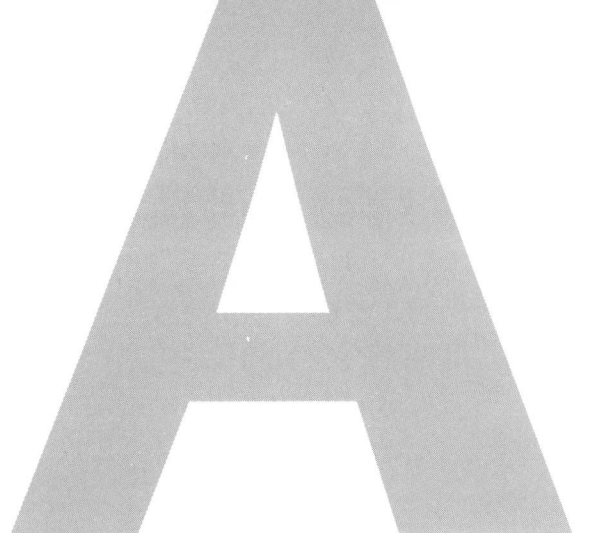

This appendix lists the properties available for Delphi components. Most components listed are available on the Component palette. Some component classes, such as TApplication, don't appear on the Component palette but are included here as a reference. A solid dot (•) marks the existence of a property for the component named in the column.

Table A.1 lists the properties available for visual components (see Chapter 4, "Using Visual Components"). Table A.2 lists the properties available for non-visual components (see Chapter 5, "Using Non-Visual Components"). Table A.3 lists the properties available for data components (see Chapter 6, "Using Data-Bound Components").

Appendix A

Table A.1 Visual Component Property Matrix

Property	TBevel	TBitBtn	TButton	TCheck-Box	TCombo-Box	TControl-ScrollBar	TDraw-Grid	TEdit	TForm	TGraphic-Control	TGroup-Box	TImage
ActiveControl									•			
ActiveMDIChild									•			
ActivePage												
Align	•	•	•	•	•	•	•	•	•		•	•
Alignment				•								
AllowAllUp												
AllowGrayed				•								
AutoEnable												
AutoOpen												
AutoRewind												
AutoScroll												
AutoSelect								•				
AutoSize								•				
Autosize												•
BackgroundColor												
BevelInner												
BevelOuter												
BevelWidth												
BorderIcons									•			
BorderStyle							•	•	•			
BorderWidth												
BoundsRect	•	•	•		•		•			•		•
Brush		•	•	•	•		•	•	•		•	•
Cancel		•	•									
Canvas					•		•		•			•

Properties **463**

	TLabel	TList-Box	TMedia-Player	TMemo	TNote-book	TOut-line	TPanel	TRadio-Button	TScroll-Bar	TScroll-Box	TShape	TSpeed-Button	TString-Grid	TTabSet
					•									
	•	•		•	•	•	•	•	•	•	•	•	•	•
	•		•				•	•						
												•		
			•											
			•											
			•											
														•
				•										
	•			•										
														•
							•							
							•							
							•							
		•		•		•	•			•			•	
							•							
	•	•	•	•	•	•	•				•		•	•
		•	•	•	•	•	•	•	•	•	•			
		•				•							•	•

(continues)

Table A.1 Continued

Property	TBevel	TBitBtn	TButton	TCheck-Box	TCombo-Box	TControl-ScrollBar	TDraw-Grid	TEdit	TForm	TGraphic-Control	TGroup-Box	TImage
Capabilities												
Caption		•	•	•					•		•	
Cells												
Center												•
CharCase								•				
Checked				•								
ClassName										•		
ClassParent										•		
ClientHandle									•			
ClientHeight	•	•	•	•	•		•	•	•	•	•	•
ClientOrigin	•	•	•	•	•		•	•	•	•	•	•
ClientRect	•	•	•	•	•		•	•	•	•	•	•
ClientWidth	•	•	•	•	•		•	•	•	•	•	•
Col							•					
ColCount							•					
Color		•	•	•	•		•	•	•		•	
ColoredButtons												
Cols												
Columns												
ColWidths							•					
ComponentCount	•	•	•	•	•	•	•	•	•	•	•	•
ComponentIndex	•	•	•	•	•	•	•	•	•	•	•	•
Components	•	•	•	•	•	•	•	•	•	•	•	•
ControlCount		•	•	•	•		•	•	•		•	•
Controls		•	•	•	•		•	•	•		•	•
Ctl3D		•		•	•		•	•	•		•	

Properties

	TLabel	TList-Box	TMedia-Player	TMemo	TNote-book	TOut-line	TPanel	TRadio-Button	TScroll-Bar	TScroll-Box	TShape	TSpeed-Button	TString-Grid	TTabSet
			•											
	•						•	•				•		
													•	
								•						
								•						
								•						
	•	•	•	•	•	•	•	•	•	•	•	•	•	•
	•	•	•	•	•	•	•	•	•		•	•	•	•
	•	•	•	•	•	•	•	•	•	•	•	•	•	•
	•	•	•	•	•	•	•	•	•	•	•	•	•	•
													•	
													•	
	•	•		•		•	•	•						
			•											
													•	
		•												
													•	
	•	•	•	•	•	•	•	•	•	•	•	•	•	•
	•	•	•	•	•	•	•	•	•	•	•	•	•	•
	•	•	•	•	•	•	•	•	•	•	•	•	•	•
		•	•	•	•	•	•	•	•	•			•	•
		•	•	•	•	•	•	•	•	•			•	•
		•		•		•		•	•	•			•	

(continues)

Table A.1 Continued

Property	TBevel	TBitBtn	TButton	TCheck-Box	TCombo-Box	TControl-ScrollBar	TDraw-Grid	TEdit	TForm	TGraphic-Control	TGroup-Box	TImage
CurItem												
Cursor		•	•	•	•		•	•	•		•	•
Default		•	•									
DefaultColWidth							•					
DefaultDrawing							•					
DefaultRowHeight							•					
DeviceID												
DeviceType												
Display												
DisplayRect												
DitherBackground												
Down												
DragCursor		•	•	•	•		•	•			•	•
DragMode		•	•	•	•		•	•			•	•
DropDownCount					•							
Enabled	•	•	•	•	•		•	•	•	•	•	•
EnabledButtons												
EndMargin												
EndPos												
Error												
ErrorMessage												
FileName												
FirstIndex												
FixedColor							•					
FixedCols							•					
FixedRows							•					

Properties

	TLabel	TList-Box	TMedia-Player	TMemo	TNote-book	TOut-line	TPanel	TRadio-Button	TScroll-Bar	TScroll-Box	TShape	TSpeed-Button	TString-Grid	TTabSet
						•									
	•	•	•	•	•	•	•	•	•	•	•	•	•	•
													•	
													•	
													•	
			•											
			•											
			•											
			•											
														•
												•		
	•	•		•		•	•	•	•	•	•			
	•	•		•		•	•	•	•	•	•			
	•	•	•	•	•	•	•	•	•	•	•	•	•	•
			•											
														•
			•											
			•											
			•											
			•											
														•
													•	
													•	
													•	

(continues)

Table A.1 Continued

Property	TBevel	TBitBtn	TButton	TCheckBox	TComboBox	TControlScrollBar	TDrawGrid	TEdit	TForm	TGraphicControl	TGroupBox	TImage
FocusControl												
Font		•	•	•	•		•	•	•		•	
FormStyle									•			
Frames												
Glyph		•										
GridLineWidth							•					
GroupIndex												
Handle		•	•	•	•		•	•	•		•	•
Height	•	•	•	•	•		•	•	•	•	•	•
HelpContext		•	•	•	•		•	•	•		•	•
Helper									•			
Hint	•	•	•	•	•		•	•	•		•	•
HintColor												
HintPause												
HorzScrollBar									•			
Icon									•			
Increment						•						
IntegralHeight												
ItemCount												
ItemHeight					•							
ItemIndex					•							
ItemSeparator												
Items					•							
KeyPreview									•			
Kind		•				•						
LargeChange												

Properties **469**

TLabel	TList-Box	TMedia-Player	TMemo	TNote-book	TOut-line	TPanel	TRadio-Button	TScroll-Bar	TScroll-Box	TShape	TSpeed-Button	TString-Grid	TTabSet
•													
•	•		•		•	•	•		•		•	•	•
		•											
											•		
												•	
											•		
	•	•	•	•	•	•	•	•	•			•	•
•	•	•	•	•	•	•	•	•	•	•	•	•	•
	•	•	•		•	•	•	•	•				
•	•	•	•		•	•	•	•	•	•	•	•	•
						•							
						•							
									•				
	•												
					•								
	•				•								
	•												
					•								
	•				•								
								•					
								•					

(continues)

Appendixes

Table A.1 Continued

Property	TBevel	TBitBtn	TButton	TCheckBox	TComboBox	TControlScrollBar	TDrawGrid	TEdit	TForm	TGraphicControl	TGroupBox	TImage
Layout		•										
Left	•	•	•	•	•		•	•	•	•	•	•
LeftCol							•					
Length												
Lines												
MDIChildCount									•			
MDIChildren									•			
Margin		•				•						
Max												
MaxLength								•				
Menu									•			
Min												
ModalResult		•	•						•			
Mode												
Modified								•				
MultiSelect												
Name	•	•	•	•	•	•	•	•	•	•	•	•
Notify												
NotifyValue												
NumGlyphs												
ObjectMenuItem									•			
Objects												
Options							•					
OutlineStyle												
Owner	•	•	•	•	•	•	•	•	•	•	•	•
PageIndex												

Properties

	TLabel	TList-Box	TMedia-Player	TMemo	TNote-book	TOut-line	TPanel	TRadio-Button	TScroll-Bar	TScroll-Box	TShape	TSpeed-Button	TString-Grid	TTabSet
												•		
	•	•	•	•	•	•	•	•	•	•	•	•	•	•
													•	
			•											
				•		•								
												•		
									•					
			•											
									•					
			•											
			•											
		•												
	•	•	•	•	•	•	•	•	•	•	•	•	•	•
			•											
			•											
												•		
													•	
													•	
					•									
					•									
	•	•	•	•	•	•	•	•	•	•	•	•	•	•
					•									

(continues)

Appendix A

Table A.1 Continued

Property	TBevel	TBitBtn	TButton	TCheckBox	TComboBox	TControlScrollBar	TDrawGrid	TEdit	TForm	TGraphicControl	TGroupBox	TImage
Pages												
Parent	●	●	●	●	●		●	●	●	●	●	●
ParentColor				●	●		●	●			●	
ParentCtl3D				●	●		●	●			●	
ParentFont		●	●	●	●		●	●			●	
PasswordChar								●				
Pen												
Picture												●
PictureClosed												
PictureLeaf												
PictureMinus												
PictureOpen												
PicturePlus												
PixelsPerInch									●			
PopupMenu		●	●	●	●		●	●	●		●	●
Position						●			●			
PrintScale									●			
Range						●						
ReadOnly								●				
Row							●					
RowCount							●					
RowHeights							●					
Rows												
Scaled									●			
ScrollBars												
ScrollPos						●						

Properties

	TLabel	TList-Box	TMedia-Player	TMemo	TNote-book	TOut-line	TPanel	TRadio-Button	TScroll-Bar	TScroll-Box	TShape	TSpeed-Button	TString-Grid	TTabSet
					•									
	•	•	•	•	•	•	•	•	•	•	•	•	•	•
	•	•		•		•	•	•		•			•	
		•		•		•			•	•			•	
	•	•		•		•	•			•			•	•
											•			
						•								
						•								
						•								
						•								
						•								
	•	•		•		•	•	•	•	•			•	
			•						•					
				•										
						•							•	
													•	
													•	
													•	
				•									•	

(continues)

Table A.1 Continued

Property	TBevel	TBitBtn	TButton	TCheck-Box	TCombo-Box	TControl-ScrollBar	TDraw-Grid	TEdit	TForm	TGraphic-Control	TGroup-Box	TImage
Scrollbars							•					
SelCount												
SelLength					•			•				
SelStart					•			•				
SelText					•			•				
Selected												
SelectedColor												
SelectedItem												
Selection							•					
Shape	•											
Shareable												
ShowHints												
Showing		•	•	•	•		•	•	•		•	•
SmallChange												
Sorted					•							
Spacing		•										
SpeedBar									•			
Start												
StartMargin												
StartPos												
State				•								
StatusBar									•			
Stretch												•
Style	•	•				•						
TabHeight												
TabIndex												

TLabel	TList-Box	TMedia-Player	TMemo	TNote-book	TOut-line	TPanel	TRadio-Button	TScroll-Bar	TScroll-Box	TShape	TSpeed-Button	TString-Grid	TTabSet
	•												
			•										
			•										
			•										
	•												
													•
					•								
												•	
										•			
		•											
						•							
	•	•	•	•	•	•	•	•	•	•	•	•	•
								•					
	•												
											•		
			•										
													•
			•										
	•				•								•
													•
													•

(continues)

Table A.1 Continued

Property	TBevel	TBitBtn	TButton	TCheckBox	TComboBox	TControlScrollBar	TDrawGrid	TEdit	TForm	TGraphicControl	TGroupBox	TImage
TabOrder		•	•	•	•		•	•	•		•	•
TabStop		•	•	•	•		•	•	•		•	•
TabStops							•					
Tabs												
Tag	•	•	•	•	•	•	•	•	•	•	•	•
Text					•			•				
TileMode									•			
TimeFormat												
Top	•	•	•	•	•		•	•	•	•	•	•
TopIndex												
TopRow							•					
TrackLength												
TrackPosition												
Tracks												
Transparent												
UnselectedColor												
VertScrollBar									•			
Visible	•	•	•	•	•	•	•	•	•	•	•	•
VisibleButtons												
VisibleColCount							•					
VisibleRowCount							•					
VisibleTabs												
Wait												
WantTabs												
Width	•	•	•	•	•		•	•	•	•	•	•
WindowMenu									•			

TLabel	TList-Box	TMedia-Player	TMemo	TNote-book	TOut-line	TPanel	TRadio-Button	TScroll-Bar	TScroll-Box	TShape	TSpeed-Button	TString-Grid	TTabSet
	•	•	•	•	•	•	•	•	•			•	•
	•	•	•	•	•	•	•	•	•			•	•
												•	
													•
•	•	•	•	•	•	•	•	•	•	•	•	•	
			•										
		•											
•	•	•	•	•	•	•	•	•	•	•	•	•	•
	•												
												•	
		•											
		•											
		•											
•													
													•
								•					
•	•	•	•	•	•	•	•	•	•	•	•	•	•
		•											
												•	
												•	
												•	
		•											
			•										
•	•	•	•	•	•	•	•	•	•	•	•	•	•

(continues)

Table A.1 Continued

Property	TBevel	TBitBtn	TButton	TCheck-Box	TCombo-Box	TControl-ScrollBar	TDraw-Grid	TEdit	TForm	TGraphic-Control	TGroup-Box	TImage
WindowState									•			
WordWrap												

Table A.2 Non-Visual Component Property Matrix

Property	TAppli-cation	TColor-Dialog	TDDE-Client-Conv	TDDE-Client-Item	TDDE-Server-Conv	TDDE-Server-Item	TDirec-tory-ListBox	TDrive-Combo-Box	TFile-ListBox	TFilter-Combo-Box	TFont-Dialog	TMain-Menu
Active												
ActiveControl												
ActiveForm												
Align							•	•	•	•		
Alignment												
AutoActivate												
AutoMerge												•
AutoPopup												
AutoSize												
BorderStyle												
BoundsRect							•	•	•	•		
Break												
Brush							•	•	•	•		
Canvas							•		•			
Caption												
ChangeDefault												
Checked												
ClientHeight							•	•	•	•		
ClientOrigin							•	•	•	•		

Properties **479**

TLabel	TList-Box	TMedia-Player	TMemo	TNote-book	TOut-line	TPanel	TRadio-Button	TScroll-Bar	TScroll-Box	TShape	TSpeed-Button	TString-Grid	TTabSet
•			•										

TMenu	TMenu-Item	TOLE-Container	TOpen-Dialog	TPopup-Menu	TPrint-Dialog	TPrinter-Setup-Dialog	TSave-Dialog	TScreen	TTimer
		•							
								•	
								•	
		•							
				•					
		•							
				•					
		•							
		•							
		•							
	•								
		•							
	•								
					•	•			
	•								
		•							
		•							

(continues)

Table A.2 Continued

Property	TAppli-cation	TColor-Dialog	TDDE-Client-Conv	TDDE-Client-Item	TDDE-Server-Conv	TDDE-Server-Item	TDirec-tory-ListBox	TDrive-Combo-Box	TFile-ListBox	TFilter-Combo-Box	TFont-Dialog	TMain-Menu
ClientRect							●	●	●	●		
ClientWidth							●	●	●	●		
Collate												
Color		●					●	●		●		
Columns							●					
Command												
ComponentCount	●	●	●	●	●	●	●	●	●	●	●	●
ComponentIndex	●	●	●	●	●	●	●	●	●	●	●	●
Components	●	●	●	●	●	●	●	●	●	●	●	●
ConnectMode				●								
ControlCount							●	●	●	●		
Controls							●	●	●	●		
ConvertDlgHelp												
Copies												
Count												
Ctl3D		●					●	●		●	●	
Cursor							●	●	●	●		
Cursors												
DDEConv				●								
DDEItem				●								
DDEService			●									
DDETopic			●									
DefaultExt												
Device											●	
Directory									●			

Properties **481**

	TMenu	TMenu-Item	TOLE-Container	TOpen-Dialog	TPopup-Menu	TPrint-Dialog	TPrinter-Setup-Dialog	TSave-Dialog	TScreen	TTimer
			●							
			●							
						●				
		●								
	●	●	●	●	●	●	●	●	●	●
	●	●	●	●	●	●	●	●	●	●
	●	●	●	●	●	●	●	●	●	●
			●							
			●							
			●							
						●				
		●								
			●	●				●		
			●							
									●	
			●				●			

(continues)

Table A.2 Continued

Property	TApplication	TColorDialog	TDDEClientConv	TDDEClientItem	TDDEServerConv	TDDEServerItem	TDirectoryListBox	TDriveComboBox	TFileListBox	TFilterComboBox	TFontDialog	TMainMenu
DirLabel							•					
DirList								•				
DragCursor							•	•	•	•		
DragMode							•	•	•	•		
Drive							•	•				
Enabled							•	•	•	•		
ExeName	•											
FileEdit									•			
FileEditStyle												
FileList							•					
FileName									•			
FileType									•			
Files												
Filter										•		
FilterIndex												
Font							•	•	•	•	•	
Fonts												
FormCount												
FormatChars				•								
Forms												
FromPage												
GroupIndex												
Handle	•						•	•	•	•		•
Height							•	•	•	•		
HelpContext		•					•	•	•	•	•	

Properties **483**

	TMenu	TMenu-Item	TOLE-Container	TOpen-Dialog	TPopup-Menu	TPrint-Dialog	TPrinter-Setup-Dialog	TSave-Dialog	TScreen	TTimer
		•	•						•	
				•				•		
				•				•		
				•				•		
				•				•		
				•				•		
									•	
									•	
									•	
						•				
		•								
	•	•	•		•					
			•					•		
		•	•	•		•	•	•		

(continues)

Table A.2 Continued

Property	TAppli-cation	TColor-Dialog	TDDE-Client-Conv	TDDE-Client-Item	TDDE-Server-Conv	TDDE-Server-Item	TDirec-tory-ListBox	TDrive-Combo-Box	TFile-ListBox	TFilter-Combo-Box	TFont-Dialog	TMain-Menu
HelpFile	●											
Hint	●						●	●	●	●		
HistoryList												
InitialDir												
InPlaceActive												
IntegralHeight							●		●			
Interval												
ItemCount												
ItemHeight							●		●			
ItemIndex							●	●	●	●		
Items								●	●	●		●
Left		●					●	●	●	●	●	
Lines				●		●						
MainForm	●											
Mask									●	●		
MaxPage												
MinPage												
Modified												
MultiSelect									●			
Name	●	●	●	●	●	●	●	●	●	●	●	●
ObjClass												
ObjDoc												
ObjItem												
Options		●									●	
Owner	●	●	●	●	●	●	●	●	●	●	●	●

Properties

	TMenu	TMenu-Item	TOLE-Container	TOpen-Dialog	TPopup-Menu	TPrint-Dialog	TPrinter-Setup-Dialog	TSave-Dialog	TScreen	TTimer
		•								
				•				•		
				•				•		
			•							
									•	
		•								
	•	•			•					
			•							
						•				
						•				
			•							
	•	•	•	•	•	•	•	•	•	•
			•							
			•							
			•							
				•		•		•		
	•	•	•	•	•	•	•	•	•	

(continues)

Table A.2 Continued

Property	TAppli-cation	TColor-Dialog	TDDE-Client-Conv	TDDE-Client-Item	TDDE-Server-Conv	TDDE-Server-Item	TDirec-tory-ListBox	TDrive-Combo-Box	TFile-ListBox	TFilter-Combo-Box	TFont-Dialog	TMain-Menu
Parent							•	•	•	•		
ParentColor							•	•	•	•		
ParentCtl3D							•	•	•	•		
PInitInfo												
ParentFont							•	•	•	•		
PixelsPerInch												
PopupMenu							•	•	•			
PrintRange												
PrintToFile												
SelLength								•		•		
SelStart								•		•		
SelText								•		•		
Selected							•		•			
ServerConv						•						
Service-Application				•								
ShortCut												
ShowGlyphs									•			
Showing							•		•	•		
TabOrder							•	•	•	•		
TabStop							•	•	•	•		
Tag	•	•	•	•	•	•	•	•	•	•	•	•
Terminated	•											
Text				•		•		•		•		
TextCase								•				

Properties **487**

	TMenu	TMenu-Item	TOLE-Container	TOpen-Dialog	TPopup-Menu	TPrint-Dialog	TPrinter-Setup-Dialog	TSave-Dialog	TScreen	TTimer
		•	•							
			•							
			•							
									•	
						•				
						•				
		•								
			•							
			•							
	•	•		•	•	•	•	•	•	•

(continues)

Appendix A

Table A.2 Continued

Property	TAppli-cation	TColor-Dialog	TDDE-Client-Conv	TDDE-Client-Item	TDDE-Server-Conv	TDDE-Server-Item	TDirec-tory-ListBox	TDrive-Combo-Box	TFile-ListBox	TFilter-Combo-Box	TFont-Dialog	TMain-Menu
Title	•											
ToPage												
Top		•					•	•	•	•	•	
TopIndex							•		•			
Visible							•	•	•	•		
Width							•	•	•	•		
Zoom												

Table A.3 Data Component Property Matrix

Property	TDBCheckBox	TDBComboBox	TDBEdit	TDBGrid	TDBImage	TDBLabel	TDBListBox	TDBMemo
Active								
Align	•	•	•	•	•	•	•	•
Alignment	•					•		•
AllowGrayed	•							
AutoCalcFields								
AutoDisplay					•			
AutoEdit								
AutoScroll								
AutoSelect			•					•
AutoSize			•			•		•
AutoUnload								
BOF								
BackgroundColor								
BorderStyle			•	•	•		•	•

Properties

	TMenu	TMenu-Item	TOLE-Container	TOpen-Dialog	TPopup-Menu	TPrint-Dialog	TPrinter-Setup-Dialog	TSave-Dialog	TScreen	TTimer
				•				•		
						•				
			•							
		•	•							
			•					•		
			•							

	TDBNavigator	TDBRadioGroup	TDataSource	TDatabase	TQuery	TReport	TTable	TTableList
				•	•		•	
	•	•						•
					•			
			•					
								•
						•		
					•		•	
								•

(continues)

Table A.3 Continued

Property	TDBCheckBox	TDBComboBox	TDBEdit	TDBGrid	TDBImage	TDBLabel	TDBListBox	TDBMemo
BoundsRect		•		•		•	•	
Brush	•	•	•	•	•		•	•
Buttons								
CanModify								
Canvas				•			•	
Caption	•					•		
Center					•			
Checked	•							
ClientHeight	•	•	•	•	•	•	•	•
ClientOrigin	•	•	•	•		•	•	•
ClientRect	•	•	•	•		•	•	•
ClientWidth	•	•	•	•	•	•	•	•
Color	•	•	•	•	•	•	•	•
Columns							•	
ComponentCount	•	•	•	•	•	•	•	•
ComponentIndex	•	•	•	•	•	•	•	•
ComponentState								
Components	•	•	•	•	•	•	•	•
Connected								
ControlCount	•	•	•	•			•	•
Controls	•	•	•	•			•	•
Ctl3D	•		•	•	•		•	•
Cursor	•	•	•	•	•	•	•	•
DataSet								
DBHandle								
DBLocale								

TDBNavigator	TDBRadioGroup	TDataSource	TDatabase	TQuery	TReport	TTable	TTableList
•							
•	•						•
	•						
				•		•	
	•						
•	•						•
•	•						•
•	•						•
•	•						•
	•						
	•						
•	•	•		•	•		•
•	•	•		•	•		•
		•		•			
•	•	•		•	•		•
					•	•	
•	•						•
•	•						•
	•						
•	•						•
		•					
				•		•	
				•			

(continues)

Table A.3 Continued

Property	TDBCheckBox	TDBComboBox	TDBEdit	TDBGrid	TDBImage	TDBLabel	TDBListBox	TDBMemo
DataField	•	•	•		•	•	•	•
DataSource	•	•	•	•	•	•	•	•
DatabaseName								
DesignInfo								
Designer								
DetailFields								
DitherBackground								
DragCursor	•	•	•	•	•	•	•	•
DragMode	•	•	•	•	•	•	•	•
DropDownControl		•						
EOF								
EditText			•					
Enabled	•	•	•	•	•	•	•	•
EndMargin								
EndPage								
Exclusive								
FieldCount				•				
Fields				•				
FirstIndex								
FixedColor				•				
FixedCols				•				
FixedRows				•				
FocusControl						•		
Font	•	•	•	•	•	•	•	•
Handle	•	•	•	•			•	•
Height	•	•	•	•	•	•	•	•

Properties

	TDBNavigator	TDBRadioGroup	TDataSource	TDatabase	TQuery	TReport	TTable	TTableList
		•						
	•	•			•			
			•	•	•		•	
			•		•			
					•			
							•	
								•
	•	•						
	•	•						
					•		•	
	•	•	•					•
								•
						•		
			•				•	
						•	•	
						•	•	
								•
		•						•
	•	•			•	•		•
	•	•						•

(continues)

Table A.3 Continued

Property	TDBCheckBox	TDBComboBox	TDBEdit	TDBGrid	TDBImage	TDBLabel	TDBListBox	TDBMemo
HelpContext	•	•	•	•	•		•	•
Hint	•	•	•	•	•	•	•	•
HintColor								
HintPause								
IndexFieldCount								
IndexFields								
IndexName								
IndexTag								
InitialValues								
IntegralHeight							•	
ItemHeight		•					•	
ItemIndex		•					•	
Items		•					•	
Left	•	•	•	•	•	•	•	•
Lines								•
Local								
Locale								
MasterFields								
MasterSource								
MaxLength			•					•
MaxRecords								
Modified			•					•
Name	•	•	•	•	•	•	•	•
Options				•				
Owner	•	•	•	•	•	•	•	•
ParamCount								

TDBNavigator	TDBRadioGroup	TDataSource	TDatabase	TQuery	TReport	TTable	TTableList
	•						•
	•						•
•							
•							
				•			
				•			
		•				•	
		•				•	
					•		
	•						
	•						
•	•						•
				•			
					•	•	
		•				•	
		•				•	
					•		
					•	•	
•	•	•		•	•		•
•	•	•		•	•		•
				•			

(continues)

Appendix A

Table A.3 Continued

Property	TDBCheckBox	TDBComboBox	TDBEdit	TDBGrid	TDBImage	TDBLabel	TDBListBox	TDBMemo
Params								
Parent	●	●	●	●	●	●	●	●
ParentColor	●	●	●	●	●	●	●	●
ParentCtl3D	●	●	●	●	●		●	●
ParentFont	●	●	●	●	●	●	●	●
Password								
PasswordChar			●					●
Picture					●			
PopupMenu	●	●	●	●	●	●	●	●
Prepared								
PrintCopies								
ReadOnly	●	●	●	●	●		●	●
RecordSize								
ReportDir								
ReportHandle								
ReportName								
RequestLive								
ResultSetLive								
SQL								
ScrollBars								●
SelCount							●	
SelLength		●	●					●
SelStart		●	●					●
SelText		●	●					●
Selected							●	
SelectedColor								

Properties

TDBNavigator	TDBRadioGroup	TDataSource	TDatabase	TQuery	TReport	TTable	TTableList
				•			
•	•						•
	•						
•	•						
	•						
			•	•		•	
•	•						
				•			
					•		
	•		•			•	
				•		•	
					•		
					•		
					•		
				•			
				•			
				•			
							•

(continues)

Table A.3 Continued

Property	TDBCheckBox	TDBComboBox	TDBEdit	TDBGrid	TDBImage	TDBLabel	TDBListBox	TDBMemo
SelectedField				●				
Selection				●				
Showing	●	●	●				●	
ShowHints								
Sorted		●					●	
StartMargin								
StartPage								
State	●							
StmtHandle								
Stretch					●			
Style		●					●	
TabHeight								
TabIndex								
TabOrder	●	●	●	●	●		●	●
TabStop	●	●	●	●	●		●	●
TableName								
Tabs								
Tag	●	●	●	●	●	●	●	●
Text		●	●					●
TextChanged								
TextLen								
TitleFont				●				
Top	●	●	●	●	●	●	●	●
TopIndex							●	
TopRow				●				
TransHandle								

TDBNavigator	TDBRadioGroup	TDataSource	TDatabase	TQuery	TReport	TTable	TTableList
●	●						
●							
							●
					●		
				●		●	
				●			
							●
							●
							●
●	●						●
●	●						●
						●	
							●
●	●	●		●	●		●
				●			
				●			
				●			
●	●						●
						●	

(continues)

Table A.3 Continued

Property	TDBCheckBox	TDBComboBox	TDBEdit	TDBGrid	TDBImage	TDBLabel	TDBListBox	TDBMemo
TransIsolation								
Transaction								
Transparent						•		
UniDirectional								
UnselectedColor								
Value								
ValueChecked	•							
ValueUnchecked	•							
Visible	•	•	•	•	•	•	•	•
VisibleButtons								
VisibleTabs								
WantTabs								•
Width	•	•	•	•	•	•	•	•
WordWrap						•		•

Properties

	TDBNavigator	TDBRadioGroup	TDataSource	TDatabase	TQuery	TReport	TTable	TTableList
					•			
							•	
					•			
								•
		•						
	•	•						•
	•							
								•
	•	•						•

Appendix B
Events

This appendix contains three tables that list the events available for Delphi components. Most components listed are available on the Component palette. Some component classes, such as TApplication, don't appear on the Component palette but are included as a reference. A solid dot (•) marks the existence of an event for the component named in the column.

Table B.1 lists the events available for visual components (see Chapter 4, "Using Visual Components"). Table B.2 lists the events available for non-visual components (see Chapter 5, "Using Non-Visual Components"). Table B.3 lists the events available for data components (see Chapter 6, "Using Data-Bound Components").

Table B.1 Visual Component Event Matrix

Event	TBevel	TBit-Btn	TButton	TCheck-Box	TCombo-Box	TControl-ScrollBar	TDraw-Grid	TEdit	TForm	TGraphic-Control	TGroup-Box	TImage
OnActivate									•			
OnChange					•			•				
OnClick		•	•	•			•		•		•	•
OnClose									•			
OnCloseQuery									•			
OnCollapse												
OnColumnMoved							•					
OnDblClick				•			•	•	•		•	•
OnDragDrop		•	•	•	•		•	•	•		•	•
OnDragOver		•	•	•	•		•	•	•		•	•
OnDrawCell							•					
OnDrawItem					•							
OnDrawTab												
OnDropDown					•							
OnEndDrag		•	•	•	•		•	•			•	•
OnEnter		•	•	•	•		•	•	•		•	
OnExit		•	•	•	•		•	•	•		•	
OnExpand												
OnGetEditText							•					
OnKeyDown		•	•	•	•		•	•	•			
OnKeyPress		•	•	•	•		•	•	•			
OnKeyUp		•	•	•	•		•	•	•			
OnMeasureItem					•							
OnMeasureTab												
OnMouseDown		•	•	•			•	•	•		•	•

Events

	TLabel	TList-Box	TMedia-Player	TMemo	TNote-book	TOut-line	TPanel	TRadio-Button	TScroll-Bar	TScroll-Box	TShape	TSpeed-Button	TString-Grid	TTab-Set
				•					•					•
	•	•	•	•		•	•	•	•	•			•	•
						•								
													•	
	•	•		•		•	•			•		•	•	
	•	•		•		•	•	•	•		•		•	
	•	•		•		•	•	•	•		•		•	
													•	
		•				•								
														•
	•	•		•		•	•	•	•		•		•	•
		•	•	•	•	•		•	•				•	•
		•	•	•	•	•		•	•				•	•
						•								
													•	
		•		•		•		•	•				•	
		•		•		•		•	•				•	
		•		•		•							•	
		•												
														•
	•	•		•		•	•	•		•	•	•	•	

(continues)

Table B.1 Continued

Event	TBevel	TBit-Btn	TButton	TCheck-Box	TCombo-Box	TControl-ScrollBar	TDraw-Grid	TEdit	TForm	TGraphic-Control	TGroup-Box	TImage
OnMouseMove		•	•	•			•	•	•		•	•
OnMouseUp		•	•	•			•	•	•		•	•
OnNotify												
OnPaint									•			
OnPostClick												
OnResize									•			
OnRowMoved							•					
OnScroll												
OnSelectCell							•					
OnSetEditText							•					
OnTopLeft-Changed							•					

Table B.2 Non-Visual Component Event Matrix

Event	TAppli-cation	TColor-Dialog	TDDE-Client-Conv	TDDE-Client-Item	TDDE-Server-Conv	TDDE-Server-Item	TDirec-tory-ListBox	TDrive-Combo-Box	TFile-ListBox	TFilter-Combo-Box	TFont-Dialog	TIndex-List
OnActivate	•											
OnApply											•	
OnChange				•		•		•	•	•		
OnClick							•	•	•	•		
OnClose				•		•						
OnDblClick							•	•	•	•		
OnDeactivate	•											
OnDragDrop							•	•	•	•		
OnDragOver							•	•	•	•		

Events

	TLabel	TList-Box	TMedia-Player	TMemo	TNote-book	TOut-line	TPanel	TRadio-Button	TScroll-Bar	TScroll-Box	TShape	TSpeed-Button	TString-Grid	TTab-Set
	•	•		•		•	•	•		•	•	•	•	
	•	•		•		•	•	•		•	•	•	•	
			•											
			•											
										•				
													•	
									•					
													•	
													•	
													•	

	TMain-Menu	TMenu	TMenu-Item	TOLECon-tainer	TOpen-Dialog	TPopup-Menu	TPrint-Dialog	TPrinter-Setup-Dialog	TSave-Dialog	TScreen	TTimer
				•							
			•								
				•							
				•							
				•							

(continues)

Table B.2 Continued

Event	TApplication	TColorDialog	TDDEClientConv	TDDEClientItem	TDDEServerConv	TDDEServerItem	TDirectoryListBox	TDriveComboBox	TFileListBox	TFilterComboBox	TFontDialog	TIndexList
OnDropDown							•	•		•		
OnEndDrag							•	•	•	•		
OnEnter							•	•	•			
OnException	•											
OnExecuteMacro					•							
OnExit							•	•	•	•		
OnHelp	•											
OnHint	•											
OnIdle	•											
OnKeyDown							•	•	•	•		
OnKeyPress							•	•	•	•		
OnKeyUp							•	•	•	•		
OnMessage	•											
OnMouseDown							•		•			
OnMouseMove							•		•			
OnMouseUp							•		•			
OnOpen				•		•						
OnPopup												
OnStatusLineEvent												
OnTimer												

	TMain-Menu	TMenu	TMenu-Item	TOLEContainer	TOpen-Dialog	TPopup-Menu	TPrint-Dialog	TPrinter-Setup-Dialog	TSave-Dialog	TScreen	TTimer
				•							
				•							
				•							
				•							
				•							
				•							
				•							
				•							
				•							
						•					
				•							•

Table B.3 Data Component Event Matrix

Event	TDBCheckBox	TDBComboBox	TDBEdit	TDBGrid	TDBImage	TDBLabel	TDBListBox	TDBMemo
AfterCancel								
AfterClose								
AfterDelete								
AfterEdit								
AfterInsert								
AfterOpen								
AfterPost								
BeforeCancel								
BeforeClose								
BeforeDelete								
BeforeEdit								
BeforeInsert								
BeforeOpen								
BeforePost								
OnCalcFields								
OnChange		•	•					•
OnClick	•	•			•	•	•	•
OnColEnter				•				
OnColExit				•				
OnDataChange								
OnDblClick		•	•	•	•	•	•	•
OnDragDrop	•	•	•	•	•	•	•	•
OnDragOver	•	•	•	•	•	•	•	•
OnDrawCell				•				
OnDrawItem		•					•	

Events

TDBNavigator	TDBRadioGroup	TDataSource	TDatabase	TQuery	TReport	TTable	TTableList
				•		•	
				•		•	
				•		•	
				•		•	
				•		•	
				•		•	
				•		•	
				•		•	
				•		•	
				•		•	
				•		•	
				•		•	
				•		•	
				•		•	
				•		•	
	•						•
•	•						•
			•				
•	•						
•	•					•	
•	•					•	

(continues)

Table B.3 Continued

Event	TDBCheckBox	TDBComboBox	TDBEdit	TDBGrid	TDBImage	TDBLabel	TDBListBox	TDBMemo
OnDrawTab								
OnDropDown		•						
OnEndDrag	•	•	•	•	•	•	•	•
OnEnter	•	•	•	•	•		•	•
OnExit	•	•	•	•	•		•	•
OnKeyDown	•	•	•	•	•		•	•
OnKeyPress	•	•	•	•	•		•	•
OnKeyUp	•	•	•	•	•		•	•
OnLogin								
OnMeasureItem		•					•	
OnMeasureTab								
OnMouseDown	•		•	•	•	•	•	•
OnMouseMove	•		•	•	•	•	•	•
OnMouseUp	•		•	•	•	•	•	•
OnNewRecord								
OnOpen								
OnResize								
OnStateChange								
OnUpdateData								

TDBNavigator	TDBRadioGroup	TDataSource	TDatabase	TQuery	TReport	TTable	TTableList
							•
•	•						•
•	•						•
•	•						•
			•				
							•
	•						
	•						
	•						
					•	•	
						•	
•							
		•					
		•					

Appendix C
Methods

This appendix contains three tables that list the methods available for Delphi components. Most components listed are available on the Component palette. Some component classes, such as TApplication, don't appear on the Component palette but are included as a reference. A solid dot (•) marks the existence of a method for the component named in the column.

Table C.1 lists the methods available for visual components. Table C.2 lists the methods available for non-visual components. Lastly, table C.3 lists the methods available for data components. Chapter 4, "Using Visual Components," provides more information on visual components. Chapter 5, "Using Non-Visual Components," discusses non-visual components, and Chapter 6, "Using Data-Bound Components," provides more information on data components.

Table C.1 Visual Component Method Matrix

Property	TBevel	TBitBtn	TButton	TCheckBox	TComboBox	TControlScrollBar	TDrawGrid	TEdit	TForm	TGraphicControl	TGroupBox	TImage
Add												
ArrangeIcons									●			
Back												
BeginDrag	●	●	●	●	●		●	●		●	●	●
BeginUpdate												
BringToFront	●	●	●	●	●		●	●	●	●	●	●
CanFocus		●	●	●	●		●		●		●	
Cascade									●			
CellRect							●					
ChangeActiveControl									●			
CheckActiveControl									●			
ClassName	●	●	●	●	●	●	●	●	●		●	●
ClassParent	●	●	●	●	●	●	●	●	●		●	●
ClassType	●	●	●	●	●	●	●	●	●		●	●
Clear					●			●				
ClearSelection								●				
ClientToScreen	●	●	●	●	●		●	●	●	●	●	●
Close									●			
CloseQuery									●			
CopyToClipboard								●				
Create	●	●	●	●	●		●	●	●	●	●	●
CutToClipboard								●				
Delete												

Methods **517**

TLabel	TList-Box	TMedia-Player	TMemo	TNote-book	TOut-line	TPanel	TRadio-Button	TScroll-Bar	TScroll-Box	TShape	TSpeed-Button	TString-Grid	TTabSet
					•								
		•											
•	•	•	•	•	•	•	•	•	•	•	•	•	•
					•								
•	•	•	•	•	•	•	•	•	•	•	•	•	•
	•	•	•	•	•	•	•	•	•		•	•	•
												•	
•	•	•	•	•	•	•	•	•	•	•	•	•	•
•	•	•	•	•	•	•	•	•	•	•	•	•	•
•	•	•	•	•	•	•	•	•	•	•	•	•	•
		•		•	•								
			•										
•	•	•	•	•	•	•	•	•	•	•	•	•	•
		•											
			•										
•	•	•	•	•	•	•	•	•	•	•	•	•	•
			•										
					•								

(continues)

Table C.1 Continued

Property	TBevel	TBitBtn	TButton	TCheck-Box	TCombo-Box	TControl-ScrollBar	TDraw-Grid	TEdit	TForm	TGraphic-Control	TGroup-Box	TImage
Destroy	•	•	•	•	•	•	•	•	•	•	•	•
Dragging	•	•	•	•	•		•	•	•	•	•	•
Eject												
EndDrag	•	•	•	•	•		•	•		•	•	•
EndUpdate												
Find-Component	•	•	•	•	•	•	•	•	•	•	•	•
Free	•	•	•	•	•	•	•	•	•		•	•
FullCollapse												
FullExpand												
GetDataItem												
GetItem												
GetSelText-Buf								•				
GetTextBuf	•	•	•	•	•		•	•	•	•	•	•
GetTextItem												
GetTextLen	•	•	•	•	•		•	•	•	•	•	•
Handle-Allocated		•	•	•	•		•		•		•	
HandleNeeded		•	•	•	•		•		•		•	
Hide	•	•	•	•	•		•	•	•	•		•
Insert												
Insert-Component	•	•	•	•	•	•	•	•	•	•	•	•
Insert-Control	•	•	•	•	•		•	•	•		•	
Invalidate	•	•	•	•	•		•	•	•	•		•
ItemAtPos												

Methods

	TLabel	TList-Box	TMedia-Player	TMemo	TNote-book	TOut-line	TPanel	TRadio-Button	TScroll-Bar	TScroll-Box	TShape	TSpeed-Button	TString-Grid	TTabSet
	•	•	•	•	•	•	•	•	•	•	•	•	•	•
	•	•	•	•	•	•	•	•	•	•	•	•	•	•
			•											
	•	•	•	•	•	•	•	•	•	•	•	•	•	•
						•								
	•	•	•	•	•	•	•	•	•	•	•	•	•	•
	•	•	•	•	•	•	•	•	•	•	•	•	•	•
						•								
						•								
						•								
						•								
				•										
	•	•	•	•	•	•	•	•	•	•	•	•	•	•
						•								
	•	•	•	•	•	•	•	•	•	•	•	•	•	•
			•	•	•	•	•	•	•	•		•	•	•
			•	•	•	•	•	•	•	•		•	•	•
	•	•	•	•	•	•	•	•	•	•	•	•	•	•
						•								
	•	•	•	•	•	•	•	•	•	•	•	•	•	•
		•	•	•	•	•	•	•	•	•	•		•	
	•	•	•	•	•	•	•	•	•	•	•	•	•	•
		•												•

(continues)

Table C.1 Continued

Property	TBevel	TBitBtn	TButton	TCheck-Box	TCombo-Box	TControl-ScrollBar	TDraw-Grid	TEdit	TForm	TGraphic-Control	TGroup-Box	TImage
ItemRect												
LoadFromFile												
LoadFromStream												
MouseToCell							•					
Move												
Next									•			
Open												
PasteFromClipboard								•				
Pause												
PauseOnly												
Play												
Previous									•			
Print									•			
Refresh	•	•	•	•	•		•	•	•	•	•	•
RemoveComponent	•	•	•	•	•	•	•	•	•	•	•	•
Repaint	•	•	•	•	•		•	•	•	•	•	•
Resume												
Rewind												
Save												
SaveToFile												
SaveToStream												
ScaleBy		•	•	•	•		•	•	•	•	•	•
ScreenToClient	•	•	•	•	•		•	•	•	•	•	•
ScrollBy		•	•	•	•		•	•	•		•	

Methods **521**

TLabel	TList-Box	TMedia-Player	TMemo	TNote-book	TOut-line	TPanel	TRadio-Button	TScroll-Bar	TScroll-Box	TShape	TSpeed-Button	TString-Grid	TTabSet
													•
					•								
					•								
												•	
					•								
		•											
		•											
			•										
		•											
		•											
		•											
		•											
•	•	•	•	•	•	•	•	•	•	•	•	•	•
•	•	•	•	•	•	•	•	•	•	•	•	•	•
•	•	•	•	•	•	•	•	•	•	•	•	•	•
		•											
		•											
		•											
					•								
					•								
•	•	•	•	•	•	•	•	•	•	•	•	•	•
•	•	•	•	•	•	•	•	•	•	•	•	•	•
	•		•	•	•	•	•		•				•

(continues)

Table C.1 Continued

Property	TBevel	TBitBtn	TButton	TCheck-Box	TCombo-Box	TControl-ScrollBar	TDraw-Grid	TEdit	TForm	TGraphic-Control	TGroup-Box	TImage
ScrollInView									●			
SelectAll					●			●				
SelectNext												
SendToBack	●	●	●	●	●		●	●	●	●	●	●
SetBounds	●	●	●	●	●		●	●	●	●	●	●
SetFocus		●	●				●	●	●		●	
SetParams												
SetSelTextBuf								●				
SetTextBuf	●	●	●	●	●		●	●	●	●	●	●
SetUpdateState												
Show	●	●	●	●	●		●	●	●	●		●
ShowModal									●			
StartRecording												
Step												
Stop												
Tile									●			
Update	●	●	●	●	●		●	●	●	●		●

Methods

	TLabel	TList-Box	TMedia-Player	TMemo	TNote-book	TOut-line	TPanel	TRadio-Button	TScroll-Bar	TScroll-Box	TShape	TSpeed-Button	TString-Grid	TTabSet
										●				
				●										
														●
	●	●	●	●	●	●	●	●	●	●	●	●	●	●
	●	●	●	●	●	●	●	●	●	●	●	●	●	●
		●	●	●		●	●	●		●			●	●
									●					
				●										
	●	●	●	●	●	●	●	●	●	●	●	●	●	●
						●								
	●	●	●	●	●	●	●	●	●	●	●	●	●	
			●											
			●											
			●											
	●	●	●	●	●	●	●	●	●	●	●	●	●	●

Appendix C

Table C.2 Non-Visual Component Method Matrix

Method	TApplication	TColorDialog	TDDEClientConv	TDDEClientItem	TDDEServerConv	TDDEServerItem	TDirectoryListBox	TDriveComboBox	TFileListBox	TFilterComboBox	TFontDialog	TMainMenu
Add												
BeginDrag							•	•	•	•		
BringToFront							•	•	•	•		
CanFocus							•	•	•	•		
ClassName	•	•	•	•	•	•	•	•	•	•	•	•
ClassParent	•	•	•	•	•	•	•	•	•	•	•	•
ClassType	•	•		•	•	•	•	•	•	•	•	•
Clear							•	•	•	•		
Click												
ClientToScreen							•	•	•	•		
CloseLink				•								
CopyToClipboard						•						
Create	•	•	•	•	•	•	•	•	•	•	•	•
CreateForm	•											
Delete												
Destroy	•	•	•	•	•	•	•	•	•	•	•	•
Dragging							•	•	•	•		
EndDrag							•	•	•	•		
Execute		•									•	
ExecuteMacro				•								
ExecuteMacroLines				•								
FindComponent	•	•	•	•	•	•	•	•	•	•	•	•
FindItem												•
Free	•	•	•	•	•	•	•	•	•	•	•	•

Methods **525**

TMenu	TMenu-Item	TOLEContainer	TOpenDialog	TPopupMenu	TPrintDialog	TPrinterSetupDialog	TSaveDialog	TScreen	TTimer
	•								
		•							
		•							
•	•	•	•	•	•	•	•	•	•
•	•	•	•	•	•	•	•	•	•
•	•	•	•	•	•	•	•	•	•
	•								
		•							
		•							
•	•	•	•	•	•	•	•	•	•
	•								
•	•	•	•	•	•	•	•	•	•
		•							
		•							
			•	•	•	•	•		
•	•	•	•	•	•	•	•	•	•
	•		•	•					
•	•	•	•	•	•		•	•	•

(continues)

Table C.2 Continued

Method	TApplication	TColorDialog	TDDEClientConv	TDDEClientItem	TDDEServerConv	TDDEServerItem	TDirectoryListBox	TDriveComboBox	TFileListBox	TFilterComboBox	TFontDialog	TMainMenu
GetItemPath							•					
GetTextBuf							•	•	•	•		
GetTextLen							•	•	•	•		
HandleAllocated							•	•	•	•		
HandleException	•											
HandleNeeded							•	•	•	•		
HelpCommand	•											
HelpContext	•											
HelpJump	•											
Hide							•	•	•	•		
IndexOf												
Insert												
InsertComponent	•	•	•	•	•	•	•	•	•	•	•	•
InsertControl							•	•	•	•		
Invalidate							•	•	•	•		
ItemAtPos							•		•			
ItemRect							•		•			
LoadFromFile												
Merge												•
MessageBox	•											
Minimize	•											
NormalizeTopMosts	•											
OLEObjAllocated												

Methods **527**

	TMenu	TMenu-Item	TOLECon-tainer	TOpen-Dialog	TPopup-Menu	TPrint-Dialog	TPrinter-Setup-Dialog	TSave Dialog	TScreen	TTimer
			•							
			•							
		•								
		•								
	•	•	•	•	•	•	•	•	•	•
			•							
			•							
			•							

(continues)

Table C.2 Continued

Method	TApplication	TColorDialog	ClientConv	TDDEClientItem	TDDEServerConv	TDDEServerItem	TDDEtoryListBox	TDirecComboBox	TDriveListBox	TFileComboBox	TFilterTFontDialog	TMainMenu
OpenLink			•				•					
PokeData			•									
PokeDataLines			•									
Popup												
ProcessMessages	•											
Refresh							•	•	•	•		
Remove												
RemoveComponent	•	•	•	•	•	•	•	•	•	•	•	•
Repaint							•	•	•	•		
RequestData				•								
Restore	•											
RestoreDefault	•											
RestoreTopMosts	•											
Run	•											
SaveToFile												
ScaleBy							•	•	•	•		
ScreenToClient							•	•	•	•		
ScrollBy							•	•	•	•		
SelectAll									•			
SendToBack							•	•	•	•		
SetBounds							•	•	•	•		
SetFocus							•	•	•	•		
SetLink				•								
SetTextBuf							•	•	•	•		

Methods **529**

	TMenu	TMenu-Item	TOLECon-tainer	TOpen-Dialog	TPopup-Menu	TPrint-Dialog	Setup-Dialog	TPrinter-TSave Dialog	TScreen	TTimer
					•					
			•							
		•								
	•	•	•	•	•	•	•	•		
			•							
			•							
			•							
			•							
			•							
			•							
			•							

(continues)

Table C.2 Continued

Method	TApplication	TColorDialog	TDDEClientConv	TDDEClientItem	TDDEServerConv	TDDEServerItem	TDirectoryListBox	TDriveComboBox	TFileListBox	TFilterComboBox	TFontDialog	TMainMenu
Show							●	●	●	●		
ShowException	●											
Terminate	●											
Unmerge												●
Update							●	●	●	●		

Table C.3 Data Component Method Matrix

Method	TDBCheckBox	TDBComboBox	TDBEdit	TDBGrid	TDBImage	TDBLabel	TDBListBox	TDBMemo
ActiveBuffer								
Append								
ApplyRange								
BeginDrag	●	●	●	●	●	●	●	●
BringToFront	●	●	●	●	●	●	●	●
BtnClick								
CanFocus	●	●	●	●		●	●	●
Cancel								
CancelRange								
Canvas								
ClassName	●	●	●	●	●	●	●	●
ClassParent	●	●	●	●	●	●	●	●
ClassType	●	●	●	●	●	●	●	●
Clear		●	●				●	●
ClearRecord								
ClearSelection			●					
Click								

Methods **531**

TMenu	TMenu-Item	TOLEContainer	TOpenDialog	TPopupMenu	TPrintDialog	TPrinterSetupDialog	TSaveDialog	TScreen	TTimer
		•							
		•							

TDBNavigator	TDBRadioGroup	TDataSource	TDatabase	TQuery	TReport	TTable
				•		•
				•		•
				•		•
•	•					
•	•					
•						
•	•					
				•		•
				•		•
•	•				•	
•	•				•	
•	•				•	
				•		•
•						

(continues)

Table C.3 Continued

Method	TDBCheckBox	TDBComboBox	TDBEdit	TDBGrid	TDBImage	TDBLabel	TDBListBox	TDBMemo
ClientToScreen	•	•	•	•	•	•	•	•
Close								
CloseApplication								
CloseReport								
Columns								
Commit								
Connect								
CopyToClipboard			•		•			
Create	•	•	•	•	•	•	•	•
CutToClipboard			•		•			
Delete								
Destroy	•	•	•	•	•	•	•	•
DestroyComponents								
DisableControls								
Disconnect								
Dragging	•	•	•	•	•	•	•	•
Edit								
EditKey								
EditRangeEnd								
EditRangeStart								
EnableControls								
EndDrag	•	•	•	•	•	•	•	•
ExecSQL								
FieldByName								

Methods

TDBNavigator	TDBRadioGroup	TDataSource	TDatabase	TQuery	TReport	TTable
	•					
			•	•		•
					•	
					•	
	•					
				•		•
				•	•	•
•	•	•	•	•	•	•
				•		•
•	•	•	•	•	•	•
		•		•		
				•		•
				•		•
•	•					
				•		•
				•		•
				•		•
				•		•
				•		•
•	•					
				•		
				•		•

(continues)

Table C.3 Continued

Method	TDBCheckBox	TDBComboBox	TDBEdit	TDBGrid	TDBImage	TDBLabel	TDBListBox	TDBMemo
FindComponent	•	•	•	•	•	•	•	•
FindField								
First								
Free	•	•	•	•	•	•	•	•
FreeBookmark								
GetAsBoolean								
GetAsFloat								
GetAsInteger								
GetAsString								
GetAttributes								
GetBookmark								
GetCurrentRecord								
GetSelTextBuf			•					•
GetTextBuf	•	•	•	•	•	•	•	•
GetTextLen	•	•	•	•	•	•	•	•
GotoBookmark								
GotoCurrent								
GotoKey								
HandleAllocated	•	•	•	•		•	•	•
HandleNeeded	•	•	•	•		•	•	•
Hide	•	•	•	•	•	•	•	•
Insert								
InsertComponent	•	•	•	•	•	•	•	•
InsertControl	•	•	•	•			•	•
Invalidate	•	•	•	•	•	•	•	•

TDBNavigator	TDBRadioGroup	TDataSource	TDatabase	TQuery	TReport	TTable
•	•	•		•	•	
				•		
				•		•
•	•				•	
				•		•
						•
						•
						•
						•
						•
				•		•
				•		•
•	•					
•	•					
				•		•
			•			•
				•		•
•	•					
•	•					
•	•					
				•		•
•	•		•	•	•	
	•					
•	•					

(continues)

Table C.3 Continued

Method	TDBCheckBox	TDBComboBox	TDBEdit	TDBGrid	TDBImage	TDBLabel	TDBListBox	TDBMemo
ItemAtPos							●	
ItemRect							●	
Last								
Lookup								
MoveBy								
Next								
Open								
ParamByName								
PasteFrom Clip-board			●					
Post								
Prepare								
Print								
Prior								
RecalcReport								
RecordModified								
Refresh	●	●	●	●	●	●	●	●
RemoveComponent	●	●	●	●	●	●	●	●
Repaint	●	●	●	●	●	●	●	●
RollBack								
Run								
RunMacro								
ScaleBy	●	●	●	●			●	●
ScreenToClient	●	●	●	●	●	●	●	●
ScrollBy	●	●	●	●			●	●
SelectAll		●	●					●

Methods **537**

TDBNavigator	TDBRadioGroup	TDataSource	TDatabase	TQuery	TReport	TTable
				•		•
				•		
				•		•
				•		•
			•	•		•
				•		
				•		•
				•		
					•	
					•	•
					•	
						•
•	•			•		
•	•	•		•	•	
•	•					
				•		•
					•	
					•	
•	•					
•	•					
•	•					

(continues)

Table C.3 Continued

Method	TDBCheckBox	TDBComboBox	TDBEdit	TDBGrid	TDBImage	TDBLabel	TDBListBox	TDBMemo
SelectNext								
SendToBack	•	•	•	•	•	•	•	•
SetAsBoolean								
SetAsFloat								
SetAsInteger								
SetAsString								
SetBounds	•	•	•	•	•	•	•	•
SetFocus		•	•	•			•	•
SetKey								
SetRangeEnd								
SetRangeStart								
SetSelTextBuf			•					•
SetTextBuf	•	•	•	•	•	•	•	•
SetVariable								
Show	•	•	•	•	•	•	•	•
StartTransaction								
UnPrepare								
Update	•	•	•	•	•	•	•	•
UpdateControls								
UpdateRecord								
ValidateEdit			•					

Methods **539**

TDBNavigator	TDBRadioGroup	TDataSource	TDatabase	TQuery	TReport	TTable
•	•					
						•
						•
						•
						•
•	•					
•	•					
				•		•
				•		•
				•		•
•	•					
					•	
•	•					
				•		•
				•		
•	•					
						•
				•		•

Appendixes

Appendix D
Constants

In general programming terms, a value that can't change at runtime is called a *constant*. In Delphi, a constant is a term that's used to describe a language construct type or a Delphi assigned value. Constants are used for management of object properties as well as for method, function, and procedure argument values.

Built-In Named Constants

In Delphi, object properties can use a wide range of constant values. To make a panel named testPanel red in color, for example, the following code can be used, setting the color property of testPanel with the constant value for red:

```
testPanel.Color = $0000FF;
```

Property values may be referenced in the same manner as well:

```
if testPanel.Color = $FF0000 {Blue}
    then ...
```

An advantage of Delphi over other Windows development environments, such as Visual Basic and Access, is that Delphi provides the programmer with unique names for a multitude of different constant values. This makes your programming efforts much easier by enabling you to remember descriptive words instead of values between -*xxx* and *yyy*. The previous code examples become much more readable when you use constant names as opposed to their actual values:

```
testPanel.Color := clRed;

if testPanel.Color = clBlue
    then messageBox('The panel is blue', 'Color Info', MB_OK);
```

Tables D.1 through D.10 show constants by their group.

Table D.1 BorderIcons Constants

Defining Class: *TBorderIcons*
Applies To: *TForm*

Name	Description
biSystemMenu	Adds a system menu to a form
biMaximize	Adds maximize button to form's title bar
biMinimize	Adds minimize button to form's title bar

Table D.2 BorderStyle Constants

Defining Classes: *TBorderStyle, TFormBorderStyle*
Applies To: *TForm and Other Visual Classes*

Name	Description
bsDialog	Use Windows dialog border for forms.
bsSingle	Use single pixel border (any object).
bsNone	Don't use a border (any object).
bsSizeable	Use Windows resizable window border for forms.

Table D.3 Color Constants

Defining Class: *TColor*
Applies To: Multiple Visual Classes

Name	Description
clBlack	Black
clMaroon	Maroon
clGreen	Green
clOlive	Olive green
clNavy	Navy blue
clPurple	Purple

Built-In Named Constants

Name	Description
clTeal	Teal
clGray	Gray
clSilver	Silver
clRed	Red
clLime	Lime green
clBlue	Blue
clFuchsia	Fuchsia
clAqua	Aqua
clWhite	White
clBackground	Current color of your Windows background
clActiveCaption	Current color of title bar of active window
clInactiveCaption	Current color of title bar of inactive windows
clMenu	Current background color of menus
clWindow	Current background color of windows
clWindowFrame	Current color of window frames
clMenuText	Current color of text on menus
clWindowText	Current color of text in windows
clCaptionText	Current color of text on title bar of active window
clActiveBorder	Current border color of active window
clInactiveBorder	Current border color of inactive windows
clAppWorkSpace	Current color of the application work space
clHighlight	Current background color of selected text
clHightlightText	Current color of selected text
clBtnFace	Current color of a button face
clBtnShadow	Current color of a shadow cast by a button
clGrayText	Current color of text that's dimmed
clBtnText	Current color of text on a button

Table D.4 Cursor Shape Constants

Defining Class: *TCursor*
Applies To: All Classes

Name	Description
crDefault	The default pointer that looks like an arrow (same as crArrow)
crArrow	A pointer that looks like an arrow (same as crDefault)
crCross	A cross-hair cursor made up of two intersecting lines
crIBeam	An I-beam cursor
crSize	A cursor made up of four arrowheads: one points up, one points down, one points left, and one points right
crSizeNESW	A cursor made up of two arrowheads: one points northeast, the other points southwest
crSizeNS	A vertical cursor made up of two arrowheads: one points up, one points down
crSizeNWSE	A diagonal cursor made up of two arrowheads: one points northwest, one points southeast
crSizeWE	A horizontal cursor made up of two arrowheads: one points left, and one points right
crUpArrow	A cursor made up of an arrow that points up
crHourglass	A cursor resembling an hourglass, used when the system is busy
crNoDrop	A cursor used to show that a drag-and-drop operation isn't applicable for the underlying area
crHSplit	A cursor indicating that a horizontal split can occur
crVSplit	A cursor indicating that a vertical split can occur

Table D.5 Font.Pitch Constants

Defining Class: *TFontPitch*
Applies To: *TFont*

Name	Description
fpDefault	Use the default font pitch for the font specified in the object's Name property.
fpFixed	Use Fixed pitch.
fpVariable	Use Variable pitch.

Table D.6 Font.Style Constants

Defining Class: *TFontStyles*
Applies To: *TFont*

Name	Description
fsBold	The font is boldfaced.
fsItalic	The font is italicized.
fsUnderline	The font is underlined.
fsStrikeout	The font is displayed with a horizontal line through the middle of it.

Table D.7 FormStyle Constants

Defining Class: *TFormStyle*
Applies To: *TForm*

Name	Description
fsNormal	The form is neither an MDI parent window nor an MDI child window.
fsMDIChild	The form is an MDI child window.
fsMDIForm	The form is an MDI parent window.
fsStayOnTop	The form will stay on top of other forms, even when it doesn't have focus.

Table D.8 Position Constants

Defining Classes: *TPosition*, **Integer**, **Longint**
Applies To: *TForm*, *TMediaPlayer*, *TScrollBar*

Name	Description
poDesigned	The form appears positioned on-screen and with the same height and width as it was left at design time.
poDefault	The form appears at a position on-screen and with a height and width determined by Delphi. Each time you run the application, the form moves slightly down and to the right. The right side of the form is always near the far right side of the screen, and the bottom of the form is always near the bottom of the screen, regardless of the screen's resolution.
poDefaultPosOnly	The form appears in the size you created it in at design time, but Delphi chooses its position on-screen. Each time you run the application, the form moves slightly down and to the right. When the form can no longer move down and to the right and still keep the same size while remaining entirely visible on-screen, the form displays at the top left corner of the screen.
poDefaultSizeOnly	The form appears at the position you left it at design time, but Delphi chooses its size. The right side of the form is always near the far right side of the screen, and the bottom of the form is always near the bottom of the screen, regardless of the screen's resolution.
poScreenCenter	The form remains the size you left it at design time but is positioned in the center of the screen.

Table D.9 Form PrintScale Constants

Defining Class: *TPrintScale*
Applies To: *TForm*

Name	Description
poProportional	The form is printed so that it maintains the same size that it has on-screen (the same number of pixels per inch is used).
poPrintToFit	The form is printed using the same screen proportions, but in a size that just fits the printed page.
poNone	No special scaling occurs; therefore, the printed form and how the form appears on-screen may have somewhat different proportions.

Table D.10 Form WindowState Constants

Defining Class: *TWindowState*
Applies To: *TForm*

Name	Description
wsNormal	The form appears neither maximized nor minimized (restored).
wsMaximized	The form is maximized.
wsMinimized	The form is minimized.

Index

Symbols

- (hyphen) menu separator bars, 113
; (semi-colon) terminator, 419-421
< (less than) relationship operator, 368
<= (less than or equals) relationship operator, 368
<> (not equal) relationship operator, 140
= (equals) relationship operator, 368
> (more than) relationship operator, 368
3-D effects (forms), 198-199

A

About Box forms, creating, 206-207
abstract methods, 81-82
accelerator keys (menus), 114
action queries, 342-343
Active property
   queries, 137
   tables, 135
ActiveControl property (forms), 194
ActiveMDIChild property (MDI), 222
Add command (Utilities menu), 348-349
Add dialog, 349
Add Fields dialog, 150
Add New Alias dialog, 130
Add Page dialog, 160
Add Table command (Query menu), 344
Add Table dialog, 138
Add to Project dialog, 166
Add utility (Database Desktop), 348-349
Add Watch command (Run menu), 434
Additional page (Component palette), 33
aliases (databases), 128-129
   connections to remote databases, 130-132
   creating, 129-130
Aliases command (File menu), 129
Align property (memos), 92
Alignment property (memos), 92
allocating memory (pointer data type), 62
AllowAllUp property (speed buttons), 95
AllowResize property (headers), 104
Alpha data type (Paradox fields), 311
ancestors, defaults, 72
Answer Sort command (Properties menu), 345
Answer Table command (Properties menu), 338
Answer Table Properties dialog, 338
ANSWER tables
   fields
      check marks, 339-340
      conditions, 340
      sorting, 345
   properties, 338
Application Icon dialog, 448
applications
   code, 234-235
      event-handlers, 235
      procedures, 235
   compiling, 446
   databases
      BDE (Borland Database Engine), 239-240
      components, 242-245
      creating, 238-239
      naming conventions, 240-241
      testing, 248
   delivering
      databases, 453-456
      executables, 446-451
      ReportSmith runtime version, 456-457
      VBXs, 453

applications

forms, inserting, 43
Help files, 451-453
icons
   creating, 449-450
   launching, 450-451
   selecting, 447-449
MDI (Multiple Document Interface), 218
   child forms, 218-221
   methods, 223-227
   parent forms, 218-221
   properties, 222-223
   referencing child forms, 221-222
messages, 438-439
pausing, 438
ReportSmith, runtime version, 456-457
resetting, 438
running, 430-431
runtime information, 80
SDI (Single Document Interface), 228
   family windows, 228-229
   master windows, 229-231
templates, 231-233
units, inserting, 43-44
see also projects
Apply buttons (Font dialogs), 124
ArrangeIcons method, 224-225
ARRAY data type (InterBase fields), 323
arrays (open arrays), 69-70
AS operator (queries), 341
assignment operators, 419-421
assignment statements, 49
Autocreate forms, 207-208
AutoEnabled property (media player), 107
Autoincrement data type (Paradox fields), 311
automatic type conversion, 63
AutoScroll property (forms), 195

Autoselect property
   edit boxes, 91
   maskEdit boxes, 91
   memos, 91
AutoSize property
   forms, 100
   labels, 90
averages (reports), 382

B

background colors (forms), 198
BackgroundColor property (color grids), 103
BASIC programming language, 57
BatchMove, 148
BCD (Binary Coded Decimal) data type (Paradox fields), 311
BDE (Borland Database Engine), 127-128, 239-240
   Configuration Utility, 129-130
   configuring, 456
   installation, 454-455
bevels, 101-102
BiGauge VBX control, 110, 185
biMaximize constant, 542
biMinimize constant, 542
Binary Coded Decimal data type (Paradox fields), 311
Binary data type
   dBASE fields, 320
   InterBase fields, 323
   Paradox fields, 311
BiPict VBX control, 110, 185
BiSwitch VBX control, 109-110, 185
biSystemMenu constant, 542
bit buttons, 95
bit maps (components), 166, 172
BLANK operator (queries), 341

BLOB data type (InterBase fields), 323
Boolean data type, 60-61
BorderIcons constants, 542
BorderIcons property (forms), 195-196
borders (forms), 196-198
BorderStyle constants, 542
BorderStyles property (forms), 196-198
Borland Database Engine, *see* BDE
Borrow Table Structure dialog, 318
breakpoints, 427-428
   comments, 427
   conditional breakpoints, 430
   disabling, 429
   enabling, 429
   list window, 428-429
   pass count, 429
   temporary breakpoints, 430
Breakpoints command (View menu), 427
Browse dialog, 451
Browse Gallery dialog, 206, 210, 219
Browse Objects window (Browser), 281
Browse Symbol dialog, 292
Browser, 176
   Browse Objects window, 281
   configuring, 303-305
   customizing, 55
   Details pane, 279, 302
   Enter key, 299-300
   filters, 281
      Constants filter, 281-282
      Functions/Procedures filter, 283
      hints, 295
      Inherited filter, 285
      Private filter, 286
      Properties filter, 285
      Protected filter, 286
      Public filter, 286
      Published filter, 286

Types filter, 284
Variables filter, 284
Virtual filter, 286
global symbols, 289-291
info line, 295-296
Inheritance tab, 298
Inspector pane, 279, 302
navigating (keyboard shortcuts), 300-302
Object Tree, 287
collapsing, 304
expanding, 304
qualified symbols, 293-294
References tab, 298
Scope tab, 296-297
sizing panes, 302
SpeedMenu, 287-296
symbols, 292
finding, 299
history lists, 296
sorting, 294-295
viewing previous symbols, 296
units, 288-289
Browser command (View menu), 176, 280
Brush property (shapes), 101
bsDialog constant, 542
bsNone constant, 542
bsSingle constant, 542
bsSizeable constant, 542
bugs, *see* errors
Build All command (Compile menu), 171, 446
buttons, 94-95
Apply button (Font dialog), 124
bit buttons, 95
Browser
History button, 296
Previous button, 296
Maximize buttons (forms), 195-196
Minimize buttons (forms), 195-196
radio buttons, 96
speed buttons, 95
byte integer data type, 60

ByteBool Boolean data type, 61
Bytes data type (Paradox fields), 311

C

C programming language, 57
CALC COUNT operator (queries), 341
CALC operator (queries), 341
CALC SUM operator (queries), 341
CalcMean() function, 69-70
calculations
fields (tables), 274-275
reports, 382
Call Stack command (View menu), 437
Call Stack window (Debugger), 437-438
Cancel Changes command (Record menu), 334
Canvas property (paintboxes), 100
Caption property
BiSwitch, 109
menus, 113-114
captions
group boxes, 97
menus, 113
panels, 97
Cascade method, 225-226
Case statement, 68-69
Cells property (string grids), 94
central processing unit, *see* CPU
CHANGETO operator (queries), 341
char data type, 61
CHAR data type (InterBase fields), 323
Character command (Format menu), 378
Character data type (dBASE fields), 320

Chart property (TKChart control), 110
check boxes, 94, 96
check marks
ANSWER tables, 339-340
menus, 117
Checked property (menus), 117
clActiveBorder constant, 543
clActiveCaption constant, 543
clAppWorkSpace constant, 543
clAqua constant, 543
class methods, 73-74
classes
databases
naming conventions, 240-241
TDataSet class, 244
exception-handling, 403
exception object classes, 399-401
constructors, 400-401
declaring, 405-406
descending classes, 402
properties, 402
forward class declaration, 80-81
pointers, 79
clBackground constant, 543
clBlack constant, 542
clBlue constant, 543
clBtnFace constant, 543
clBtnShadow constant, 543
clBtnText constant, 543
clCaptionText constant, 543
clFuchsia constant, 543
clGray constant, 543
clGrayText constant, 543
clGreen constant, 542
clHighlight constant, 543
clHightlightText constant, 543
ClientHeight property (forms), 198

clients (DDE)

clients (DDE)
  conversations, 119
  items, 119-120
ClientWidth property (forms), 198
clInactiveBorder constant, 543
clInactiveCaption constant, 543
clLime constants, 543
clMaroon constant, 542
clMenu constant, 543
clMenuText constant, 543
clNavy constant, 542
clOlive constant, 542
Close command (File menu), 165, 326
Close method, 226
closing tables, 326
clPurple constant, 542
clRed constant, 543
clSilver constant, 543
clTeal constant, 543
clWhite constant, 543
clWindow constant, 543
clWindowFrame constant, 543
clWindowText constant, 543
code
  applications, attaching, 234-235
    event-handlers, 235
    procedures, 235
  Component Expert, 167-168
  dead code elimination, 42
  step into, 431-432
  step over, 432
Code Editor window, 29-30, 42-44, 54
ColCount property (string grids), 94
collapsing Object Tree (Browser), 304
Color constants, 542-543
Color dialogs, 123
color grids, 103
Color property
  Color dialogs, 123

forms, 198
ColoredButtons property (media player), 107
colors
  background colors (forms), 198
  Color dialogs, 123
columnar reports, 360
columns
  reports
    grouping, 380-382
    moving, 376
  tables
    moving, 328-329
    rotating, 329
    sizing, 326-327
Columns property (DirectoryListBoxes), 105
combo boxes, 93-94, 121
command buttons (SpeedBar), 33
commands
  Compile menu
    Build All, 171, 446
    Compile, 420
    Syntax Check, 420
  Edit menu (Undo), 334
  File menu
    Aliases, 129
    Close, 165, 326
    Merge, 130
    New, 360
    New Component, 165
    New Form, 43, 206, 219
    New Project, 44, 218
    New Unit, 43
    Open, 325
    Open Project, 51
    Remove File, 210
    Run, 356
    Save File As, 44, 50, 166
    Save Project As, 51
  Format menu (Character), 378
  Insert menu (Picture), 379
  Messages menu (WinSight)
    Options, 442

Selected Windows, 442
Options menu
  Environment, 35, 54, 209
  Gallery, 212
  Install Components, 34, 156
  Open Library, 37
  Project, 54, 207, 417
Properties menu
  Answer Sort, 345
  Answer Table, 338
  Delete, 331
  Restore, 331
Query menu
  Add Table, 344
  Execution Options, 345
  Remove Table, 344
Record menu
  Cancel Changes, 334
  Delete, 335
  Insert, 335
  Lock, 336
  Post/Keep Locked, 336
  Unlock, 336
Run menu
  Add Watch, 434
  Evaluate/Modify, 435
  Program Pause, 438
  Program Reset, 438
  Run, 53, 431
  Run to Cursor, 430
  Step Over, 430, 432
  Trace Into, 431
Table menu (Restructure Table), 324
Tools menu
  Report Query, 365
  Sorting, 370
Utilities menu
  Add, 348-349
  Copy, 349
  Delete, 350
  Empty, 335, 351
  Info Structure, 353
  Passwords, 351
  Rename, 352
  Sort, 352
  Subtract, 354

controls **553**

View menu
  Breakpoints, 427
  Browser, 176, 280
  Call Stack, 437
  Edit Data, 333
  Forms, 43
  Object Inspector, 53
  Project Manager, 50, 166, 209, 220
  Project Source, 30, 50
  Run Query, 338
  SpeedBar, 34
  Toggle Form/Unit, 46
  Toolbar, 358
  View Data, 333
  Watches, 433
  Window List, 29
comments (breakpoints), 427
comp real data type, 60
compatibility of variable data types, 63
Compile command (Compile menu), 420
Compile menu commands
  Build All, 171, 446
  Compile, 420
  Syntax Check, 420
compile-time errors, 387
compiling applications, 446
Compiling dialog, 156, 182
COMPLIB.DCL file, 154-155
Component Expert, 164-168
Component palette, 31, 33
  components
    deleting, 36, 158-159
    inserting, 37
    moving, 36, 159
    rearranging, 36
  creating, 37
  Help, 35
  maximizing, 34-35
  minimizing, 34-35
  pages
    Additional page, 33
    Data Access page, 34, 241

    Data Controls page, 34, 241
    deleting, 36, 158-159
    Dialogs page, 34
    inserting, 36, 160
    rearranging, 36
    renaming, 159-160
    Samples page, 34
    Standard page, 33
    System page, 34
    VBX page, 34
component writing, 163-164
components
  bit maps, 166, 172
  creating, 164-167
  databases, 240-245
  DCL (Dynamic Component Library) files, deleting, 161-162
  DCR (Dynamic Component Resource) files, 172
  editing, 164-167, 173-175
  HLP (Help) files, 172-173
  KWD (keyword) files, 172-173
  libraries, installation, 170-171
  messages (design time), 181-182
  PAS files (source files), 172
  private members, 168
  projects
    deleting, 166
    inserting, 166
  properties
    declaring, 178
    defaults, 179-181
  protected members, 169
  public members, 169
  published members, 169
  registration, 169-170
  saving, 166
  testing, 182-184
ComponentState property, 182
conditional breakpoints, 430

conditions (ANSWER fields), 340
Configuration Utility (BDE), 129-130
configuring
  BDE (Borland Database Engine), 456
  Browser, 303-305
  Debugger, 425-426
  Turbo Debugger, 440
connections to remote databases with aliases, 130-132
ConnectMode property (DDE), 119
constants, 541
  BorderIcons, 542
  BorderStyle, 542
  Color, 542, 543
  Cursor Shape, 544
  Font.Pitch, 545
  Font.Style, 545
  Form PrintScale, 546
  Form WindowState, 547
  FormStyle, 545
  Position, 546
Constants filter (Browser), 281-282
constructors
  Create, 400
  CreateFmt, 400-401
  CreateRes, 400-401
  CreateResFmt, 400-401
  virtual constructors, 80
context-sensitive help, 201
control boxes (forms), 195-196
controls
  databases, 240-241
  VBX controls, 184-186
    BiGauge, 110, 185
    BiPict, 110, 185
    BiSwitch, 109-110, 185
    Component palette, 34
    delivering, 453
    inserting, 109
    installation, 186-188
    TKChart, 110, 185
    wrapper, 188-189

conversations (DDE), 119-120
Copy command (Utilities menu), 349
Copy dialog, 349
Copy utility (Database Desktop), 349-350
copying tables, 349-350
counting records in reports, 382
CPUs, 55
crArrow constant, 544
crCross constant, 544
crDefault constant, 544
Create a New Report dialog, 360
Create constructor, 400
Create dBASE for Windows Table dialog, 319
Create INTRBASE Table dialog, 322
Create New Table Link dialog, 367
Create Paradox 5.0 for Windows Table dialog, 310-318
Create Table dialog, 310-319, 322
CreateFmt constructor, 400-401
CreateRes constructor, 400-401
CreateResFmt constructor, 400-401
crHourglass constant, 544
crHSplit constant, 544
crIBeam constant, 544
crNoDrop constant, 544
crosstab reports, 360
crSize constant, 544
crSizeNESW constant, 544
crSizeNS constant, 544
crSizeNWSE constant, 544
crSizeWE constant, 544
crUpArrow constant, 544
crVSplit constant, 544
Ctl3D property (forms), 198-199
Cursor property (forms), 199

Cursor Shape constants, 544
cursors (forms), 199
custom property editors, 164
Customize Installation dialog, 457
customizing
 Browser, 55
 Code Editor window, 54
 Component palette, 158-161

D

Data Access page (Component palette), 34, 241
Data Controls page (Component palette), 34, 241
data encryption, *see* encryption
data types
 fields
  dBASE tables, 320
  InterBase tables, 322-323
  Paradox tables, 311
 variables, 59-60
  automatic type conversion, 63
  Boolean, 60-61
  char, 61
  compatibility, 63
  integer, 60
  PChar, 62
  pointer, 62
  real, 60
  string, 62
  typecasting, 63-65
data-entry fields, 151
data-entry forms, 263-266
Database Desktop, 307
 Add utility, 348-349
 ANSWER tables
  check marks (fields), 339-340
  conditions (fields), 340

properties, 338
 sorting fields, 345
columns
 moving, 328-329
 rotating, 329
 sizing, 326-327
Copy utility, 349-350
Delete utility, 350
Empty utility, 351
headers, 328
Info Structure utility, 353
Passwords utility, 351
queries, 337
 action queries, 342-343
 example elements, 343-344
 execution options, 345-346
 joined tables, 344
 opening, 346
 operators, 341-342
 QBE (Query By Example), 337-338
 saving, 346-347
 SQL scripts, 347-348
 wild cards, 341
Query window, 338
records
 deleting, 335
 inserting, 335
 locking, 336
 posting, 336-337
 unlocking, 336
Rename utility, 352
rows, 327-328
Sort utility, 352
starting, 308
Subtract utility, 354
tables
 closing, 326
 creating, 309-310
 dBASE tables, 319-322
 editing, 332-337
 InterBase tables, 322-324
 navigating, 331-332
 opening, 325-326
 Paradox tables, 310-318
 properties, 330-331

restructuring, 324
scroll lock, 329
Database Login dialog, 135
DatabaseName property (tables), 133
databases, 146
  aliases, 128-129
    connections to remote databases, 130-132
    creating, 129-130
  BatchMove, 148
  BDE (Borland Database Engine), 239-240
  classes
    naming conventions, 240-241
    TDataSet class, 244
  components, 240-245
    DataSources, 134-135, 245
    DBCheckBox, 151
    DBComboBox, 151
    DBEdit, 150
    DBGrid, 149-150
    DBImage, 151
    DBListBox, 151
    DBLookupCombo, 152
    DBLookupList, 152
    DBMemo, 151
    DBNavigator, 150, 257-258
    DBRadioGroup, 151
    DBText, 150
    TField, 243-244
  controls, 240-241
  creating, 238-239
  delivering, 453-456
  demos, 127, 129-130
  grids, 245-246
    creating, 246-247
    editing, 249-254
  passwords, 135, 146
  queries, 135-136
    runtime, 143-144
    saving, 142-143
    SQL (Standard Query Language), 136-137, 254-258
    starting, 142-143
    Visual Query Builder, 138-144

stored procedures, 146-147
tables, 133-135, 149-150
testing, 248
Databases dialog, 143
DATAFORM.DPR project, 238
DATAGRID.DPR project, 238
DataSet Designer, 249-254, 270-272
DataSources (databases), 134-135, 150, 245
Date data type
  dBASE fields, 320
  InterBase fields, 323
  Paradox fields, 311
dBASE tables
  creating, 319
  data types (fields), 320
  Field Roster, 320
  indexes, 321
  record locking, 321-322
DBCheckBox, 151
DBComboBox, 151
DBD, *see* **Database Desktop**
DBEdit, 150
DBGrid, 149-150
DBImage, 151
DBListBox, 151
DBLookupCombo, 152
DBLookupList, 152
DBMemo, 151
DBNavigator (databases), 150, 257-258
DBRadioGroup, 151
DBText, 150
DCL (Dynamic Component Library) files, 154-155, 163
  creating, 156-158
  deleting components, 161-162
DCR (Dynamic Component Resource) files, 172
DDE (Dynamic Data Exchange), 118-119
  clients
    conversations, 119
    items, 119-120

  servers
    conversations, 120
    items, 120
    macros, 120
DDEConv property (DDE), 119
DDEItem property (DDE), 119
dead code elimination, 42
Debugger
  breakpoints, 427-428
    conditional breakpoints, 430
    disabling, 429
    enabling, 429
    list window, 428-429
    pass count, 429
    temporary breakpoints, 430
  Call Stack window, 437-438
  code
    step into, 431-432
    step over, 432
  configuring, 425-426
  debug information (projects), 280-281
  Watch List window, 433
    SpeedMenu, 434-435
    variables, 433-435
declaring
  classes
    exception object classes, 405-406
    forward class declaration, 80-81
  functions, 65-67
  procedures, 65-67
  properties, 178
DefaultColWidth property (string grids), 94
DefaultExt property (Open/Save dialogs), 121
DefaultRowHeight property (string grids), 94
defaults
  ancestors, 72
  command buttons (SpeedBar), 33
  Font dialogs, 124
  forms, 213

properties, 179-181
templates (forms), 210-211
Define Field dialog, 271
defining exceptions, 405-412
Delete command
  Properties menu, 331
  Record menu, 335
  Utilities menu, 350
Delete dialog, 350
Delete utility (Database Desktop), 350
deleting
  command buttons (SpeedBar), 33
  components
    Component palette, 36, 158-159
    DCL (Dynamic Component Library) files, 161-162
    projects, 166
  forms, 210-211
  links (tables in report queries), 368
  pages (Component palette), 36, 158-159
  properties (tables), 331
  records
    action queries, 342-343
    tables, 335
  tables, 350, 367
  templates (forms), 212-213
  variables (Debugger Watch List window), 435
delivering applications
  databases, 453-456
  executables, 446-451
  ReportSmith runtime version, 456-457
  VBXs, 453
Delphi Installation dialog, 454
DELPHI.INI file, 155
Demos directory, 51
dependent tables (Paradox, listing), 318

descending classes (exception object classes), 402
design-time messages, 181-182
Detail window (WinSight), 442
Details pane (Browser), 279
  Enter key, 299-300
  sizing, 302
DeviceType property (media player), 107
dialogs, 120
  Add, 349
  Add Fields, 150
  Add New Alias, 130
  Add Page, 160
  Add Table, 138
  Add to Project, 166
  Answer Table Properties, 338
  Application Icon, 448
  Borrow Table Structure, 318
  Browse, 451
  Browse Gallery, 206, 210, 219
  Browse Symbol, 292
  Color dialogs, 123
  Compiling, 156, 182
  Component Expert, 164-168
  Copy, 349
  Create a New Report, 360
  Create dBASE for Windows Table, 319
  Create INTRBASE Table, 322
  Create New Table Link, 367
  Create Paradox 5.0 for Windows Table, 310-318
  Create Table, 310-319, 322
  Customize Installation, 457
  Database Login, 135
  Databases, 143
  Define Field, 271
  Delete, 350

Delphi Installation, 454
Edit Breakpoint, 429
Edit Class Name, 187
Edit Template Info, 213
Empty, 351
Enter Password(s), 351
Environment Options, 35, 54-55, 209
Evaluate/Modify, 435-437
Expression, 141
Field Link Designer, 273
Find dialogs, 125
Font dialogs, 123-124
Gallery Options, 212
Install Components, 37, 109, 156, 161, 171
Install VBX, 186
Join, 140
New Program Object, 450
New Report Style, 363
Open dialogs, 120-123
Open Report, 356
Password Security, 316
Picture, 379
Print dialogs, 124-125
Print Setup dialogs, 124-125
Program Item Properties, 451
Project Options, 54, 207, 418
Query Option, 345
Referential Integrity, 315
Remove from Project, 210
Rename, 352
Rename Page, 159
Replace dialogs, 125-126
Report Query, 364-365
ReportSmith Installation Options, 457
Restructure, 353
Save As, 50
Save dialogs, 120-122
Save File, 166
Save Form Template, 211
Save Project As, 51
Save Query, 142
Save Table As, 318, 324
Select File, 324, 353
Select Table To Be Added, 365

Sort Answer, 345
Sort Table, 352
SpeedBar Editor, 32
String List Editor, 136
Structure Information, 353
Subtract, 354
Table Columns, 368-370
Table Language, 317
Table Lookup, 313
Table Type, 309, 319, 322
View Form, 43
Watch Properties, 434
Dialogs page (Component palette), 34
dimensions (forms), 198
dimming menu items, 116
directives
override, 82
private, 168
protected, 169
public, 169
published, 169
Directory property
directoryListBoxes, 105
fileListBoxes, 104
directoryListBoxes, 105
disabling
breakpoints, 429
forms, 199
menu items, 116
variables (Debugger Watch List window), 435
DOUBLE data type (InterBase fields), 323
double real data type, 60
draw grids, 103
Drive property
directoryListBoxes, 105
driveComboBoxes, 106
driveComboBoxes, 106
Dynamic Component Library files, see DCL files
Dynamic Component Resource files, see DCR files
Dynamic Data Exchange, see DDE
dynamic methods, 81

E

edit boxes, 91, 121
Edit Breakpoint dialog, 429
Edit Class Name dialog, 187
Edit Data command (View menu), 333
Edit menu commands (Undo), 334
Edit Template Info dialog, 213
editing
components, 164-167, 173-175
fields, 149-150
grids, 249
customization popup menu, 249-250
DataSet Designer, 250-254
links (report query tables), 368
properties with Object Inspector, 47-48
tables, 149-150, 332
Edit mode, 333
Field View mode, 333-334
report queries, 367
undoing edits, 334-335
text (reports), 379
variables, 435-437
EditMask property (maskEdit boxes), 92
editors
custom property editors, 164
Fields Editor, 149
icon editors, 449
Input Mask editor, 92
SQL Editor, 259-263
String List Editor, 102, 136
Empty command (Utilities menu), 335, 351
Empty dialog, 351

Empty utility (Database Desktop), 351
Enabled property
forms, 199
headers, 104
menus, 116
EnabledButtons property (media player), 107
enabling
breakpoints, 429
forms, 199
variables (Debugger Watch List window), 435
encryption (Paradox tables), 316-317
Enter key (Browser), 299-300
Enter Password(s) dialog, 351
entering text in reports, 379
Environment command (Options menu), 35, 54, 209
Environment Options dialog, 35, 54-55, 209
equals (=) relationship operator, 368
error checking, 412
errors
compile-time errors, 387
error checking, 412
GPF (General Protection Fault) errors, 443
handling, 393-397, 412
logic errors, 387, 424
preventing, 412
runtime errors, 387-389, 423-424
syntax errors, 416-422
finding, 417-422
preventing, 422
UAE (Unrecoverable Application Errors), 443
Evaluate/Modify command (Run menu), 435
Evaluate/Modify dialog, 435-437

event handlers

event handlers, 25-26, 235
event-driven
  programming, 18-19
events, 24-25
  code, 48-49
  custom events, 178-179
  inspecting, 40-42
  OnApply, 124
  OnChange, 119
  OnClick, 90
  OnExecuteMacro, 120
  OnFind, 125
  OnReplace, 126
  OnTimer, 118
  properties (object fields), 177
Events page (Object Inspector), 40-42
example elements (queries), 343-344
exception object classes, 399-400
  constructors
    Create, 400
    CreateFmt, 400
    CreateRes, 400-401
    CreateResFmt, 400-401
  declaring, 405-406
  descending classes, 402
exceptions, 388-389
  defining, 405-412
  handling, 390
    class level, 403
    IDE (Integrated Development Environment), 391-392
    termination code, 392-393
    try..except blocks, 389-391
    try..finally blocks, 389-391
  messages, 404
  raising, 389, 398-399
  RTL (runtime library), 389
  volatile data, 390
executables
  debug information, 446-447

icons
  creating, 449-450
  lauching, 450-451
  selecting, 447-449
Execution Options command (Query menu), 345
expanding Object Tree (Browser), 304
experts
  Component Expert, 164-168
  Form Expert, 213-214
Expression dialog, 141
expressions (format strings), 436
extended real data type, 60
extensions (files) in dialogs, 121

F

Field Link Designer dialog, 273
Field Roster
  dBASE tables, 320
  InterBase tables, 322-323
  Paradox tables, 310-312
fields
  ANSWER tables
    check marks, 339-340
    conditions, 340
    sorting, 345
  calculations, 274-275
  data-entry, 151
  dBASE tables, 320
  editing, 149-150
  graphics, 151
  inserting, 149-150, 270-272
  InterBase tables
    data types, 322-323
    naming, 322
  memo fields, 151
  Paradox tables
    data types, 311
    naming, 310
  report query tables, 368-370
  text, 150

Fields Editor, 149
File menu commands
  Aliases, 129
  Close, 165, 326
  Merge, 130
  New, 360
  New Component, 165
  New Form, 43, 206, 219
  New Project, 44, 218
  New Unit, 43
  Open, 325
  Open Project, 51
  Remove File, 210
  Run, 356
  Save File As, 44, 50, 166
  Save Project As, 51
FileEditStyle property (Open dialogs), 121
FileListBoxes, 104-105
FileName property
  fileListBoxes, 104
  media player, 107
  Open dialogs, 121
files
  COMPLIB.DCL, 154-155
  DCL (Dynamic Component Library) files, 154-155, 163
    creating, 156-158
    deleting components, 161-162
  DCR (Dynamic Component Resource) files, 172
  DELPHI.INI, 155
  extensions, inserting in dialogs, 121
  GAUGE.VBX file, 185
  history lists (Open dialogs), 122-123
  HLP (help) files, 172-173
  KWD (keyword) files, 172-173
  masks (Open/Save dialogs), 122
  names (Open dialogs), 121
  PAS, 172
  PICT.VBX file, 185
  SWITCH.DCR file, 188
  SWITCH.DCU file, 188

functions

SWITCH.VBX file, 185
TKCHART.VBX file, 185
FileType property (fileListBoxes), 104
Filter property
  filterComboBoxes, 106
  Open dialogs, 122
  Save dialogs, 122
filterComboBoxes, 106-107
FilterIndex property, 122
filters
  Browser, 281
    Constants filter, 281-282
    Functions/Procedures filter, 283
    hints, 295
    Inherited filter, 285
    Private filter, 286
    Properties filter, 285
    Protected filter, 286
    Public filter, 286
    Published filter, 286
    Types filter, 284
    Variables filter, 284
    Virtual filter, 286
  Open dialogs, 122
  Save dialogs, 122
Find dialogs, 125
  OnFind event, 125
  text, 125
finding
  symbols (Browser), 299
  syntax errors, 417-422
FindText property
  Find dialogs, 125
  Replace dialogs, 125
fitting reports on a page, 374-376
FixedCols property (string grids), 94
FixedRows property (string grids), 94
Float data type (dBASE fields), 320
FLOAT data type (InterBase fields), 323
focus (forms), 194
FocusControl property (labels), 90
Font dialogs, 123
  Apply buttons, 124
  defaults, 124
Font property
  Font dialogs, 124
  forms, 200
Font.Pitch constants, 545
Font.Style constants, 545
fonts
  forms, 200
  reports, 378
footers (reports), 381
ForegroundColor property (color grids), 103
Form Experts, 213-214
Form PrintScale constants, 546
form reports, 360
Form window, 29, 42-44
Form WindowState constants, 547
Format menu commands (Character), 378
format strings in expressions, 436
FormatChars property (DDE), 119
Formatted Memo data type (Paradox fields), 311
forms
  3-D effects, 198-199
  About Box forms, 206-207
  Autocreate forms, 207-208
  borders, 196-198
  colors (background), 198
  control boxes, 195-196
  creating, 43
  cursors, 199
  data-entry forms, 263-266
  defaults, 213
  deleting, 210-211
  dimensions, 198
  disabling, 199
  display options, 204-205
  enabling, 199
  focus, 194
  fonts, 200
  Form Experts, 213-214
  Gallery, 54
  Help, 201-202
  keyboard navigation, 202
  LineItem forms, 266-277
  Maximize buttons, 195-196
  MDI (Multi-Document Interface) forms, 200
  menus, 203-204
  Minimize buttons, 195-196
  moving, 203
  naming, 44, 203
  objects
    inserting, 45-46
    selecting, 46-47
  placement order, 201
  scaling, 203-204
  scroll bars, 195, 202
  SDI (Single Document Interface) forms, 201
  templates, 209-210
    creating, 211-212
    defaults, 210-211
    deleting, 212-213
    naming, 211
    renaming, 213
  text, 200
  windows, 205
Forms command (View menu), 43
FormStyle constants, 545
FormStyle property
  forms, 200-201
  MDI, 223
forward class declaration, 80-81
fpDefault constant, 545
fpFixed constant, 545
fpVariable constant, 545
fsBold constant, 545
fsItalic constant, 545
fsMDIChild constant, 545
fsMDIForm constant, 545
fsNormal constant, 545
fsStayOnTop constant, 545
fsStrikeout constant, 545
fsUnderline constant, 545
functions
  CalcMean( ), 69-70
  declaring, 65-67

RegisterComponents(), 169
Result variable, 70
return type, 70-71
Functions/Procedures filter (Browser), 283

G

Gallery, 54
Gallery command (Options menu), 212
Gallery Options dialog, 212
GAUGE.VBX file, 185
General Protection Fault errors, *see* GPF errors
global symbols (Browser), 289-291
glyphs
    buttons, 95
    outlines, 102
GPF (General Protection Fault) errors, 443
GraphEx project, 416
Graphic data type (Paradox fields), 311
graphics
    buttons, 95
    fields, 151
    outlines, 102
    reports, 379-380
    speed buttons, 95
    see also images
grayed state
    check boxes, 96
    menu items, 116
grids, 245-246
    color grids, 103
    creating, 246-247
    draw grids, 103
    editing, 249
        customization popup menu, 249-250
        DataSet Designer, 250-254
    string grids, 94
    tables, 134-135, 149-150
group boxes, 97

GroupIndex property (speed buttons), 95
grouping columns in reports, 380-382

H

handling
    errors, 393-397, 412
    events, 235
    exceptions, 390
        class level, 403
        IDE (Integrated Development Environment), 391-392
        termination code, 392-393
        try..except blocks, 389-391
        try..finally blocks, 389-391
headers, 104
    reports, 381
    tables, 328
Height property (forms), 198
Help, 35
    components, 172-173
    context-sensitive help, 201
    Help files (applications), 451-453
HelpContext property (forms), 201-202
hiding
    menu items, 117
    SpeedBar, 34
Hint property (menus), 115-116
hints
    filters (Browser), 295
    menu items, 115-116
History button (Browser), 296
history lists
    Browser, 296
    files in Open dialogs, 122-123

HistoryList property (Open dialogs), 122
HLP files, 172, 173
HorzScrollBar property
    forms, 202
    scroll boxes, 100
hyphen (-) menu separator bars, 113

I

icon editors, 449
icons
    creating, 449-450
    launching, 450-451
    selecting, 447-449
IDAPI, *see* BDE
IDE (Integrated Development Environment) and exception-handling, 391-392
images, 100
indexes
    dBASE tables, 321
    InterBase tables, 323
    Paradox tables
        primary indexes, 312
        secondary indexes, 314-315
    properties, 76-79
info line (Browser), 295-296
Info Structure command (Utilities menu), 353
Info Structure utility (Database Desktop), 353
inheritance (methods), 176-177
Inheritance tab (Browser), 298
Inherited filter (Browser), 285
Input Mask editor, 92
Insert command (Record menu), 335
Insert menu commands (Picture), 379

inserting
  command buttons
    (SpeedBar), 33
  components
    Component palette,
      37
    projects, 166
  fields
    DataSet Designer,
      270-272
    tables, 149-150
  forms, 43
  graphics (reports),
    379-380
  menu items (menu bar),
    31
  methods, 177-178
  objects (forms), 45-46
  pages (Component
    palette), 36, 160
  records
    action queries,
      342-343
    tables, 335
  tables (report queries),
    365
  units, 43-44
  Visual Basic controls, 109
inspecting
  events, 40-42
  properties, 39-40
Inspector pane (Browser),
  279
  Enter key, 299-300
  sizing, 302
Install Components
  command (Options
  menu), 34, 156
Install Components dialog,
  37, 109, 156, 161, 171
Install VBX dialog, 186
installation
  BDE (Borland Database
    Engine), 454-455
  components (libraries),
    170-171
  ReportSmith, runtime
    version, 457
  SQL links, 455-456
  VBX controls, 186-188

integer data type, 60
InterBase Local Server
  database, 130-132
InterBase tables
  creating, 322
  Field Roster, 322-323
  fields
    data types, 322-323
    naming, 322
  indexes, 323
  naming, 324
  saving, 324
interfaces
  MDI (Multiple Document
    Interface)
    child forms, 200,
      218-222
    methods, 223-227
    parent forms, 200,
      218-221
    templates, 231-233
  Open dialogs, 121
  SDI (Single Document
    Interface)
    family windows,
      228-229
    forms, 201
    master windows,
      229-231
    templates, 231-233
  VBX wrapper, 188-189
Interval property (timers),
  118

J-K

Join dialog, 140
joins (tables), 272-273
  Add utility, 348-349
  queries, 344
keyboard shortcuts
  Browser, 300-302
  menus, 114
KeyPreview property
  (forms), 202
keys
  accelerator keys (menus),
    114

  Enter key (Browser),
    299-300
  forms, 202
  shortcut keys
    Browser, 300-302
    menus, 114
  Tab key, 108-109
keyword files, 172-173
Kinds property (bit
  buttons), 95

L

label reports, 360
labels, 90
launching applications
  with icons, 450-451
Left property (forms), 203
less than (<) relationship
  operator, 368
less than or equals (<=)
  relationship operator,
  368
libraries
  component installation,
    170-171
  RTL (runtime library),
    389
  VCL (Visual Components
    Library), 154
LIKE operator (queries),
  341
LineItem forms, 238,
  266-277
LINEITEM.DPR project,
  238
Lines property
  memos, 92
  outlines, 102
links
  DDE (Dynamic Data
    Exchange)
    clients, 119-120
    servers, 120
  tables, 276-277
  report queries, 367
list boxes, 93
list window (breakpoints),
  428-429

listing dependent tables (Paradox), 318
listings
   2.1 Source Code for the APP1.DPR Project File, 52
   2.2 Source Code for the APP1 Unit, 52-53
   7.1 A Code Template for Your Component, 167-168
Lock command (Record menu), 336
locking records, 321-322, 336
logic errors, 387, 424
Logical data type (dBASE fields), 320
Logical data type (Paradox fields), 311
LoginPrompt property (databases), 146
LONG data type (InterBase fields), 322
Long Integer data type (Paradox fields), 311
LongBool Boolean data type, 61
longing integer data type, 60
lookup tables (Paradox), 313-314

M

macros (DDE), 120
Main window, 29-37
Mask property (fileListBoxes), 104
maskEdit boxes, 91-92
   MaxLength property, 91
   PasswordChar property, 91
   ReadOnly property, 91
masks
   Open dialogs, 122
   Save dialogs, 122
MasterFields property
   queries, 144-145
   tables, 144-145
MasterSource property
   queries, 144-145
   tables, 144-145
Maximize buttons (forms), 195-196
maximizing
   Component palette, 34-35
   SpeedBar, 35
maximum values, calculating in reports, 382
MaxLength property
   edit boxes, 91
   maskEdit boxes, 91
   memos, 91
MaxPage property
   Print dialogs, 125
   Print Setup dialogs, 125
MDI (Multiple Document Interface), 218
   forms
      child forms, 200, 218-222
      parent forms, 200, 218-221
   methods, 223-227
   properties, 222-223
   templates, 231-233
MDIChildCount property, 222
MDIChildren property, 222
media player, 107-108
Memo data type
   dBASE fields, 320
   Paradox fields, 311
memo fields, 151
memory, allocating to pointer data type, 62
memos, 91
menu bars
   inserting menus, 30-31
   ReportSmith, 357
Menu Designer, 112-113
Menu property (forms), 203
menus
   accelerator keys, 114
   captions, 113
   creating, 111-113
   forms, 203
   items
      checking, 117
      disabling, 116
      hiding, 117
      hints, 115-116
      moving, 115
      names, 113
      popup menus, 108, 204
      separators, 113
      shortcut keys, 114
      submenus, 115
Merge command (File menu), 130
message property (exception object classes), 402
message-handling methods, 82-85
MessagePtr property (exception object classes), 402
messages
   applications, 438-439
   components (design time), 181-182
   exceptions, 404
Messages menu commands (WinSight)
   Options, 442
   Selected Windows, 442
methods
   abstract methods, 81-82
   class methods, 73-74
   dynamic methods, 81
   inheritance, 176-177
   inserting, 177-178
   MDI (Multiple Document Interface), 223-227
   message-handling methods, 82-85
   overriding, 175-178
   pointers, 74-75
   polymorphism, 286
Minimize buttons (forms), 195-196
minimizing
   Component palette, 34-35
   SpeedBar, 35

Open dialogs 563

minimum values,
  calculating in reports,
    382
MinPage property
  Print dialogs, 125
  Print Setup dialogs, 125
ModalResult property
  (bit buttons), 95
Mode property
  (BatchMove), 148
Money data type
  (Paradox fields), 311
monitors, 55
more than (>) relationship
  operator, 368
moving
  columns
    reports, 376
    tables, 328-329
  components (Component
    palette), 36, 159
  forms, 203
  menu items, 115
Multiple Document
  Interface, *see* MDI

N

Name property
  forms, 203
  tables, 133
naming
  conventions (databases),
    240-241
  fields
    InterBase tables, 322
    Paradox tables, 310
  files (Open dialogs), 121
  forms, 44, 203
  menus, 113
  projects, 51
  tables
    InterBase tables, 324
    Paradox tables, 318
  templates (forms), 211
  units, 44
navigating
  Browser, 300-302
  DataSource, 150
  forms with keyboard, 202
  records (tables), 257-258
  tables, 331-332
nesting
  menus, 115
  try blocks, 396-397
New command (File
  menu), 360
New Component
  command (File menu),
    165
New Form command (File
  menu), 43, 206, 219
New Program Object
  dialog, 450
New Project command
  (File menu), 44, 218
New Report Style dialog,
  363
New Unit command (File
  menu), 43
Next method, 226
not equal (<>) operator,
  140
NOT operator (queries),
  341
notebooks, 98
Notify property (media
  player), 107
NotifyValue property
  (media player), 107
Number data type (dBASE
  fields), 320
Number data type
  (Paradox fields), 311

O

ObjClass property (OLE
  containers), 108
ObjDoc property (OLE
  containers), 108
object classes, *see* classes
object fields (event
  properties), 177
Object Inspector command
  (View menu), 53
Object Inspector window,
  29, 38-42
    editing properties, 47-48
  pages
    Events page, 40-42
    Properties page, 39-40
Object Tree (Browser), 287
  collapsing, 304
  expanding, 304
object-oriented
  programming (OOP),
    20-21
objects, 21-22
  ancestors, defaults, 72
  creating, 22
  inserting in forms, 45-46
  new object models, 71
  protected parts, 72
  references, 72-73, 79
  selecting, 46-47
  virtual constructors, 80
ObjItem property
  (OLE containers), 108
OLE containers, 108
OLE data type
  dBASE fields, 320
  Paradox fields, 311
on..do statements
  (try..except error-
  handling blocks), 394
OnApply event, 124
OnChange event, 119
OnClick event, 90
one-to-many relationships
  (tables), 144-145
OnExecuteMacro event,
  120
OnFind event, 125
OnReplace event, 126
OnTimer event, 118
OOP (object-oriented
  programming), 20-21
open arrays, 69-70
Open command (File
  menu), 325
Open dialogs
  combo boxes, 121
  creating, 120-121
  edit boxes, 121
  file extensions, 121
  file masks, 122
  file names, 121
  history lists (files),
    122-123

564 Open Library command (Options menu)

Open Library command
  (Options menu), 37
Open Project command
  (File menu), 51
Open Report dialog, 356
opening
  projects, 51-53
  queries, 346
  reports, 356
  tables, 325-326
operators
  assignment operators,
    419-421
  queries, 341-342
  relationship operators,
    368
Options command
  (Messages menu)
  (WinSight), 442
Options menu commands
  Environment, 35, 54, 209
  Gallery, 212
  Install Components, 34,
    156
  Open Library, 37
  Project, 54, 207, 417
Options property
  Color dialogs, 123
  Font dialogs, 124
  Open dialogs, 123
  Print dialogs, 125
  Print Setup dialogs, 125
  Save dialogs, 123
  string grids, 94
outlines, 102-103
OutlineStyle property
  (outlines), 102
override directive, 82
overriding methods,
  175-178

P

PageIndex property
  (notebooks), 98
pages
  Component palette,
    33-34
      Data Access page, 241

Data Controls page,
  241
deleting, 36, 158-159
inserting, 160
rearranging, 36
renaming, 159-160
notebooks, 98
Object Inspector window
  Events page, 40-42
  Properties page, 39-40
reports, fitting on a page,
  374-376
Pages property
  (notebooks), 98
paintboxes, 100-101
palettes, see Component
  palette
panels, 97
Paradox tables, 310
  creating, 318
  dependent tables, listing,
    318
  Field Roster, 310-312
  fields
    data types, 311
    naming, 310
  indexes
    primary indexes, 312
    secondary indexes,
      314-315
  lookup tables, 313-314
  naming, 318
  passwords, 316-317
  referential integrity,
    315-316
  saving, 318
  table languages, 317
  validity checks, 312
Params property (stored
  procedures), 147
ParentFont property
  (forms), 200
PAS files, 172
Pascal, 57-59
pass count (breakpoints),
  429
Password Security dialog,
  316
PasswordChar property
  edit boxes, 91

maskEdit boxes, 91
memos, 91
passwords
  databases, 135, 146
  Paradox tables, 316-317
  tables, 351
Passwords command
  (Utilities menu), 351
Passwords utility
  (Database Desktop), 351
pausing applications, 438
PChar data type, 62
Pen property (shapes), 101
PICT.VBX file, 185
Picture command
  (Insert menu), 379
Picture dialog, 379
Picture property (images),
  100
PixelsPerInch property
  (forms), 203-204
poDefault constant, 546
poDefaultPosOnly
  constant, 546
poDefaultSizeOnly
  constant, 546
poDesigned constant, 546
pointer data type, 62
pointers
  classes, 79
  methods, 74-75
polymorphism, 175, 286
pOn property (BiSwitch
  control), 109
poNone constant, 546
poPrintToFit constant, 546
poProportional constant,
  546
popup menus, 108, 204
PopUpMenu property
  (forms), 204
poScreenCenter constant,
  546
Position constants, 546
Position property
  forms, 204-205
  scroll boxes, 100
  scrollbars, 99
Post/Keep Locked
  command (Record
  menu), 336

properties

posting records, 336-337
preventing errors, 412, 422
Previous button (Browser), 296
Previous method, 227
primary indexes (Paradox tables), 312
Print dialogs, 124-125
Print Setup dialogs, 124-125
PrintRange property
   Print dialogs, 125
   Print Setup dialogs, 125
private directive, 168
Private filter (Browser), 286
private members (components), 168
ProblemTableName property (BatchMove), 148
procedures
   declaring, 65-67
   references, 235
   stored procedures, 146-147
Program Item Properties dialog, 451
Program Pause command (Run menu), 438
Program Reset command (Run menu), 438
programming
   event-driven programming, 18-19
   object-oriented programming (OOP), 20-21
   top-down programming, 18
   visual programming, 21
programming blocks, 67
Progress property (timers), 118
Project command (Options menu), 54, 207, 417
Project Manager, 50, 208-209
Project Manager command (View menu), 50, 166, 209, 220

Project Manager window, 44
Project Options dialog, 54, 207, 418
Project Source command (View menu), 30, 50
projects, 49-50
   components
      deleting, 166
      inserting, 166
   creating, 44-45
   DATAFORM.DPR, 238
   DATAGRID.DPR, 238
   debug information, 280-281
   GraphEx project, 416
   LINEITEM.DPR, 238
   naming, 51
   opening, 51-53
   running, 53
   saving, 50-51
   SQLEDIT.DPR, 238
   see also applications
properties, 23
   Active
      queries, 137
      tables, 135
   ActiveControl (forms), 194
   ActiveMDIChild, 222
   Align (memos), 92
   AllowAllUp (speed buttons), 95
   AllowResize (headers), 104
   AutoEnabled (media player), 107
   AutoScroll (forms), 195
   Autoselect
      edit boxes, 91
      maskEdit boxes, 91
      memos, 91
   AutoSize
      forms, 100
      labels, 90
   BackgroundColor (color grids), 103
   BorderIcons (forms), 195-196
   BorderStyles (forms), 196-198

Brush (shapes), 101
Canvas (paintboxes), 100
Caption
   BiSwitch, 109
   menus, 113-114
Cells (string grids), 94
Chart (TKChart control), 110
Checked (menus), 117
ClientHeight (forms), 198
ClientWidth (forms), 198
ColCount (string grids), 94
Color
   Color dialogs, 123
   forms, 198
ColoredButtons (media player), 107
Columns (DirectoryListBoxes), 105
components
   declaring, 178
   defaults, 179-181
ComponentState, 182
ConnectMode (DDE), 119
Ctl3D (forms), 198-199
Cursor (forms), 199
DatabaseName (tables), 133
DDEConv (DDE), 119
DDEItem (DDE), 119
DefaultColWidth (string grids), 94
DefaultExt
   Open dialogs, 121
   Save dialogs, 121
DefaultRowHeight (string grids), 94
DeviceType (media player), 107
Directory
   directoryListBoxes, 105
   fileListBoxes, 104
Drive
   directoryListBoxes, 105
   driveComboBoxes, 106

565

properties

editing (Object Inspector), 47-48
EditMask (maskEdit boxes), 92
Enabled
  forms, 199
  headers, 104
  menus, 116
EnabledButtons (media player), 107
events (object fields), 177
FileEditStyle (Open dialogs), 121
FileName
  fileListBoxes, 104
  media player, 107
  Open dialogs, 121
FileType (fileListBoxes), 104
Filter
  filterComboBoxes, 106
  Open dialogs, 122
  Save dialogs, 122
FilterIndex (filters), 122
FindText
  Find dialogs, 125
  Replace dialogs, 125
FixedCols (string grids), 94
FixedRows (string grids), 94
FocusControl (labels), 90
Font
  Font dialogs, 124
  forms, 200
ForegroundColor (color grids), 103
FormatChars (DDE), 119
FormStyle (forms), 200-201
  properties (MDI), 223
GroupIndex (speed buttons), 95
Height (forms), 198
HelpContext (forms), 201-202
Hint (menus), 115-116
HistoryList (Open dialogs), 122

HorzScrollBar
  forms, 202
  scroll boxes, 100
indexed properties, 76-79
inspecting, 39-40
Interval (timers), 118
KeyPreview (forms), 202
Kinds (bit buttons), 95
Left (forms), 203
Lines
  memos, 92
  outlines, 102
LoginPrompt (databases), 146
Mask (fileListBoxes), 104
MasterFields
  queries, 144-145
  tables, 144-145
MasterSource
  queries, 144-145
  tables, 144-145
MaxLength
  edit boxes, 91
  maskEdit boxes, 91
  memos, 91
MaxPage
  Print dialogs, 125
  Print Setup dialogs, 125
MDIChildCount, 222
MDIChildren, 222
Menu (forms), 203
Message (exception object classes), 402
MessagePtr (exception object classes), 402
MinPage
  Print dialogs, 125
  Print Setup dialogs, 125
ModalResult (bit buttons), 95
Mode (BatchMove), 148
Name
  forms, 203
  tables, 133
Notify (media player), 107
NotifyValue (media player), 107

ObjClass (OLE containers), 108
ObjDoc (OLE containers), 108
ObjItem (OLE containers), 108
Options
  Color dialogs, 123
  Font dialogs, 124
  Open dialogs, 123
  Print dialogs, 125
  Print Setup dialogs, 125
  Save dialogs, 123
  string grids, 94
OutlineStyle (outlines), 102
PageIndex (notebooks), 98
Pages (notebooks), 98
Params (stored procedures), 147
ParentFont (forms), 200
PasswordChar
  edit boxes, 91
  maskEdit boxes, 91
  memos, 91
Pen (shapes), 101
Picture (images), 100
PixelsPerInch (forms), 203-204
pOn (BiSwitch control), 109
PopUpMenu (forms), 204
Position
  forms, 204-205
  scroll boxes, 100
  scrollbars, 99
PrintRange
  Print dialogs, 125
  Print Setup dialogs, 125
ProblemTableName (BatchMove), 148
Progress (timers), 118
read-only, 76, 79
ReadOnly
  edit boxes, 91
  maskEdit boxes, 91
  memos, 91

Query window (Database Desktop)   567

ReplaceText (Replace dialogs), 125
RowCount (string grids), 94
Scaled (forms), 203-204
ScrollBars (memos), 92
SelectedColor (tab sets), 98
ServerConv (DDE), 120
ServiceApplication (DDE), 119
set members, 94
Shape (bevels), 102
ShortCut (menus), 114
SQL (queries), 136
StoredProcName (stored procedures), 147
Stretch (forms), 100
StretchBit (BiPict control), 110
Style
   bevels, 102
   shapes, 101
   tab sets, 98
syntax, 75-76
TableName (tables), 133
tables
   deleting, 331
   saving, 330-331
Tabs
   notebooks, 98
   tab sets, 98
TabStop, 108-109
Text (memos), 92
TextCase (driveComboBoxes), 106
TextPosition (BiSwitch control), 110
Top (forms), 203
UnselectedColor (tab sets), 98
Value (DDE), 120
VertScrollBar
   scroll boxes, 100
   forms, 202
Visible
   forms, 205
   MDI, 223
   menus, 117

Wait (media player), 107
Width (forms), 198
WindowMenu (forms), 205
WindowState (forms), 205
WordWrap
   labels, 90
   memos, 92
write-only, 76, 79
xGapStyle (TKChart control), 110
zGapStyle (TKChart control,) 110
see also appendixes A, B, and C for a complete listing of properties
Properties filter (Browser), 285
Properties menu commands
   Answer Sort, 345
   Answer Table, 338
   Delete, 331
   Restore, 331
Properties page (Object Inspector), 39-40
protected directive, 169
Protected filter (Browser), 286
protected members (components), 169
protected parts (objects), 72
public directive, 169
Public filter (Browser), 286
public members (components), 169
published directive, 169
Published filter (Browser), 286
published members (components), 169
purging records, 351

Q

QBE (Query By Example), 337-338

qualified symbols (Browser), 293-294
queries, 135-136, 337
   action queries, 342-343
   ANSWER tables
      check marks (fields), 339-340
      conditions (fields), 340
      properties, 338
      sorting fields, 345
   example elements, 343-344
   execution options, 345-346
   join tables, 344
   opening, 346
   operators, 341-342
   properties
      Active property, 137
      MasterFields property, 144-145
      MasterSource property, 144-145
      SQL property, 136
   QBE (Query By Example), 337-338
   report queries, 363-365
      fields, 368-370
      tables, 365-370
   runtime, 143-144
   saving, 142-143, 346-347
   SQL (Standard Query Language), 254
      scripts, 347-348
      SELECT statements, 254-255
      statements, 136-137
      writing, 255-256
   starting, 142-143
   Visual Query Builder, 138-144
   wild cards, 341
Query menu commands
   Add Table, 344
   Execution Options, 345
   Remove Table, 344
Query Option dialog, 345
Query window (Database Desktop), 338

568 radio buttons

R

radio buttons, 96
raise keyword, 398-399
raising exceptions, 389, 398-399
read-only properties, 76, 79
ReadOnly property
 edit boxes, 91
 maskEdit boxes, 91
 memos, 91
real data types, 60
rearranging Component palette, 36
Record menu commands
 Cancel Changes, 334
 Delete, 335
 Insert, 335
 Lock, 336
 Post/Keep Locked, 336
 Unlock, 336
records
 action queries, 342-343
 counting (reports), 382
 dBASE tables, locking, 321-322
 deleting, 335
 inserting, 335
 locking, 336
 navigating, 257-258
 posting, 336-337
 purging, 351
 unlocking, 336
reducing, *see* minimizing
references
 objects, 72-73, 79
 procedures, 235
References Tab (Browser), 298
referential integrity (Paradox tables), 315-316, 318
Referential Integrity dialog, 315
RegisterComponents() function, 169
registration (components), 169-170

relationship operators, 368
relationships (tables)
 one-to-many relationships, 144-145
 report queries, 368
remote database connections, 130-132
Remove File command (File menu), 210
Remove from Project dialog, 210
Remove Table command (Query menu), 344
Rename command (Utilities menu), 352
Rename dialog, 352
Rename Page dialog, 159
Rename utility (Database Desktop), 352
renaming
 pages (Component palette), 159-160
 tables, 352
 templates (forms), 213
Replace dialogs, 125
 OnReplace events, 126
 text, 125
ReplaceText property (Replace dialogs), 125
Report Query command (Tools menu), 365
Report Query dialog, 364-365
report window (ReportSmith), 358-359
reports
 calculations, 382
 columnar reports, 360
 columns
  grouping, 380-382
  moving, 376
 creating, 360
 crosstab reports, 360
 fitting on a page, 374-376
 footers, 381
 form reports, 360
 graphics, 379-380
 headers, 381
 label reports, 360
 opening, 356

 queries, 363-365
  fields, 368-370
  tables, 365-370
 records, counting, 382
 sorting, 370-373, 383
 styles, 362-363
 text
  editing, 379
  entering, 379
  fonts, 378
  selecting, 377
ReportSmith, 355-356
 menu bars, 357
 report window, 358-359
 ribbons, 357, 359
 rulers, 358-359
 runtime version, 456-457
 starting, 356
 title bars, 358
 toolbars, 357-358
ReportSmith Installation Options dialog, 457
resetting applications, 438
Restore command (Properties menu), 331
Restructure dialog, 353
Restructure Table command (Table menu), 324
restructuring tables, 324
Result variable (functions), 70
return type (functions), 70-71
ribbons (ReportSmith), 357, 359
rotating columns (tables), 329
RowCount property (string grids), 94
rows (tables), 327-328
RTL (runtime library), 389
rulers (ReportSmith), 358-359
Run command (File menu), 356
Run command (Run menu), 53, 431
Run menu commands
 Add Watch, 434
 Evaluate/Modify, 435

SpeedBar

Program Pause, 438
Program Reset, 438
Run, 53, 431
Run to Cursor, 430
Step Over, 430, 432
Trace Into, 431
Run Query command (View menu), 338
Run to Cursor command (Run menu), 430
running applications, 53, 430-431
runtime errors, 387-389, 423-424
 exceptions, 388-389
  handling, 389-399
  messages, 404
  raising, 389, 398-399
  termination code, 392-393
  volatile data, 390
runtime information (applications), 80
runtime library, *see* **RTL**

S

Samples page (Component palette), 34
Save As dialog, 50
Save dialogs
 creating, 120-121
 file extensions, 121
 file masks, 122
Save File As command (File menu), 44, 50, 166
Save File dialog, 166
Save Form Template dialog, 211
Save Project As command (File menu), 51
Save Project As dialog, 51
Save Query dialog, 142
Save Table As dialog, 318, 324
saving
 components, 166
 projects, 50-51
 properties (tables), 330-331

queries, 142-143, 346-347
SQL scripts, 348
tables
 InterBase tables, 324
 Paradox tables, 318
templates (applications), 233
Scaled property (forms), 203-204
scaling forms, 203-204
Scope tab (Browser), 296-297
scroll boxes, 99-100
scroll lock (tables), 329
scrollbars, 99
 forms, 195, 202
 memos, 92
ScrollBars property (memos), 92
SDI (Single Document Interface), 228
 family windows, 228-229
 forms, 201
 master windows, 229-231
 templates, 231-233
secondary indexes (Paradox tables), 314-315
Select File dialog, 324, 353
SELECT statement (SQL), 254
Select Table To Be Added dialog, 365
Selected Windows command (Messages menu) (WinSight), 442
SelectedColor property (tab sets), 98
selecting
 objects, 46-47
 text (reports), 377
 windows, 53-54
semi-colon (;) terminator, 419-421
separators (menus), 113
ServerConv property (DDE), 120
servers (DDE), 120
ServiceApplication property (DDE), 119
set members (properties), 94

Shape property (bevels), 102
shapes, 101
sharing
 event-handlers, 235
 procedures, 235
SHORT data type (InterBase fields), 322
Short data type (Paradox fields), 311
shortcut keys
 Browser, 300-302
 menus, 114
ShortCut property (menus), 114
shortint integer data type, 60
Single Document Interface, *see* **SDI**
single real data type, 60
sizing
 Browser panes, 302
 columns (tables), 326-327
 headers (tables), 328
 rows (tables), 327-328
Sort Answer dialog, 345
Sort command (Utilities menu), 352
Sort Table dialog, 352
Sort utility (Database Desktop), 352
sorting
 fields (ANSWER tables), 345
 reports, 370-373, 383
 symbols (Browser), 294-295
 tables, 352
Sorting command (Tools menu), 370
source (syntax errors), finding, 421-422
specifiers (CreateFmt constructor), 401
speed buttons, 95
SpeedBar, 30, 32-33
 command buttons, 33
 hiding, 34
 maximizing, 35
 minimizing, 35

SpeedBar command
  (View menu), 34
SpeedBar Editor dialog, 32
SpeedMenu
  Browser, 287-296
  Watch List window
    (Debugger), 434-435
SpeedMenu (Menu
  Designer), 112
SQL (Standard Query
  Language), 254
  scripts, 347-348
  statements, 136-137
    SELECT, 254
      Visual Query Builder,
        138-144
  writing queries, 255-256
SQL Editor, 259-263
SQL links, installation,
  455-456
SQL property (queries), 136
SQLEDIT.DPR project, 238
Standard page
  (Component palette), 33
starting
  Database Desktop, 308
  queries, 142-143
  ReportSmith, 356
  Turbo Debugger, 439
  WinSight, 441
  WinSpector, 443
statements
  assignment statements,
    49
  case, 68-69
  on..do statements
    (try..except error-
    handling blocks), 394
  SQL statements (queries),
    136-137
    SELECT, 254
      Visual Query Builder,
        138-144
  terminators, 419-421
"step into" code, 431-432
"step over" code, 432
Step Over command
  (Run menu), 430, 432
stored procedures, 146-147

StoredProcName property
  (stored procedures), 147
Stretch property (forms),
  100
StretchBit property (BiPict
  control), 110
string data type, 62
string grids, 94
String List Editor, 102, 136
structure information
  (tables), 353
Structure Information
  dialog, 353
Style property
  bevels, 102
  shapes, 101
  tab sets, 98
styles (reports), 362-363
submenus, 115
subtotals, calculating in
  reports, 382
Subtract command
  (Utilities menu), 354
Subtract dialog, 354
Subtract utility (Database
  Desktop), 354
subtracting tables, 354
SWITCH.DCR file, 188
SWITCH.DCU file, 188
SWITCH.VBX file, 185
symbols (Browser), 292
  filtering, 281-286
  finding, 299
  global symbols, 289-291
  history lists, 296
  info line, 295-296
  inheritance, 298
  qualified symbols,
    293-294
  scope, 296-297
  sorting, 294-295
  source code references,
    298
  viewing previous
    symbols, 296
syntax
  errors, 416-422
    finding, 417-422
    preventing, 422
  properties, 75-76

Syntax Check command
  (Compile menu), 420
System page (Component
  palette), 34

T

Tab key, 108-109
tab sets, 98
Table Columns dialog,
  368-370
Table Language dialog,
  317
table languages (Paradox
  tables), 317
Table Lookup dialog, 313
Table menu commands
  (Restructure Table), 324
Table Type dialog, 309,
  319, 322
TableName property
  (tables), 133
tables, 133-134
  ANSWER tables
    check marks (fields),
      339-340
    conditions (fields), 340
    properties, 338
    sorting fields, 345
  closing, 326
  columns
    moving, 328-329
    rotating, 329
    sizing, 326-327
  copying, 349-350
  creating, 309-310
  dBASE tables
    creating, 319
    Field Roster, 320
    indexes, 321
    record locking,
      321-322
  deleting, 350
  editing, 332
    Edit mode, 333
    Field View mode,
      333-334
    undoing edits,
      334-335

fields
    calculations, 274-275
    data-entry, 151
    editing, 149-150
    graphics, 151
    inserting, 149-150, 270-272
    memo fields, 151
    text, 150
grids, 134-135, 149-150
headers, sizing, 328
InterBase tables
    creating, 322
    Field Roster, 322-323
    indexes, 323
    naming, 324
    saving, 324
joins, 272-273
    Add utility, 348-349
    queries, 344
linking, 276-277
navigating, 331-332
opening, 325-326
Paradox tables, 310
    creating, 318
    dependent tables, 318
    Field Roster, 310-312
    indexes, 312, 314-315
    lookup tables, 313-314
    naming, 318
    passwords, 316-317
    referential integrity, 315-316
    saving, 318
    table languages, 317
    validity checks, 312
passwords, 351
records
    action queries, 342-343
    deleting, 335
    inserting, 335
    locking, 336
    navigating, 257-258
    posting, 336-337
    purging, 351
    unlocking, 336
relationships, 144-145
renaming, 352

report queries, 365
    deleting, 367
    editing, 367
    fields, 368-370
    inserting, 365
    links, 367
    relationships, 368
restructuring, 324
rows, sizing, 327-328
scroll lock, 329
sorting, 352
structure information, 353
subtracting, 354
Tabs property
    notebooks, 98
    tab sets, 98
TabStop property, 108-109
TDataSet class (databases), 244
templates
    applications, 231-233
        creating, 233
        saving, 233
    forms, 209-210
        creating, 211-212
        defaults, 210-211
        deleting, 212-213
        naming, 211
        renaming, 213
temporary breakpoints, 430
termination code (exceptions), 392-393
terminators (semi-colon ; terminator), 419-421
testing
    components, 182-184
    databases, 248
text
    fields, 150
    Find dialogs, 125
    forms, 200
    memos, 92
    Replace dialogs, 125
    reports
        editing, 379
        entering, 379
        fonts, 378
        selecting, 377

Text property (memos), 92
TextCase property (DriveComboBoxes), 106
TextPosition property (BiSwitch control), 110
TField (databases), 243-244
three-dimensional effects (forms), 198-199
Tile method, 227
Time data type (Paradox fields), 311
timers, 117-118
Timestamp data type (Paradox fields), 311
title bars (ReportSmith), 358
TKChart VBX control, 110, 185
TKCHART.VBX file, 185
TODAY operator (queries), 341
Toggle Form/Unit command (View menu), 46
toggling menu items, 117
Toolbar command (View menu), 358
toolbars
    buttons, 95
    ReportSmith, 357-358
    speed buttons, 95
Tools menu commands
    Report Query, 365
    Sorting, 370
Top property (forms), 203
top-down programming, 18
totals, calculating in reports, 382
Trace Into command (Run menu), 431
try..except exception-handling blocks, 389-391, 393-394
    nesting, 396-397
    on..do statement, 394-396
try..finally exception-handling blocks, 389-391, 396-397

572 Turbo Debugger

Turbo Debugger, 439-441
  configuring, 440
  starting, 439
typecasting, 63-65
typed pointer data types, 62
Types filter (Browser), 284

U

UAE (Unrecoverable Application Errors), 443
Undo command (Edit menu), 334
undoing edits, 334-335
units
  Browser, 288-289
  creating, 43-44
  naming, 44
Unlock command (Record menu), 336
unlocking records, 336
Unrecoverable Application Errors, see UAE
UnselectedColor property (tab sets), 98
untyped pointer data types, 62
Utilities menu commands
  Add, 348-349
  Copy, 349
  Delete, 350
  Empty, 335, 351
  Info Structure, 353
  Passwords, 351
  Rename, 352
  Sort, 352
  Subtract, 354

V

validity checks (Paradox tables), 312
Value property (DDE), 120
VARCHAR data type (InterBase fields), 323

variables
  data types, 59-60
    automatic type conversion, 63
    Boolean, 60-61
    char, 61
    compatibility, 63
    integer, 60
    PChar, 62
    pointer, 62
    real, 60
    string, 62
    typecasting, 63-65
  editing, 435-437
  Result variable (functions), 70
  viewing, 435-437
  Watch List window (Debugger), 433-434
    deleting, 435
    disabling, 435
    editing, 435
    enabling, 435
Variables filter (Browser), 284
VBX controls, 184-186
  Component palette, 34
  delivering, 453
  inserting, 109
  installation, 186-188
  BiGauge, 110, 185
  BiPict, 110, 185
  BiSwitch, 109-110, 185
  TKChart, 110, 185
  wrapper, 188-189
VCL (Visual Components Library), 154
VertScrollBar property
  forms, 202
  scroll boxes, 100
View Data command (View menu), 333
View Form dialog, 43
View menu commands
  Breakpoints, 427
  Browser, 176, 280
  Call Stack, 437
  Edit Data, 333
  Forms, 43
  Object Inspector, 53

Project Manager, 50, 166, 209, 220
Project Source, 30, 50
Run Query, 338
Speedbar, 34
Toggle Form/Unit, 46
Toolbar, 358
View Data, 333
Watches, 433
Window List, 29
viewing variables, 435-437
virtual constructors, 80
Virtual filter (Browser), 286
Visible property
  forms, 205
  MDI, 223
  menus, 117
Visual Basic, 21, 57
Visual Basic eXtension controls, see VBX controls
Visual Components Library, see VCL
visual programming, 21
Visual Query Builder, 138-144
volatile data, 390

W

Wait property (media player), 107
Watch List window (Debugger), 433
  SpeedMenu, 434-435
  variables, 433-434
    deleting, 435
    disabling, 435
    editing, 435
    enabling, 435
Watch Properties dialog, 434
Watches command (View menu), 433
Width properties (forms), 198
wild cards (queries), 341
Window List command (View menu), 29

WindowMenu property (forms), 205
windows
    Browse Objects window (Browser), 281
    Call Stack window (Debugger), 437-438
    Code Editor window, 29-30, 42-44, 54
    Detail window (WinSight), 442
    Form window, 29, 42-44
    forms, 205
    list window (breakpoints), 428-429
    Main window, 29-37
    Object Inspector window, 29, 38-42
    Project Manager window, 44
    Query window (Database Desktop), 338
    report window (ReportSmith), 358-359
    selecting, 53-54
    Watch List window (Debugger), 433
        SpeedMenu, 434-435
        variables, 433-435
WindowState property (forms), 205
WinSight, 441-442
    Detail window, 442
    starting, 441
WinSpector, 443-444
word integer data type, 60
WordBool Boolean data type, 61
WordWrap property
    labels, 90
    memos, 92
write-only properties, 76, 79
writing SQL queries, 255-256
wsMaximized constant, 547
wsMinimized constant, 547
wsNormal constant, 547

X-Y-Z

xGapStyle property (TKChart control), 110
zGapStyle property (TKChart control), 110

Highest quality.
Under budget.
On time.

Down to Earth.

Brickhouse Data Systems, Inc. believes in making you look good. Our highly skilled programming staff can give you a head start on your next Delphi development project. Give us a call and let us help you deliver your system on time, under budget, and with the highest quality possible.

BorlandConnections
Developer Member

Brickhouse Data Systems, Inc.
765 Park Avenue
Bound Brook, NJ 08805-1508

Phone: (908) 563-6844
CompuServe: 71760,2720

- Consulting
- Expert Software Craftsmanship
- Custom Solutions and Integrations
- Rapid Application Development
- Client/Server Database Systems
- LAN Applications

Highest quality.
Under budget.
On time.

Down to Earth.

Brickhouse Data Systems, Inc. believes in making you look good. Our highly skilled programming staff can give you a head start on your next Delphi development project. Give us a call and let us help you deliver your system on time, under budget, and with the highest quality possible.

BorlandConnections
Developer Member

Brickhouse Data Systems, Inc.
765 Park Avenue
Bound Brook, NJ 08805-1508

Phone: (908) 563-6844
CompuServe: 71760,2720

- Consulting
- Expert Software Craftsmanship
- Custom Solutions and Integrations
- Rapid Application Development
- Client/Server Database Systems
- LAN Applications

GET CONNECTED
to the ultimate source of computer information!

The MCP Forum on CompuServe

Go online with the world's leading computer book publisher! Macmillan Computer Publishing offers everything you need for computer success!

Find the books that are right for you!
A complete online catalog, plus sample chapters and tables of contents give you an in-depth look at all our books. The best way to shop or browse!

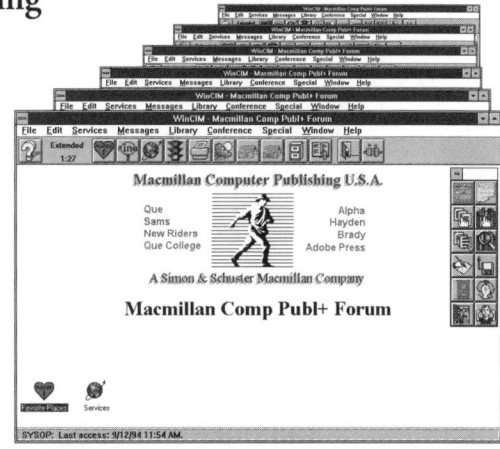

- ➤ Get fast answers and technical support for MCP books and software
- ➤ Join discussion groups on major computer subjects
- ➤ Interact with our expert authors via e-mail and conferences
- ➤ Download software from our immense library:
  - ▷ Source code from books
  - ▷ Demos of hot software
  - ▷ The best shareware and freeware
  - ▷ Graphics files

Join now and get a free CompuServe Starter Kit!

To receive your free CompuServe Introductory Membership, call **1-800-848-8199** and ask for representative #597.

The Starter Kit includes:
- ➤ Personal ID number and password
- ➤ $15 credit on the system
- ➤ Subscription to *CompuServe Magazine*

Once on the CompuServe System, type:

GO MACMILLAN

for the most computer information anywhere!

PLUG YOURSELF INTO...

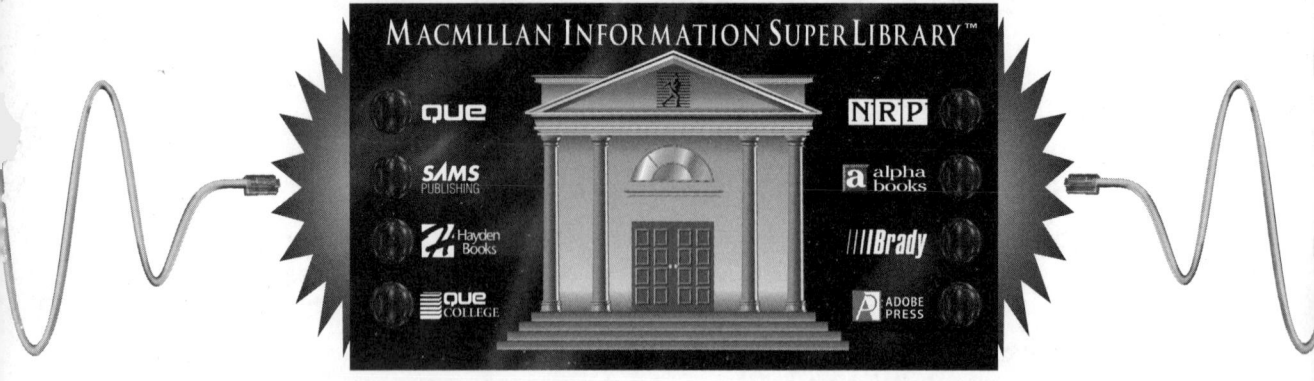

THE MACMILLAN INFORMATION SUPERLIBRARY™

Free information and vast computer resources from the world's leading computer book publisher—online!

FIND THE BOOKS THAT ARE RIGHT FOR YOU!

A complete online catalog, plus sample chapters and tables of contents give you an in-depth look at *all* of our books, including hard-to-find titles. It's the best way to find the books you need!

- **STAY INFORMED** with the latest computer industry news through our online newsletter, press releases, and customized Information SuperLibrary Reports.
- **GET FAST ANSWERS** to your questions about MCP books and software.
- **VISIT** our online bookstore for the latest information and editions!
- **COMMUNICATE** with our expert authors through e-mail and conferences.
- **DOWNLOAD SOFTWARE** from the immense MCP library:
    - Source code and files from MCP books
    - The best shareware, freeware, and demos
- **DISCOVER HOT SPOTS** on other parts of the Internet.
- **WIN BOOKS** in ongoing contests and giveaways!

TO PLUG INTO MCP:

GOPHER: gopher.mcp.com
FTP: ftp.mcp.com

WORLD WIDE WEB: http://www.mcp.com

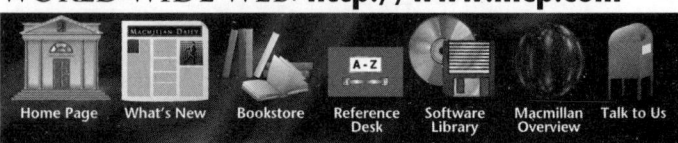